# FLORIDA
## ALMANAC

## 2000-2001

By Del Marth and Martha J. Marth
Edited by Bernie McGovern

**PELICAN PUBLISHING COMPANY**
Gretna 2000

First published 1983 by
Pelican Publishing Company, Inc., as the "Fifth Edition"
Fifth edition: 1983-84
Sixth edition: 1986-87
Seventh edition: 1988-89
Eighth edition: 1990-91
Ninth edition: 1992-93
Tenth edition: 1995-96
Eleventh edition: 1997-98
Twelfth edition: 1998-99
Thirteenth edition: 1999-2000
Fourteenth edition: 2000-2001
Fourteenth edition, second printing: 2000-2001

ISSN: 0361-9796
ISBN: 1-56554-768-3 (hardcover)
ISBN: 1-56554-769-1 (paperback)
*The 2000-2001 edition has been updated*
*by the editors of Pelican Publishing Company, Inc.,*
*and any errors made by them*
*are their responsibility.*

Printed in the United States of America
Published by Pelican Publishing Company, Inc.
1000 Burmaster Street, Gretna, Louisiana 70053

# CONTENTS

# PREFACE

The *Florida Almanac,* now in its fourteenth edition, was first produced in 1972 in response to a newspaper editor's complaint about the lack of one source for information on the state. Subsequent editions have grown to reflect Florida's increasing population, laws, university enrollments, sports activities, zip codes, and landmarks.

Over the years this almanac has become the most widely used and quoted reference book about the state. It is now an essential part of any family, academic, corporate, and political reference shelf.

The *Florida Almanac* also is much used around the nation by people planning to relocate to the state. They are eager to learn all about their exciting future home.

We thank the many people whose interest in the state has prompted them to purchase each of the previous twelve editions so that they may stay on top of new developments. To those of you who are reading the *Florida Almanac* for the first time, we can promise that you will find much fascinating information contained in these pages.

THE EDITORS

# INTRODUCTION
## THE SUNSHINE STATE

Florida is a peninsula of superlatives, geographically and socially. For example:
- Florida is the youngest part of the continental United States—the nation's last land mass, say geologists, to emerge from the ocean.
- The state has more tidal shoreline than any other except Alaska.
- With 53 inches of annual rainfall, Florida is one of the wettest states, yet it is in the same latitudinal belt as great deserts such as the Sahara and the Arabian.
- The state has the country's largest number of first-magnitude springs (27), which are defined as discharging at least 100 cubic feet of fresh water per second.
- Within the state's boundaries are 7,800 lakes, the largest being the 448,000-acre Lake Okeechobee, the nation's second largest freshwater lake wholly within the U.S.
- Florida's southern tip is only 1,700 miles from the Equator, yet two-thirds of the nation's population is within a two-day drive of the state.
- The state's 58,560 square miles make it larger than England and Wales combined, and if the Continental Shelf around Florida were raised by just 500 feet, Florida would double in size.
- Because Jacksonville is directly south of Cleveland and Pensacola directly south of Chicago, Florida is more a Midwestern than an Eastern state, yet all but a portion of the Panhandle is in the Eastern Time Zone.
- The state misses being within the Tropic Zone by less than 100 miles.
- Florida lightning packs more punch than lightning anywhere else, a robust bolt sending out an average current of 45,000 amps, enough to momentarily supply the electrical needs of 300 homes.
- Cities in the Panhandle may record two dozen days a year of below-freezing temperatures, but, 800 miles to the south, the Miami airport has recorded only four winter seasons with freezing temperatures since 1952.
- Florida is the nation's fourth most populous state, with 14.9 million people, yet nearly half of the state is covered with uninhabited forests.
- Regions such as Tampa/St. Petersburg have an unusually high number of days with thunderstorms, more than 100, yet St. Petersburg, between 1967 and 1969, registered a record 768 consecutive days of sunshine.
- Florida, over the centuries, has belonged to five different nations—Spain, England, France, the Confederacy, and the United States.

- Eight Indian tribes—the Timucuan, Tocobaga, Apalachee, Tequesta, Calusa, Ais, Seminole, and Miccosukee —have called Florida their home.
- The state has 34 major rivers, including the famous Suwannee and the unusual north-flowing St. Johns.
- More available groundwater flows beneath Florida than under any other state, all of it stored in major aquifers.
- Florida beaches, if arranged to lie in a straight line, would extend 1,800 miles.
- Of the state's 67 counties, 31 have populations under 50,000.
- The 1990 federal census revealed that Florida had 9 of the nation's 11 most rapidly growing metropolitan areas. Indicators are that the offical 2000 census will hold similar prospects.
- Since 1955, nearly two-thirds of Florida's new residents have moved to the state from New York, Ohio, New Jersey, Pennsylvania, Illinois, Michigan, and Georgia.

Undeniably, Florida stands out among North American locales as uniquely blessed with natural resources, a sensational climate, and a rich history. Such amenities, no doubt, explain why the state is growing, according to census data, at a net rate of 600 people each day.

# ───── CLIMATE AND WEATHER ─────

Florida's official nickname, the "Sunshine State," reflects the economic importance of climate to its visitors and residents. Often called Florida's most important natural resource, the climate is usually pleasant and uniform. General climatic conditions range from a zone of transition between temperate and sub-tropical conditions in the extreme northern interior to the tropical climate found in the Florida Keys. The chief factors affecting the state's climate are latitude, proximity to the currents of the Atlantic Ocean and the Gulf of Mexico, and numerous inland lakes.

Summers throughout the state are long, warm, and relatively humid. Winters, although punctuated with periodic invasions of cool to occasionally cold air, are mild due to the southerly latitude (between 24° 20' and 31°N) and relatively warm adjacent seawaters.

Coastal areas in all sections of Florida average slightly warmer temperatures in winter and cooler ones in summer than do inland points at the same latitude. The Gulf Stream, which flows around the western tip of Cuba through the Florida Straits and northward around the lower east coast, exerts a warming influence to the southern east coast because of the prevailing easterly winds in that area.

## TEMPERATURE

In winter, southern Florida is one of the warmest places on the United States mainland. Summers generally are hot throughout the state, although sea breezes tend to modify the climate along the coastal areas. Even though southern Florida is 400 miles closer to the tropics than northern Florida, it has fewer hot days each summer because of the sea breezes. Summer heat is tempered in all areas by frequent afternoon or early evening thunderstorms. These showers, which occur on the average of about half of the summer days, are accompanied frequently by a rapid 10- to 20-degree drop in temperature, resulting in comfortable weather for the remainder of the day.

Because most of the large-scale wind patterns affecting Florida have passed over water surfaces, hot drying winds seldom occur.

The highest recorded temperature was 109 degrees at Monticello on June 29, 1931.

## AVERAGE ANNUAL TEMPERATURES FOR SELECTED LOCATIONS

| Location | Minimum | Maximum |
|---|---|---|
| Daytona Beach | 61 | 80 |
| Fort Lauderdale | 67 | 84 |
| Fort Myers | 64 | 84 |
| Gainesville | 58 | 82 |
| Jacksonville | 59 | 79 |
| Key West | 73 | 83 |
| Lakeland | 61 | 82 |
| Melbourne | 63 | 81 |
| Miami | 69 | 83 |
| Naples | 64 | 85 |
| Ocala | 59 | 83 |
| Orlando | 62 | 83 |
| Pensacola | 59 | 77 |
| St. Petersburg | 66 | 82 |
| Sarasota | 62 | 83 |
| Tallahassee | 56 | 79 |
| Tampa | 63 | 82 |
| West Palm Beach | 67 | 83 |

In Florida, more people die from excessive heat than from lightning. Medical experts explain that the human body temperature rises dangerously when hot days combine with high relative humidity because perspiration cannot evaporate and cool the body.

A National Weather Service Heat Index chart defines how hot the weather is on a given day. The chart combines Fahrenheit air temperature and relative humidity.

### HEAT INDEX CHART
#### Percentage of Relative Humidity

|   |     | 30 | 35 | 40 | 45 | 50 | 55 | 60 | 65 | 70 | 75 | 80 | 85 | 90 | 95 |
|---|-----|----|----|----|----|----|----|----|----|----|----|----|----|----|----|
| T |     |    |    |    |    |    |    |    |    |    |    |    |    |    |    |
| E | 115 | 135 | 143 | 151 |    |    | APPARENT TEMPERATURE | | | | | | | | |
| M | 110 | 123 | 130 | 137 | 143 | 150 |    |    |    |    |    |    |    |    |    |
| P | 105 | 113 | 118 | 123 | 129 | 135 | 142 | 149 |    |    |    |    |    |    |    |
| E | 100 | 104 | 107 | 110 | 115 | 120 | 126 | 132 | 138 | 144 |    |    |    |    |    |
| R | 95  | 96 | 98 | 101 | 104 | 107 | 110 | 114 | 119 | 124 | 130 | 136 |    |    |    |
| A | 90  | 90 | 91 | 93 | 95 | 96 | 98 | 100 | 102 | 106 | 109 | 113 | 117 | 122 |    |
| T | 85  | 84 | 85 | 86 | 87 | 88 | 89 | 90 | 91 | 93 | 95 | 97 | 99 | 102 | 105 |
| U | 80  | 78 | 79 | 79 | 80 | 81 | 81 | 82 | 83 | 85 | 86 | 86 | 87 | 88 | 89 |
| R | 75  | 73 | 73 | 74 | 74 | 75 | 75 | 76 | 76 | 77 | 77 | 78 | 78 | 79 | 79 |
| E | 70  | 67 | 67 | 68 | 68 | 69 | 69 | 70 | 70 | 70 | 70 | 71 | 71 | 71 | 71 |

The chart's apparent temperatures are readings in shady, light-wind conditions. For full sunshine, calculate a 15-degree increase.

Elderly persons and small children, or persons who are on certain medications, overweight, or have an alcohol habit are particularly vulnerable to heat stress.

Symptoms and treatment of various levels of heat stress are:

Sunburn—Skin redness, swelling, pain, blisters, fever, and headaches. Ointments help mild cases; more severe sunburns should receive medical help.

Cramping—Occurs in legs and occasionally in the abdomen. Gentle massage may help, as do sips of mild (teaspoon of salt to 8 oz. of water) salt water. If persistent, see a doctor.

Heat Exhaustion—Marked by profuse sweating, weak pulse, and severe fatigue. Skin may appear pale and feel cold and clammy. Fainting and vomiting signal greater severity. Person should be moved to cool location, preferably air-conditioned, where cool compresses should be applied. Continuing symptoms require medical attention.

Sunstroke—High (106°) temperature, rapid and strong pulse, and hot, dry skin. Once a victim is moved to a cool location, medical help should be summoned while cool, wet compresses are applied. This condition can be fatal.

## FROST

Although average minimum temperatures during the coolest months range from the middle 40s in the north to the middle 50s in the south, no place on the mainland is entirely safe from frost or freezing. With few exceptions, these cold waves seldom last more than two or three consecutive days. It is rare for temperatures to remain below freezing throughout the day anywhere in the state. On the first night of a cold wave there usually is considerable wind which, because of the continual mixing of the air, prevents marked temperature differences between high and low ground. By the second night, winds usually have subsided and radiational cooling under clear skies accelerates the temperature drop after sundown.

Some winters, often several in succession pass without widespread freezing in the southern areas. The most distressing winters to the agriculture industry are those with more than one severe cold wave, interspersed with periods of relative warmth. The later freezes almost always find vegetation in a tender stage of new growth.

Noteworthy cold spells of the 20th century were in January 1905, December 1906, December 1909, February 1917, January 1928, December 1934, January 1940, February 1947, the winter of 1957-58, December 1962, January 1977, January 1981, January 1982, Christmas 1983, January 1985, and Christmas 1989. It was the 1962 freeze that killed many tropical palms and Australian pines throughout the central part of the state, but the most severe freezes recorded in the state were those of 1894, 1895, 1899, 1983, 1985, and 1989. Lowest recorded Florida temperature was 2 degrees below zero at Tallahassee on February 13, 1899.

One of the longest and the most widespread freezes occurred at Christmas in 1989. Freezing temperatures penetrated as far south as Miami. Falling snow and sleet on December 23 forced the closing of icy interstate highways and airports in most of north and central Florida. The freezing temperatures and fallen snow lingered through December 25, causing power outages statewide.

## HUMIDITY AND FOG

Florida's humid climate is attributed to the fact that no point in the state is more than 60 miles from salt water and no more than 345 feet above sea level.

Humidity is the degree of wetness or dryness of the air and is measured by a percentage ratio called "relative humidity." This is a ratio of the amount of moisture and temperature at a given spot to the maximum amount (99 percent) of moisture that could be contained by the same air at the same spot. The warmer the air becomes, the more moisture it can hold. Therefore a person can feel stickier on a warm day with 80 percent humidity than on a cold day with the same humidity.

The climate of Florida is humid. Inland areas with greater temperature extremes enjoy slightly lower relative humidity, especially during hot weather. On the average, variations in relative humidity from one place to another are small.

Heavy fogs are usually confined to the night and early-morning hours when the humidity range is about 85 to 95 percent. Fogs are more prevalent in the late fall, winter, and early spring months. They occur on the average about 35 to 40 days per year over the extreme northern portion; 25 to 30 days per year in the central portion; and less than 10 days per year in the extreme southern areas. These fogs usually dissipate soon after sunrise. Heavy daytime fog is seldom observed in the state.

## AIR POLLUTION

Southeast Florida has the worst air pollution problem in the state, reports the U.S. Environmental Protection Agency. Second worst is the Tampa Bay Area, and third worst is the Jacksonville area. The agency blames it on ozone, caused chiefly by car emissions. Ozone is a form of oxygen produced when sunshine cooks hydrocarbons and nitrogen oxides, with 70 percent of the key ozone ingredients coming from auto exhausts. Six urban counties—Broward, Duval, Hillsborough, Miami-Dade, Palm Beach, and Pinellas—require bi-annual inspections for auto emissions.

## PREVAILING WINDS

Prevailing winds over the southern peninsula are southeast and east. Over the remainder of the state, wind directions are influenced locally by convectional forces inland and the "land and sea breeze" effect near the coast. Consequently, prevailing directions are somewhat erratic but, in general, follow a pattern of northerly in winter and southerly in summer. March and April are, on average, the windiest months. High local winds of short duration occur occasionally with thunderstorms in summer and with cold fronts moving across the state in other seasons. Average annual wind speed in Florida is 8.6 mph.

## RAINFALL

The state's rainfall is varied both in annual amount and in seasonal distribution. Individual rainfall measuring stations have annual averages from about 50 to 65 inches. In the Florida Keys, annual averages are only about 40 inches. The main areas of high annual rainfall are in the extreme northwestern counties and at the southeastern end of the peninsula. Many localities have received more than 100 inches in a calendar year. In contrast, most localities received less than 40 inches in a calendar year.

Although the state average rainfall is 53 inches (averaging 150 billion gallons of water daily), evaporation reduces the "available" rainfall amount to about 40 inches annually.

In the summer "rainy season" there is close to a 50-50 chance some rain will fall on a given day. During the remainder of the year, the chances are much less, some rain being likely on one or two days per week. The seasonal distribution changes somewhat from north to south. In the northwestern counties

## WINDCHILL

| | | Degrees Fahrenheit | | | | | | | | | | | |
|---|---|---|---|---|---|---|---|---|---|---|---|---|---|
| | | 0 | 75 | 65 | 55 | 45 | 35 | 30 | 25 | 20 | 15 | 10 | 5 | 0 |
| W | 0 | 75 | 65 | 55 | 45 | 35 | 30 | 25 | 20 | 15 | 10 | 5 | 0 |
| I | 5 | 74 | 64 | 53 | 43 | 33 | 27 | 21 | 16 | 12 | 7 | 1 | -6 |
| N | 10 | 69 | 58 | 45 | 34 | 21 | 16 | 9 | 2 | -2 | -9 | -15 | -22 |
| D | 15 | 68 | 56 | 42 | 29 | 16 | 11 | 1 | -6 | -11 | -18 | -25 | -33 |
| | 20 | 67 | 54 | 40 | 26 | 12 | 3 | -4 | -9 | -17 | -24 | -32 | -40 |
| M | 25 | 66 | 52 | 36 | 23 | 7 | 0 | -7 | -15 | -22 | -29 | -37 | -45 |
| P | 30 | 65 | 50 | 34 | 21 | 5 | -2 | -11 | -18 | -26 | -33 | -41 | -49 |
| H | 35 | 65 | 49 | 33 | 20 | 3 | -4 | -13 | -20 | -27 | -35 | -43 | -52 |
| | 40 | 65 | 49 | 32 | 19 | 1 | -4 | -15 | -22 | -29 | -36 | -45 | -54 |

The chart shows the wind chill factor for exposed skin, your face, for example, on a brisk, windy day. To read the chart find the air temperature on the top line, then locate the wind speed in the column on the left. Follow the wind speed line over to the temperature column and read the approximate chill on your bare skin.

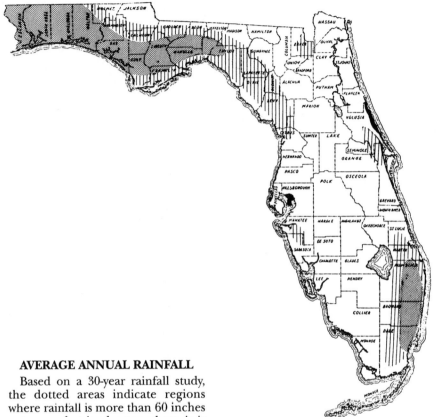

## AVERAGE ANNUAL RAINFALL

Based on a 30-year rainfall study, the dotted areas indicate regions where rainfall is more than 60 inches a year, and striped areas where it is 56-60 inches annually. The small, darkened areas in Hillsborough and Volusia counties receive under 48 inches, as do the Florida Keys. The remainder of the state records an annual 56 inches.

or Panhandle, there are two wet periods: late winter or early spring, and again during summer, and one pronounced low point, October-November. A secondary low point occurs in April and May. On the peninsula, the most striking features of the seasonal distribution are the dominance of summer rainfall (generally more than half the average annual total falls in the four-month period June through September) and the rather abrupt start and end of the summer "rainy season."

Most localities have at some time experienced two-hour rainfalls in excess of three inches, and 24-hour amounts of near or greater than 10 inches.

### Record 24-Hour Rainfalls

| Year | Location | Amount (inches) |
|------|----------|-----------------|
| 1941 | Trenton . . . . . . . . . . .30 |
| 1950 | Yankeetown . . . . . . . .38.7 |
| 1950 | Cedar Key . . . . . . . . .34 |
| 1969 | Fernandina Beach . . .22 |
| 1980 | Key West . . . . . . . . . .23.3 |

The above totals, with the exception of the Key West and the Fernandina Beach figures, occurred in connection with a tropical disturbance or hurricane. Maximum daily rainfall has been reported in all months except December and February, but more than 60 percent of extreme rainfall has occurred in September and October.

Areas in the state with the least annual rainfall are Niceville in the western Panhandle, with 3.6 inches, and the Keys and other south Florida areas such as the counties of Monroe, Collier, Hendry, and interior regions of Lee County, which tally an annual rainfall of just 1.3 inches.

## THUNDERSTORMS

Florida is the thunderstorm capital of the nation. A study by the National Oceanic and Atmospheric Administration shows Fort Myers averages 100 days with lightning annually, the Tampa Bay area, 90, and Miami, 76. The so-called "lightning belt" in Florida is an area from between Orlando and Tampa south along the west coast to Fort Myers and east to Lake Okeechobee. One study revealed 120 days of thunderstorms occurred in one year within a 50-mile radius of Tampa.

Few of the state's thunderstorms last more than two hours. They are attributed to hot, wet air close to the ground combined with an unstable atmosphere. An average lightning bolt lasts just a thousandth of a second and packs around 30,000 degrees Fahrenheit in a one-inch channel that can deliver a shock in the 6,000-25,000-amp range. But Florida's lightning frequently packs a walloping 45,000 amperes. Researchers believe Florida lightning is particularly powerful because it is born of tall, more highly charged storm-cloud formations.

The state has the nation's worst record of deaths by lightning, with storms occurring nearly every day from June to September, usually in the afternoon. In 1998, lightning killed eight and injured 45. Since 1960, lightning has killed an annual average of 10 and injured 45 in Florida. Lightning is the leading weather cause of death in Florida, responsible for more than half of all such fatalities.

### Florida Lightning Deaths

| Location | Percentage |
|----------|------------|
| In an open field . . . . . . . . . .27% |
| Under a tree . . . . . . . . . . . . .13% |
| On water . . . . . . . . . . . . . . . .25% |
| Using heavy equipment . . . . .6% |
| On a golf course . . . . . . . . . .3% |
| Unknown or unreported . . .25% |

Lightning injuries to trees appear to be governed by the voltage of the charge, the moisture content of the tree, and the species of the tree. "Hot" bolts—those with temperatures above 25,000 degrees—will make an entire tree burst into flames; "cold" lightning can make a tree explode, as it strikes at 20,000 miles per second. Tall trees or those growing alone in open areas, and trees with roots in moist soils or those growing along water, are most likely to be struck. Some species are more resistant to lightning strikes than others. Commonly hit are oak, pine, and maple. Experts point out that trees high in oil, such as birch and beech, are poor conductors of electricity, but oaks and pines have high starch contents, making them good conductors. Deep-rooted and decaying trees also appear more susceptible to lightning. Some trees are known to have been hit by lightning up to seven times.

Experts suggest that the following precautions be taken during a thunderstorm:

1. Avoid using electrical appliances, especially the telephone. Lightning can strike telephone lines and utility poles and the current may be carried through the wires.

2. Avoid water—whether it's in the shower, at the beach, or out on your boat. Water conducts electricity and lightning tends to strike the highest point on a plain. Your boat or your body could be the highest point on a level area. If you are out on your boat, take extra precautions and head for a protected shoreline or marina if possible.

3. If outside, especially on a golf course or other open area such as a ball field, seek shelter anywhere but under trees. These are primary lightning targets. If no shelter is available, lie low in the deepest ground depression around.

4. Never hold onto any lightning attractants such as golf clubs, metal tennis rackets, or fishing poles. Avoid proximity to other electrical conductors such as wire fences, clotheslines, or metal pipes.

5. If riding in a car, stay inside but avoid touching any metal parts.

6. A tingling sensation or your hair standing out from your head may indicate a bolt is close to striking nearby. Drop to the ground and lie flat.

7. Be aware of the lightning season—July to August is the peak period—and schedule outdoor activities for times other than the mid-afternoon, when most thunderstorms occur.

8. In the event someone is struck by lightning, cardiopulmonary resuscitation must be administered immediately.

## SNOW

Snowfall in Florida is rare. The greatest recorded snowfalls in Florida occurred on the same date, February 13, in 1899 and 1958. In 1899, four inches were measured at Lake Butler in Union County, and one-half inch at Bartow in Polk County. In 1958, most of Florida west of the Suwannee River received two to three inches of snow while areas east of the river and north of about Latitude 30 degrees measured one to two inches. Three inches measured at Tallahassee in February 1958 is the greatest ever recorded there since records began in 1886.

It's doubtful, however, that Florida ever experienced as wide-ranging a snowfall as occurred in the winter of 1977. Recorded as the most consistently cold January on record, the first month of that year saw the appearance of snow all the way from the Georgia border into Miami. Traces were measured in Broward and Miami-Dade counties, in Palm Beach, and in Miami Beach for the

## FROST LINES

Average dates of last killing spring frosts in Florida.

Average dates of first killing fall or winter frosts in Florida.

first time. A half-inch was measured in the Tampa Bay area, and an inch in St. Augustine and parts of Volusia County. Snow and sleet fell on three different days during that month in 1977 in Jacksonville. And in Fort Myers, recordkeepers recorded snowflakes during that spell for only the fourth time in its history. Pensacola also measured an inch, and Orlando reported snow on two consecutive days.

## DROUGHT

Drought is a prolonged period of below normal or expected precipitation. The annual cycle of temperature and rainfall leads to seasonal droughts in many areas of the state. Drought conditions in south Florida occur every year that winter rainfall is even slightly below normal. In north Florida, a seasonal drought occurs most often in fall and spring.

A study of several regions of the state from 1980 to 1982, when compared against a 30-year mean (1951-1980), revealed a decline in rainfall for the Pensacola, Tallahassee, Jacksonville, and Lake Okeechobee areas. By contrast, that same study revealed a rise in rainfall for the Fort Myers and West Palm Beach areas.

The most severe lack of rainfall was recorded for the Pensacola area during the years 1889-1894, when three consecutive years recorded less than 45 inches of rainfall.

## EARTHQUAKES

Florida is relatively free of earthquakes, thanks to the limestone base that supports the land and tends to act as a shock absorber for any subterranean shifting that might occur. Nevertheless, some earthquakes have been recorded in the state, all of a minor magnitude. The earliest recorded and most severe quake occurred January 12, 1879, near St. Augustine. Tremors lasted about 10 minutes and covered a 25,000-square-mile area from Savannah, Georgia, southward to Daytona Beach. Damage was limited to falling plaster in some buildings.

Six other earthquakes were recorded in the state, but only one was outside the state's northern region. The latter occurred December 22, 1945, when Miami Beach residents reported tremors but no damage. Authorities later determined that the tremors were actually vibrations associated with an earthquake centered in Cuba.

Altogether, there have been between 30 and 40 tremors reported in Florida since 1879. Only seven were confirmed by seismographic recording and the others were written off as the result of explosions and sonic booms.

A 250-year review of the state's seismic activity by the University of Florida indicates fewer bona fide seismic events than previously thought. Just as with the 1945 Miami Beach tremors, seismic experts report that most of Florida's so-called quakes were really vibrations felt in connection with activity outside the state or were explosions that could not be verified. Two authentic quake tremors, according to university seismologists, occurred in 1973 and 1975 in the Daytona and Sanford areas when the earth's crust made a minor adjustment. Florida has no active faults, no emerging volcanoes, and no growing mountain ranges, which are the geological prerequisites to most major earthquake activity.

The University of Florida, in Gainesville, is headquarters for the state's network of seismographic recording stations affiliated with the national network that monitors earthquake activity. The Florida network includes seismographic recording stations in Gainesville, the Oscar Scherer State Recreation Area near Sarasota, the Everglades National Park, and Wakulla Springs in Florida, and one station in Waycross, Georgia.

## TORNADOES

April, May, and June are considered peak periods for tornadoes. Florida, with 20 twisters a year, ranks eighth in the nation's annual numbers of tornadoes. Fortunately, many of Florida's tornadoes are the weaker, waterspout type of storm. The more severe tornadoes, associated with a squall line, occur mainly in Florida's Panhandle during February and March.

Tornadoes can surpass hurricanes in deadly force. The counterclockwise, upward movement of air within the twister causes rapid expansion, cooling, and condensation, which contribute to the formation of the dark cloud of the tornado funnel. A tornado is seen most often in muggy, oppressive weather when large thunderstorms are apparent. Rain, hail, and flashes of lightning may precede the storm. Inside the funnel, air pressure is so low it can cause structures to explode. Destructive paths of tornadoes average about a quarter-mile wide and 16 miles long, although many in Florida are shorter. Tornadoes travel from southwest to northeast.

---

### Tornado Categories

For the purpose of study, weather researchers rate tornadoes based on miles per hour of wind speed and damage that can be expected to result from the storm.

| Rating | Category | Wind Speed | Damage |
|--------|----------|------------|--------|
| Weak | F-0 | 40- 72 | Light |
| Weak | F-1 | 73-112 | Moderate |
| Strong | F-2 | 113-157 | Significant |
| Strong | F-3 | 158-206 | Severe |
| Violent | F-4 | 207-260 | Disastrous |
| Violent | F-5 | 261-318 | Incredible |

In addition, seven other tornado categories exist, at least for research purposes. These categories range from F-6 to F-12 and have wind speeds from 319 mph to the speed of sound.

Fortunately, Florida tornadoes are rarely recorded as doing more than moderate damage.

Over water, a tornado takes the form of a waterspout. It is safe boating practice to stay away from any thunderstorm cell, especially any so-called "anvil-shaped" clouds whose level bases can form the deadly swirling winds.

If a tornado is spotted, move away from it. Persons in open country should seek a depression and hide inside it. In a house, residents are advised to open windows to help balance the air pressure and then move to a secure location such as a bathroom or another room centrally situated within the house.

If tornado conditions are present, weather forecasters will issue warnings or watches on emergency broadcasting stations. A "tornado watch" means tornadoes and severe thunderstorms are possible in the area; a "tornado warning" means a tornado has been detected in the area.

**Florida Tornado Deaths**

## HURRICANES

Florida and other Gulf and Atlantic coastal states lie in the general path of tropical hurricanes. Most of these vicious storms spawn in the Caribbean Sea or in an area east of the Lesser Antilles in the Atlantic Ocean.

Florida's vulnerability varies with the progress of the hurricane season. August and early September tropical storms normally approach the state from the east or southeast, but as the season progresses into late September and October, the region of maximum hurricane activity concerning Florida shifts to the western Caribbean. Most storms that move into Florida approach from the south or southwest, entering the Keys, the Miami area, or along the west coast.

Caused by wind rushing toward a low-pressure area, hurricanes take the form of huge doughnuts. In the northern hemisphere, high winds revolve counterclockwise around a calm center or "eye." The movement is clockwise in the southern hemisphere.

The lowest sea level pressure ever recorded in an Atlantic storm was 26.22 inches measured inside Hurricane Gilbert on September 13, 1988. It was the most intense storm ever measured in the Western Hemisphere. Its highest sustained winds measured 183 mph. Gilbert's destructive path took it across Jamaica, the Cayman Islands, and the Yucatan Peninsula, making final landfall on the northern Mexican coast. The second lowest barometric reading, 26.35 inches, occurred at Long Key in the Florida Keys on September 2, 1935. This occurred during the infamous "Labor Day Hurricane," when maximum winds were not recorded because wind-measuring equipment was blown down before the peak of the storm was reached. Engineers calculated that winds of 200 to 250 mph would have been required to account for some of the damage caused.

Ranging from 60 to 1,000 miles in diameter, a hurricane is defined by winds of more than 74 mph, accompanied by heavy rains, extremely large waves, and dangerously high tides. Immediately outside the eye, winds may surge as high as 125 to 150 mph or more, blowing rain in horizontal sheets. The storm itself has forward movement and can travel very slowly or at speeds of more than 60 mph.

Once a hurricane is formed it poses a multiple threat to people and property in its path. Wind, rain, waves, and storm surge are its four most destructive forces. Any one of these forces is capable of causing severe damage.

Hurricane rains often come as a blessing to parched lands, but they may also come too fast and cause wholesale flooding and destruction. The average hurricane will drop some six inches of water over a given area. The extremes of this average range from practically no rain to downpours measured in feet.

After an average of 8 to 10 days of blowing, the normal hurricane dies by either running too far from the tropical latitudes of its birth, or by advancing over land. Uneven land masses hinder the free flow of winds and fail to offer the supply of moisture the storm needs to keep going. Many hurricanes lose their punch while still at sea and hit land classified only as tropical storms (winds under 74 mph).

## How to Estimate Wind Speeds (mph)

| | | |
|---|---|---|
| Calm | . . . . . .under 1 | . .Smoke rises straight up, nothing moves |
| Light air | . . . . . . . .1-3 | . .Smoke drifts, leaves barely move |
| Light breeze | . . . . .4-7 | . .Wind is felt on face |
| Gentle breeze | . . .8-12 | . .Wind extends light flags |
| Moderate | . . . . .13-18 | . .Small breeze, branches move |
| Fresh breeze | . . .19-24 | . .Small trees move, small crests on waves |
| Strong breeze | . .25-31 | . .Large branches move, twigs break, moss falls, wires hum |
| Moderate gale | .32-38 | . .Large trees move, difficulty walking |
| Fresh gale | . . . . .39-46 | . .Small and weakened limbs fall |
| Strong gale | . . . .47-54 | . .Slight structural damage |
| Whole gale | . . . .55-63 | . .Small trees uprooted, much damage |
| Storm | . . . . . . .64-74 | . .More damage |
| Hurricane | 75+ | . .Severe, life-threatening damage |

Hurricanes form over all tropical oceans except the South Atlantic and the eastern South Pacific. A hurricane is called a "willy-willy" in Australia, a cyclone in the Indian Ocean region, a typhoon in the western Pacific Ocean, and a *baguio* in the Philippines. *Hurricane* is derived from the Carib Indian word *huracan* (meaning the "evil spirit"), which is now the Spanish word for such storms.

The Gulf of Mexico and the eastern seaboard produce an average of 10 hurricanes annually. As few as 2, and as many as 20, have been recorded in individual years.

In 1898, during the term of President McKinley, the United States established meteorological stations in the West Indies to keep watch on low-pressure areas and establish a warning system for the U.S. mainland. Today the National Hurricane Center is located in Miami and, aided by reports from ships at sea, hurricane reconnaissance aircraft, radar detection equipment, and satellite reports, weathermen follow each tropical disturbance closely. The months of June through October are considered to be the hurricane season, but late hurricanes have occurred. Hurricane Alice, for example, formed off the Windward Islands in January 1955.

## STORM TERMS USED BY THE NATIONAL WEATHER SERVICE

**Advisory**—A method for disseminating hurricane and storm data to the public every six hours.

**Special Advisory**—A warning given anytime there is a significant change in weather conditions or change in warnings.

**Intermediate Advisory**—A method of updating regular advisory information every two to three hours as necessary.

**Gale Warning**—Wind speeds of 39 to 54 mph expected.

**Storm Warning**—Wind speed of 55 to 74 mph expected.

**Tropical Disturbance**—An unsettled area of thunderstorms moving in the tropics.

**Tropical Depression**—A low-pressure area with rotary circulation of clouds and winds up to 38 mph.

**Tropical Storm**—Counterclockwise cloud circulation with winds from 39 mph to 73 mph. At this time the storm is assigned a name.

**Hurricane Watch**—A hurricane may threaten the area.

**Hurricane Warning**—A hurricane is

expected to strike the area within 24 hours or less.

**Hurricane**—A tropical storm that reaches winds of 74 mph.

**Storm Surge**—Domes of water caused when strong and swirling winds combine with low atmospheric pressure to cause sea level to rise. There are higher than normal waves on the top of the storm surge, but the term "tidal wave" is incorrect.

## HURRICANE CATEGORIES

Hurricane intensity is measured in one of five categories, each determined by the maximum velocity of the winds leading the frontal system. Categories change frequently as wind speeds increase or die down, and forecasters refer to hurricanes as being upgraded or downgraded from one category to another. The categories are as follows:

| | |
|---|---|
| **Category 1:** | 74- 95 mph |
| **Category 2:** | 96-110 mph |
| **Category 3:** | 111-130 mph |
| **Category 4:** | 131-155 mph |
| **Category 5:** | over 155 mph |

### Hurricane Names

Early Spanish explorers named the severe storms they experienced after certain saints on whose special days the hurricanes first appeared. Much later, these storms were identified by latitude and longitude. The next method of identification was use of phonetic alphabet letters: Able for A (the first hurricane), Baker for B, and so on.

By 1953, the weather bureau began naming the storms with female names, still following the alphabet. Origin of naming storms after females is obscure, but some say it is based on the World War II servicemen's practice of naming Pacific storms after their wives or sweethearts. Protests from women became so strong by 1978 that the following year every other storm was given a male name.

Names of minor hurricanes may be reused a good number of years later, but to avoid confusion, the National Hurricane Center has a policy of permanently retiring the name of any storm that takes a heavy toll in lives and/or property.

### Worst Florida Hurricanes

A study of the entry points and direction of the motion of hurricanes passing over Florida between 1885 and 1980 reveals some regions are more susceptible to hurricanes than others. South Florida and the Panhandle are the most susceptible.

**1848:** September 25—Unnamed hurricane entered at the Tampa Bay area and destroyed Fort Brooke.

### Retired Hurricane Names

| | |
|---|---|
| 1954: Carol, Hazel, Edna | 1974: Carmen |
| 1955: Janet, Connie, | 1975: Eloise |
|     Diane, Ione | 1977: Anita |
| 1957: Audrey | 1979: David, Frederick |
| 1960: Donna | 1980: Allen |
| 1961: Carla | 1983: Alicia |
| 1963: Flora | 1985: Elena, Gloria |
| 1964: Cleo, Dora, Hilda | 1988: Gilbert, Joan |
| 1965: Betsy | 1989: Hugo |
| 1967: Beaulah | 1992: Andrew |
| 1969: Camille | 1995: Luis, Marilyn, Opal, Roxanne |
| 1970: Celia | 1996: Cesar, Frank, Hortense |
| 1972: Agnes | 1998: Georges, Mitch |

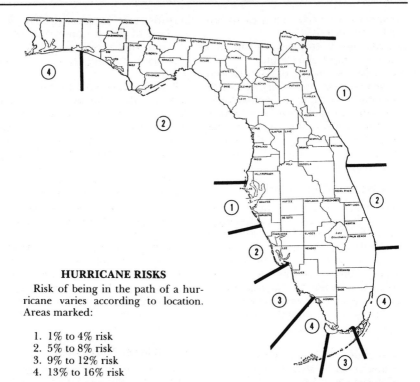

**HURRICANE RISKS**

Risk of being in the path of a hurricane varies according to location. Areas marked:

1. 1% to 4% risk
2. 5% to 8% risk
3. 9% to 12% risk
4. 13% to 16% risk

**1894:** September 18-30—Entered south of Fort Myers and passed across state to exit in Atlantic Ocean south of Daytona Beach.

**1896:** September 22-October 1—Entered at Cedar Key, moving northeastward to Pennsylvania. Claimed more than 100 lives and damage to Florida estimated at $7 million.

**1919:** September 2-14—Classified as one of the great storms of the century. The Florida Keys were severely damaged before the storm died in the Gulf of Mexico.

**1921:** October 21-31—One of the most severe storms to strike the central west coast. Entered at Tarpon Springs and slowly passed into the Atlantic between St. Augustine and Daytona Beach. Adequate warnings kept loss of life to eight persons; damage estimates ranged from $2 to $10 million.

**1926:** September 6-22—Miami, in the storm's direct path, received the worst damage in the city's history.

Three miles of dike along Lake Okeechobee failed to stand against floodwaters of 10-12 feet at Moore Haven and up to 5 feet at Clewiston. More than 250 people were drowned near Clewiston and more than 130 at Moore Haven. Property damage was estimated, statewide, at between $27 and $37 million.

**1928:** September 16—Struck Palm Beach with gusts up to 130 mph. It moved inland over an earthen dike, pushing a wall of water over settlements at Belle Glade, Pahokee, South Bay, Pelican Bay, Canal Point, and surrounding areas. The final loss of life was tallied at a staggering 1,770 by the Red Cross, although the U.S. Department of Commerce estimate was closer to 2,000 persons.

**1935:** August 31-September 8—The "Labor Day Hurricane" that is still considered the most severe in terms of wind velocity, central pressure, and resulting storm tides. It passed over the Keys and moved up the Gulf to enter at Cedar Key. Red Cross estimated the dead at 409.

**1944:** October 13-21—Entered near Sarasota, followed a northeasterly course to the Atlantic south of Jacksonville, and reentered Georgia. This large hurricane extended 200 miles to the east and 100 miles to the west of its eye. Damages were among the highest ever recorded with crop losses estimated at $63 million. Evacuation is credited with keeping the death toll at 18, 9 of whom were seamen who drowned when their boat capsized.

**1945:** September 12-19—Noted for damage caused to Richmond Air Force Base near Homestead, when hangars caught fire. Property losses estimated at between $30 and $35 million.

**1960:** August 29-September 13—Hurricane Donna is rated as second in intensity to the Labor Day Hurricane, with winds gusting to 175 mph. Total damage estimate was more than $140 million, including $60 million to the state's citrus crop. Twelve persons were killed, 144 hospitalized and another 1,000 injured.

**1964:** August 25-29—Hurricane Cleo directly struck Miami and then cut a path up the east coast of Florida and into the south Atlantic states. This storm left an estimated $128 million damage in its wake.

**1965:** September 8-15—Hurricane Betsy entered through the Keys and Miami and exited into the Gulf heading northwest. Before dying in Louisiana, Betsy killed 74 persons.

**1975:** September 23—Hurricane Eloise hit Florida's Panhandle with winds up to 135 mph. Only one death was attributed to the storm, but property damage between Panama City and Fort Walton totaled about $100 million and 17,000 residents in the area were left homeless.

### Hurricanes in Recent Years

**1985:** Eleven named storms blew out of the Atlantic and the Gulf,

killing 30 people. Tropical Storm Bob formed in late September and cut across Florida at Fort Myers, dumping heavy rains. Hurricane Elena formed August 29 in the Caribbean, moved around in the Gulf, and battered the state's west coast from St. Petersburg to Pensacola, forcing the evacuation of 1.2 million people and causing $1 billion in damage. Tropical Storm Isabel came ashore weakly October 10 at Jacksonville. The year's final storm, Kate, hit Florida's Panhandle and killed four persons. The National Hurricane Center called 1985 the worst year yet in terms of damage, with an estimated $4 billion nationally.

**1986:** One of the weakest seasons on record with just six named storms, only one hitting Florida. Hurricane Charley swept across the mainland starting at Florida's Panhandle and emerged off South Carolina, killing three.

**1987:** The first Hurricane Floyd crossed the tip of south Florida with 80 mph winds, doing little damage in another quiet year.

**1989:** Although remembered for Hurricane Hugo, only 1 of 11 named storms brushed Florida, Tropical Storm Karen, which blew through the Florida Straits and gave up.

**1990:** Again, only one storm hit Florida. Tropical Storm Marcos formed near Key West, then dumped heavy rains on St. Petersburg.

**1992:** Only one hurricane made landfall in the contiguous U.S.—but it was Hurricane Andrew. The storm proved to be unprecedented in its economic devastation along a route from the northwestern Bahamas, across the southern Florida peninsula, to south-central Louisiana. With damage in the U.S. estimated at $30 billion, Andrew is the most expensive natural disaster in U.S. history. As a Category 4 storm, it caused 26 deaths in and around Miami, and left 250,000 people homeless. Andrew became a hurricane on August 22. Maximum sustained surface wind speed for Andrew by the time it hit Florida two days later, near Homestead Air Force Base, was estimated at 112 miles per hour, with gusts near 134 miles per hour. Andrew faded away finally by August 28, leaving its mark in the history books.

**1994:** Although fewer tropical storms and only three hurricanes developed during this season, it nonetheless ended with a bang— Hurricane Gordon, which caused massive flooding throughout the state. Tropical Storm Alberto began the season, developing in early July in the Caribbean and later causing an estimated $40 million in flood damage in six Panhandle counties. It stalled over Georgia and killed 31 there. Later in the month, Tropical Storm Beryl brushed into the Panhandle with 35-mph winds and rain, causing even more flooding. In Georgia and South Carolina, Beryl was worse—spawning tornadoes and injuring 36. Hurricane Gordon was just barely a hurricane. Born November 8 off the tip of Nicaragua, it zigzagged as a tropical storm through the Caribbean, killing more than 500 in Haiti before snaking west to east across Florida, where it battered homes and crops. Gordon then meandered up the East Coast, turned around, crossed its own earlier path, and died as a tropical storm again. Its rains were estimated to have caused eight storm-related deaths in the U.S. and caused at least $336 million in damage to the state's agriculture industry.

**1995:** The year was the busiest tropical storm season since 1933 and the third worst since record-keeping began in 1871. There were 19 storms, 11 of them hurricanes. Sixteen of them bothered Florida not at all. But the other three bothered the entire state greatly. The season had just opened when Hurricane Allison appeared almost without warning off the Gulf Coast and stayed there, cre-

ating 20-foot waves and leaving 1.4 million people without power. It finally came ashore at Florida's Big Bend, but was a comparatively light blow. However, to a state still rattled by the memory of 1992's devastating Hurricane Andrew, and with three years' worth of new and inexperienced population, the first storm of the season seemed like an omen. There was nearly a month of peaceful weather but on August 2, Hurricane Erin, which formed just two days before, hit Vero Beach with flooding rains and an unusually high number of tornadoes. Two major ships sank off the coast and 1 million people lost power. Landfall brought a technical lull to Erin, which was downgraded to tropical storm status. Still a fierce storm, however, it kept coming across the peninsula south of Orlando and north of Tampa to emerge in the Gulf of Mexico the next day. Having dropped enough rain to have, in popular thought, single-handedly ended Central Florida's 20-year drought, Erin almost immediately recharged over the Gulf's warm waters, regaining its hurricane status. Expected to continue west farther into the Gulf, Erin instead headed north and slammed into Florida's Panhandle. In 48 hours, it had hammered Florida's east coast, west coast, and south coast. Perhaps because the state ordered the evacuation of three-quarters of a million residents, Erin killed only 11 people. It caused $700 million in property damage. Hurricane Opal formed on September 27, and was viewed from afar as Central America's problem, which, after killing 50 there, would continue heading west. But like Erin, it recharged in the Gulf and headed north toward the U.S. Opal crashed into the Florida Panhandle October 4 near Ft. Walton Beach with sustained winds of 125 mph and gusts of 145. It tore a swath through 120 miles of beaches and brought havoc to Pensacola before traveling on and up into Alabama, finally dying in

North Carolina. It killed 9 more, despite the evacuation of 100,000 coastal residents. In Florida alone (15 counties were declared federal disaster areas) it caused $1.8 billion in damage. It was the third most destructive storm in Florida's recorded history.

**1996:** No hurricanes hit Florida during 1996 and only one tropical storm reached its shores, even though the Atlantic and Caribbean hurricane alleys were their busiest since 1961 with 13 named storms, six of them Category 3 or higher. The season began with Hurricane Bertha roaring toward the peninsula. But after 500,000 people evacuated the east coast, the storm veered north to miss Florida completely, doing damage instead to the Carolinas. It remained quiet until Tropical Storm Josephine, an obscure low-pressure system languishing in the Gulf of Campeche, came to life October 4 and immediately raced across the Gulf of Mexico to hit the underpopulated Big Bend area at St. Marks on October 7. Moving so quickly, it did little direct damage. However, its accompanying rains flooded the Jacksonville area far to the east. Josephine's trailing winds coupled with high tides also caused heavy flooding in the Tampa Bay area. Less than two weeks later, Hurricane Lili threatened Florida. Having killed 8 in Central America, Lili slammed into Cuba October 19. Key West, Florida's island city most vulnerable to storms and closer to Cuba than to the Florida mainland, prepared for the worst, including the prospect of evacuation along the two-lane multibridge Overseas Highway. But Lili never came. Instead it took an unusual track to the east, passing through the central Bahamas before going upward and onward into the Atlantic. Just the near miss, however, brought flooding to an already saturated Palm Beach area.

**1997:** The season got off to a late and lazy start but got serious with Danny, one of the most unusual storms in history. A small disturbance in the Gulf of Mexico just south of New Orleans, it became a tropical storm July 17 and passed over the barrier Grand Isle, Louisiana, leaving heavy flooding in its wake. It became a minimal hurricane the next day and traveled along Mississippi's very short shore before standing off and then entering Mobile Bay, Alabama, on July 19, as its winds passed back and forth over the 75 mph mark. The following day, it finally moved north over land, into Alabama and Mississippi, downgraded to a tropical depression. It had left 30 inches of rain along the way and 41 inches at Mobile Bay, with heavy flooding from Louisiana to the Florida Panhandle. Although its winds were minimal, it left the ground so saturated that its relatively small hurricane breezes toppled big trees rooted only in mud. But the storm wasn't over. Its "remnants" traveled through Georgia, the Carolinas, and Virginia and left floods along its path. When it entered the Atlantic Ocean at Norfolk July 24, it immediately resumed its tropical storm status and traveled up the coast to hit Cape Cod before disappearing in the North Atlantic. The storm in all its aspects had killed six. The rest of Florida got its 1997 quota of rain when a September weather phenomenon put it in the path of an ongoing deluge. Sandwiched between two strong but stationary weather fronts, a low in the Gulf of Mexico, and a high in the Atlantic, Florida became the only escape route for a western Caribbean but non-tropical weather system that poured more than a foot of rain onto the peninsula in less than 36 hours. The deluge overpowered sewer systems and caused coastal, river, and creek flooding. One person drowned and scores were injured, including six downed by lightning.

**1998:** Florida got its first hurricanes since 1995 with the 1998 storm season which saw the state hit by two, Earl and Georges, battered by a third,

Frances, and scared witless by a fourth, Mitch. Tropical Storm Earl formed August 31 in the Bay of Campeche and headed for New Orleans. But off the Louisiana coast it turned 90 degrees and headed east along the Gulf Coast and achieved hurricane status. Traveling parallel to the coast, it brought high winds and rain to Louisiana, Mississippi, Alabama, and Florida's panhandle. A large, gangly, disorganized hurricane, Earl dropped torrential rains on a line between Montgomery and Macon before it even came on shore at Panama City, making it Florida's first hurricane of the season. It killed two commercial fishermen who were within sight of but never made Panama City. Earl also carried an unusual band pattern that formed an extensive eastward tail that whipped Florida's peninsula with storms, tornadoes, and heavy rains even as Earl faded away up the U.S. mainland. Storm damage in Florida was estimated to be relatively light at less than $25 million. A week later, on September 9, Tropical Storm Frances formed in the western gulf and aimed at Texas. But instead of heading west, it went north, causing heavy flooding in Houston on September 11. Like Hurricane Earl, Frances had a very wide band pattern and its eastern side inundated New Orleans and spread heavy rains into Florida's western panhandle. Tropical Storm Georges formed September 16 off the Cape Verde islands and reached hurricane status the following day, quickly displaying all the characteristics of a major and classic storm. Georges hit the U.S. Virgin Islands and Puerto Rico the next day, killing 5. Both were declared disaster areas. On September 22, it continued on to Hispanola. Key West began evacuations, calling on tourists and visitors to leave while they could, over the two-lane highway connecting it with the mainland. There are no hurricane shelters in Key West. The next day, hurricane warnings went up for the keys and both South Florida coasts, and 80,000 were ordered off the Keys as Georges hit the east coast of Cuba and headed west across the length of the island. The storm killed more than 300 in the Caribbean. As wind and rain threatened the bridges of U.S. Highway 1, evacuation of the Keys ended on September 24 with remaining residents told to find what shelter they could. Georges hit Key West at dawn the next day with the eye passing over the city at midday, the first time the city had experienced an eye since Inez in 1966. Both the city and the other keys were hard hit by the storm but there were no deaths or serious casualties. The storm left most of the city's famous houseboat population homeless and the city without power. Damage to Key West and the keys was heavy, with 20,000 structures damaged. A tornado was spawned as far north as Cutler Ridge and 200,000 homes lost power, bringing to the greater Miami area the spectre of 1992's Hurricane Andrew. The rain shield ran as far north as Sebring. On Florida's west coast, more than a half million people as far north as Citrus County came under a mandatory evacuation order and those on the flood-prone coast obeyed. But after passing the keys Georges did not fulfill the worst fears (a direct turn north), but instead slowly continued its west northwest passage over the Dry Tortugas and entered the Gulf of Mexico just far enough away from Florida's Gulf Coast to keep rain, wind, and flood to a minimum. Georges slowly rose up the Gulf, threatening Louisiana, Mississippi, or the Florida Panhandle. It came to the virtual stop, building strength before smashing into land at Biloxi, Mississippi at dawn on September 28, deliving high winds and copious rainfall. Almost immediately, Georges declined into tropical storm status but the rains kept coming. Pensacola, on the eastern side of the hurricane, registered two feet of rain as the storm with steadily declining winds turned into Alabama and into Georgia. Rivers flowing into the state quickly overflowed. The Blackwater River, which floods at 11 feet, ran at a record 26 feet. More than 200 people were rescued by the National Guard on the Florida Panhandle. The Panhandle's barrier islands took the brunt. Dunes only recently restored after 1995's Hurricane Opal were again destroyed. Navarre Beach in Santa Rosa County briefly disappeared under water. Heavy rains continued the following day. On September 30, 15 days after Georges formed, what remained of the eye moved over the Panhandle, drenching Georgia while its last bands raked the northern Peninsula of Florida. Both ends of the state were declared disaster areas. Florida's second primary election was delayed a week in Monroe County. In its more than two week run, Georges caused $2 billion in damage, half in the Caribbean, half in the Keys and northern Gulf. Mitch was not only the worst storm of the season; it may have been the worst storm of the century. It began innocently enough as a low-pressure system in the Caribbean and became a tropical storm October 22, a thousand miles south of Jamaica. That night it became a hurricane and by October 26 it was a Category 5 storm, the most severe, heading north. But before hitting Jamaica, it veered due west and settled in just off the coast of Honduras, where it remained October 27-28 as a 350-mile wide, Category 4 hurricane. Then it came on shore. Although diminished back to being a tropical storm, Mitch dropped more than five feet of rain on Honduras for two more days, killing more than 8,000, with anoter 11,000 missing and presumed dead. More than 1.5 million people were left homeless. The Honduran infrastructure was destroyed and the nation faced both famine and pesti-

lence. In neighboring Guatemala and Nicaragua, 2,000 more people died. Although further diminished by mountainous terrain, Mitch's fury reached the Central American Pacific Coast. Then it turned back and began moving north up Mexico's Yucatan Peninsula, emerging into the Gulf of Mexico as a tropical storm again on November 3. Heading east, it streaked toward Florida, which it hit the morning of November 5. It came ashore near Naples and rushed through southern Florida on a path toward the Bahamas and then out into the north Atlantic. The lower peninsula received five inches of rain in just a few hours but the storm caused only light damage, except at Key Largo where, accompanied by tornadoes, it destroyed homes on the island. However, no lives were lost in Florida.

**1999:** Tropical storms teased technology and fooled Florida forecasters, causing a crisis in confidence in the state's weather warning system. Hurricane Floyd, the largest storm in recorded history, approached Florida and set off the largest evacuation in the American experience. As a tropical storm, Floyd formed September 9 in the Atlantic. Five days later, it was a monster, a Category 4 hurricane with 155-mph winds. It also reached gigantic proportions—650 miles across and covering 170,000 square miles, an area capable of holding five Hurricane Andrewses. While it pummeled the Bahamas, its gale force winds extended across the state and into the Gulf of Mexico and its forces so menaced Florida's east coast that 1.3 million people were evacuated and, for the first time, the entire east coast of Florida fell under a hurricane warning at the same time. Disney World closed for the first time in its history, along with all other major attractions in the Orlando area. But the next day, Floyd passed Florida, raking the coast but doing relatively little damage, causing few injuries and never making landfall. The greatest injury was done by looters along the evacuated eastern half of the peninsula. Tropical Storm Harvey formed September 19 in the Gulf of Mexico. It was a strange, fast-moving, one-sided storm with all its fury in front of it as it headed for Tampa Bay. But in the middle of the night, it turned south along the Gulf Coast, raking it with rain before coming ashore at Everglades City. By the time its eye was over the Everglades, it was producing just a rainy day in Miami. Already burned, forecasters immediately downplayed the impact of Tropical Storm Irene when it formed October 13, south of Cuba. It became a hurricane the next day, hitting Cuba, and October 15 saw its eye over Key West, flooding the island city and causing extensive damage. The storm came ashore at Flamingo at the tip of the state and, still downplaying its Category 1 minimal hurricane status, forecasters plotted it to go right up the center of the peninsula, causing all inland areas to batten down. But when Irene reached Lake Okeechobee, it veered east. It exited at Boca Raton October 16, cutting a very narrow swath on the mainland. However, that brief visit by a minimal hurricane flooded southeast Florida, caused more than $100 million in damage and killed five. Federal and private forecasters were hit by charges that they deceived public safety officials and the public overtly in the case of Floyd, and by never hinting in the cases of Harvey and Irene that they didn't have a clue where the storms were headed.

### 2000 Hurricane Names

Alberto, Beryl, Chris, Debby, Ernesto, Florence, Gordon, Helene, Isaac, Joyce, Keith, Leslie, Michael, Nadine, Oscar, Patty, Rafael, Sandy, Tony, Valerie, William.

### 2001 Hurricane Names

Allison, Barry, Chantal, Dean, Erin, Felix, Gabrielle, Humberto, Iris, Jerry, Karen, Lorenzo, Michelle, Noel, Olga, Pablo, Rebekah, Sebastien, Tayna, Van, Wendy.

### October Busiest Month

Despite their association with summer, tropical storms and hurricanes occur most frequently in October in Florida. The "hurricane season" is from June 1 through November 30.

The monthly breakdown of such storms that have affected Florida from 1885 through 1998 follows.

June . . . . . . . . . . . . . . . . . . . . . . .25
July . . . . . . . . . . . . . . . . . . . . . . .15
August . . . . . . . . . . . . . . . . . . . . .37
September . . . . . . . . . . . . . . . . . . .54
October . . . . . . . . . . . . . . . . . . . .55
November . . . . . . . . . . . . . . . . . . .9

## THE GREENHOUSE EFFECT ON FLORIDA

Scientists studying the Earth's atmosphere and climate predict that if pollution trends continue at present or higher rates for another 50 or 100 years, the Earth will grow warmer. Estimates are that such warming would not have to be much—just three or four degrees—to melt portions of the polar ice caps. The result would be a rising of ocean levels by approximately 15 feet due to ice runoff, a situation that could be disastrous for Florida.

The state could lose up to one-fourth of its landmass if this were to occur. Melting of the polar ice caps would result in, for Florida, wetter summers, warmer temperatures, more flooding, and fewer wetlands. Fish, mangroves, and the citrus industry all would migrate north. Scientists believe the greenhouse effect is now occurring because increasing amounts of carbon dioxide are being released into the atmosphere from the burning of fossil fuels such as coal and petroleum. Projections indicate a continuing greenhouse effect is likely to raise the level of the ocean, thereby increasing shore erosion, inundating coastal wetlands, and worsening flood problems. In addition, certain species of fish off the state's coasts would either die or move to cooler waters.

Most experts fear little can be done to halt this warming trend.

## LOWEST RAINFALL

The lowest average monthly rainfall ranges from 3.6 inches at Niceville in the western Panhandle to 1.3 inches at several locations in southwestern Florida and the Keys. October tends to have the least rainfall in extreme northern Florida, whereas November is the month of least average rainfall in central Florida and along the Gulf coast.

## SNOW FROM THE ARCTIC

A particularly heavy and widespread snowfall occurred in Florida in February 1899. Weather experts have dubbed this event the "Great Arctic Outbreak of 1899."

## HURRICANE FURY

Hurricane experts always worry that Florida residents will ignore weather warnings because they underestimate the power of these tropical storms. Eyewitnesses who survived the September 1935 Florida Keys Labor Day Hurricane, however, record being lifted by winds into trees, and of seeing homes floating off their foundations. Estimated to have been surpassed in strength only by Hurricane Gilbert, the 1935 storm killed 409 people, many by drowning or from being struck by flying debris.

## HORSES AND HURRICANES

Humans aren't the only beings at risk in a hurricane. Horses are, too. Equine safety officials advise that horses should be evacuated 72 hours before a storm is due. Within 72 hours of a storm, however, they should not be moved because livestock trailers are unstable in high winds. Facing hurricane-force winds, horses fare better in large open pastures, ideally more than five acres but no smaller than one acre. Such pastures should be free of debris, power lines, and free-standing items that would fly in high winds. Pastures should have a fresh supply of drinking water.

# GEOGRAPHY

## PHYSICAL FEATURES

Florida has an area of 58,560 square miles of which 4,308 square miles are water. The 22nd state in size, its geographic center is 12 miles northwest of Brooksville, in Hernando County.

Because of Florida's peninsular shape, no part of the state is more than 60 miles from salt water.

The state's highest point, 345 feet, is in the Panhandle, in northern Walton County. Its lowest is sea level. Landform regions have been divided into four sections, but the division between each is hazy. The regions are as follows:

**1. Northwest Plateau and the Tallahassee Hills.** This original flat upland is dissected by many streams. In some places nothing is left of the plateau.

**2. Central Highlands.** At most places flat and at others hilly, this landform is studded by lakes and sinkholes. The four ridges that border this area are thought to be ancient beach ridges.

**3. Coastal Lowlands.** Generally quite flat and covered with flatwoods.

**4. Southern Lowlands.** Of the Everglades type, a swamp-sink flatland. Former beach ridges paralleling the coast are quite common for many miles inland.

## GEOLOGICAL FORMATIONS

The first critical observations on the geology of Florida were made in 1846 in the vicinity of Tampa. The years since then have been fruitful in the field of Florida geology. Subsurface formations have been explored by many deep borings, made chiefly in the search for petroleum.

Floridian Plateau is the name applied to the great projection of the continent of North America that separates the deep water of the Atlantic Ocean from the deep water of the Gulf of Mexico. This definition includes not only the state of Florida but an equally great or greater area that lies submerged beneath water less than 300 feet deep. The plateau terminates at the Florida Keys, where the southern end drops off steeply into the Straits of Florida.

The Floridian Plateau apparently has always formed part of the continental mass, as distinguished from the deep sea. Its earliest history indicates links with the Caribbean islands. This can be seen in the shape and direction of the peninsula today. The geological story of Florida is complex, but for sake of simplicity it can be broken down into six periods:

**1. Mountains.** Hundreds of millions of years ago, south Florida was an arc of volcanic mountains. These ancient precambrian formations were then buried. In Highlands County they are now 13,000 feet below the surface. *(Paleozoic)*

**2. Limestone.** Limestone sediment was deposited on the plain caused by erosion of the ancient mountains. Their weight caused further sinking of the land, and over a period of about a hundred million years, thousands of feet of limestone was formed. *(Mesozoic and Early Tertiary)*

**3. Marls and Phosphate.** The limestone layers arched and Florida rose above the ocean waters. Erosion leveled this plain and it submerged slightly, forming marshes and lagoons. *(Late Tertiary)*

**4. Ice Age.** When the ice sheet covered much of Canada and the northern United States, Florida became cool and rainy. Because so much of the earth's supply of water was piled up in glaciers, the sea level around the world lowered, leaving much of the Continental Shelf (now covered by the Gulf of Mexico) exposed, and Florida became twice the size it is today. Many animals—bears, wolves, saber-toothed tigers, mastodons, and other prehistoric creatures— roamed over this large landmass. *(Pleistocene)*

**5. Terraces.** During the melting and reforming of the northern ice sheet, the sea level rose and fell, cutting bluffs and terraces into the land. The climate was drier than before and winds built dunes on many of the newly-formed terraces. *(Pleistocene and Holocene)*

**6. Florida Today.** The land is still being worn away by rain, rivers, waves, and wind. Underground water dissolves the limestone and forms caves and sinkholes. The land continues to change with the east coast building up and the west coast sinking.

## SINKHOLES

Geologists classify sinkholes into two types: solution sinkholes and collapse sinkholes. Both occur as a result of natural erosion of the state's underlying bed of limestone.

*Solution sinkholes* occur most often where overlying soil touches limestone. As the limestone underpinning erodes, the surface soil begins sinking gradually, the terrain often forming a bowl-shaped depression. A pond or marsh may form in the resultant bowl. *Collapse sinkholes* are usually more violent and occur when an

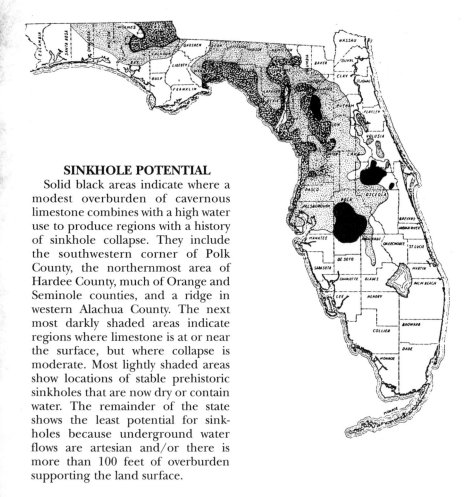

## SINKHOLE POTENTIAL

Solid black areas indicate where a modest overburden of cavernous limestone combines with a high water use to produce regions with a history of sinkhole collapse. They include the southwestern corner of Polk County, the northernmost area of Hardee County, much of Orange and Seminole counties, and a ridge in western Alachua County. The next most darkly shaded areas indicate regions where limestone is at or near the surface, but where collapse is moderate. Most lightly shaded areas show locations of stable prehistoric sinkholes that are now dry or contain water. The remainder of the state shows the least potential for sinkholes because underground water flows are artesian and/or there is more than 100 feet of overburden supporting the land surface.

## ANATOMY OF A SINKHOLE

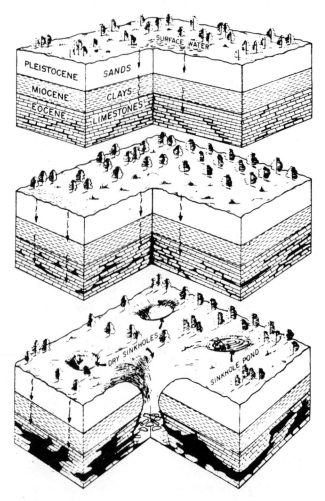

underground cavern can no longer support the ground above it and a hole suddenly opens.

Groundwater plays a vital role in all sinkhole development. During periods of prolonged drought, for instance, a low water level in the supporting limestone may prompt a collapse of land triggered by a loss of buoyancy, gravity, and water pressure. Similarly, sinkholes may occur after heavy rains, causing groundwater circulation in underground limestone caverns to become active and exert pressure on weak joints and cracks.

The area in Florida least likely to suffer sinkholes is south Florida, from slightly north of the Lake Okeechobee area south to the Keys. In this region, artesian pressures are at or above land surface while limestone formations are deep. But any area of Florida is capable of producing sinkholes, for the depressions form wherever the roof of an underground cavern is unstable. Excessive pumping of water during a drought, outside stresses such as heavy traffic, or an increase in heavy buildings can trigger the collapse of an area's limestone support system.

New sinkholes are reported at a rate of 300 to 400 each year in Florida, but most, perhaps 4,000 annually, go unnoticed. Many are less than 20 feet wide and occur in isolated areas. The largest sinkhole recorded in Florida occurred in 1981 at Winter Park. It reached a width of 300 feet and a depth of 100 feet, swallowing a house, six vehicles, part of a swimming pool, and portions of two streets. Damage totaled $4 million. Only one death has been attributed to a sinkhole. In 1959 a well driller was buried when the ground caved in under him near Keystone Heights.

Currently there are no means by which sinkhole development can be predicted. Many Florida homeowners buy "sinkhole insurance," but it is not necessary or recommended in all areas of the state.

---

### THE DEVIL'S MILLHOPPER

Florida's oldest sinkhole, a tourist attraction, is the Devil's Millhopper in northwest Gainesville. Geologists estimate the sink was formed nearly 20,000 years ago. It is 117 feet deep, its sides covered from top to bottom by vegetation. The sink got its name after fossilized bones and teeth were found in the bottom and visitors termed the hole the lair of the devil. Once owned by the University of Florida, the sink and surrounding 63 acres were deeded in the 1970s to the state. The Devil's Millhopper is now a "State Geological Site," the only one in Florida. To accommodate visitors, the state in 1976 built a 221-step wooden stairway from top to bottom.

---

### CAVES

With all the sinks and limestone in Florida, there is only one large cave— Florida Caverns. This cave is three miles north of Marianna in the Panhandle section.

Smaller caves exist near Brooksville, Ocala, and Gainesville. Bat Cave east of Gainesville, Devil's Head east of Lake City, and Natural Bridge Cave in Jackson County are three of the better known small caves.

### SOILS

Florida soils are generally sandy with underlying clay or limestone layers. With the exception of those areas with a high water table, drainage in such soils is good.

Leaching is a problem in sandy soils and soil nutrients must be replaced by the use of fertilizer or cover crops. Sandy soils also tend toward acidity and liming may be necessary for certain crops. Peat is sometimes added to soils low in humus.

The Florida farmer finds that even on mediocre soils, the combination of good till and the Florida climate makes agriculture one of the state's most prosperous industries.

In general, there are eight soil types in Florida:

**1. Western Highlands Ultisols—** Level to sloping loamy and sandy soils, with loamy subsoils that are well drained. Used for field crops, pastures, and forestry.

**2. Western Highlands Untisols—** Nearly level to sloping thick sands that drain excessively. Field crops, pastures, and forestry are primary uses.

**3. Central Ridge Entisols—**Nearly level to sloping thick sands used for field crops, watermelons, and citrus in the south.

**4. Central Ridge Alfisols and Ultisols—**Gently sloping, well-drained sand with loamy subsoils underlain by phosphatic limestone. Used primarily for field crops, tobacco, vegetables, pastures, and citrus in the south.

**5. Flatwoods Spodosols**—Nearly level and somewhat poorly drained sandy soils with dark, sandy subsoil layers. Mostly used for pastures, vegetables, flowers, forest products, and citrus. It is the predominate soil type in Florida, but is considered only good to poor for homesites.

**6. Soils of Organic Origin**—Level, very poorly drained organic soils underlain by marl or limestone. Primarily used for sugarcane, vegetables, pastures, and sod. Located primarily south of Lake Okeechobee and classified as very poor for homesites and urban development.

**7. Soils of Recent Limestone Origin**—Level, very poorly drained marly, sandy soils underlain by limestone. Used for winter vegetables. Found primarily in southernmost reaches of state and classified as poor for homesites and urban development.

**8. Miscellaneous Coastal**—Beaches, tidal marshes, and swamps. Dominated by sloping sandy beaches and sand dunes. Primarily used for recreation and wildlife. It is highly variable as homesites and for urban development.

## BEACHES AND COASTLINE

Sand beaches account for more than 1,000 miles of the state's Atlantic Ocean and Gulf of Mexico coastlines. These beaches continue to be listed by tourists as a major reason for vacationing in Florida.

Unfortunately, a study by geologists in the 1980s found that some Florida beaches lose as much as 28 feet of sand annually to erosion. Although the study also found that the sea sometimes gives back as much as 16 feet at other beaches, the state's beaches are still eroding at an average of 3 feet a year.

No studies have been reported on how much beach is lost on barrier islands that have been heavily developed with hotels and houses. State officials regularly discuss limiting or banning construction on barrier islands but public outcry, particularly by owners of beachfront property, so far has muffled any action.

For decades, the state has experimented with various types of barriers to prevent beach erosion. Tried have been permeable groins, wooden piers, concrete walls, and jetties, but none have shown marked success. The result is that many eroded beaches, particularly those used for recreation, have had to be replenished with sand dredged from off shore.

In the past decade, beach erosion has been most severe in the Panhandle and Big Bend areas. Geologists blame it on a series of tropical storms and hurricanes that have struck that part of the state.

Despite the erosion, Florida's beaches continue to be rated some of the most attractive in the nation. A ranking of the nation's beaches by Florida International University coastal researcher Stephen Leatherman had seven Florida beaches among the top 20 in 1999. Measured were sand softness, water and air temperatures, water currents, safety, amenities, pests, access, crime, litter, and number of sunny days.

Florida's top beach sites were: St. Joseph Peninsula State Park, near Port St. Joe; Perdido Key State Recreation Area, near Pensacola; Cape Florida State Recreation Park, near Miami; Fort De Soto Park, near St. Petersburg; Caladesi Island State Park, near Clearwater; St. George Island State Park, near Eastpoint; and Siesta Beach, off Sarasota.

Bahia Honda State Recreation Area, Grayton Beach State Recreation

*(continued on next page)*

area, and St. Andrews State Recreation Area were each previously named the nation's best beach and are no longer eligible for the list.

South Beach, in Miami, and Clearwater Beach were named among the best "city" beaches; Crescent Beach, on Siesta Key, among the best walking beaches, and Captiva Island, off Fort Myers, among the most romantic beaches.

## SAND

Florida's Panhandle has the whitest beaches in the world. They are made of sand that is 99.4 percent pure crystal that traveled from the area of what is now the Appalachian Mountains to the shores of the Gulf of Mexico at the conclusion of the Ice Age. The stretch of gulf front running from approximately Pensacola to Panama City has become known as the Emerald Coast because of the bright green color of the water over the glistening white sand.

Central Florida gulf beaches are composed of a combination of calcium carbonate from crushed sea animals and quartz. Beaches along the Atlantic Coast are formed by heavy deposits of crushed shell and are noted for their large grains.

South Florida sand is a mixture of quartz and crushed coral.

## AQUIFERS

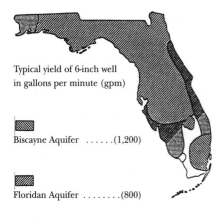

Typical yield of 6-inch well in gallons per minute (gpm)

Biscayne Aquifer . . . . . .(1,200)

Floridan Aquifer . . . . . . . .(800)

Other aquifers . . . . .(300 gpm)

## PRINCIPAL SOURCES OF GROUNDWATER

Studies reveal that Florida has more available groundwater than any other state. This is because nearly all of the state sits atop groundwater reservoirs called aquifers. These aquifers are of two types—*artesian* and *nonartesian*.

An *artesian* aquifer is one that contains water under sufficient pressure to rise above the top of the containing ground formation. A *nonartesian* aquifer is one that contains water that is not confined so that the upper water surface (water table) is free to rise and fall.

Six primary aquifers have been identified in Florida with the state's principal groundwater source being the artesian Floridan Aquifer. It supplies most of the state's water users. Five other more superficial or intermediate aquifers overlie the Floridan Aquifer.

**FLORIDAN AQUIFER** is dubbed Florida's "rain barrel" by hydrologists. This aquifer measures an estimated 82,000 square miles. Only in the westernmost part of the Panhandle and the southwesternmost regions of the state is the Floridan Aquifer's importance supplanted by other aquifers. And along most of the Atlantic and Gulf coastal areas, the aquifer contains highly mineralized or brackish water.

The Floridan Aquifer includes the Lake City, Avon Park, and Ocala Limestones, all of the Eocene Age; the Suwannee Limestone of the Oligocene Age; and the Tampa Limestone and permeable parts of the Hawthorn Formation of the Miocene Age. In some areas the Floridan Aquifer is exposed at the surface, but over much of the state it lies beneath several hundred feet of sediments.

Well yields in the Floridan Aquifer average about 1,500 gallons per minute and range from several hundred gallons per minute to more than 10,000 gallons per minute, depending mainly on well size, depth, and location.

Natural recharge of the state's primary aquifer is divided by hydrologists into four categories:

1. Areas of generally no recharge under natural conditions, which includes about 45 percent of the state. This occurs because the level to which water will rise in a tight well casing is actually above the land surface and thus classified as an artesian flow area.

2. Areas of very low recharge. These are areas where the aquifer's confining beds are relatively impermeable and often more than 25 feet thick. Recharge occurs at rates of less than two inches per year.

3. Areas of very low to moderate recharge of from two to ten inches annually. Low to moderate recharge occurs because both the water table and the level to which water will rise in a tightly-encased well are at or near land surface.

4. Areas of high recharge, which includes about 15 percent of the state. This occurs primarily in well-drained upland areas—porous sand ridges such as are found in western Alachua and Marion counties, nearly all of Gilchrist and Suwannee counties, and portions of Orange and Lake counties. These areas recharge at a rate estimated at between 10 and 20 inches per year.

Additional high recharge of the Floridan Aquifer takes place in areas where drainage occurs through sinkholes, such as in portions of Pasco, Polk, and Hernando counties.

**BISCAYNE AQUIFER** is a non-artesian aquifer that underlies about 3,200 miles of Miami-Dade, Broward, and Palm Beach counties. It is the sole source of water for these heavily populated areas. A highly permeable, wedge-shaped formation that ranges from 100 to 250 feet thick along the coast, the aquifer thins considerably from southeastern Palm Beach County to where it nears the Big Cypress Swamp in the state's southern interior.

This aquifer is recharged primarily by rainwater and from the canal system that extends outward from Lake Okeechobee. Because of its permeability, the Biscayne Aquifer is especially prone to outside contamination. And because it comes in direct contact with the ocean, the aquifer is susceptible to saltwater intrusion.

**CHOKOLOSKEE AQUIFER** is situated in southwestern Florida. This aquifer is recharged largely by local rainfall. It underlies about 3,000 miles of the Big Cypress Swamp and the coastal regions of Collier, Lee, and Monroe counties, where it is the prime source of water. The extreme eastern and southern reaches of this aquifer are most permeable. Urban development and agricultural use is rapidly depleting fresh water in this aquifer and increasing the intrusion of salt water.

**HAWTHORN FORMATION AND TAMPA LIMESTONE** are primary water sources for those southwestern Florida stretches that lie outside of the Chokoloskee Aquifer. It is not in direct contact with the Floridan Aquifer and supplies only about 2 percent of the publicly used water in Florida.

**SAND AND GRAVEL AQUIFER** lies beneath approximately 2,400 square miles at the tip of the state's Panhandle, principally in Escambia and the western half of Santa Rosa counties. It is also a secondary water source of Okaloosa and Walton counties. Wedge shaped, with thicknesses up to 700 feet, this formation is primarily recharged by local rainfall.

**UNDIFFERENTIATED AQUIFERS** are a collection of unspecified water sources that include beds of sand, shell, sandstone, dolomite, clay-like sands, and limestone. These important water containers span Florida's east coast from Duval County south to portions of Palm Beach County, and inland to Hendry, Glades, Collier, and Monroe counties, and on the west coast to parts of Lee, Charlotte, and Sarasota counties. The undifferentiated aquifers are estimated by hydrologists to supply about 7 percent of the water for public use.

## FUTURE WATER SUPPLY

As the state's population mounts, there is increasing disharmony over the state's water resources. Many counties must institute rationing when water tables drop.

Fortunately, the state overall has an abundant quantity of potable water, but supply is unevenly distributed. Meanwhile the demand for Florida's water swells. In 1980 (the latest available complete survey period), the state ranked 20th overall in the amount of fresh water it consumes. It was projected to rise to the ninth-ranked water consumer by the year 2000.

Only small amounts of water are used by people for drinking or for cooking—less than a gallon per day per person. Far heavier is the use of water for washing, cleaning, and removing waste—750 gallons per day in 1980 for each Florida resident.

Not so surprising is the fact that heavily populated Miami-Dade, Broward, Pinellas, Hillsborough, Palm Beach, Duval, and Orange counties used 68 percent of the water withdrawn in the state for public use in 1980.

Irrigation is the largest overall user of Florida's fresh water. More than 2 million Florida acres are irrigated each year using more than 3 billion gallons daily. It is used primarily on citrus, pasture, sugarcane, truck crops, corn, watermelons, and tobacco.

Of total water, both fresh and saline, thermoelectric power generation is the biggest user. In 1980, 16 billion gallons per day were used to generate power in the state. However, of that amount, nearly 90 percent of it was saline. An unfortunate byproduct of this use of saline water is that it is returned to sensitive estuaries. Thus, estuarine life is killed because of the heated wastewater returned from the generating system is often too hot for estuary life survival.

Other Florida industries, the 1980 survey reported, consumed 781 million gallons daily. Pulp and paper production used 210 million gallons per day, the largest industrial consumer. While industry does not rank as the heaviest user of Florida's water supplies, it tends to render much of its wastewater unusable—unable to be purified for reuse or even disposed of safely.

In 1980, Florida's water requirements to support human needs were increasing at the rate of 50 million gallons per day, but awareness of present and future water problems is also increasing. Florida's five water management districts keep a close eye on growth trends and conservation measures. Citizens also are growing more protective of their rivers, lakes, and wetlands. As an example, in 1988 voters approved the Blue Belt Amendment, which would permit a homeowner with high water recharge property to receive a tax break. *(Source: Water Resources Atlas of Florida)*

## WETLANDS

*Wetlands* is a generic term used to describe any of many different ecosystems that are periodically inundated by fresh or salt water. These would be swamps, marshes, bogs, and overflowed lands.

In Florida, wetlands are categorized as cypress ponds, prairies, floodplains, river swamps, forested freshwater wetlands such as hammocks, freshwater marshes, wet prairies, salt marshes, and mangrove swamps. These soggy areas are crucial habitats for fish and wildlife food sources, nurseries, and breeding areas. It is estimated that 20 percent of all the state's endangered plants and animals depend on wetlands for survival.

In addition, wetlands play a major role in improving water quality by trapping nutrients, toxins, and disease-producing microorganisms. Other wetland functions include erosion protection, flood runoff, and storage.

State officials estimate that between 1850 and 1973, Florida suffered a 60 percent loss in its wetlands. That trend continues. Types of wetlands include:

**HAMMOCKS,** a word of Indian derivation that approximates the meaning of "jungle." The essential characteristic of a hammock is its thick tangle of vegetation. Two kinds of hammocks exist in Florida: high (light soil) and low (heavy soil). Both are extremely fertile. The largest bodies of rich hammock lands are to be found in Levy, Alachua, Marion, Hernando, and Sumter counties. Gulf Hammock in Levy and adjoining counties comprises perhaps the largest body of rich land in the state. Leon, Gadsden, Jefferson, Madison, and Jackson counties also have large areas of high, rolling hammock lands.

Trees in low hammocks are predominately cypress. Live oaks, hickory, magnolia, and other hardwoods grow in the high hammock areas.

**CYPRESS STRANDS,** best known of which are the Fakahatchee Strand and Corkscrew Swamp, both in south Florida. With their canopies of cypress, some more than 100 feet tall, the strands harbor a rich range of plant-life including orchids, bromeliads, vines, and ferns. Strands are prime breeding sites for birds and mammals.

**FRESHWATER MARSH,** of which the vast Everglades is Florida's primary example. It is unique in the world. As home to alligators and other animals such as the rare Florida Panther, such wetlands maintain a complex cycle of water, grasses, and fire—all necessary to retain ecological balance. Hardy grasses form muck, which supports other plant life. As water tables fluctuate naturally, these grasses grow wet or dry.

During dry seasons, organic matter decomposes. When wet, the decomposed matter releases nutrients. Gradually the grass humus expands, held in check only by naturally-occurring fires. Artificial manipulation of water levels through use of canals and drainage systems greatly interferes with the critical natural flow of freshwater marshes.

**MANGROVE SWAMPS,** where mangrove plants thrive in salt water and serve as protective breeding habitats for fish and shellfish. The plants prevent soil erosion. In Florida, several varieties of mangroves grow along the east coast from St. Augustine south, around the state's tip, and up the west coast to the Cedar Key area. Once viewed as a developer's headache, many of the state's mangrove swamps have been routinely removed. In recent years the value of mangrove areas has become known and they are protected by law.

**ESTUARIES** abound in Florida. They form when freshwater and seawater combine and are characterized by tidal fluctuations. Spring water gets progressively saltier as it flows toward the ocean or the Gulf of Mexico. Saline "zones" form, each a unique system of plants and animals. Frogs, aquatic insects, and microscopic single-celled plants and animals live near the spring. Jellyfish, flounder, sea stars, and barnacles prefer salty water. Brackish waters in between are home to crabs, tall grasses, turtles, and water birds such as egrets and ospreys.

Florida environmentalists are concerned about the state's estuaries. Because of the salinity zone factor, the balance of natural areas is critical. Problems affecting estuaries are dredging, flood control, overheated nuclear power plant discharges, and loss of spring water to supply growing populations.

## FORESTS

At one time Florida was nearly 90 percent forest. Very little of this virgin forest is left because lumbering was one of the state's earliest industries. Almost all of today's pine is second or third growth, but whether pine or otherwise, about 50 percent of Florida remains in forestland.

Florida's mixed vegetation reflects the state's location on the border of the tropics. Soils, drainage, and latitude are the primary controls over what trees may be growing where. Nearly half of the species of trees native to the United States are found in Florida, but the palmetto and the pitch pine are the only trees found on both the southern and northern borders of the state.

## LAKES

Florida has about 7,800 lakes, many of which are still unnamed. They range in area from mere one-acre ponds to mighty Lake Okeechobee, which measures 448,000 acres.

Nearly all of Florida's lakes are natural, having originated either as sinkholes, as sea-bottom depressions, or as erosion points of rivers. More than one-third of the state's lakes are to be found in just four of the 67 counties—Lake, Orange, Osceola, and Polk. The following is a list of Florida lakes of 1,000 acres or more in size:

| Name of Lake | Size (Acres) |
|---|---|
| **Alachua County** | |
| Ledwith Lake | 1,785 |
| Levy Lake | 4,556 |
| Little Lochloosa Lake | 2,642 |
| Lochloosa Lake | 5,705 |
| Lake Newnan | 7,427 |
| Orange Lake | 12,706 |
| Paynes Prairie Lake | 4,292 |
| **Baker County** | |
| Ocean Pond | 1,774 |
| **Bay County** | |
| Deerpoint Lake | 5,000 |
| **Bradford County** | |
| Lake Sampson | 2,042 |
| Little Santa Fe | 1,135 |
| Santa Fe Lake | 4,721 |
| **Brevard County** | |
| Lake Poinsett | 4,334 |
| Lake Washington | 4,362 |
| Lake Winder | 1,496 |
| South Lake | 1,101 |
| **Broward County** | |
| Conservation Area 2 Lake | 134,400 |
| Conservation Area 3 Lake | 585,280 |
| **Citrus County** | |
| Tsala Apopka Lake | 19,111 |
| **Clay County** | |
| Doctors Lake | 3,397 |
| Kingsley Lake | 1,652 |
| Lake Geneva | 1,630 |
| Sand Hill Lake | 1,263 |
| **Collier County** | |
| Lake Trafford | 1,494 |
| **Flagler County** | |
| Lake Disston | 1,844 |
| **Gadsden County** | |
| Lake Talquin | 8,850 |
| **Gulf County** | |
| Dead Lake | 3,655 |
| Lake Wimico | 4,055 |
| **Highlands County** | |
| Lake Istokpoga | 27,692 |
| Lake Jackson | 3,412 |
| Lake Josephine | 1,236 |
| Lake June-in-Winter | 3,504 |
| Lake Placid | 3,320 |
| **Indian River County** | |
| Blue Cypress Lake | 6,555 |
| **Jackson County** | |
| Jim Woodruff Reservoir | 37,500 |
| Ocheesee Pond | 2,225 |

**Jefferson County**

| | |
|---|---|
| Lake Miccosukee | 6,226 |

**Lake County**

| | |
|---|---|
| Lake Beauclair | 1,111 |
| Lake Dora | 4,475 |
| Lake Dorr | 1,533 |
| Lake Eustis | 7,806 |
| Lake Griffin | 16,505 |
| Lake Harris | 13,788 |
| Lake Louisa | 3,634 |
| Lake Minnehaha | 2,261 |
| Lake Minneola | 1,888 |
| Lake Norris | 1,131 |
| Lake Yale | 4,042 |
| Little Lake Harris | 2,739 |
| Okahumpka Swamp | 3,226 |

**Leon County**

| | |
|---|---|
| Lake Iamonia | 5,757 |
| Lake Jackson | 4,004 |

**Levy County**

| | |
|---|---|
| Lake Rousseau | 3,657 |

**Madison County**

| | |
|---|---|
| Hixtown Swamp | 9,776 |

**Marion County**

| | |
|---|---|
| Lake Kerr | 2,830 |
| Lake Weir | 5,685 |
| Sellers Lake | 1,050 |

**Orange County**

| | |
|---|---|
| Bay Lake | 1,060 |
| Big Sand Lake | 1,110 |
| Johns Lake | 2,417 |
| Lake Apopka | 30,671 |
| Lake Butler | 1,665 |
| Lake Conway | 1,075 |
| Lake Hart | 1,850 |
| Lake Mary Jane | 1,158 |
| Lake Tibet | 1,198 |

**Osceola County**

| | |
|---|---|
| Alligator Lake | 3,406 |
| Cat Lake | 2,080 |
| Cypress Lake | 4,097 |
| East Lake Tohopekaliga | 11,968 |
| Econlockhatchee River Swamp | 4,108 |
| Lake Conlin | 6,281 |
| Lake Gentry | 1,791 |
| Lake Hatchineha | 6,665 |
| Lake Jackson | 1,020 |
| Lake Kissimmee | 34,948 |

| | |
|---|---|
| Lake Marian | 5,739 |
| Lake Tohopekaliga | 18,810 |
| (Unnamed Lake) | 3,778 |

**Palm Beach County**

| | |
|---|---|
| Conservation Area 1 Lake | 141,440 |
| Lake Okeechobee | 448,000 |

**Pinellas County**

| | |
|---|---|
| Lake Tarpon | 2,534 |

**Polk County**

| | |
|---|---|
| Ariana Lake | 1,026 |
| Crooked Lake | 5,538 |
| Lake Arbuckle | 3,828 |
| Lake Buffum | 1,543 |
| Lake Clinch | 1,207 |
| Lake Eloise | 1,160 |
| Lake Hamilton | 2,162 |
| Lake Hancock | 4,519 |
| Lake Livingston | 1,203 |
| Lake Marion | 2,990 |
| Lake Mattie | 1,078 |
| Lake Parker | 2,272 |
| Lake Pierce | 3,729 |
| Lake Rosalie | 4,597 |
| Lake Weohyakapka | 7,532 |
| Reedy Lake | 3,486 |
| Tiger Lake | 2,200 |

**Putnam County**

| | |
|---|---|
| Crescent Lake | 15,960 |
| Levy's Prairie | 1,938 |
| Little Lake George | 1,416 |

**Seminole County**

| | |
|---|---|
| Lake Jessup | 10,011 |
| Puzzle Lake | 1,300 |

**Sumter County**

| | |
|---|---|
| Lake Panasoffkee | 4,460 |

**Volusia County**

| | |
|---|---|
| Gopher Slough | 1,088 |
| Lake Ashby | 1,030 |
| Lake Dexter | 1,902 |
| Lake George | 46,000 |
| Lake Harney | 6,058 |
| Lake Monroe | 9,406 |
| Lake Woodruff | 2,200 |

**Washington County**

| | |
|---|---|
| The Deadening Lakes | 2,538 |
| Pate Pond | 1,045 |
| Pine Log Swamp Pond | 1,056 |

## SPRINGS

The stratified components of Florida's peninsula—mainly basal rock, limestone, and clays—and the unique limestone cap thousands of feet deep that extends over most of the state, provide Florida with a steady flow of fresh water. Tens of thousands of years ago, when the peninsula emerged from the sea for the last time, these rocks and the sandy soil trapped the salt water. But centuries of heavy rains forced the salt below sea level and today Florida's heavy annual rainfall floats on top of this ancient seawater with little mixing. The groundwater collects in the porous limestone layer, forming a statewide underground reservoir. These reservoirs are called aquifers and they underlie almost all of Florida.

Many of Florida's lakes and springs are supplied by these underground aquifers. There are two kinds of springs—the *seepage spring* that is formed when the ground surface dips below the water table, and the *artesian spring* that receives its water through deep fissures or well-like channels that may run 100 feet or more below the surface. The water is forced up into these springs by the tremendous pressures of its accumulated weight in the aquifers below. When this outlet is near the top, the water in the spring bubbles on the surface. Outlets deep below are not reflected on the surface, but the water gushes out, unseen, with tremendous force, at the opening.

Some of Florida's lakes are simply sinks and are directly affected by the amount of rainfall. During dry seasons, the "lake" becomes a pond, a mud bed, or it may dry up completely. These disappearing lakes are common throughout the state. Some lake basins were formed by the sea in low places that were formerly ocean floors, some are fed by artesian springs, while still others are created when the wind cuts through the sand to make a sea level channel to a depression.

There are 320 known springs in Florida and they are found in 46 of the 67 counties. Twenty-seven of that total are classified as *first magnitude* springs. In a first magnitude spring, water flows at a rate of at least 100 cubic feet per second. More than a dozen springs are to be found offshore along Florida's coast. These *submarine* springs simply emerge below sea level and if large enough will create a boil that can be seen at the water's surface. Several submarine springs have been identified in the Atlantic Ocean off Crescent Beach. Six are in the Gulf near Wakulla, 4 lie near Pasco County, and 1 is adjacent to Lee County.

So-called *pseudo-springs* are not true springs, but are actually flows from artesian wells of depths of 1,000 or more feet. There are 7 pseudo-springs, all in south Florida. They are Carlsbad Spa Villas in Broward County, Hot Springs in Charlotte County, Hurricane Lodge and the Mineral Springs in Miami-Dade County, Shangri-La Motel Health Resort and Warm Spring Spa in Lee County, and Pennecamp in Monroe County.

Following are major springs by county:

**Alachua County**
Glen Springs
Hornsby Spring
Magnesia Spring
Poe Spring

**Bay County**
Gainer Springs
Pitts Spring

**Bradford County**

Helbronn Spring
**Calhoun County**
Abes Spring

**Citrus County**
Blue Spring
Chassahowitska
    Springs
Crystal River Springs
Homosassa Springs

Ruth Spring
**Clay County**
Green Cove Spring
Wadesboro Spring

**Columbia County**
Bell Springs
Ichetucknee Spring

**Dixie County**
Copper Spring

Little Copper Spring
Guaranto Spring
McCrabb Spring

**Escambia County**
Mystic Springs

**Gadsden County**
Chattahoochee
Spring
Glen Julia Springs

**Gilchrist County**
Bell Springs
Blue Springs
Ginnie Springs
Hart Springs
Lumber Camp
Springs
Otter Springs
Rock Bluff Springs
Sun Springs
Townsend Spring

**Gulf County**
Dalkeith Springs

**Hamilton County**
Alapaha Rise
Holton Spring
Morgan Spring
White Springs

**Hernando County**
Bobhill Springs
Little Springs
Salt Spring
Weeki Wachee Spring

**Hillsborough County**
Buckhorn Spring
Eureka Springs
Lettuce Lake Spring
Lithia Springs
Six Mile Creek
Spring
Sulphur Springs

**Holmes County**
Jackson Spring
Ponce de Leon
Springs
Vortex Blue Spring

**Jackson County**
Black Spring

Blue Springs
Blue Hole Spring
Bosel Spring
Daniel Springs
Double Spring
Gadsen Spring
Hays Spring
Mill Pond Spring
Springboard Spring
Sand Bag Spring
Waddells Mill Pond
Spring

**Jefferson County**
Wacissa Springs
Group:
Big Spring
Gerner Springs
Blue Spring
Buzzard Log
Springs
Minnow
Spring
Cassidy Spring
Springs No. 1
and 2
Thomas Spring
Log Springs
Allen Spring
Horsehead
Spring

**Lafayette County**
Allen Mill Pond
Spring
Blue Spring
Convict Spring
Fletcher Spring
Mearson Spring
Owens Spring
Perry Spring
Ruth Spring
Steinhatchee Spring
Troy Springs
Turtle Spring

**Lake County**
Alexander Springs
Apopka Spring
Blue Spring
Bugg Spring
Camp La No Che
Spring
Holiday Springs
Messant Spring

Seminole Springs

**Leon County**
Horn Spring
Natural Bridge
Spring
Rhodes Spring
St. Marks Spring

**Levy County**
Blue Springs
Fannin Springs
Manatee Springs
Wekiva Springs

**Liberty County**
White Springs

**Madison County**
Blue Spring
Pettis Spring
Suwanacoochee
Spring

**Marion County**
Juniper Springs
Orange Springs
Rainbow Springs
Salt Springs
Silver Springs
Silver Glen Springs
Fern Hammock
Springs
Wilson Head Spring

**Nassau County**
Su-No Wa Spring

**Orange County**
Rock Springs
Wekiva Springs
Witherington Spring

**Pasco County**
Crystal Springs
Horseshoe Spring
Magnolia Springs
Salt Springs

**Pinellas County**
Health Spring

**Putnam County**
Beacher Springs
Mud Spring
Nashua Spring
Satsuma Spring
Forest Spring
Welaka Spring
Whitewater Springs

**LOCATION OF SPRINGS**

**Santa Rosa County**
Chumuckla Springs
**Sarasota County**
Little Salt Spring
Warm Mineral
Springs
**Seminole County**
Clifton Spring
Elder Spring
Heath Spring
Lake Jessup Spring
Miami Springs
Palm Springs
Sanlando Springs
Starbuck Spring
**Sumter County**
Fenny Springs
Gum Springs
**Suwannee County**
Bonnett Spring
Branford Springs
Charles Springs

Ellaville Spring
Falmouth Spring
Little River Springs
Peacock Springs
Royal Spring
Running Springs
Suwannee Springs
Thomas Spring
Tilford Spring

**Taylor County**
Carlton Spring
Ewing Spring
Hampton Springs
Iron Spring
Waldo Springs

**Union County**
Worthington Springs

**Volusia County**
Blue Spring
Gemini Springs
Green Springs

Ponce de Leon
Springs
Seminole Springs
**Wakulla County**
Grays Rise
Indian Springs
Kini Spring
Newport Springs
Panama Mineral
Springs
River Sink Spring
Spring Creek Springs
Wakulla Springs

**Walton County**
Euchee Springs
Morrison Spring

**Washington County**
Beckton Springs
Blue Spring
Cypress Spring
Blue Springs
Williford Springs

## FIRST MAGNITUDE SPRINGS

| | Avg. Flow Cubic Ft. Per Second | Temp. °F | Discharge Cubic Ft. Per Second |
|---|---|---|---|
| **Alachua County** | | | |
| Hornsby Spring | 163 | 73 | 76-250 |
| **Bay County** | | | |
| Gainer Springs | 159 | 72 | 131-185 |
| **Citrus County** | | | |
| Chassahawitska Springs | 139 | 74 | 32-197 |
| Crystal River Springs | 878 | 75 | * |
| Homossassa Spring | 192 | 73 | 125-257 |
| **Columbia County** | | | |
| Ichetucknee Springs | 358 | 73 | 241-578 |
| **Hamilton County** | | | |
| Alapaha Rise | 508 | — | — |
| Holton Spring | 482 | — | — |
| **Hernando County** | | | |
| Weeki Wachee Spring | 176 | 74 | 101-275 |
| **Jackson County** | | | |
| Blue Springs | 190 | 70 | 56-287 |
| **Jefferson County** | | | |
| Wacissa Group | 374 | 69 | 255-596 |
| **Lafayette County** | | | |
| Troy Springs | 166 | 72 | 148-206 |
| **Lake County** | | | |
| Alexander Springs | 120 | 74 | 74-162 |
| **Leon County** | | | |
| Natural Bridge Spring | 106 | 68 | 79-132 |
| St. Marks Spring | 519 | 69 | 310-950 |
| **Levy County** | | | |
| Fannin Springs | 102 | 72 | 64-137 |
| Manatee Springs | 181 | 72 | 110-238 |
| **Madison County** | | | |
| Blue Spring | 123 | 70 | 78-145 |
| **Marion County** | | | |
| Rainbow Springs | 788 | 73 | 487-1,230 |
| Silver Springs | 823 | 73 | 539-1,290 |
| Silver Glen Springs | 112 | 73 | 90-129 |
| **Suwannee County** | | | |
| Falmouth Spring | 125 | 70 | 60-159 |
| **Volusia County** | | | |
| Blue Spring | 162 | 73 | 63-214 |
| **Wakulla County** | | | |
| Kini Spring | 176 | 70 | — |
| River Sink Spring | 164 | 70 | 102-215 |
| Spring Creek Springs | 2,000 | 73 | * |
| Wakulla Springs | 375 | 70 | 25-1,870 |

*Tidal-affected discharge

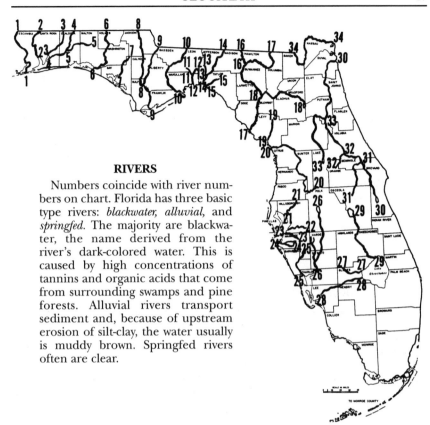

## RIVERS

Numbers coincide with river numbers on chart. Florida has three basic type rivers: *blackwater, alluvial,* and *springfed.* The majority are blackwater, the name derived from the river's dark-colored water. This is caused by high concentrations of tannins and organic acids that come from surrounding swamps and pine forests. Alluvial rivers transport sediment and, because of upstream erosion of silt-clay, the water usually is muddy brown. Springfed rivers often are clear.

| Map No. | River | Length in Miles | Drainage Area in Sq. Miles | Type |
|---|---|---|---|---|
| 22 | Alafia | 25 | 335 | Blackwater |
| 9 | Apalachicola | 94* | 17,200 | Alluvial |
| 14 | Aucilla | 60* | 747 | Blackwater/Springfed |
| 3 | Blackwater | 49* | 860 | Blackwater |
| 28 | Caloosahatchee** | 75 | 1,378 | Blackwater |
| 8 | Chipola | 89 | 781 | Springfed |
| 6 | Choctawhatchee | 100* | 4,676 | Alluvial |
| 7 | Econfina Creek | 36 | 435 | Blackwater |
| 15 | Econfina | 43 | 239 | Blackwater |
| 31 | Econlockhathcee | 36 | 129 | Blackwater |
| 2 | Escambia | 54* | 4,233 | Alluvial |
| 27 | Fisheating Creek | 51 | 436 | Blackwater |
| 21 | Hillsborough | 56 | 690 | Blackwater |
| 29 | Kissimmee | 134*** | 2,945 | Blackwater |
| 23 | Little Manatee | 38 | 222 | Blackwater |
| 24 | Manatee | 35 | 357 | Blackwater |
| 25 | Myakka | 68 | 235 | Blackwater |
| 10 | Ochlockonee | 102* | 1,720 | Alluvial |
| 33 | Oklawaha | 79 | 2,970 | Blackwater/Springfed |

| 26 | Peace | 106 | 1,367 | Blackwater |
| 1 | Perdido | 58 | 925 | Blackwater |
| 30 | St. Johns | 273 | 8,840 | Mixed type with springs |
| 12 | St. Marks | 36 | 535 | Springfed |
| 34 | St. Mary's | 127 | 1,480 | Springfed |
| 18 | Santa Fe | 76 | 1,520 | Springfed |
| 5 | Shoal | 37 | 499 | Blackwater |
| 17 | Suwannee | 177* | 9,630 | Blackwater/Springfed |
| 19 | Waccasassa | 29 | 610 | Blackwater |
| 13 | Wacissa | 12 | 99 | Springfed |
| 11 | Wakulla | 10 | 0 | Springfed |
| 32 | Wekiva | 14 | 189 | Springfed |
| 16 | Withlacoochee (N) | 23* | 2,120 | Blackwater/Springfed |
| 20 | Withlacoochee (S) | 86 | 1,710 | Blackwater/Springfed |
| 4 | Yellow | 61* | 1,365 | Blackwater |

*Distances from mouth to Florida state line.
**The Caloosahatchee is classified a canal because of its locks.
***Before river was rechanneled. The Kissimmee is being restored to its original state.

### THE GREEN SWAMP

One of the last remaining wilderness areas of Florida is the Green Swamp, 850 square miles of wet marshland, sand hills, thick forests, rivers, and lakes in the center of the state. The swamp is bounded by Brooksville, Clermont, Haines City, Lakeland, and Zephyrhills. It is of unique hydrologic significance and the headwaters of four major Florida rivers–the Hillsborough, Oklawaha, Peace, and Withlacoochee. From the swamp's surface water runoff and its base flow comes the initial flow of the four rivers. In addition, the huge Lake Okeechobee and the Everglades are dependent on the Green Swamp through the Kissimmee River system.

Beneath the swamp is one of Florida's greatest water sources. Its underground streams supply 70 percent of all the water used in the state and about 90 percent of the water supply for central Florida. Most importantly, the highest groundwater altitude in Florida is within the Green Swamp, a factor that creates pressure on groundwaters to flow into low-pressure metropolitan areas in all four directions. Without this constant

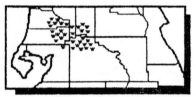

pressure from the swamp, salt water would force its way into the underground caverns or aquifers that hold so much of the state's freshwater.

Much of the Green Swamp region has been set aside for natural water storage, with other portions opened up for recreation. But environmentalists fear not enough of the region has been closed off to development, and are urging the Southwest Florida Water Management District to purchase for the state larger tracts within the swamp. So far, the district has bought 55,000 of the swamp's 544,000 acres.

Besides the Green Swamp's vast underground water reservoir, its visible features also are of immense importance to many Floridians. The region is the habitat of an enormous variety of plants and animals, some of which depend completely on wetlands.

# MINERALS

Florida has a varied mineral base, but most of all there is phosphate. The state is host to not one but two of the world's largest deposits of phosphate ore, enabling Florida to be the supplier of 75 percent of this nation's fertilizer and other phosphate needs while supplying 25 percent of the world's demand.

The smaller of the two phosphate fields is located in Hamilton County in north Florida on the Georgia border. The larger is centered in Polk and Hillsborough counties in west central Florida and spills over into Hardee and Manatee counties. Because of the central field's size and its proximity to Tampa Bay, most of the state's phosphate processing and transport operations are located there as well.

Phosphate, a natural chemical compound containing phosphorus and oxygen, is found in phosphate rock, usually combined with calcium and magnesium. Phosphate also occurs in bone ash and vegetable mold. Given Florida's geology and its ever-changing landscape through the millennia, huge phosphate deposits are no surprise. Phosphates are considered essential for the growth of plants and animals. They are primarily used in the manufacture of fertilizers.

In addition to phosphate rock mining and fertilizer manufacturing operations, firms in the field produce sulfuric acid, phosphoric acid, triple superphosphate, ammoniated phosphates, feed phosphates, recovered fluoride products, and other by-products. There is no synthetic phosphate.

Of the Florida phosphate rock mined, 90 percent is used to make fertilizer. Five percent is used in animal-feed supplements. The remainder is used in a variety of products including vitamins, soft drinks, toothpaste, light bulbs, film, bone china, flame-resistant fabric, optical glass, and other consumer products.

### Florida Phosphate Rock Mined
### (in million metric tons)

| | | | |
|---|---|---|---|
| 1998......34.0 | 1992......36.2 | 1970......28.3 | 1910.......2.1 |
| 1997......32.8 | 1991......36.2 | 1960......12.4 | 1900.......0.7 |
| 1996......35.3 | 1990......35.5 | 1950.......8.2 | 1890.......0.5 |
| 1995......33.8 | 1985......39.0 | 1940.......3.9 | |
| 1994......29.9 | 1980......43.0 | 1930.......3.3 | |
| 1993......25.2 | 1975......39.0 | 1920.......3.4 | |

Because phosphate rock is insoluble, it must be converted into a finished product for subsequent use.

### Major Finished Phosphate Product Production—1998
### (short tons)

Diammonium Phosphate (DAP)............................10,769,666
Superphosphoric Acid......................................662,081
Triple Super Phosphate (TSP) ............................1,274,937
Phosphoric Acid...........................................158,522
Monoammonium Phosphate (MAP) ........................2,340,330

Although 34 million metric tons of phosphate rock were mined in 1998, the rock was taken from only 5,839 acres of land. Phosphate mining companies own outright or hold mineral rights to 495,474 acres of Florida land.

Since 1971, the state has levied a severance tax on the phosphate industry and has collected more than $1.3 billion. In 1998, $60.6 million was levied. A mandated portion of the taxes, the first $10 million, collected goes to the state's fund to buy environmentally sensitive land. The remaining monies go into a land reclamation fund, the state general revenue fund, to the counties in which mining is conducted, and to the independent Florida Institute of Phosphate Research created by the Florida legislature in 1978 to both aid and monitor phosphate operations in the state.

Because phosphate mining scars the land and phosphate mining and processing require vast amounts of water, the phosphate industry is under constant monitoring by private environmental groups and public agencies.

Since 1975, Florida law has required that all mined land must be reclaimed. More than $282 million has been spent in the last decade on mandatory and non-mandatory reclamation projects with mining concerns meeting or surpassing reclamation deadlines. Since 1980, 17 million trees have been planted as part of reclamation projects and thousands of acres of reclaimed mine-owned land has been donated to the state and other public agencies for recreational use. Meeting state requirements, however, is not limited to reclaiming land for that level of use. Reclaimed phosphate land is suitable for residential, commercial, industrial, and agricultural use as well.

It takes 576 gallons of water to mine a ton of phosphate rock today. But in 1991, the same production required 1,185 gallons. Today, 95.4 percent of the water used in the mining process is reused; 92.1 percent of the water used in the manufacturing process is recycled for reuse.

Florida's other plentiful minerals include sand, limestone, peat, and several varieties of clay, especially in Gadsden and Putnam counties, including brick clay, kaolin used for pottery, and the rare and valuable "fuller's earth." Most sand and gravel is mined and moved rather than processed. It also is the handy and economical base of Florida's cement industry. Sand that is processed contains viable amounts of ilumenite, rutile, and zircon.

### Other Non-Fuel Mineral Production in Florida
### (in thousand metric tons)

|                               | 1993   | 1994   | 1995   | 1996   | 1997   |
|-------------------------------|--------|--------|--------|--------|--------|
| Clays                         | 407    | 430    | 421    | 433    | 465    |
| Peat                          | 219    | 206    | 294    | 288    | 244    |
| Sand and Grave (construction) | 22,800 | 16,600 | 19,300 | 20,500 | 19,300 |
| Sand and Gravel (industrial)  | 504    | 540    | 547    | 535    | 515    |
| Stone (crushed)               | 64,900 | 66,300 | 68,000 | 70,000 | 70,200 |

Florida also has some oil on shore, with two fields east of Fort Myers and another, the best known, at Jay in Santa Rosa County. Most of Florida's reserves, however, are believed to be offshore on both the Atlantic and the Gulf coasts. But getting it and getting at it has been stymied by an ongoing struggle between the state and oil producers over whether it should be explored for off Florida's beaches. The state's concerns are both ecological and economic. A major oil spill, it is believed, would not only foul Florida's fragile coastal ecology, it could well ruin more than one season of the state's most valuable tourist trade by befouling its alluring beaches. Oil companies recently have won court victories over a 20-year state ban on oil drilling offshore but the issue is far from resolved.

In 1997, Florida became home to a world's record deposit of one of the rarest minerals, fulgurite. Fulgurite is a glassy tube formed below ground when the ground is hit by lightning. The bolt melts sand, which when cooled forms tubes surrounding the lightning's path. University of Florida scientists carefully unearthed a two-branch fulgurite on the grounds of Camp Blanding. One branch was 16 feet long, the other 17 feet. Recovered in one piece, Florida claimed the world's record. The previous record was held by a one-prong fulgurite measuring 13 feet.

# FLORIDA HISTORY

## EXPLORATION AND COLONIZATION

Scholars estimate the first human inhabitants of Florida arrived about 10,000 B.C. Little is known of these early Indian settlers because there are no surviving written records until the arrival of Juan Ponce de Leon in 1513. Between March 27 and April 2 of that year the Spanish explorer sighted the Florida coast and made landfall in the vicinity of present day St. Augustine.

It is believed that other Spaniards, and perhaps Englishmen, explored the coastal waters between 1487 and 1513, but crudely drawn maps from that era are not conclusive.

The name Florida is credited to Ponce de Leon, who selected it because of the "many cool woodlands" he saw and because the discovery was made during the Spanish Feast of the Flowers.

In 1521, Ponce de Leon returned to establish a plantation colony for Spain. The settlement was short-lived, but it marked Europe's first attempt to colonize the New World. Nearly two decades later, Spanish explorer Hernando De Soto landed somewhere between Fort Myers and Tampa, leaving a trail of dead Indians and sacked villages between that area and the Mississippi River, which he is credited with discovering. He died along the river soon afterward.

While in Florida, De Soto found Juan Ortiz, a Spanish soldier who had accompanied intermediate explorer Panfilo de Narvaez and had been held captive by Indians. Ortiz's knowledge of his Indian captors enabled scribes accompanying the De Soto expedition to elaborate on their Florida adventures. Their notes would provide future historians with their first knowledge of the land's native inhabitants of that era.

Early Spanish explorers and would-be colonizers found neither the gold nor glory they were seeking in Florida, but their efforts were not entirely wasted. The strategic geographical importance of the Florida peninsula in the Spanish dreams of empire gained military and political recognition. Conquests in Central and South America were bringing big dividends of silver, gold, and jewels into the mother country's treasury. To carry the loot to King Philip II, the Spanish treasure fleet sailed from Mexico and other points along the Caribbean coast, following the Gulf Stream along Florida's southern and eastern coasts. But pirates were often waiting for the heavily laden vessels to sail into the Florida straits. Between buccaneers and hurricanes, many of the Spanish galleons learned that the Florida Keys opened the door to Davy Jones' Locker.

Another attempt at colonization in Florida had been undertaken by Spanish explorer Tristan de Luna in 1559. He established a settlement on Pensacola Bay that year, but it was abandoned two years later when a storm wrecked most of his fleet.

Florida's geographical advantages became apparent to France so that in 1562 Jean Ribaut was dispatched to establish a colony for religious freedom from which Frenchmen could prey on the Spanish plate fleet. Two years later, Rene de Goulaine de Laudoniere built Fort Caroline near the mouth of the St. Johns River, known to the French as the River of May.

The intrusion threw the Spanish court into a royal temper. King Philip promptly commissioned Pedro Menendez de Aviles, captain-general of the armed fleet, to rout the French and set up a haven for shipwrecked sailors. In August 1565, Menendez sailed into a harbor he called San Augustin and the following month he established the first permanent settlement in what is now the United States.

Menendez and his troops succeeded in wiping out the French through a series of massacres typical of the period. The French-built Fort Caroline was renamed San Mateo and converted into a Spanish outpost after its capture.

While European armies battled for physical possession of Florida, European missionaries battled for the souls of the natives. Unfortunately, the Indians could not, or chose not to, distinguish a clergyman from a soldier. The first priest known to die for his faith in Florida was Frey Luis Cancer de Barbasto, a Dominican missionary killed by Indians near Tampa Bay in 1549. Despite discouraging losses, efforts to convert the Indians to Christianity were in full swing by 1566. Jesuit and Franciscan friars had hoisted the fallen banner and humbly ministered to their half-heathen, half-Christian flocks.

Meanwhile, in Europe, the French were fuming over the loss of Fort Caroline and Dominque de Gourgues was ordered to lead an expedition to avenge the massacres. He successfully executed both his orders and the Spanish garrison of San Mateo before returning to France.

Spain's loss of the outpost failed to halt its advance in the New World. It established a colonial pattern of forts and missions from Florida to Rappahannock, Virginia. As her power in the New World grew, however, her prestige among her peers was dwindling. In 1586, Sir Francis Drake sacked and burned the Spanish settlement of St. Augustine, and two years later English sailors routed the proud Spanish Armada, paving the way for more British encroachments upon Spanish territory.

## WIDENING HORIZONS, 1600-1800

Despite these losses, Spain remained entrenched in the southeastern portion of North America, prompting the English to concentrate their settlements on the upper eastern seaboard. The English settled Jamestown in 1607, followed by the Pilgrim landing at Plymouth Rock in 1620. In succeeding decades, the English moved steadily southward, pushing the northern border of Spanish Florida closer to the present-day state line. By 1670, the British had moved into South Carolina, making nearby Spanish outposts easy prey for marauding English colonists.

By the end of the 17th century Spain found her position threatened on all sides. The English were moving down from the north and the French were moving up the Gulf coast to the west. Fortifications were built at Pensacola to guard against French encroachment.

England wanted Florida to round out her seaboard colonies, so in 1702 Gov. James Moore of South Carolina set sail with that objective in mind. His forces staged a two-month siege of St. Augustine during which the town was captured, but the Spanish held the well-fortified Castillo de San Marcos. After a futile bombardment of the Castillo's impenetrable walls, Moore's fleet withdrew.

To the west, in 1719, the French captured Pensacola from the Spanish. But the English threat soon united Spain and France and the colony was returned to the Spanish. During this period, the French occupied the Gulf coast west of Pensacola.

Meanwhile, British Gen. James Oglethorpe founded the colony of Georgia in 1732. For eight years it was the buffer between the British-owned Carolinas and Spanish-owned Florida, but in 1740 Oglethorpe struck. He seized outlying Spanish forts and bombarded Castillo de San Marcos. For 27 days the siege continued, but lack of water and provisions, coupled with the July sun and hordes of insects, forced him to withdraw.

Unable to successfully penetrate Florida from the north, the English tried another strategy. During the Seven Years' War (1756-63) England captured Havana, Cuba. To get Cuba back, England forced Spain to relinquish Florida.

England found Florida mostly wilderness. St. Augustine was a city of only 900 houses, and Pensacola in the 18th century had grown little beyond its original settlement. The English did acquire a fort, San Marcos de Apalache, near the St. Marks River, but the rest of the peninsula was largely unexplored.

The new government made elaborate plans to attract settlers. To govern the territory, England divided Florida into two provinces, east Florida with the capital at St. Augustine, and west Florida with Pensacola as its capital. A plantation economy was established and the first Florida exports began to trickle across the Atlantic. For the first time Florida was experiencing a measure of economic and political security.

Elsewhere on the continent, conditions were far from peaceful. British rule was new in Florida and accepted by the settlers who remained, but the citizens of the northern colonies were moving to free themselves from the stranglehold of King George III of England. Throughout the Revolutionary War, Florida remained loyal to the Crown and became a haven for several thousand wealthy Tories. The newcomers established plantations in east Florida and soon assumed a position of leadership in the territory's affairs. But British ownership was not to last long.

In 1783, Spain evened a 20-year score by capturing the British-owned Bahamas. To regain the islands, England returned Florida to Spain.

The last significant event of the 18th century for Florida was the Pinckney Treaty between the United States and Spain in 1795. It set the northern boundary of Florida at the 31st parallel.

## THE AMERICANIZATION OF FLORIDA, 1800-1865

Spain's second attempt to gain a foothold in North America was doomed from the start. British plantation owners left when the Union Jack was lowered, and Florida began leaning toward annexation by the United States. In Europe, Napoleon was threatening the already-weakened mother country. Finally, in 1819, Spain and the U.S. began negotiations to transfer the Spanish colony to the United States of America. Two years later, the Stars and Stripes became the fourth national flag to fly over Florida.

At the time, Florida had some 4,300 inhabitants, nearly all clustered along the coasts at Pensacola, St. Marks, Key West, St. Augustine, and Fernandina Beach. Two or three hundred more settlements were scattered throughout north Florida. The rest of the land belonged to the Indians. Virtually all of the former Spanish colonists had emigrated and the cultural patterns of the settlements were becoming Americanized.

With the lure of virgin land as bait for new residents, Florida's provisional governor, Andrew Jackson, set out to remove the Indians to the central part of the peninsula. As this was accomplished, settlers began to immigrate from both the United States and the Bahamas. In 1822, when the area gained official territorial status, Florida began to grow. A capital site was selected in 1824 and a year later the new town, Tallahassee, was settled by immigrants from Georgia, Virginia, and North Carolina. By 1830 the population of the new territory had reached 35,000.

As in the west, Florida's Indian problems mounted as more and more white settlers moved in. An 1832 pact with the Seminole tribe, which had drifted into Florida some 80 years earlier, seemed to solve the problem when the Indians agreed to migrate west of the Mississippi River. Despite the truce, however, a group of warriors led by Chief Osceola was tired of being forced to vacate their own land. They rebelled in 1835. Indian war parties attacked Fort King near Ocala and ambushed two companies of U.S. troops near

Bushnell. The latter encounter is remembered as the Dade Massacre.

The Second Seminole War (1835-42) was costly to both sides. The ranks of the Indians were decimated and they, in turn, killed about 2,500 soldiers and an unknown number of settlers. In the end, 3,824 Indians and Negroes were relocated in Arkansas. Another 100 or so Seminoles remained hidden in the Everglades. Osceola, who had entered an American camp under a flag of truce, was imprisoned and died in a military jail.

The war over, Florida concentrated on its preparations for statehood. The Tallahassee to St. Marks and the St. Joseph-Lake Wimico railroads had been completed, and the agricultural pattern of the plantation system was established. With the Indian situation resolved, the territory boomed. By the time Florida attained statehood in 1845 the population had grown to 65,500. Most of the leaders who were to fashion the state's future were southern plantation owners.

In 1855, the General Assembly passed the first Internal Improvement Act, which used swamp, overflow, and other land ceded to the state by the federal government to stimulate an intrastate system of railroads and canals. Interest in cross-state canals as a system of transportation had been generated 25 years earlier and the idea still appeals to some Floridians today.

As the slavery issue assumed national proportions, a new national political party arose to challenge the Democrats, but it gained little support in Florida. As the Whig Party disintegrated, southerners moved into the Democratic camp, leaving the strength of the newly organized Republican Party to the northern states. With the election of Republican Abraham Lincoln as president in 1860, the Florida Legislature rushed through an act for a constitutional convention to meet at Tallahassee and appropriated $100,000 for state troops. The census that year listed Florida's population as 140,000, of which nearly 45 percent was black.

Florida withdrew from the Union on January 10, 1861, and the War Between the States began in April. During the next four years, Florida furnished 15,000 troops for the Confederate Army, a Florida militia, plus salt, beef, bacon, and cotton to the Southern army. Another 1,290 Floridians served in the Union forces. Supply lines from Florida to the Confederate forces further north were saved when Confederates defeated a Union force at Olustee in north central Florida. And during the final months of the war, home guards and cadets saved Tallahassee from capture by turning back invading Union forces at the Battle of Natural Bridge. Thus, Tallahassee was the only Confederate capital east of the Mississippi River to escape capture.

At war's end, Federal troops entered Tallahassee on May 10, 1865. Ten days later the American flag again flew over the Florida Capitol. A Florida constitutional convention convened October 25, 1865, to annul the Ordinance of Secession and declare that slavery no longer existed. Nonetheless, a Floridian's right to vote remained restricted to "free white male persons of 21 years or more, but none others."

## RECONSTRUCTION, 1865-1900

The conclusion of the war left the Republicans in power in both the northern and southern states. Florida became part of the Third Military District under a military governor and the state was ordered to draft a new constitution. The 1868 document granted equal suffrage to all races, initiated a uniform system of free schools, provided for an enlightened criminal code, and furnished a measure of protection for workers. It also ended military rule. The civil government was formally reinstated on July 4, 1868, but the state's political destiny remained in the hands of newcomers and newly enfranchised voters.

Eight years later, Florida's electoral

votes were the decisive factor in placing Republican Rutherford B. Hayes in the White House, but the Democrats regained control of enough state offices to end carpetbag rule when federal troops were withdrawn in 1877.

While the state struggled to adjust politically, the people were learning to live without the slaves, who had constituted a large part of the wealth and labor economy of the plantation system. Many former planters tried to reestablish their position by hiring former slaves, but the old holdings gradually gave way to small tracts worked by tenant farmers.

While once prosperous coastal towns and railroads were bankrupt, other industries were born and flourished in the post-war economy—among them were timber, shipping, and cattle. In addition, cigar makers emigrated from Cuba to Key West and then to Tampa. Key West also lost its grip on the sponge fisheries when a group of Greek divers settled Tarpon Springs. Mining became an important industry with the discovery of phosphate in the Peace River Valley in 1881.

An infant citrus industry began spreading throughout the state, but severe freezes in 1894 and 1895 killed or damaged most of the groves. Many north Florida growers were forced to take up other occupations. The freeze loss provided an incentive for remaining Florida citrus growers to develop better and hardier strains. Their success eventually projected the state into the nation's top citrus producer.

As the economic welfare of Floridians increased, the state's natural blessings were attracting a growing number of tourists and sportsmen, many of whom remained to contribute to the peninsula's rapid growth. Florida's population more than doubled between 1870 and 1890, and by 1900 had passed the half-million mark.

The Reconstruction constitution forced upon the State Legislature in 1868 was replaced by a more democratic document adopted in 1885. It made cabinet and supreme court posts and all county offices, except the county commissioner, elective. It created the State Board of Education and authorized the establishment of Normal schools. The 1885 constitution remained the basis of Florida government for 84 years.

## THE 20TH CENTURY

Despite its rapid population increase in the final decades of the 19th century, Florida could not begin to develop its vast resources without an intrastate transportation system. So large land grants were given to men like Henry Plant, who promptly built 600 miles of railroad track, opening the southwestern portion of the state, and to Henry Flagler, who laid lines extending the length of the state's east coast and into the Florida Keys. But neither man limited his interest to railroads; each built luxury hotels to accommodate the influx of tourists his railroad would carry, thus contributing to the phenomenal growth of the state's tourism industry.

By 1917, the state was ready to embark on a major road-building program to supplement the railroads. In 1924, Connors Highway connected West Palm Beach and Okeechobee City, where the new highway met the road to Tampa. Four years later the Tamiami Trail cut through the lower Everglades to join the booming west and lower east coasts. Railroads, too, pushed on during this period with lines being built around both sides of Lake Okeechobee. The expanding transportation system, together with the availability of automobiles, fostered the great Florida land boom of the 1920s.

The boom's opening shot was an advertising campaign that brought thousands of land speculators to the state. It was fired in 1919, by Carl Fisher of Miami Beach. He had dredged enough sand from the bottom of Biscayne Bay to turn a mangrove swamp into an inviting seashore. He then set out to sell it to the American public as the rising national economy was giving them more spare time and extra cash.

As word of the fabulous land and unbelievable bargains spread northward, a restless Yankee population swarmed into Florida to buy, to speculate, and to settle. By the summer of 1925 land fever had become epidemic and Florida had become a coast-to-coast real estate office. Men became millionaires in a matter of weeks or months, but the wealth was all on paper—titles, mortgages, options, and promissory notes. When the bona fide buyers with cash in the bank gave out, the boom collapsed like the bubble it was.

In its wake came the Great Depression that followed the stock market crash of 1929. During the 1930s, Florida's progressive pace stabilized, concentrating on scientific and technological advances to cure old ills rather than to undertake new projects. When World War II broke out, the state became a military training camp and an embarkation center for men and supplies. Many servicemen who were stationed in Florida at some time during their tour of duty returned with their families when the war was over.

In recent years the peninsula that was a pawn in the battles between the most powerful nations of Europe for three centuries has become one of the nation's fastest growing states. According to the 1990 census, Florida ranked fourth among states in population, a place it is expected to maintain with the 2000 census. Native industries continue to play an important role in the world market, and the state has become the nation's leader in space exploration and research. Meanwhile, the famous Florida climate and wide range of attractions continue to make the state one of the most popular resort destinations in North America.

## CHRONOLOGY

**10,000-8,000 B.C.**—First human inhabitants migrate to the Florida peninsula from southern Georgia.

**8,000 B.C.-A.D. 1500**—Aboriginal Indian tribes settle in small communities. Tribes from the north are joined by migrating natives of Cuba and Mexico bringing variations in ethnic culture.

**1500**—European seamen explore coastal waters and islands surrounding Florida.

**1513**—Juan Ponce de Leon becomes the first known explorer to disembark on Florida soil, probably somewhere between present-day St. Augustine and Jacksonville.

**1516-42**—Expeditions by Spanish explorers Miruelo (Pensacola), Pineda (Gulf coast), Ponce de Leon (Charlotte Harbor), Narvaez (Gulf coast north of Tampa Bay), and De Soto (march from central west coast through interior to Mississippi River).

**1549**—Dominican priest Frey Luis Cancer de Barbaso first churchman to die for his faith in the New World (near Tampa Bay).

**1559**—De Luna expedition attempts settlement at Pensacola.

**1562**—Attempted Huguenot settlement at Port Royal.

**1564**—Rene de Laudoniere of France builds Fort Caroline near the mouth of the St. Johns River and establishes Huguenot colony.

**1565**—Pedro Menendez de Aviles of Spain founds St. Augustine and captures Fort Caroline, renaming it San Mateo.

**1568**—De Gourgues avenges the French massacre at Fort Caroline.

**1586**—British adventurer Sir Francis Drake razes St. Augustine.

**1600**—The 17th century becomes noted for the spread of Spanish colonization throughout Florida and up the eastern seaboard, the rise of English interest in the strategic value of the Florida peninsula, and Indian rebellions leading to the construction of some of the state's earliest fort settlements.

**1679**—Spanish construct the first Fort St. Marks (San Marcos de Apalache) at the junction of the St. Marks and Wakulla rivers.

**1698**—Pensacola founded by the Spaniard Arriola.

**1702**—British Gov. James Moore of South Carolina invades Florida and lays unsuccessful siege on St. Augustine.

**1719**—Pensacola captured by the French, recaptured by the Spanish, then recaptured by the French.

**1723**—Pensacola restored to Spain by alliance pact with France.

**1740**—British Gen. James Oglethorpe siege of St. Augustine unsuccessful.

**1743**—Oglethorpe continues raids into Florida.

**1756**—Start of Seven Years' War between Spain and England during which British capture Havana, Cuba.

**1763**—Spain relinquishes Florida to England to ransom Havana.

**1763-76**—British establish plantation colonies in Florida.

**1776-80**—Florida remains loyal to England during American Revolution and provides a haven for thousands of wealthy Tories.

**1783**—England returns Florida to Spain in exchange for the Bahamas and Gibraltar. British loyalists emigrate.

**1785-95**—Spanish-American border disputes precipitate Spain's subsequent withdrawal from Florida.

**1795**—Spain relinquishes its claim to the northern part of West Florida.

**1800**—Spain cedes Louisiana to France.

**1803**—Louisiana Purchase. U.S. claims West Florida.

**1810**—Rebellion in West Florida following Napoleon's brother Joseph assuming the Spanish throne. Republic of West Florida proclaimed.

**1813**—Gen. Andrew Jackson drives British out of Pensacola.

**1818**—Brief First Seminole War centers around Gen. Jackson's invasion of Spanish Florida.

**1819**—Negotiations with Spain to transfer Florida to U.S. begin.

**1821**—U.S. acquires Florida, Andrew Jackson provisional governor.

**1822**—Congressional Act providing for a Florida governor and a 13-member legislature signed into law by President Monroe. William P. DuVal becomes first territorial governor.

**1823**—Tallahassee selected as site of new capital because of its location midway between Pensacola and St. Augustine.

**1824**—First Legislature meets in log cabin near site of present Capitol.

**1830**—Beginning of first land boom with settlers arriving by steamboat. In one decade, Florida's population increases from 15,000 to 34,000.

**1835**—Dade Massacre marks beginning of Second Seminole War.

**1836**—Florida's first railroads begin operation.

**1837**—Osceola captured. Dies at Fort Moultrie, Charleston, S.C., the following year. Battle of Okeechobee on Christmas Day is last major engagement of the Second Seminole War.

**1838-39**—Convention at St. Joseph drafts constitution in anticipation of statehood. Construction of Capitol begins.

**1840**—Florida's population estimated at 54,000.

**1841**—Yellow fever epidemic.

**1842**—U.S. declares Second Seminole War ended; 3,824 Indians and blacks relocated in Arkansas. Some 300 Seminoles remain in Florida and are assigned to reservations.

**1845**—Statehood. First governor William D. Moseley; first congressman, David Yulee. Census lists 66,500 Floridians.

**1849-50**—Coastline surveyed. Sections and townships laid out by General Land Office. Population 88,000.

**1851**—Dr. John Gorrie of Apalachicola patents artificial ice maker.

**1855**—General Assembly establishes first Internal Improvement Fund of $1 million.

**1860**—Following election of President Lincoln, Florida Legislature convenes to enact a constitutional convention and appropriate $100,000 for state troops. First east-west railroad completed between Fernandina and Cedar Key. Population: 140,000.

**1861**—Florida secedes from the Union (Jan. 10). State forces seize Fort Clinch, Fort Marion (Castillo de San Marcos), Fort Barrancas, Fort McRee, the Pensacola Navy Yard, and the arsenal at Chattahoochee.

**1861-65**—Florida furnishes salt, beef, and bacon for the Confederate Army, as well as 15,000 volunteer soldiers, 5,000 of whom are killed or die of wounds or disease.

**1865**—War Between the States ends with Union victory. Slavery abolished, and Florida put under military rule.

**1868**—New state constitution drafted and accepted by the U.S. government. Civil government resumes and Harrison Reed elected governor. Equal suffrage granted to races. Free school system established.

**1870**—Population: 188,000.

**1873**—Despite a depression, 50,000 tourists visit Silver Springs.

**1876**—Democrats regain control of state offices. Internal Improvement Fund bankrupt.

**1877**—Federal troops withdraw, ending carpetbag rule.

**1877-81**—Term of Gov. G. F. Drew ends Reconstruction. Population: 270,000.

**1881**—Philadelphia industrialist Hamilton Disston buys 4 million acres of Everglades to free Internal Improvement Fund of debt and opens way for development of south Florida. Phosphate discovered in Peace River Valley.

**1883-85**—Era of railroads. Henry B. Plant opens the west coast; Henry M. Flagler penetrates the east coast. Both men build luxury hotels to accommodate their rail passengers.

**1885**—Constitutional Convention. Cabinet posts, Supreme Court seats, and most county offices made elective. Normal schools established.

**1888**—Phosphate mining begins. Yellow fever epidemic leads to creation of State Board of Health.

**1889**—Poll tax introduced to hamper black voting.

**1890**—Population: 397,000.

**1891**—Railway mileage increases from 500 miles in 1884 to 2,560.

**1894-95**—Citrus boom in north central Florida hit by frosts; industry moves southward.

**1897**—State Railroad Commission established.

**1898**—Spanish-American War. Army camps set up in Miami, Tampa, and Jacksonville. Thousands of soldiers returning to northern homes advertise Florida.

**1900**—Population: 530,000.

**1901**—Primary election law replaces convention system of nominating candidates for public office.

**1904**—Flagler begins rail line to Key West.

**1905**—Buckman Act consolidates universities into University of Florida in Gainesville, Florida State College for Women in Tallahassee, and Florida Agricultural and Mechanical College in Tallahassee (for blacks). Everglades Drainage District created.

**1908**—Ocala and Choctawhatchee National Forests established.

**1910**—Population: 752,000.

**1912**—First train into Key West.

**1913**—First Corrupt Practices law enacted. Maximum allowable expenditure for candidates seeking the governorship or a U.S. Senate seat set at $4,000.

**1914**—World's first scheduled airline service starts between St. Petersburg and Tampa. Naval air station built at Pensacola.

**1915**—State takes first steps to assume responsibility for highway system. Carl Fisher dredges Biscayne Bay.

**1917-18**—First World War. Florida used for training camps and shipbuilding; 42,000 Floridians serve in Armed Forces.

**1920**—Population: 968,000.

**1922**—First state radio broadcasting station, WDAE, Tampa.

**1923**—Use of state convicts in private enterprise abolished following death of prisoner in a commercial camp. Eradication of tick fever in cattle begins.

**1926**—Hurricane swamps Miami and Lake Okeechobee. The Florida boom busts, presages Great Depression.

**1927**—Maximum expenditures for governorship and U.S. Senate candidates upped from $4,000 to $15,000; for congressmen from $2,000 to $4,000; for cabinet posts from $2,500 to $5,000. Sugarcane plantations at Clewiston begin on large scale.

**1928**—Tamiami Trail opens from Tampa to Miami. Heavy loss of life at Okeechobee in wake of hurricane.

**1929**—Key West-Havana air service marks start of Pan American's Latin American routes. President Coolidge dedicates Bok Tower.

**1930**—Population: 1,568,000.

**1931**—Using part of gasoline tax, Legislature secures bonds for roads and bridges. Pari-mutuel wagering at dog and horse tracks legalized.

**1933**—Chicago mayor Anton J. Cermak fatally wounded in Miami during attempt on Franklin D. Roosevelt's life. Beer sales legalized.

**1935**—Overseas railroad converted to highway. Fred and Ma Barker slain by federal agents in Oklawaha.

**1937**—Poll tax abolished.

**1939**—Highway Patrol created.

**1940**—Parole Commission created by Legislature. Florida plays host to 2.5 million tourists. Population: 1,897,000.

**1941**—World War II begins. Florida used for training camps and recuperation centers, plus shipbuilding and

tooling industries; 250,000 Floridians serve in Armed Forces.

**1942**—Constitutional amendment pledges 2 cents of gas tax for 50 years to retire county road and bridge bonds.

**1943**—Cigarette tax enacted to replace revenue lost on wartime horse and dog racing.

**1945**—Florida celebrates 100 years of statehood. Sin tax increased to provide more money for state institutions and schools.

**1947**—Minimum Foundation Program enacted. Two state universities, FSU and UF, become coeducational. President Truman dedicates Everglades National Park.

**1949**—Sales tax initiated during special Legislative session. State bills overhaul election laws, raise standards for fresh and canned citrus products, and require farmers and ranchers to keep livestock off highways. Jim Woodruff Dam construction begins.

**1950**—Frozen citrus concentrate becomes major industry. Population: 2,771,000.

**1954**—Sunshine Skyway toll bridge (15.2 miles) across Lower Tampa Bay connects St. Petersburg with Manatee County.

**1955**—Construction on Florida Turnpike begins.

**1957**—Educational TV authorized. Funds appropriated for expansion of junior college system and construction of University of South Florida at Tampa.

**1958**—First satellite (*Explorer I*) placed in orbit from Cape Canaveral. First domestic jet airline passenger service in the U.S. inaugurated by National Airlines between New York and Miami.

**1959**—Fidel Castro assumes power in Cuba, starting massive immigration of Cubans to Florida.

**1960**—Hurricane Donna socks the Florida Keys and central peninsula. Population: 4,925,000.

**1961**—Commander Alan B. Shepherd, Jr. completes first U.S.

manned suborbital space flight from Cape Canaveral on May 5.

**1962**—Lt. Col. John H. Glenn becomes first American in orbit (February 20), circling earth three times in Mercury capsule *Friendship 7*.

**1963**—Maj. Leroy Gordon Cooper orbits earth 22 times in final and longest flight of Project Mercury. State constitution amended to authorize sale of state bonds for building programs at colleges and vocational schools, and for conservation. Governor and cabinet elections changed to non-presidential years. President Kennedy visits Tampa days before he is assassinated in Dallas November 22. Cape Canaveral's name changed to Cape Kennedy by presidential decree.

**1964**—Hurricane Cleo causes more than $115 million in property damage. Two new state universities established: Florida Atlantic University in Boca Raton and University of West Florida in Pensacola.

**1965**—Maj. Edward H. White becomes first American to walk in space (June 3). University system Board of Regents established. American Football League franchise awarded to Miami Dolphins.

**1966**—First soft landing on surface of moon by an unmanned spacecraft launched from Cape Kennedy. Claude R. Kirk becomes first Republican governor since 1877. Announcement of $300-million Walt Disney World to be built near Orlando. Hurricane Inez howls across Caribbean, Florida, and Mexico.

**1967**—Three U.S. astronauts killed in fire aboard *Apollo I* on Cape Kennedy grounds. Apportionment efforts by Legislature ended by Federal Court rulings setting boundaries of Senate and House districts and ordering new elections.

**1968**—Constitution revised by Legislature for first time since 1885 and ratified by voters. Republican presidential convention at Miami Beach nominates Richard M. Nixon.

Teachers lose statewide walkout for a school budget increase.

**1969**—Crew of *Apollo II* first humans to walk on the moon (July). Florida legislators vote themselves a pay raise from $1,200.00 to $12,000.00 per year. Florida schools integrated amid marches, lawsuits, and federal threats.

**1970**—Major oil spill in Tampa Bay makes ecology a prime campaign issue. Reubin Askew elected governor.

**1971**—Gov. Askew gets passage of $100-million corporate profits tax. Overcrowded Raiford State Prison scene of the worst prison riot in Florida's history. Walt Disney World opens in Orlando.

**1972**—State's 1968 anti-abortion law is liberalized. Federal panel declares Florida's voter residency requirements unconstitutional. State is among first to hold its presidential primary and Independent George Wallace is top vote-getter. Democrats nominate George McGovern, and Republicans President Nixon, during their national conventions in Miami Beach.

**1973**—Defendants in the Gainesville Eight conspiracy case found innocent of charges of plotting violence during the 1972 Republican National Convention. Florida becomes one of three states to recognize 18 as the legal age. Three separate Skylab missions rocket nine men into space, last of the manned space flights prior to space shuttle vehicles. Miami Dolphins win Super Bowl VII, completing only undefeated season in NFL history.

**1974**—Energy crisis and gas shortages prompt Gov. Askew to lower maximum speed limit to 55. Daylight saving time is enacted to conserve energy. Red Tide hits Florida's west coast causing millions of dollars of damage in fish kills. Legislature grants additional $5,000.00 homestead exemption to Florida residents over 65 years of age. U.S. Supreme Court rules Florida's 61-year-old right-to-reply law is an unconstitutional violation of freedom of the press. U.S. Sen. Edward Gurney indicted by grand jury on charges of bribery, perjury, and conspiracy. Tampa gets National Football League franchise. Gov. Askew reelected. Dolphins win second straight Super Bowl.

**1975**—January jobless rate hits 25-year high of 8.3 percent, by November peaks at 13 percent. South Vietnam refugees aarive at Eglin Air Force Base, number 10,000 by mid-year. Law calls for updated stickers to be added to old license tags. Gov. Askew chooses a black U.S. Magistrate, Joseph Hatchett, for Supreme Court vacancy. Eight Panhandle counties declared disaster area because of heavy August rains. U.S. Senator Gurney acquitted on five felony charges, jury hung on other two charges. Hurricane Eloise hits Panhandle September 23, killing one and causing estimated $52 million damage.

**1976**—U.S. Supreme Court upholds Florida's death penalty. Construction of new state Capitol under way—controversy over razing of old Capitol results in its preservation. New pro football team Tampa Bay Buccaneers fumble way through first season, losing all 14 league games.

**1977**—Florida Senate again rejects Equal Rights Amendment passage, 21-19. Legislature passes bill permitting use of controversial drug laetrile in cancer treatment. Dade County led by citrus promotion queen Anita Bryant, rejects ordinance giving "equal rights" to homosexuals. Sunshine Amendment requiring many state and county officeholders to disclose their financial statements takes effect.

**1978**—Club-wielding attacker creeps into Florida State University sorority house and kills two coeds; police arrest Theodore Bundy. Chlorine gas kills eight when tanker train derails near Youngstown.

Darkhorse Democrat Bob Graham elected governor. Proposal for casino gambling on Miami Beach voted down.

**1979**—State Supreme Court decides interest rates on home mortgages may climb above 10 percent without violating state usury laws. Former Florida Power Corp. Board Chairman Angel P. Perez sentenced to six months in oil-pricing scandal. Chemical-laden train derails near Crestview, forcing evacuation of 5,000 residents. State Supreme Court authorizes use of cameras and recording equipment in courtrooms. Torrential May rain dumps up to 16 inches on Tampa Bay area in 12-hour period, killing five and causing $22 million damage in St. Petersburg. John Arthur Spinkelink becomes 197th person executed in Florida electric chair. Miami jury finds Theodore Bundy guilty of FSU coed murders and the attempted murder of three other coeds on same night. Bundy sentenced to death.

**1980**—Coast Guard buoy tender Blackthorn with 50 men aboard collides with 605-foot oil tanker Capricorn in Tampa Bay, killing 23 Coast Guardsmen. Bundy convicted of murdering 12-year-old Kimberly Leach of Lake City. Freighter Summit Venture strikes Sunshine Skyway bridge across Tampa Bay, collapsing southbound span, spilling Greyhound bus, truck, and passenger cars into bay, killing 35. Four ex-Miami policemen acquitted in death of black insurance executive Arthur McDuffie; verdict spawns three days of rioting in Miami's Liberty city area; National Guard sent in, 16 persons killed, 370 injured. November rain dumps 23 inches on Key West in 24 hours. Mass exodus of refugees from Cuba; 140,000 enter south Florida during the year.

**1981**—Unofficial 1980 census puts state's population at 9,740,000, a 41 percent increase since 1970, earning the state four new congressional seats.

Severe January cold ruins nearly 20 percent of citrus crop. State decides to build taller, wider Sunshine Skyway bridge across Tampa Bay at cost of $215 million. U.S. Rep. Richard Kelly, 5th District Republican, found guilty of accepting bribe in Abscam case. Cocoa Beach condominium under construction collapses, killing 11 workmen. Space shuttle *Columbia* launched April 12 on maiden voyage, becoming first reusable spacecraft. Boatload of Haitian refugees founders near Hillsboro Beach, 33 drown.

**1982**—Hard January freezes prompt governor to declare emergency in citrus industry. Legislature approves increase in state sales tax to 5 percent, reapportions state senate and representative districts, realigns congressional districts to accommodate four additional congressmen, and again votes down ERA amendment.

**1983**—Federal judge upholds state's literacy test requiring that high school students be functionally literate before graduating. Mass murderer Gerald Stano admits killing eight Florida women, is sentenced to death. Jacksonville Bulls new team in United States Football League. Quietest hurricane season in 50 years ends. Record freezes statewide over Christmas holidays hit hard at citrus and vegetable crops. Miami policeman shoots black man in video arcade, setting off three days of rioting.

**1984**—Governor says 1983 Christmas freezes damaged 30 percent of crops in half the state's counties. Report sets citrus loss in 1983 Christmas freeze at $1 billion. Former Gov. Askew withdraws as Democratic presidential candidate. Jury finds Miami policeman Luis Alvarez innocent of manslaughter in riot-causing shooting of black man. Serial murderer Christopher Wilder, a Boynton Beach millionaire, kills self in New Hampshire to prevent capture. Miami opens $1 billion Metro rail system. University of Florida football team

charged with 107 NCAA violations, coach Charlie Pell resigns; team wins SEC title for first time, ruled ineligible for Sugar Bowl because of violations. Infestation of alleged citrus canker spreads through state groves. Orlando's Joe Kittinger becomes first solo balloonist to cross Atlantic. Orlando gains USFL franchise, hires Northern Illinois coach Lee Corso. Three Pensacola abortion clinics bombed.

**1985**—Temperatures hover below freezing for 36 hours in most widespread January cold spell in century. Legislature raises drinking age back to 21. Forest fires burn 150,000 acres, destroy 200 homes, mostly in Flagler and Volusia counties. Rosemary Barkett becomes first woman appointed to Florida Supreme Court. Florida Gators stripped of SEC title for NCAA violations.

**1986**—Seven astronauts killed at Cape Canaveral when *Challenger* space shuttle explodes after launch; all manned space missions cancelled for next two and a half years. Legislature approves Sunday parimutuel racing. Two FBI agents killed and five wounded at Miami shootout. Gov. Bob Graham elected U.S. senator replacing Paula Hawkins. Tampa Republican Bob Martinez elected governor. USFL cancels 1986 football season.

**1987**—Lt. Gov. Wayne Mixson sworn in as governor for three days to fill office between Senator Graham's January 3 move to Washington and Governor-elect Martinez's inauguration on January 6. Miami and Orlando awarded National Basketball Association franchises. Legislature passes and governor signs $770 million tax hike, largest in state's history. Palm Bay supermarket sniper William Cruse kills 6 and wounds 14. State allows 65 mph speed on 60 percent of Florida's interstate system. New state lottery game approved by governor. Pope John Paul II visits Miami. Special legislative session repeals 5 percent service tax. Lawton Chiles announces he will not seek reelection to U.S. Senate.

**1988**—Legislature approves increasing general sales tax from 5 to 6 percent. Willy Darden, 14 years on death row, electrocuted. *Jacksonville Journal* and *Miami News* newspapers fold. Weeklong September rain causes north and central state flooding, seven die. Shuttle *Discovery* launched, first since *Challenger* disaster. Connie Mack defeats U.S. Rep. Buddy McKay for Lawton Chiles's U.S. Senate seat. New NBA franchise team Miami Heat wins first game after 17 defeats.

**1989**—Three days of rioting in Miami's black neighborhoods leaves three dead. Serial killer Ted Bundy, 42, executed in January after 10-year legal battle. University of Florida basketball team wins Southeastern Conference for first time. Legislature in special session declines to pass pro-life bill. U.S. Rep. Claude Pepper, 88, dies in May. Brutal murder of Bradley McGee, 2, by Lakeland stepfather prompts demand for reform of child abuse cases handled by Department of Health and Rehabilitative Services. NCAA violations in University of Florida's athletic program topples basketball coach Norm Sloan and football coach Galen Hall. Former University of Florida quarterback and Heisman Trophy winner Steve Spurrier named as new UF football coach. John Lombardi named University of Florida president. State's worst drought in 27 years brings mandatory water restrictions to south Florida in the fall. Devastating cold front hits state at Christmas, closing airports and interstates and causing statewide power outages.

**1990**—Panama's president, Manuel Noriega, brought to Miami in January for trial on drug charges. Joe Robbie, Miami Dolphins founder, dies in January. Flooding Panhandle rivers in March force evacuation of 2,000 homes. Owners/players contract dispute delays spring training baseball season. St. Petersburg's Suncoast Dome opens in March. Jacksonville gunman James Pough, 42, kills 10 people in loan-office rampage in June, the worst mass murder by a single gunman in Florida history. Roswell Gilbert, 81-year-old inmate convicted of mercy killing his ailing wife in 1985, is released from prison. Five college students in Gainesville brutally murdered by unknown attacker. Iraq's invasion of Kuwait results in massive state National Guard and Army Reserve unit call-up. Nation's thrift scandal begins toppling savings and loan associations, including Miami's giant CenTrust. Florida State University, an independent in college sports, joins Atlantic Coast Conference. Florida Supreme Court upholds right-to-die case. Rock group 2 Live Crew charged with obscenity in Broward County nightclub appearance. Lotto awards record $106 million jackpot. NCAA Committee on Infractions in September places University of Florida basketball and football programs on two-year probation. State gasoline prices soar to seven-year high. Former U.S. Senator Lawton Chiles soundly defeats Republican incumbent Bob Martinez in gubernatorial race. Fall encephalitis outbreak in 27 counties causes 10 deaths among 213 cases. Outgoing Gov. Martinez in November named nation's drug czar. Tampa awarded National Hockey League franchise.

**1991**—Miami-based Eastern Airlines closes. Former Gov. LeRoy Collins, 82, dies. Dale Lick named new Florida State University president. Former U.S. Sen. George Smathers donates record $20 million to University of Florida library system. Legislature approves $29.3 billion state budget, including $164 million in new taxes. New Department of Elder Affairs created. Queen Elizabeth II visits, confers honorary knighthood on Tampa resident Gen. Norman Schwarzkopf. Five Navy bombers found by treasure salvors are determined not to be the "Lost Squadron" of Bermuda Triangle fame that went down in 1945 off the coast of Florida. Leon County prosecutors charge 24 Florida legislators with not reporting dozens of lobbyist-financed vacation trips. Two University of Florida female students found murdered in their Gainesville apartment, Newberry carpet cleaner Allan Davis, 29, is arrested. Miami (and Denver) awarded new National League baseball franchises. The 1990 Census puts Florida's population at 12,937,926, a 34 percent increase from 1980. Amtrak train derails near Palatka, injuring 50.

**1992**—Former Panama leader Gen. Manuel Noriega convicted in Miami federal court on drug conspiracy charges. Four killed by tornadoes in Pinellas Park, with $32 million in damages. Ander Crenshaw, senator from Jacksonville, becomes first Republican senate president in 118 years. Orlando judge grants 12-year-old a divorce from his parents. Hurricane Andrew, a Category 4 storm, slams into southeast Florida, killing 85 throughout its entire course and, in the U.S., causing $30 billion in damages.

**1993**—March "no-name" storm spawns at least 50 tornadoes throughout state. Tides and high winds cause 51 deaths and $620 million in damages in 21 counties. Two Cleveland Indians baseball players are killed and one injured when their powerboat runs into a Clermont lake dock in the dark. Jacksonville wins National Football League franchise. State Attorney Janet Reno becomes U.S. attorney general. Seminole Indian Bingo Hall in Tampa opens 24-hour poker parlor, first in state. Black New York stockbroker severely burned by two men later convicted in the racially motivated attack. British tourist killed at interstate rest stop; four teens accused, with the youngest aged 13. Three-ship collision in Gulf off St. Petersburg spills 328,000 gallons of oil

that pollutes 16 miles of beaches. Amtrak train and gasoline tanker collide near Fort Lauderdale, killing six and injuring 15. Pro-life protestor Michael Griffin fatally shoots Dr. David Gunn at Pensacola abortion clinic.

**1994**—Ringling Bros. circus train derails near Orlando, killing two. Florida State University wins national championship football title. Danny Rolling convicted of 1990 murders of five Gainesville college students and sentenced to death. Florida legislature approves compensation for 1923 massacre of six black residents and razing of Rosewood. World Cup Soccer games held in Orlando's Citrus Bowl. Dr. John Britton and volunteer escort shot to death by Paul Hill at Pensacola abortion clinic. Oba Chandler convicted of 1989 deaths of three Ohio tourists found bound and drowned in Tampa Bay.

**1995**—Gov. Lawton Chiles filed suit against the tobacco industry to recover $1.2 billion Florida had spent in treating smoking-related illness among its population covered by Medicaid over the preceding five years. The state supreme court curbed further the practice of "ambulance chasing" by lawyers. Walt Disney World announced yet another addition to its three parks near Orlando, but rival Universal Studios matched it with its own expansion. Despite budget cutbacks and program uncertainties, NASA launched six shuttle flights from its Cape Kennedy complex. St. Petersburg was awarded an American League baseball team, the Tampa Bay Devil Rays. Malcolm Glazer bought the Tampa Bay Buccaneers NFL franchise from a trust established for that purpose by late owner Hugh Culverhouse. Glazer immediately demanded a new stadium from local government under the threat of moving the team.

**1996**—Cuban MiG fighter jets brought down two unarmed civilian planes in February and killed four

American members of the anti-Castro Brothers to the Rescue flying out of Miami. The action spurred passage of the Helms-Burton Law toughening the U.S. economic boycott of Cuba. ValuJet Flight 592 went down in the Everglades, killing 110. Investigators determined that improperly labeled oxygen generators burst into flame in the cargo hold and engulfed the doomed airliner. It disappeared beneath the swamp; only 36 bodies were recovered and identified. The U.S. Supreme Court overturned the federal Indian Gaming Act of 1988 when, citing the 11th Amendment, it said the Seminole Nation of Florida could not sue the State of Florida for refusing to negotiate "in good faith" on the issue of gambling. Separately, it told Florida to redraw its Third Congressional District, claiming it was racially gerrymandered. The state did and incumbent Corrine Browne was reelected. Racial tension returned to Florida in October when a white St. Petersburg police officer shot and killed a suspected African-American drug dealer in a stolen car following a routine traffic stop, sparking two nights of rioting. The unrest was repeated three weeks later when a grand jury ruled the shooting justified. Declaring that healthy students are better learners, Florida became the first state to mandate the re-inoculation of all students, requiring those entering the seventh grade to take a new round of immunization shots. Florida cast its 25 electoral votes for Democrat Bill Clinton for president but gave Republicans a majority in the Florida House for the first time in 122 years. The Republicans had captured the Florida Senate for the first time since Reconstruction in 1994 and retained it in the fall election. Tampa voters approved a half-cent sales tax increase to boost schools and public safety and, not incidentally, build a new football stadium. The National Football League rewarded Florida by awarding nearly back-to-back Super Bowls to the state with Miami's new stadium hosting the 1999 game and Tampa's the 2001 outing. Citing mismanagement and corruption, the state declared a "financial emergency" in Miami and stepped in with a powerful panel of oversight experts after investigators found the city to be an undisclosed $68 million in debt, with bankruptcy a prospect. The city's bonds were reduced to junk status.

**1997**—An armored truck crash on an interstate overpass in Miami spilled $500,000.00 in cash and $149,000.00 in food stamps onto the roadway below where residents rushed to help. Only $20.38 was recovered. Low-stakes poker rooms at the state's pari-mutuel facilities became legal, an effort to prop-up horse tracks, dog tracks, and Jai-Alai frontons in the face of competition from the Lottery, cruise ships, and from high-stakes bingo games and casino operations run by the Seminole Indian Tribe of Florida. Meanwhile, the Seminoles sued the federal government for failing to require Florida Gov. Lawton Chiles to sign a compact with the tribe allowing it to operate full gambling casinos. Florida gun laws were castigated by President Clinton after a 69-year-old Palestinian, who purchased a semiautomatic pistol in the state after establishing minimum residency, used it to kill one and injure six in a deliberate shooting incident in New York. Tobacco companies agreed to a settlement negotiated directly by Gov. Chiles requiring them to pay the state $11.3 billion and drastically reduce their merchandising in the state. A major maverick tornado hit the streets of downtown Miami, but just the streets. It danced carefully among the high rises before crossing the MacArthur Causeway, doing the same on Miami Beach and heading out to sea. There were no injuries and little damage. As the hurricane season opened with no storm in sight, Florida was attacked by nature anyway. Mediterranean fruit flies and the equally feared citrus canker bacteria struck Central Florida citrus groves; at the same time, southern pine beetles attacked the Ocala National Forest and other north Florida woodlands. Despite the manifestation, a huge citrus crop was forecast. The U.S. Supreme Court upheld the boundaries of Florida's State Senate District 21, held by James Hargett, D-Tampa, allowing it to weave through urban areas in three Tampa Bay counties. Florida's Senators Bob Graham-D and Connie Mack-R came to the aid of the state, which had been stung by court reversals that lifted its oil drilling ban, proposing federal legislation to prevent offshore drilling. Rallying behind Miami, the state put its resources behind the city's effort to host the Pan-American Games as a gateway to Tampa hosting the Olympic Games in the first half of the 21st century. The World Series-winning Florida Marlins baseball team was put up for sale when owner Wayne Hizinger complained he was not making enough money. Key West, claiming a common-law trademark, said it would fight any attempt by Ernest Hemingway's heirs to put a crimp in its image or activities involving the late author. The Rev. Henry Lyons of St. Petersburg, president of the National Baptist Convention, found himself between a rock and a hard place when his wife was arrested for setting fire to a $700,000 waterfront home he owned with another woman. A judge declared "Ol' Sparky," the state's electric chair, to be functioning in good order and to not constitute cruel and unusual punishment. Death-row inmates went to court after flames appeared to shoot out from the head of Pedro Medina, executed earlier in the year. Three high-ranking Florida executives of Columbia/HCA, a nationwide hospital chain, were indicted on federal charges of Medicare fraud. Sentinel chickens alerted health officials to the return of mosquito-borne St. Louis encephalitis in central Florida. A 1990 outbreak killed 11. In what was described as the largest bank merger in American history, NationsBank of Charlotte, N.C., purchased Barnett Banks of Florida for $14.6 billion to create the third largest U.S. bank. The Jacksonville Port Authority was fined by the federal government for dealing directly with Cuba on renewed trade if and when a U.S. boycott against the Communist island is lifted. It marked the first time a government agency was reprimanded for such dealings. In September, the scandal-plagued City of Miami survived an attempt to abolish it when an overwhelming 85 percent of voters elected to keep the 101-year-old city intact. Schools sent thousands of middle-school students home and told their parents to keep them there until they complied with stringent new inoculation rules. The Florida Cabinet, under court order to reconsider its earlier decision to ban the introduction of the oil-tar fuel Orimulsion to the state, sent the issue back to the court for its own reconsideration. The court had earlier approved it. University of Florida football coach Steve Spurrier, already the highest paid coach in college football agreed to a new contract through 2002 paying a minimum of $1.9 million annually. It represented a $1 million raise for Spurrier, whose 1996 Gators were national champions. Forty-year-old University of South Florida fielded its first football team and won its first game 80-3 over Kentucky Wesleyan before more than 49,000 fans. Elvin Martinez, the longest-serving member of the Florida Legislature, retired to accept the governor's appointment as a judge. Possession of tobacco products by a minor became a crime. A "common pocket knife" is not a weapon under Florida law; the state supreme court castigated school officials and dismissed charges against a 14-year-old girl who carried one to school and violated a "weapons ban." Criticism turned to outrage when the Department of Family Services admitted that five children under its protection had died from abuse or neglect within a month. The tobacco industry settled for $349 million the first-ever class-action "second-hand smoke" suit. The action was brought by airline flight attendants in Miami.

**1998**—The year was one of one natural disaster after another: record tornadoes, unprecedented forest fires, recurring blights, and the return of hurricanes. The worst tornado storm in the history of Florida killed 42 people and injured more than 250 in March. At least three nighttime "supercells," Level Three twisters swirling at more than 200 mph, accompanied by at least four other "minor by comparison" tornadoes, travelled in parallel from Gulf to Atlantic and took more lives at one time than any Florida tornado incident in recorded history. Devastated were Daytona Beach, Winter Garden, Sanford, Kissimmee, and Titusville. Kissimmee accounted for most of the dead and injured. Medflies again invaded and despite public outcry, officials took to the skies with malathion to contain them. Despite aerial spraying, the trapped fly count continued to rise. The medfly is a crop-destroying insect able to turn more than 200 varieties of fruit and vegetables into mush. In addition to the aerial spraying, millions of sterile medflies were released into the affected areas. In October, they were declared eradicated again. During the medfly period, scattered incidents of citrus canker appeared in the state's groves. The two are not linked. Despite the blights, the Florida citrus crop was headed for a record $244 million crop, but drought took care of that prospect and forecasts were for a 20 percent decline in the crop instead. The value of citrus groves continued a decade-long decline. Lightning over a drought stricken northeast Florida brought devastating forest and grass fires that just kept spreading, prompting a 4th of July fireworks ban statewide and the evacuation of the entire population of Flagler County and most of the populations of Brevard and Volusia Counties. The mass exodus was prompted when three separate fires moved toward combining into a massive firestorm. The fires, which raged in every Florida county except Monroe, destroyed nearly a half-million acres, including 49,000 acres in Flagler County alone. More than 200 buildings were destroyed. The fire closed a 100-mile section of I-95 and both I-10 and I-4 had sporadic closures. The fires did not cease to be a problem until summer rains began in mid-July. No one was killed in the fires but more than 100 were injured. Property damage was more than $392 million. Despite disaster and adversity, Florida drew a record 48 million visitors during the year. Jeb Bush, who narrowly lost the governorship to Lawton Chiles eight years before, won a landslide victory for the office over Lt. Gov. Buddy MacKay, giving the Republicans both the governor's office and both houses of the legislature for the first time since Reconstruction. MacKay, however, did become governor for 23 days when Chiles died in December. Floridians, who have historically declined to change their constitution via popular vote, swept a dozen amendments on the ballot into the basic charter and fundamentally changed both Florida's unique form of government by eliminating half the statewide elected Cabinet offices and its traditional politics by opening its primaries. Judi Buenoano was executed 27 years after she killed her husband with arsenic to gain his insurance money, the first women to be executed by the state in 150 years. Florida attorney general Bob Butterworth warned American Family Publishers to stop mailing "deceptive" and "reprehensible" sweepstakes pitches from the state and to its residents. He said the letters informed people that they were "winners" when they were not. Major sweepstakes are operated from Tampa. When nothing much happened, Butterworth declared that American Family Publishers had crossed the line into "unlawful deception" and sued the company, Time Customer Service, and two celebrity spokesmen, Ed McMahan and Dick Clark, seeking millions of dollars in fines. Former Miami police officer Grant Snowden, once "Officer of the Year," was freed after serving 12 years in prison on a sexual abuse conviction that a federal appeals court discredited and overturned. His conviction, in 1986, came at the height of nationwide sexual child abuse hysteria. He was prosecuted by now U.S. Attorney General Janet Reno. Freddie Lee Pitts and Wilbert Lee, two Floridians who spent 12 years in prison after twice being wrongfully convicted of murder, were awarded $500,000.00 each plus legal expenses authorized by the Legislature. They were pardoned by Gov. Reubin Askew in 1975. Lawrence Singleton, accused of killing a Tampa prostitute and known to be the man who raped a California teen-ager, cutting off her arms with an ax and leaving her to die, was found guilty and was sentenced to death. The Rev. Henry Lyons of St. Petersburg, president of the National Baptist Convention, was indicted by the State of Florida on a three-count information alleging theft, swindle, and extortion. Lyons, who declined to resign from his post as head of the nation's largest black religious organization, was then indicted on 56 counts by a federal grand jury. Adam Herbert is the first African-American to be named chancellor of the state university system. A U.S. Senate committee rejected Florida State Senator Daryl Jones, nominated by President Clinton to be Secretary of the Air Force. The Senate approved former university regent Paul L. Cejas as ambassador to Belgium. Joe Carollo convinced an appeals court that massive absentee voter fraud robbed him of the office he should have won outright in 1997 and took the reins as mayor of Miami, ousting former mayor Xavier Suarez. Carollo won the first primary but was 155 votes short of the majority needed to avoid a runoff. Suarez had won the absentee vote by a 2-1 ratio in the primary, depriving Carollo of the primary win. Suarez then took the runoff on election day. Suarez spent four months in office and his tenure was described as erratic. He declared the city's financial emergency a "fantasy," although the city continues to operate under state oversight. The court saw no doubt that there was election fraud involved in the absentee voting. A lower court had previously seen it, too, and had ordered a new election. The appeals court nixed an election by throwing out 5,000 absentee ballots and installed Carollo. The Florida Supreme Court affirmed the ruling, leaving Carollo in office for the full term through 2001. There was no evidence linking Suarez to the fraud. The court action did not stop a state investigation of the election or prevent a variety of vote integrity safeguards from being installed around the state. The Legislature mandated classical music be played every day in all state-funded childcare and educational programs. Shoppers welcomed a sales tax holiday on clothes for a week just before school started. New laws made more than a quarter of a million children eligible for state-subsidized healthcare, increased the minimum intangible property tax required to actually trigger payment, thus removing 180,000 Floridians from the burden, renewed a requirement passed after Hurricane Andrew preventing property insurance companies from dropping more than 5 percent of their customers in a given year, made a false report of child abuse a felony, and required law enforcement to notify day care centers within 48 hours if a sexual predator takes up residence within a mile of them. Trial in a class action suit involving 100,000-200,000 people against the tobacco industry got underway. Sought was $25 billion in compensatory and punitive damages. The state opened negotiations with the tobacco industry to collect an additional $1.7 billion under a provision of their tobacco settlement allowing the state to collect more if other states did. The state continued to battle lawyers who represented it over the $257 million they say they are owed. Florida learned it would not get to levy a tax or clamp down for bootlegging on out-of-state firms selling beer and wine to Floridians via mail order. The 11th U.S. Circuit Court of Appeals denied the state access to federal courts on the matter. The governor's decision to allow a Jai-Alai tax reform to become law came too late for the Tampa fronton, which closed after 45 years. St. Petersburg's Sunken Gardens, was put on the sales block for development. But the city declared the property, which has drawn tourists for decades, a historic site, hampering any transaction. The giant Knight-Ridder newspaper company, owner of the *Miami Herald* and one of only two Fortune 500 companies in south Florida, announced it would abandon its Miami headquarters for one in California where it owns the *San Jose Mercury News*. Walt Disney World opened its fourth theme park, the $800 million Animal Kingdom, and became the largest employer of staff in one place with 50,000 workers. Rival Universal Studios, meanwhile, readied its $1-billion Islands of Adventure park, with plans for two more Orlando parks early in the next century. Down the road, Anhauser-Busch's Sea World

announced it, too, would add a new interactive theme park adjacent to its present facility. Pepsi entered the juice market against Coca-Cola's Minute Maid brand by purchasing Bradenton's Tropicana from Seagram's. Tropicana controls 40 percent of the market. America's first orbiting astronaut, John Glenn, 77, returned to space aboard the shuttle *Discovery*. A nine-year-old boy was taken by a shark off Vero Beach, the first shark death in Florida waters in a decade. The state received a $4.1 million grant through the National Oceanographic and Atmospheric Administration to find a way to predict the appearance of red tide. The Florida Cabinet again rejected Orimulsion as a power plant fuel in Florida and Florida Power and Light, the advocate, announced it would no longer pursue the program. Democratic U.S. Senator Bob Graham and Republic Senator Connie Mack proposed federal legislation to keep oil companies seeking to drill off Florida's coasts at bay. Scientists could not explain the appearance of a band of cold water off the Panhandle coast in mid-summer that produced fish kills. The state told the City of St. Petersburg it wants to purchase 454 acres of land in Hernando County, which includes Weeki Wachee Springs, to ensure the springs and its surroundings remain in public hands. The springs, home to the popular "mermaid" tourist attraction, would remain that, at least until 2020, when the 50-year-old attraction's lease expires. St. Petersburg bought the springs more than 60 years ago to ensure its water supply. The Seminole Tribe of Florida, frustrated in its efforts to expand its casino operations and despairing of federal intervention, offered the state a 45 percent share of the profits if it would allow the tribe to convert their high-stakes bingo halls in Tampa, Immokolee, Hollywood, and Brighton into full casinos and allow the tribe to expand its gambling operations to Miami, Orlando, Jacksonville, and Coconut Creek. Governor Lawton Chiles warned U.S. Secretary of the Interior Bruce Babbitt, who could grant the Seminoles' wish under federal rules, to stay out of the state's business. Pensacola launched a year-long celebration of its founding 440 years ago and its refounding 300 years ago. Marjory Stoneman Douglas, 108-year-old grande dame credited with saving the Everglades and effectively starting the modern conservation movement with her book, *River of Grass,* died at her Miami home. The FBI arrested eight men and two women in Miami on charges of spying for Cuba. It was the first breaking of a Cuban spy ring in the 40 years of hostility between the U.S. and Communist Cuba. The FBI said the ring was a Havana-run counterintelligence operation engaging in infiltrating and monitoring U.S. military facilities and operations in Florida. The U.S. Coast Guard declared virtually all of peninsula Florida's coast a "security zone" requiring all boats of less than 150 ft. in length to get a permit to make trips to Cuba. A major fire endangered more than 2,500 people aboard the 12-story, $275 million *Ecstasy* cruise ship. No passengers were injured but 50 crewmembers suffered smoke inhalation. The ship's proximity to land, just off its Miami port, to rescuers, and fire fighting equipment saved both the ship and the passengers, officials said. The drama played off Miami Beach. Despite warnings, rip tides off Daytona Beach forced lifeguards to rescue 421 swimmers in two days. The previous rescue high at Daytona Beach was set in 1976 when nearly 400 were pulled from the surf in one day. Daytona's Volusia County employs more than 200 lifeguards. Miss Florida Lissette Gonzalez may not have won the 1998 Miss America title but a Floridian took the prize anyway. Nicole Johnson, of Seminole in Pinellas County, competing as Miss

Virginia, won the title. In baseball, the Tampa Bay Devil Rays began play in the American League, while in the National League, the World Champion Florida Marlins went from first to worst after trading away most of the members of its winning team. Jacksonville University opened its inaugural football season.

**1999**—The first week of the year greeted Floridians with the coldest weather in three years, with a hard freeze in central Florida. Jeb Bush was sworn in as only the third Republican governor of the 20th Century, and the first with a Republican legislature since Reconstruction. The legislature then passed a $48.9 billion dollar budget, including a billion dollar tax cut, declared a second-annual and extended "sales tax holiday," and allocated billions more in spending for education and social services. The Republicans also honored late Democratic Gov. Lawton Chiles by establishing both the Lawton Chiles Trail, commemorating the late Democratic governor's famous "Walkin' Lawton" campaign walk from Pensacola to Key Largo, and a $1.7 billion Lawton Chiles Endowment, based on the $13-billion tobacco company settlement personally negotiated by Chiles. Earnings from the fund will perpetually fund health needs and research. Florida's radical, new, and already famous education voucher plan was inaugurated, grading schools and allowing children in failing schools to take state money with them if they wished to change schools, public or private. Two Pensacola schools were judged to have failed, but less than 100 children chose to take the vouchers and make a move. Of those, approximately half went to other public schools, while the others choose private facilities. According to the 1999 evaluations, nearly 80 other public schools were in dire danger of being declared failures in 2000. Taking advantage of another option offered by the legislature, two entire school districts, Hillsborough and Volusia, became the nation's first "charter school districts," allowing them to operate outside the traditional norms. Polk County mandated a strict school uniform policy for elementary and middle school students, with no options for parents. Although considered rural, Polk administers the nation's 45th largest school district and the policy affects more than 60,000 students. In an effort to hire more minority teachers, Palm Beach County schools recruited six new teachers from Spain. The Florida Supreme Court upheld a 1992 amendment vote to limit the terms of state legislators, and the cabinet and Lieutenant Governor to no more than eight consecutive years. Forty percent of the legislature will not be allowed on the ballot for re-election in 2000. Popular Republican U.S. Senator Connie Mack surprised all with an announcement that he would not seek another term in 2000, setting off a flurry of activity in both parties. President Clinton named short-term former Gov. Buddy MacKay a special envoy to Latin America. Former Florida House Speaker Volley ("Bo") Johnson was convicted, along with his wife, for failing to report income from lobbyists during his term. The judge turned away the pleas of "good character" witnesses and sentenced him to 2 years in prison; his wife received 15 months. The judge said they committed crimes, not errors. Florida's most famous piece of furniture, the 76-year-old "Ol' Sparky", the electric chair, was retired. The concept was not. "New Sparky" is bigger and sturdier, to accommodate today's larger death-row inmates and said to be "more comfortable." One woman and 237 men sat in the fatal seat. Four women and 370 men were scheduled to use the new version. The first to die on the new furniture was 344-pound Allen Lee Davis. His nosebleed on execution set off a new "cruel and unusual" debate. The state Supreme Court ruled, again, the method constitutional. The U.S. Supreme Court, however, agreed to hear the argument that the chair constituted cruel and unusual punishment, effectively ending capital punishment in the state until it does. Seven death-row inmates had died, but only Davis from execution. Five died of natural causes, and 1 in an altercation with guards. The high court granted a new trial to a man convicted of a murder-for-hire scheme and told the prosecutors it was getting tired of having to grant new trials and overturning convictions because of "egregious and inexcusable prosecutorial misconduct." In addition, the court complained, it found trial errors in 83 percent of first-time death penalty appeals, up from 77 percent in 1998. It also ruled that a man mugged while changing a tire is covered by his auto insurance. Attacks "are an ageless and foreseeable hazard associated with the use of a vehicle." Justice Leander Shaw harkened to the dangers faced by vulnerable wayfarers from highwaymen and desperados and "these villains are with us still." Rev. Henry Lyons of St. Petersburg resigned from his post as president of the National Baptist Convention after being found guilty in state court of racketeering and grand theft. He was sentenced to 5½ years in state prison. He pleaded guilty to five federal counts as well under a plea bargain, and received 51 months under the federal charges to run concurrently with his state sentence. He was also ordered to make $5.25 million in restitution. Meeting in Tampa, the convention elected Rev. William J. Shaw of Philadelphia to replace Lyons. Brazil's economic problems worried state businessmen. Brazil is Florida's largest foreign trading partner, accounting for 20 percent of the state's exports and 3 percent of its economy. Brazil is also a major tourist provider to Florida. Attractions offered discount deals to Canadians similar to those made to

Florida residents when the annual migration of "Snowbirds" was crimped by a weak Canadian economy and a falling Canadian dollar. St. Joe Company of Jacksonville, the state's largest private landowner, said it would sell 800,000 of its 1 million acres of timberland in northwest Florida. The huge land package was put together by Alfred I. DuPont and his brother-in-law, power-broker Ed Ball, following the bust of the Florida Boom in 1926. Carolina Power & Light of Raleigh bought Florida Progress, parent company of Florida Power, the state's second largest and most expensive electric utility, with 1.3 million customers, for $5.3 billion. Archeologists poured over an Indian stone circle amidst Miami office buildings and towering apartments near the mouth of the Miami River. Either Tequestas or breakaway Mayans were thought to be responsible for the site. Believed to date from 1100 A.D., with probable religious significance, artifacts indicate it was also and perhaps exclusively a trade center when Miami was a major pre-Columbian port. The county stopped development of the site and the state is negotiating to buy it. Meanwhile, the state filed suit against the federal Department of the Interior after the agency published rules that would allow the Seminole Indians to operate full gambling casinos and vowed to take the case all the way to the U.S. Supreme Court. Alabama joined Florida in the suit. The Miccosukee Tribe continued to build modern homes on their reservation overlooking Everglades National Park, despite pressure from environmentalists and government regulators to remain picturesque. Archaeologists found a mass grave containing the remains of an estimated 2,500 people at Pensacola. They believe the people died in waves of violence and disease over a period from 1698 to 1719, when French, Spanish, and Indians fought over the site. More than 250 antiquities, stolen from a Corinth, Greece, museum in 1990, were recovered in Miami. A bacterial meningitis outbreak centered in Palatka felled nine and killed one. Putnam County officials inoculated more than 13,000 to stymie the outbreak. Circus star Mario Zacchini, the last living member of the original Flying Zacchinis, and inventor of the "human cannonball" attraction, died, as did Marion Bowman, abbot of St. Leo Monastery and founder of St. Leo University. The gruff and colorful Benedictine prelate was a Democratic Party power-broker and oft-time bane of the Catholic Church. St. Petersburg's Derby Lane canceled races for the first time in its 74-year history after six greyhounds died of pneumonia and a hundred others fell ill with a virus infection popularly called "kennel cough." Other tracks around the state and tracks in several other states declared quarantines and placed a watch on the health of their animals. Dogs also died at tracks at Daytona and West Palm Beach. Unable to stop the spread of dreaded citrus canker in south Florida, where it had killed more than 100,000 trees, the state proposed a $165-million fight against it, including building a mile-wide "firebreak" in Broward County, from the Atlantic to the Everglades. Georgia is famous for its Okefenokee Swamp, but when it went up in flames, it was in the little known Florida portion of the great wilderness. 53,000 acres burned away, 50,000 of them in Florida. With rainfall measuring less than half that of the previous year, devastating forest fires returned to the state for the second consecutive year. The governor declared a state of fire emergency, adding the National Guard to firefighters already battling seasonal blazes. Harsh weather, drought, and wildfires had a negative effect on the state's considerable and illegal marijuana crop, forcing more planters indoors. Miami-Dade and Pinellas

Counties led the state in homegrown crops. The 1999 orange crop was forecast to be 23 percent smaller than 1998's record harvest, but a bumper 2000 crop is also forecast. Red Tide appeared simultaneously off all three Florida coasts for the first time on record. The blooms occurred off Pensacola, Tampa Bay, and Jacksonville. Oriental fruit flies, yet another menace to Florida agriculture, showed up in Hillsborough and Volusia Counties, on opposite sides of the peninsula, but were not found in concentration. Unlike Mediterranean Fruit Flies, attacked with the controversial Malathion poison, the new menace was tempted with a poisonous bait developed in the 1920s and sprayed closely, primarily on utility poles. Quincy Farms, the major north Florida mushroom producer, signed a labor contract with the United Farm Workers, its first in Florida. Two swarms of African bees were destroyed in bait hives at the Jacksonville port, marking the first time they've made it ashore. Officials have found 17 swarms aboard ships since 1983. The state maintains 500 bait hives at ports, along I-10, and on its borders. A contagious respiratory disease was believed to have killed more than 100 gopher tortoises, a Florida species of special concern. Meanwhile, American crocodiles were nesting in Biscayne Bay north of Homestead for the first time in a century. After years of battling with the powerful Lykes interests, the state won 9,000 acres of creek bed and 9,000 acres of adjacent land from the company, which had closed the waterway and its environs to the public. Although the company had been vilified by environmentalists for a decade, the state, in taking title to the land and reaffirming the public's interest in the waterway, found it was unlikely it could afford to keep the area in the pristine state maintained by the company. Monroe County Sheriff Rick Roth accepted a $25 mil-

lion check from the U.S. Customs Service, his department's share of the $50 million seized from a drug dealer, the largest currency seizure in Customs' history. The reward was the highest ever paid to a local agency by the federal government. Monroe deputies discovered the horde in the offshore bank accounts of a convicted marijuana merchant. Miami-Dade joined New Orleans, Chicago, and other cities in suing gun manufacturers for the cost of gun-related deaths and injuries. Broward County joined Monroe County in offering health benefits for "domestic partners." A state investigation found no evidence of price fixing for Passover matzo in Florida. Following a successful campaign in California, the Civil Rights Initiative movement came to Florida seeking to eliminate public preferences for minorities. Officials approved a plan to build the world's second largest desalinization plant on Tampa Bay to produce 25 million gallons of drinking water daily. Miami-Dade voters crushed a measure to raise the sales tax in the county to 7.5 percent. St. Petersburg purchased the venerable Sunken Gardens attraction near downtown and designated it a botanical garden until it figured out what to do with it. City voters also gave it the okay to sell the Weeki Wachee Springs attraction in Hernando County. The springs were once seen as the long-range solution to the city's drinking water problems. A 42-year-old Orlando woman died 72 days after being shot and paralyzed by her 68-year-old mother, who feared her daughter planned to put her in a nursing home. The daughter received court permission to disconnect the respirator that kept her alive. Prosecutors passed on answering the question raised when they declined to prosecute the mother for murder. She was charged with attempted murder based on the original shooting. More than four dozen airline service employees were arrested at Miami

International Airport and accused of smuggling narcotics and weapons from Latin American and distributing them around the U.S. A Miami jury found against the nation's biggest tobacco companies in the first class-action case to reach a verdict, finding the companies conspired to hide the dangers and addictive qualities of tobacco. A corporation, SabreTech Inc., was charged with 110 counts of third-degree murder and second-degree manslaughter in the 1996 ValueJet crash in the Everglades. Three employees were also charged with conspiracy. The Miami-Dade state attorney's office alleged oxygen canisters illegally transported on the plane by the company caused a fire leading to the crash. Coast Guard policy that required Cuban sea-borne refugees be maced, blasted with hoses, and physically restrained from reaching land within site of beach-goers drew heavy fire from the Miami Cuban community, which witnessed the incident, both for the action and the policy which prompted it. Cubans reaching land are allowed to stay. Those stopped at sea are returned via Guantanamo Bay. A Clearwater man filed suit against the state lottery, charging its 900-telephone number for lottery results is an illegal violation of the state's public records law, amounting to selling the records for $0.77 per minute. The lottery gets more than 200,000 calls a month on the line and the average call last 90 seconds. The suit asks for class action status. The lottery has collected $6.3 million from the calls, equal to the average one-week jackpot. The state began publishing some of its materials, not only in English and Spanish, but in Creole as well. State First Lady Columba Bush was stopped by customs officials at Atlanta's airport and fined for failure to declare $19,000.00 worth of Paris clothes and jewelry. She said she was afraid her husband would be angry at the extent of her shopping spree. A Miami woman, whose husband is charged with espionage, filed a personal injury lawsuit against the Republic of Cuba, charging the marriage was a sham to cover spying activities. She charged the Cuban government with sexual assault. Additional charges were filed in the spy case against the ten in custody and the four still at large. The Tampa Bay Devil Rays baseball team canceled plans to moves its Double AA minor league team from Orlando to Tallahassee after the venerable Southern League balked at moving one of its teams from a major market. Wade Boggs of the Devil Rays got his 3,000th hit, and became the first player in history to hit that mark with a home run. The Junior Pan American track and field events and the Pan Am Junior Judo championships were driven from Miami to Olympic-bidding Tampa after Cuban activists persuaded local officials to cancel the events if Cuba participated. Cuba did not. Miami subsequently dropped its bid to host the 2007 Pan American Games. The state gave Vero Beach $7.5 million to help the city buy and maintain the Los Angeles Dodgers spring training facility and keep the team from moving to Arizona. Former state Education Commissioner Betty Castor resigned as president of the University of South Florida to head a national educational organization. Controversial John Lomdardi resigned as president of the University of Florida to join the faculty after yet another dust-up involving generous raises for his subordinates. Both Lombardi and Castor won high praise for dramatic increases in research revenues to their respective universities during their tenures. Florida State University replaced the University of Florida as the nation's top party school according to the annual Princeton Review rankings. The University of Florida placed second. Officials were not amused. After years of dismissing abominable tales of Florida's "skunk ape," the Collier County Tourist Development Council allocated $44,000.00 to promote and "research" the beast. Tallahassee's Lake Jackson disappeared one night—again. The 4000-acre lake drained down a sinkhole as it has before on what scientists believe is a 25-year cycle. Although the area is noted for its caverns, where the water goes is a mystery.

## MINORCANS AT NEW SMRYNA

Encouraged by Scotsman Andrew Turnbull, settlers from the island of Minorca sailed to Florida and formed a farming colony in the New Smryna area during the late 1700s. Although the colony hoped to successfully cultivate silk, wine, honey, and olives, indigo became the Minorcans' primary cash crop.

## FLORIDA'S WILD WEST

A little-known aspect of Florida life in the 1800s is its similarity to the Wild West. De Soto County was on a par with Dodge City as the site of frequent cattle wars, rustling, and hangings.

## MILLIONS FORGOTTEN

Over the years hundreds of Floridians die leaving millions of dollars in money, jewelry, coins, and other valuables in their homes or safe deposit boxes with no heirs to claim them. As a result, in 1961, the Florida Disposition of Unclaimed Property Act was enacted. It requires banks, savings and loan associations, insurance companies, fiduciaries, governmental units, and various businesses and trustees to report any abandoned property to the state comptroller. This abandoned property is held by Florida and out-of-state corporations for seven years, and by financial institutions for 10 years, per the state law. Meanwhile, the comptroller's office is required to make an effort to find the owners or heirs by listing the names of the owners of any unclaimed property, money, and deposits in legal advertisements in Florida newspapers. The ads run twice a month each January. Because of the ads, 40 percent of the abandoned valuables are claimed by rightful parties. The balance is turned over to the state school fund. Contents of safe deposit boxes are handled differently; if the owner or heirs do not claim the box within seven years, the contents are sold at public auction and the proceeds given to the school fund.

## CALENDAR OF TRADITIONAL ANNUAL FESTIVALS

Specific dates for the following annual events are available through area chambers of commerce.

**January**
Epiphany Day at Tarpon Springs
Florida Keys Renaissance Faire at Key West
Carillon Festival, Bok Tower Gardens, at
    Lake Wales
Brooksville Raid Festival at Brooksville
**February**
Battle of Olustee at Olustee
Hoggetown Medieval Faire at Gainesville
Gasparilla Invasion and Parade at Tampa
Edison Pageant of Light at Fort Myers
Florida State Fair at Tampa

**March**
Gasparilla Sidewalk Art Festival at Tampa
Battle of Natural Bridge at Woodville
Italian Renaissance Fair at Miami
Manatee Heritage Week at Bradenton
Festival of States at St. Petersburg
Strawberry Festival at Plant City
**April**
Ribfest and Hot Air Balloon Rally at
    Melbourne
Seafood Festival at Fort Lauderdale
Rodeo and Festival at Odessa

*(continued on next page)*

*(continued from previous page)*

Indian River Festival at Titusville
Conch Republic Celebration at Key West
Sugar Festival at Clewiston
**May**
Roaring Twenties Days at Sebring
**June**
Southwest Florida Wine Fair at Captiva Island
**July**
Hemingway Days Festival at Key West
**August**
Boca Festival Days at Boca Raton
**September**
Union Garrison Weekend at Fernandina Beach
Days in Spain at St. Augustine
**October**
Hispanic Heritage Festival at Miami

Rattlesnake Festival at San Antonio
John's Pass Seafood Festival at Madeira Beach
"Jeannie" Auditions and Ball at White Springs
Peanut Festival at Williston
Broward Navy Days and Fleet Week at Port Everglades
**November**
Jazz Festival of South Walton at Seaside
National Native American Festival at Jacksonville
French Film Festival at Sarasota
**December**
King Mango Strut at Coconut Grove
Victorian Seaside Christmas at Amelia Island
Lighted Boat Parade at St. Petersburg

## LIGHTNING

A cloud-to-ground lightning stroke can be up to nine miles long.

## MILES OF FRESH WATER

Florida has 3 million acres of freshwater lakes and 12,000 miles of streams and rivers. From those waters over 250 different species of freshwater fishes have been collected.

# ARCHAEOLOGY

Although there were no dinosaurs in Florida, the state's fossil history goes back an estimated 50 million years. While scientists believe that Florida did not rise from the sea until about 25 million years ago, remains of sea creatures such as sea urchins, sharks, primitive manatees, sea turtles, and snakes can be found in the state's limestone deposits.

As the sea level declined and more of Florida's land mass was exposed, mammals began migrating into the still-forming peninsula. Fossil remains of such animals as the saber-tooth cat, a giant land tortoise, rhinoceroses, small three-toed horses, camel-like creatures, alligators, a primitive bear, and deer or antelope-type animals may be found in various regions of the state.

As a result of rising and lowering sea levels, fossil remains often are a mix of land and sea creatures.

## FIRST FLORIDIANS

The earliest migrations of humans to Florida is thought to have occurred about 10,000 years ago. Bones of animals known to have lived at that time have been found bearing stone spear points, proof that human hunters existed. Further evidence that humans indeed lived in Florida at least 8,000 years ago was found in 1983 in a peat bog near Titusville. Called the Windover Site, the site yielded more than 120 human skulls.

Remarkably, the bog had preserved the skulls of the long dead men, women, and children. The remains had been wrapped in cloth, and brain tissue in the skulls was in good enough condition to be studied by scientists. Skeletons of the early inhabitants revealed many with broken bones and bone infections. One hip joint was found imbedded with a spear point.

Scientists estimate that the first organized settlements in Florida probably occurred about 7,000 years ago. A variety of shellfish remains, piled high by the early Indians mark settlements which were usually along river valleys. Evidence further suggests the humans were nomadic.

Pottery dating back 3,000 to 4,000 years has shown that Florida's inhabitants had some trade with Indians in Alabama and Georgia because some pottery remains are made of materials not found in Florida. A few centuries later, what is believed to be additional migration into Florida brought a change in tools and cooking or eating utensils.

Later findings indicate that some time near the start of the Christian age Florida's inhabitants began building burial mounds and using copper for decorative and practical purposes. Archaeologists estimate that by the time the first white explorations occurred in Florida there were at least six basic Indian groups or subgroups on the peninsula. Population figures for these early people vary widely. The least number estimated is 10,000; missionaries with explorers wrote of between 16,000 and 34,000. Modern scholars tend toward higher numbers, possibly as high as nearly a million. This high number is disputed, however, by some archaeologists who claim the physical evidence from Indian sites does not indicate such a vast population.

Following are major Indian groups known to have inhabited Florida:

**TIMUCUANS** lived throughout the north-central regions, in areas today occupied by Cape Canaveral, Ocala, Gainesville, and Jacksonville, and in the Suwannee River valley region west to the Aucilla River. They were reported by Spanish explorers as strong, handsome people of some height. Other explorers labeled the Timucuans as stubborn, perhaps because they resented the Spanish use of them as cargo bearers, a task considered women's work by the Indians. In addition, religious missionaries outlawed such Timucuan enjoyments as ball games and dancing and had declared the traditional medicine men off limits.

**TOCOBAGA** may have been a branch of the Timucua who lived from about Tarpon Springs south to Sarasota. Some confusion exists because at least one explorer claimed the Tocobaga lived along north Florida's Wacissa River. This is disputed by modern anthropologists who maintain this more northerly group was a small band of about 300 Tocopaca, not Tocobaga, who lived in the St. Marks River area.

**APALACHEE** occupied the region from the Aucilla River west to the Ochlockonee River, north into Georgia and south to the Gulf of Mexico. Today's Tallahassee was center of the Apalachee territory.

Historians report that it was rumors of Apalachee gold that lured Spanish explorers Narvaez in 1528 and De Soto in 1539. The natives these explorers met were prosperous and ferocious. In fact, the Spanish had been warned not to venture into Apalachee lands for the northern tribe quartered and burned intruders. As for the rumored riches, it is likely the metal the Apalachee possessed was copper, not gold. In 1647, the Apalachee warred against the Spanish, killing three friars and the Spanish governor's lieutenant and his family. The reason for the revolt appears to have been the Indians' fear of ever-growing numbers of Spanish intruders and their missions. Several non-Apalachee Indian groups lived within Apalachee territory, including the Tama, Yamasee, Capara, and Chine.

**TEQUESTA** lived in the region from today's Pompano Beach to Cape Sable, where it is thought they mingled with the Calusa. Evidence suggests the Tequesta ate the usual berries, sea grapes, palm nuts, and prickly pears but also fed on manatees, deer, and land and sea turtles. Although the Tequesta were considered less warlike than other Indians, they were hostile to whites and took a heavy toll on any shipwreck survivors they encountered. Indians from this region are thought to have made dugout canoe trips to Cuba.

**CALUSA** occupied territory ranging from Tampa Bay and Charlotte Harbor south to Cape Sable and likely into the Lake Okeechobee area. Archaeological evidence suggests the Calusa were non-agricultural and, as mariners, dined principally on fish and shellfish. Like the Tequesta, the Calusa traveled to Cuba and Hispanola. This Indian group also is known by the names of Calos or Carlos.

**AIS** lived along coastal areas in the region of the Indian River, Cape Canaveral, and St. Lucie River. A branch of this tribe has been cited as the rescuers of Quaker Jonathan Dickinson when his ship wrecked off Hobe Sound in East Florida. Despite the rescue, Dickinson later recounted in his book, *God's Protecting Providence*, that the Indians stripped Dickinson's party of men, women, and children of their clothing. After months of wilderness hardships, they made their way to St. Augustine.

The original tribes gradually faded away. Many Indians died initially from Old World diseases contracted during first contact, and again later with colonization. But assimilation took the greatest toll on an identifiable Indian population. Beyond St. Augustine, settled- and organized-Florida, over 300 years of Spanish influence, became a Mestizo society, growing ever more European with each generation. Much of that society emigrated when faced with 20 years of British rule. The rest left en masse, primarily for Cuba, when the U.S. took possession.

## ADVENT OF THE SEMINOLES

In 1750, Creek Chief Secoffee led his people into Florida from Georgia. They had broken with their old nation in the north, formed a strong confederation, and were now known as Seminoles, or "runaway." Also part of the Seminole Nation were the last of the old, aborigine tribes such as the Yamasee (driven from the Carolinas) and the Oconee, who migrated from the Apalachicola region.

In the early 1700s, Creek Indians sided with the British against the Spanish and launched raids from Georgia into Florida as far south as the Everglades. When the British replaced the Spanish in Florida, the Indians welcomed their British friends and together they formed a unified confederation.

This was not to last, however, and in 1783, when the Spanish regained possession of Florida, the Indians once again were fighting with whites. Some of the friction resulted from runaway slaves who were given refuge by the Indians; other unrest was caused by the Indians' British friends.

In late 1817, at the start of what is known as the First Seminole War, the U.S. government ordered the army's Andrew Jackson to take personal charge of the campaign against the Indians, their British allies, and the Spanish. Jackson promised President Monroe to have the job done within 60 days.

By April 1818, Jackson had traveled to Apalachicola and St. Marks and then marched eastward toward the Suwannee River. At the settlement of Old Town (on U.S. 19 today, near Chiefland), Jackson court martialed two Britishers for aiding the Indians—Robert Ambrister, who was shot, and Alexander Arbuthnot, who was hanged.

Jackson soon headed back toward Pensacola, where he arrived in May 1818 to occupy the city and take over Fort Barrancas. But upon arrival he learned that the executions of Ambrister and Arbuthnot had led to demands by Britain for an apology. Congress debated the matter for nearly a month, but never voted to censure Jackson, who enjoyed the support of Secretary of State John Quincy Adams.

Within three years, Florida was transferred from Spain to the United States and by 1822, with Florida a newly-designated U.S. territory, Andrew Jackson became its first governor. But friction between white settlers and the Seminoles continued and in 1823 an Indian conference convened in December at Moultrie Creek near St. Augustine, during which an Indian treaty was negotiated. It set aside lands north of Charlotte Harbor and south of Ocala exclusively for Seminole Indians. The Indians, in exchange for giving up the lands to the north that they held and a promise to not provide refuge for runaway slaves, also gained tools, livestock, cash, and a year's ration of meat, corn, and salt.

The Treaty of Moultrie Creek was only a year old when President Monroe began speaking out against Indians in every part of the country, urging their removal to reservations. Meanwhile, in Florida, the Seminoles were having difficulties with the terms of the Moultrie Creek treaty. They did not like the treaty-prescribed land, which had been stricken by a drought. And they continued to harbor runaway slaves, or so white slave owners contended. As U.S. policy toward Indians everywhere became more strident, federal representatives in 1827 tried to interest the Seminoles into moving from Florida, to lands further west.

James Gadsden, a government representative, called a meeting of the Seminole Indians at Paynes Landing on the Oklawaha River and convinced seven chiefs to sign away the benefits of the earlier Treaty of Moultrie Creek. During the meeting, the Indians agreed, wittingly or not, to accept $13,000.00 apiece and to move west by November 1833. But two chiefs later charged that they had not signed the agreement and they considered the Treaty of Moultrie Creek still in effect. Nevertheless, the U.S. government insisted the Seminoles be prepared to move west by January 1836.

The Indians were not cooperative, however, and for several reasons. Whites murdered Indian chief Charley Emathla, blaming the slaying on Chief Osceola, and U.S. soldiers had captured Osceola's wife, contending she was a fugitive slave. Foreseeing another war, other chiefs and their families fled to U.S. forts for protection, an influx that created further uneasiness among white settlers.

In 1835, the expected Second Seminole War broke out and it was to last for seven years. Seminole factions began attacking a number of sites, including the Simmons plantation in Micanopy, plantations in Matanzas, and settlement buildings in New Smyrna. Then, in December 1835, Indians ambushed Gen. Wiley Thompson and a lieutenant outside of Fort King at Ocala. That same day, an Indian ambush caught Maj. Francis Dade and two companies of soldiers at Bushnell as they were marching from Fort Brooke in Tampa to Fort King. Major Dade was killed by the first shot and a total of 103 soldiers died. The event became known among whites as the Dade Massacre.

News of Dade's fate prompted activation and enlargement of Florida's militia. In January 1836 the U.S. government sent 14 companies of soldiers under the leadership of Gen. Winfield Scott to join the territory's militia. Much of the Indian militancy occurred until 1837 under the leadership of Osceola, who is quoted as having said, "Your men will fight and so will we, until the last drop of Seminole blood has moistened the dust of his hunting ground."

But in 1837, Osceola and another leader, Coacoochee, agreed to arbitrate the hostilities. As the two rode into St. Augustine under a flag of truce sent to Osceola by Gen. Thomas Jesup, Jesup ordered the pair captured and they were taken to St. Augustine's Fort Marion (Castillo de San Marcos). Coacoochee escaped, but Osceola died.

During the next year, U.S. troops pushed the Indians further south and in December of that year a major skirmish provided then-Col. Zachary Taylor with the only major U.S. victory against the Indians. Taylor's victory triggered the shipment of nearly 3,000 Seminoles out of Florida to areas west of the Mississippi River. Isolated Indian raids continued until November 1841, when Coacoochee, the most powerful Indian leader since Osceola, finally gave up. In 1842 the Second Seminole War was declared over.

The 300 or so Seminoles who did not move west fled into the Everglades. In 1851, they regrouped under another chief, Billy Bowlegs. He had gone to Washington and New York that year to listen to rationales by white leaders for total Indian emigration. But he returned unpersuaded, and in 1855 a group of his followers attacked a group of white surveyors. Further Indian raids were made on settlers and forts in the Sarasota area, in Hillsborough County, and at Fort Meade. Skirmishes continued through 1857 in what became known as Bowlegs' War or the Third Seminole War. But in 1858 Bowlegs surrendered, and the U.S. government quickly deported him from Florida via steamer from Egmont Key. His followers fled into the Big Cypress area and to the Everglades in south Florida.

Succeeding generations of Seminoles, now several thousand in number, still live there today, under a truce signed with the U.S. government in 1934. They have divided into two groups, the "Reservation

Seminoles," who live on or near four federal reservations: one in Big Cypress, in Hendry County south of Lake Okeechobee; another in Brighton, in Glades County northwest of Lake Okeechobee; one near Hollywood, in Broward County north of Miami; and a fourth, small reservation outside Tampa, in Hillsborough County. A second and smaller group, the "Trail Seminoles," better known as the Miccosukees, number near 400 and live on a 76,000-acre reservation about 25 miles west of Miami. They are recognized as a separate tribe. The Indians and the white populace in Florida no longer war against each other, but disputes continue, often over the Indians' sovereign status. These days, however, both sides turn their conflicts over to attorneys.

## OSCEOLA

The American Indian Osceola is one of Florida's most enchanting historical figures, romanticized to near legend. Osceola's origins remain murky. By some accounts he was born "Billy Powell" near Tuskegee, Ala., in about 1804. His father, William Powell, was an English Indian trader from Virginia. Osceola's part Creek mother is listed as Polly Copinger Powell.

Diaries and other reports describe Osceola as 5 feet, 10 inches tall, thin, with reddish-brown hair. He probably was left-handed.

In about 1813 Polly and son Billy moved to Florida, possibly because of increasing Indian and government conflicts. Sometime after 1818, Billy Powell became "As-se-he-ho-lar," ("Ussa Yaholo" or "Asi yaholo"), which was Anglicized as "Osceola." The name translates to "black drink" or the "black drink singer," reportedly because Osceola not only tolerated quantities of "asi," a ceremonial holly brew, but robustly hollered "yaholo," a traditional post-drink whoop.

During the 1820s, white settlers immigrated to Florida and Indian raids escalated. Osceola was an influential leader among Creeks and Seminoles, but never was a chief.

Precisely what moved Osceola to militancy may never be known. One source says Osceola became enraged over mistreatment of his wife, Morning Dew, by Indian Agent Wiley Thompson. This is unsubstantiated by more modern historians.

But enmity did exist between Osceola and Thompson. In June 1835, Thompson pushed Osceola to sign a treaty that would remove Florida Indians from their lands. Military journals report that Osceola insulted, and perhaps threatened, Agent Thompson.

Thompson had Osceola arrested, but freed him after he signed the treaty. The following November Osceola was implicated in the murder of Indian Charley Emathla, a white sympathizer. One month later, an Osceola-led raid on Fort King left Agent Thompson dead.

Indian attacks continued until October 1837, when Osceola was duped into a peace parley at Fort Peyton, near St. Augustine. Instead of negotiating, Gen. Thomas Jesup arrested Osceola.

On Dec. 31, 1837, an ill and weary Osceola was transferred from St. Augustine's Fort Marion (Castillo de San Marcos) to Fort Moultrie in Charleston (S.C.) harbor. Despite his failing health, Osceola was noted as being popular and good-natured. On Jan. 30, 1838, he died at age 34 from quinsy, an acute throat infection. (continued on next page)

*(continued from previous page)*

Two more events occurred before Osceola was buried. One, a death cast was made of his upper body. And, second, Fort Moultrie surgeon Frederick Weedon removed Osceola's head and kept it at his home until it became part of a New York Medical College-Museum collection.

Legend has attributed the beheading of Osceola to retribution—that Dr. Weedon's wife, Mary Thompson Weedon, was related to the slain Indian Agent Thompson. But Florida historian Patricia Wickman found no link between Mary Weedon and Agent Thompson.

In 1967, vandalism forced the National Park Service to dig up Osceola's grave. A headless skeleton, verified as Osceola's, was found in the grave. Archaeologist John Griffin, who examined Osceola's body at that time, said the head was likely removed for scientific study. He said, "Craniology or phrenology were popular studies at the time of Osceola's death."

No one knows what happened to Osceola's head. The New York collection burned in 1865 and no records have been found that verify the head was actually with the burnt collection.

Weedon's diary says Osceola's deathbed request was to be buried in Florida. Several failed attempts have been made since 1930 to bring his body to Florida. But because Osceola was in federal custody at the time he died, the National Park Service has chosen to retain this famous Floridian in South Carolina.

## FOLKLORE

Florida abounds with folklore because of four basic heritages—"Crackers," Blacks, Latins, and Indians. "Crackers" were the original white settlers, thought to have come from Alabama and Georgia. Two theories persist about the origin of the word. One is that the term is a shortened version of "corn cracker"; the other, more popular theory, suggests that the term is derived from "whip cracker." Early Floridians drove cattle with bullwhips that could be heard cracking for long distances. Cracking of whips was not only useful for moving herds or for driving teams of oxen and mules hauling timbers, but was also an enjoyable pastime at which settlers became proficient.

Much "cracker" folklore has been lost but, like many other peoples, their fishing, hunting, planting, and doctoring were conducted on the basis of superstition. Fence posts, for example, were never set in moonlight.

Likewise, Florida Indians created elaborate ceremonies to bring them good luck and good times. Building a canoe, for example, was a hallowed event. As for weather, Seminoles still believe they can forecast hurricanes by studying sawgrass blooms.

Blacks brought voodoo to the mainland from the Bahamas and West Indies, and today voodoo rituals are still practiced nearly everywhere in Florida. Among the Latins in Tampa, a widely popular cone of incense would be burned to reveal, in its ashes, a number that foretold the current bolita winner. Bolita (little ball), introduced to Tampa by Cubans, was a lottery that spawned superstitions, including interpretations of dreams and the symbolism of numbers.

Folklore also involved medicinal beliefs. Below are Florida folk medicines, some with a possible scientific basis:

| Common Name | Use | Common Name | Use |
|---|---|---|---|
| Onion | antiseptic | Catnip | for colic |
| Virginia snake root | stimulant or tonic, for headache and ring-worm | Pine tree | antiseptic |
| | | Wild cherry | cough syrup |
| Cabbage | for carbuncles | Black root | Indian purgative |
| | | Red oak | for diarrhea |
| Buttonwood | for fever | Post oak | Indian poultice |
| Jerusalem oak | anthel-mintic | | |
| | | Sumac | Indian poultice |
| Stargrass | laxative and emetic | Trumpet plant | for smallpox |
| Gopher or fevergrass | for fever | | |
| Dog fennel | diaphoretic | Sassafras | a tonic |
| Black walnut | for ground itch | Queen's delight | emetic or purgative |
| Low bush myrtle | incites coughing | Deer tongue | diaphoretic |
| | | Prickly ash | for syphilis |

## COWBOY TRIBUTE

Morgan Bonapart ("Bone") Mizell remains one of Florida's most famous cowboys. Born in 1863 near Horse Creek in what was then Manatee County (now De Soto County), Bone became renowned for his wit and mischievous pranks. Celebrated cowboy artist Frederick Remington portrayed Bone in the painting *A Cracker Cowboy*. After a lifetime of owning and working cattle, Bone died in 1921 in a train depot at Fort Ogden, Florida. He is buried in Joshua Creek Cemetery near Arcadia, and a historical marker at Zolfo Springs' Pioneer Park was erected in 1974 to honor him.

## MOST SOUTHERN STATE

Florida's northernmost point lies more than 100 miles south of California's southern border, and the southern tip of Florida is 1,700 miles from the equator, closer than any other part of the continental U.S.

## DISTANCE AND DIRECTIONS

Jacksonville is 837 miles west of the northern shore of Maine. It is also nearly due south of Cleveland. A line drawn directly south from Maine almost bisects the Panama Canal, and virtually all of South America lies east of that line.

# NATIONAL MONUMENTS AND MEMORIALS

**CASTILLO DE SAN MARCOS NATIONAL MONUMENT,** in St. Augustine, encompasses the oldest masonry fort existing in the U.S., dating from the Spanish colonial period. The Castillo is a symmetrically shaped, four-sided structure surrounded by a moat 40 feet wide. Entrance into the fort is by drawbridge. The outer walls are 16 feet thick at the base and taper to nine feet at the top. They are constructed of coquina blocks cemented together by oyster lime mortar. Beautifully arched casements and interesting cornices testify to the workmanship and imagination of the Spanish builders. The fort contains guardrooms, a jail, living quarters for the garrison, storerooms, and a chapel. Nearly all the rooms open onto a 10,000 square foot court.

Impregnable San Marcos was constructed because of international rivalry over Florida. Spain claimed the area both by papal grant and the discoveries (1513) of Juan Ponce de Leon in his quest for land to compensate his loss of the Puerto Rico governorship. St. Augustine, founded in 1565 as a military outpost to strengthen the Spanish claim to Florida and to protect Spain's trade route from the rich Caribbean areas to the mother country, was first attacked by the French and later by British freebooters. With the founding of Charleston in 1670 and the menace of English colonists only 200 miles away, the Spanish began construction on the present stone fort at the north entrance to St. Augustine harbor in 1672. The massive fort was intended to replace the last of nine successive wooden forts on the site. Its baptism by fire came in 1702 when South Carolinians unsuccessfully besieged it. Continued attacks by the English colonists to the north ended in 1740

when General Oglethorpe of Georgia failed to capture the fort after a 38-day siege. However, in 1763, England secured Florida by terms of the Treaty of Paris and occupied the Castillo from July 21, 1763, to July 12, 1784.

After 21 years of British occupation, Florida was returned to Spain in exchange for the Bahama Islands. Florida remained a Spanish colony until 1821, when the U.S. acquired the territory by treaty and the payment of $5 million to American citizens for claims against Spain. Under the U.S. government, the Castillo was renamed Fort Marion in honor of Francis Marion, the Revolutionary War hero.

The fort became a U.S. military prison during the Second Seminole War. Among the prisoners were Osceola, the famous Indian leader, and Coacoochee, who made a spectacular escape through the bars of the casement. Except for a short Confederate occupation, the fort was periodically again used as a prison in 1875-77, 1886-87, and in 1898.

Castillo de San Marcos was declared a national monument in October 1924. Though the fort has lost its military usefulness, the powder magazine (dubbed the dungeon by the public), the shot furnace, the guardrooms, and the chapel are of continuing interest. From the massive walls a visitor can see the old City Gate and the narrow streets of the quaint city that it protected for 149 years.

**DE SOTO NATIONAL MEMORIAL** is five miles west of Bradenton, along the shores of the Manatee River where it enters Tampa Bay. It is a large stone monument and park commemorating Hernando De Soto's landing on the Florida west coast and his captaining of the first major exploration of the southern U.S. (1539-43).

Columbus had given Spain an early

claim to the New World and its wealth, and her warriors penetrated the newfound continent with amazing rapidity. Hardy and courageous men, loyal to King and Church, they built some 200 towns in America long before the first English colony was attempted in North Carolina.

De Soto was a typical Spanish conquistadore. Charles V appointed him governor of Cuba and Adelantado (leader) to "conquer, pacify and populate" the North American continent. He landed with his army at Tampa Bay, on the west coast, assigned 100 men to guard the camp, and sent ships back to Cuba for supplies. On July 15, 1539, he began the 4,000-mile northward march through unknown lands and forests. The expedition of about 1,000 men was plagued by heat, hunger, and hostile Indians but along the way De Soto seized village chieftains and forced them to supply food, carriers, and guides.

De Soto spent his first winter near the present site of Tallahassee. Setting forth in the spring of 1540, his army marched to the Savannah River, reached the Xuala region of western South Carolina, then moved up in North Carolina and across the Great Smoky Mountains to Tennessee. Finding no treasure, the weary men turned south, marching into Alabama. Here, powerful Tascalusa, Lord of the Mobile Indians, hid his anger when the Spanish seized him and agreed to furnish 400 carriers as soon as the army reached Mabila. But instead of carriers, warriors greeted De Soto and a fierce battle ensued. The Spanish suffered crippling losses in men, horses, and supplies.

De Soto had planned to go south to the Gulf of Mexico and meet his supply ships but, fearing that many of his men would desert to the ships, he turned his army north again and continued his exploration.

Hoping to find the rumored wealth of Pachaha Province, the expedition crossed the Mississippi River on hastily constructed barges and pushed into Arkansas. But De Soto found no gold so he turned west, then south, to winter on the west bank of the Ouachita River. Discouraged and ill, De Soto returned to the Mississippi River in the spring, planning to settle at a seaport and refit for a westward advance. But he died on May 21, 1542 and was buried in the Mississippi. Remnants of his expedition eventually reached Cuba by way of Mexico under the leadership of Luis de Moscoso. The De Soto National Memorial, established in 1949, embraces 25 acres on the Manatee River shore.

**FORT CAROLINE NATIONAL MEMORIAL,** 10 miles east of the city of Jacksonville, is a 119-acre park on the St. Johns River. It was established in 1953 to commemorate an attempt by the French to settle in Florida. Here the French and Spaniards vied for supremacy at the beginning of the first century of American colonization.

As part of his plan to strengthen France by uniting Catholic and Huguenot against the traditional Spanish enemy, Admiral Gaspard de Coligny sought to establish French bases in North America. In the 1560s he sent out an expedition under Jean Ribault, a man of exceptional experience and ability. The expedition touched along the St. Johns River near Mayport, then sailed north to leave a small garrison at Port Royal, South Carolina. But civil war in France prevented reinforcement and, after much suffering, the garrison survivors built a crude craft and returned home.

That same decade the French made a second attempt to settle Florida's east coast, under the leadership of Rene de Laudoniere. Three vessels set out from Havre De Grace conveying some 300 people to the new land. Of this number, 110 were sailors, 120 were soldiers, and the rest artisans, servants, and a few women—but no farmers. As a colony site, the French chose a broad, flat knoll on the shore about five miles upstream from the mouth of the St. Johns River. With the help of Timucuan Indians under Chief Saturiba, the colonists built a triangular fort of earth and wood. They named it Fort Caroline, in honor of King Charles IX.

Greed, mutiny, and famine combined to destroy the efforts of French colonization. And finding neither gold nor silver mines in Florida, a number of the men became impatient with wilderness life. After stealing three vessels, they set forth to prey upon the ships carrying treasure from Mexico and the Indies to Spain.

Before being captured by the Spaniards, the mutineers had seized four ships and plundered a Cuban town. During the same period, the winter of 1564-65, the settlers remaining at Fort Caroline nearly died of starvation. In desperation, they decided to repair a vessel and return to France. As the mutineers had proven, the French colony at Fort Caroline was a threat to Spanish commerce and a possible base for an attack on the Indies. While the French rulers claimed the settlement was in French territory, the Spaniards considered it a pirate's nest on Spanish land. Spain's King Philip II decided to commission Pedro Menendez de Aviles to "explore and colonize Florida" and sent an armada to drive out "settlers and corsairs" of all nations not subject to Spain. But another fleet was already on the high seas. Frenchman Jean Ribault had left France with reinforcements for the settlers and arrived at Fort Caroline just as the colonists were about to sail back to France.

Five days later, part of the Spanish fleet reached the St. Johns River and found the French united. The Spanish fleet offered battle, which the French declined. So the Spanish retreated to the St. Augustine harbor to await the remainder of their forces. As the Spanish unloaded stores and supplies, the French fleet drew up for a fight. But a low tide prevented the French from entering the harbor to get at the Spaniards. Before the tide turned, a storm blew up and drove the French fleet ashore in the Matanzas Inlet area just south of St. Augustine.

With the French ships being driven ashore by a gale, Menendez decided to march overland and swept down on unguarded Fort Caroline. After capturing it, he marched back south and successfully attacked the survivors of the shipwrecked French fleet (see Fort Matanzas).

Occupying Fort Caroline, the Spanish changed its name to San Mateo. But in 1568, the French, seeking revenge, landed a force north of the St. Johns River commanded by Dominique de Gourgues. Gourgues, enlisting the Indians as allies, wiped out the Spanish garrison at the fort and burned much of it.

The actual site of Fort Caroline no longer exists because its meadow and part of the bluff washed away after the river channel was deepened in the years following 1880. In addition to the park, the memorial includes a visitors' center with a museum in which is shown a replica of Fort Caroline.

**FORT JEFFERSON NATIONAL MONUMENT** is the largest 19th century coastal fort built in the U.S. It is 68 miles west of Key West at Tortugas Harbor on Garden Key in the "Dry Tortugas." At one time it was considered the "Key to the Gulf of Mexico."

Surrounded by a moat 70 feet wide and 30 feet deep, the six-sided brick fort has a perimeter of one-half mile and covers most of the 16-acre Garden Key. From base to crown, its eight-foot-thick walls stand 50 feet high, its massive foundations resting on coral rock and sand 10 feet below sea level. It has three gun tiers designed for 450 cannons, and was intended to garrison 1,500 men. Within the court are the foundations of the three-story officer and enlisted men's quarters, unfinished powder magazines, and two restored buildings.

Started by the U.S. in 1846, construction went on for nearly 30 years but was never completed. Obstacles were almost insurmountable—ships, money, and cargoes were lost in making the hazardous 1,500-mile voyage from eastern seaports. In addition, workmen found it difficult to withstand the subtropical heat, disease, and poor food. The site also was regularly swept by hurricanes.

The selection of Garden Key for the great fort was inevitable. Past this point sailed ships carrying the growing commerce of the Mississippi Valley and there were still keen memories of Gen. Andrew Jackson's fight with the British at New Orleans. Britain, too, in the mid-1800s was developing her West Indies possessions. And Texas, a new republic, seemed about to form an alliance with France or England and thus provide Europeans a foothold on the Gulf Coast.

Despite its strategic location, however, the fort never played a significant role in American history. The British ceased to be a threat in the northern Gulf region after their disastrous invasion attempt at New Orleans in 1815. Fort Jefferson was only half-completed when war broke out between the North and South, but to prevent its seizure by Florida secessionists, federal troops hurriedly occupied it. Following the war, little more was done to complete the fort. Engineers realized that the foundation was not resting on solid coral reef but upon sand and coral boulders washed up by the sea. The huge structure settled and walls began to crack.

For almost 10 years after the war, the uncompleted Fort Jefferson was used as a prison. Among the prisoners sent there were four of the so-called "Lincoln Conspirators," those accused of plotting with John Wilkes Booth to kill the president and prominent members of his Cabinet.

Because of hurricane damage and persistent yellow fever outbreaks, Fort Jefferson finally was abandoned in 1874. It was reactivated briefly in 1898 as a naval base and was the departure point for the ill-fated battleship *Maine,* which was blown up in Havana Harbor soon afterward. The mysterious explosion was blamed on Spain and precipitated the Spanish-American War. The fort has seen only sporadic and brief military use since World War I.

**FORT MATANZAS NATIONAL MONUMENT,** on Rattlesnake Island, is 14 miles south of St. Augustine across the Matanzas River, opposite the southern tip of Anastasia Island. The fort, of coquina blocks cemented together with oyster lime mortar, has two main levels. The garrison climbed a removable ladder to enter the fortification at the first level—a gun deck some 16 feet above the ground. The second level is a 30-foot two-story tower extending the length of one side and containing a small powder magazine and two guardrooms. Drinking water was stored in a cistern in the lower level. The monument covers an area of 298 acres, and includes Rattlesnake Island and the southern tip of Anastasia Island. It is typical of north Florida dune country with a heavy low growth of scrub and palmetto.

Near Fort Matanzas a decisive episode in the Franco-Spanish struggle for Florida occurred in 1565. A fleet of 300 Huguenots, under the leadership of Jean Ribault, unsuccessfully attacked the area's Spanish soldiers centered around the new settlement of St. Augustine. A storm blew the fleet ashore south of that area and the crew was hunted down by Pedro Menendez de Aviles, the founder of St. Augustine. Menendez killed all but a few of the 300 shipwrecked survivors. Thus, Matanzas, which means "slaughter" in English, received its name.

The value of the Matanzas site as a

warning outpost was proved early when runners raced from the tip of the island to St. Augustine in 1683 with word of the approach of pirate bands set on sacking the city. And during a 1740 attack on the St. Augustine area, the Matanzas Inlet proved to be an invaluable lifeline for provisions from Havana for the garrison at nearby Castillo de San Marcos. Realizing the importance of continued control of the inlet, the Spanish built the present-day Fort Matanzas in 1742, but under great difficulty. Long pilings had to be driven into the mud to support the stones that had been transported by boat from the King's Quarry on Anastasia Island. The English finally gained control of Fort Matanzas, along with the rest of Florida, by the Treaty of 1763, only to trade it all back to Spain for the Bahama Islands in 1784. By the time Florida was ceded to the U.S. by Spain in 1821, the interior of Fort Matanzas was mostly ruins.

The Fort Matanzas area was designated a national monument in 1924 and put under the supervision of the National Park Service. The service stabilized the fort and constructed a headquarters building on Anastasia Island and landing wharves on the river.

## FORTS AND BATTLEFIELDS

From the period of Spanish exploration to the end of Reconstruction following the War Between the States, Florida's history can be traced through its military installations.

To conquer the Florida frontier, Spain depended in part on Christianity but it soon learned it had to back up its missions with fortified outposts. Encroaching on the peninsula were the British and the French. To thwart their invasion, Spain chose to construct a super fort. It became the famous Castillo de San Marcos at St. Augustine. So well did it do its job that it preserved Spanish authority long after Spain's boundaries in

Florida had dwindled and its inner outposts had fallen to the enemy.

Remnants of the first period of Christian Florida consist primarily of 300-year-old skeletons of former fortresses built by the English, the French, and the Spanish as each attempted to establish a foothold in Florida. In addition to major military centers, many small outposts stretched across north Florida and along the coasts. Most of these left only a name in a government report carefully preserved in the national archives.

A second outcropping of military posts began during the first Seminole War and continued through the Billy Bowlegs War of the early 1850s. The First Seminole War—as some historians call Gen. Andrew Jackson's campaign of 1817-18—was more of an American attempt to crush Europeans, notably the British, than it was to quell an Indian uprising. It was fought against Indians (who had been planning for years to rebel), runaway slaves, and the English army, which encouraged and supplied the insurgents.

The second and major Seminole War lasted from 1835 to 1842 and ended in a stalemate. It was almost over on Christmas Day 1837 when Col. Zachary Taylor's army defeated a large Seminole force at the Battle of Okeechobee. The Florida frontier was relatively quiet for almost two years when Gen. Alexander Macomb, commander-in-chief of the U.S. Army, led the assembled chiefs to believe the land to which they were to be deported would be a permanent home instead of the temporary quarters he planned.

News of the betrayal reached the Seminole villages in south central Florida and the reaction was immediate and final. A trading post being built on the Caloosahatchee River was attacked and 17 dragoons were killed and scalped. This led to the reactivation of many forts and supply posts and to Taylor's promptly establishing

53 new outposts in the trouble zones. Only a few of these frontier military posts can be considered forts under the true definition. Most were stockades or blockhouses manned by 20 or 30 soldiers, in many instances Florida volunteers, who didn't consider the army a full-time job.

Nonetheless, the development of Florida can be traced to and from these small safety islands. Many present cities and towns grew up around a minor military post and some still bear the name of the army officer who built or commanded the fort. Listed are some of the more familiar military sites that played a role in Florida's history.

**CASTILLO DE SAN MARCOS** (See National Monuments and Memorials.)

**FORT BARRANCAS,** at Pensacola Harbor, was built by the U.S. between 1839 and 1845. A bricked tunnel connects it with Batteria de San Antonio, which was built in 1797 on the approximate site of two earlier wooden forts, one constructed by d'Arriola in 1698, the other by the British about 1771.

**FORT BROOKE,** Tampa, was a pioneer log outpost built in 1823. It was named for its first commander, Col. George Brooke, and played a strategic role in the early part of the Second Seminole War. The base also served as an embarkation point for Indians being shipped out of the state. As the fighting shifted to southern Florida, the center of military activity was transferred to Fort Myers.

**FORT CAROLINE** at St. John's Bluff was built by French explorer Laudoniere in 1564. More than two centuries later, the English established a settlement near the bluff and named it St. John's Town. It provided a Tory refuge during the final months of the Revolutionary War, then declined during the second period of Spanish rule. By 1817 most of its 300 buildings had disappeared

and the fort had washed into the river. (See National Monuments and Memorials.)

**FORT CLINCH,** on Amelia Island, was begun in 1847 and completed in 1851. It was garrisoned by both Confederate and Union forces during the War Between the States, then by U.S. troops for six years during Reconstruction. The fort, named in honor of Gen. D. L. Clinch, one of the Union officers who captured Fort Gadsden and later helped conclude the Seminole War, was reactivated briefly during the Spanish-American War in 1898.

**FORT DADE and BATTLEFIELD,** off U.S. 301 at Bushnell, was the site of the first major battle of the Second Seminole War. In December 1835 Maj. Francis L. Dade and a detachment of several officers and 102 men left Fort Brooke (Tampa) for Fort King (Ocala). On the morning of the 28th, the company was marching along the Withlacoochee River near the present town of Bushnell when it was ambushed by a Seminole war party led by Chiefs Alligator, Juniper, and Micanope. The major and 106 of his men were killed. Of an estimated 180 warriors, 3 were killed and 5 wounded.

**FORT DE SOTO,** at the mouth of Tampa Bay, was built on Mullet Key in 1898 and armed with eight 12-inch mortars that never fired a shot at an enemy. As early as 1849, the key, along with nearby Egmont and Passage keys, were recommended by Col. Robert E. Lee, later of Confederate Army fame, as a coastal defense in Florida. During the War Between the States, federal forces were stationed on Mullet Key as a blockade headquarters for the area and a haven for Union sympathizers. The fort as built at the turn of the century remains. During both World Wars, the federal government made use of the fort and Mullet Key; during World War I it was activated as a Coast

Artillery Training Center, and in World War II it was used as an Air Corp Gunnery and Bombing Training Center. It now is part of a vast park.

**FORT GADSDEN,** also known as Fort Blount, was at Buck's Siding in the Panhandle area and built in 1814 by Indians and runaway slaves, with considerable help from the British. In July 1816, U.S. forces attacked the outpost and on the fourth day of battle a hot cannonball landed in the powder magazine and blew up the fort. Only 60 of its 334 occupants escaped instant death, many of the casualties being women and children. Two of the 3 white men who escaped injury were executed by command of Gen. Andrew Jackson.

**FORT GEORGE ISLAND,** near the mouth of the St. Johns River, was orginally a Spanish outpost and mission. It was subsequently the object of attack by the French, the British, and the soon-to-be Americans.

**FORT JEFFERSON** (See National Monuments and Memorials.)

**FORT KING,** at Ocala, was established as an Indian trading post in 1825. Two years later the post was garrisoned with troops and renamed Fort King. The site, which lies about two miles east of the present city of Ocala, was the scene of the ambush of Gen. Wiley Thompson and his aide in December 1835. The event, together with the simultaneous Dade Massacre, started the Second Seminole War.

**FORT LAUDERDALE,** on the approximate site of the present-day city, was a stockade built at New River by Maj. William Lauderdale in 1838. Originally one of many outposts built along military paths during the Seminole wars, the fort and vicinity was settled in 1895 and grew into one of the most popular playgrounds on the east coast.

**FORT MATANZAS** (See National Monuments and Memorials.)

**FORT McREE** was built shortly after Fort Pickens to protect the opposite side of the channel. Ruins of its orginal brick foundation are still visible at low tide. The present channel flows across the old parade grounds.

**FORT PICKENS,** on the western tip of Santa Rosa Island, once guarded the eastern entrance to Pensacola Harbor. The pentagonal structure was completed in 1834 and at one time was the third largest fort in the U.S. Apache Chief Geronimo and his followers were imprisoned here in 1886.

**FORT ST. MARKS,** at St. Marks, was built in 1739, the fourth fort to be constructed on the apex of a peninsula formed by the junction of the St. Marks and the Wakulla rivers. The Spanish were the first to fortify the site in 1677. Subsequently, the fort was destroyed (once by pirates), rebuilt, and occupied by British, Indian, and American garrisons.

**MARIANNA BATTLEFIELD,** near Marianna, now displays a monument in its Confederate Park to commemorate the defense of the town by a force composed largely of boys, wounded soldiers, and old men on September 27, 1864. Sixty of the Home Guards were killed or wounded and another 100 captured by Union forces.

**NATURAL BRIDGE BATTLEFIELD** is one of two celebrated Confederate battle sites in Florida. In March 1865, Union forces planned to capture Fort St. Marks, then move into Tallahassee, the state's capital. But due to a combination of Confederate resistance and shoals, the federal assault failed. When the landing force could not cross the bridge at Newport, it tried again at Natural Bridge. The only defense the state could muster consisted of a few Confederate regulars, the Home Guard, cadets from West Florida Seminary (now Florida State University), and a few children and old men. Good planning stopped the Union troops and Tallahassee became the only Southern capital east of the

Mississippi to escape federal conquest. This, the last battle in Florida of the War Between the States, is commemorated by a monument, battlefield markers, and a display of old Confederate earthworks.

**OKEECHOBEE BATTLEFIELD** was the scene of the final major engagement of the Second Seminole War. On Christmas Day 1837 Col. Zachary Taylor and 1,067 regulars defeated a Seminole force estimated at 400 men. The encounter took place along the northeastern shore of the famous inland lake. The price of the American victory was 26 dead and 112 wounded. The Seminole toll was 11 dead, 14 wounded.

**OLUSTEE BATTLEFIELD** is located on U.S. 90 between Olustee and Sanderson. Florida escaped most of the physical devastation suffered by the Confederacy, but the state did play a significant role as the breadbasket of the Southern armies. To cut this breadline, the Union army marched toward the peninsula's rich agricultural area in February 1864. On February 20, Confederate troops defeated Union forces at Ocean Pond near Olustee, thus saving Florida's interior lines of supply and confining Union soldiers to the coast. The battle between the evenly matched forces (North, 5,000 officers and men; South, 5,200 officers and men) lasted six hours. It cost the North 203 killed, 1,152 wounded, and 506 missing; the South suffered 93 dead, 847 wounded, and 6 missing.

**WITHLACOOCHEE BATTLE-FIELDS** were the site of several decisive battles of the Seminole War, all along the Withlacoochee River. Three days after the Dade Massacre in December 1835, Gen. D. L. Clinch, with 280 regular soldiers and 500 militia, was attacked by a a Seminole war party at the river just north of the junction of the present-day Marion, Sumter, and Citrus counties. The Indians were repulsed but not defeated.

When news of the fighting reached Army officials, Gen. Edmund Gaines and 700 troops were diverted from New Orleans to defend Fort Brooke in Tampa. Gen. Winfield Scott was given command of the armies dispatched to rout the Seminoles. Both generals battled Osceola's forces in the tri-county corner, General Gaines in February 1836 and General Scott the following month. But neither army was able to pursue its quarry into the dense swamps and hammocks of central Florida. By using the guerrilla warfare tactics that enabled inferior American forces to sap the strength of the English during the Revolutionary War, the Seminoles were able to stall their inevitable defeat for seven years.

The only other significant encounter in the area occurred in November 1836 when Gen. Richard K. Call attacked an Indian encampment in the Big Wahoo Swamp a few miles northeast of the Dade Battlefield. Reinforced by 1,200 troops, the Florida forces chased the Seminoles until the soldiers were "waist deep" in the swamp and could no longer follow.

## FORTIFIED OUTPOSTS

**FORT ALABAMA** was the site of the outpost on the Hillsborough River between Tampa and Zephyrhills that supported old Fort Brooke. It was built in 1836 on the site of Burnt Bridge, the bridge crossed by Major Dade and his men on their way to the Dade Massacre. The bridge was burned by Indians, then rebuilt and burned twice more before it was abandoned.

**FORT ANN** was a Second Seminole War outpost near present day Titusville.

**FORT ANNUTTGELIEA** was an outpost established in 1840 to protect Hernando County settlers in event of an Indian attack.

**FORT ARMSTRONG** was a stockade built in 1836 on the site of the Dade Battlefield.

**FORT ARBUCKLE**, built in 1850, was part of the ring of civilian and military posts created to protect settlers in the interior sections of southwestern Florida.

**FORT BLOUNT** was a stockade built by settlers in the Bartow area during the Second Seminole War.

**FORT CASEY** was built in 1850 on an elevated key in Charlotte Harbor. It was distinguished by two coconut trees visible at a great distance.

**FORT CENTER** was a crude, wooden fort near the western extremity of Lake Okeechobee used during the Seminole conflicts.

**FORT CHRISTMAS,** on the St. Johns River, 80 miles north of the Okeechobee Battleground, was constructed beginning on Christmas Day 1837.

**FORT CHOKONIKLA,** built in 1849, was part of a network of stockades constructed to protect inland settlers between Fort Myers and Fort Meade during Indian uprisings.

**FORT CROSS** was built in 1838 as a fortified outpost west of the upper reaches of the Withlacoochee River near Brooksville.

**FORT CUMMINGS** was a military post 16 miles southwest of Davenport in Polk County, built in 1839.

**FORT DALLAS,** erected on the Miami River in 1836, was used to guard against the Everglades Seminoles for almost two decades. The city of Miami grew from its site.

**FORT DEFIANCE** was a small outpost near Micanopy, used briefly during the summer of 1836.

**FORT DENAUD,** an outpost up the Caloosahatchee River from Fort Myers and built in 1837, was reactivated during the latter part of the Second Seminole War.

**FORT DIEGO** was one of several outlying outposts of Castillo de San Marcos on the St. Johns River. It was captured by General Oglethorpe of Georgia during his assault on St. Augustine in 1740.

**FORT DRANE,** between Tallahassee and the Withlacoochee River, was built on the plantation of Gen. D. L. Clinch following the Dade Massacre. It served as a district headquarters and was the scene of numerous Indian battles before being abandoned in 1836.

**FORT DRUM,** near LaBelle, was abandoned before the Billy Bowlegs War and later burned by Indians.

**FORT DULANY** was a supply depot near the mouth of the Caloosahatchee River in Lee County. It was built in 1837 as part of the network of outposts necessitated by the Second Seminole War.

**FORT FANNIN** on the Suwannee River was established in 1838. Numerous arrowheads and shark-tooth fishhooks found on a nearby bluff indicate it was once an Indian village.

**FORT FOSTER** was the name given to the rebuilt Fort Alabama.

**FORT FRASER,** near Lake Hancock in Polk County, was built in 1837 to provide protection for nearby settlers.

**FORT GARDINER** on the Kissimmee River near the northern shores of Lake Okeechobee was built by Col. Zachary Taylor in December 1837 as a base from which to fight the Indians gathering at the lake.

**FORT GATLIN,** in present-day Orlando, was established in 1837 and named in honor of Dr. John S. Gatlin, a U.S. Army physician who died in the Dade Massacre.

**FORT GREEN** was one of several outposts along the Peace River during the Billy Bowlegs War. The Hardee County settlement that grew up around it bears its name.

**FORT HARLEE** was near Waldo on the Santa Fe River.

**FORT HARTSUFF** was part of an

outpost network between Fort Myers and Fort Meade for the defense of area settlers from Indian attacks. It was named after Lt. George L. Hartsuff, a topographical engineer, and is the site of present-day Wauchula.

**FORT HARVIE** was the original name of the outpost that became Fort Myers. It was built in 1841 and abandoned a year later.

**FORT HEILEMAN** was a principal depot for the U.S. Army in the late 1830s. It was at the fork of the north and south branches of Black Creek at Ga rey's Ferry (now Middleburg).

**FORT HOOKER** was another of the Peace River fortifications built during the Second Seminole War. It was 16 miles north of Fort Meade and garrisoned by Florida Volunteers.

**FORT JUNIPER** was on the site now occupied by the Juniper Lighthouse. A stockade built in 1838 by Hobe Sound settlers, its records reveal 678 Indians and Negroes were imprisoned at the fort before it was abandoned in 1842.

**FORT KEAIS** was part of the southwestern interior chain activated during the resumption of hostilities in the Second Seminole War. It was in the Big Cypress south of Fort Denaud.

**FORT KISSIMMEE** was a stockade built near a trouble spot during the Billy Bowlegs War.

**FORT LANE** was a militia center built in 1837, 10 miles south of Fort Mellon.

**FORT LLOYD** was an outpost northeast of the site of the Battle of Okeechobee.

**FORT MAITLAND,** built in 1838, was named for Capt. William S. Maitland. The city of Maitland was built on its site.

**FORT MARION** was the American name for Castillo de San Marcos. (See National Monuments and Memorials.)

**FORT MASON** was a stockade built in 1837 on the shores of Lake Eustis.

**FORT McCOY** was an outpost 20 miles northeast of Ocala.

**FORT MEADE,** built on the Peace River during the Second Seminole War, was named for Lt. George Meade, who later gained fame at the Battle of Gettysburg.

**FORT MELLON** is marked today by a stone monument in Sanford. Built in 1837, it became a trading post called Mellonville.

**FORT MITCHELL** was a two-story blockhouse east of Ocala built in 1814 to protect a rebel "American" settlement defying Spanish rule. It was named for Gov. David Mitchell of Georgia.

**FORT MOSE,** an outlying outpost for Castillo de San Marcos, was captured by Gen. Oglethorpe during his 1740 siege of St. Augustine. It was retaken by the Spanish, and was manned by runaway slaves from plantations in the British Carolinas.

**FORT MYAKKA** was built in 1849 to protect settlers from Indian forays.

**FORT MYERS** was built in 1850 on the site of the old Fort Harvie, which had been a temporary post during the Second Seminole War. It was named by Gen. David Twiggs in honor of his future son-in-law, Gen. Abraham C. Myers.

**FORT OGDEN** was an old Indian fort built in 1841, now the site of the town by the same name.

**FORT PEYTON** was a fort and blockhouse built near Moultrie in 1836. In 1837, Osceola, the great Seminole leader, was en route to the fort under the Indian equivalent of a flag of truce when he was captured. A marker about a mile from the post preserves the site of his betrayal.

**FORT PICOLATA,** a small fort on the St. Johns River, was captured by Gen. Oglethorpe en route to St. Augustine. Retaken by the Spanish, the fort was rebuilt with two swivel guns. In 1765 it was selected for the festive meeting between East Florida governor James Grant and the Indians to set Indian boundaries.

**FORT PIERCE**, erected between 1838 and 1842, served as an U.S. Army headquarters and was named in honor of Lt. Col. Benjamin Pierce, a brother of President Franklin Pierce.

**FORT POINSETT,** on Cape Sable was built in 1836 to protect the southern coast.

**FORT ST. ANDREWS** was an English outpost built on Cumberland Island during Gen. Oglethorpe's encroachments on Spanish territory in 1734.

**FORT ST. FRANCIS DE PUPA,** near Green Cove Springs, suffered the same misfortunes as its sister outpost, Fort Picolata. Built by the Spanish in 1737, Fort St. Francis was destroyed by the British forces of Gen. Oglethorpe in 1740, then rebuilt by the Spanish. The original wooden structures of both St. Francis and Picolata were replaced with two-story coquina buildings with two swivel guns mounted on the roof. During the 1760s, the two forts were garrisoned by British soldiers whose primary job was to keep the Indians on the west side of the St. Johns River.

**FORT SAN LUCIA** was in the vicinity of Jensen Beach and built by the Spanish in 1568. Indians killed so many of the Spaniards that the surviving soldiers mutinied and retreated into St. Augustine.

**FORT SAN NICHOLAS** is now only a gray stone marker about three miles east of U.S. 1 in Jacksonville. The site of the fort, built by the Spanish Gov. Don Manuel de Monteano about 1740, lies 1,500 feet north of the St. Johns River.

**FORT SCOTT** was built in 1816 at the junction of the Flint, Chattahoochee, and Apalachicola rivers to store supplies brought in from New Orleans and to provide defense against Indian and black tribal members.

**FORT SIMMONS,** built in 1841, superseded Fort Denaud on the Caloosahatchee River and was situated about five miles below the previous fort so as to bypass a sandbar that prevented the passage of steamboats.

**FORT STARKE** was established in 1840 at the mouth of the Manatee River as part of an outpost network guarding against Seminoles.

**FORT SULLIVAN** was another Seminole War stockade, built in 1839, 11 miles east of Lake Thonotosassa in Hillsborough County.

**FORT TAYLOR** served as a way station for travelers. It was a military camp built during the 1880s about 25 miles north of Tampa on the road to Brooksville.

**FORT T.B. ADAMS** was a supply depot on the north bank of the Caloosahatchee River across from Fort Denaud.

**FORT THOMPSON** was a Seminole War fort and supply depot on the Caloosahatchee River that was reactivated during the Billy Bowlegs War. After the War Between the States, the area was settled by Capt. F. A. Hendry, who became a successful rancher and for whom the county is named.

**FORT WACAHOOTA,** a Seminole War outpost, originally had been the site of the Mission Francisco de Potato. The fort was established in the 17th century but no trace of either the fort or the mission remains.

**FORT WALTON,** on the site of present-day Fort Walton, was built during the Seminole War and was used by the Confederate Army during the War Between the States.

**FORT WEADMAN** was an outpost eight miles west of St. Augustine.

**FORT WILLIAM** was an English stockade built on Cumberland Island during Gen. Oglethorpe's raids of the mid-1700s.

# LANDMARKS ON NATIONAL REGISTER OF HISTORIC PLACES
## (By County)

The National Register of Historic Places is an official list of historically significant sites and property throughout the country that is compiled by the National Park Service. Listed are districts, sites, buildings, structures, and objects that have been identified and documented as being significant to American history, architecture, archaeology, engineering, and culture.

**Alachua County**
Newnansville Town Site
Hotel Thomas
Rochelle School
Neilson House
Matheson House
Bailey House
Buckman Hall
Epworth Hall
Kanapaha (Haile Plantation)
McKenzie House
Thomas Hall
Rawlings House
U.S. Post Office, Gainesville
Anderson Hall
Newell Hall
Bryan Hall
Peabody Hall
Library East
Floyd Hall
Flint Hall
Women's Gym
N.E. Gainesville Residential District
Baird Hardware Co. warehouse
Star Garage
Micanopy Historic District
Boulware Springs Waterworks
Rolfs Hall
Newberry Historic District
S.E. Gainesville Residential District
Univ. of Fla. Campus Historical District
P. K. Yonge School
Old WRUF Radio Station
Evinstin Store and Post Office
Pleasant Street Historic District
Melrose Historic District
Cox Furniture Store and Warehouse
Dixie Hotel

**Baker County**
Olustee Battlefield
Burnsed Blockhouse
Old Baker County Courthouse

**Bay County**
McKenzie House

**Bradford County**
Bradford County Courthouse
Call Street Historic District

**Brevard County**
Launch Complex 39
St. Gabriel's Episcopal Church
Old Haulover Canal
Melbourne Beach Pier
Porcher House
Fla. Power & Light Co. Ice Plant
Cape Canaveral AF Station Launch
Windover
St. Joseph's Catholic Church
Wager House
Judge Robbins House
Spell House
Pritchard House
Titusville Commercial District
St. Luke's Episcopal Church
Alladin Theater
Barton Avenue Residential District
Community Chapel of Melbourne Beach
Hill House
Indian Fields
Persimmon Mound
Rockredge Drive Residential District
Valencia Subdivision Residential District
Whaley Citrus Packing House

**Broward County**
Lock 1, North New River Canal
New River Inn
Stranahan House
Hillsboro Inlet Light Station

Oakland Park Elementary School
Sample Estate-McDougald House
Bonnet House
Davie School
Seaboard Airline RR Station
Young Home
Deerfield School
Cap's Place
Old Dillard High School
U.S. Car #1

## Calhoun County

Cayson Mound and Village
Old County Courthouse

## Charlotte County

Freeman House
Big Mount Key
Charlotte High School
Old First National Bank of Punta
    Gorda
Icing Station at Bull Bay
Punta Gorda Atlantic Coast Line
    Depot
Punta Gorda Ice Plant
Punta Gorda Residential District
Punta Gorda Woman's Club
Smith Building
Villa Bianca
West Coast Fish Company Cabin
Willis Fish Cabin

## Citrus County

Crystal River Indian Mounds
Mullet Key
Fort Cooper
Yulee Sugar Mill Historic Memorial
Florida City Historic District

## Clay County

Clark-Chalker House
St. Margaret's Episcopal Church
St. Mary's Episcopal Church
Clay County Courthouse
Bubba Midden
Princess Mound
Haskell-Long House
Budington House
Methodist Episcopal Church
Frisbee House
Chalker House
Middleburg Historic District
Green Cove Springs Historic District
Winterbourne House

## Collier County

Turner River Site
Smallwood Store
Seaboard Coast Line RR Depot
C. J. Ostl Site
Sugar Pot Site
Halfway Creek Midden
Hinson Mounds
Platt Island
Palm Cottage
Burns Lake Site
Plaza Site
Naples Historic District
Keewaydin Club

## Columbia County

Henderson House
Fort White School Historic District
Hotel Blanche
Columbia County High School
Duncan House
Lake Isabella Historic Residential
    District

## De Soto County

Arcadia Historic District

## Dixie County

Garden Patch Archaeological Site

## Duval County

Grand Site
Kingsley Plantation House
Catherine Street Fire Station
Old St. Luke's Hospital
Red Bank Plantation
Riverside Baptist Church
Yellow Bluff Fort
Fort Caroline National Memorial
Epping Forest
Masonic Temple
Jacksonville Free Public Library
St. James Building
Jacksonville Terminal Complex
Dyal-Upchurch Building
Porter House
Klutho House
Florida Theatre
Brewster Hospital
Morocco Temple
St. John's Lighthouse
St. Andrews Episcopal Church
Bethel Baptist Institutional Church
Sammis House

El Modelo Block
Centennial Hall—Edward Waters
  College
Stanton School
Lane-Towers House
Riverside Historic District
Florida Baptist Building
3325 Via De La Reina
3335 Via De La Reina
3500 Via De La Reina
3609 Via De La Reina
3685 Via De La Reina
3703 Via De La Reina
3764 Ponce De Leon Avenue
7144 Madrid Avenue
7207 Ventura Avenue
7217 Ventura Avenue
7227 San Pedro
7245 San Jose Boulevard
7246 San Carlos
7246 St. Augustine Road
7249 San Pedro
7288 San Jose Boulevard
7306 St. Augustine Road
7317 San Jose Boulevard
7330 Ventura Avenue
7356 San Jose Boulevard
7400 San Jose Boulevard
San Jose Administration Building
San Jose Country Club
San Jose Hotel
San Jose Estates Gatehouse
Springfield Historic District
The Village Store
Title and Trust Company of
  Florida Building
Avondale Historic District
310 West Church Street
  Apartments
Carling Hotel
Casa Marina Hotel
Church of the Immaculate
  Conception
Grover-Stewart Drug Company
  Building
Little Theater
Mount Zion AME
Plaza Hotel
South Atlantic Investment
  Corporation Building
Woman's Club of Jacksonville
Young Men's Hebrew Association

**Escambia County**
Fort Barrancas Historic District
Lavalle House
L & N Marine Terminal Building
Dorr House
Fort George
Old Christ Church
Fort Pickens
Pensacola Historic District
Pensacola Lighthouse and Keepers
  Quarters
American National Bank Building
L & N Passenger Station
St. Michael's Creole Benevolent
  Society
Saenger Theatre
Jones House
Perdido Key Historic District
St. Joseph's Church Complex
San Carlos Hotel
Thiesen Building
Pensacola Hospital/Sacred Heart
  Hospital
Edmunds Apartment House
Crystal Ice Co. Building
North Hill Preservation District
Plaza Ferdinand VII
Alger-Sullivan Lumber Co.
  Residential District
King-Hooton House
Pensacola Naval Air Station
  Historic District
Pensacola Hospital

**Flagler County**
Bulow Plantation Ruins
Bunnell State Bank Building
Marine Studios

**Franklin County**
Porter's Bar
Yent Mound
Pierce Site
Fort Gadsden Historic Memorial
Raney House
Trinity Episcopal Church
Cape St. George Light
Crooked River Lighthouse
Apalachicola Historic District
*Governor Stone* (schooner)

**Gadsden County**
Willoughby House

Quincy Historic District
Old Philadelphia Presbyterian
  Church
Quincy Library/Academy
Judge White House
Love House
McFarlin House
Stockton-Curry House
Shelfer House
Quincy Woman's Club
U.S. Arsenal Officer's Quarters
Davis House

**Gulf County**
  *USS Montgomery* (snagboat)

**Hamilton County**
  United Methodist Church
  Old Hamilton County Jail

**Hardee County**
  Paynes Creek Massacre Fort
    Chokonikla
  Carlton Estate

**Highlands County**
  Seaboard Airline Depot, Old
    Sebring
  Hainz House
  Harder Hall
  Vinson House
  Sebring House
  Sebring Downtown Historic
    District
  Avon Park Historic District
  Central Station
  Highlands County Courthouse
  Lake Placid A.C.L. RR Depot

**Hillsborough County**
  Floridan Hotel
  Cockroach Key
  Fort Foster
  Circulo Cubano De Tampa
  Egmont Key
  El Pasaje Hotel/Cherokee Club
  Tampa Bay Hotel
  Ybor Factory Building
  Masonic Temple #25
  Hillsboro State Bank Building
  Mosely Homestead
  Hutchinson House
  Union RR Station
  Stovall House
  George Miller House/Woman's
    Club
  Leiman House

Johnson-Wolff House
El Centro Español of West Tampa
Federal Building/U.S.
  Courthouse/Postal Station
Old School House
Taliaferro/Ward House
Tampa Theatre
Tampa City Hall
Ybor City Historic District
Plant City Union Depot
Kress Co. Building
Centro Asturiano
Anderson-Frank House
El Centro Español De Tampa
Plant City High School
Hyde Park Historic District
West Tampa Historic District
Tampania House
Upper Tampa Bay Archaeological
  District
LeClaire Apartments
Curtis House
Palmerin Hotel
36 Columbia Drive
Spanish Apartments
Bay Isle Commercial Building
Seminole Heights Historic District
161 Bosporous Avenue
190 Bosporous Avenue
36 Aegean Avenue
53 Aegean Avenue
59 Aegean Avenue
84 Adalia Avenue
97 Adriatic Avenue
100 W Davis Blvd.
116 W Davis Blvd.
200 Corsica Avenue
131 W Davis Blvd.
Episcopal House of Prayer
124 Baltic Circle
125 Baltic Circle
132 Baltic Circle
202 Blanca Avenue
220 Blanca Avenue
418 Blanca Avenue
301 Caspian Street
North Plant City Residential
  District
Palace of Florence Apartments
Tampa Free Public Library

**Indian River County**
  Spanish Fleet Survivors and Salvors
    Camp

Pelican Island National Wildlife
  Refuge
Vero RR Station
Lawson House
Judge Gregory House
Old Palmetto Hotel
Vero Beach Community Building
Vero Theater

## Jackson County

Waddell's Mill Pond Site
Ely-Criglar House
Erwin House
Great Oaks/Bryan Mansion
Pender's Store
Theophilus West House
Russ House

## Jefferson County

San Juan De Aspalaga Mission
San Joseph De Ocuya Mission
San Miguel De Asile Mission
Palmer-Perkins House
Wirick-Simmons House
Lyndhurst Plantation
Asa May House
Denham-Lacy House
Lloyd RR Depot
Perkins Opera House
Turnbull-Ritter House
Dennis-Coxetter House
Lloyd-Bond House
Lloyd Historic District
Palmer House
Monticello Historic District

## Lake County

Bowers Bluff Middens Site
Kimball Island Midden Site
Howey House
Holy Trinity Episcopal Church
Mote Morris House
Clifford House
Donnelly House
Lakeside Inn
Clermont Woman's Club
Ferran Park/Alice McClelland
  Memorial Band Shell
Mount Dora A.C.L. RR Station
Pendleton House
Woman's Club of Eustis

## Lee County

Boca Grande Quarantine Station
Mound Key—Koreshan State Park
Demere Key

Josslyn Island
Pineland Site
Koreshan Unity Settlement
Sanibel Lighthouse
Sanibel Lighthouse Keeper's
  Quarters
Charlotte Harbor and Northern RR
Murphy-Burroughs House
Henry Ford Estate
Jewett-Thompson House
Alderman House
Boca Grande Lighthouse
Journey's End
Lee County Courthouse
Fort Myers Downtown Commercial
  District
Buckingham School
Punta Gorda Fish Company Ice
  House
Dunbar School
Thomas Edison Winter Estate
Fish Cabin at White Rock Shoals
Hendrickson Fish Cabin at Captiva
  Rocks
Ice House at Captiva Rocks
Ice House at Point Blanco
Larsen Fish Cabin at Captiva Rocks
Leneer Fish Cabin at Captiva
  Rocks
Norton Fish Cabin at Captiva
  Rocks
Whidden Fish Cabin at Captiva
  Rocks

## Leon County

Lake Jackson Mounds
San Luis de Talimali Mission
Escambe
Union Bank
Bellevue
Cascades Park
Goodwood
The Grove (Governor Call House)
Brokaw-McDougall House
The Columns
Walker Library
Natural Bridge Battlefield
Pisgah United Methodist Church
First Presbyterian Church
Calhoun Street Historic District
Park Avenue Historic District
Caroline Brevard Grammar School
Carnegie Library
Gilmore Riley House

Gallies Hall & Buildings
St. Johns Episcopal Church
Old City Water Works
Exchange Bank Building
George Lewis II House
Magnolia Heights Historic District
Woman's Club of Tallahassee
Bradley's County Store Complex
Gov. John Martin House
Tall Timbers Plantation District
Los Robles Gate
Covington House
Coles Farmhouse
Old Florida State Capitol
Fort Braden School
Leon High School
Tallahassee Historic District

**Levy County**
Island Hotel
Cedar Keys Historic Site

**Liberty County**
Yon Mound and Village
Gregory House/Torreya State Park
Otis Hare

**Madison County**
Wardlaw-Smith House
Dial-Goza House
First Baptist Church
Bishop-Andrews Hotel

**Manatee County**
Madira Bickel Mounds
Gamble Mansion
De Soto National Memorial
Original Manatee County
     Courthouse
Bradenton Carnegie Library
Braden Castle Park District
Seagate (Crosley House)
Woman's Club of Palmetto
Palmetto Historic District
Whitfield Estates/Broughton
     Street Historic District

**Marion County**
Coca-Cola Bottling Plant
Mount Zion AME Church
Ritz Apartments
Marion Hotel
McIntosh Historic District
Ocala Historic District

Tuscawilla Park Historic District
Orange Springs Church
Townsend House
Dunnellon Boomtown Historic
     District
Smith House
Ayer House
Gen. Robert Bullock House
Josselyn House
Lake Weir Yacht Club

**Martin County**
House of Refuge at Gilbert's Bar
Lyric Theater

**Miami-Dade County**
Cape Florida Lighthouse
El Jardin
Florida Pioneer Museum
Miami City Hospital (Bldg. 1)
Olympia Theatre
Ransom School
Anderson General Merchandise
     Store
Venetian Pool
Vizcaya
Munroe House
Grand Concourse Apartments
Adams House
Clune Building
Trinity Episcopal Cathedral
Warner House
Opa-Locka Co. Administration
     Building
Hurt Building
Opa-Locka RR Station
Osceola Apartment Hotel
Kampong Estate
Long House
Homestead (Cooper) Public
     School
Coral Gables Congregational
     Church
Freedom Tower
Gesu Church
Halissee Hall
Hialeah Park Race Track
Coral Gables City Hall
Plymouth Congregational Church
First Coconut Grove School House
Hervey Allen Study
Miami Woman's Club
Miami-Biltmore

Arch Creek Historic and
  Archaeological Site
Douglas Entrance
Dr. James Jackson's Office
Pan American Seaplane Base
U.S. Post Office and Courthouse,
  Miami
Woman's Club of Coconut Grove
Beth Jacob Social Hall
Miami Beach Architectural District
Fire Station #4
Congress Building
Charles Deering Estate
Silver Palm School House
Coral Gables Police and Fire
  Station
Opa-Locka Bank
Offshore Reefs Archaeological
  District
273 NE 98th Street
276 NE 98th Street
253 NE 99th Street
310 NE 99th Street
389 NE 99th Street
553 NE 101st Street
561 NE 101st Street
1291 NE 102nd Street
10108 NE 1st Avenue
577 NE 96th Street
540 NE 96th Street
353 NE 91st Street
357 NE 92nd Street
477 NE 92nd Street
145 NE 95th Street
Curtiss House
Hequembourg House
Millard-McCarthy House
Fla. East Coast RR Locomotive
  #153
Baird House
Cravero House
Crouse House
Etheredge House
Griffiths House
Haislip House
Helm Stores and Apartments
Helms House
Higgins Duplex
King Truck Factory and Showroom
Root Building
Taber Duplex
Tinsman House

Tooker House
Wheeler House
South River Drive Historic
  District
Entrance to Central Miami
Meyer-Kiser Building
Palm Cottage
Priscilla Apartments
Central Baptist Church
Coral Gables Elementary School
Dade Courthouse
Old U.S. Post Office and
  Courthouse
Brickell Mausoleum
City of Miami Cemetery
DuPont Building
Walgreen's Drugstore
Fire Station #2
Security Building
Hahn Building
Kentucky Home
Shoreline Arcade
City National Bank Building
Huntington Building
Ingraham Building
Southside School
Dorsey House
Mt. Zion Baptist Church
J & S Building
Lyric Theater
121 NE 100th Street
361 NE 97th Street
284 NE 96th Street
287 NE 96th Street
262 NE 96th Street
107 NE 96th Street
257 NE 91st Street
384 NE 94th Street
431 NE 94th Street
Algonquin Apartments
Martina Apartments
S & S Sandwich Shop
Venetian Causeway
Atlantic Gas Station
Coral Gables House
Greater Miami AME Church
Greenwald Steam Engine #1058
MacFarland Homestead Historic
  District
Old Spanish Monastery
Rock Gate
St. John's Baptist Church

**Monroe County**

Indian Key
San Jose Wreck
Old Post Office and Customshouse
Fort Zachary Taylor
Martello Gallery
Sand Key Lighthouse
Gato House
Porter House
The Armory
Bat Tower
Ft. Jefferson National Monument
Hemingway House
U.S. Coast Guard Headquarters
West Martello Tower
Little White House
Overseas Highway and Railway
	Bridge
Rock Mound Site
Key West Historic District
U.S. Naval Station Historic District
*Western Union* (schooner)
Carysport Lighthouse
Pidgeon Key Historic District
Adderley House
*HA 19* (Japanese midget submarine)
Thompson Fish House

**Nassau County**

Fort Clinch
"Tabby" House/Lewis House
Bailey House
Fairbanks House
Fernandina Beach Historic District
Palmer House
Merrick-Simmons House
Old Fernandina Historic Site

**Okaloosa County**

Fort Walton Mound
Gulfview Hotel Historic District

**Okeechobee County**

Okeechobee Battlefield
Freedman-Raulerson House

**Orange County**

Maitland Art Center
Old Orlando RR Depot
Rodgers Building
Bridges House
Phillips House
First Church of Christ Scientist
Tinker Building

Waterhouse House
Comstock-Harris House
Withers-Maguire House
Waite-Davis House
Apopka Seaboard Air Line Railway
	Depot
Brewer House
Carroll Building
Huttig Estate
Lake Eola Heights Historic District
Ryan & Co. Lumber Yard
Twin Mounds Archaeological
	District

**Osceola County**

Osceola County Courthouse
Colonial Estate
Desert Inn
First United Methodist Church
Kissimmee Historic District
Old Holy Redeemer Catholic
	Church

**Palm Beach County**

Jupiter Inlet Historic and
	Archaeological Site
Big Mound City
Bingham-Blossom House
Whitehall (Flagler House)
Breakers Hotel Complex
Jupiter Inlet Lighthouse
Paramount Theatre Building
Seaboard Coastline RR Passenger
	Station
Brelsford House/The Banyans
Florida East Coast Passenger
	Station
Boynton Women's Club
Boca Raton Old City Hall
Palm Beach Winter Club
	Administration Building
Kelsey City City Hall
Mar-A-Lago National Historic
	Landmark
Gulf Stream Hotel
U.S. Beach Post Office
Hibiscus Apartments
Dixie Court Hotel
Mickens House
Palm Beach Daily News Building
Vineta Hotel
Seaboard Airline RR Station
Warden House

Old Lake Worth City Hall
Norton House
Aiken House
Boynton School
Hatch's Department Store
Northwest Historic District
Northwood Historic District
Old Palm Beach Jr. College
  Building
Palm Beach Mercantile Company
Sundy-Shaw House
Viz Mizner
West Palm Beach National Guard
  Armory

**Pasco County**

Dade City Depot
Baker House
Jeffries House

**Pinellas County**

Weedon Island
Safety Harbor
Fort De Soto Batteries
Bay Pines
Andrews Memorial Chapel
Don Ce Sar Hotel
South Ward School
Roebling Estate
Belleview Biltmore Hotel
Safford House
Williams House
Vinoy Park Hotel
U.S. Post Office
Douglas House
Veillard House
Snell Arcade/Rutland Building
St. Petersburg Public Library
Dennis Hotel
Alexander Hotel
Ducros House
Cleveland Street Post Office
Casa de Muchas Flores
Boone House
Central High School
St. Petersburg Lawn Bowling Club
Casa Coe da Sol
Arcade Hotel
Potter House
Studebaker Building
Johnson Building/Pinellas Hotel
Harbor Oaks Residential District
First Methodist Church

Old Tarpon Springs City Hall
Old Tarpon Springs High School
Pass-A-Grille Historic District
*St. Nicholas III* (boat)
The *N.K. Symie* (boat)
Sponge-hooking boat *Duchess*
*St. Nicholas VI* (boat)
Arfaras Sponge Packing House
*Cretekos* (sponge-diving boat)
Tarpon Springs Historic District

**Polk County**

Casa de Josefina
Bok Mountain Sanctuary and
  Singing Tower
South Florida Military College
Christ Episcopal Church
Swearington House
Holland House/The Gables
Florida Southern College
Lake Mirror Promenade
South Lake Morton Historic
  District
El Retiro
Polk County Courthouse
Bullard House
Tillman House
Johnson House
Dixie Walesbilt Hotel
Lake Wales City Hall
First Baptist Church
Church of the Holy Spirit
Atlantic Coastline RR Depot
Chalet Suzanne
Lake Wales Commercial District
Bartow Downtown Commercial
  District
Beacon Hill/Alta Vista Residential
  District
Central Grammar School
Downtown Haines City
  Commercial District
East Lake Morton Residential
  District
Haines City National Guard
  Armory
Mountain Lake Colony House
Mountain Lake Estates Historic
  District
Northeast Bartow Residential
  District
Polk Hotel
Polk Theater and Office Building

South Bartow Residential District
St. Mark's Episcopal Church

## Putnam County

Mount Royal
Melrose Women's Club
Bronson-Mulholland House
Hubbard House
St. Marks Episcopal Church
Old ACL Union Depot
Palatka South Historic District
Palatka North Historic District

## St. Johns County

Castillo de San Marcos National
    Monument
St. Augustine Historic District
St. Augustine Alligator Farm
    Historic District
Gonzalez-Alvarez House
Fort Matanzas National Monument
Alcazar Hotel
Avero House
Fish Island
Cathedral of St. Augustine
Lindsley House
Rodriquez-Sanchez House
Sanchez Powder House
Llambias House
Spanish Coquina Quarries
Ximenez-Fatio House
O'Reilly House
Hotel Ponce de Leon
Markland
Grace United Methodist Church
St. Augustine Lighthouse
Old St. Johns County Jail
Bridge of Lions
Abbott Tract Historic District
Model Land Co. Historic District
Lincolnville Historic District
Xavier-Lopez House
Shell Bluff Landing
Solla-Carcaba Cigar Factory
Villa Zorayda

## St. Lucie County

Fort Pierce
St. Lucie High School
Casa Caprona/Markent
    Apartments
Cresthaven
St. Lucie Village Historic District
Hammond House

Hurston House

## Santa Rosa County

St. Mary's Episcopal Church
Louisville & Nashville Depot
Ollinger-Cobb House
Thomas Creek Archaeological
    District
Arcadia Sawmill and Dam
Bagdad Village Historic District
Milton Historic District
*Bethune Blackwater* (schooner)
Florida State Road #1
Mt. Pilgrim African Baptist Church

## Sarasota County

Osprey Archaeological and
    Historic Site
Little Salt Springs
Warm Mineral Springs
Whitfield Estates
Williams House
Sarasota Woman's Club
Reagin House
Halton House
City Waterworks
South Side School
Bay Haven School
*Sarasota Herald* Building
Cables-Ringling Estates Historic
    District
Field Estate
Hotel Venice
Atlantic Coastline Passenger Depot
Bacon & Tomlin, Inc.
Burns Court Historic District
DeCanizares House
DeMarcay Hotel
Edwards Theatre
Frances-Carlton Apartments
Kress Building
Purdy House
Roth Cigar Factory
Sarasota County Courthouse
Sarasota High School
*Sarasota Times* Building
U.S. Post Office—Federal Building
Wilson House
Myakka School House
Lemon Bay Woman's Club
Levillain-Letton House
Blalock House
Venice RR Depot
Edgewood Historic District

Armada Road Multi-family District
Venezia Park Historic District
Bacheller-Brewer Model Home
Estate
Bickel House
Corrigan House
Eagle Point Historic District
Earle House
El Patio Apartments
710 Armada Road South
Keith Estate
Dr. Kennedy House
Rigby's La Plaza Historic District
Sanderling Beach Club
Thoms House
Triangle Inn

**Seminole County**

Sanford Commercial District
Bradlee-McIntyre House
Longwood Village Hotel
Sanford Grammar School
Old Fernald-Laughton Memorial
Hospital
Sanford Residential District
Longwood Historic District
St. James AME Church

**Sumter County**

Dade Battleground Historic
Memorial
Thomas R. Pierce House

**Suwannee County**

Hull-Hawkins House
Old Live Oak City Hall
Blackwell House
Union Depot & ACL Freight
Station

**Taylor County**

Main Post Office
Taylor County Jail

**Union County**

Townsend Building

**Volusia County**

Bethune-Cookman College
Nocoroco (Tomoka State Park)
Turtle Mound
New Smyrna Sugar Mill Ruins
DeBary Hall
Ponce de Leon Inlet
Lighthouse

Ormond Hotel
Dunlawton Plantation/Sugar Mill
Bar
The Casements
All Saints Episcopal Church
Stetson Mansion
Mary McLeod Bethune House
DeLand Hall
Kress Building
Anderson Price Memorial
Library
The Abbey
Rogers House
Lippincott Mansion
Merchants Bank
Downtown DeLand Historic
District
El Real Retiro
South Beach Street Historic
District
Ross Hammock Site
Women's Club
Dix House
The Porches
Rowallan
The Hammocks
Talahloka Hotel
Anderson Lodge
Casements Annex
Old DeLand Memorial
Hospital
Thurman House
New Smyrna Beach Historic
District
Barberville Central High School
Blodgett House
Donnelly House
El Pino Parque Historic District
Gamble Place Historic District
Holly Hill Municipal Building
Kling House
Lake Helen Historic District
Olds Hall
Southern Cassadaga Spiritualist
Camp Historic District
Spruce Creek Mound Complex
Stetson University Campus Historic
District
Stevens House
Strawn Historic Agricultural
District
Strawn Historic Citrus Packing
House District

U.S. Post Office
West DeLand Residential
   District
White Hall
Young Memorial Library

**Wakulla County**
Fort San Marcos de Apalachee
Bird Hammock
Old Wakulla County
   Courthouse
St. Marks Lighthouse

Sopchoppy High School Gym
Wakulla Springs Archaeological
   and Historic District

**Walton County**
Sun Bright/Catts House
Chautauqua Hall of Brotherhood
DeFuniak Springs Historic District

**Washington County**
Moss Hill Church
South Third Street Historic District

# COUNTIES

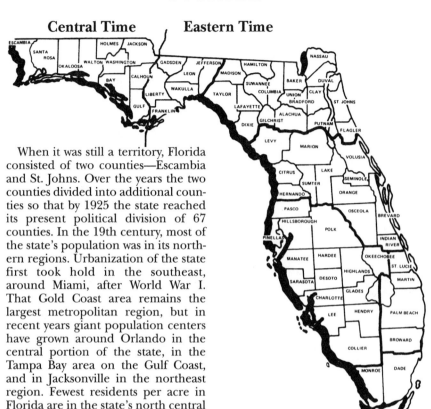

**Central Time**  **Eastern Time**

When it was still a territory, Florida consisted of two counties—Escambia and St. Johns. Over the years the two counties divided into additional counties so that by 1925 the state reached its present political division of 67 counties. In the 19th century, most of the state's population was in its northern regions. Urbanization of the state first took hold in the southeast, around Miami, after World War I. That Gold Coast area remains the largest metropolitan region, but in recent years giant population centers have grown around Orlando in the central portion of the state, in the Tampa Bay area on the Gulf Coast, and in Jacksonville in the northeast region. Fewest residents per acre in Florida are in the state's north central and northwest sections. Greatest growth in the past decade has been along the Gulf Coast, from Citrus County south to Collier County. The population around Orlando also has mushroomed primarily because of major entertainment attractions there. With an estimated 14.9 million persons in the state in 1999, Florida is the nation's fourth most populous state.

All Florida is divided into two time zones. The Apalachicola River marks the boundary between the Eastern and Central time zones in the state. Most of North Florida and the entire peninsula are on Eastern time, while all west of the river is on Central time. Counties in the Central Time Zone are Jackson, Calhoun, Gulf, Holmes, Washington, Bay, Walton, Okaloosa, Santa Rosa, and Escambia.

## ORIGIN OF COUNTY NAMES

**Alachua**—Indian term meaning "grassy."

**Baker**—for Judge James M. Baker.

**Bay**—from St. Andrew's Bay.

**Bradford**—for Capt. Richard Bradford, first Florida officer killed during the War Between the States.

**Brevard**—for Dr. Theodore W. Brevard, author of the North Carolina Declaration of Independence.

**Broward**—for Gov. Napoleon B. Broward.

**Calhoun**—for U.S. Sen. John C. Calhoun.

**Charlotte**—for the harbor.

**Citrus**—for the state's citrus industry.

**Clay**—for statesman Henry Clay.

**Collier**—for landowner Barron G. Collier.

**Columbia**—for Christopher Columbus.

**De Soto**—for Spanish explorer Hernando De Soto.

**Dixie**—for the popular term applied to the South.

**Duval**—for Gov. William P. DuVal.

**Escambia**—Indian term meaning "barter."

**Flagler**—for state developer Henry Flagler.

**Franklin**—for Benjamin Franklin.

**Gadsden**—for James Gadsden, aide to Gen. Andrew Jackson.

**Gilchrist**—for Gov. Albert H. Gilchrist.

**Glades**—for Everglades.

**Gulf**—for the Gulf of Mexico.

**Hamilton**—for Alexander Hamilton.

**Hardee**—for Gov. Cary A. Hardee.

**Hendry**—for early resident Capt. Francis A. Hendry.

**Hernando**—for explorer Hernando De Soto.

**Highlands**—for geography of the county.

**Hillsborough**—for English Earl of Hillsborough.

**Holmes**—for an early resident.

**Indian River**—for Indian River.

**Jackson**—for Gen. and Pres. Andrew Jackson, first American Governor of Florida.

**Jefferson**—for Pres. Thomas Jefferson.

**Lafayette**—for the Marquis de Lafayette.

**Lake**—for the many lakes in the county.

**Lee**—for Gen. Robert E. Lee.

**Leon**—for explorer Ponce de Leon.

**Levy**—for David Levy Yulee, state's first U.S. senator.

**Liberty**—for the right of U.S. citizens.

**Madison**—for Pres. James Madison.

**Manatee**—for marine mammal.

**Marion**—for Gen. Francis Marion of the Revolutionary War.

**Martin**—for Gov. John W. Martin.

**Miami-Dade**—for its principal city and for Maj. Francis L. Dade, killed in Second Seminole War.

**Monroe**—for Pres. James Monroe.

**Nassau**—for German Duchy of Nassau.

**Okaloosa**—Indian word for "black water."

**Okeechobee**—for Lake Okeechobee, Indian word for "big water."

**Orange**—in honor of citrus crop.

**Osceola**—for Seminole Indian leader.

**Palm Beach**—for palms on beaches.

**Pasco**—for U.S. Sen. Samuel Pasco.

**Pinellas**—Spanish for "Point of Pines."

**Polk**—for Pres. James Polk.

**Putnam**—for Benjamin Alexander Putnam, adjutant to Gen. Zachary Taylor in Second Seminole War.

**St. Johns**—from St. Johns River, called by Spanish explorers "San Juan Baptista."

**St. Lucie**—for Catholic Church saint.

**Santa Rosa**—for Catholic Church saint.

**Sarasota**—Indian word referring to "Point of Rocks" on Gulf.

**Seminole**—for the Indian tribe of that name.

**Sumter**—for Gen. Thomas Sumter of the Revolutionary War.

**Suwannee**—Indian word meaning "echo."

**Taylor**—for Gen. Zachary Taylor.

**Union**—for unity.

**Volusia**—for settler named Volus.

**Wakulla**—Indian word for spring meaning "mystery."

**Walton**—for a prominent Georgia colonel.

**Washington**—for Pres. George Washington.

## FORMATION OF COUNTIES

Gen. Andrew Jackson, while serving as military governor of Florida, divided the peninsula into counties by an ordinance which read, in part:

"All the country lying between the Perdido and Suwaney rivers, with all islands therein, shall form one county to be called Escambia.

"All the country lying east of the river Suwaney, and every part of the ceded territories not designated as belonging to the former county, shall form a county to be called St. Johns."

The ordinance establishing the first counties was dated July 21, 1821. One year later the territorial council, forerunner of the present state legislature, began dividing the original two counties and adding more. From that time until 1925 seldom did a session of the legislature or, before statehood, the council, pass without at least one new county being added.

Date of formation in the following chart is the date of final action by the council or legislature in approving the county. Where the same date is indicated, order was determined by the order listed in the law.

| Rank | County | County Seat | Date Formed |
|------|--------|-------------|-------------|
| 1 | Escambia | Pensacola | July 21, 1821 |
| 2 | St. Johns | St. Augustine | July 21, 1821 |
| 3 | Jackson | Marianna | August 12, 1822 |
| 4 | Duval | Jacksonville | August 12, 1822 |
| 5 | Gadsden | Quincy | June 24, 1823 |
| 6 | Monroe | Key West | July 3, 1823 |
| 7 | Leon | Tallahassee | December 29, 1824 |
| 8 | Walton | De Funiak Springs | December 29, 1824 |
| 9 | Alachua | Gainesville | December 29, 1824 |
| 10 | Nassau | Fernandina Beach | December 29, 1824 |
| 11 | Orange | Orlando | December 29, 1824 |
| 12 | Washington | Chipley | December 9, 1825 |
| 13 | Jefferson | Monticello | January 20, 1827 |
| 14 | Madison | Madison | December 26, 1827 |
| 15 | Hamilton | Jasper | December 26, 1827 |
| 16 | Columbia | Lake City | February 4, 1832 |
| 17 | Franklin | Apalachicola | February 8, 1832 |
| 18 | Hillsborough | Tampa | January 25, 1834 |
| 19 | Miami-Dade | Miami | February 4, 1836 |
| 20 | Calhoun | Blountstown | January 26, 1838 |
| 21 | Santa Rosa | Milton | February 18, 1842 |
| 22 | Hernando | Brooksville | February 24, 1843 |
| 23 | Wakulla | Crawfordville | March 11, 1843 |
| 24 | Marion | Ocala | March 14, 1844 |
| 25 | Brevard | Titusville | March 14, 1844 |
| 26 | Levy | Bronson | March 10, 1845 |

| 27 | Holmes | Bonifay | January 8, 1848 |
| 28 | Putnam | Palatka | January 13, 1849 |
| 29 | Sumter | Bushnell | January 8, 1853 |
| 30 | Volusia | De Land | December 29, 1854 |
| 31 | Manatee | Bradenton | January 9, 1855 |
| 32 | Liberty | Bristol | December 15, 1856 |
| 33 | Lafayette | Mayo | December 23, 1856 |
| 34 | Taylor | Perry | December 23, 1856 |
| 35 | Suwannee | Live Oak | December 21, 1858 |
| 36 | Bradford | Starke | December 31, 1858 |
| 37 | Clay | Green Cove Springs | December 31, 1858 |
| 38 | Baker | Macclenny | February 8, 1861 |
| 39 | Polk | Bartow | February 8, 1861 |
| 40 | Osceola | Kissimmee | May 12, 1887 |
| 41 | Lee | Fort Myers | May 13, 1887 |
| 42 | De Soto | Arcadia | May 19, 1887 |
| 43 | Lake | Tavares | May 27, 1887 |
| 44 | Citrus | Inverness | June 2, 1887 |
| 45 | Pasco | Dade City | June 2, 1887 |
| 46 | St. Lucie | Fort Pierce | May 24, 1905 |
| 47 | Palm Beach | West Palm Beach | April 30, 1909 |
| 48 | Pinellas | Clearwater | May 23, 1911 |
| 49 | Bay | Panama City | April 24, 1913 |
| 50 | Seminole | Sanford | April 25, 1913 |
| 51 | Broward | Fort Lauderdale | April 30, 1915 |
| 52 | Okaloosa | Crestview | June 13, 1915 |
| 53 | Flagler | Bunnell | April 28, 1917 |
| 54 | Okeechobee | Okeechobee | May 8, 1917 |
| 55 | Hardee | Wauchula | April 23, 1921 |
| 56 | Highlands | Sebring | April 23, 1921 |
| 57 | Charlotte | Punta Gorda | April 23, 1921 |
| 58 | Glades | Moore Haven | April 23, 1921 |
| 59 | Dixie | Cross City | April 25, 1921 |
| 60 | Sarasota | Sarasota | May 14, 1921 |
| 61 | Union | Lake Butler | May 20, 1921 |
| 62 | Collier | East Naples | May 8, 1923 |
| 63 | Hendry | La Belle | May 11, 1923 |
| 64 | Martin | Stuart | May 30, 1925 |
| 65 | Indian River | Vero Beach | May 30, 1925 |
| 66 | Gulf | Port St. Joe | June 6, 1925 |
| 67 | Gilchrist | Trenton | December 4, 1925 |

## ANNUAL PRICE LEVEL INDEX
### (1998)

The Florida Price Level Index measures the cost of living in each county compared to a statewide average. It is compiled each year by the Department of Education and is computed by pricing 117 items that consumers normally use. These items fall into five categories—food, transportation, housing, clothing and recreation, and health and personal services. The "index" column following indicates how much above or below the state average (100) it costs to maintain a fixed, specified standard of living in each county. The column marked "rank" compares a county's cost of living with the other 66 counties.

For example, Miami-Dade County is the second most expensive county in which to live; its 107.23 index says the cost of living in Miami-Dade County is 7.23 percentage points higher than the state average. The purpose of the index is to establish a differential formula for state contributions to its school systems. Each county is a unified school district.

| County | Index | Rank | County | Index | Rank |
|--------|-------|------|--------|-------|------|
| Alachua | .95.19 | .27 | Lee | .97.80 | .15 |
| Baker | .92.17 | .51 | Leon | .97.50 | .17 |
| Bay | .94.29 | .37 | Levy | .90.83 | .62 |
| Bradford | .91.80 | .57 | Liberty | .90.35 | .64 |
| Brevard | .97.92 | .14 | Madison | .92.63 | .46 |
| Broward | .105.80 | .3 | Manatee | .99.22 | .10 |
| Calhoun | .89.90 | .65 | Marion | .94.16 | .39 |
| Charlotte | .96.52 | .20 | Martin | .97.96 | .13 |
| Citrus | .92.19 | .49 | Miami-Dade | .106.28 | .2 |
| Clay | .96.01 | .22 | Monroe | .112.43 | .1 |
| Collier | .100.99 | .7 | Nassau | .94.78 | .32 |
| Columbia | .91.63 | .59 | Okaloosa | .95.14 | .28* |
| De Soto | .93.16 | .41* | Okeechobee | .95.48 | .25 |
| Dixie | .92.18 | .50 | Orange | .99.04 | .12 |
| Duval | .97.28 | .18 | Osceola | .96.56 | .19 |
| Escambia | .93.16 | .41* | Palm Beach | .102.69 | .6 |
| Flagler | .94.85 | .31 | Pasco | .95.44 | .26 |
| Franklin | .94.31 | .36 | Pinellas | .103.74 | .4 |
| Gadsden | .93.07 | .44 | Polk | .94.58 | .30 |
| Gilchrist | .92.02 | .52 | Putnam | .92.28 | .48 |
| Glades | .95.66 | .23 | St. Johns | .99.18 | .11 |
| Gulf | .91.98 | .55 | St. Lucie | .94.47 | .34 |
| Hamilton | .91.96 | .56 | Santa Rosa | .91.55 | .60 |
| Hardee | .92.01 | .53 | Sarasota | .102.90 | .5 |
| Hendry | .94.46 | .35 | Seminole | .99.48 | .9 |
| Hernando | .93.26 | .40 | Sumter | .89.66 | .66 |
| Highlands | .94.51 | .33 | Suwannee | .91.76 | .58 |
| Hillsborough | .100.86 | .8 | Taylor | .95.14 | .28* |
| Holmes | .92.72 | .45 | Union | .91.30 | .61 |
| Indian River | .97.64 | .16 | Volusia | .95.64 | .24 |
| Jackson | .90.55 | .63 | Wakulla | .92.53 | .47 |
| Jefferson | .94.26 | .38 | Walton | .92.00 | .54 |
| Lafayette | .93.12 | .43 | Washington | .89.64 | .67 |
| Lake | .96.14 | .21 | *Tied | | |

## COUNTY PROFILES

**ALACHUA**
Area: 961 square miles
Approx. elev: 165 ft.
Avg. temps: 57 Jan.
            81 Aug.
Avg. annual rain: 50 in.
1980 pop: 151,348
1990 pop: 181,596
1998 est. pop: 198,662

In the north central section of the state, Alachua County is most noted as the site of the state's major higher education facility, the University of Florida. Education is the county's foremost "industry," with its estimated 34,000 students comprising nearly half the population of the county's major city, Gainesville.

Biggest private sector employers are hospitals, although numerous technological firms have settled in the area because of the university's presence. Major transportation into the county is via I-75 and the Gainesville Regional Airport.

Besides Gainesville, the county seat, incorporated areas include Alachua, Archer, Hawthorne, High Springs, LaCrosse, Micanopy, Newberry, and Waldo. One of the county's most scenic unincorporated areas is the settlement of Cross Creek, the home of Marjorie Kinnan Rawlings.

Alachua is particularly endowed with natural beauty. Sprinkled liberally through the rolling, heavily treed landscape are springs, rivers, nature walks, a major botanical garden, a vast prairie, and archaeological sites.

## BAKER

Area: 588 square miles
Approx. elev: 129 ft.
Avg. temps: 55 Jan.
　　　　81 Aug.
Avg. annual rain: 49.27 in.
1980 pop: 15,289
1990 pop: 18,486
1998 est. pop: 21,103

On the Florida-Georgia border, Baker County is primarily an agricultural county. The Battle of Olustee, one of the state's most important battles during the War Between the States, was fought in the county. Numerous small streams flow through Baker, providing excellent fishing, as does the bordering St. Mary's River. Quail, deer, and turkey also are found in its vast forests.

Nearly one-half of the lightly populated county's area is dominated by the Osceola National Forest, one of three in the state. In addition, a large portion of Baker's northern region is composed of valuable wetlands, much of which have been and are being purchased by the state and the Nature Conservancy to prevent their development.

Agricultural products are its residents' primary source of income. Major transportation into the county is I-10.

It is served by Jacksonville International Airport in adjacent Duval County.

Incorporated places include Macclenny, the county seat, and Glen Saint Mary.

## BAY

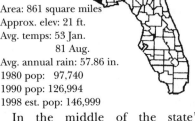

Area: 861 square miles
Approx. elev: 21 ft.
Avg. temps: 53 Jan.
　　　　81 Aug.
Avg. annual rain: 57.86 in.
1980 pop:　97,740
1990 pop: 126,994
1998 est. pop: 146,999

In the middle of the state's Panhandle, on the Gulf of Mexico, Bay County is a favorite tourist site because of its outstanding beaches. Most of its population clusters around its spacious bays—St. Andrew, West Bay, North Bay, and East Bay—and St. Andrew Sound. Long, narrow barrier islands shield the mainland from the Gulf. Adjoining the county's major populated center, Panama City, is Tyndall Air Force Base.

During World War II, Panama City was a major shipbuilding center. Today, the county still depends for much of its employment and economic resources on nearby military activities. As a result, many pensioned military persons have chosen the area for their retirement.

Bay County also entertains large tourist populations because of its miles of beaches (the area has been referred to as the Miracle Strip). St. Andrew's State Recreation Area in Bay County is one of the state's 113 parks and among its most visited.

Major private employers include hospitals and paper and chemical manufacturers. Transportation into the county is via I-10 and the Panama City/Bay County Regional Airport.

Largest incorporated places are Panama City, the county seat, and Callaway, Lynn Haven, Springfield, and Parker.

## BRADFORD

Area: 305 square miles
Approx. elev: 150-180 ft.
Avg. temps: 60 Jan.
           81 Aug.
Avg. annual rain: 49.40 in.
1980 pop: 20,023
1990 pop: 22,515
1998 est. pop: 24,777

One of the state's smallest, Bradford County is a land-bound region in northeast Florida in which truck crops, tobacco, timber, and livestock play an important economic role. Largest private employers include manufacturers of mineral sand, work clothing, and wood products. Transportation routes serving the county are I-10 and I-75. The nearest airport is 24 miles distant, the Gainesville Regional Airport.

A primary asset of Bradford County is its location, a pleasant hour's drive from the recreation, historical sites, and shopping amenities in Jacksonville, St. Augustine, and Gainesville.

Largest incorporated places are Starke, the county seat, and Lawtey, Hampton, and Brooker.

## BREVARD

Area: 1,310 square miles
Approx. elev: 6-26 ft.
Avg. temps: 62 Jan.
           81.5 Aug.
Avg. annual rain: 50.74 in.
1980 pop: 272,959
1990 pop: 398,978
1998 est. pop: 466,093

The U.S. space program is the focal point of Brevard County, which is in the central part of the peninsula fronting on the Atlantic Ocean. Long and narrow, Brevard is 72 miles from north to south, but only 20 miles wide. Cape Canaveral is within its borders.

Brevard's economic health for decades has been tied to the U.S. space program, but annually more of its future is being oriented toward its massive coastline, which is attracting increasing numbers of new residents.

The majority of its population is sidled up to the Indian River, a major state waterway on the western shore of the Kennedy Space Center complex. Brevard's percentage of population growth the past decade exceeded the state's percentage of increase.

Largest employers are electronics and aerospace manufacturers. Transportation into the county includes I-95 and Melbourne Regional Airport.

Largest incorporated places are Melbourne, Palm Bay, Cocoa, Rockledge, and Titusville, the county seat.

## BROWARD

Area: 1,220 square miles
Approx. elev: 8 ft.
Avg. temps: 68.6 Jan.
           82 Aug.
Avg. annual rain: 65.19 in.
1980 pop: 1,014,043
1990 pop: 1,255,488
1998 est. pop: 1,503,407

Part of the Gold Coast, Broward County's vast metropolitan area runs up its eastern shores on the Atlantic Ocean. The majority of the county's square miles, however, are inland, in the eastern portion of the unpopulated Everglades.

Despite this marked contrast between eastern and western Broward that results in much of the county being sparsely populated, Broward has more than 1,000 people per square mile. That ranks it as the second most populated and second most densely populated of the 67 counties.

Major private employers are in financial services, telecommunications, radio products, and computers. Transportation routes into Broward include I-75, I-95, and the Florida Turnpike, plus air service at Fort Lauderdale/Hollywood International Airport.

Largest incorporated places are Fort Lauderdale, the county seat, and

Hollywood, Pompano Beach, Coral Springs, and Plantation.

## CALHOUN

Area: 567 square miles
Approx. elev: 51 ft.
Avg. temps: 53 Jan.
        81.5 Aug.
Avg. annual rain: 58.94 in.
1980 pop:  9,294
1990 pop: 11,011
1998 est. pop: 12,420

A rural county with few people, Calhoun County is tucked in the Panhandle a short distance from the Gulf of Mexico and the Georgia and Alabama borders. It is primarily forests and wetlands, and largely undeveloped.

A variety of small industries include trucking, flowers, clothing, and wood products, all with fewer than 150 employees.

Two of Calhoun's greatest assets are rivers—the mighty Apalachicola, which outlines the county's eastern border, and the Chipola, which bisects the county. Both provide abundant recreational activities.

Transportation needs are served by I-10 and the Tallahassee Regional Airport, located 50 miles to the east.

Largest incorporated places are Blountstown, the county seat, and Altha.

## CHARLOTTE

Area: 832 square miles
Approx. elev: 3 ft.
Avg. temps: 64 Jan.
        81.9 Aug.
Avg. annual rain: 52.55 in.
1980 pop: 59,115
1990 pop: 110,975
1998 est. pop: 134,899

On the southwest coast, fronting on the Gulf of Mexico, Charlotte County is only 17 miles from north to south, but has approximately 120 miles of shoreline. It is one of the state's fastest-growing counties, in part because of its wide-ranging waterfront.

Both the Myakka and Peace rivers

flow through it and into expansive Charlotte Harbor, on whose shores sits Punta Gorda, the county seat. West of the harbor is a fast-developing peninsula protected from Gulf storms by numerous barrier islands, including Gasparilla. Nearby Lemon Bay, Placida Harbor, and Gasparilla Sound are excellent fishing grounds.

Health care facilities are among the largest private employers in the county. Major transportation routes are I-75 and U.S. 41. Air service is at the Southwest Florida Regional Airport 25 miles to the south in adjacent Lee County.

Because Charlotte and its adjoining county to the south, Lee, are among the state's fastest growing, the area enjoys a new four-year university, Florida Gulf Coast University.

Largest populated centers are Punta Gorda, the county seat, and Port Charlotte.

## CITRUS

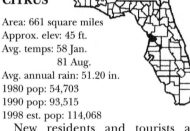

Area: 661 square miles
Approx. elev: 45 ft.
Avg. temps: 58 Jan.
        81 Aug.
Avg. annual rain: 51.20 in.
1980 pop: 54,703
1990 pop: 93,515
1998 est. pop: 114,068

New residents and tourists are attracted to Citrus County, a region with its western boundary on the Gulf of Mexico and its eastern area dominated by the Withlacoochee State Forest and Tsala Apopka Lake.

The largest private employer is a nuclear power plant, but others include health care facilities and retailers. I-75 and U.S. 41 are major motor routes into the county. Nearest major airport is Tampa International 65 miles to the south.

Recreation opportunities abound in Citrus County, which has dozens of freshwater lakes, rivers, springs, wildlife refuges, and parks. The county is most famous for its many manatees, an endangered mammal. Sometimes called sea cows, the gentle manatees have made the county's Crystal River one of their favorite eating and mating grounds.

Largest incorporated places are Inverness, the county seat, and Crystal River.

## CLAY

Area: 644 square miles
Approx. elev: 25-150 ft.
Avg. temps: 55.4 Jan.
　　　　　 81.3 Aug.
Avg. annual rain: 53.42 in.
1980 pop:　67,052
1990 pop: 105,986
1998 est. pop: 137,455

Its eastern border fronting on the St. Johns River, Clay County is a neighbor of sprawling Duval County to its north. The doubling of Clay's population during the past decade is attributed in large part to its proximity to Duval and the popular recreation county, St. Johns.

The U.S. Army has a large facility, Camp Blanding, in the western area of Clay. Private employment is in industries producing concrete and asphalt, lumber and wood chips, minerals, and dairying. Routes with spurs into the county include I-95, I-10, and U.S. 17. Jacksonville International Airport, 33 miles to the north, is the nearest major air facility.

Numerous sulphur springs near the St. Johns River have been thought to have medicinal benefits and, say some, may have been the springs sought by Ponce de Leon.

Largest incorporated places are Orange Park, Green Cove Springs, the county seat, and Keystone Heights.

## COLLIER

Area: 2,119 square miles
Approx. elev: 4 ft.
Avg. temps: 67.8 Jan.
　　　　　 82.4 Aug.
Avg. annual rain: 51.40 in.
1980 pop:　85,791
1990 pop: 152,099
1998 est. pop: 199,436

Known for its 10,000 islands, Collier County and its Everglades region offer one of the last large strands of cypress in the U.S. The Everglades dominate much of Collier, thus, development has been almost exclusively along the county's western boundary, on the Gulf of Mexico.

In the 1800s, Seminole Indians, in flight after losing battles with the U.S. Army, settled in the Everglades. Today a majority of the estimated 2,000 Seminoles in Florida live in Collier.

Major private employers are in health services and lodging. Major roads into the county are I-75 and U.S. 41. Nearest major air service is at Southwest Florida Regional Airport in Lee County to the north.

Largest incorporated places are Naples and Everglades City. County seat is in East Naples.

## COLUMBIA

Area: 789 square miles
Approx. elev: 200 ft.
Avg. temps: 55.6 Jan.
　　　　　 81 Aug.
Avg. annual rain: 49.88 in.
1980 pop: 35,399
1990 pop: 42,613
1998 est. pop: 52,956

Among Columbia County's great natural resources are the Osceola National Forest and the bordering Suwannee River. The famous river enters Florida from the Okefenokee Swamp in Georgia near the Columbia County line, which borders the Peach State.

Largest private employers are in asphalt paving and mobile home manufacturing and sales. The county is home to the Florida Sports Hall of Fame.

Both I-10 and I-75 enter the county, but the nearest major airport, the Gainesville Regional Airport, is 42 miles to the south.

A popular visitor stop is the beautiful Ichetucknee River that provides swimming and canoeing. Its nearly three miles of slowly flowing spring water also make it one of the world's finest tubing sites.

Largest incorporated places are Lake City, the county seat, and Fort White.

## DE SOTO

Area: 721 square miles
Approx. elev: 56 ft.
Avg. temps: 63 Jan.
        82 Aug.
Avg. annual rain: 50.66 in.
1980 pop: 19,039
1990 pop: 23,865
1998 est. pop: 24,820

A cattle and citrus region, De Soto is an inland county nearer the Gulf of Mexico than the Atlantic Ocean. It is primarily rural, sparsely populated, and proud of its annual All-Florida Rodeo held twice each year.

Flowing through De Soto is one of Florida's two dozen major rivers, the Peace. It is a mecca for fishing and canoeing.

Private industry includes citrus, packing houses, and agriculture. I-75 is the primary driving route into the county, and, for air service, travelers favor the Sarasota/Bradenton Airport 53 miles to the northeast.

Arcadia, the county seat, is the only notable populated city in De Soto County.

## DIXIE

Area: 709 square miles
Approx. elev: 42 ft.
Avg. temps: 55.2 Jan.
        81.4 Aug.
Avg. annual rain: 58.20 in.
1980 pop: 7,751
1990 pop: 10,585
1998 est. pop: 12,959

One of the state's least densely populated counties with about 15 persons per square mile, Dixie County fronts on the Gulf of Mexico but it does not have wide, attractive beaches. Instead, the region is more a favorite with deer, turkey, and wild pig hunters than with tourists.

Timber companies are Dixie's largest private employers. The major road into the county is U.S. 19, and air service is available 60 miles to the east at Gainesville Regional Airport.

The county's history includes a battle at Old Town on U.S. 19, once a large Indian village where Chief Billy Bowlegs encountered Andrew Jackson during Indian uprisings. Prior to the Civil War, Old Town was the site of a factory where Spanish moss was turned into clean, economical stuffing for mattresses and furniture.

Incorporated places are Cross City, the county seat, and Horseshoe Beach.

## DUVAL

Area: 840 square miles
Approx. elev: 25 ft.
Avg. temps: 55.2 Jan.
        81.4 Aug.
Avg. annual rain: 58.20 in.
1980 pop: 570,981
1990 pop: 672,971
1998 est. pop: 735,733

Tucked into the northeast corner of Florida, Duval has one of the nation's largest ports, used heavily by the U.S. Navy. During World War II, the port at Jacksonville was a busy military embarkation point. It still is a busy military site for the Air Force and Navy.

In 1967 the city of Jacksonville and Duval County consolidated into one large political entity, making Jacksonville the state's most populous city and, in land area, the world's largest city. Coursing through downtown Jacksonville is one of the world's few northerly flowing rivers, the St. Johns.

Largest private industries in Duval are retailing, banking, health care, insurance, communications, and shipping. I-10 and I-95 enter the county, as do U.S. 1 and U.S. 90. Jacksonville International Airport provides air service.

Notable areas include the urban core formerly known as Jacksonville, the government center, as well as Jacksonville Beach, Atlantic Beach, Neptune Beach, and Baldwin.

## ESCAMBIA

Area: 762 square miles
Approx. elev: 20 ft.
Avg. temps: 53 Jan.
        81 Aug.
Avg. annual rain: 58.60 in.
1980 pop: 233,794
1990 pop: 262,798
1998 est. pop: 282,303

Spain, France, and England all owned portions of Escambia County at one time. It is the state's most western county and, unlike most of Florida, is in the Central Time Zone. It is separated on the west from Alabama by the Perdido River; its southern boundaries front on the Gulf of Mexico.

Perdido Key and Santa Rosa Island stand between the Gulf and the county's major city, Pensacola. Also on the waterfront is the Pensacola Naval Air Station.

Pensacola is considered by many to be a military town because of its air station and Eglin Air Force Base in adjoining Santa Rosa County.

Health care, chemicals, and paper products, along with tourism, are Escambia's chief industries. The major route into the county is I-10, with air service provided by Pensacola Regional Airport.

Largest incorporated places are Pensacola, the county seat, and Century.

## FLAGLER

Area: 504 square miles
Approx. elev: 0-22 ft.
Avg. temps: 58.6 Jan.
        81.6 Aug.
Avg. annual rain: 50.74 in.
1980 pop: 10,913
1990 pop: 28,701
1998 est. pop: 47,455

Noted for its miles of pristine beaches, Flagler County is along the Atlantic Ocean on Florida's northeast coast.

Among its superlatives is the fact that Flagler, over the course of the past decade, was Florida's fastest-growing county.

Yacht building, tourism, and land development are the county's major industries. I-95 and U.S. 1 pass through the county. Air service is available 30 miles south at Daytona Beach Regional Airport.

Largest incorporated places are Flagler Beach, Bunnell, the county seat, and Beverly Beach.

## FRANKLIN

Area: 565 square miles
Approx. elev: 0-24 ft.
Avg. temps: 53.7 Jan.
        81.7 Aug.
Avg. annual rain: 58.36 in.
1980 pop: 7,661
1990 pop: 8,967
1998 est. pop: 10,079

Sparsely populated Franklin County, in the Panhandle, is separated from the Gulf of Mexico by Apalachicola Bay and the offshore St. George Island. Its interior is noted for the vast acreage of the Apalachicola National Forest and Tate's Hell Swamp.

Seafood is the county's primary industry. Passing near Franklin County is I-10. Its residents use air service at the Tallahassee Regional Airport 75 miles to the northeast.

Largest incorporated places are Apalachicola, the county seat, and Carrabelle.

## GADSDEN

Area: 523 square miles
Approx. elev: 250-300 ft.
Avg. temps: 53.7 Jan.
        80.4 Aug.
Avg. annual rain: 56.02 in.
1980 pop: 41,565
1990 pop: 41,105
1998 est. pop: 44,043

Bordering the Georgia state line, Gadsden County was settled by wealthy slave owners, and the county is still famous for its large plantations and tobacco crop. The county harbors the huge Woodruff Dam.

Mostly rural, Gadsden lost population during the 1980s, but it has rebounded in the past decade.

Private employers include wholesale food distributors, mushroom growers, and makers of lumber, wire and nails, and furniture. Motoring routes into the county include I-10 and U.S. 90. Nearest air service is 20 miles away, at the Tallahassee Regional Airport.

Largest incorporated places are Quincy, the county seat, and Chattahoochee, Havana, Gretna, and Midway.

## GILCHRIST

Area: 348 square miles
Approx. elev: 63 ft.
Avg. temps: 56.2 Jan.
            81.2 Aug.
Avg. annual rain: 54.76 in.
1980 pop: 5,767
1990 pop: 9,667
1998 est. pop: 13,791

A region of clear springs and rivers, Gilchrist County in north central Florida curves around both the Suwannee and Santa Fe rivers. It is a largely agricultural county, growing watermelons and dotted with dairies. It was the last of the state's counties to be formed.

Dairying and tourism are the county's primary industries. Because of its many crystal-clear springs, its rivers, and its uncrowded conditions, Gilchrist also is becoming a favorite homesite for retirees and for persons employed in nearby Gainesville. It is one of the few counties not traversed by a U.S. highway or Interstate. Nearest air service is 45 miles east at the Gainsville Regional Airport.

Largest incorporated places are Trenton, the county seat, Bell, and Fannin Springs.

## GLADES

Area: 898 square miles
Approx. elev: 8-22 ft.
Avg. temps: 64 Jan.
            81.2 Aug.
Avg. annual rain: 49.95 in.
1980 pop: 5,992
1990 pop: 7,591
1998 est. pop: 8,492

One of five counties bordering Lake Okeechobee, Glades also is the site of a large Seminole Indian reservation. Most of Glades' few residents live along the lakeshore. Its hinterland is occupied mostly by the Fisheating Creek Wildlife Refuge and Management Area.

Glades' largest product is sugarcane, although sizable dairy herds were evident in past decades until strict pollution requirements forced many to shut down.

U.S. 27, once the principal route through Florida, is the sole major highway through the county.

Moore Haven, the only significant city in Glades County, is the county seat.

## GULF

Area: 578 square miles
Approx. elev: 15 ft.
Avg. temps: 53.7 Jan.
            81.7 Aug.
Avg. annual rain: 58.36 in.
1980 pop: 10,658
1990 pop: 11,504
1998 est. pop: 13,476

Once an important cotton-shipping area, Gulf County also was the site of the state's first Constitutional Convention. It took place in 1838 in Port St. Joe, a city that was destroyed by a Yellow Fever epidemic and a tidal wave in 1841.

Gulf is a Panhandle county, fronting on the Gulf of Mexico. But much of its shoreline is sheltered by St. Joseph Peninsula.

Paper is the county's biggest industry, followed by the transportation of crude oil, magnesium, and coal. The county's major motoring route is U.S. 98. Air service is available 40 miles to the west at the Panama City/Bay County Regional Airport.

Largest incorporated places are rebuilt Port St. Joe, the county seat, and Wewahitchka.

## HAMILTON

Area: 515 square miles
Approx. elev: 152 ft.
Avg. temps: 53.7 Jan.
            81 Aug.
Avg. annual rain: 49.51 in.
1980 pop:  8,761
1990 pop: 10,930
1998 est. pop: 12,651

Site of the Stephen Foster Memorial and state park on the Suwannee River, Hamilton County in north Florida shares its northern boundary with the state of Georgia. It is a small, lightly populated county, much of it covered by forests.

The primary private employer is the phosphate industry, although the county does have numerous vegetable-producing operations. The major thoroughfare through Hamilton is I-75, entering Florida from Georgia. The nearest large airport is Jacksonville International some 90 miles to the east

Canoeing the Suwannee River's whitewater shoals and the Withlacoochee River, the county's western boundary, are popular recreational activities.

Largest incorporated places are Jasper, the county seat, Jennings, and White Springs.

## HARDEE

Area: 630 square miles
Approx. elev: 55 ft.
Avg. temps: 63 Jan.
            82.3 Aug.
Avg. annual rain: 58.07 in.
1980 pop: 20,357
1990 pop: 19,499
1998 est. pop: 21,046

Rural and locked into the south central section of the state, Hardee County is a citrus and cattle region. The county also calls itself the nation's cucumber capital.

Although agriculture in Florida is second in state income only to tourism, farm-rich Hardee did not share in the state's population growth in the 1980s. It, like one other county, lost population.

Largest industries are citrus growing and packing, and cattle ranching. The major highway through Hardee is U.S. 17, and the nearest air service is available either at Tampa International in adjoining Hillsborough County or at the Sarasota/Bradenton Airport in nearby Sarasota County.

Largest incorporated places are Wauchula, the county seat, Bowling Green, and Zolfo Springs.

## HENDRY

Area: 1,189 square miles
Approx. elev: 12 ft.
Avg. temps: 64 Jan.
            81.2 Aug.
Avg. annual rain: 52.22 in.
1980 pop: 18,599
1990 pop: 25,773
1998 est. pop: 29,357

Touching on Lake Okeechobee, Hendry County is best known for its rich mucklands and sugar refineries. Big Cypress Seminole Indian reservation is in the county's southeast tip.

Sugar processing is by far the county's largest private industry, although employers also include truck farmers and citrus growers.

The county's only major highway is U.S. 27, which runs along its northern boundary. Closest air service is 40 miles distant at the Southwest Regional Airport near Fort Myers.

Largest incorporated places are Clewiston and La Belle, the county seat.

## HERNANDO

Area: 508 square miles
Approx. elev: 175 ft.
Avg. temps: 59.8 Jan.
             81 Aug.
Avg. annual rain: 55.76 in.
1980 pop:   44,469
1990 pop: 101,115
1998 est. pop: 127,227

On the Gulf of Mexico and north of the Tampa Bay area, Hernando County has been one of the state's fastest-growing counties. A considerable portion of the Withlacoochee State Forest is in the county, as is the famous Weekee Wachee Spring attraction.

Health care, electronics, mining and minerals, and tourism provide the county's economic base. I-75 passes through the county's eastern section, U.S. 19 through its western region. Nearest major air service is at Tampa International 45 miles to the south.

Largest incorporated area is Brooksville, the county seat.

## HIGHLANDS

Area: 1,119 square miles
Approx. elev: 150 ft.
Avg. temps: 63.2 Jan.
             81.8 Aug.
Avg. annual rain: 52.22 in.
1980 pop: 47,526
1990 pop: 68,432
1998 est. pop: 75,206

Named for its rolling countryside, Highlands County in the south central area of Florida is the home of Sebring and that city's famous 24-hour auto endurance race. Near another of its cities, Avon Park, was a World War II air base that is now a tract for practice bombing.

The county is also dotted with lakes, the largest being Lake Istokpoga near the city of Lake Placid. The county also is home to Highlands Hammock State Park, one of the nation's outstanding natural parks, with 3,800 acres of forests and plants.

Largest private employers are in health care, citrus, boat manufacturing, banking, and lawn supplies.

Major highways crossing the county are, from east to west, U.S. 98, and from north to south, U.S. 27. Air service is available at Orlando International 80 miles to the north.

Incorporated places include Sebring, the county seat, Avon Park and Lake Placid.

## HILLSBOROUGH

Area: 1,062 square miles
Approx. elev: 15-121 ft.
Avg. temps: 60.4 Jan.
             81.5 Aug.
Avg. annual rain: 48.48 in.
1980 pop: 646,960
1990 pop: 834,054
1998 est. pop: 925,277

Site of one of the state's most populous cities, Tampa, Hillsborough County on the state's west coast fronts on Tampa Bay, which funnels into the Gulf of Mexico. Tampa was once known as the Cigar City, and cigars still are hand-rolled in some parts of the city, but Tampa in the past 30 years has become a primary service and financial center in the South.

Hillsborough also has a substantial international port in Tampa Bay and has what many travelers consider to be the nation's finest air terminal, Tampa International Airport.

Enthusiastic sports fans are entertained by all of professional sports' major leagues and by being the center of baseball's spring training sites.

Private industry includes communications, air services, food processing and shipping, retail and banking headquarters, and tourist attractions such as Busch Gardens. Hillsborough also is home to the University of South Florida, second largest of the state's ten universities.

Major arteries into Hillsborough County include I-75 and I-4, and U.S. 41 and 301.

Incorporated places in the county are Tampa, the county seat, Plant City, and Temple Terrace.

## HOLMES

Area: 484 square miles
Approx. elev: 120 ft.
Avg. temps: 53.3 Jan.
            81.6 Aug.
Avg. annual rain: 57.40 in.
1980 pop: 14,723
1990 pop: 15,778
1998 est. pop: 18,622

Holmes County is in the Panhandle, bounded on the north by Alabama, and is one of the state's smallest counties in size and population.

Rural and landlocked, Holmes depends on private employers in the clothing and health care fields for its economic base.

The major highway through Holmes is U.S. 90. Nearest air service is 45 miles away at Dothan, Alabama.

Largest incorporated places are Bonifay, the county seat, and Ponce de Leon, Esto, Westville, and Noma.

## INDIAN RIVER

Area: 549 square miles
Approx. elev: 25 ft.
Avg. temps: 63.4 Jan.
            81.3 Aug.
Avg. annual rain: 52.84 in.
1980 pop: 59,896
1990 pop: 90,208
1998 est. pop: 99,155

Indian River County is halfway down the peninsula of Florida on the Atlantic Ocean and is most famous for its citrus products. Development has been along its eastern shore, with much of its increasing population settling across a causeway from the mainland to the ocean beachfront. The Indian River separates the mainland from the beach communities. Health care, airplane manufacturing, and citrus are the county's major industries.

Motoring routes into the county include I-95, U.S. 1, U.S. A1A, and the Florida Turnpike. Air service is available at the Vero Beach Municipal

Airport and, 45 miles to the north, in adjacent Brevard County at Melbourne Regional Airport.

Largest incorporated places are Vero Beach, the county seat, and Sebastian, Indian River Shores, Fellsmere, and Orchid.

## JACKSON

Area: 938 square miles
Approx. elev: 120 ft.
Avg. temps: 52.6 Jan.
            81 Aug.
Avg. annual rain: 54.69 in.
1980 pop: 39,154
1990 pop: 41,375
1998 est. pop: 45,660

Jackson County is the only Florida county to border two states, Alabama and Georgia. It also is home to three waterways—the Chattahoochee, the Flint, and the Apalachicola rivers.

The county also is known for Florida Caverns, a 1,217-acre state park. Indians used the caverns as refuge during skirmishes with U.S. Army troops, and those fleeing troops during the War Between the States also hid out in the underground chasms.

Major private industries in Jackson include the manufacturing of clothing, furniture, washing machines, and lumber. I-10 traverses the county, as does U.S. 90. The nearest airline service is 35 miles distant, at Dothan, Alabama.

Largest incorporated places are Marianna, the county seat, and Graceville, Sneads, Cottondale, and Malone.

## JEFFERSON

Area: 609 square miles
Approx. elev: 202 ft.
Avg. temps: 53.5 Jan.
            80.5 Aug.
Avg. annual rain: 56.74 in.
1980 pop: 10,703
1990 pop: 11,296
1998 est. pop: 12,952

Jefferson County is the only county to extend from the Georgia state line to the Gulf of Mexico. Its largest city, and county seat, Monticello, is noted for its 19th-century architecture.

Like many north Florida counties, it is sparsely populated, mostly agricultural, and the rich solitude of its forests and streams remains largely undiscovered by tourists and retirees.

Major private employers are in clothing, nurseries, dairying, and food production. I-10 and U.S. 90 traverse the county. Nearest air service is 23 miles distant at the Tallahassee Regional Airport.

## LAFAYETTE

Area: 554 square miles
Approx. elev: 69 ft.
Avg. temps: 55.2 Jan.
          81.4 Aug.
Avg. annual rain: 58.24 in.
1980 pop: 4,035
1990 pop: 5,578
1998 est. pop: 6,225

Considering Florida's tremendous growth since World War II, it is a near marvel that an area in the state more than 500 square miles in size has so few residents. Yet that is Lafayette County, in north central Florida.

One of the state's least densely populated counties, with only 10 people per square mile, Lafayette is known primarily for its hunting and fishing.

Flat and wooded, the county has numerous natural attractions, including numerous springs adjacent to the famous Suwannee River that carves out Lafayette's eastern boundary. Employment, besides in agriculture (primarily dairying), centers on firms that build boats, pack seafood, and harvest timber.

The major artery into the county is U.S. 27. Air service is available at Gainesville Regional Airport about 65 miles to the east.

Mayo is the county's only incorporated city, and is the county seat.

## LAKE

Area: 1,163 square miles
Approx. elev: 124 ft.
Avg. temps: 59.7 Jan.
          82.4 Aug.
Avg. annual rain: 47.47 in.
1980 pop: 104,870
1990 pop: 152,104
1998 est. pop: 202,207

Centrally located in the state between the Gulf of Mexico and the Atlantic Ocean, Lake County is noted for its citrus groves and the estimated 1,440 lakes that dot its rolling landscape. Some residents swear that the county's relatively high altitude combined with its lakes produce warm winters and cool summers.

Major lakes such as Griffin, Yale, Eustis, Harris, Louisa, and Apopka make for excellent fishing in the county. Other recreational activity centers on the Ocala National Forest in Lake's northeast corner.

Major private employment is in the citrus industry, but employers include those in metal fabrication, concrete, and mobile home construction.

The Florida Turnpike and U.S. 27 are the county's major thoroughfares. Orlando International Airport, 45 miles distant, provides the nearest air service.

Largest incorporated places are Leesburg, Eustis, Mount Dora, Clermont, and Tavares, the county seat.

## LEE

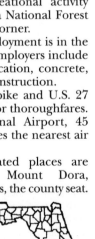

Area: 1,005 square miles
Approx. elev: 7 ft.
Avg. temps: 63.8 Jan.
          81.5 Aug.
Avg. annual rain: 52.39 in.
1980 pop: 205,266
1990 pop: 335,113
1998 est. pop: 392,895

A well-known tourist center, Lee County is dominated by its major city, Fort Myers, famous as the winter home of inventor Thomas Edison. The southwest county fronting on the Gulf of Mexico also is known for its pair of enchanting offshore barrier islands, Sanibel and Captiva.

Lee's rapid growth, coupled with that of its northern neighbor Charlotte County, led to Lee being named as the site for the state's 10th four-year university, Florida Gulf Coast University.

The county's many bays and long coastline, along with the Caloosahatchee River (a waterway extending to the state's east coast), make Lee a paradise for water enthusiasts.

Major private employers are in health care, communications, foliage growing, and land developing.

Thoroughfares into the county include I-75 and U.S. 41. Residents are served by the area's Southwest Florida Regional Airport.

Largest incorporated places are Cape Coral, Sanibel, North Fort Myers, and Fort Myers, the county seat.

## LEON

Area: 696 square miles
Approx. elev: 192 ft.
Avg. temps: 51.7 Jan.
          80.8 Aug.
Avg. annual rain: 55.17 in.
1980 pop: 148,655
1990 pop: 192,493
1998 est. pop: 216,978

In what is known as the Big Bend area of the state and adjacent to the Georgia state line, Leon County is the site of the state's capital, Tallahassee. The site was so chosen because, at the time of achieving statehood in 1845, most Floridians lived in north Florida, and Tallahassee was midway between Pensacola and St. Augustine. It was the only state capital east of the Mississippi River not captured by Union forces during the War Between the States.

Leon is an old South county, with roads and farmland shaded by large oaks heavily draped in Spanish moss. Favorite fishing and boating spots are the Ochlockonee River, Lake Talquin, Lake Jackson, Lake Miccosukee, and the Apalachicola National Forest,

which occupies roughly one-third of the county.

Largest employer is the state government and the two state universities in Tallahassee—Florida State and Florida A&M. Sizable private employers include those in health care, publishing, and printing.

Major roads into the county include I-10, U.S. 90, and U.S. 27. The county has its own airport, Tallahassee Regional.

Largest incorporated place is Tallahassee, both the county seat and the state capital.

## LEVY

Area: 1,137 square miles
Approx. elev: 13-82 ft.
Avg. temps: 57.9 Jan.
          82 Aug.
Avg. annual rain: 45.30 in.
1980 pop: 19,870
1990 pop: 25,923
1998 est. pop: 31,796

A large, forested region, Levy County is a north central county on the Gulf of Mexico. Its famous offshore island, Cedar Key, used to be the southern terminus of the state's first railroad and now is a popular tourist retreat.

One of the state's most popular parks, Manatee Springs, is in Levy, along the Suwannee River that separates Levy from Dixie County.

Aside from agriculture and timber, private employers are few and mostly in services. The primary highway through Levy is U.S. 19, which runs southward from Tallahassee near the Georgia line to the Tampa Bay area. Air service is some 60 miles to the east, at Gainesville Regional Airport.

Largest incorporated places are Williston, Chiefland, Inglis, Cedar Key, and Bronson, the county seat.

## LIBERTY

Area: 845 square miles
Approx. elev: 116 ft.
Avg. temps: 53 Jan.
          81.5 Aug.
Avg. annual rain: 58.94 in.
1980 pop: 4,260
1990 pop: 5,569
1998 est. pop: 6,759

Liberty, a small Panhandle county, is sparsely populated in part because so much of its area is devoted to forests and wildlife. Its quiet Southern charm makes it a paradise for woodlands lovers and botanists. The Apalachicola National Forest takes up more than half the county. Another large section is the Telogia Creek Wildlife Management Area. Torreya State Park also covers 1,063 acres of Liberty.

Adding to the county's undeveloped character is the Apalachicola River, Liberty's western boundary, and the Ochlockonee River, its eastern boundary. The Apalachicola River at one time was the main commercial water route through Florida from Georgia and Alabama to the Gulf of Mexico.

Largest employers are in health care and forestry. I-10 passes through Liberty County, but the nearest air service is 45 miles distant at the Tallahassee Regional Airport.

Bristol is the largest incorporated area and the county seat.

## MADISON

Area: 708 square miles
Approx. elev: 133 ft.
Avg. temps: 54.8 Jan.
          81.3 Aug.
Avg. annual rain: 52.50 in.
1980 pop: 14,894
1990 pop: 16,569
1998 est. pop: 17,652

Another largely agricultural Georgia border county, Madison County was on the route that Spanish explorer Hernando De Soto took northward into the U.S. hinterland.

Near the county's main city, Madison, stood the Spanish mission of Santa Helena de Machaba. Madison County, like many north Florida counties, is geologically and socially more characteristic of the Deep South than of the Florida most tourists know, meaning urbanized regions such as Orlando, Tampa Bay, and Miami.

Major private industries are in processed meats, poultry, and the manufacture of wheel covers, plywood, and furniture. I-10 and U.S. 90 are the county's primary highways and air service is available in the adjoining county at Tallahassee Regional Airport.

Incorporated places include Greenville, Lee, and Madison, the county seat.

## MANATEE

Area: 772 square miles
Approx. elev: 9-17 ft.
Avg. temps: 61.5 Jan.
          81.2 Aug.
Avg. annual rain: 54.60 in.
1980 pop: 148,442
1990 pop: 211,707
1998 est. pop: 239,682

Historians believe Spanish explorer Hernando De Soto landed in Florida in Manatee County along the Manatee River near where it empties into the Gulf of Mexico.

The western region of this centrally located coastal county, including Anna Maria Island, is becoming heavily developed while the county's eastern section remains agricultural.

Many residents find the commute from Manatee to the metropolitan area of Pinellas County across Tampa Bay a pleasant, scenic drive over one of the nation's most beautiful bridges, the Sunshine Skyway.

Major private employers produce citrus juice and boats, and provide health services. Thoroughfares through Manatee include I-75 and U.S. 41. Air service is provided by the Sarasota/Bradenton Regional Airport.

Largest incorporated areas are Bradenton, the county seat, and Palmetto, Holmes Beach, Longboat Key, and Bradenton Beach.

## MARION

Area: 1,652 square miles
Approx. elev: 100 ft.
Avg. temps: 58.6 Jan.
        81 Aug.
Avg. annual rain: 51.94 in.
1980 pop: 122,488
1990 pop: 194,833
1998 est. pop: 241,513

Marion County has become widely known as "Thoroughbred Country." Because of its peculiar limestone base soil, this central Florida county has proven an ideal place to breed and raise racehorses, several of them Kentucky Derby winners.

Marion, one of the state's fastest-growing counties, is the site of several nationally familiar attractions, including Silver Springs. Within its boundaries also is a large section of the Ocala National Forest.

Besides Thoroughbred breeders, private employers in Marion include those in electronics, health care, fire and rescue equipment, van conversions, rubber hoses, and communication equipment.

Major thoroughfares are I-75, U.S. 441, and U.S. 27. Metropolitan air service is available to the southeast at Orlando International Airport or to the north at Gainesville Regional Airport.

Incorporated areas include Ocala, the county seat, and Belleview, Dunnellon, Reddick, and McIntosh.

## MARTIN

Area: 582 square miles
Approx. elev: 14 ft.
Avg. temps: 65 Jan.
        81.8 Aug.
Avg. annual rain: 49.79 in.
1980 pop:  64,014
1990 pop: 100,900
1998 est. pop: 115,940

On the lower east coast, Martin County is sandwiched by the Atlantic Ocean on the east and Lake Okeechobee on the west. Primary development of the county has occurred along the ocean coast.

Residents take pride in the county's small but varied wildlife population, its high sand dunes along the shoreline, and its Hobe Sound National Wildlife Refuge.

Health care and aerospace, along with tourism, are the county's major private industries. Motor routes into Martin County include I-95, U.S. 1, and the Florida Turnpike. Air service is available 45 miles distant at Palm Beach International Airport.

Incorporated areas include Stuart, the county seat, and Sewalls Point, Ocean Breeze Park, and Jupiter Island.

## MIAMI-DADE

Area: 2,109 square miles
Approx. elev: 15 ft.
Avg. temps: 68 Jan.
        82 Aug.
Avg. annual rain: 57.77 in.
1980 pop: 1,625,979
1990 pop: 1,937,094
1998 est. pop: 2,152,437

Heart of the Gold Coast and most famous of Florida's regions is Miami-Dade County, its new and increasingly popular name recognizing its largest city and county seat. The area has become a truly cosmopolitan county, largely because of the influx of Cubans, West Indians, and Latin Americans. For years, Miami was Florida's most populous city, but that title now belongs to Jacksonville's consolidated Duval County.

Its large, mixed population has attracted several professional sports franchises, including basketball's Miami Heat, football's Miami Dolphins, baseball's Florida Marlins, and hockey's Florida Panthers.

Like most east coast counties, Miami-Dade is heavily developed along its coast and sparsely populated in its western region because of massive wetlands.

Major private employers are centered on airlines, department stores, communications, banking, transportation, and food service.

Highways into the County include I-95, U.S. 1, and the Florida Turnpike. The area is served by Miami International Airport.

Other incorporated places are Hialeah, Miami Beach, North Miami, and Coral Gables.

## MONROE

Area: 1,418 square miles
Approx. elev: 10 ft.
Avg. temps: 70 Jan.
          83.6 Aug.
Avg. annual rain: 38.03 in.
1980 pop: 63,098
1990 pop: 78,024
1998 est. pop: 81,203

The majority of Monroe County's land area is on the southwest tip of the Florida peninsula and separated from the county's Florida Keys, which comprise Monroe's main population centers.

The county portion on the mainland is largely undeveloped and includes the Everglades National Park. The Florida Keys portion stretches some 100 miles into the Straits of Florida, which divide the Atlantic Ocean from the Gulf of Mexico.

Significant points of interest dot the Keys. They are the site of John Pennekamp Coral Reef State Park, featuring 100 square miles of living coral, and a half dozen wildlife refuges and other state parks. Dominating the county's seven Dry Tortugas Islands is the 19th-century Fort Jefferson, a massive coastal fort.

The Keys, particularly Key West, have blossomed from a sleepy, tropical paradise into a bustling, populated spa where fishing, boating, and "good times" are primary pursuits.

Monroe is primarily a tourist area with few sizable employers or businesses. Access to the county is via U.S. 1, and air service is available at Key West International Airport or at Miami International to the north.

Incorporated areas include Key Colony Beach, Layton, and Key West, the county seat.

## NASSAU

Area: 671 square miles
Approx. elev: 22 ft.
Avg. temps: 55.6 Jan.
          81.5 Aug.
Avg. annual rain: 48.50 in.
1980 pop: 32,894
1990 pop: 43,941
1998 est. pop: 55,349

In the northeasternmost tip of the state, Nassau County is bordered on the east by the Atlantic Ocean, and on the north and west by the state of Georgia. The St. Mary's River forms the boundary between Georgia and Nassau County.

Nassau is steeped in history, and the area around one of its major attractions, Fort Clinch, has been under eight different flags.

Paper products and tourism are the area's primary economic ventures. Interstates 95 and 10, U.S. highways 1, 23, and 301, and State Highway A1A are the major thoroughfares into and through the county. The nearest airport, 25 miles to the south, is Jacksonville International.

Incorporated areas include Hilliard, Callahan, and Fernandina Beach, the county seat.

## OKALOOSA

Area: 998 square miles
Approx. elev: 4-300 ft.
Avg. temps: 51.4 Jan.
          80.3 Aug.
Avg. annual rain: 63.70 in.
1980 pop: 109,920
1990 pop: 143,776
1998 est. pop: 169,289

Eglin Air Force Base embraces

more than half of Okaloosa, but the Panhandle county also is well known for its miles of beaches along the Gulf of Mexico and Choctawhatchee Bay. Its northern boundary is the state of Alabama. Development is restricted to the county's southeastern and central regions. Through the northern reaches flow the Yellow and Blackwater rivers, the latter coursing through the Blackwater River State Forest.

The beaches of Okaloosa are prized for their white quartz sand, a much finer and whiter sand than that found on beaches in central and southern Florida.

Largest private employers are in electronics and health care. Major roads into the county are I-10, U.S. 98, and U.S. 90. Flights are available from the Okaloosa County Air Terminal.

Incorporated areas include Fort Walton Beach, Niceville, Valparaiso, Destin, and Crestview, the county seat.

## OKEECHOBEE

Area: 780 square miles
Approx. elev: 27 ft.
Avg. temps: 63.3 Jan.
       81.3 Aug.
Avg. annual rain: 47.90 in.
1980 pop: 20,264
1990 pop: 29,627
1998 est. pop: 31,158

Named for the great lake that it borders, Okeechobee County in south central Florida is primarily agricultural. Its farms have rich organic soil and are noted for their winter vegetable crops.

Lake Okeechobee also provides commercial fishing. A shallow lake— its average depth measured at 14 feet—it is the largest U.S. lake without a natural outlet. The lake could be considered the county's sole tourist attraction since lake fishing is good the year around.

Okeechobee's economic base depends on agriculture and dairying,

with the result that it has few sizable industries other than those associated with land use. Both the Florida Turnpike and U.S. 441 service motorists to the area. Air service is 56 miles distant at Palm Beach International Airport.

Largest incorporated area is Okeechobee, the county seat.

## ORANGE

Area: 1,003 square miles
Approx. elev: 106 ft.
Avg. temps: 60.7 Jan.
       82 Aug.
Avg. annual rain: 52.35 in.
1980 pop: 471,660
1990 pop: 677,491
1998 est. pop: 805,537

Once noted almost entirely as a citrus center, Orange County, in central Florida, has been transformed over the past two decades into a highly urbanized area because of the many large tourist attractions that have located in its area, particularly Walt Disney World.

The millions of tourists flocking into Orange each year need not worry much about accommodations, because the county has more hotel rooms than New York City. The county also boasts major private industries such as aerospace, communications, publishing, health care, and banking. Highways into the county include I-4, the Florida Turnpike, U.S. 17, and U.S. 441. The local airport is Orlando International Airport.

Largest incorporated areas are Winter Park, Ocoee, Apopka, Maitland, and Orlando, the county seat.

## OSCEOLA

Area: 1,467 square miles
Approx. elev: 69 ft.
Avg. temps: 61.3 Jan.
　　　　　82 Aug.
Avg. annual rain: 50.06 in.
1980 pop: 49,287
1990 pop: 107,728
1998 est. pop: 145,666

Over the years Osceola County in central Florida has been devoted to cattle raising, but the county is rapidly being urbanized because of its proximity to Walt Disney World and other major attractions.

Cattle raising in past years covered two-thirds of Osceola, and the city of Kissimmee has been known as the "cow capital of Florida."

Western Osceola County is made up of Lake Kissimmee and the Kissimmee River, both important to the region's water resources.

Tourism, houseware products, electronics, molded injections, and food distribution, in addition to ranching, are the county's major industries.

I-4 and the Florida Turnpike are the county's primary roadways, with air service provided by nearby Orlando International Airport.

Incorporated areas include St. Cloud and Kissimmee, the county seat.

## PALM BEACH

Area: 2,578 square miles
Approx. elev: 0-20 ft.
Avg. temps: 67.2 Jan.
　　　　　81.7 Aug.
Avg. annual rain: 59.44 in.
1980 pop: 573,125
1990 pop: 863,518
1998 est. pop: 1,032,625

Largest in size of all Florida counties, Palm Beach County runs to extremes—populous cities on the Atlantic coast and lush vegetable farms in its western region.

West Palm Beach on the inland waterway, and Palm Beach on the oceanfront, are well known to most tourists, but few visitors or residents venture into the county's vast hinterland that contains thousands of square miles of wetlands, wildlife refuges, and the Everglades.

Major private employers produce jet engines, computers, and sugar. I-95, the Florida Turnpike, U.S. 1, and A1A are the county's major roads. Air service is available at Palm Beach International Airport.

Incorporated areas include Boca Raton, Boynton Beach, Delray Beach, Riviera Beach, and West Palm Beach, the county seat.

## PASCO

Area: 772 square miles
Approx. elev: 0-100 ft.
Avg. temps: 60.3 Jan.
　　　　　81 Aug.
Avg. annual rain: 55 in.
1980 pop: 194,123
1990 pop: 281,131
1998 est. pop: 325,824

In the past 20 years large tracts that once were Pasco County farmland have been subdivided to provide homes for new residents in this fast-growing region in central Florida on the Gulf of Mexico.

Migration in past years has been mostly retirees, but more young families are moving in because the county's growth is fueling numerous service industries.

Being adjacent to the metropolitan Tampa Bay area, Pasco also is home to thousands of workers who commute daily to St. Petersburg, Tampa, and Lakeland.

Major industries include citrus products, health care, and retailing. Highways traversing Pasco are U.S. 19 and I-75. The nearest sizable airport is Tampa International, 35 miles to the south.

Incorporated areas include New Port Richey, Zephyrhills, Port Richey, St. Leo, San Antonio, and Dade City, the county seat.

## PINELLAS

Area: 309 square miles
Approx. elev: 0-75 ft.
Avg. temps: 62 Jan.
     82.7 Aug.
Avg. annual rain: 54.53 in.
1980 pop: 728,409
1990 pop: 851,659
1998 est. pop: 878,231

A peninsula on the Florida peninsula, Pinellas County is nearly surrounded by water. To the east and south is Tampa Bay, to the west a string of barrier islands and the Gulf of Mexico. Pinellas has long been a favorite tourist and retirement center, but in the past decade has been luring electronic industries for a more varied economic base.

Its major city, St. Petersburg, fronts on Tampa Bay and many rate the city's waterfront park facilities as the state's finest. A mile from the city's waterfront is the domed Tropicana Field, built at a cost of $138 million, home to the new major league baseball team, the Tampa Bay Devil Rays.

Pinellas' vast waterfront, running south from Tarpon Springs past barrier islands and into Tampa Bay, has always been a major beacon for tourism. The unusual geography of the county also keeps attracting new residents, the result being that Pinellas is Florida's most densely populated county, with nearly 3,000 people per square mile.

Largest private employers are in publishing, electronics, computers, and communications. Major highways into the county are I-275 and U.S. 19. St. Petersburg/Clearwater International Airport is mid-county; 15 miles to the east is Tampa International Airport.

Largest cities are St. Petersburg, Dunedin, Largo, Tarpon Springs, Pinellas Park, and Clearwater, the county seat.

## POLK

Area: 2,048 square miles
Approx. elev: 115-215 ft.
Avg. temps: 61 Jan.
     81.8 Aug.
Avg. annual rain: 49.21 in.
1980 pop: 321,652
1990 pop: 405,382
1998 est. pop: 452,584

Midway between Tampa and Orlando, in central Florida, is Polk County, largest producer of citrus in the state.

A large county in size, Polk has varied assets for residents and tourists. Lakes proliferate in the region, the county is home to one of Florida's first major attractions, Cypress Gardens, as well as the Frank Lloyd Wright-designed Florida Southern College, and, together with Highlands County, it accommodates the military by providing it the Avon Park Bombing Range.

Polk's proximity to the Tampa Bay area and the Orlando area also has abetted the county's rapid population growth.

Besides citrus, major industries include phosphate mining, trucking, building supplies, and tourist attractions. I-4 and U.S. 27 are major routes through Polk County. Air service is available in the adjacent counties at Tampa International Airport and Orlando International Airport.

Incorporated areas include Lakeland, Winter Haven, Haines City, Lake Wales, and Bartow, the county seat.

## PUTNAM

Area: 879 square miles
Approx. elev: 5 ft.
Avg. temps: 65 Jan.
     81.8 Aug.
Avg. annual rain: 49.79 in.
1980 pop: 50,549
1990 pop: 65,070
1998 est. pop: 70,419

Known for its bass fishing and azalea gardens, Putnam County in northeast Florida sidles along the St. Johns River. It is only 22 miles inland from the Atlantic Ocean, and 52 miles south of Jacksonville.

Part of the Ocala National Forest occupies Putnam, but the county is most sloganized as the "Bass Fishing Capital of the World." It is also famous for Ravine State Gardens, 182 acres of sub-tropical foliage highlighted by more than 100,000 azalea plants.

Major industries are pulp and paper making, and manufacturing of furniture, plywood, bags, boats, and concrete pipe.

The primary motoring route through Putnam is U.S. 17. Air service is available 70 miles to the north at Jacksonville International Airport.

Incorporated areas include Crescent City, Interlachen, Pomona Park, Welaka, and Palatka, the county seat.

## ST. JOHNS

Area: 660 square miles
Approx. elev: 0-27 ft.
Avg. temps: 57 Jan.
80.7 Aug.
Avg. annual rain: 48.25 in.
1980 pop: 51,303
1990 pop: 83,829
1998 est. pop: 116,147

Steeped in exploration history, St. Johns County in northeast Florida on the Atlantic Ocean was fought for by the Spanish, the French, the English, and the Americans. The area around St. Augustine, the oldest city in the U.S., was first visited by Spanish explorer Ponce de Leon in 1513. The Castillo de San Marcos at St. Augustine is one of the best-preserved specimens of Middle Ages military architecture found in the New World.

Miles of unspoiled oceanfront beaches in St. Johns have been "discovered" only in recent years, with the result that the county population grew 63 percent in the 1980s.

Tourism is a major industry, as are aeronautics, aluminum extrusion, auto parts manufacturing, and health food preparation. Major travel routes through the county are I-95, U.S. 1, and A1A. Air service is 46 miles to the north at Jacksonville International Airport.

Incorporated places include Hastings, St. Augustine Beach, and St. Augustine, the county seat.

## ST. LUCIE

Area: 626 square miles
Approx. elev: 5 ft.
Avg. temps: 65 Jan.
81.8 Aug.
Avg. annual rain: 49.79 in.
1980 pop: 87,182
1990 pop: 150,171
1998 est. pop: 179,178

On the Atlantic Ocean, halfway down the peninsula, St. Lucie County has become a haven for tourists and new residents along its oceanfront, while its interior reaches remain used for citrus and truck crop production. St. Lucie's population growth rate has outpaced that of the state.

The Indian River separates the county's mainland from the main barrier island, Hutchinson.

Major private employers are in health care, communications, retailing, and citrus concentrate. Roadways traversing St. Lucie include I-95, the Florida Turnpike, and U.S. 1. Air service is available 60 miles to the south at Palm Beach International Airport.

Incorporated places include Port St. Lucie, St. Lucie Village, and Fort Pierce, the county seat.

## SANTA ROSA

Area: 1,152 square miles
Approx. elev: 10 ft.
Avg. temps: 53.8 Jan.
80.5 Aug.
Avg. annual rain: 58.85 in.
1980 pop: 55,988
1990 pop: 81,608
1998 est. pop: 117,322

Situated in the extreme northwest Panhandle, Santa Rosa County is bounded on the north by Alabama and on the south by the Gulf of Mexico. To its west is the busy Escambia River, and much of its eastern acreage is taken up by the Blackwater River State Forest.

Frontage on Santa Rosa Sound, part of the state's Intracoastal Waterway, is the county's main draw, although the county's economic base depends also on Eglin Air Force Base in the county's eastern region. The Yellow and Blackwater rivers also course through the eastern area, emptying into East and Escambia bays.

Principal private industries include clothing, chemicals, medical services, oil and gas products, and agriculture. Motor routes into the county include I-10, U.S. 90, and U.S. 98, with air service provided by Pensacola Regional Airport 23 miles away in adjoining Escambia County.

Major incorporated areas are Jay, Gulf Breeze, and Milton, the county seat.

## SARASOTA

Area: 563 square miles
Approx. elev: 18 ft.
Avg. temps: 61.5 Jan.
        80 Aug.
Avg. annual rain: 57.11 in.
1980 pop: 202,251
1990 pop: 277,776
1998 est. pop: 303,400

Famous for its cultural activities and attractions such as the Ringling Museum of Art, Sarasota County on the central west coast of Florida also has some of the state's finest Gulf of Mexico beaches.

The county is known for its attractive barrier islands such as St. Armands Key, Longboat Key, Siesta Key, and Casey Key. All have been heavily developed the past 20 years. Population growth of the county also has spread eastward during the past decade into the county's woodlands, which feature the popular Myakka River State Park.

Tourism is a major industry, as are retailing, electronics, health care,

banking, and real estate development. Major arteries into the county are I-75 and U.S. 41.

Incorporated areas include Venice, North Port, Longboat Key, and Sarasota, the county seat.

## SEMINOLE

Area: 352 square miles
Approx. elev: 25 ft.
Avg. temps: 61.6 Jan.
        82 Aug.
Avg. annual rain: 50.51 in.
1980 pop: 179,752
1990 pop: 287,529
1998 est. pop: 350,859

One of Florida's smaller counties, Seminole County is in the upper portion of central Florida near but not on the Atlantic Ocean. Its proximity to Orange County, with its Walt Disney World and other major attractions, and Brevard County with its space center, has changed Seminole County from an agricultural region to a cluster of small urban centers.

Seminole's population growth is attributed to its proximity to the ocean and Orlando, and to a trio of large lakes plus the St. Johns River, which defines the county's eastern boundary.

Industries include communications, food, electronics, housing, and telephone equipment. Motor routes through the county include I-4 and U.S. 17. Air service is available 15 miles away at Orlando International Airport.

Incorporated areas include Altamonte Springs, Winter Springs, Casselberry, Longwood, and Sanford, the county seat.

## SUMTER

Area: 574 square miles
Approx. elev: 70 ft.
Avg. temps: 58.4 Jan.
        81 Aug.
Avg. annual rain: 51.44 in.
1980 pop: 24,272
1990 pop: 31,577
1998 est. pop: 40,426

Many Florida visitors pass through Sumter County near the center of Florida's peninsula because it is the northern terminus of the Florida Turnpike. It has been known for decades for mining, principally limestone.

The Dade Massacre occurred here in 1835. A confrontation between Indians and the U.S. Army, it touched off the Second Seminole War in Florida. One of the state's four national military cemeteries, the Withlacoochee National Cemetery, is at Bushnell.

Besides mining, industries include rail transportation, trucking, meat products, pipe and tube manufacturing, and metal production. Both the Florida Turnpike and I-75 traverse Sumter County, whose residents find the nearest air service 40 miles away at Orlando International Airport.

Incorporated areas include Wildwood, Coleman, Center Hill, Webster, and Bushnell, the county seat.

## SUWANNEE

Area: 687 square miles
Approx. elev: 109 ft.
Avg. temps: 55.6 Jan.
            81 Aug.
Avg. annual rain: 49.60 in.
1980 pop: 22,287
1990 pop: 26,780
1998 est. pop: 32,665

Suwannee County is named after the famous river that forms the county's western boundary. Sparsely populated, the county is typical of many north Florida counties that have avoided over-population yet are rich in forests, rivers, lakes, and numerous clear springs.

Suwannee is best known among skin divers, fishermen, and hunters, but in recent years has attracted retirees from population centers such as Tampa, St. Petersburg, and Miami.

Major employers are in poultry, mining, boat manufacturing, and ornamental plants. I-10, I-75, and U.S.

90 are major roads through the county. Air service is available 60 miles away at Gainesville Regional Airport.

Incorporated places are Live Oak, the county seat, and Branford.

## TAYLOR

Area: 1,052 square miles
Approx. elev: 47 ft.
Avg. temps: 55.8 Jan.
            81.4 Aug.
Avg. annual rain: 58.24 in.
1980 pop: 16,532
1990 pop: 17,111
1998 est. pop: 18,849

Calling itself the "Forest Capital of the World," Taylor County on the upper west coast of Florida has a vast Gulf of Mexico shoreline, but is known primarily as a county in which some 75 percent of its land area is in commercial forests.

Taylor also is popular among hunters, for much of the county is devoted to, besides forests, wildlife management refuges.

Industries include pulp and cellulose, construction, fencing and mulch, pyrotechnics, and lumber. The primary highway through the county is U.S. 19. Air facilities are available at Tallahassee Regional Airport 55 miles to the north.

Perry, the county seat, is the county's only sizable incorporated population center.

## UNION

Area: 245 square miles
Approx. elev: 141 ft.
Avg. temps: 55.9 Jan.
            81.4 Aug.
Avg. annual rain: 49.40 in.
1980 pop: 10,166
1990 pop: 10,252
1998 est. pop: 12,423

Smallest of all Florida counties, Union County in north central Florida devotes most of its land to commercial forests. It also has several large state prison facilities, so that most of the county's labor force is employed by the state.

Industries center on lumber, clothing, trucking, and health care. No major highways traverse Union County, only state roads, and air service is 25 miles to the south at Gainesville Regional Airport.

Incorporated places are Worthington Springs, Raiford, and Lake Butler, the county seat.

## VOLUSIA

Area: 1,207 square miles
Approx. elev: 40 ft.
Avg. temps: 59.3 Jan.
　　　　　81.5 Aug.
Avg. annual rain: 53.36 in.
1980 pop: 258,762
1990 pop: 370,712
1998 est. pop: 423,409

Tourism is one of Volusia County's biggest assets, brought about primarily by the famous hard sand beaches at Daytona Beach. The county, on the northeast coast, has a vast Atlantic Ocean shoreline and is within a short distance of major attractions in Orange County and the space center in adjacent Brevard County.

Development has occurred on the county's east coast and in its western reaches, the central area dotted primarily by wetlands and wildlife refuges.

Primary industries are medical supplies, electronics, citrus juices, acoustics, plastic, and transportation. I-4 and I-95 pass through Volusia County, as do U.S. 1 and U.S. 92. The county has its own air services at Daytona Beach International Airport.

Incorporated areas include Daytona Beach, Port Orange, Ormond Beach, New Smyrna Beach, and DeLand, the county seat.

## WAKULLA

Area: 635 square miles
Approx. elev: 8 ft.
Avg. temps: 54.2 Jan.
　　　　　81.4 Aug.
Avg. annual rain: 54.03 in.
1980 pop: 10,887
1990 pop: 14,202
1998 est. pop: 18,652

A heavily wooded, sparsely populated region, Wakulla County in the Panhandle is famous for one of the world's largest spring basins. Much of the county is part of the Apalachicola National Forest, while its southern boundary on the Gulf of Mexico is noted for fishing and seafood.

Industry is as sparse as the population, with commercial fishing providing much of the area's revenue.

U.S. 90 runs across the county, which is served by air by the Tallahassee Regional Airport 25 miles to the north.

Incorporated places are Sopchoppy and St. Marks. The community of Crawfordsville is the county seat.

## WALTON

Area: 1,135 square miles
Approx. elev: 266-345 ft.
Avg. temps: 52.8 Jan.
　　　　　80.8 Aug.
Avg. annual rain: 65.70 in.
1980 pop: 21,300
1990 pop: 27,760
1998 est. pop: 37,410

The highest elevation in Florida is in Walton County, at a site 345 feet above sea level. Much of the western portion of this Panhandle county is included in the sprawling Eglin Air Force Base.

Walton County is bordered on the north by Alabama, and on the south by the Gulf of Mexico. Its most famous attraction is Grayton Beach State Recreational Area, 356 acres of beach, sloping sand dunes, pine woodlands, and lakes.

Industries include poultry, clothing, orthopedic supplies, and health care. Major motoring routes through the county are I-10 and U.S. 90. Air service is available 35 miles away at Okaloosa County Air Terminal.

Incorporated places are Freeport, Paxton, and DeFuniak Springs, the county seat.

## WASHINGTON

Area: 611 square miles
Approx. elev: 75 ft.
Avg. temps: 52.5 Jan.
         81.2 Aug.
Avg. annual rain: 60.20 in.
1980 pop: 14,509
1990 pop: 16,919
1998 est. pop: 20,292

Travelers through this modestly populated Panhandle county can become confused because the shape of Washington County is such that motorists leave Washington, enter Holmes County, then find themselves re-entering Washington County.

The county is populated by small towns, their surroundings devoted mostly to farms and rural pursuits. Its western boundary is the Choctawhatchee River.

Private employers include makers of bed products, clothing, and turbine engines. I-10 and U.S. 90 cross the northern section of the county. Air travelers pick up flights 40 miles distant at the Panama City/Bay County Regional Airport.

Incorporated places are Vernon, Caryville, Wausau, Ebro, and Chipley, the county seat.

## HURRICANE EVACUATION

Florida counties have hurricane evacuation plans established, but experts point out that such evacuations would likely take hours. In Key West, for instance, where only the Overseas Highway is available to motorists, officials estimate it would take more than 16 hours to remove a hurricane-threatened population. Panama City's limited access to the mainland would require more than 22 hours to completely evacuate, and it would take about 15 hours, estimate the experts, to move St. Petersburg/Clearwater residents safely inland.

## PIEDMONT FLORIDA

Five Florida counties, Jackson, Gadsden, Leon, Jefferson, and Madison, all near the Georgia border, were dubbed "Piedmont Florida" by the 19th-century writer Sidney Lanier. This 150-mile stretch is one of the state's most beautiful regions, with rich red clay soils, numerous lakes, springs, and lush hills that display brilliant autumn colors.

## RICHEST TOWN

Jupiter Island, in Martin County, is the richest town in America based on median home prices, according to Worth magazine. The median home price in Jupiter Island in 1997-98 was $1.7 million, $100,000.00 more than the median price of a home in the previous "richest city," Aspen, Colorado.

# FORESTS

Florida's forests occupy 42 percent of the state's total land area. Over the past 50 years, however, Florida has experienced nearly a six-fold increase in population, particularly in the southeast. Land use changes associated with this population growth and urban buildup gradually have reduced the size of the state's forest resources.

With about 35 million acres of land, Florida has 14.6 million acres classed as commercial forestland. About 49 percent of this commercial timber acreage is held by thousands of private owners, 31 percent by timber interests. The most heavily forested area is the northwest section of the state, where commercial forests occupy 75 percent of the land area. Northeast Florida also is heavily forested, with 70 percent of its land occupied by commercial forests. Much timberland in this section of the state has been cleared for pasture. The net loss of commercial forests in the past decade has been 332,000 acres. Reforesting involves planting 135 million trees per year.

Pulpwood remains Florida's leading forest product, accounting for about 61 percent of each year's total timber output, or 4.5 million cords. Sawlogs account for 29 percent of the harvest, with 805 million board feet. More than 55,000 persons are directly employed by industries based on forest production in the state including 135 sawmills and more than a thousand wood-products manufacturers. Forestry is an $8.5 billion annual industry in the state.

## *NATIONAL FORESTS*

**APALACHICOLA NATIONAL FOREST** was established in 1936, and covers 557,000 acres in the northern section of the state. It is primarily a pine hardwood forest, and offers natural sinks, bottomland, and hardwood swamps along large rivers. The forest rivers and tributaries provide miles of fishing, mainly bass, bream, and perch. Other popular forest pursuits are hunting for quail, deer, and bear, as well as boating and swimming. Camping and picnic sites are numerous and hotels are not far away in the nearby towns of Apalachicola, Blountstown, Bristol, and Tallahassee.

**CHOCTAWHATCHEE NATIONAL FOREST,** in the Panhandle's Okaloosa and Walton counties, was deeded to the federal park system near the turn of the century, but in the 1940s much of its acreage was transferred to the War Department for use as Eglin Air Force Base. Only about 1,000 acres of the forest now remain outside the base. Rocky Bayou State Recreation Area, a state park, is in the forest so most of the forest's recreational activities are administered by the state park system.

**OCALA NATIONAL FOREST,** established in 1908, is a camper's paradise, mainly because of two famous springs, Juniper and Alexander. Other springs and large clear-flowing streams are scattered throughout the forest's 366,000 acres. A sub-tropical wilderness, the Ocala offers much botanical growth among its palms, hardwoods, and pines. Annual large game hunts are permitted in the forest by the wildlife management. Hunting camps, plus swimming and camping sites, are plentiful. Commerical accommodations are nearby just outside the forest.

**OSCEOLA NATIONAL FOREST,** near Jacksonville and Lake City, with 170,000 acres, is the smallest of the three major national forests. It is flat country, abundant with ponds, sinks, and cypress swamps, and a state breeding ground for game. Hunting of deer, quail, and dove is permitted but controlled. Best fishing is for bass, perch, and bream. Camping and picnicking sites are available.

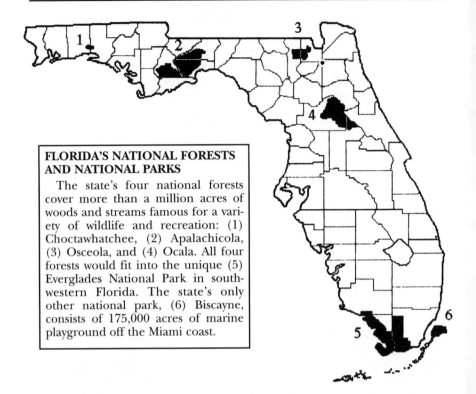

**FLORIDA'S NATIONAL FORESTS AND NATIONAL PARKS**

The state's four national forests cover more than a million acres of woods and streams famous for a variety of wildlife and recreation: (1) Choctawhatchee, (2) Apalachicola, (3) Osceola, and (4) Ocala. All four forests would fit into the unique (5) Everglades National Park in southwestern Florida. The state's only other national park, (6) Biscayne, consists of 175,000 acres of marine playground off the Miami coast.

### NATIONAL SEASHORES

**CANAVERAL NATIONAL SEASHORE** is a largely undeveloped wetland covering 57,000 acres in parts of two counties, Volusia and Brevard, next door to the Kennedy Space Center. Established by Congress in 1975, the preserve offers 26 miles of beaches along the Atlantic Ocean that include Playalinda, Apollo, and Klondike.

**GULF ISLANDS NATIONAL SEASHORE,** including Perdido Key, are offshore islands preserved by a 1971 congressional act setting aside these 139,776 acres along the northwest Florida Gulf coast. The acreage includes white-sand beaches and sea-oat-covered dunes along the shores of Escambia, Santa Rosa, and Okaloosa counties. Outstanding beaches include 14 miles of shoreline on Perdido Key, 17 miles of Gulf frontage at Fort Pickens, and 18 miles of beachfront on Santa Rosa Island.

### NATIONAL PRESERVES

**BIG CYPRESS NATIONAL PRESERVE** was set aside by Congress in 1974 as a buffer zone to the northwest section of the adjacent Everglades National Park. Subtropical plant and animal life abounds in the preserve, the ancestral home of the Seminole and Miccosukee Indians.

### NATIONAL PARKS

**BISCAYNE NATIONAL PARK** was set aside in 1968 as a national monument. Its 181,500 acres of water, reefs, and barrier islands were renamed a national park in 1980. Only 5 percent of the park consists of land, making it the largest marine park under the protection of the National Park Service. In the southern portion of Miami-Dade County, Biscayne is best known for tropical fish, shipwrecks, living coral, and birds, and is a haven for scuba diving, fishing, and boating. Four presidents also have used the park as a vacation site.

**EVERGLADES NATIONAL PARK,** sprawling over more than 1.4 million acres, is the largest subtropical wilderness in the U.S. Concern for the Everglades led Congress in 1947 to declare the area in Florida's southern tip as a national park, the first park ever established for purely ecological reasons. Among the park's resources

are more than 300 species of birds, 1,000 varieties of seed-bearing plants, 120 species of trees, 25 different types of orchids, 465,000 acres of sawgrass or freshwater marsh, and 230,000 acres of mangrove forest. All but 7 percent of the Everglades' million-plus acres are designated as wilderness. For park visitors, each season has its own advantage. The winter dry season is the best time to see abundant wildlife, while the summer's wet months provide calmer waters and better fishing.

---

### NATIONAL SANCTUARY

**FLORIDA KEYS MARINE SANCTUARY** was established by Congress in 1990 and is the nation's ninth and largest U.S. marine sanctuary, covering 2,600 nautical square miles. The designation calls Florida's coral reefs, mangrove islands, and seagrass beds "the marine equivalent of the tropical rain forests." Beginning at Biscayne National Park southeast of Miami, the sanctuary stretches along the Atlantic Ocean side of the Florida Keys all the way to Fort Jefferson National Monument some 70 miles west of Key West. On the Gulf of Mexico side, the sanctuary runs from Fort Jefferson to Everglades National Park on the tip of the Florida Peninsula. Boundaries of the sanctuary end where the water reaches a depth of 300 feet, which is about 10 miles out from shore on either side of the Keys.

---

### STATE FORESTS

During the Great Depression, the federal government bought thousands of Florida acres for reclamation and resettlement projects. They became the nucleus of the state's forest system. Today, more than 800,000 Florida acres are set-aside as state forests. In all, there are 36 such forests. They are:

| State Forest | Acreage | County |
|---|---|---|
| Blackwater River | 189,594 | Santa Rosa/Okaloosa |
| Withlacoochee | 154,368 | Citrus/Hernando/Pasco/Sumter |
| Tate's Hell | 131,256 | Franklin/Liberty |
| Picayune Strand | 55,473 | Collier |
| Goethe | 49,989 | Levy |
| Okaloacoochee Slough | 31,486 | Collier/Hendry |
| Tiger Bay | 23,425 | Volusia |
| Jennings | 20,623 | Clay |
| Lake Wales Ridge | 20,235 | Polk |
| Lake George | 19,610 | Volusia |
| Seminole | 19,368 | Lake |
| Lake Talquin | 16,327 | Gadsden/Leon |
| Point Washington | 15,180 | Walton |
| Twin Rivers | 14,775 | Hamilton/Madison/Suwanee |

| | | |
|---|---|---|
| Etoniah Creek | .8,554 | .Putnam |
| Myakka | .8,532 | .Charlotte/Sarasota |
| Pine Log | .6,911 | .Bay/Washington |
| Little-Big Econ | .4,980 | .Seminole |
| Ralph E. Simmons | .3,638 | .Nassau |
| Ross Prairie | .3,527 | .Marion |
| Cary | .3,413 | .Nassau/Duval |
| Big Shoals | .1,666 | .Hamilton |
| Deep Creek* | .380 | .St. Johns |
| Carl Duval Moore | .306 | .Putnam |
| Watson Island* | .276 | .St. Johns |
| Choctawhatchee | .235 | .Washington |
| Porter Pond* | .80 | .Washington |
| Woodville | .73 | .Leon |
| Holopaw* | .58 | .Osceol |
| Bruner Bay* | .40 | .Washington |
| Holmes Creek* | .40 | .Washington |
| Loblolly | .40 | .Washington |
| Tupelo* | .40 | .Washington |
| Cottage Hill | .31 | .Escambia |
| Gillis Road* | .20 | .Santa Rosa |

*Currently not accessible to public due to location.*

## SPECIES OF TREES

Florida is the most prolific tree flora state in the continental United States. There are about 314 species growing in this state, comprising almost half of all the varieties in North America north of Mexico.

The state's tree flora can be divided into four primary divisions: sweet gum, gum maple, tulip tree, and slash pine in the north; a southern division composed of longleaf pine, magnolia, and cypress; a Caribbean representation including royal palm, mahogany, and gumbo limbo; and an endemic representation such as Florida yew, dune holly, and Florida hickory.

Pine species generally are the most prolific, valuable, and versatile of all Florida tree species. Following are some of the most common trees found in the state.

**AMERICAN BEECH** occurs in alluvial soils in middle and western Florida. It is found scattered among other hardwood trees and sometimes makes small groups in pure stands. It drops its leaves in autumn but is one of the most beautiful of all trees, in summer or winter. The bark of this trees is perhaps its most distinctive characteristic, remaining an unbroken light gray throughout the tree's life. Wood of this tree is very hard and is of some value as lumber, although it will not stand up to weather or to being in soil.

**ACACIA** grows to only about 20 feet in height, but is a favorite in the southern regions in the state as a decorative tree. Its fernlike leaves and puffy, golden flowers make it pretty; its branches bear thorns. If kept trimmed, the acacia may also be used as a hedge.

**AMERICAN ELM,** sometimes called White Elm, is a famous shade tree that ranges from New England to the Rocky Mountains and southward to Texas. In low ground on riverbanks it is found in Florida in the Everglades. It reaches an average height of 60 to 70 feet and a diameter of four to five feet. The elm's wood is heavy, hard, strong, and difficult to split. It is used for wheel hubs, saddle trees, boats, barrel hoops, and as veneer for baskets and crates.

**AMERICAN HOLLY** is a Florida native evergreen that is becoming increasingly rare. It seldom reaches more than 30 feet tall, and has been considerably cut for Christmas decoration. Its leaves feature spiny points and in the fall it bears a red or yellow berry. Wood of the larger trees is favored for cabinetry.

**AMERICAN SWEETGUM,** or Red or Sweet Gum, is a large valuable forest tree. It occurs on hammocks, rich river bottoms, and in swamps, as well as on drier lands as far south as Cape Canaveral and Tampa Bay. It is usually abundant in second growth on old fields and in cut-over woods. In the fall its coloring is brilliant, ranging from pale yellow through orange and red to a deep bronze. Wood of this tree is not durable, but is used for flooring, interior finish, and for pulp.

**BALD CYPRESS** is a swamp-dwelling tree found throughout the South. It can grow to 150 feet tall and is a member of the pine family. This tree's unusual feature is a "knee" that emerges from the water. These knees release oxygen and provide the mother tree with carbon dioxide. Bald cypress will grow on dry land, but do not have knees in this case. These trees are virtually immune to serious pests and diseases. The wood is very durable and good for use in contact with soil and weathers very well for use in shingles or siding.

**BIGLEAF MAGNOLIA** is a magnolia with extraordinarily large leaves, 20 to 30 inches long with a 10-inch width. The tree is medium-sized, reaching a height of 30 to 40 feet, with a straight trunk up to 12 to 16 inches in diameter, ending in stout, noticeably wide-spreading branches. The tree is sparsely found over western and middle Florida in good soils with plenty of moisture. Flowers of this magnolia are white, nine to 12 inches across, with a pleasant fragrance.

**BOXELDER** is a tree found sparsely in north Florida and in the upper part of the peninsula. It favors hammocks and riverbanks and is a true maple with the difference that it has a compound leaf. It is a tree of medium size, rarely reaching over 24 inches in diameter and 60 to 70 feet in height. It has been planted for shade because in good soil it grows rapidly. It is not long-lived or generally satisfactory for any purpose and reproduces quickly. It is often destroyed by grazing or cultivation.

**BUCKWHEAT TREE,** or Titi, a small tree, is common along Florida's swamps, ponds, and bays. In such areas it often forms dense thickets over the coastal region and somewhat inland over the pine barrens. Titi occasionally reach a height of 40 feet, but usually do not exceed 25 feet. The trunk is small, inclined, or crooked, and divides at a height of 10 to 15 feet into numerous branches.

**CABBAGE PALMETTO** is a member of the palm family. It is named from its large leaf-bud or "cabbage" at the top of the trunk, which can be cooked and eaten as a vegetable. The loss of the bud causes a branching, if not the tree's death. Like lilies, grasses, and corn, the palms grow outward from many bundles of tissues located centrally within the trunk. This is unlike the growth of pines, gums, oaks, and many other trees that yearly form a ring of wood. Cabbage Palmetto can grow 50 to 80 feet high with a straight, clear trunk up to two feet in diameter, covered with shallow ridges and fissures. It grows in sandy soil or hammocks over most of the coast, including the Keys north to the Apalachicola River.

**CAROLINA LAURELCHERRY** is a handsome tree with dark green leaves and much-planted for ornamental purposes. The laurel cherry, or mock orange, is native as far south as Biscayne Bay and the Kissimmee River. It prefers riverbanks and the borders of hammocks, and is abundant in the Orange County area. The trunk is straight or leaning, up to 40 feet in height. It is also some 10 inches in diameter, but the wood has no special uses.

**CHICKASAW PLUM** is found from central Florida north, usually in woodlands and hammocks. It is a spectacular spring flowering tree, with branches covered in small white blooms that precede the emergence of new leaves. In summer, a reddish-yellow berry becomes a favorite of birds. Although the fruit is acidic and sour, some persevering cooks create a tasty jam with it. These trees grow to about 25 feet tall.

**COMMON PERSIMMON,** often called "simmon," is well known throughout the southern United States. It is usually medium sized, rarely exceeding 60 feet in height and 18 inches in diameter, and occurs throughout the state. It prefers open, sandy woods and is most abundant in old fields, though it may be found on hammocks and rich bottomlands. Timber from this tree is valued for making golf-stick heads.

**COMMON SASSAFRAS** is a small, aromatic tree, usually not over 40 feet in height or one foot in diameter. It is found throughout northern and central parts of the state in woods and fields and is one of the first broad-leaf trees to come up on abandoned fields, where the seeds are dropped by birds. It is closely related to red bay and the camphor tree of Japan. The root of this tree yields an aromatic oil used for flavoring.

**CUBAN ROYAL PALM,** a common native tree of Florida, is found along the shore and on some of the nearby Everglade Keys of southernmost Florida. It is a majestic palm that has been extensively planted in south Florida. The same tree is native and similarly widely planted for ornament and shade in Cuba and elsewhere. The tree rises to a height of some 80 to 120 feet on a trunk some two feet in diameter with an enlarged base giving it an appearance of stability.

**FALSEMANGROVE,** also called Buttonwood or White Mangrove, is a tree of the muddy tidal shores of bays and lagoons from Cape Canaveral on the east coast and Cedar Key on the west coast, south over the Keys, reaching greatest abundance and largest size in or near Monroe County. It attains heights up to 60 feet and diameters up to 20 inches, although generally smaller. Wood of this tree contains high amounts of tannin, used for tanning leather.

**FLORIDA FISHFUDDLETREE,** or Jamaica Dogwood, is one of the most abundant tropical trees and most valuable timber producers in subtropical Florida. It occurs on hammocks over the coastal shores and Keys from Bay Biscayne to Cape Sable. The tree grows rapidly and reaches heights up to 50 feet with trunks from two or three feet in diameter.

**FLORIDA MAPLE,** or Southern Sugar Maple, closely resembles the well-known northern sugar maple, and extends into the state from Georgia and Alabama. It is found on hammocks and good forest soil, reaching a height rarely over 50 feet, with a trunk up to two feet in diameter. Leaves turn yellow or scarlet during autumn.

**FLORIDA POISONTREE,** or Hog Gum, is a very common, medium-sized tree with poisonous properties. It is found on hammocks along the shores south from Bay Biscayne and over the Keys. It reaches heights of 30 to 40 feet with a short trunk up to two feet in diameter. The bark exudes a milky caustic or burning juice. It has emetic or purgative properties.

**FLOWERING DOGWOOD,** prevalent north of Orange County, is one of the state's most spectacular flowering trees. It is one of the most popular landscaping trees and its flowering habits tend to overwhelm the fact that its wood is valuable. This tree can be found on a wide variety of soils and will bloom heavily in gardens, street plantings, or in forests. In

Florida west of the Ocklockonee River, an occasional fragrant specimen can be found; and a few rare trees bloom with pink or a light red color.

**HAMMOCK HICKORY,** or Florida Pignut, is a common hickory on the hammocks of Florida north of the Everglades. The tree usually reaches 40 to 80 feet, with a trunk of one to two feet in diameter. It is covered with medium gray, comparatively thin bark close and tight to the tree, and is broken into shallow furrows and small ridges. The branchlets are bright reddish-brown and smooth, which is one of the guides for identifying this tree.

**HAWTHORN** shows up with a number of species distributed throughout north and central portions of the state. About 50 species are known to occur in Florida on the poorest, richest, shallowest, and deepest soil regions, as well as on limestone hills or rich bottom and swamp land. Most forms have a common likeness, possessing thorns and bearing white blossoms and red or yellow fruit. Some species are planted as ornamentals, but otherwise the group is of little commercial value.

**JUNGLEPLUM,** Mastic or Wild Olive, is a large, valuable timber tree growing along the state's coast from Brevard and Lee counties south into the Keys. It grows to 70 feet high with a large, straight trunk from three to four feet in diameter. Fruit of this tree is enjoyed by some people and its wood is used for boat building.

**LAUREL OAK,** a common but beautiful oak, is generally distributed and found on stream banks except in the extreme southern regions of the state. Laurel Oaks can reach 100 feet with a three- to four-foot diameter. It is especially valued as a shade tree.

**LINDEN,** also called Basswood or Wahoo, is a distinctive forest tree that appears in at least four species over northern or central Florida and into the Panhandle. They are common and valuable timber trees that attain heights of 70 feet and diameters of two feet. Outer bark from this tree is used for making rough camp buildings.

**LIVE OAK** can be found throughout Florida except for some of the Keys. Its habit of spreading, sometimes to 100 feet, makes it a striking shade tree. Live oak trunks may be three to four feet in diameter and divide into many limbs. This tree is slow growing but highly desirable.

**LOBLOLLY PINE** is also called Oldfield Pine and is an important tree throughout most of the South. Loblolly is most common in north Florida, often along streams and rivers, but can be found from central Florida northward. Loblolly has much shorter needles than slash pine and the needles grow three in a sheath. The loblolly cone is very prickly and elongated.

**LONGLEAF PINE** is a striking tree found throughout the state. As its name suggests, the needles of this tree are from 10 to 15 inches long. Wood of this pine is a favorite because it is strong and durable. The tree's gum is used to produce rosin, tar, and turpentine. It is also called the pitch pine, the yellow pine, and the southern pine.

**PIGEON SEAGRAPE,** or Pigeon Plum, is the only tree member of the buckwheat family of plants. It is a large tree, up to 70 feet in height with a tall, straight trunk up to two feet in diameter. It is found most often on hammocks of the Keys, but its range is from Cape Canaveral around to Cape Sable.

**POND APPLE** is abundant near waterways and along the borders of Lake Okeechobee. Also called the Alligator Apple, it is related to the paw paw, and grows to a height of 50 or 60 feet. It has a sturdy, often buttressed base, and a short, clear trunk that is often irregularly shaped. This tree's fruit is yellow when ripe and is aromatic, but does not taste good and is not recommended for eating.

**PUMPKIN ASH** grows in deep-river swamps of central and western Florida. It reaches heights of nearly 100 feet with a somewhat slender trunk of up to three feet in diameter. It resembles tupelo or cypress in that its trunk has an enlarged base.

**RED MULBERRY** trees occur nearly throughout the state and are the state's only native mulberry. White and black mulberry species are also found in the state but they were imported from elsewhere. This tree rarely grows higher than 50 feet with a trunk that is two feet in diameter. Fruit is a dark red, almost black color, and is sweet and edible. The tree is a particular favorite of birds.

**REDBUD** is an exotic-looking tree, especially in spring when its branches are covered in tiny pinkish-red blooms. It prefers the northern regions of the state, but a few individuals can be found as far south as Tampa. It is an ideal candidate for beautification projects along streets or highways as it requires very little maintenance.

**RIVER RED GUM** is one of several Eucalyptus introduced from Australia. It is tall—110 feet—with a shapely form. This tree has been used for reforestation because it grows so rapidly, about 10-15 feet per year. It is tolerant of poor soil and makes a good shade tree in the warmer regions of the state, south of a line from Tampa to Vero Beach.

**SAND PINE** flourishes in very sandy soils throughout Florida, except in the hottest areas. It is most abundant in the eastern and central portions of the peninsula. Two varieties of this pine are found in Florida: the Choctawhatchee and the central or Ocala type, which is found in the Ocala National forest.

**SHORTLEAF PINE** is also called the yellow or rosemary pine. It is widely distributed throughout the South and is found most often in north Florida. Once mature, this tree has a tall, straight trunk and an oval crown and may reach heights of 60 feet and a diameter of about two and one-half feet.

**SLASH PINE** is a fast-growing tree common to all of Florida. Second growth stands of slash pine form a large part of the state's pine forests. This pine is an excellent timber tree and its gum is used to produce turpentine and other products.

**SOUTHERN MAGNOLIA** is a beautiful forest tree that occurs naturally in the hammocks and swamps of Florida. It attains heights generally of 60 to 80 feet and has a trunk diameter of about four feet. It is also called the Evergreen Magnolia and bears beautiful flowers that are white with a lavender center and a pleasing aroma.

**SOUTHERN RED CEDAR** occupies the same range and is often confused with West Indies Juniper. This tree is evergreen, fragrant, and occurs through most of the state south to Sarasota County. It tolerates a wide range of soils and reaches heights of up to 50 feet. Its aromatic woods are used to line closets and chests.

**SOUTHERN WAXMYRTLE** attains a height of about 40 feet and is found over most of the state. It is a small tree with a slender upright trunk and its spreading branches form a round-shaped head. It is found largely in swampy areas.

**TURKEY OAK** is found abundantly throughout the scrub woodlands of Florida. It is usually no taller than 20 or 30 feet, although a few individuals reach 60 feet in height. Its leaves are deeply divided into three or five lobes and are quite characteristic of only this tree. Its wood is used primarily for fuel. Another name for this oak is Blackjack. Usually growing with this oak is another oak that is dubbed a "turkey" oak, but which has oblong leaves and is more properly termed "bluejack" or Upland Willow Oak.

**WEST INDIAN MAHOGANY** can attain a height of 50 feet. It is deciduous and found only in south Florida. It is fast growing and provides ample shade with spreading, densely foliaged branches. Wood of this tree tends to be brittle and may be damaged during hurricanes.

**WEST INDIES JUNIPER** is common in the state except in the southern areas. It also is called Red Cedar and its aromatic heartwood is used to make closet linings and cedar chests. Durable, especially in contact with the soil, this tree provides long-lasting fence posts or poles.

**WHITE OAK** is a shapely oak that can reach 100 feet tall. It is an important timber tree with a trunk diameter of two or three feet. It is found in the middle and western parts of Florida. In open fields, this tree develops a broad crown and reaching limbs and can be a most attractive shade tree.

## A POTPOURRI OF PALMS

The world boasts some 4,000 species of palms and while Florida has only a small percentage of that number, perhaps several hundred, it does have more than any other state. In fact, most of the palms native to the U.S. are found in Florida. They range from dwarf shrubby types to magnificent trees reaching 100 feet tall. Some species are erect in habit of growth, others are leaning; some have but a single trunk, others have numerous stems forming clumps of different sizes.

All palms can be divided according to leaf type into two main classes: pinnate or feather leaved, and palmate or fan leaved. By far the larger number of species belong to the pinnate class.

The greatest threat to Florida's palm trees is a disease called lethal yellowing that has struck hard at coconut palms and numerous other species, including the Christmas palm and the date palm. The disease hit Florida in 1955, spreading from Key West to the mainland. In the 1970s it had killed an estimated 5 million palms in the Miami area, including 90 percent of the city's coconut palms.

The disease is caused by microorganisms carried from tree to tree by insects called planthoppers. The planthopper feeds on palm leaves and injects the organism into the tree much the way a mosquito injects malaria into humans. Signs of an affected coconut palm are the rapid loss of both mature and immature coconuts, followed by the palm's flower buds dying and blackening in their pods. The palm's fronds then turn yellow and fall, leaving only a rotting trunk.

Plant pathologists have found no way of stopping the disease, but are experimenting with antibiotics and insecticides. They have also discovered that Florida's most popular turf grasses are ideal hosts for planthoppers, while Caribbean turf grasses are not. The disease now has spread from Miami's east coast to the west coast area of Fort Myers, and experts fear it will move south toward Naples. Both communities have voluminous stands of coconut palms.

As the trees sicken and die, tree experts are urging residents to replant with Malayan Dwarf and the hybrid Maypan palms, both proven resistant to lethal yellowing. Like the coconut palms now under siege, which are classified as the Jamaica tall coconut palm, the two recommended replacement types also grow coconuts. Royal Palm and Cabbage Palmetto, native to Florida, also appear immune.

## CHAMPION TREES

Hundreds of tree species thrive in Florida because of the diversity of its climate. The American Forestry Association, along with the Florida Department of Agriculture and Consumer Services, seeks to locate and record the largest specimens of each species.

Some species known to grow in the state have never been nominated and thus may not appear on this list of national champion trees in Florida. Anyone wishing to nominate a tree should contact the local county forester.

The champion tree list that follows is compiled by the American Forestry Association in cooperation with Florida officials. It lists those trees in Florida that are known to be of record size nationally.

Measurements are given in inches for circumference, in feet for height, and in feet for average crown spread. To determine the largest tree, one point is allowed for each inch of circumference, each foot of height, and each four feet of average crown spread.

| Species | Circ. (in.) | Height (ft.) | Spread (ft.) | Location |
|---|---|---|---|---|
| Alvaradoa, Mexican | 32 | 35 | 14 | Miami |
| Bayberry, Southern | 49 | 31 | 27 | Fort George Island |
| Black mangrove | 86 | 61 | 42 | Everglades National Park |
| Blackbeard, catclaw | 122 | 88 | 63 | Sarasota County |
| Blolly, longleaf | 55 | 48 | 14 | Florida Keys |
| Boxwood, Florida | 24 | 27 | 16 | Monroe County |
| Buccaneer Palm | 30 | 23 | 10 | Biscayne National Park |
| Buckwheat tree | 73 | 58 | 30 | Wakulla County |
| Bumelia, tough | 41 | 41 | 28 | Amelia Island |
| Bustic, willow | 41 | 56 | 23 | Miami-Dade County |
| Butterbough | 52 | 45 | 31 | Biscayne National Park |
| Button mangrove | 136 | 41 | 65 | Palm Beach |
| Buttonbush | 49 | 23 | 22 | High Springs |
| Buttonwood | 174 | 51 | 68 | Palm Beach |
| Byrsonima, Key | 62 | 15 | 30 | Monroe County |
| Cajeput tree | 201 | 62 | 54 | Hollywood |
| Camphor tree (tie) | 368 | 72 | 102 | Hardee County |
| Camphor tree (tie) | 366 | 68 | 131 | Zephyrhills |
| Canella | 19 | 29 | 18 | Biscayne National Park |
| Caper, Jamaica | 25 | 15 | 20 | Lee County |
| Cedar, Southern red | 193 | 80 | 59 | Alachua County |
| Cherry, West Indies | 65 | 53 | 50 | Miami |
| Chinkapin, Allegheny | 84 | 60 | 63 | Putnam County |
| Cinnecord | 14 | 20 | 24 | Monroe County |
| Clusai, Florida | 52 | 27 | 28 | Martin County |
| Coral bean | 38 | 22 | 25 | Lee County |
| Cupania, Florida | 18 | 27 | 17 | Monroe County |
| Cypress pine, blue | 186 | 57 | 58 | Bradenton |
| Cyrilla, swamp | 46 | 52 | 28 | Washington County |
| Dahoon, myrtle | 67 | 46 | 35 | Lawtey |
| Darling plum | 17 | 40 | 11 | Florida Keys |

| | | | | |
|---|---|---|---|---|
| Devilwood | .35 | .46 | .27 | .Putnam County |
| Dogwood, swamp | .15 | .23 | .24 | .Palatka |
| Doveplum | .66 | .45 | .28 | .Miami |
| Elder, Florida | .34 | .20 | .14 | .Gainesville |
| Elm, cedar | 102 | .118 | .66 | .Silver River |
| Elm, Florida | 158 | .94 | .54 | .Alachua County |
| Falsemastic | 105 | .70 | .80 | .Florida Keys |
| Fiddlewood, Florida | .46 | .39 | .29 | .Miami-Dade County |
| Fig, Fla. strangler | .288 | .80 | .76 | .Miami-Dade County |
| Fig, shortleafed | .245 | .41 | .57 | .Monroe County |
| Fishpoison tree | 101 | .41 | .48 | .Lee County |
| Flowerface (tie) | .20 | .12 | .15 | .Broward County |
| Flowerface (tie) | .16 | .16 | .14 | .Broward County |
| Fringetree | .42 | .41 | .31 | .Suwannee County |
| Geiger tree | .50 | .25 | .23 | .Lee County |
| Guiana plum | .23 | .31 | .28 | .Coral Gables |
| Gumbo limbo (tie) | .97 | .63 | .66 | .Miami-Dade County |
| Gumbo limbo (tie) | .124 | .36 | .55 | .Miami Shores |
| Hawthorn, beautiful | .23 | .44 | .30 | .Tallahassee |
| Hawthorn, parsley | .16 | .33 | .23 | .Gainesville |
| Hawthorn, yellow | .47 | .30 | .36 | .Levy County |
| Holly, Carolina | .14 | .25 | .18 | .Jacksonville |
| Holly, tawnberry | .40 | .55 | .22 | .Miami-Dade County |
| Hypelate | .58 | .38 | .35 | .Monroe County |
| India almond | 135 | .61 | .71 | .Monroe County |
| Laurelcherry, Carolina | .127 | .47 | .55 | .Lakeland |
| Lidflower, pale | .18 | .33 | .19 | .Monroe County |
| Lignum vitae, rough | .56 | .37 | .26 | .Biscayne National Park |
| Loblolly bay | 161 | .94 | .52 | .Ocala National Forest |
| Lysiloma bahama | .96 | .79 | .42 | .Homestead |
| Mahogany, W. Indies | .130 | .70 | .59 | .Lee County |
| Manchineel | .47 | .39 | .34 | .Monroe County |
| Mango | .73 | .40 | .43 | .Pompano Beach |
| Mangrove, red | .77 | .75 | .41 | .Everglades National Park |
| Milkbark | .38 | .41 | .20 | .Monroe County |
| Oak, Chapman | .81 | .45 | .50 | .Ocala National Forest |
| Oak, laurel | .258 | .80 | .114 | .Okaloosa County |
| Oak, myrtle (tie) | .51 | .48 | .54 | .Clearwater |
| Oak, myrtle (tie) | .69 | .36 | .35 | .Fort Clinch State Park |
| Oak, sand live | 184 | .82 | .88 | .Gainesville |
| Oak, water | 266 | .128 | .79 | .Calhoun County |
| Oysterwood | .13 | .24 | .11 | .Monroe County |
| Palmetto, cabbage | .45 | .90 | .14 | .Highlands Hammock State Park |
| Paradise tree | .78 | .62 | .47 | .Fort Lauderdale |
| Paurotis palm | .13 | .32 | .28 | .West Palm Beach |
| Pepper tree, Brazil | 166 | .35 | .52 | .Broward County |

| | | | | |
|---|---|---|---|---|
| Pinckneya | 12 | 32 | 16 | Orange Springs |
| Pine, sand (tie) | 78 | 103 | 46 | Wekiva Springs State Park |
| Pine, sand (tie) | 83 | 106 | 38 | Pasco County |
| Pine, So. Fla. slash | 120 | 69 | 56 | Sarasota County |
| Poisontree, Florida | 63 | 63 | 72 | Miami-Dade County |
| Pondapple | 125 | 44 | 47 | Miami |
| Prickly ash, lime | 42 | 25 | 31 | Lee County |
| Redberry, eugenia | 58 | 45 | 25 | Miami-Dade County |
| Royal palm, Florida | 78 | 80 | 32 | Homestead |
| Sapodilla | 99 | 50 | 29 | Miami |
| Satinleaf | 65 | 42 | 37 | Miami |
| Satinwood, W. Indies | 43 | 20 | 30 | Florida Keys |
| Saw palmetto (tie) | 26 | 17 | 11 | Withlacoochee State Forest |
| Saw palmetto (tie) | 27 | 21 | 8 | Fort Pierce |
| Seagrape | 90 | 57 | 69 | Miami |
| Seven-year apple | 11 | 25 | 11 | Homestead |
| Shaving Brush | 109 | 31 | 67 | Boynton Beach |
| Silverpalm, Florida(tie) | 19 | 27 | 6 | Florida Keys |
| Silverpalm, Florida (tie) | 22 | 22 | 6 | Florida Keys |
| Soapberry, wingleaf | 85 | 70 | 39 | Paynes Prairie Preserve |
| Soldier wood | 22 | 41 | 13 | Monroe County |
| Staggerbush | 29 | 40 | 21 | Orange Home |
| Stopper, Simpson | 53 | 32 | 34 | Hollywood |
| Strongback, Bahama | 24 | 28 | 23 | Monroe County |
| Sumac, Southern | 13 | 22 | 15 | Arcadia |
| Tallowwood | 16 | 25 | 21 | Biscayne National Park |
| Tamarind | 157 | 60 | 82 | Monroe County |
| Tetrazygia, Florida | 16 | 41 | 19 | Miami-Dade County |
| Thatchpalm, Florida (tie) | 18 | 23 | 6 | Monroe County |
| Thatchpalm, Florida (tie) | 12 | 28 | 2 | Hollywood |
| Torchwood (tie) | 16 | 22 | 15 | Monroe County |
| Torchwood (tie) | 12 | 24 | 13 | Miami-Dade County |
| Tupelo, Ogeechee | 201 | 60 | 61 | Columbia County |
| Viburnum, possumhaw | 12 | 26 | 9 | Fort McCoy |
| Viburnum, Walter | 22 | 30 | 23 | Gainesville |
| White mangrove | 63 | 34 | 27 | Chokoloskee Island |
| Yew, Florida | 25 | 20 | 26 | Torreya State Park |

## Florida Forever

The new Florida Forever program, the nation's largest conservation land program, passed by the 1999 Florida Legislature, provides $300 million a year for 10 years. It includes $105 million for water resource development to be divided among the state's water management districts; $105 million for land acquisition; $72 million to buy urban parkland and for other capital projects in existing parks; $4.5 million to the Florida Greenways and Trails program to buy land; $4.5 million to manage state lands; an equal amount to manage state forests; and another $4.5 million on other projects.

## FLORIDA TRAIL SECTIONS MAP

**THE FLORIDA TRAIL**
Completed  ▬▬▬▬▬
Proposed ● ● ● ● ● ● ●

### FLORIDA TRAIL

A hiking trail through Florida—
from the Everglades to the
Blackwater River State Park near
Pensacola—is being carved out by
ardent outdoors people. When finished, the trail will cover 1,300 miles
through the wilderness areas of the
Sunshine State. To date, some 1,000
miles have been completed.

The dream in the 1960s of a
Miami real estate salesman and
photographer, James A. Kern, the
trail is a two-and-a-half-foot-wide
natural footpath without gravel. It is
marked by an orange blaze and
winds through varied topography
from the Big Cypress Swamp in
southwest Florida to the hardwood
forests of north Florida. Longest
completed section is a 250-mile
stretch from the Ocala National
Forest north and then west through
the Osceola National Forest.
Another large segment follows the
Suwannee River. The trail is being
created by the Florida Trail
Association and other concerned
groups.

# SPANISH MOSS

Sometimes called Southern moss, Florida moss, and even "old man's beard," Spanish moss is a member of the bromelaceae family of plants, best known of which is the pineapple. An air plant, it needs no roots, but traps and absorbs water through its leaves. For food, the moss combines water with carbon dioxide from the air and manufactures its own food by photosynthesis. Spanish moss is not a parasite on trees, but uses trees only for mechanical support.

In the summer, the long strands of moss produce tiny yellow-green flowers. When ripe seeds are cast off they are spread by the wind to other trees nearby. In high winds, thousands of pieces of the plant will be snapped off and carried great distances. Some will be forcefully driven into cracks in trees and telephone poles, others will be stopped by buildings, rooftops, and other structures, where they grow into mature, healthy plants. Scientists believe hurricanes, with their tremendous winds, are a major means of spreading Spanish moss.

Hardwoods, especially live oaks, are most likely to harbor the moss though no tree is immune to it. In north Florida, for example, pecan groves must be de-mossed regularly if they are to produce their best nut crops. Pecan trees, like live oaks, offer excellent growing conditions for the moss because they provide open crowns and horizontal branches.

Of course, too much moss in any tree is not good. Because it can absorb several times its own weight in water when it rains, moss tends to make branches sag, split, and break off under its great weight. At the same time, its rain-holding characteristic can be an asset to the tree. Moss reduces rain runoff and holds water in reserve so that when a dry season hits, the trapped water slowly evaporates, creating an air of humidity around the tree.

Scientists attribute other good effects to Spanish moss. It blocks out much sunlight, they explain, and thereby influences the type of ground plants that grow under trees. Without this shade, some ground species would not exist, while others would become more numerous. They explain tree-living creatures also would be affected by the absence of moss in Florida. Several species use the moss for roosting and rearing of their young; others, like the warblers, carry away the plant for nesting material. Even raccoons and squirrels make use of the moss for nest building or protective cover.

Harvesting moss was a big industry in Florida at one time. At the industry's peak in 1936, dozens of gins dried, combed, and sold the plant. Collected by hand, usually with the aid of a hook or blades, the moss was piled in large heaps or buried in long, shallow pits. This allowed the gray outer portions of the strands to rot away, and what remained was a central black fiber, tough and resilient. It was used to fill cushions of automobiles and railway coach seats, mattresses, chairs, couches, even horse collars. The industry thrived until the late 1950s when the cheaper foam upholstering materials were invented.

Today, the gins are gone, and the fear is that Spanish moss may eventually follow. Scientists first noted trouble in 1968 in Manatee County, where moss began dying in large bunches. Soon reports came in from Orlando, Ocala, Tampa, and Leesburg that the moss there, too, was dying. The prevalent theory as to the cause is air pollution.

A University of Florida professor explains, "Spanish moss is ultrasensitive to airborne pollutants, and these pollutants are readily picked up by the

*(continued on next page)*

fuzzy surface of the moss." If the die-off continues, Florida could lose all its Spanish moss, a disturbing prospect . . . and a rather unattractive one to those who associate moss-draped oaks with the romantic Old South.

## POISONOUS PLANTS

Florida's wide variety of flora harbors numerous poisonous plants. Following is a list and description of such plants most frequently encountered. Fortunately, most have such an unpleasant taste or consistency that it is not likely anyone would chew them for long or swallow any part of them. Should a person do so, however, and begin suffering effects, a call or trip to the nearest poison control center would be wise.

**ANGEL'S TRUMPET** is a beautiful flowering plant with a long history in folklore as having hallucinogenic properties. In fact, the flower and seeds deliver a deadly poison that has killed numerous Florida teenagers in the 1990s.

**AZALEA** is a popular landscaping plant, but all of the plant is poisonous if eaten.

**BARBADOS NUT,** also called French Purge Nut or Curcas Bean, is a coarse annual plant or small tree up to 15 feet tall. The leaves are thick, six inches or more wide, heart-shaped or coarsely three to five-lobed. All cases of poisoning have occurred from eating the seeds.

**BITTERWEED** is a flowering plant that ranges in height from six inches to three feet. Leaves are about an inch long, very narrow, and found on multiple stems and branches. Flowers look like black-eyed susans, with yellow petals, but the centers are also yellow. It is found primarily in north and central Florida along roadsides and in fields. As its name suggests, it tastes bitter, but all parts of the plant are poisonous.

**BOXWOOD** is an ornamental shrub rarely over five feet tall with bright green, shiny leaves. Both the bark and leaves of this shrub contain an alkaloid substance that causes severe abdominal pain, and in some instances, convulsions.

**BRACKEN FERN** is a long-stemmed, coarse fern found most often in open woods or in fields from Lake Okeechobee north. Its leaves are lacy and form a clearly triangular shape. Livestock may be poisoned by this plant if it is accidentally baled with hay.

**CAROLINA JESSAMINE** is a showy vine featuring dark, oval leaves that are one-half to two and one-half inches long. This plant often is used in landscaping as it is an evergreen and bears clusters of fragrant yellow trumpet-like flowers all summer. The flowers, leaves, and roots contain a poison that can affect nerve endings of the body. Also called the Evening Trumpet Flower.

**CASTOR BEAN,** also called Palma Crista or Castor Oil Plant, is a robust annual herb growing to the size of a small tree. The strong stems are green or red to purple. Leaves are star-shaped with five to nine or more lobes, thin and finely toothed along the margin. Castor bean contains a poisonous principle, ricin, which is a true protein, plus ricinoleic acid and oliec acid. This plant also is used as an ornamental and is abundant as a wild plant in the Lake Okeechobee area.

**CRAPE JASMINE** is a rather succulent shrub, three to eight feet tall. The flowers, one to two inches across, are produced in small clusters. They are pure white with a yellowish tubular base. The roots, bark, and flower may be harmful if eaten.

**CROATALARIA** ranges from three to six feet tall and is found all over the state. It has large, waxy leaves four to seven inches long that may have a bristle at the tip. A spike of yellow flowers grows snapdragon-like on a stalk within the plant. Livestock may be poisoned by this plant, which is often found in abandoned or neglected fields.

**CROWN OF THORNS** is a low-growing shrub with thorny stems and branches. They are purplish in color and armed with numerous stiff, sharp-pointed spines. The milky sap or latex is quite irritating to the skin of some people. The root contains an unclassified toxic substance.

**DEADLY NIGHTSHADE** is a two-foot-tall plant with black berries and white flowers. All parts are poisonous if eaten.

**DIEFFENBACHIA,** or Dumb Cane, is a tender house plant. The green stems, three to six feet tall, are fleshy and the green leaves, usually a foot long, may be spotted. Chewing or swallowing any of these parts, which contain calcium oxalate, is quite harmful and can cause severe swelling of the throat or tongue.

**ELDERBERRY** is a widespread plant featuring small white flowers and purple berries, but its roots, bark, stem, and leaves are poisonous if eaten.

**ELEPHANT EAR** is a large-leaved plant that can reach enormous proportions. It is a favorite for Florida landscapes and is often seen in the wild. Ironically, it is a food source in some parts of the tropical world. But its roots and rhizomes require very careful and knowledgeable preparation. Raw, all parts of this plant deliver a stinging toxin. It is one of the most frequently reported causes of plant poisoning in Florida.

**ERYTHRINA** leaves and flowers, when cooked, are edible, but its raw seeds are highly poisonous.

**GLORIOSA,** or Climbing Lily, is a tender, herbaceous plant. The weak stems, upright at first, attain a height of five to seven feet. The numerous narrow leaves grow in pairs all along the stem. These leaf ends act as tendrils, twining around any suitable support. Each flower is crinkled along the edges, is yellow or yellow and red in color, or becomes red all over as the flower fades. All parts of this plant are poisonous, with the highest concentration of toxic materials in the tubers. Death has been reported to have occurred within four hours after tubers were eaten.

**HYDRANGEA** is a stiff, stout shrub 3 to 12 feet tall. The flowers are borne at the end of the stems in dense, rounded clusters sometimes a foot in diameter. The individual flowers are pink, blue, or almost white. All parts of the plant are poisonous.

**JIMSON WEED,** also called Jamestown Weed or Thorn Apple, is a large annual weed, three to five feet tall, with several widespreading branches near the top of the stem. The erect flowers are short-stalked, funnel-shaped, and white or pale bluish-purple in color. All parts of the plant, particularly the seeds, are poisonous. Children have been poisoned by eating the fruit or sucking the flowers.

**LANTANA** is a native Florida shrub that is increasingly used as an ornamental. It reaches three to five feet in height. Oval leaves, pointed at one end, are scalloped along the edges and toxic. Children may be attracted by the dainty flowers of white, yellow, pink, orange, or scarlet that are clustered into tiny "bouquets." Immature berries are deadly.

**LARKSPUR (ANNUAL OR ROCKET)** is an upright annual garden plant grown for its flowers. Young plants form dense rosettes 5 to 10 inches across. Flowers vary in color from white to pink, rose, blue, or purple, or may be striped. The fruits are urn-shaped capsules. All plant parts are poisonous.

**LARKSPUR (HARDY)** is a perennial plant often used in flower gardens. The pale blue flowers scattered along the flowering stems are slender-stalked. If eaten in large quantities it could be hazardous.

**MANGO** is a large, tropical fruit tree that grows up to 60 feet in height. Because mango is related botanically to poison ivy, susceptible individuals who come in contact with the plant can develop a dermatitis similar to ivy poisoning. Handling any part of the plant may result in the poisoning. Many people are not affected by mangos; in fact, it is an unusually delicious fruit that can be purchased at supermarkets. But those persons suffering a reaction to mangos may lessen the poisoning effect by cooking the fruit, which destroys its inflammatory contents.

**MILK BUSH,** also called Pencil Cactus or Malabartree, is a shrub or small, multi-branched tree up to 15 feet tall. On old plants the trunk, three inches or more in diameter, is grayish but all of the rest of the plant is green. The twigs are produced in whorl-like clusters at the ends of each flush of growth. If eaten, the plant parts are reputed to be dangerously toxic. It has been used as a fish poison in its native India.

**MISTLETOE** has white berries that, if eaten, can cause acute stomach pains, cramps, vomiting, and heart failure.

**OLEANDER (COMMON)** is a woody shrub or small tree from 5 to 25 feet in height. The flowers vary in color from white through pink, creamy yellow, rose, and deep red. All plant parts are poisonous if eaten. One leaf is reported to be sufficient to kill an adult. Children may be poisoned by carrying flowers around in their mouths in play. Some people have suffered poisoning after eating frankfurters roasted on oleander stems. Inhaling smoke from burning oleander stems and leaves has caused symptoms of poisoning.

**POINSETTIA,** a favorite holiday plant, has leaves and seeds that can cause burning, inflammation, and blistering if eaten.

**POKEWEED,** also called Poke or Pokeberry, is a robust herbaceous plant growing six feet tall. The lower leaves are a foot or more long, gradually diminishing until the upper leaves are about three inches in length. All are spear-shaped. The flowers, produced all summer, are white. The flattened, purple-black, juicy berries contain several seeds. All plant parts, particularly the berries and roots, are considered toxic. Symptoms occur about two hours after the plant has been consumed. The young sprouts of this plant, called Poke (or Polk) Salad, are edible as greens, but harvesting and cooking them is best left to the experts.

**PRIMROSE (TOP)** is a winter-flowering greenhouse ornamental plant with leaves growing in a dense rosette. Individual leaves are nearly round, two to four inches long, and heart-shaped at the base. The pale pink to rose-colored flowers are produced at the top of the flower stalk. Handling primrose plants results in an itching dermatitis in some individuals. The irritation resembles ivy-poisoning but is usually less severe.

**PRIVET (LIGUSTRUM)** is a glossy shrub or small tree, 5 to 25 feet tall, and commonly used as a hedge plant. Records of poisonings by privet seem to be rare in the U.S., but in Europe children have died from eating the plant's fruits.

**RHUBARB** is a popular garden plant. Its stalk is edible, but leaf blades are toxic if eaten.

**ROSARY PEA,** also called Crabeye or Jequirity Pea, is a woody vine climbing to a height of 10 to 20 feet on other plants, arbors, or other support. The pods split along one side and show the two rows of bright red seeds that are black on one end. One seed thoroughly chewed and swallowed is sufficient to cause fatal poisoning of an adult.

**RUBBER PLANT,** used for interior decoration, contains latex in its stems and leaves that can cause burning, itching and blistering.

**STINGING NETTLE** is found in sandy areas, and its stiff hairs inject an irritant causing redness, intense itching, and swelling.

**TREE TOBACCO** is a shrub or small tree 10 to 15 feet tall with tubular flowers that either are erect or drooping, and borne in open clusters or panicles. The individual flowers, one to two inches long, are yellow or greenish yellow, and only slightly flared open at the ends. Cattle are reported to have been poisoned by this plant.

**TRUMPET VINE** has leaves and flowers that are poisonous if touched, resulting in skin inflammation and burning.

**TUNG-OIL TREE,** also called Tung Tree or Tung Nut, is a small, deciduous tree with smooth bark. The leafstalk bears two reddish or brownish glands or small knobs close to the leaf blades. The flowers are produced in large clusters before the leaves appear. They are pale pink or white and have reddish-brown bases. The fruits are nearly global and dark green, later turning brown. Each fruit contains three to seven large, hard, rough-coated seeds with white flesh. Cases of tung poisoning have occurred from eating the nuts.

**WATER HEMLOCK** grows in water and, if eaten, all parts of the plant can cause nausea, delirium, convulsions, and even death.

**WILD CHERRY** leaves contain cyanide poisoning that can cause convulsions and coma.

**YELLOW ALLAMANDA** is a vigorous vine or weak-stemmed shrub with leafy stems growing as much as 15 feet in a season. The large yellow flowers are produced in clusters near the ends of the branches. In Florida the plant, especially the fruit, has acquired the reputation of being dangerously poisonous. No known poison has been extracted from the plant but it would be best left alone anyway.

**YELLOW OLEANDER** is a shrub with a dense crown. Its dark leaves are three to six inches long, about a quarter-inch wide, glossy above, and paler beneath. The yellow to dull orange flowers are produced in small clusters near the tips of the twigs. The fruits are somewhat triangular. All plant parts are poisonous if eaten.

---

## ORPHANED BIRDS

Orphaned baby birds are best left alone, according to Florida bird expert Herbert Kale. He says that parent birds are generally near and need no human assistance unless the baby is in obvious danger. Baby birds can be picked up and placed safely in a nearby shrub or tree. Handling babies will not prompt parent birds to abandon their fledgling—that is a myth, Kale says.

---

## ENDANGERED REFUGES

The 7,500-acre National Key Deer Wildlife Refuge in the western Florida Keys and the 145,000-acre Loxahatchee National Wildlife Refuge west of Boynton Beach are among the 10 most endangered wildlife sanctuaries in the U.S. because of nearby commercial development and inappropriate recreational activities. The refuges are home to Key deer, bald eagle, manatee, peregrine falcon, wood stork, and hundreds of plant varieties, including the Key tree cactus.

# FLOWERS

They don't call Florida "Florida" for nothing. Discoverer Ponce de Leon was so overwhelmed by the extent and variety of the flora he encountered that he named the area, and subsequently the state, "Florida"—the land of flowers.

Today, botanists have identified more than 3,500 species of plant life in the state, providing an explosion of color throughout the year. Whether native, imported or escaped, or representing the southern reaches of northern temperate-zone flowering plants or the northernmost outpost of the flowers of the tropics, most of the world's flowering plants thrive in some part of the state.

Gardening is a major activity of Floridians, especially new Floridians, although they may have to change the timing, care, and feeding of their favorite flowers from "back home." Flower shows are regularly held throughout the state and are heavily attended. The annual explosion of simple phlox along roadsides and in open fields is a tourist attraction similar to the turning of the leaves in northern climes.

The flowers of Florida can be divided into native plants and imported plants. The native plants include those endemic to Florida, temperate plants for which Florida is the southernmost range, and tropical plants for which Florida is the northernmost range. Many plants imported for landscaping have escaped into the wild. Some fare poorly, others have taken on a new and evolving life. Others still have become nuisance plants.

## NATIVE FLOWERS

| | | |
|---|---|---|
| Duck Potato | Sedge | Black Ti-ti |
| Arrowhead | White Bracted Sedge | Ti-ti |
| Colic Root | Day Flower | St. John's Wort |
| Yellow Colic Root | Pink Spiderwort | Hypericum |
| Wild Onion | Spiderwort | Tartflower |
| Devil's Bit | Hat Pins | Dwarf Huckleberry |
| String Lily | Bog Buttons | Hairy Laurel |
| Dogtooth Violet | Wild Rice | Fetterbush |
| Spider Lily | Canna | Indian Pipes |
| Alligator Lily | Arrowroot | Wild Azalea |
| Pine Lily | Star Anise | Shiny Blueberry |
| False Garlic | Pawpaw | Low Bush Blueberry |
| Wake Robin | Flag Pawpaw | Rosemary |
| Bellwort | Sweet Shrub | Snowbell |
| Atamasco Lily | Spice Bush | Marlberry |
| Crow Poison | Carolina Bay | Florida Violet |
| Snakeroot | Peperomia | Long-leaf Violet |
| Manfreda | Lizard's Tail | Field Pansy |
| Yucca | Columbine | Sea Rocket |
| Redroot | Leather Flower | Waltheria |
| Goldcrest | Rue Anemone | Poppy Mallow |
| Catbrier | Prickly Poppy | Swamp Mallow |
| Purple Flat Iris | Watershield | Salt March Mallow |
| Southern Blue Flag | Lotus | Turk's-cap |
| Blue-eyed Grass | Water Lily | New Jersey Tea |
| Golden Club | Loblolly Bay | Spurge |
| Cattail | Possum Haw | Tread Softly |
| Yellow-eyed Grass | Yaupon | Pineland Croton |
| Pickerel Weed | Sweet Pepperbush | Painted Leaf |

Jimson Weed
Narrow Leaf Ground
    Cherry
Seaside Ground Cherry
Common Nightshade
Horse Nettle
Blodgett's Nightshade
Creeping Morning
    Glory
Annual Phlox
Cardinal Flower
Glades Lobelia
Venus' Looking-glass
Oxalis
Crane's Bill
Locust Berry
White Bachelor-button
Tall Milkwort
Large-Flower Polygala
Candyweed
Polygala
Winged Sumac
Red Buckeye
Prickly Pear
Pink Purslane
Bloodleaf
Chickweed
Wild Buckwheat
Red Chokeberry
Gopher Apple
Hog Plum
Swamp Rose
Sand Blackberry
White Indigo
Pineland Baptisia
Cassia
Rabbit Bells
Dalea
Summer Farewell
Beggar's Lice

Lupine
Dollar-weed
Pencil Flower
Tephrosia
Oak-leaf Hydrangea
Virginia Willow
Sundew
Dew Threads
Tall Meadow Beauty
Ludwigia
Primrose Willow
Evening Primrose
Button Bush
Diodia
Beach Creeper
Firebush
Partridge Berry
Richardia
Pineland Allamanda
Blue Star
Wild Allamanda
Seaside Gentian
Gatesby Gentian
Sabatia
Agalinis
False Foxglove
Water Hyssop
Buchnera
Indian Paint Brush
Lousewort
Seymeria
Beech Drops
Orobanche
Meadow Parsnip
Florida Elder
Possom Haw
Black Haw
Sky-flower
Scorpion-tail
Puccoon

Beauty Berry
Lantana
Blue Porterweed
Conradina
Lion's Ear
Blue Sage
Tropical Sage
Lyre-leaf Sage
Skullcap
Hedge-nettle
Frost Aster
White-top Aster
Sea Myrtle
Honeycomb Head
Greeneyes
Spanish Nettles
Bigelowia
Sea Daisy
Deer Tongue
Thistle
Tickseed
Swamp Coreopsis
Ageratum
Flat-topped Goldenrod
Gaillardia
Garberia
Rabbit Tobacco
Bitterweed
Beach Sunflower
Rayless Sunflower
Blazing Star
Roserush
Barbara's Buttons
Palafoxia
Golden Aster
Camphor Weed
Blackroot
Sow Thistle
Stokesia
Ironweed

## IMPORTED FLOWERS

Brazilian Elodia
Spanish Bayonet
Water Hyacinth
Mexican Poppy
Banana Water Lily
Pimpernel

Annatto
Begonia
Watercress
Wild Radish
Poinsettia
Angel Trumpet

Nightshade
Wahlenbergia
Puncture Weed
Alligator Weed
Mock Strawberry
Crimson Clover

| Lavender Scallops | Mullen | Verbena |
| Life Plant | English Plantain | Chamomile |
| Primrose | Bush Dogwood | Tasselflower |
| Butterfly Bush | Angelica | Cat's Ear |
| Madagascar Periwinkle | Japanese Honeysuckle | Wild Marigold |
| Oleander | Glorybower | |

Florida is also home to many endangered flowers protected by either federal or state law. While many have become very rare, other protected flowers, rare elsewhere, are known to grow in abundance in Florida. Either way, protected flowers may not be disturbed.

### ENDANGERED FLOWERS

| Celestial Lily | Delicate Ionopsis | Trumpets |
| Spider Orchid | Rose Pogonia | White Top Pitcher Plant |
| Pale Grass Pink | White Fringed Orchid | Hooded Pitcher Plant |
| Grass Pink | Crested Fringed Orchid | Sweet Pitcher Plant |
| Thickroot Orchid | Snowy Orchid | Pine-sap |
| Rosebud Orchid | Scarlet Ladies Tresses | Chapman's |
| Spring Coral Root | Fragrant Ladies Tresses | Rhododendron |
| Shell Orchid | Lesser Ladies' Tresses | Halberd Leaf Violet |
| Dingy Epidendrum | Grass-leaf Ladies' | Yellow Rhexia |
| Green-fly Orchid | Tresses | Tetrazygia |
| Rigid Epidendrum | Vanilla Orchid | Red Mangrove |
| Long-horned Orchid | Quail-Leaf | Black Mangrove |
| Water-spider Orchid | Texas Anemone | Sea Lavender |

### GARDENING

Florida is also home to numerous flowering trees; brilliantly flowering vines, ferns, and bromeliads; plants which fruit rather than flower; and a wide variety of natural grasses and herbs.

The state's perennial plants are likely to show up almost any time, almost anywhere. But for gardeners who prefer order in their lives and in their gardens, it takes long experience or reeducation to make a garden grow in the way the gardener expects and desires. What worked back home is unlikely to work in Florida.

The first observation a gardener will make is that Florida's soil is basically sand, requiring careful preparation for success. The gardener must also be aware of where in Florida the garden is located. Much of what thrives in the Everglades will not survive in the Panhandle and vice versa. Central Florida treads the thin line between the two extremes, enjoying both the benefits and the dangers of being caught in the middle. Florida also has some interesting pests that also vary from one region to another.

Still, most Florida gardeners will find themselves and their plots overrun with color.

Again depending on location, many flowering favorites can be planted almost any time. This monthly schedule, starting at the beginning of the year, indicates Florida's earliest prudent planting dates. The further north one plants, the later seeds, bulbs, cuttings, and plants should go into the ground. Gardeners should also be aware of a plant's salt tolerance. Nowhere in Florida is very far from the coast.

## MONTHLY PLANTING SCHEDULE

### January-February

**Flowers**
Aster
Baby's Breath
Bachelor Button
Balsam
Calendula
Candyturf
Carnation
Cosmos
Cockscomb
Daisy
Forget-Me-Not
Gaillardia
Globe Amaranth
Hollyhock
Lace Flower
Larkspur
Lobelias
Lupins
Marigolds
Morning Glory
Nasturtium
Pansy
Periwinkle
Petunia
Phlox
Pinks
Poppies
Portulacas
Salvia
Scabiosa
Snapdraggon
Statice
Stock
Strawflower
Sweet Pea
Sweet William
Verbenas

**Bulbs**
Amaryllis
Caladium
Callas
Cannas
Dahlias
Gladiolus
Iris
Lillies
Narcissus
Tuberose
Zephyranthes

### March-April

**Flowers**
Zinnias

**Bulbs**
Archimines
Begonias
Caladiums
Gloxinias

### May

**Flowers**
Four-o'clock

### June

**Flowers**
Dianthus

### July

Your "spring" planting is now complete, but it's still not too late to plant Cosmos, Cockscomb, Gailladias, Salvia, Strawflowers, Verbenas, and Zinnias.

### August

**Flowers**
Tithonias

### September-October

**Flowers and Bulbs**

Much of what was planted in January-February can be planted again, with the exception of Larkspur and Morning Glory. Plant Pansy, Periwinkle, Petunia, Phlox, Poppies, and Portulacas late in this period rather than early. Bulbs that can again go back into the ground in October include Amaryllis, Callas, Gladiolus, Lillies, Narcissus, and Zephyranthes. October is also the time to put Eucharis and Gloriosas into the ground.

### November-December

**Flowers and Bulbs**

Keep on planting. Again, what was good for January and February is good for November-December, with the exceptions of Larkspur, Morning Glory, and Pinks. You can continue to plant Dianthus but not Zinnias. You may continue your bulb planting with Amaryllis, Callas, Gladiolus, Lilies, and Zephyranthes. This also is the time to add Dahlia Tubers and Easter Lilies.

The hurricane season continues through November, but real summer is pretty much over. Near the end of the year, earlier is better than later in much of Florida.

Many casual gardeners prefer to plant by cuttings using the old standbys: Hibiscus, Azalea, Crepe Jasmin, and Poinsettias. In much of Florida it really is just a matter of snipping off the end of an existing plant, sticking it in the ground, going away, and coming back to find a magnificently flowering plant.

### FREEZE AND FROST

Frost and hard freeze (28 degrees

for more than four hours) is a regular occurrence in north Florida, which has a winter. Both are rare in south Florida and unheard of in extreme south Florida. But they are likely occurrences at various points of winter in central Florida. Frost and even a light freeze can be handled often by simply covering plants. But a hard freeze leaves devastation, or apparent devastation. The first instinct of gardeners, especially those new to Florida, is to cut back and even uproot the damage. Don't. The first order of business is to pick up only loose debris and then live with an unsightly garden, because much of what appears dead is not. Many plants will come back either from apparently dead stalks or from the roots, but not if they are cut back and subjected to another freeze. March 1, when the danger of freeze and frost is most likely over, has become the unofficial "cut back" day in much of Florida.

## WATER

Many areas of Florida are under water restriction of one type or another. Violations carry penalties, usually fines. Because of the summer heat and the inherent tendency of many plants to wither in that heat and under the direct rays of the sun, many gardeners, especially those new to Florida, tend to overwater. Those same plants, however, come back almost daily when the heat is broken and the sun is blocked, most often by regular, even daily, rain. Overwatering in Florida not only tempts the law, but it can kill the garden.

# STATE PARKS

Florida's state park system, consisting of more than 100 recreational areas, is among the nation's finest. The parks offer fishing, boating, camping, backpacking, swimming, skin diving, scuba diving, horseback riding, cycling, nature and canoe trails, and scores of historic sites.

Many of the parks front on the Atlantic Ocean or the Gulf of Mexico, providing a variety of landscapes. In the Panhandle are mounds of white sand dunes, while the state's subtropical southern tip is famous for its coral reefs and mangroves.

Coursing through the parks are more than two dozen rivers, each explorable by boat, canoe, or tubing. Along the shore grow record-sized trees and rare plants, some lining ravines and sinkholes. More than 300 springs, many of them acquired by the state for public use and preservation, are found at park sites in north and north central Florida.

All state parks open at 8 A.M. and close at sunset year round; museum hours are 9 A.M. to noon, and 1 to 5 P.M., with some closed two days a week.

Freshwater and saltwater fishing licenses are required, and can be purchased at a county tax collector's office or from a local bait and tackle shop.

Park visitors bringing their own horses into a park that offers riding trails must bring proof of their horse's negative Coggins test.

Following is a brief profile of each park. The accompanying map and code are included for quick reference to parks in different regions of the state.

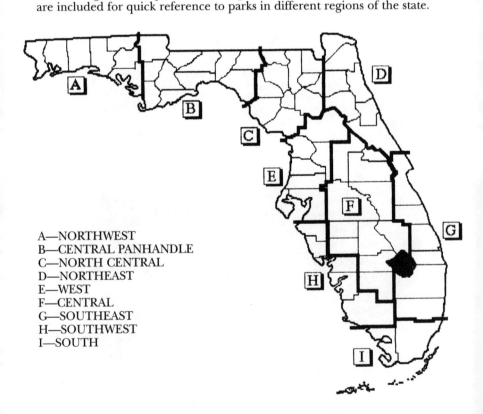

A—NORTHWEST
B—CENTRAL PANHANDLE
C—NORTH CENTRAL
D—NORTHEAST
E—WEST
F—CENTRAL
G—SOUTHEAST
H—SOUTHWEST
I—SOUTH

## A—NORTHWEST

**BIG LAGOON STATE RECRE-ATION AREA,** in Escambia County, is noted for its sandy beaches and salt marshes, important habitats for numerous birds and animals. An observation tower at the east beach offers a panoramic view of Big Lagoon and Gulf Islands National Seashore across the Intracoastal Waterway. Available are swimming, fishing, boating, camping, and picnicking. The park is on County Road 292A, 10 miles southwest of Pensacola.

**BLACKWATER RIVER STATE PARK,** in Santa Rosa County, features one of the world's purest sandbottom rivers. The park's pristine conditions are especially attractive to nature lovers. The river and its banks offer camping, picnicking, fishing, boating, and canoeing.

**CONSTITUTION CONVENTION STATE MUSEUM,** in Gulf County, commemorates the work of 86 territorial delegates who drafted Florida's first constitution. The site, St. Joe, was a boomtown created in 1835 to compete as a trading port with the town of Apalachicola. It vanished, however, in the mid-1800s when besieged by yellow fever and storms. The museum is at 200 Allen Memorial Way, Port St. Joe.

**EDEN STATE GARDENS,** in Walton County, was the property of an early Florida lumbering family. Visitors may tour both the Southern mansion and surrounding grounds. A picnic area is provided. The gardens are in Point Washington off U.S. 98 on County Road 395.

**FALLING WATERS STATE RECRE-ATION AREA,** in Washington County, gets its name from its most dramatic feature, a 67-foot waterfall. On the site is a 100-foot-deep sink into which flows a small stream. The area covers 155 acres, and offers camping, picnicking, and nature trails. The park is three miles south of Chipley off State Road 77A.

**GRAYTON BEACH STATE RECRE-ATION AREA,** in Walton County, is one of northwest Florida's most popular parks because its 336 acres offers all types of recreational activity, including surf fishing. The park is near Grayton Beach on State Road 30A south of U.S. 98.

**HENDERSON BEACH STATE RECREATION AREA,** in Okaloosa County, is among the state's new parks and features 1.3 miles of white sand beach along the Gulf of Mexico. Available are picnic facilities, a pavilion, and a boardwalk. The park is just east of downtown Destin on U.S. 98.

**PERDIDO KEY STATE RECRE-ATION AREA,** in Escambia County, is a 247-acre barrier island near Pensacola on the Gulf of Mexico. It not only protects the mainland from storms, but provides a habitat for shorebirds and other coastal animals. Popular are its wide, white sand beaches and rolling sea-oat-covered dunes. The park is 15 miles southwest of Pensacola off State Road 292.

**PONCE DE LEON SPRINGS STATE RECREATION AREA,** in Holmes County, is the site of several natural springs. The sources of the main spring are two flows from a limestone cavity. The two flows produce 14 million gallons of crystal-clear water daily, all of which empties into the Choctawhatchee River and from there into the nearby Gulf of Mexico. The park is a half-mile south of U.S. 90 on County Road 181A.

**ROCKY BAYOU STATE RECRE-ATION AREA,** in Okaloosa County, is known as a peaceful camping, hiking, and fishing area, its 357 acres noted for extensive sandpine forests and plant and animal life. The park is five miles east of Niceville on State Road 20.

**ST. ANDREWS STATE RECRE-ATION AREA,** in Bay County, consists of 1,260 acres and offers waterfront camping. Fishing is popular off two piers, jetties, and offshore. Picnic sites are provided on the Gulf beach and on Grand Lagoon. The park is three miles east of Panama City off State Road 392.

## B—CENTRAL PANHANDLE

**DEAD LAKES STATE RECREATION AREA,** in Gulf County, is a floodplain formed when sand bars created by Apalachicola River currents cut off the flow into the region of the nearby Chipola River, resulting in high water that killed thousands of trees. Animal life abounds in the area, which also provides excellent fishing, boating, and camping. The park is one mile north of Wewahitchka off State Road 71.

**ECONFINA RIVER STATE PARK** is located on the Gulf of Mexico, consists of 3,377 acres of greatly varied landscapes, from pine flatlands, to oak/palm forests, to broad expanses of salt marsh dotted with pine islands, and offers spectacular vistas and scenic beauty. Primary recreational activities include picnicking, canoeing, boating, and fishing. Unimproved hiking and equestrian trails are also available. It is located in Taylor County at the end of SR 14, south of U.S. 98.

**FLORIDA CAVERNS STATE PARK,** in Jackson County, is 1,280 acres of hammock, floodplain, and limestone outcroppings that feature a series of connecting caves. Guided tours of the caves are given daily. Other activities include picnicking, camping, swimming, fishing, boating, and horse trails. The park is three miles north of Marianna on State Road 167.

**FOREST CAPITAL STATE MUSEUM,** in Taylor County, celebrates the importance of forestry to the region. The museum is filled with exhibits of different kinds of woods, and depicts the techniques used to harvest forests. The museum is south of Perry on U.S. 19.

**FORT GADSDEN STATE HISTORIC SITE,** in Liberty County, was a War of 1812 battle site. The fort is long gone, destroyed in an assault upon it by gunboats, but a miniature replica of it is displayed. The park is six miles southwest of Sumatra off State Road 65.

**JOHN GORRIE STATE MUSEUM,** in Franklin County, cites the work of John Gorrie, a leading Apalachicola citizen in the early 1800s who invented an ice machine to cool rooms. Some credit him with discovering air conditioning. A replica of his machine is in the museum. The park is on Sixth Street in Apalachicola off U.S. 98.

**LAKE JACKSON MOUNDS STATE ARCHAEOLOGICAL SITE,** in Leon County, is a complex of six Indian earth temple mounds. Guided tours and interpretive programs are available. The park is off U.S. 27 two miles north of I-10 in Tallahassee.

**MACLAY STATE GARDENS,** in Leon County, once owned by Alfred and Louise Maclay, was made into ornamental gardens open to the public by Mrs. Maclay after her husband's death. In 1953 she donated the gardens to the state. Open all year, the gardens' blooming season is between January and May. Picnicking, boating, and swimming are also available. The park is five miles north of the state capital in Tallahassee, a half-mile north of I-10 on U.S. 319.

**NATURAL BRIDGE BATTLEFIELD STATE HISTORIC SITE,** in Wakulla County, is the site of a confrontation between Union and Confederate forces during the Civil War. Union forces arriving in Apalachee Bay planned to move north and take Tallahassee. The two sides fought at the natural bridge spanning the St. Marks River. After several hours fighting, Union forces retreated. The park is six miles east of Woodville off State Road 363.

**OCHLOCKONEE RIVER STATE PARK,** in Wakulla County, is a 392-acre setting of grassy ponds and oak thickets, ideal for wildlife. Picnicking, boating, and fishing are available along the river's banks. The park is four miles south of Sopchoppy on U.S. 319.

**RIVER BLUFF PICNIC SITE,** in Leon County, was formed in 1927 when the Jackson Bluff Dam was built on the Ochlockonee River. The area is thickly forested, harbors plentiful wildlife, and has excellent fishing grounds. Nature walks, boating, and, of course, picnicking are also available. The park is 20 miles west of Tallahassee on Vause Road off State Road 20.

**ST. GEORGE ISLAND STATE PARK,** in Franklin County, is a coastal barrier island adjacent to the Gulf of Mexico and Apalachicola Bay. Nine miles of beaches make up the park, which is noted for bird watching, swimming, camping, picnicking, hiking, and shelling. Boardwalks and observation platforms aid visitors in enjoying the area. The park is on St. George Island 10 miles southeast of Eastpoint off U.S. 98.

**ST. JOSEPH PENINSULA STATE PARK,** in Gulf County, offers miles of natural beach in the 2,516-acre park bordered by St. Joseph Bay and the Gulf of Mexico. The park provides excellent bird watching, camping, fishing, hiking, boating, and swimming. The park is near Port St. Joe off County Road 30-E near U.S. 98.

**SAN MARCOS DE APALACHE STATE HISTORIC SITE,** in Wakulla County, is the site of the first fort built at the junction of the Wakulla and St. Marks rivers. On the site is a museum featuring exhibits and history of the original fort. The park is in St. Marks off State Road 363.

**TALLAHASSEE-ST. MARKS HISTORIC RAILROAD STATE TRAIL,** in Wakulla County, is the first of many Rails-to-Trails projects being developed in Florida. Once the longest-operated railroad in Florida, used to transport cotton and other products to the Gulf coast, the old railbed now is an improved trail for cyclists, hikers, joggers, and horseback riders. The park is on State Road 363 just south of Tallahassee.

**THREE RIVERS STATE RECREATION AREA,** in Jackson County, is at the meeting of the Apalachicola, Flint, and Chattahoochee rivers. In its midst is Lake Seminole, noted for bass, panfish, and catfish angling. The area also is a favorite for picnicking, camping, hiking, and boating. The park is two miles north of Sneads on State Road 271.

**TORREYA STATE PARK,** in Liberty County, is named for a rare species of tree that grows only along the Apalachicola River bluffs. Special about the park is its steep, 150-foot bluffs along the Apalachicola. Available are amenities for camping, hiking, and picnicking. The park is 13 miles north of Bristol on State Road 12.

**WAKULLA SPRINGS STATE PARK,** in Wakulla County, is the site of one of the world's largest and deepest springs. The Wakulla Springs Lodge and Conference Center offers excellent, comfortable accommodations overlooking the spring, and glassbottom boats that cruise the park. Picnicking, swimming, scuba diving, and snorkeling are favorite visitor activities. The park is 14 miles south of Tallahassee on State Road 267.

### C—NORTH CENTRAL

**CEDAR KEY STATE MUSEUM,** in Levy County, celebrates the days Cedar Key thrived as the terminus of the state's first cross-state railroad. The track was used to ship cotton, lumber, and turpentine to Fernandina on the east coast. These days Cedar Key is attractive to tourists as a rustic island best known for fishing. The museum is in Cedar Key on Museum Drive off State Road 24.

**DEVIL'S MILLHOPPER STATE GEOLOGICAL SITE,** in Alachua County, is the state's only geological park. It features a giant sinkhole, into which visitors may descend via a wooden staircase. The park is two miles northwest of Gainesville off State Road 232.

**GAINESVILLE-HAWTHORNE STATE TRAIL** stretches 17 miles from Gainesville's Boulware Springs Park, through the Paines Prairie State Preserve and the Lockloosa Wildlife Management Area to Hawthorne. The recreational trail is designed for walking, cycling, and horseback riding. Parking is provided at the two trailheads, at Gainesville's Boulware Springs Park on S.E. 15th Street in Gainesville, and near U.S. 301 at Hawthorne.

**ICHETUCKNEE SPRINGS STATE PARK,** in Columbia County, is rated by some as the world's finest site for tubing. A tributary of the Santa Fe River, the Ichetucknee is an outstanding riverfront park that offers canoeing, swimming, scuba diving, hiking, picnicking, nature study, and, of course, tubing. The park has two entrances. The north entrance is four miles northwest of Fort White off State Roads 47 and 238. The south entrance is east of Fort White off U.S. 27.

**MANATEE SPRINGS STATE PARK,** in Levy County, is the site of a first magnitude spring that flows into the nearby Suwannee River. More than 2,000 park acres provide hiking, camping, swimming, canoeing, fishing, and scuba diving. The park is six miles west of Chiefland at the end of State Road 320 off U.S. 98.

**MARJORIE KINNAN RAWLINGS STATE HISTORIC SITE,** in Alachua County, is in the famous community of Cross Creek, the home of novelist Marjorie Kinnan Rawlings. Her home and its grounds are preserved as a historic site. The park is in Cross Creek off State Road 325.

**O'LENO STATE PARK,** in Alachua County, is bisected by the Santa Fe River, which disappears underground in the park only to resurface miles to the south where it flows into the Suwannee River. In Depression days, the Civilian Conservation Corps built the park, including its pavilions and still-in-use suspension bridge. It is a unique spot for swimming, canoeing, fishing, hiking, and horseback riding. Numerous cabins, plus a dining hall and kitchen, are available to groups. The park is six miles north of High Springs on U.S. 441.

**OLUSTEE BATTLEFIELD STATE HISTORIC SITE,** in Baker County, is the site of a Civil War battle between Union and Confederate troops. The site is marked by a trail and signs. Every February the battle, which claimed nearly 3,000 casualties, is reenacted on the grounds. The park is two miles east of Olustee on U.S. 90.

**PAYNES PRAIRIE STATE PRE-SERVE,** in Alachua County, is 18,000 acres of prairie, marsh pine flatwoods, hammocks, swamps, and ponds, all teeming with wildlife. Activities for visitors include camping, fishing, swimming, picnicking, hiking, and bridle trails. The park is south of Gainesville on U.S. 441.

**PEACOCK SPRINGS STATE RECREATIONAL AREA,** in Columbia County, includes two major springs and numerous sinks and depressions. It has one of the continent's longest underwater cave systems. Swimming, picnicking, and diving are popular. The park is 16 miles southwest of Live Oak on State Road 51.

**SAN FELASCO HAMMOCK STATE PRESERVE,** in Alachua County, is 6,000 acres of hammock, limestone outcrops, sinkholes, and springs. Park rangers offer group hikes. Riders may take horses in the park upon request. The park is four miles northwest of Gainesville on State Road 232.

**STEPHEN FOSTER STATE FOLK CULTURE CENTER,** in Hamilton County, pays homage to composer Stephen Foster, who penned the official state song. It is bordered by the Suwannee River, and is the site each year of folk festivals and programs. The park is in White Springs off U.S. 41 N.

**SUWANNEE RIVER STATE PARK,** in Suwannee County, is 1,800 acres at the junction of the Withlacoochee and Suwannee rivers. Wildlife is abundant, and visitors can enjoy camping, fishing, canoeing, hiking, and swimming. The park is 13 miles west of Live Oak off U.S. 90.

**WACCASASSA BAY STATE PRESERVE/CEDAR KEY SCRUB STATE PRESERVE,** in Levy County, is 35,000 acres of salt marsh, wooded islands, and tidal creeks. Many endangered species still live in the preserves, making the area of special interest to environmentalists. The preserves are nine miles east of Cedar Key on State Road 24.

### D—NORTHEAST

**AMELIA ISLAND STATE RECREATION AREA,** in Nassau County, is 200 acres of unspoiled beach along the Atlantic Ocean. It is an ideal area for picnicking, hiking, and coastal fishing. The park is seven miles north of Little Talbot Island State Park, off A1A.

**ANASTASIA STATE RECREATION AREA,** in St. Johns County, is an excellent bird watching park, with numerous salt and freshwater species along the coastal shores and in the lagoons and tidal marshes. Ocean swimming and surfing are popular sports. The park is at St. Augustine Beach off A1A at State Road 3.

**BIG TALBOT ISLAND STATE PARK,** in Duval County, is a barrier island suited to a variety of recreation, including swimming, picnicking, surfing, hiking, and fishing. The park is 20 miles east of downtown Jacksonville on A1A.

**BLUE SPRING STATE PARK,** in Volusia County, is adjacent to the St. Johns River and to Blue Spring Run, both offering boating and fishing. The park also is a winter home for the endangered manatee, which can be seen from an observation platform. The park is two miles west of 17-92 on French Avenue in Orange City.

**BULOW CREEK STATE PARK,** in Flagler County, was once the site of two plantations. Today it is a pleasant oasis with a nature trail showing off a variety of plant and animal life. The park is off old Dixie Highway near the Volusia/Flagler County line.

**BULOW PLANTATION RUINS STATE HISTORIC SITE,** in Flagler County, once was the site of a plantation growing sugarcane and cotton. It was destroyed in the Second Seminole War. Picnicking, fishing, and canoeing are available near the ruins. The park is three miles west of Flagler Beach on State Road 100 and south off County Road 2001.

**DE LEON SPRINGS STATE RECREATION AREA,** in Volusia County, is named for the park's second magnitude springs, around which visitors may swim, picnic, and canoe. The park is in De Leon at the junction of Ponce De Leon and Burt Parks roads.

**FAVER-DYKES STATE PARK,** in St. Johns County, is a tranquil, 752-acre park that runs along an aquatic preserve, Pellicer Creek. The creek area teems with wildlife. Fishing, picnicking, and hiking are favorite activities. The park is 15 miles south of St. Augustine at the junction of I-95 and U.S. 1.

**FORT CLINCH STATE PARK,** in Nassau County, was the site of a fort built nearly two centuries ago to protect shipping in the adjacent St. Mary's River. The fort was occupied by both Union and Confederate forces during the Civil War. It is one of the state's oldest parks, its structures built by the Civilian Conservation Corps in the 1930s. The site's 1,100 acres offer camping, swimming, surf and pier fishing, and hiking. The park is near Fernandina Beach off A1A.

**FORT GEORGE STATE CULTURAL SITE,** on Fort George Island, home to another of the units in the Talbot Islands GEOpark complex, has been occupied continuously by man for over 5,000 years, and traces remain of each occupation period. Several plant species occur here, far beyond their normal range, and Mount Cornelia, at 65 feet, is the highest point along the Atlantic coast south of Sandy Hook, New Jersey. Bicycling or hiking are activities along the island's tree-lined and canopied roads and trails. The site lies approximately 16 miles east of downtown Jacksonville on State Road A1A, or 3 miles south of Little Talbot Island State Park.

**GAMBLE ROGERS MEMORIAL STATE RECREATION AREA,** at Flagler Beach, is bordered by the Atlantic Ocean to the east and the Intracoastal Waterway on the west. This 144-acre, shadeless park offers coastal camping, picnicking, boating, fishing, nature trailing, and scenic relaxation. Its 34 modern campsites are on the Atlantic and are among the most popular in the state. Reservations may, and should be, made eleven months in advance. The beach is a nesting home to several species of endangered turtles. Boating facilities are on the Intracoastal. The park is located 3 miles south of Flagler Beach and 18 miles north of Daytona Beach on Hwy. A1A, which divides the park.

**GOLD HEAD BRANCH STATE PARK,** in Clay County, is a 1,562-acre site built on sand hills. Ravines cut through the rolling hills and are cooled by a spring-fed stream that flows into Lake Johnson. Four trails course through the park, whose

buildings were erected by the Civilian Conservation Corps. Available is swimming, boating, fishing, camping, and hiking. The park is six miles northeast of Keystone Heights on State Road 21.

**GUANA RIVER STATE PARK,** in St. Johns County, may have been where Ponce de Leon first landed, historians believe. It is 2,400 acres offering seven different plant communities, from beach frontage to interior hammocks. Swimming and surfing are available on the Atlantic Ocean, and fishing and boating on the Guana River. The park is north of St. Augustine off A1A.

**HONTOON ISLAND STATE PARK,** in Volusia County, once was home to the Timucuan Indians, a boatyard, a cattle ranch, and a pioneer family. Its 1,650 acres are accessible only by private boat or by ferry. Camping, nature study, boating, picnicking, cabin rental, and fishing are available. The park is six miles west of DeLand off State Road 44.

**KINGSLEY PLANTATION STATE HISTORIC SITE,** in Duval County, is one of the few remaining examples of the South's plantation system in Florida and is the oldest plantation house in the state. It was built in 1817 on land granted to John McQueen by the King of Spain. The park is near Fort George off A1A.

**LITTLE TALBOT ISLAND STATE PARK,** in Duval County, is a barrier island on the Atlantic coast that offers five miles of wide beaches, sand dunes, and salt marshes. The site is busy with wild animals, particularly along the adjacent Fort George River. Recreation includes fishing, camping, hiking, picnicking, surfing, and swimming. The park is 17 miles northeast of Jacksonville off A1A.

**NEW SMYRNA SUGAR MILL RUINS STATE HISTORIC SITE,** in Volusia County, was the site of a large plantation sugar mill that was attacked and destroyed by Indians during the Second Seminole War. The park is west of State Road 44 and south of Mission Drive in New Smyrna Beach.

**RAVINE STATE GARDENS,** in Putnam County, were created in 1933 by a federal works project at the site of a steep ravine. The ravine occurred from water flowing under sandy ridges along the west bank of the St. Johns River. Peak flowering season is spring. The park is off Twigg Street in Palatka.

**TOMOKA STATE PARK,** in Volusia County, is graced with huge oaks where the Tooka and Halifax rivers merge. Park activities include camping, hiking, fishing, boating, and picnicking. The park is three miles north of Ormond Beach on North Beach Street.

**WASHINGTON OAKS STATE GARDENS,** in Flagler County, is a 380-acre park bounded by the Matanzas River and the Atlantic Ocean. Its beach is unique to Florida in that it is boulder-strewn, the result of ocean waves washing away at the sand. Visitors can enjoy fishing, picnicking, and strolling through ornamental gardens. The park is three miles south of Marineland off A1A.

### E—WEST

**ALAFIA RIVER STATE RECREATION AREA,** is at Picnic in southeast Hillsborough County. The state's newest park has opened 200 of its 7,000 acres of reclaimed phosphate land to the public. The park for picnickers and hikers is on State Road 39 south of Lithia.

**ANCLOTE KEY STATE PRESERVE,** in Pinellas County, features four miles of beach, an 1887 lighthouse, and active wildlife habitats. This pristine preserve provides swimming and nature study, but camping is primitive. This park is three miles off Tarpon Springs and is accessible only by private boat.

**CALADESI ISLAND STATE PARK,** in Pinellas County, is one of the Gulf coast's few undeveloped barrier islands. Arrivals are by private boat or a ferry that operates from nearby Honeymoon Island. Swimming, shell collecting, and strolling the nature trails are favorite activities. Boaters must register before sundown to stay overnight. This park is southwest of the city of Dunedin.

**CRYSTAL RIVER STATE ARCHAEOLOGICAL SITE,** in Citrus County, features a pre-Columbian Indian mound complex dating back to 200 B.C. The site is heavily wooded. Methods used to excavate the mounds, as well as artifacts from the site, are on display. The park is at 3400 N. Museum Point in Crystal River.

**DADE BATTLEFIELD STATE HISTORIC SITE,** in Sumter County, provides a history lesson to visitors who learn how more than 100 soldiers were killed in a battle that launched Florida's Second Seminole War. An interpretive trail and visitor's center are set among pine flatwoods. Picnickers are welcome. The park is off State Road 476 west of Highway 301.

**EGMONT KEY STATE PARK** guards the mouth of Tampa Bay. Its past is mainly military and strategic. Visitors can swim from its beaches or walk its historic sites. The island is a haven for the gopher tortoise and other species. Although nowhere near it, the key is in Hillsborough County, and located in the Gulf, directly west before the bay. It is accessible only by private boat and activities are heavily monitored.

**FORT COOPER STATE PARK,** in Citrus County, was a refuge during the Second Seminole War and is situated in a hardwood forest dotted with swamp and marsh. Ten miles of trails delight nature lovers and equestrians. Fishing, picnicking, swimming, and canoeing also are available. During April, a Seminole Indian War reenactment is portrayed by park personnel. The park is on State Road 39 two miles southeast of Inverness.

**HILLSBOROUGH RIVER STATE PARK,** in Hillsborough County, was developed by the Civilian Conservation Corps in the 1930s. Nearly 3,000 acres afford a range of natural beauty. Fort Foster in the park is a working fort with personnel living on the site as people did in the 1830s. The park is 12 miles north of Tampa and six miles south of Zephyrhills on U.S. 301.

**HOMOSASSA SPRINGS STATE WILDLIFE PARK,** in Citrus County, accents Florida's unique wildlife. A display exhibits black bears, alligators, wild birds, and small mammals. In an underwater viewing station, visitors can watch endangered manatees that live at the spring. The park is at Homosassa Springs off U.S. 19 about five miles south of Crystal River.

**HONEYMOON ISLAND STATE RECREATION AREA,** in Pinellas County, provides diverse ecosystems, from tidal marsh to pinelands. It offers fishing, swimming, picnicking, and boating. The site has been a favorite leisure spot since 1939 when the island, originally called Hog Island, was developed. The park is at the west end of State Road 586 north of Dunedin.

**LITTLE MANATEE RIVER STATE RECREATION AREA,** in Hillsborough County, highlights a river that takes canoers more than four miles through this park. Horseback-riding enthusiasts can enjoy miles of trails in this 1,638-acre facility. The park is four miles south of Sun City Center off U.S. 301 on Lightfoot Road.

**RAINBOW SPRINGS STATE PARK,** once the site of the old tourist attraction, is Florida's third largest spring. The springs start the Rainbow River. The park's azalea gardens, the river wetlands, and sand hill pine forest are home to many species of plants and animals. Man has been at the springs for 10,000 years. Activities include camping, swimming, picnicking, canoeing, and tubing. The azalea gardens bloom in February and March.

The park is located 3 miles north of Dunellon, off U.S. Hwy. 41. The camping entrance is located 2½ miles north of Marion County, on Road 484 off Dunellon's SW 180th Ave.

**SILVER RIVER STATE PARK,** in Marion County, is 2,300 acres featuring 14 different plant communities, plus riverbeds and springs. Silver Springs is at the headwater of the Silver River, which flows into the Oklawaha River. Amenities are limited. The park is a mile south of Silver Springs on County Road 35.

**WEEDON ISLAND STATE PRESERVE,** in Pinellas County, aims to protect some of the region's last stands of mangrove swampland. Once citrus groves, the island has a rich archaeological history. Hiking, picnicking, fishing, and nature study are the main activities. The park is off Gandy Boulevard west of Gandy Bridge.

**WITHLACOOCHEE STATE TRAIL** is located on Croom Rital Road, off State Road 50, a mile east of I-75, in Ridge Manor. It currently consists of a 46-mile paved stretch of railroad right-of-way that has been converted to a recreation area suitable for hiking, biking, and horseback riding enthusiasts. The trail runs 6 miles south to Trilby, and 40 miles north through the Withlacoochee State Forest and along the Withlacoochee River, then continues north through Floral City, Inverness, Citrus Springs, and ends at Gulf Junction, just south of Dunellon. Entry with parking is available at eight locations along the way.

**YBOR CITY STATE MUSEUM,** in Hillsborough County, focuses on Tampa's rich Latin history in a building that once housed a bakery. A unique and colorful culture, as well as world-renowned cigars, are entertainingly featured. The museum is at the corner of 9th Avenue and 19th Street in Tampa.

**YULEE SUGAR MILL RUINS STATE HISTORIC SITE,** in Citrus County, offers a glimpse of plantation Florida when slaves worked David Yulee's 5,100 acres to produce sugar. Yulee served in the U.S. Congress before the Civil War. The park is on State Road 490 west of U.S. 1 in Homosassa.

## F—CENTRAL

**HIGHLANDS HAMMOCK STATE PARK,** in Highlands County, is a 3,800-acre site that was acquired for the public in the 1930s when local residents feared the extensive hammock would be turned into farm land. Park facilities were built by the Civilian Conservation Corps. Walking the boardwalks through the park exposes visitors to wildlife and various plant communities. The available recreation consists of hiking and horse trails. The park is four miles west of Sebring on State Road 634.

**LAKE GRIFFIN STATE RECREATION AREA,** in Lake County, is best noted for its bass fishing. Camping, canoeing, and nature study also attract visitors. The park is on U.S. 441 in Fruitland Park.

**LAKE KISSIMMEE STATE PARK,** in Polk County, is on the shores of Lakes Kissimmee, Rosalie, and Tiger, all of which offer outstanding fishing, boating, and camping. Hiking along 13 miles of trails brings visitors in contact with deer, eagles, cranes, and turkeys. An 1876 "cow camp" is re-created on the grounds. The park is 15 miles east of Lake Wales off State Road 60.

**LAKE LOUISA STATE PARK,** in Lake County, is 1,790 acres on the shores of Lake Louisa. The lake, on the rim of the Green Swamp, is part of a chain of lakes that connect to the Palatkahah River. The park is noted for its hardwood forests, marshes, swamps, streams, and hammocks. Swimming, picnicking, fishing, and canoeing are popular. The park is two miles off State Road 561 on Lake Nellie Road.

**LOWER WEKIVA RIVER STATE RESERVE,** in Seminole County, is noted for its blackwater streams and wetlands, which provide habitat for

bear, otter, wood stork, cranes, and alligators. It is a 4,636-acre park bordering two miles of St. Johns Creek and four miles of the Wekiva River and Blackwater Creek. It is rich in plant life. Available are canoeing, camping, hiking, and horse trails. The park is nine miles west of Sanford on State Road 46.

**PAYNES CREEK STATE HISTORIC SITE,** in Hardee County, commemorates a fort and trading post established here to protect early white settlers from Seminole Indian attacks. The structures were abandoned after a malaria outbreak. Exhibits about the Seminoles and the fort and trading post are on the grounds. Picnicking and fishing are available. The park is a half mile east of Bowling Green on State Road 664A.

**ROCK SPRINGS RUN STATE PRESERVE,** in Lake County, features 12 miles of unspoiled frontage on the Wekiva River and Rock Springs Run. Hiking, primitive backpacking, camping, nature study, canoeing, and horseback riding are permitted. The park is in Sorrento on State Road 46 via State Road 433.

**TENOROC STATE RECREATION AREA,** in Polk County, is a fish habitat and quality recreation site transformed from a reclaimed phosphate mining operation. Bass fishing is excellent. A picnic pavilion is available with reservations. The park is northeast of Lakeland on State Road 33A.

**TOSOHATCHEE STATE RESERVE,** in Orange County, is a huge site of 28,000 acres and 19 miles on the St. Johns River. Its biological diversity accounts for varied wildlife among the marshes, swamps, flatwoods, and hammocks. Popular are backpacking, canoeing, fishing, camping, and limited hunting. The park is in Christmas on Taylor Creek Road.

**WEKIWA SPRINGS STATE PARK,** in Orange County, is 6,397 acres, holding 13 miles of hiking trails. The park's springs are the headwaters for the Wekiwa River, which flows 15 miles into the St. Johns River. Activities include swimming, canoeing, picnicking, and camping. Horse trails also are available. The park is near Apopka on Wekiwa Springs Road off State Road 434 or 436.

## G—SOUTHEAST

**FORT PIERCE INLET STATE RECREATION AREA,** in St. Lucie County, is a 340-acre spa along the Atlantic Ocean and Intracoastal Waterway that is excellent for swimming, picnicking, hiking, and surfing. Bird watchers are entertained by numerous species on adjacent Jack Island. The park is four miles east of Fort Pierce via the north Causeway to Atlantic Beach Boulevard.

**HUGH TAYLOR BIRCH STATE RECREATION AREA,** in Broward County, is a 180-acre oasis in the Fort Lauderdale metropolitan area. It is nestled between the Atlantic Ocean and the Intracoastal Waterway. Swimming, picnicking, fishing, canoeing, and hiking are available. For joggers the park provides a two-mile run. Facilities include cabins, meeting and dining rooms, and a kitchen. The park is on East Sunrise Boulevard off A1A in Fort Lauderdale.

**JOHN D. MACARTHUR BEACH STATE PARK,** in Palm Beach County, is a barrier island fronting on the Atlantic Ocean. Its mixture of hammock, mangroves, and rare plant species beckons visitors, as do its excellent swimming, fishing, snorkeling, and shell collecting. The park is three miles south of the intersection of U.S.1 and PGA Boulevard on A1A.

**JOHN U. LLOYD BEACH STATE RECREATION AREA,** in Broward County, is a 244-acre site dotted by sand dunes, coastal hammocks, and mangroves. Recreation is abundant, including ocean swimming, fishing from jetties, hiking, boating, and picnicking. The park is in Dania off A1A.

**JONATHAN DICKINSON STATE PARK,** in Martin County, is a mammoth site of woods, mangroves, swamps, plants, and wildlife. At 10,328 acres, it is one of the state's largest parks. It is home to the Loxahatchee River, designated a national wild and scenic river, on which tours are given aboard a 30-passenger boat. Recreation includes fishing, boating, hiking, cycling, and canoeing. Horse trails wind through the grounds. The park is 12 miles south of Stuart on U.S. 1.

**SEBASTIAN INLET STATE RECREATION AREA,** in Brevard County, offers jetties into the Atlantic Ocean, a beach area, and the Indian River, all famous for fishing for snook, bluefish, redfish, and Spanish mackerel. Campsites along the inlet provide water and electricity. Swimming, surfing, boating, and scuba diving are popular sports. For the less active, a visitor's center features information about a nearby wrecked Spanish treasure fleet. Bird watchers also are treated to countless shore and wading birds. The park is in Melbourne Beach on A1A.

**ST. LUCIE INLET STATE PARK,** in Martin County, is a barrier island accessible only by private boat. Visitors may stroll along a 3,300-foot boardwalk through coastal hammocks lush with palms, ferns, and wild fruit. Miles of Atlantic Ocean beachfront are perfect for swimming, fishing, and picnicking. The park is in Port Salerno and is reached by boat across the Intracoastal Waterway.

**THE BARNACLE STATE HISTORIC SITE,** in Broward County, is named after a home on the grounds called The Barnacle. Visitors may tour the home and picnic on the grounds. A footpath leads visitors to the early Coconut Grove of the 1880s, before Miami was developed. The park is at 3485 Main Highway in present-day Coconut Grove.

## H—SOUTHWEST

**CAYO COSTA STATE PARK,** in Lee County, is called by some the state's most beautiful subtropical beach park. Cayo Costa is an island, accessible only by private boat or ferry, that is one island in a barrier chain that protects the Florida mainland from storms blowing in from the Gulf of Mexico. The island shelters Pine Island South and Charlotte Harbor with miles of beaches, pine forests, hammocks, and mangrove swamps. Birds proliferate, and shell collecting is ideal during the winter months. Other recreation includes swimming, fishing, boating, picnicking, and primitive camping. The park is on Cayo Costa Island, directly south of Boca Grande.

**COLLIER-SEMINOLE STATE PARK,** in Collier County, is best known for the many threatened and endangered species that populate this park in the Everglades region. Vegetation is characteristic of the coastal forests of the Yucatan and the West Indies. A six-mile nature trail takes visitors into the park's hinterland, which is popular with primitive campers. Fishing and boating are available. The park is 17 miles south of Naples on U.S. 41.

**DELNOR-WIGGINS PASS STATE RECREATION AREA,** in Collier County, is a tropical setting on the Gulf of Mexico. It is a narrow barrier island offering swimming, fishing, boating, picnicking, and cycling. Separating the park from the mainland are mangrove swamps and tidal creeks. The park is six miles south of Bonita Springs on County Road 901 off U.S. 41.

**DON PEDRO ISLAND STATE RECREATION AREA,** in Charlotte County, is a barrier island park between Little Gasparilla Island and Knight Island. It is reached only by private boat. Recreation includes picnicking, shelling, swimming, fishing, and nature study. Park docks are provided on the bay side via a channel south of the Cape Haze powerline crossing.

**FAKAHATCHEE STRAND STATE PRESERVE,** in Collier County, is a major drainage slough of the Big Cypress Swamp. Forests of cypress, royal palms, and epiphytic plants may be greater than in any other region of Florida. Besides extremely rare plants, the park is home to abundant wildlife including rarely seen Florida black bears, Florida panthers, and wood storks. Facilities are minimal, with only a boardwalk and hiking trails providing access into the interior. The park is west of Copeland on Janes Memorial Scenic Drive.

**GAMBLE PLANTATION STATE HISTORIC SITE,** in Manatee County, features the only plantation home in south Florida. It once was headquarters for an extensive sugar plantation. After the Civil War, the Confederate secretary of state took refuge here before fleeing to England. Today, the mansion and its 16 acres are kept in the style of a 19th-century plantation. Picnicking on the grounds is permitted. The park is in Ellenton on U.S. 301.

**GASPARILLA ISLAND STATE RECREATION AREA,** in Lee/Charlotte counties, is a barrier island on the Gulf of Mexico that, legend has it, was a base for the infamous pirate Jose Gaspar. Picnicking, swimming, fishing, and shelling during winter months are popular activities. The park can be reached via the Boca Grande Causeway at Placida and County Road 775.

**KORESHAN STATE HISTORIC SITE,** in Lee County, once was the "New Jerusalem" of the followers of Koreshanity, a religion based on celibacy, separation of sexes, and communal ownership of all property. The community took shape in 1894, but by 1961 was down to four members, who deeded the site to the state. Guided walks and campfire programs are scheduled, and camping, fishing, and boating are available. The park is at Estero on U.S. 41.

**LAKE MANATEE STATE RECREATION AREA,** in Manatee County, is a 556-acre park on three miles of Lake Manatee's south shore. Mostly woods and marshes, the acreage does offer swimming, camping, fishing, boating, and picnicking. The park is 15 miles east of Bradenton on State Road 64.

**LOVERS KEY STATE RECREATION AREA,** in Lee County, remains relatively undeveloped with few facilities. It is part of Black Island and Inner Key, both on the Gulf of Mexico, and is best known for wildlife and natural recreation opportunities. The park is between Fort Myers Beach and Bonita Beach on County Road 865.

**MYAKKA RIVER STATE PARK,** in Sarasota County, covers 45 square miles and is the state's largest park. It is named for the Myakka River, which flows for 12 miles through its grounds. It has a large wildlife population. The natural landscape includes hammocks, marshes, sloughs, abundant plants, and the Upper Myakka Lake. Available are camping, backpacking, fishing, horse trails, and canoeing. The park is 12 miles east of Sarasota on State Road 72.

**OSCAR SCHERER STATE RECREATION AREA,** in Sarasota County, is home to several declining species such as the scrub jay, indigo snake, and gopher tortoise. Swimming is popular in a freshwater lake, and fishing and canoeing are available in the park's tidal creek. The park is two miles south of Osprey on U.S. 41.

## I—SOUTH

**BAHIA HONDA STATE RECREATION AREA,** in Monroe County, is Florida's southernmost park, boasting plants and animal species closely aligned with the Caribbean. It has excellent swimming on both its shores—the Atlantic Ocean and Florida Straits. Also offered are camping, boating, and fishing. The park is 12 miles south of Marathon.

**BILL BAGGS CAPE FLORIDA STATE RECREATION AREA,** in Miami-Dade County, is a 406-acre park that fills to capacity early each day. It is on the southern tip of a barrier island, Key Biscayne. Picnicking and hiking are favorite activities. The park is south of downtown Miami on Key Biscayne off the Rickenbacker Causeway.

**CHEKIKA STATE RECREATION AREA,** in Miami-Dade County, is 640 acres in the east Everglades, and was named after a Seminole Indian who was hunted down in the area by the U.S. Army during the Second Seminole War. Largely hammocks and wetlands, the acreage is home to hundreds of bird and animal species, some of them endangered. Hiking, camping, picnicking, fishing, and swimming are available. The park is 11 miles north of Homestead on State Road 27.

**FORT ZACHARY TAYLOR STATE HISTORIC SITE,** in Monroe County, is named for the president in office when this fort was being built. It took 21 years to complete the three-story fortification, which during the Civil War remained in Union hands. Swimming and fishing are available around the fort. The park is at Key West at Southard Street on Truman Annex.

**INDIAN KEY STATE HISTORIC SITE,** in Monroe County, is an island reached only by private boat. It was inhabited by Indians for centuries, but became the site of a ship salvaging business in the early 1800s. A prosperous island, its development was halted in 1840 when the settlement was burned by Indians during the Second Seminole War. Remains of the key's early history still can be seen. The park is on the ocean side of U.S. 1 at Mile Marker 78.5.

**JOHN PENNEKAMP CORAL REEF STATE PARK,** in Monroe County, covers 70 nautical square miles of coral reefs, seagrass beds, and mangroves. The underwater park is Florida's most popular, drawing a million visitors a year. It was established to preserve the only living coral reef in the U.S. Park submerged land covers 53,661 acres, and offers snorkeling, swimming, fishing, and boating. Uplands of 2,350 acres are home to rare plants. The park is north of Key Largo at Mile Marker 102.5.

**LIGNUMVITAE KEY STATE BOTANICAL SITE,** in Monroe County, is an example of life decades ago in the Florida Keys. The park is a 280-acre island featuring trees native to tropical forests. On the grounds and open to the public is the Matheson House, whose owner bought and developed the island in 1919. Access is by private or charter boat. The park is one mile west of U.S. 1 at Mile Marker 78.5.

**LONG KEY STATE PARK,** in Monroe County, is halfway down the chain of Florida Keys, and is billed as a sun-drenched tropical paradise. Tropical trees and marine and birdlife are abundant and observable along two nature trails. Fishing, camping, swimming, picnicking, canoeing, and hiking are offered. The park is at Mile Marker 67.5 on the Overseas Highway.

**NORTH SHORE STATE RECREATION AREA,** in Miami-Dade County, is nearly surrounded by urban Miami Beach. Years ago it was a city park, but it has been deeded to the state. A mere 40 acres, it offers plenty of recreation, including swimming, picnicking, biking, and hiking. The park is east of Collins Avenue between 79th and 87th streets.

**OLETA RIVER STATE RECREATION AREA,** in Miami-Dade County, is an oasis in heavily urbanized North Miami. Mangrove forests and aquatic areas offer biking, picnicking, fresh and saltwater fishing, canoeing, and swimming along a 1,200-foot beach on the Oleta River and Intracoastal Waterway. The park is at 3400 NE 163rd Street.

**SAN PEDRO UNDERWATER ARCHAEOLOGICAL PRESERVE** is under 18 feet of water. The *San Pedro,* a 287-ton, Dutch-built ship that sailed and sank as part of the New Spain fleet in 1733, was rediscovered in the 1960s in Hawk Channel. It is among the most picturesque of the 1733 wreck sites, due to her location in a white sand pocket surrounded by turtle grass. A large pile of ballast stones, 90-feet long and 30-feet wide, marks her final resting place. The site has been enhanced with seven replica cannons, an anchor, and an information plaque. It is located approximately 1.25 nautical miles south from Indian Key at LORAN coordinates 14082.1 and 43320.6. Anchoring is at mooring buoys to prevent anchor damage to the site.

## FEES AND REGULATIONS

**Entrance Fees** **Charge**

Vehicle and driver (up to 8 people) ...........................$3.25

Selected Parks ...........................................$4.00

Each additional passenger ..................................$1.00

Selected Parks, single occupant vehicle .........................$2.00

Pedestrian, bicyclist ........................................$1.00

Honor Parks, per vehicle .............................$2.00 to $4.00

Children, under age 6 .......................................free

Food Stamp card holders ...............................half-price

Bus Tours .................the lesser of $33.00 or $0.75 cents per person

*Special and annual Individual and Family passes available.*

**Picnic Pavilions**

Group rental is available, with fees ranging from $20 to $150 depending on park and size of pavilion.

**Miscellaneous Charge**

Museum fee—per person ...................................$1.00

Boat launching-per boat (selected parks) .................$2.00 to $4.00

**Cabins**

Eight Florida state parks offer vacation cabins. The cabins are situated in pristine settings and are convenient to other park facilities and use areas. Parks offering cabins are Gold Head Branch, Jonathan Dickinson, Oleta River, Myakka River, Bahia Honda, Blue Spring, Hontoon Island, Cayo Costa, and St Joseph. Charges range from $50.00 per day to $110.00 per day and reservations are taken.

**Camping**

Camping fees vary according to season, length of stay, site location, extra vehicles, electricity use, and extra persons. Reservations may be made in person or by phone, and are accepted between 8 A.M. and 5 P.M. no more than 60 days in advance, with the exception of Gamble Rogers at Flagler Beach. Of the 43 camping parks, 9 do not accept reservations, sites being made available on a first-come, first-served basis.

**Pets in the Parks**

Pets in Florida's state parks are restricted from certain park areas for sanitary reasons and to ensure a more relaxing retreat for visitors. Pets are not allowed in the camping areas, on beaches, in concession facilities, and may be restricted in other designated park areas such as wildlife sanctuaries. Where pets are allowed they must be kept on a 6-foot, hand-held leash. Service dogs are welcome in all areas of the parks.

**Management and Protection**

Florida State Parks are managed as natural systems. All plant and animal life is protected in state parks. Hunting, livestock grazing, and timber removal are not permitted. Natural resources may not be removed, defaced, mutilated, or molested. For safety, animals are not to be fed. Intoxicants and firearms are prohibited from state parks.

# WILDLIFE

No state offers a variety of wildlife as diverse as Florida. Its subtropical climate is suited to creatures found nowhere else in the contiguous U.S., from the placid and endearing manatees to the aggressive and feared alligators and crocodiles. Even the state's birds are enticingly different from winged creatures found elsewhere. Below are details on some of the more famous, and notorious, residents of the state's woods, rivers, lakes, and shores.

## MAJOR SPECIES OF MAMMALS

**ARMADILLOS** are a good example of an exotic species run amok in Florida. The large armadillo population resulted from animals migrating from Texas and being intentionally released. The nine-banded armadillo now lives everywhere in Florida except the Everglades and coastal islands. About house cat-sized, armadillos are uniquely hard-shelled. They grow to nearly three feet long and can weigh 14 pounds. They burrow and their tunnels can also house rats, opossums, snakes, and spiders. Mostly nocturnal, armadillos forage all night for insects and grubs. They always bear four young of the same sex that are born in March and April. Although their sharp-toed front feet cause extensive lawn damage, they help the state by their greedy consumption of many grubs and insects. Some people eat armadillos and report the taste to be like pork. However, armadillos are the only mammals besides humans that are vulnerable to leprosy, and are now used in leprosy vaccine research. For this reason, it is recommended that contact with them be avoided.

**BAT** species in Florida include the gray myotis, keen myotis, mastiff, big brown, eastern pipistrel, red, hoary, Seminole, eastern yellow, evening, eastern big-eared, and Mexican free-tailed. Some species such as the evening and yellow bats may live alone or in small groups in trees, without attracting much attention. Colonial bats such as the Mexican freetailed will gather by the thousands in caves or other hollow outcroppings.

Caves serve as maternity wards for such species as the gray myotis, which bears one to three young, usually from May to July. Bats eat insects by the thousands during each evening's outing. Moths, mosquitoes, and other insects are the bats' diet staple. Like any mammal, bats can carry rabies, although their secretive habits make them less likely than dogs to spread the disease to humans. Florida has no indigenous vampire bats.

**BLACK BEARS** are limited mostly to unpopulated wilderness areas of the state, primarily in the Osceola National Forest, the Apalachicola National Forest, on the Georgia border in the Okefenokee Swamp, and increasingly are found in the southern parts of the state, including the Everglades. Bears make dens beneath trees, in hollow logs, or in caves or rock outcroppings. Females generally bear one to three cubs every other year and the young remain with their mother for about 12 months. The bears' diet ranges from berries and plants to insects and small mammals. They will invade camping areas and garbage sites in search of food. An adult male black bear may roam a territory of 15 miles. Bears have moderately good hearing and an excellent sense of smell. The Florida black bear is a subspecies of other black bear species.

**BOBCATS** are found nearly everywhere in the unpopulated regions of Florida. Scrappy hunters with razor-sharp claws and needle-like teeth, bobcats prefer a diet of birds and small mammals, although occasionally opportunistic individuals may raid chicken coops. A litter of two to four kittens are usually born in spring and leave their mother within a year. This cat's fur is varying shades of brown and its distinctive bobtail makes it easy to identify. Most bobcats weigh between 15 and 35 pounds and travel alone, unless with kittens, on a range of 25 to 50 miles. Stealth and keen eyesight are the major aids to this primarily nocturnal animal.

**COYOTE** populations are growing in Florida, with all of the state's 67 counties now believed to provide habitat to these wild canines. Coyotes are durable newcomers. Males weigh about 30 pounds and females weigh 20 to 25. After mating in January and February, female coyotes bear 5 to 10 pups, and occasionally mate with domestic dogs to produce what are called "coy dogs." Food is rarely a problem for coyotes because they eat virtually anything and have a particular liking for watermelon. Florida farmers are concerned about losing livestock to coyotes and blame the wild canines for losses of chickens, goats, pigs, sheep, and calves. But Smithsonian Institution studies reported the coyote's diet is similar to that of foxes, with prey primarily being small rodents such as rabbits. It is legal in Florida to hunt coyotes and they may be trapped with steel leg-hold traps if a proper permit has been obtained from the Florida Fish and Wildlife Conservation Commission. Coyote pens afford a legal new sporting use of captive coyotes, which are chased by dogs until they are killed or escape.

**FLORIDA PANTHERS** are Florida's most highly endangered species, with a population estimated at just 50. Florida's panther is a unique relative of the mountain lion or puma found in other states. The state's largest wild cat, it is identified by a kinked tail, some white spotting, and a peculiar swirl of fur in the middle of its back.

The panther is a good-sized cat, about six feet long, standing 24 to 28 inches tall at the shoulder, and weigh-

ing 60 to 80 pounds (females) or 100 to 130 pounds (males). Its range is from 50 to 100 miles, and some panthers are known to have traveled 20 miles in a 24-hour period.

Habitat destruction is the prime reason for the panther's decline. It once ranged throughout the state, but now lives almost entirely in either the Big Cypress Swamp or the Everglades regions of south Florida. Human encroachment has decreased availability of food such as white-tailed deer, and many of the big cats are killed trying to cross highways.

Another snag in panther survival is the animal's low birth rate—two to four kittens every other year. Scientists recently learned that the gene pool of some panther groups is growing severely limited as the small number of animals inbreed. Long-term effects of this are not precisely known, but researchers say male panthers are revealing a high incidence of reproductive abnormality, which could affect birth rates.

In addition, a 1990 U.S. Fish and Wildlife Service study reported high levels of mercury in panthers that live in the Fakahatchee Strand and East Everglades. Scientists believe the mercury is coming from contaminated

Panther crossing sign.

small prey, such as raccoons, which the panthers eat. Mercury also reduces fertility.

During 1988 and 1989, scientists released a half-dozen sterilized Texas cougars in north Florida to study how well these cousins of the Florida panthers would survive. The cougars adapted well, but by spring 1989 most had been killed by hunters. The remaining cougars were recaptured and the study was aborted.

The U.S. Wildlife Service and the state's Fish and Wildlife Conservation Commission are now studying a new plan to breed captive Florida panthers in an effort to expand the gene pool.

The Florida panther was federally listed as endangered in 1973, and in 1976 the U.S. Fish and Wildlife Service appointed a Recovery Team to draw up a panther recovery program. The legislature named the panther to be the state animal in 1978. It is a felony to kill one in the wild, punishable by a heavy fine, lengthy imprisonment, or both. Persons are asked to report the deaths of Florida panthers by calling 1-800-342-8105.

**FLYING SQUIRRELS** are tennis ball-sized cousins of the common gray squirrel and are found from north Florida south to the Lake Okeechobee area. These tiny rodents are exceedingly shy and nocturnal. They do not fly like birds, but rather glide from a high branch to a lower limb through use of a skin flap that balloons out from the body. A glide of about 80 feet is optimum. They nest in tree cavities, and mate in February, March, June, and July, with two to six young born slightly more than a month after mating. They eat insects, bird eggs, seeds, and nuts. Their primary predators are owls.

**FOX** in Florida are either of the gray or red variety. The gray fox is found throughout the state. Only 15 inches tall, it has a silvery gray coat highlighted with reddish brown on its underbelly, legs, under its bushy tail, and around its white face. A hallmark is the black stripe atop the length of its tail. The gray fox is a good climber and will scramble up a tree to be rid of pursuers.

The red fox is found in north Florida to Polk County. It is vividly orangish-red with a white underbelly, black feet, and a white tail tip.

These small members of the dog family are mostly nocturnal. After mating in February or March, they bear litters of three to seven pups. Foxes eat almost anything, including acorns, birds, eggs, small mammals, and insects. They den in hollow logs or in ground burrows.

**KEY DEER** are confined to Florida's Keys, with most of the population on Big Pine Key. These "toy" members of the white tail deer family weigh 50-80 pounds and are only two feet tall. They are thought to have miniaturized as a result of adapting to their reduced range, where smaller rather than larger deer survived to breed. Key deer numbered just 50 animals in 1947, but protection has increased their numbers to about 300 today. Development, highway traffic, and dogs continue to threaten their future. They eat grasses, shrubs, and twigs in the wild, but humans often feed the endearing creatures unusual foods, but to do so is a violation of state and federal law. Key deer bear one to two young once a year.

**MINK,** a valuable fur-bearing animal, exists in Florida in two subspecies—the Florida mink in northern areas, and the Everglades mink in the southern region. Minks inhabit the state's freshwater marshes where such food as fish, frogs, turtles, snakes, birds, insects, and mice are available. Female minks bear a single litter of three to four young, usually in May. The Everglades mink is protected from human hunters but not from such natural predators as bobcats, owls, hawks, and foxes.

**OPOSSUMS,** the state's only marsupial, can be found throughout the state's woodlands. They seek shelter in old logs or brushpiles and are nocturnal hunters of berries, eggs, insects, and carrion. Opossum are prolific and may bear up to 14 young once or twice a year, which are carried in a stomach pouch for the first two months of their lives. Young 'possums later travel on their mother's back. Adult opossums are often hunted for their meat, which has a high nutritional value.

**POCKET GOPHERS** are often called salamanders by Florida natives. True salamanders are amphibians, while pocket gophers are small mammals about half the size of a rat. It is easy to see the gopher's work—mounds of piled sand. Seeing the worker is more difficult because gophers are solitary and nocturnal. Male gophers dig yards-long tunnels that intersect with females' tunnels. In spring, litters of three to seven babies are born. Gophers feed on roots and other vegetation, and are rated beneficial by most researchers. Gopher tunneling aerates and turns soil over.

**WEST INDIAN MANATEES,** once thought to be mermaids, are Florida's most renowned and endangered marine mammals. A specimen grows from 10 to 13 feet long and weighs between 1,200 and 3,500 pounds. Manatees are slow-moving creatures who enjoy the warmth of Florida's rivers in winter. The walrus-like animals have no fear of man and spend their days placidly grazing the water surface, ingesting about 100 pounds of river grass daily. This dietary habit exposes the manatee to the propeller blades of boats, and nearly every animal seen bears the scars. For that reason, waterways known to be frequented by manatees are marked as "no wake" or "idle" zones and some stretches are off limits to all boating.

Besides boaters, increasing numbers of divers present a harassment to the giant sea cow. Some fishermen also discard fishing lines in water and subject the manatees to entanglement. Fishhooks have been found in the lips of manatees.

Laws have been enacted under the Manatee Sanctuary Act that proclaim the entire state of Florida as a refuge and sanctuary for manatees. It is illegal for any person to kill, molest, or knowingly cause physical harm to a manatee. Violations are a first-degree misdemeanor and punishment can bring a maximum penalty of one year in prison, a fine of $20,000, or both.

Manatee-saving actions, besides slow boat speed, urged by the Florida Fish and Wildlife Conservation Commission, include:

—Wearing polarized glasses while operating a boat to make it easier to see a manatee swimming under water

—Staying in marked boating channels, the depth of which helps protect manatees

—Keeping boats out of seagrasses where manatees graze

—No approaching or touching of manatees by divers

Manatees reproduce very slowly, with females bearing one calf every three to five years. The manatee population, established by annual count, stood at 2,022 in 1998 and 2,353 in 1999. Death rates have been 120 in 1985, 206 in 1990, 174 in 1991, 162 in 1992, 145 in 1993, 193 in 1994, and 201 in 1995. But in 1996, the record year, 415 manatees died, with more than half attributed to the most virulent outbreak of Red Tide in Florida's history. In 1997, 242 manatees died, in 1998, 231. Recent studies indicate manatees may be much more intelligent than previously thought.

To report injured or killed manatees, persons are asked to call 1-800-DIAL-FMP (1-800-342-5367).

**WHITETAIL DEER** are a normally shy and retiring species that has adapted to the state's increasing human population. They live throughout the state, except in the most urbanized areas. Deer are browsers and eat twigs, acorns, shrubs, fungi, and grass. They generally bear two fawns once or twice a year. Because they enjoy leafy plants, deer can cause considerable damage to crops if their numbers grow large. This often occurs because natural predators such as wolves and panthers are no longer available to balance the population. In-season hunting is a partial control over deer populations in specified areas of the state.

## MAJOR SPECIES OF REPTILES AND SNAKES

**ALLIGATORS** were once relentlessly hunted for their hides, and had become nearly extinct in Florida by the 1960s. In 1967, the federal government declared alligators to be an Endangered Species and prohibited gator hunting and the sale of hides. The alligator responded and by the mid-1970s, the reptile numbers soared to an estimated half-million. In 1977, the alligator's status was upgraded from "endangered" to "threatened," which legalized the killing of the creatures if they were deemed dangerous. Today, the alligator is a Species of Special Concern and the state sanctions tightly regulated hunts to keep a check on alligator numbers.

Scientists estimate the alligator has undergone few physical changes in the past 200 million years. It is highly adapted to watery habitats of the southeastern U.S. In size, the alligator can grow up to 16 feet, although a 19-foot record length is listed in some references. Well-formed jaws provide ample crushing power for the alligator to eat about anything it wants at a rate of 150 to 200 pounds a day, except during the winter months' dormancy period. Usual diet includes fish, frogs, birds, and snakes, although larger alligators will take raccoons, muskrats, large wading birds, and an occasional wild hog.

With its thick, rudder-like tail and eyes that are protected by a clear lid, the alligator is adept in or under water and can remain submerged for up to a half-hour. On land, the alligator is most commonly seen basking in the sun. An aroused alligator, however, can move with amazing speed to seize prey or to protect its nest.

Egg-laying reptiles, alligators generally nest in piles of plant debris mounded up along the bank of a waterway. Nests can measure four to seven feet in diameter and contain a dozen or more eggs. Only an estimated 20 percent of the eggs survive to hatch and predators such as birds, bass, and other alligators take a toll on hatchlings.

Although alligators can be dangerous, they provide a great benefit to creatures with whom they share the wilds. Holes dug by alligators soon become water sources for all animals during droughts. And birds nesting near an alligator nest reap the benefit of a watchful mother alligator that keeps raccoons and other predators from the vicinity. Alligators also feed on the poisonous cottonmouth water moccasins and help control the snake's population.

As Florida's population grows, the alligator's habitat shrinks. The result is that thousands of "nuisance" alligator calls are made to state game officials when wandering alligators are found in carports, swimming pools, storm drains, or on lawns. Wildlife officers relocate creatures less than four feet in length to the more remote swamplands.

Alligators will seek food wherever they find it, so ducks, pets, and even small children may be attacked. Game officials report that since 1948 nearly 250 unprovoked alligator attacks on humans have occurred. Nine deaths have been linked to alligators. Parents and homeowners living near natural alligator habitats are warned to keep children and pets under a watchful eye and to report immediately any alligator sightings that could result in life-threatening situations.

The largest alligator documented by Florida game officials was a 1,043-pounder removed in 1989 from Orange Lake in Alachua County. It measured 13 feet, 10½ inches long, and produced 294 pounds of meat and 15 feet of hide for a total of $2,500 in wholesale value. The longest alligator, taken in 1997 from Lake Monroe near Sanford, measured a fraction over 14 feet. A state-operated annual alligator harvest is held each fall, with about 200 participants issued permits. In recent years, alligator hides have sold for about $42 per foot, with meat selling for roughly $5 per pound.

**CROCODILES** often are confused with alligators, but can be distinguished by their pointier snout and two large teeth protruding from both sides of the snout. Crocodiles are listed by both the state and federal governments as an Endangered Species, and the only place in the United States where they are found is at the most southerly tip of Florida—in the Everglades, around the Florida Keys, and near Biscayne Bay.

Crocodiles bury their eggs in sand mounds and the females usually return to the nests at night. The number of eggs range between 21 and 56, and they hatch in about three months. These reptiles are slightly smaller than alligators, attaining an average length of 10 feet (a record length is 15 feet). They are ferocious fighters, however, and people should avoid approaching them. Their diet is basically the same as alligators: any living creature within reach of its powerful jaws is fair game.

**GOPHER TORTOISES,** large land turtles, have been plodding, natural inhabitants of Florida for centuries. Just 30 years ago, more tortoises than people lived in the state. Today, it is estimated Florida is home to about 1 million tortoises, but their numbers are dwindling as habitats are being gobbled up by developers. The crea-

tures have been listed by the state as a Species of Special Concern since 1978.

Gopher tortoises (called gophers by native Floridians) live in deep burrows in open fields or woodlands. The holes also provide housing for burrowing owls, opossums, toads, indigo snakes, pine snakes, frogs, and mice—some of which are only found in tortoise burrows.

Gopher breeding begins when they are 10 to 15 years old. Females lay 5 to 10 hardshelled eggs in a sand mound near the burrow between February and September. Eggs hatch after about three months, but the hatchlings are preyed upon by many animals, including fire ants, raccoons, and armadillos. Gopher tortoises can live up to 60 years.

Few tortoises live that long. Many are killed when their burrows are excavated to find rattlesnakes during scheduled hunts known as "round-ups," although researchers claim few rattlesnakes live in gopher holes. Hunting gophers, however, is prohibited.

**SEA TURTLES** of five species are to be found in Florida's coastal water. They are:

• **Leatherback Turtle**—the largest of sea turtles. It can mature at six feet in length and weigh up to 1,300 pounds. It is easily identified by its top shell, which is divided longitudinally into six sections by prominent ridges called keels. Coloring is predominately black with white spots.

Leatherbacks have strong front flippers that aid it as a long-distance swimmer in the open sea. These turtles are known to travel more than 3,000 miles to nesting sites. Jellyfish is a staple of leatherbacks and the discovery of deep-water jellyfish in turtle stomachs has led to the belief that these turtles dive to great depths. Leatherbacks range throughout the Atlantic, Pacific, and Indian oceans and some nest in Florida each year.

This turtle's flesh is not particularly tasty. Although some slaughter for meat occurs, the biggest threat to its survival is the taking of eggs for food. They do not thrive in captivity.

• **Green Turtle**—likely the most economically important sea turtle. It is typically about 39 inches long and weighs about 300 pounds. It gets its name from its green coloring, although some locals generically refer to it as the black turtle. Green turtles are found in the Atlantic, Pacific, and Indian oceans, but usually in warm climates. They are known to migrate 1,400 miles in open ocean to reach nesting sites, some of which are along Florida's Atlantic coast. They are plant feeders, grazing on seagrass and sometimes on algae. Green turtles are in danger from human consumption of turtle meat and eggs, and use of turtle leather and shell. Many of these turtles drown in shrimp trawls.

• **Loggerhead Turtle**—a reddish-brown turtle that grows to a length of about 38 inches and a weight of from 200 to 350 pounds. The turtle is named for its large-sized head. Loggerheads are slow swimmers who range about 500 miles out to sea. Florida's nesting population is sizable, with most placing their eggs along the Atlantic coast from Volusia County south to Broward County, and on the west coast in the Cape Sable area. The loggerhead diet is varied and includes crabs, shrimp, jellyfish, and plant matter. Humans have long enjoyed these turtles for food; raccoons enjoy the turtle eggs. Shrimp trawlers and destruction of habitat are other key threats to loggerheads.

• **Kemp's Ridley**—the most endangered of sea turtles. It is a cream and black creature, small in comparison to other sea turtles, measuring about 30 inches long and weighing 85 to 100 pounds. For decades, Kemp's Ridleys were often seen in southeastern waters but the whereabouts of their nesting sites were a mystery. In 1947, a Mexican engineer's film revealed ridleys nested on a remote sand bar beach off the Mexican coast. Numbers have so declined, however, that the 1947 population estimate of 40,000 turtles has been reduced to between 400 and 600 females.

Some scientists estimate that at the present rate ridleys will be extinct in 20 years. Conservation efforts since 1978 on the part of Mexico and the U.S. include beach patrols and tagging. Still, numbers decline. In October 1988, 55 dead ridleys washed up on beaches in Nassau and St. Johns counties. Many scientists blame the shrimping industry for drowning ridleys and other sea turtles in nets. The ridley's diet includes fish, jellyfish, crustaceans, swimming crabs, and mollusks.

• **Hawksbill Turtle**—readily identified by its birdlike beak. The hawksbill grows to a length of three feet and weighs about 100 pounds when mature. It is found throughout the world in shallow waters where it dines on vegetation and may consume sponges.

Only a few Florida nesting sites have been documented, most of them on offshore reefs and in the Keys. These turtles historically have been prized for their attractively marked shells used for ornaments or jewelry, especially in Japan, to which an estimated 40 percent of the Caribbean based hawksbill turtle shell is shipped. Most serious depletion of hawksbill population occurs in southeast Asia, where some 65,000 turtles are killed each year for their shells.

Declining sea turtle numbers prompted the federal government in 1988 to enact a law requiring use of Turtle Excluder Devices (TEDS) in Florida waters from May 1 through August 31. These devices allow sea turtles to escape from shrimp trawling nets and are required on all domestic trawlers over a certain length plying U.S. coastal waters. Stiff penalties await those who do not conform to the regulations.

Currently, the leatherback, Kemp's Ridley, and hawksbill turtles are included on federal Endangered Species lists, and the green turtle is Endangered on the state's list. They are protected by federal and state laws, so it is illegal to import, sell, or transport these turtles or their products in interstate or foreign commerce without special permits. It is also unlawful to tamper with nesting turtles or eggs.

**SNAKES** are plentiful in Florida. The state has more snake species than any other. By far, most varieties are harmless consumers of worms, lizards, and frogs. Only six species in Florida are poisonous, three of them members of the rattlesnake family. All six are capable of causing painful bites that are seldom fatal. Nationally, for example, of the approximate 6,000 persons bitten by poisonous snakes each year, fewer than a dozen die. Most bites occur during the warm spring and summer months when the snakes are most active.

The best precaution that can be taken against being bitten by poisonous snakes is to familiarize yourself with these species and give them a wide berth when you see them. Memorize what they look like, where their habitats are most likely to be found, and always look down toward the ground when treading in the woods and swamplands they habitate. Whenever possible, step over, rather than on, hollow logs, debris piles, and other likely snake nesting sites. As a rule, snakes are more afraid of us than we are of them and will normally run from us, but don't count on it in all cases. They will bite if stepped on, molested, cornered, or if they are defending a nest. When hiking in the woods or swamps, thick high boots are recommended. When cleaning up long-standing piles of wood, boards, leaves, trash, or other debris around the house or farm, turning them with a long-handled rake at first is safer than reaching in with your bare hands.

If a snakebite does occur, there are recommended immediate procedures that can and should be taken prior to admission to the hospital. These emergency procedures are often published in brochures given out free by pharmacies, hospitals, state agencies, or other public service organizations. These brochures should be kept in a convenient location in the house and carried on all outings into snake habitats.

Florida's poisonous snakes are:

• **Diamondback Rattlesnake**—the largest, most dangerous snake native to Florida. Its large body size, quantity of venom, aggressive defensive tactics, and blazingly accurate striking speed make it a snake to be treated with utmost respect.

The diamondback is recognized by a distinctive pattern of yellow-bordered, diamond-shaped body markings. Brittle, button-shaped segments form a rattle at the end of the tail. The arrow-shaped head is much wider than the neck.

Found in every county in Florida, the diamondback also inhabits many of the coastal islands. It may be encountered in almost any habitat, but most commonly frequents palmetto flatlands, pinewoods, abandoned fields, and brushy, grassy areas. In most situations the snake is difficult to spot because its color pattern blends into the background.

When disturbed the rattler assumes a defensive posture with body coiled, head and neck raised, rattle free and elevated to sound a warning. From

this stance, if the target is close, the rattler can repeatedly deliver a stabbing strike. Its optimum striking distance is from one-third to more than one-half its body length.

Recurving fangs lying folded inside the roof of the rattler's mouth become erect when the mouth is opened wide during a strike. As the fangs pierce a victim, pressure is exerted on poison sacs and the venom is pumped into the wound. The rattler does not have to be coiled to strike; it can strike from any position, in any direction. When disturbed or when protecting a nest, it may sound a warning rattle, but not always.

Diamondback rattlers shed skin three to five times a year, depending on the amount of food it takes in, which governs its growth. A new segment is added to the rattle at each shedding, a phenomenon that allows herpitologists to estimate a rattler's age. Although it may attain a length of more than eight feet, it is rare to find a rattler longer than seven feet. Rattlesnakes feed mainly on small mammals such as rabbits, squirrels, rats, mice, shrews, and sometimes birds.

Rattlers bear 9 to 15 young at a time. Newborn rattlers are equipped with venom and the fangs to inject it.

This species is commercially valued for its hide, meat, and venom, and for exhibition purposes. It renders valuable service to farmers by preying on crop-destroying rodents. Besides large birds, the rattler's natural predators include the indigo snake and the scarlet king snake.

• **Canebrake Rattlesnake**—found mainly in north Florida, but reported as far south as Alachua County. This snake is the southern counterpart of the timber rattler found in other parts of the U.S.

The canebrake is recognized by a grayish-brown or pinkish-buff color, with dark bands across its body, an orange or rusty-red stripe down the middle of its back, and a brown or black tail that bears a rattle. As with other rattlers, the canebrake's head is much wider than its neck, but it is more slender than the average diamondback. Florida specimens rarely measure more than five feet long.

This snake is commonly found in flatwoods, river bottoms and hammocks, and may be found in abandoned fields and around farms. During hot weather, it may seek low, swampy ground.

• **Pygmy Rattlesnake**—also called the ground rattler. It is commonly found in all of Florida's counties and on some offshore islands. Its rattle is small and slender and produces a buzzing sound like an insect. This signal can be heard from no more than a few feet away.

Stout-bodied for its diminutive size of less than 18 inches, the pygmy is gray and prominently marked with roundish dusky-colored spots. At the base of its head, red spots alternate with black along the midline on the back.

Pygmy rattlers feed on small frogs, lizards, mice, and other snakes. Like other members of the pit viper family, it does not lay eggs, but gives birth to live young.

These snakes are encountered primarily in wetlands, in palmetto flatwoods, or in areas of slash pine and wire grass. For its size, the pygmy rattler has a feisty disposition and is quick to strike. Its bite produces pain and swelling that normally subsides in a few days. It can be fatal to humans under some circumstances, but no deaths from a pygmy rattler bite have been recorded.

• **Cottonmouth (Water Moccasin)**—the only poisonous water-dwelling snake in North America. The cottonmouth is a pit viper that has no rattles and grows to a large size, usually more than five feet. Most Florida specimens average about three feet and are found in every county and on many coastal islands.

Coloring of the cottonmouth varies from olive-brown to black, with or without dark crossbands on the body. It is stoutly shaped, with an abruptly tapering tail and a broad head much wider than its neck. A distinctive mark is a dark band extending from the eye to the rear of the jaw. A drooping mouthline and protective shields over its eyes give it a sullen expression.

A disturbed cottonmouth often draws into a loose coil, cocks its head up, and opens its mouth wide to reveal a white interior, hence the name cottonmouth. From this pose it lunges out in a fast strike to imbed its poisonous fangs. It usually keeps a hold on prey, chewing in order to drive its fangs deeper. It does not have to be coiled to strike, but can deliver a bite from almost any position, in or out of water. It is unpredictable and may behave calm and sluggish, or aggressive.

As a water snake, the cottonmouth is usually found along the edges of lakes, swamps, and marshes, where it hides in brushy areas or in low trees overhanging the water. It forages at night for fish, frogs, other snakes, lizards, and small mammals.

Cottonmouth young, 6 to 12 of them in the average litter, are born with poison sacs loaded and ready. The little snakes are boldly marked with red-brown crossbands and bright yellow tails. At this stage they can be mistaken for another poisonous species, the copperhead.

Poison of the cottonmouth causes much pain and swelling. But with immediate medical treatment, the bite is only occasionally fatal to humans.

• **Copperhead**—found only rarely in Florida in a few northwestern Panhandle counties. This is a primarily northern mountain and wilderness snake that hibernates in the winter. Reports of bites from this snake are rare in Florida, and no deaths have ever been attributed to the copperhead by state health agencies.

The copperhead is a handsome snake, with pinkish-tan body color and reddish-brown crossbands. The bands are wide along the sides and narrow along the back, forming something of an hourglass shape. The copper-colored head from which it receives its name is wider than the neck. Its average length is less than three feet. The copperhead's coloration is so similar to that of young cottonmouths that the two are often confused with one another.

• **Coral Snake**—brightly colored and the most deadly venomous snake in North America. Corals are related to the cobras, kraits, and mambas found in tropical countries. Fortunately, most coral snakes are shy and secretive and will not bite unless startled, tormented, or hurt. It has short fangs and a small mouth and does not strike like the pit vipers, but bites and chews to inject its poison.

Most bites from coral snakes occur when people pick up or attempt to touch one. As a result, fingers are the most frequent target for the coral's venom, although toes and other parts of the feet may be attacked if a person steps on or near the snake.

Coral snakes often are confused with the harmless scarlet king snake. Both snakes have brightly colored bands of red, black, and yellow. However, the red rings of the coral snake border the yellow, whereas the red rings of the non-poisonous king snake border black. A helpful rhyme goes: "Red touch yellow, kill a fellow; red touch black, good for Jack." The

coral snake also has a black nose; the king snake has a red nose.

The largest coral snake recorded was 47 inches long, but most specimens are less than two feet. The coral's body is small and slender, and it has a narrow head more commonly found on non-poisonous species of snakes.

Pine woods, under rotting logs or brush piles, along pond or lake borders, or dense hammock areas are the most common sites of coral snake nests. It eats frogs, lizards, and other snakes, and lays up to half a dozen eggs that hatch in two to three months.

## MAJOR SPECIES OF BIRDS

**BROWN PELICANS** are commonly seen along Florida's coast, and this expert diver is easily recognized by the large pouch underneath its long bill. Its pouch is not used to carry or store fish, but rather acts as a scooping strainer as the pelican gathers the fish.

A stocky bird, the brown pelican's wingspan can reach 90 inches. They are aggressive and noisy companions at nearly every fishing dock, where they await castoff bait or scraps of fish.

In Florida, the brown pelican is a Species of Special Concern because its numbers have declined in past decades. Studies have attributed this to the use of insecticides that, when ingested, weaken egg walls causing them to break before hatching. Brown pelicans lay two or three white eggs in a nest of sticks or grass in trees or low bushes. Some individuals may lay eggs on the ground. Loss of habitat and harassment has added to the decline of this bird's numbers. As Florida's human population has grown, and more and more coastal islands have been developed, greater numbers of Floridians are boating and fishing. These encroachments have been detrimental to the brown pelican population, currently estimated to be around 25,000.

**CRANES,** specifically the sandhill specimen, are a most spectacular Florida resident. They once were plentiful all over the United States, but today can be found only in isolated areas. These cranes stand up to four feet tall and have a wingspan of about 80 inches. After an elaborate mating ritual, the female lays two buff-colored eggs in a grassy nest in marshlands. It is a Threatened Species and experts fear it will eventually decline, as did the whooping crane.

**CRESTED CARACARA** is rapidly declining in its habitat north and west of Lake Okeechobee. This long-legged raptor stands 20 to 25 inches from head to tail and has a 4-foot wingspan. It is boldly patterned with vulture-like red skin on its face and a distinguishing crest of dark brown. Primary prey includes reptiles, other birds, mammals, and carrion. Nests are built of twigs and limbs in cabbage palms, but only 250 nesting pairs of the crested caracara, also called the Mexican eagle, are believed to exist in Florida. It is on both the state and federal threatened species lists.

**EAGLES,** the national bird, are on the increase in Florida. Wildlife officials report more than 5,200 southern bald eagle hatchings have occurred in the state in the past 20 years. Compared to other southern states, Florida has nearly double the eagle nesting territories, and populations have remained stable since reliable counts began in 1973.

Florida classifies the southern bald eagle as a Threatened Species, although the federal government has removed eagles from the Endangered list. Consequently, land development in Florida is restricted within a mile of an eagle's nest. In Florida, where wildlife officials estimate 75 percent of the eagle population lives on privately owned land, this has created land-use problems.

The state's eagle population generally mates in the fall, with about two eggs appearing in nests between October and February. The eggs require about a month to hatch and young spend nearly four months maturing. An average of one eaglet survives in most nests.

A regal bird, the southern bald eagle boasts a wingspan of up to 90 inches.

Human-eye view of some of Florida's most graceful large birds as they soar overhead. Top to bottom: bald eagle, turkey vulture, osprey, and red-tailed hawk.

Eagles are meat eaters and they prefer fresh-killed prey like rodents, squirrels, land reptiles, and other birds.

**EGRETS** of several varieties live in Florida all or most of the year. The great egret, the snowy egret, the reddish egret, and the smaller cattle egret all breed in the state.

**HERONS** such as the great blue, the great white, the tri-colored, the little blue, and the green-backed live in Florida year-round. Their plumage and grace makes them great favorites of bird lovers. Several are Species of Special Concern.

One of Florida's most famous and beautiful birds, the pink flamingo, is a member of the heron family. Once highly sought after by plume hunters, they are found in especially large numbers in the Everglades, where they are protected.

**KITES** in Florida are primarily the Everglades species. This species is a sleek gray (male) or brown (female) bird that feeds exclusively on snails and is often listed as the snail kite. It is a shy bird, seldom seen or heard, and is highly endangered because of the invasion of Florida's waterways by water hyacinths, which effectively hide snails from the kite. Recent surveys have reported sighting only 326 Everglades kites.

**OSPREYS,** hawklike brown birds, are another of Florida's Species of Special Concern. Ospreys are adept at fishing with their feet, which are equipped with sharp spikes that aid in carrying a fish back to the nest.

Wherever there is water there is likely an osprey. Nests are easily spotted masses of twigs and sticks often in trees, but just as often stuck on a light pole, a channel marker, or a telephone pole. As with other fish-eating birds, the osprey's numbers declined because of pesticide use.

**OWLS** are predominantly nocturnal and are sure to delight any camper or bird watcher. The state is home to several species, including the great horned owl, barred owls, barn owls, and burrowing owls.

Environmentally important, owls eat snakes, roaches, grasshoppers, and small rodents. Many species live in dead trees or, if possible, in vacant outbuildings. The burrowing owl, which makes its home in ground holes, is a Species of Special Concern.

**SCRUB JAYS** are a crestless and more brilliant type of jay than the common blue. The scrub jay is classified as a Threatened Species. It is to be found only in the state's more isolated areas where it feeds on insects, acorns, and berries. Scrub jays mate for life.

**SONGBIRDS** by the thousands either live in Florida or visit during winter. Major species include larks, jays, titmice, wrens, warblers, thrushes, vireos, cardinals, sparrows, orioles, mockingbirds, and finches.

**VULTURES,** winged scavengers, are often looked upon with disdain because they feed on carrion. This is a vital natural function, however, which keeps the environment healthy. Often called "nature's cleanup crew," vultures can be seen circling slowly, searching for food while riding the thermal air currents.

The turkey vulture is nearly the size of an eagle and frequents forests and farmlands. Vultures nest in fallen logs or in hollow trees, laying a couple of brown and white eggs inside the crevice with no nesting material.

Black vultures are slightly less common and are smaller than the turkey vulture but their nesting habits are similar. The species recently has come under state protection.

**WILD TURKEYS** are popular hunting fare in Florida. They are similar to domestic turkeys, but are much more wary and are of a sleeker build. They are found throughout the state, but are scarce in the Everglades. Mating activity begins in March and an average nest contains 8 to 11 eggs. Although Florida is ranked as a leading turkey hunting state, destruction of habitat is expected to affect their numbers in the wild.

**WOOD STORKS,** gracefully large wading birds, boast a wingspan of over five feet. Wings have conspicuous black marks, as does the tail. Colonies of thousands of wood storks once roosted in the cypress and mangrove swamps of Florida. This bird is listed as Endangered because its population declined rapidly from more than 70,000 in the 1930s to about 12,000 today. The primary reason for the population decrease is the draining of wetlands and logging activities, as well as the destruction of mangroves. It is North America's only true stork.

**WOODPECKERS** abound in Florida, ranging from the rather small, colorful redheaded woodpecker to the pileated woodpecker whose body is 17 inches long. The ivory-billed woodpecker is endangered and may be extinct. No reliable sightings of this magnificent bird have been reported in more than 10 years. Numbers of the red-cockaded woodpecker are also dwindling as stands of old-growth pine are timbered. This 8-inch bird lives only in live pine trees, where resin drips protect the nest from predators such as the pine snake. But it can take years for red-cockaded woodpeckers to peck out a nesting cavity, so humans are helping by installing pre-constructed nesting boxes in pine trees.

### Hooked or Tangled Sea Birds

Seabirds tangled in discarded fishing lines are not an uncommon sight along the shore of Florida. In most cases, the bird, often a pelican, has been unknowingly snared by a careless fisherman's discards. Unless attended to, the bird probably will suffer a slow, torturous death. Under no conditions should a line, nor a multiple hook, be left in a bird. Wildlife officers have some suggestions for helping a hooked bird.

They urge that the bird be captured. If the victim is in the water, a large hoop net is recommended. If on land, the victim should be gathered in a towel, shirt, blanket, or other cloth. Removing a hook is not difficult. In the case of a pelican that is hooked in the pouch below the bill, for example, hold the bill and cut off the hook barb; then back the hook out. Never cut the line and expect the bird to free itself. Leaving a trailing monofilament line on a bird can be disastrous. The bird very likely will accidentally hang itself from the line at its nightly roost.

Once the hook and line have been removed, ideally the bird should be brought to a bird sanctuary for further treatment and extended care.

To prevent hook and line injuries, several precautions should be taken. Among them: Be aware of pelicans and seabirds when fishing, and always avoid casting while birds are in the vicinity. Do not leave fishing lines unattended, especially when they are baited. Do not throw waste line overboard. And do not leave a rod with the line reeled up and hook dangling—birds often fly into dangling hooks or lines and become tangled.

Another danger to seabirds is six-pack plastic rings. Water birds and ducks have been known to stick their heads into one of the rings and not be able to shake it loose. Slow starvation often results if the plastic ring restricts feeding and flying. To discard six-pack plastic rings, cut all connections of plastic to "open" the rings and dispose of the remains in proper trash receptacles.

## VENOMOUS SPIDERS

There are few poisonous spiders in Florida. Only two species, in fact, can cause serious injury or death, but their bites are nonetheless painful and immediate hospital treatment is recommended for victims. As is the case with poisonous snakes, the best assurance against being bitten is visual recognition of the harmful species and avoiding them on sight. Observing caution around their most likely habitats is also recommended, including checking under toilet seats in unfamiliar places before sitting down.

The venomous spiders found in Florida are:

• **Brown Recluse**—most commonly found in the yard or house. Indoors, this spider prefers to hide behind books, furniture, in shoes, clothing, in folded towels, and under items left lying on the floor. Outdoors, the brown recluse, as its name implies, hides under rocks, loose bark, and any other secretive areas.

This rusty-brown spider also is called the violin spider because it has such a shape outlined in darker brown shades on its back. Including legs, the brown recluse is about the size of a half-dollar.

The source of its painful bite is a nerve poison that kills cells as it spreads through tissue. The longer the poison remains in the victim's system, the greater the tissue damage, and some severe bites may take months to heal. Instances of red blood cell destruction have been reported which resulted in kidney or liver problems in victims, particularly in children and in elderly persons. A telltale symptom of the brown recluse bite is a crusty wound that forms a reddish-purple zone on the flesh surrounding the site. Bite victims should try to remain calm, since panic results in a more rapid flow of blood and the poison carried in it through the body. Emergency hospital treatment should be sought immediately.

• **Widows**—native to Florida in four species. All are potently poisonous, but reports of serious encounters have involved only the southern black widow. The bite of these spiders is a needle-like pang that is followed in about 15 minutes by muscle cramps, usually in the shoulder, thighs, and back. Severe pain later spreads to the abdomen, and weakness and tremors follow. Breathing may grow difficult, and the skin becomes cold and clammy. In severe instances, shock and vomiting may occur. Medical treatment should be sought immediately. Treatment with antivenin is effective. Reported deaths occurred because the victim suffered from an additional health problem such as heart disease. In one case, the victim was bitten at the base of the skull and the spider's venom traveled rapidly to the brain.

Florida's widows species are:

—**Southern black widows,** a glossy black or dark reddish-brown-colored spider with a distinctively bright orange hourglass marking on the frontal abdomen. The southern black

widow is the most widespread of Florida's widow spiders and can be found in stumps, pipes, building materials, under stones, in storm sewers, in water meter boxes, and under the ledges of seawalls throughout the state.

—**Northern black widows,** which behave and appear nearly the same as the southern version, except that they have two red-orange barlike designs on the frontal abdomen instead of the more obvious hourglass. The northern widow has been found only in the state's Panhandle, usually west of Tallahassee.

—**Red widows,** which prefer the palmettos of pine scrublands in central and southeastern Florida. This is an exotic-looking spider, red everywhere except on the abdomen, which is dark brown and often has several yellow or orange spots.

—**Brown widows,** varying in color from light gray or brown to almost black. The abdomen is usually highly marked with spots or lines of white, red, and yellow. The frontal abdomen includes the classic red-orange hourglass. This spider lives in the state's southeastern coastal regions, rarely north of Daytona Beach, and prefers well-lighted haunts such as automobile service stations.

## MAJOR INSECT PESTS

**AFRICANIZED BEES** have crossed the U.S. border into Texas and are forecast to invade Florida sometime within the next decade. State agriculture officials are watching closely the movement of Africanized bees and maintain traps along Interstate 10 and at ports to monitor their eventual arrival. The newcomers could cripple Florida's bee industry by taking over the hives of more gentle European honeybees. Africanized bees produce less honey than European honeybees and are less easily managed by beekeepers, factors that could cause pollination costs to rise.

Florida bee experts say the state has a plan to minimize the impact of Africanized bees that focuses on diluting the African strain by cross-breeding.

Africanized bees have been dubbed "killers" because they have caused some 350 deaths in Latin America. Africanized bee venom is no more potent than that of other bees, but this species swarms angrily and will pursue those disturbing their nests for greater distances than their more docile European cousins. Most reported deaths have occurred because of massive numbers of stings. Africanized bees are slightly smaller and darker colored than other varieties.

**CHIGGERS** are minor Florida pests found in underbrush. They burrow under skin and can cause severe itching and possible secondary infections. Tree bark, moss, even wooden park picnic benches can harbor chiggers. Preventative insect repellents help, and an after-hiking bath is recommended. Clear nail polish dabbed on chigger bites is reputed to smother the insects.

**FIRE ANTS** are to be found throughout Florida. Contrary to many notions, fire ants are not unusually large. They measure from one-sixteenth to one-fourth of an inch long. Such small sizes belie the ferocity of this ant's sting and at least one infant death has been reported due to massive numbers of ant bites. Fire ants are reddish-black and have proportionately large heads. Their mounds or nests are excavations usually found in woods or fields and often are placed near protective shrubs, but they are a problem for homeowners' lawns as well. Some nests may contain up to a half-million ants and, when their nests are stepped on, they may swarm up the person's leg and attack in force.

These ants can cause severe problems among farmers because newly born calves, lambs, or foals may become targets of the insects, which are attracted to the mucous membranes of the young animals. Pet owners should protect newborn puppies or kittens from fire ants.

Medical problems from fire ant bites can be severe. After the initial, painful bite, secondary infection or allergic reactions may occur.

Scientists are investigating several natural fire ant eradication methods. One is the thief ant that will devour fire ant queens. Another biological control under investigation is a fungus that affects the ants. Boiling water, while initially killing some ants, will usually just prompt surviving ants to move the nest to another location. Commercial baits work well when worker ants carry the bait into the nest to the queen.

**FLEAS** affect Florida pets and their owners, especially in warm months. Dogs need frequent bathing and insecticidal sprays or dips may be necessary. Frequent vacuum cleaning as well as household flea sprays and applications of boric acid may be necessary to prevent infestations of dwellings.

**FRUIT FLIES,** particularly the Mediterranean, are the bane of Florida's citrus industry. Fruit fly (also called Medfly) infestations have damaged Florida citrus crops in the 1920s, the 1950s, the 1960s, the 1980s, and the 1990s—most recently in 1998. The fly's damage is done when larvae feed on the ripening fruit and it falls to the ground. Not only citrus is vulnerable to Medfly damage. Watermelon, papaya, Surinam cherry, and mango can be affected. There are more than 100 known species of fruit plants that Medflies infest.

In the past, the most effective means of eradicating Medflies was aerial spraying of the chemical malathion. Concern about the pesticide's effect on humans, however, has prompted further investigation into producing safer sprays and finding methods of early detection of the flies.

**LOVE BUGS** are the sticky little pests that cover Florida cars for about four weeks every May and September. They develop in moist hammocks or wooded areas where larvae or young feed on decaying vegetation. Their name derives from their flight, which occurs in mating tandem. After a couple of days, the male dies and is shaken loose by the female, who seeks out a new mate. After about three matings, the female dies. Fortunately, love bugs do not bite, sting, or feed on plants. They are simply annoying. To minimize damage to automobile paint, crushed bugs should be washed off as quickly as possible.

**MOSQUITOES** have been slapped at by Floridians since the state was discovered. It is the female mosquito that bites, for she must have a blood meal before she can produce eggs. Florida has several types of mosquitoes, all of which lay eggs in stagnant water. For that reason, old tires, tubs, or other containers should be kept drained.

Diseases that can be spread by mosquitoes include malaria, yellow fever, and encephalitis, although their occurrence is rare.

Any of Florida's woodlands and marshes harbor mosquitoes, especially in summer. A good insect repellent is advised before venturing outside, especially in the evening or in dense, shaded woods. One theory holds that body warmth attracts mosquitoes. Florida old-timers say perfume also attracts the pests.

New to Florida is the Asian Tiger. Health officials say this mosquito is highly tolerant of insecticides and carries encephalitis, yellow, and dengue fevers. It is distinctively marked with black and white stripes, and is an aggressive insect.

**ROACHES** have been around for an estimated 350 million years, and Florida is home to 56 of the known 3,500 species. A most noticeable Florida roach is the American Cockroach, called "Palmetto Bug" by polite folks. These large (up to two inches long) and speedy bugs fly well, live in palm and oak trees, and enjoy the indoors, especially kitchens. A smaller but even more common roach is the German, which is lighter colored than the American version. A third common roach is the Oriental model, which is nearly black and is about one and one-half inches long. All of these varieties shun light.

These repugnant regulars have been joined by a new roach variety, the Asian, which flies and is more silvery-colored. This new roach is attracted to light and, should it thrive, promises to put a damper on outdoor barbecues. All roaches thrive in garbage and pet food, and will eat virtually anything. Researchers report some species of roaches can live on little more than dust; others resort to cannibalism if left with nothing else to eat. Many are virtually immune to insecticides. Known natural predators of roaches include some spiders, lizards, and snakes.

**TERMITES** cause millions of dollars of damage to Florida homes each year. They are pale, antlike insects that gather in large colonies and thrive on woody fibers. Florida's native subterranean termite tends to start destruction at the foundation of a home. It also swarms at night.

A newcomer, the Formosan termite, is causing concern because it displays greater destructive habits and is, say entomologists, about 10 times more aggressive than subterranean termites. Unlike the subterranean variety, Formosan termites swarm in daytime and can devour structures from the top floor down by building long mud tubes that may actually go across concrete to reach wood. They also attack trees such as the citrus and mango, as well as sugarcane, and consume great amounts of woody materials.

Presently, Formosan termites have been found in the Miami-Ft. Lauderdale area, and in Orlando, Tampa, and Pensacola. An effective chemical control is being developed. Meanwhile, one researcher found that a foundation barrier made of uniformly particled sand seems to stop the Formosan termite. The sand particles are too large for termites to move with their jaws, yet small enough to keep the insects from squeezing through to the structure's foundation.

**TICKS** have long pestered Florida dogs and cats. A few species, such as the soft mammal tick or the Eastern wood tick, are known to spread disease. More recently, the black-legged tick, a mite-sized, hard-bodied insect, has been linked to Lyme Disease, which is thought to prompt arthritis in some affected people. Florida's warm weather provides a near year-round tick season. Insect repellent should be used and all clothing should be washed immediately after visiting the state's woodlands.

### FRESHWATER FISH

An estimated 675 strictly freshwater fish species inhabit lakes and rivers in North America, and another 100 regularly enter fresh waters in the U.S. and Canada from the sea. Floridians are told they have 115 native freshwater fish species in the state's lakes and streams, plus another 175 marine, migratory, and exotic species that invade the state's streams.

The Panhandle rivers and streams, because that area was never completely flooded thousands of years ago, retain more species of mainland fishes than the peninsula. In fact, about one-half of the native freshwater fish species of Florida occur only in, or west of, the Suwannee River system.

Containing the largest variety of freshwater species are the Apalachicola and Escambia rivers, both in the Panhandle. Wildlife officials have recorded 83 different kinds of fish in the Apalachicola and 81 in the Escambia.

Following are descriptions of some of the state's best-known species:

**BLACK BASS** in Florida are the largest in the world. Four varieties are recognized:

• **Largemouth bass** average four pounds, although 12 to 14-pound catches are not rare. Color varies according to water color, but these bass always have a dark side stripe from tail to gill. They will strike almost any artificial lure and are considered fighters.

• **Smallmouth bass** are present but have never thrived in Florida. Coloring is similar to the largemouth bass, but the smallmouth has more rows of scales and, as the name implies, a smaller mouth.

• **Spotted bass** are easily confused with largemouth, but have regular rows of black spots instead of irregular blotches below the lateral line. They are found in cool, clear streams with gravel and sand bottoms. Averages 10 inches in length.

• **Suwannee bass** are found in its namesake river and tributaries.

**BLACK CRAPPIE** is also known as Speckled Perch and is not a hot-weather fish, but does offer much sport to cane pole fishermen. A member of the sunfish family, the crappie is flat with an irregular pattern of black dots on a silver background. The average weight is 12 ounces for landed fish, but an adult specimen may reach three pounds.

**BREAM** is also called Bluegill, and like the bass, the color of this fish varies with water conditions. It is sunfish shaped and usually olive-green on the back with a purplish, chain mail effect. Best bream fishing is spring and early summer, but this fish is caught statewide year round. Both bluegill and the shellcracker bream may weigh in at three pounds. Both are popular panfish.

**CATFISH** come in three popular varieties in Florida. They are:

• **Channel cat,** slate gray to blue with a forked tail and averaging about four pounds. It is found in rivers, lakes, and waterways and is considered one of the state's best-tasting freshwater fish.

• **Bullheads,** usually weighing in at about one pound. This catfish is dark yellow or brownish and is found throughout the state. A variation of the species has a mottled gray-black coloring and reaches four pounds. Both have square-shaped tails and are edible.

• **White cat,** gray-blue with a white belly, but with no deeply-forked tail. It is found throughout the state and weighs about one pound. Known specimens have reached nine pounds, but this size is rare. It has good food value.

**GARFISH** is one of the least popular Florida fish. It is ugly and seldom eaten. When hooked, they are fighters and are just not worth the effort it takes to land them. The alligator gar is the largest and can reach 100 pounds, but averages about 18 pounds. It is found in sloughs and streams in western Florida. The longnose gar may reach 50 pounds and its average length is two feet. It is most common in central Florida, but is found in all but the southernmost regions. A third variety, spotted gars, seldom exceed five pounds and are found statewide.

**MUDFISH** is also known as Bowfin or Dogfish, and has little sport or commercial value. Its color is mottled olive and its average weight is one pound. It is found in lakes, rivers, and ponds throughout the state.

**PICKEREL,** also called Pike, comes in two types in Florida, the chain pickerel (jackfish) and the small redfin. Some outdoor writers refer to the jackfish as an eastern pickerel and say the term "chain pickerel" is a misnomer, preferring the term pike or redfin pike. The fish is a brownish-green on its back, fading to greenish-yellow on the sides and belly, with chain-like olive blotches. Average weight is eight pounds and it is found throughout the state.

**SHAD,** also called Herring, is a popular freshwater fish that makes good eating. Some shad varieties are considered gamefish and some are worthless. One of the most numerous varieties in Florida is the gizzard shad with an average size of nine inches and a three to four-pound average weight. It is inedible and used for bait. Two other members of the shad family are fairly common in Florida streams—the American (white) shad, which is bluish above with silver sides and reaches a weight of about five pounds, and the Alabama shad, which seldom exceeds one pound. Both are valued for their flesh and roe.

**STURGEON,** although nearly depleted, have been found spawning in rivers and streams entering the Gulf. Average size is three feet, although it reaches weights of several hundred pounds. It is easily recognized by bony plates that cover it. Its food value is only fair, but the sturgeon is prized for its roe, which is processed for caviar.

## SALTWATER FISH

**BARRACUDA** is a formidable fish with sharp, double-edged teeth. It is rarely dangerous unless bothered. An average barracuda in south Florida waters will weigh up to 10 pounds with 15 and 20 pounds fairly common offshore. The fish is smoky to dark gray on back and shaped like a torpedo. It is not considered edible because it occasionally dines on smaller reef fish whose organs are toxic.

**BONEFISH** is a small, inedible, powerful fish that is highly regarded by fishermen. It is the fastest of shallow water game fish and is seldom caught until it moves onto the flats for dinner. Bonefish prefer the warmer waters of southern Florida, where they grow to an average weight of about five pounds, with eight- or nine-pound fish not uncommon.

**BONITA** is a small cousin of the blue fin tuna sometimes called "little tunny." This superb game fish has been known to reach 20 pounds, but three to five pounds is average. They are caught year round in Florida. Food value is low, but the sporting fish strike and fight hard. It makes good bait for sharks and other large game fish. Gill plates of the bonita are extra sensitive and care should be used when releasing this fish.

**DOLPHIN,** not to be confused with the porpoise, is a hard striking animal usually weighing about five pounds, although 30- or 40-pounders are not rare. A surface-feeding fish, the dolphin likes warm water and its iridescent coloring seems to change when it is excited.

**JACKS** are considered by many the gamest of all reef fish, even though most Jack family fish are poor to fair in food value. They are most tasty when served smoked. The amberjack is streamlined and a powerful underwater fighter. Its average weight is 20 to 30 pounds, but catches twice that size are fairly common. The yellow or bar jack is a small cousin of the amberjack that averages between three and eight pounds.

Another variety, Jack crevelles, has been dubbed the bulldogs of the sea for the fight they wage when hooked. Their average size is just five pounds, but they seem much bigger while being hooked.

Of all the Jacks, however, the African pompano is the most prized. It is prevalent in Cuban water, averages 12 pounds, and makes an excellent trophy fish.

Other members of the Jack family are the blue runner, an avid fighter, and the permits. Permits are elusive and require patience. Their speed and agility are similar to the bonefish. Florida permit average 11 pounds, with 20 to 30 pounds considered a good day's work.

**LADYFISH** rarely exceed five pounds, but this fish is a surprisingly powerful member of the tarpon and bonefish family. It can be found in all Florida water, including brackish, and prefers the bays and channels near grass feeding beds.

**MARLIN** come in two types, the blue and the white, and both can be caught off Florida coasts. The blue averages between 150 and 200 pounds and requires an experienced angler equipped with heavy gear. This fish's spearing nose and lashing tail can be dangerous if encountered. The white marlin is smaller and not as common in Florida waters and is occasionally hooked while trolling for sailfish. Most white marlin catches are made from March to May, whereas blue marlin fishing peaks between May and July.

**REDFISH** are known by several names, such as red, bull red, puppy drum, and channel bass. It is a sporting fish and, at 10 pounds or less, is excellent table fare. The average Florida red is smaller than its northern cousins and weighs between three and eight pounds. The adult fish is solid red with a large black spot at the base of its tail, and is generally caught in shallow waters.

Recent extensive catching of this fish for use in popular Cajun recipes has forced game officials to impose severe limits on their taking. Anglers should stay current on fishing regulations and check whether or not redfish season is open.

**SAILFISH** is a most enticing and sought-after game fish that can average over seven feet in length. It was rarely caught until discovery of the drop-back technique in which the angler lets his bait drop toward the bottom for about 10 seconds. The fish supposedly thinks it has stunned or killed the bait. This delayed procedure allows the fish to inhale the live bait and the hook. Sails can be easily released by snipping the leader wire near the mouth. The hook dissolves. Badly injured fish may be served smoked.

**SHARKS** come in about 350 varieties, worldwide, but only about 24 are considered dangerous to man. Of that two dozen, only seven "man-eating" varieties are known to venture into Florida waters.

In fact, documented shark attacks are rare in the Gulf of Mexico and Atlantic Ocean, although caution while swimming is advised. Sharks are unpredictable scavengers who track their targets to within visual range and begin circling. A circling shark sometimes will spiral in and bump its nose against its prey. If the quarry does not strike back, the shark may attack. Once blood flows, more sharks will usually arrive to share the kill in a feeding frenzy.

The shark is among the most efficient killers found in nature. Rows of teeth, as many as 19, can tear prey apart. In some species, such as the great white, the upper jaw moves forward and upward to better seize, shake, and hold the victim while it prepares to eat. Sharks' skin is also dangerously abrasive and even a brush by a small shark can remove human skin and sometimes the muscle layer beneath.

The following shark varieties found in Florida are listed here in order of reported incidents of attacks:

• **Sand,** common in shallow waters, eats mostly small fish, but may bite if stepped on. Reaches a length of 8 to 10 feet.

• **Bull,** averages 9 feet, weighs about 500 pounds, and can be dangerous.

• **Mako,** considered a man-eater with an average 12-foot length. It is fast swimming and has reportedly attacked boats. Weighs approximately 1,000 pounds.

• **Hammerhead,** easily identified by its unusual head shape. It averages 9 feet.

• **Tiger,** also a man-eating shark, will attain a length of more than 15 feet and weighs about 1,800 pounds. Has been known to attack boats.

• **Lemon,** averages 9 feet long, 800 pounds weight, and is considered dangerous.

• **White,** dangerous to the point of being legendary. Averages 18 feet in length, but seen only occasionally in Florida waters. It is highly aggressive, will attack boats, and is capable of eating humans. Usual weight is about 1,700 pounds. Females generally outweigh males.

• **Black-tipped,** also called the spinner shark. It often travels in schools and leaps from the water. Common in Florida waters and may exceed 8 feet in length, but is seldom more than 150 pounds.

• **Nurse,** found in shallow waters near mangroves in Florida. Very sluggish, this shark is dangerous only when stepped on. Weighs 200-400 pounds and averages about 10 feet long.

• **Porbeagle,** prefers colder waters, averages 8 feet in length, and weighs about 400 pounds.

• **Thresher,** can exceed 15 feet in length with a weight of about 900 pounds. Usually attacks only when provoked.

• **Dogfish,** common to Florida waters and only about 4 feet long. It will bite if tormented and its sandpapery hide can scrape off human skin if it brushes past and makes contact.

The International Game Fish Association recognizes six shark species as gamefish: blue, mako, porbeagle, thresher, tiger, and white, with the mako the most popular. It gives anglers a battle with long runs and spectacular leaps.

Food value of sharks is debatable, although consumers may unknowingly purchase shark labeled as "steak-fish." The shark's liver is a source of high vitamin A content and sharkskin is used for luggage, wallets, and handbags.

**SHEEPSHEAD** is a lightly-nibbling common fish along Florida's West Coast. It tends to inhale bait and must be given time to nibble its way to the hook. It is good eating and weighs one or two pounds.

**TARPON** are a most popular and exciting fish to catch. Tarpon are acrobats and have an uncanny knack for shaking free of hooks. They are widespread along the Gulf Coast and in the Keys. The average tarpon weighs 68 pounds and the species is not considered edible. They are valued more for the sport than the palate, and tarpon "round-ups" (or "rodeos") are held in Florida and in other Gulf states.

**WAHOO** is a spunky fish rarely hooked in Florida waters. Its average weight is 15 to 20 pounds, and like its smaller cousin, the king mackerel, the wahoo's food value is good. It is a popular trophy fish.

## SALTWATER FOOD FISH

**BLUEFISH** are strong, swift fish that migrate along the Atlantic coast. Excellent eating, bluefish are most commonly caught from mid-December to May. The species is voracious while schooling and will bite anything.

**CREVELLE** is a close relative to the blue runner and pompano. It is good eating, and is most common during winter months. The fish is most abundant on Florida's west coast. Anglers catch this fish by trolling. Average weight is about a pound.

**GROUPER** is one of the largest, most widely distributed fish families in the world. Largest member of the family, the Jewfish, can weigh up to 600 pounds.

There are a number of grouper species including the Black, Yellow, Nassau, Rockhind, Gag, Rock, and Red. All are fine food, but the red is the most abundant and the most commercially important. All are found on the Gulf Coast but can be caught along the state's entire coastline. They are found mostly on offshore banks and reefs, usually near a rock bottom.

Red groupers are solitary fish and seldom school. They are caught throughout the year and, when fully grown, will weigh as much as 50 pounds.

**KINGFISH (KING MACKEREL)** is a large relative of the Spanish Mackerel and ranks as a top game fish. It is slightly less desirable than its smaller cousin for eating. Kings are most common in February and March where they are caught along both Florida coasts. The fish is a fighter and may leap 10 or more feet out of the water when hooked. Drifting over a reef using live shrimp bait is a successful way to catch king.

**LISA,** more commonly called mullet, is one of the important food fish of the South. Only menhaden and shrimp exceed catch of mullet. It has firm, tender flesh with a mild flavor. Its roe is also eaten.

Lisa (a name coined by marketers) frequent coastal waters near brackish river mouths and may be found in freshwater. There are about 100 species of Lisa, but the striped or jumping is the most abundant. White Lisa is taken in just a few locales such as the Keys.

Most often netted, Lisa or mullet are easily spotted because they jump. Best catches are from April through November with heaviest runs in September.

**POMPANO** is a choice food fish. Height of the season is from January to April, but the supply is dwindling. Pompano is a thin fish with a forked tail and is dark blue at the top, shading to bright silver on the sides. The average market size is about 24 ounces. They are found in all Florida coastal waters in areas with sandy bottoms near the shore, or in channels near flats. Anglers report success with yellow feather jigs that are bumped rapidly on the bottom or under bridges or docks. Light tackle can be used, but be ready for a fight.

**SNAPPER** include several species, all available in Gulf waters but rarely found on the Atlantic coast. Red, Yellowtail, Gray, Cubera, Dog, Schoolmaster, Mangrove, Mutton, and Vermillion are a few. Snapper is one of the most widely known of all fishes and lives offshore in rock gullies. Small specimens come close to shore. They are excellent food fish and average 5 to 10 pounds. Red snapper usually are caught in deep water with heavy rods or handlines, using cut mullet or small fish for bait.

**SNOOK,** also called the robalo or sergeant fish, is common along the southwest Florida coast. It is a good food fish. Average size is 3 to 5 pounds. Snook are found in a variety of waters and can be caught from bridges, from a boat in an inlet, or close to shore. They can be found in brackish and fresh waters. Shrimp, dead or alive, and strip-cut mullet make good bait.

**SPANISH MACKEREL** is a schooling, migrating fish found along the entire coast of Florida where it feeds on smaller fish and squid. It is a good, sporty food fish most often caught between October and March.

**TROUT,** or sea trout, belong to the croaker family and are related to the spots and drums. The Spotted sea trout, the most important of the group, is an excellent game and food fish. This fish remains in shallow waters throughout the year. Larger trout travel in large schools and swim low in the water. When close to shore, they usually come in with the tide. Trout like grass beds, sand patches, and mud flats, and are found around bays and inland waters, sometimes in the ocean.

Fishermen usually anchor, but drifting often gets results. Bait may be live shrimp, spoons, or jigs. The Gray sea trout is relatively scarce in Florida waters, occurring occasionally in the Gulf. The White or Sand trout is found only in the Gulf and is a good pan fish, about 11 to 15 inches.

## OTHER MAJOR MARINE SPECIES
### Poisonous Species
**JELLYFISH** are blobby floating creatures that periodically invade Florida's waters. Two common jellyfish varieties are the Moon Jelly and the Lion's Mane. A third, potentially dangerous type is the Portuguese man-of-war, found most often on the Atlantic coast. It floats along, its presence revealed only by a bluish air bladder that acts as a sail. Under-water, the man-of-war trails tentacle-like streamers that may be 40 feet long. These tentacles contain sensors that signal if a fish (or human) is nearby, and the tentacles literally shoot a microscopic thread that contains nerve poison.

The poison paralyzes the man-of-war's fish dinner, but usually does no more to humans than zap them with a hefty sting. Of course, some people are allergic to the toxin and, as with a bee sting, can develop complications. A chief predator of the man-of-war is the loggerhead turtle, whose tough skin and beak protect it from man-of-war toxin.

The Moon Jellyfish is whitish-clear and can inflict a tingling sting if encountered, while the pinkish-colored Lion's Mane is rarely potent enough to be of concern.

Jellyfish venom, say scientists, is protein-based and stings can quickly be relieved by use of chemicals such as ammonia or meat tenderizing powder that break down proteins. Beachwalkers should beware of stepping on them, however, since the venom remains in the tentacles even after the jellyfish are dead.

**STINGRAYS** are dangerous residents of Florida's coastal waters. Marine biologists estimate that some 1,500 people are injured by stingrays each year in the U.S., most occurring in summer when rays invade shallow waters for breeding. It usually burrows in sand or mud with only its eyes and tail exposed and is difficult to see. A serrated barb on the ray's tail contains a poison that produces a painful sting if a bather steps on it.

Stingrays are actually docile and their inflicted injuries on people are usually accidental. However, the stings can produce symptoms such as low blood pressure, rapid heartbeat, vomiting, diarrhea, and sweating. Fatalities are rare, but medical treatment should be sought immediately.

Emergency treatment should include washing the wound site with saltwater and removing the barb if it remains in the skin. Hot water for 30 to 90 minutes also reduces the pain. Swimmers and beachwalkers can lessen the risk of stepping on a stingray if they shuffle their feet as they wade. This will dislodge the ray. Fishermen catching stingrays on their lines are advised to cut the lines immediately, keeping a safe distance from the ray's whipping tail. Never attempt to bring one into a boat, live or dead.

The most common ray in Florida waters is the Southern stingray, which reaches a width of five feet and a length of about seven feet.

### Shellfish

Shellfish found in Florida waters consist of several varieties of crustaceans and mollusks. Pollution has blighted some of the ocean beds where these creatures live. Among the varieties inhabiting Florida waters are:

**BLUE CRAB,** a blue-colored crustacean found all along the Gulf Coast and the South Atlantic. It prefers brackish waters. One time-tested method for snaring these crabs is to lower a string to which a bread ball or a chunk of chicken has been attached. In shallow water, a crab will likely give the string a tug. Pull the string (and crab) up evenly and gently so the crab doesn't let go. Dump the catch in a bucket of salty water. Eat by boiling as soon as possible.

**SOFT-SHELLED CRAB** is actually a blue crab that is growing a new shell. The popular King and Dungeness crabs are not found in Florida's warm waters.

**CLAMS** in Florida are edible just as those are up north. Quahogs can be found buried in coastal mud or sand.

When hunting the clam, look for them in shallow water and at low tide along sandbars. Discard any clam that does not close when picked up. One that does not open after being steamed also should be discarded. When opening a clam, use a thin, sharp knife and place it between the shell half, cutting around the clam and twisting to pry open the shell. Then cut muscles from the two shell halves. Boiling in water about 10 minutes usually will open shells.

**CONCHS,** pronounced "konks," are found in the Keys and are among the largest in North America. The animal inside the conch shell retreats inside when approached. It can be removed by cutting the pointed end of the shell and inserting a knife. After removing, the conch must be skinned before cooking.

**COQUINA** are pretty, tiny shells found along Florida beaches and are related to oysters and clams. There is a tiny animal inside the kernel-sized shells which, if boiled in enough quantity, produces a tasty chowder broth. It is nearly impossible to rinse all the sand from coquina shells, and many people dislike coquina chowder's grit.

**LOBSTER,** Florida-style, is a cousin of the more famous Maine lobster, and is smaller, usually one to two pounds. It also lacks meat in the claw. Popularity of this tasty crawfish has led to lobster season changes, so local game and fish officials should be contacted to make sure lobster beds are open.

**OYSTER** beds once surrounded Florida on a vast scale, but habitat destruction and pollution have narrowed the commercial harvest to the Apalachicola region of the Gulf Coast. Some oyster lovers contend that summer oysters are less tasty than those harvested in cooler months, and any oysters that are open when gathered should be discarded.

**SCALLOPS** are found in shallow bays and inland waters, especially in July and August. They are feisty little mollusks and will swim away from pursuers by opening and closing their shells. The muscle is the desired edible bit of the scallop. Bay scallops are smaller than Deep Sea scallops, which are found in deeper, colder waters. It is easy to shuck a scallop by prying the shell open with a knife, cutting the pinkish muscle out, and storing it in a tub of salt water.

**SHRIMP** are probably the most popular shellfish and among the easiest to catch. Armed with a net and a light (shrimp are nocturnal), wade out to waters where shrimp school. They are constantly moving. Florida's shrimp are either pink or white. If overcooked, shrimp will be either rubbery or will have a mealy texture. The best cooking time is about five minutes in either beer or herbal-seasoned water.

**STONE CRABS** are rock-hard and have one large and one small claw. They can be found along rocks near beaches and inland waters. The usual method of taking stone crabs is a long-handled pole that has a wire hook on the end. Stone crab catches are restricted and no females may be taken. Some enthusiasts keep the meaty large claw and return the crab to the water to grow a new claw.

### Whales Along the Coasts

Anyone venturing into the deep waters some 125 miles off the Florida coasts has the chance of seeing any of a dozen whale species known to travel past the state. Unfortunately, most of these creatures go unseen unless they have stranded themselves on coastal or island beaches. Because studying whales is a difficult and often expensive scientific undertaking, not much is known about the habits of some species. But all whales, being warm-blooded mammals, give live birth, usually not more than every two years, to single young called calves.

The following whale species seen off Florida's coasts are listed as endangered by Florida's Fish and Wildlife Conservation Commission and the federal government:

• **The great sperm whale** is a giant. Males can grow to 62 feet long and weigh 35 to 51 tons. Females are usually 38 feet long and 38 tons in weight. Females give birth to one 11-to-14-foot calf after 16 months of gestation. The species eats primarily squid, shark, octopus, and seals.

• **The right whale** lacks a dorsal fin. It is a baleen whale, that is, the whale's mouth contains not teeth but horn-like material that filters tiny plankton from seawater. Up to 50 feet long and 50 feet in circumference, this species has been heavily hunted. A single calf is born after a year's gestation.

• **Humpbacked whales** average about 40 feet long with 30 tons of heft. This baleen whale is named for a triangular, fin-like bump on its back. Single calves are born after 11 months of gestation. One of the most studied whales, it is admired for its playfulness, rowdy mating games, and singing.

• **The fin whale** is an aerodynamic baleen whale that swims about 25 miles per hour. Usually 65 to 80 feet long, the species can weigh 80 tons. Calves, up to 21 feet long, are born after the whales have come south to winter. It is also called the finbacked whale.

• **The sei whale,** sometimes called the sardine whale, resembles the fin whale but is smaller. The species skims the water's surface for tiny sea creatures to eat and tends to prefer temperate climes. Its name is properly pronounced "say" whale.

Other whale and dolphin species have been found beached along Florida's coastline, including rarely seen pygmy sperm and dwarf sperm whales.

The spectacular killer whales, now popular performance animals, are actually large dolphins. Their name is deserved, as they are adept hunters of seal, tuna, penguin, sea otter, walrus, and an occasional great white shark.

Pilot whales, another member of the dolphin family, are among the most numerous of the reported strandings. An encounter with killer whales can panic a herd of pilot whales into beaching themselves, but scientists believe most beachings are due to parasite infestations.

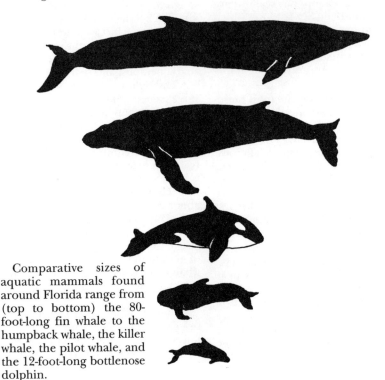

Comparative sizes of aquatic mammals found around Florida range from (top to bottom) the 80-foot-long fin whale to the humpback whale, the killer whale, the pilot whale, and the 12-foot-long bottlenose dolphin.

## CORAL REEFS

Florida's spectacular living coral reefs stretch south from Miami to the Dry Tortugas, 65 miles west of Key West. Visitors may see coral reefs first-hand by visiting Biscayne National Park, John Pennekamp Coral Reef State Park, or the Looe Key and Key Largo Marine Sanctuaries. Though reefs appear to be nothing more than rocky fish refuges, they are living creatures that support an amazing array of sea life. Florida's coral reefs are the only true coral reefs in U.S. continental waters.

Stony corals are hard-plated layers of calcium carbonate that is secreted by the coral polyp, a living animal that is a member of the jellyfish and sea anemone family. A reef is formed as the coral forms large colonies welded together by chemicals and sea algae. Coral colors range from whitish cream to green and brown.

Coral reefs support a wide assortment of other sea creatures. Spotted, striped, and peacock-hued fish varieties include the Blue Tang, Parrotfish, French Angels, Triggerfish, and Damselfishes, in all, more than 150 species of tropical fish.

(continued on next page)

Other, less recognizable species found in and around the coral reefs are sea anemones, colorful marine worms and mollusks, starfish, sponges, fans, and sea plumes. Turtles, shrimp, conchs, and octopus also frequent the reefs.

Scientists are growing increasingly concerned that the state's coral reefs are rapidly declining. Many species are displaying tumors, black band disease, and bleached patches where the coral polyps have died. A virus has begun to attack the reefs and no way has been determined to stop it.

The coral has a few natural enemies, such as fish or worms that nibble away at the polyps. Also responsible for reef destruction are recreational scuba divers. More than a half million swimmers, snorkelers, and scuba enthusiasts visit Florida's state reefs each year. With them come boat propellers, anchors, fishing, and diving gear. The sheer numbers of people who prop to rest or to take photographs on the coral kill the delicate creatures. Pollution from the burgeoning Keys with their gallons of poorly treated sewage, tons of garbage, and the petroleum contamination from the area's hundreds of boats continue to threaten the reef environment. Coral preservation was a major consideration in Florida's declaring a moratorium on offshore oil drilling. However, the 20-year-old ban was successfully challenged in court in 1996 and the state lifted it. But no drilling has taken place, and the state has taken other legal and political means to prevent it.

Should the coral reefs die, it would spell the end of an entire Florida ecosystem.

## ENDANGERED SPECIES

The Florida animals in this list are either Endangered (E), Threatened (T), or are a Species of Special Concern (SSC) because of declining numbers, as determined by the Florida Fish and Wildlife Conservation Commission. Species that are listed on both the commission's list and the list of the U.S. Fish and Wildlife Service are indicated with an asterisk.

### MAMMALS

Right whale . . . . . . . . . . . . . . . . .E*
Sei whale . . . . . . . . . . . . . . . . . .E*
Finback whale . . . . . . . . . . . . . . .E*
Florida mastiff bat . . . . . . . . . . . . .E*
Florida panther . . . . . . . . . . . . . . .E*
Humpback whale . . . . . . . . . . . . .E*
Gray bat . . . . . . . . . . . . . . . . . . .E*
Indiana bat . . . . . . . . . . . . . . . . .E*
Key deer; toy deer . . . . . . . . . . . . .E*
Key Largo cotton mouse . . . . . . . .E*
Key Largo woodrat . . . . . . . . . . . .E*

Duke's saltmarsh vole . . . . . . . . . .E*
Anastasia Island beach mouse . . .E*
Choctawhatchee beach mouse . . .E*
Perdido Key beach mouse . . . . . .E*
Sperm whale . . . . . . . . . . . . . . . .E*
West Indian manatee . . . . . . . . . .E*
Lower Keys marsh rabbit . . . . . . .E*
Silver rice rat . . . . . . . . . . . . . . . .E*
St. Andrews beach mouse . . . . . . .E
Southeastern beach mouse . . . . . .E*
Big Cypress fox squirrel . . . . . . . .T
Everglades mink . . . . . . . . . . . . . .T
Sherman's Short-tailed shrew . .SSC
Sanibel Island rice rat . . . . . . . .SSC
Florida mouse . . . . . . . . . . . . . .SSC
Sherman's fox squirrel . . . . . . .SSC
Homosassa shrew . . . . . . . . . . .SSC
Eastern chipmunk . . . . . . . . . .SSC

### BIRDS

Cape Sable seaside sparrow . . . .E*
Florida grasshopper sparrow . . . .E*
Ivory-billed woodpecker . . . . . . .E*
Kirtland's warbler . . . . . . . . . . . .E*
Wood stork . . . . . . . . . . . . . . . .E*

Snail kite . . . . . . . . . . . . . . . . . . . .E*
Bachman's warbler . . . . . . . . . . . .E*
Arctic peregrine falcon . . . . . . . . .E
Piping plover . . . . . . . . . . . . . . .T*
Bald eagle . . . . . . . . . . . . . . . . . .T
Red-cockaded woodpecker . . . . . .T
Florida scrub jay . . . . . . . . . . . . . .T*
Crested caracara . . . . . . . . . . . . . .T*
Roseate tern . . . . . . . . . . . . . . . . .T*
Southeastern snowy plover . . . . . .T
White-crowned pigeon . . . . . . . . .T
Southeastern kestrel . . . . . . . . . . .T
Florida sandhill crane . . . . . . . . . .T
Least tern . . . . . . . . . . . . . . . . . . .T
Whooping Crane . . . . . . . . . . . .SSC
Black skimmer . . . . . . . . . . . . . .SSC
Roseate spoonbill . . . . . . . . . . .SSC
Wakulla seaside sparrow . . . . . .SSC
Scott's seaside sparrow . . . . . . .SSC
Limpkin . . . . . . . . . . . . . . . . . .SSC
Burrowing owl . . . . . . . . . . . . .SSC
Worthington's marsh wren . . . .SSC
Marian's marsh wren . . . . . . . .SSC
Little blue heron . . . . . . . . . . . .SSC
Reddish egret . . . . . . . . . . . . . .SSC
Snowy egret . . . . . . . . . . . . . . . .SSC
Tricolored heron . . . . . . . . . . . .SSC
American oystercatcher . . . . . .SSC
Brown pelican . . . . . . . . . . . . . .SSC
Osprey . . . . . . . . . . . . . . . . . . . .SSC
White ibis . . . . . . . . . . . . . . . . .SSC

**FISH**

Shortnose sturgeon . . . . . . . . . . . .E*
Okaloosa darter . . . . . . . . . . . . . .E*
Blackmouth shiner . . . . . . . . . . . .E
Crystal darter . . . . . . . . . . . . . . .T
Key silverside . . . . . . . . . . . . . . .T
Atlantic sturgeon . . . . . . . . . . .SSC
Common snook . . . . . . . . . . . .SSC
Lake Eustis pupfish . . . . . . . . . .SSC
Harlequin darter . . . . . . . . . . . .SSC
Southern tessellated darter . . . .SSC
Saltmarsh topminnow . . . . . . . .SSC
Suwannee bass . . . . . . . . . . . . .SSC
Shoal bass; Chipola bass . . . . . .SSC
Bluenose shiner . . . . . . . . . . . .SSC

Mangrove rivulus . . . . . . . . . . .SSC
Key blenny . . . . . . . . . . . . . . .SSC

**AMPHIBIANS AND REPTILES**

Atlantic green turtle . . . . . . . . . .E*
American crocodile . . . . . . . . . .E*
Leatherback turtle . . . . . . . . . . .E*
Atlantic hawksbill turtle . . . . . . .E*
Atlantic ridley turtle . . . . . . . . . .E*
Striped mud turtle
(lower Fla. Keys) . . . . . . . . . . . . .E
Atlantic loggerhead turtle . . . . .T*
Eastern indigo snake . . . . . . . . .T
Atlantic salt marsh snake . . . . . .T*
Blue-tailed mole skink . . . . . . . .T*
Sand skink . . . . . . . . . . . . . . . . .T*
Big Pine Key ringneck snake . . . .T
Short-tailed snake . . . . . . . . . . . .T
Miami black-headed snake;
rimrock crowned snake . . . . . . . .T
Florida brown snake (Keys only) .T
Florida ribbon snake (Keys only) .T
American alligator . . . . . . . . . .SSC
Alligator snapping turtle . . . . .SSC
Suwannee cooter . . . . . . . . . . .SSC
Red rat snake; corn snake
(Keys only) . . . . . . . . . . . . . . .SSC
Florida Keys mole skink . . . . . .SSC
Gopher turtle . . . . . . . . . . . . . .SSC
Barbour's map turtle . . . . . . . .SSC
Georgia blind salamander . . . .SSC
Pine Barrens treefrog . . . . . . . .SSC
Florida pine snake . . . . . . . . . .SSC
Dusky gopher frog . . . . . . . . . .SSC
Florida gopher frog . . . . . . . . .SSC
Bog frog . . . . . . . . . . . . . . . . . .SSC

**INVERTEBRATES**

Schaus' swallowtail butterfly . . . . .E*
Pillar coral . . . . . . . . . . . . . . . . . .E
Stock Island tree snail . . . . . . . . . .E
Florida cave shrimp . . . . . . . . . . .T
Florida tree snail . . . . . . . . . . . .SSC
Econfina crayfish . . . . . . . . . . . .SSC
Sims Sink crayfish . . . . . . . . . . .SSC
Black Creek crayfish . . . . . . . . .SSC

---

## REPORT DEAD BIRDS

Birds are occasionally killed when they encounter toxic pesticides. If you find a number of dead birds in a single locale, report it to the local Florida Fish and Wildlife Conservation Commission office.

## WILDLIFE ALERT

Citizens witnessing violations of Florida's wildlife laws are urged to call "Wildlife Alert," a toll-free number to the Florida Fish and Wildlife Conservation Commission. Investigators are sent to the scene, and if an arrest is made, the caller is eligible for a cash reward ranging from $25 to $1,000.

The reward program was established in 1980 as the commission's way for private citizens to assist state wildlife officers in law enforcement. Reward money comes not from tax funds but from donations by conservation-minded organizations and individuals. In addition, convicted wildlife violators often are ordered by judges to contribute to the "Wildlife Alert" fund as part of their punishment.

Most rewards are given in connection with fishing and hunting regulations, with the largest money awarded those callers who give information leading to arrests of persons killing or harming the state's endangered species.

Citizens witnessing violations are asked to obtain, if possible, names, addresses, descriptions of persons and vehicles involved, and location. Toll-free numbers to call are:

| | |
|---|---|
| Lakeland | 1-800-282-8002 |
| West Palm Beach | 1-800-432-2046 |
| Panama City | 1-800-342-1676 |
| Ocala | 1-800-342-9620 |
| Lake City | 1-800-342-8105 |

## EXOTIC WILDLIFE

Florida's wildlife systems constantly change. Just as some species dwindle, others appear—either by migrating or through accidental or deliberate introduction. Climate, particularly in south Florida, provides for bountiful breeding of the exotics.

Scientists are growing concerned that exotic species will replace Florida's native species by out-breeding and out-competing native species for the available habitat and food. In addition, predators that control native species often dislike the exotics, so the new arrivals thrive while the predators go hungry.

Laws attempt to control importation and selling of exotic species in Florida, but no agency has the sole responsibility of monitoring the state's wild exotic populations. Moreover, say some biologists, such monitoring would be difficult because deciding precisely which species are native or exotic has just begun.

Scientists do know, however, that some animals imported to Florida from foreign countries are affecting the state's traditional species.

Some 23 non-native bird species thrive mostly in south Florida. Colorful and attractive, the birds delight watchers, but biologists consider the newcomers as biological pollution. So far, not much data has recorded damage caused by exotic birds such as the Spot-breasted Oriole and the Blue-gray Tanager, but some, such as the Monk Parakeet, are known fruit crop destroyers in their homelands.

The ecological or financial impact of some other imports are not yet known, but they are decidedly unwanted. The giant "Bufo" toad, popular in the pet trade, is but one of 25 species of frogs, lizards, and snakes estimated to now inhabit Florida. These large toads can poison domestic dogs.

*(continued on next page)*

*(continued from previous page)*

During the 1970s, wildlife officers near Miami captured individual specimens of Siamese, Egyptian, and Ceylonese cobras thought to have been purposely released by a religious sect.

Undesirable fish species also have easily found their way into Florida waters. They range from unwanted aquarium fish that are released by homeowners, to fish farm escapees, to species that were released to control some other unwanted biological pest.

The walking catfish strolled away from a Broward County fish farm in the 1960s and now inhabits most of south Florida's freshwater bodies. Fish farmers erect fences to prevent these catfish from preying on aquarium species.

The Spotted Tilapia, a West African fish, is presumed to have escaped from a Miami-Dade County fish farm in the 1970s. Since then, it has aggressively overtaken native fish and some studies have found some canals contain few fish species other than Spotted Tilapia.

Exotic mammals have not presented as great a problem and their presence appears to be benignly tolerated. Two colonies of Rhesus monkeys at Ocala's Silver Springs are popular residents whose threatened removal prompted citizen protest. Jaguarundi and ocelots are so shy as to be seldom noticed. Armadillos are firmly entrenched with virtually no predators.

But exotics cost money to control. The Giant African Snail, released by a North Miami resident in 1966, reproduced rapidly and soon began consuming shrubs and trees. The snails soon demanded attention when they began eating paint off stucco buildings, probably in a search for needed calcium. After two eradication programs finally seemed to work, the bill tallied nearly $650,000.00.

Wildlife officials see no end to the constant battle of incoming exotic species. Current quarantine procedures catch only an estimated 10 percent of the unwanted creatures.

## HUNTING FEES AND REGULATIONS

For the purpose of hunting in Florida, a resident is a person who has lived continuously in Florida for six months, or filed domicile papers with the county court clerk. Active military personnel stationed in Florida and full-time students in a Florida school are considered residents when purchasing a Hunting License Stamp or permit stamps.

To increase hunting safety in Florida, the state requires that any hunters born on or after June 1,1975, complete a hunter safety course before they may hunt with a firearm, bow, or crossbow. Exempt from this law are persons hunting in their county of residence, on their homestead or the homestead of their spouse or minor child, or any minor child hunting on the homestead of his or her parent.

Firearm-related hunting accidents over the past decade have totaled more than 300, 60 of them fatalities. The latest annual report revealed that in the 1996-97 season, 21 accidents occurred, four of them fatal.

### Licensing/Stamps

A Hunting License Stamp, or a Sportsman's License Stamp, is required of anyone hunting furbearing animals.

To trap furbearing animals a person must have a Trapping License Stamp.

An Archery Stamp is required in addition to a Hunting License Stamp if one wishes to participate in archery season, although such a stamp is not required for Sportsman's License holders.

For a person participating in a muzzleloading gun season, a Muzzleloading Gun Stamp is required unless that person already holds a Sportsman's License.

To hunt waterfowl, hunters must purchase a federal Migratory Bird Hunting and Conservation Stamp and a Florida Waterfowl Stamp, in addition to a Hunting License Stamp. The Florida Waterfowl Stamp is not required for Sportsman's License holders, but the federal stamp is.

For turkey hunters, a Florida Turkey Stamp must be purchased, in addition to a Hunting License Stamp, unless the hunter already has purchased a Sportsman's License.

All the above stamps, except federal waterfowl stamps, may be purchased from a county tax collector or their subagents. Subagents may charge an addition $.50 fee. Subagents are primarily hunting and fishing equipment retailers. The federal stamps are available at U.S. post offices.

Persons hunting in their county of residence, on their homestead, are not required to have a Hunting License Stamp, Turkey Stamp, Archery Stamp, Muzzleloading Stamp, or Florida Waterfowl Stamp. Nor are residents 65 years of age or more who possess a Resident Senior Citizen Hunting and Fishing Certificate. The stamps also are not required of totally and permanently disabled persons who have bought a Florida Resident Disabled Person Hunting and Fishing License, nor do children under age 16 need to purchase the stamps.

### License Costs, annual

Florida Sportsman's
License . . . . . . . . . . . . . .$ 67.50*
Statewide Hunting . . . . . .$ 12.50
Statewide Hunting/
Fishing . . . . . . . . . . . . . .$ 23.50

Non-Resident State
Hunting . . . . . . . . . . . . .$151.50**
Non-Resident 10-Day . .$ 26.50*/**
Wildlife Management
Area Stamp . . . . . . . . . . .$ 25.00
Archery Stamp . . . . . . . .$ 5.00
Muzzleloading Gun Stamp $ 5.00
Florida Waterfowl Stamp .$ 3.00
Florida Turkey Stamp . . . .$ 5.00
Resident Senior Citizen
Certificate . . . . . . . . . .No charge**
Resident Disabled Person
Certificate . . . . . . . . . .No charge
*Florida Sportsman's License does not include the Saltwater Fishing License, Federal Duck Stamp, Trapping License, or other Commercial licenses. It does include Statewide Hunting, Statewide Freshwater Fishing, Type I Wildlife Management Area Stamp, Archery Stamp, Muzzleloading Gun Stamp, Turkey Stamp, and Florida Waterfowl Stamp.
**Also available to Georgia residents with a Georgia Honorary Certificate.

### Lifetime Sportsman's License

The state now issues an all-inclusive Sportsman License, as well as a lifetime license and a five-year license to Floridians for hunting and fishing, both saltwater and freshwater.

This license is good for a sportsman's lifetime and includes hunting, fresh- and saltwater fishing, wildlife areas, archery, muzzleloading gun, turkey, Florida waterfowl, snook, and crawfish. Costs are:

| Age | Fee |
|---|---|
| 4 years or younger . . . . .$ | 401.50 |
| 5 to 12 years old . . . . . .$ | 701.50 |
| 13 to 63 years old . . . . .$ | 1,001.50 |
| 64 years or older . . . . . .$ | 13.50 |

### Lifetime License

A lifetime license for hunting includes stamps for Wildlife Management Area, archery, muzzleloading gun, turkey, and Florida waterfowl.

| Age | Fee |
|---|---|
| 4 years or younger . . . . .$ | 201.50 |
| 5 to 12 years . . . . . . . . .$ | 351.50 |
| 13 years or older . . . . . .$ | 501.50 |

## TRESPASS

A Florida hunting license does not authorize trespass. Landowner permission must be obtained before entering private land. Trespass while in possession of a firearm is punishable by imprisonment for up to five years and/or a fine up to $5,000.00.

## LEGAL METHODS OF TAKING GAMES

For taking resident game birds and mammals: Rifles, shotguns, pistols, and birds of prey (falcons, owls, and hawks) may be used. Longbows, compound bows, recurved bows, and crossbows must have a minimum draw weight of 35 pounds. Hand-held releases may be used. Broadheads must have two sharpened edges with a minimum width of 7/8 inch.

For hunting deer: Muzzleloading guns firing a single bullet must be at least .40 caliber. Those firing two or more balls must be 20-gauge or larger.

For taking migratory game birds: Shotguns (not larger than 10-gauge and plugged to a three-shell capacity with a filler, which cannot be removed without disassembling the gun), birds of prey, and bows may be used.

All other methods and equipment are prohibited.

### Florida Wildlife Harvest Data State Management Areas (1998-99 Hunting Season)

| | |
|---|---:|
| Deer | 3,951 |
| Hog | 2,656 |
| Duck | 6,238 |
| Dove | 2,000 |
| Snipe | 2,144 |
| Quail | 2,837 |
| Rabbit | 291 |
| Squirrel | 9,714 |
| Bobcat | 7 |
| Raccoon | 68 |
| Turkey | 754 |
| Woodcock | 18 |

### Bag Limits

| | Daily | Season limit | Possession |
|---|---|---|---|
| Deer (antlered) | 2 | None | 4 |
| Deer (antlerless) | 2 | Permit | 4 |
| Deer (antlerless-archery season) | 2 | None | 4 |
| Deer (antlerless-season) | 1 | 2 | 2 |
| Wild Hog | 1 | None | 2 |
| Turkey (fall season) | 1 | 2 | 2 |
| Turkey (spring season) | 1 | 2 | 2 |
| Quail | 12 | None | 24 |
| Gray Squirrel | 12 | None | 24 |
| Rabbit | 12 | None | 24 |

Raccoon, Opossum, Coyote, Nutria, Skunk, Beaver: No bag or possession limit.

Florida law prohibits hunters from shooting wildlife from rights-of-way along paved or graded roads. Penalty for violation is a $500 fine and/or 60 days in jail. It is also illegal to release dogs on road rights-of-way so that they may chase game across private property.

### Licenses via Phone

Florida hunting and fishing licenses may be obtained from anywhere in the U.S. and Canada by telephone with a credit card. A valid temporary license number is issued immediately over the phone and a hard copy will follow. There is an addition $3.95 "convenience" charge for the service which is available toll-free at 1-888-486-8356 (hunting) or at 1-888-347-4356 (fishing).

## FRESHWATER FISHING FEES AND REGULATIONS

A freshwater fishing license stamp is required for all residents between 16 and 65 years of age, and all non-residents of 16 or more years of age, to fish by any method, including cane poles.

Defined as a resident is a person who has lived in Florida for six continuous months, or who has signed a domicile certificate at the court clerk's office.

Military personnel who are home on leave in Florida for 30 days or less may sport fish without a fishing license.

The state's "cane pole law" permits a resident to fish in the county of residence without a license, but he must buy a license if cane pole fishing in a Fish Management Area.

Game fish as defined by the state include but are not limited to black bass, black crappie, bluegill, redear sunfish, warmouth, redbreast sunfish, spotted sunfish, chain pickerel, redfin pickerel, peacock bass, white bass, striped bass, and sunshine bass.

Non-game fish include bowfin, common carp, catfish, eels, gar, shad, shiners, tilapia, killifish, suckers, top-minnows, and fishes not listed as freshwater game fish and not taken for sport.

### License Costs

Resident Fishing/Hunting  . .$23.50
Resident 12-Month Fishing  . .$13.50
Sportsman's License  . . . . . . .$67.50
Non-Resident
12-Month Fishing  . . . . . . . .$31.50
Non-Resident 7-Day Fishing  .$16.50
Resident Senior Citizen
Certificate  . . . . . . . . . . .No charge*
Resident Disabled Person
Certificate  . . . . . . . . . . . .No charge
*Includes Georgia residents holding Georgia honorary certificate. All holding Georgia fishing licenses can fish in Florida's St. Mary's River and Lake Seminole.*

Sportsman's License includes all resident hunting and fishing licenses and stamps, except a few special stamps. In addition to fees above, tax collectors and authorized agents selling licenses are entitled to a $.50 to $1.00 surcharge.

The state now issues an all-inclusive sportsman license, as well as lifetime and five-year licenses to Florida residents for hunting and fishing, both saltwater and freshwater.

### Lifetime Sportsman's License

This license is good for a sportsman's lifetime and includes hunting, fresh- and saltwater fishing, wildlife areas, archery, muzzleloading gun, turkey, Florida waterfowl, snook, and crawfish. Costs are

| Age | Fee | |
|---|---|---|
| 4 years or younger  . . . .$ | 401.50 |
| 5 to 12 years  . . . . . . . .$ | 701.50 |
| 13 to 63 years  . . . . . . .$ | 1,001.50 |

### Lifetime Freshwater or Saltwater Fishing License

| Age | Fee | |
|---|---|---|
| 4 years or younger  . . . .$ | 126.50 |
| 5 to 12 years  . . . . . . . .$ | 226.50 |
| 13 years or older . . . . . .$ | 301.50 |

A five-year freshwater or saltwater fishing license costs $61.50. The five-year saltwater license does not include snook, crawfish, or tarpon.

## Bag Limits

• 5 Black Bass (largemouth, Suwannee, redeye, spotted, and shoal basses individually or total), of which only one may be 22 inches or longer in total length

• 20 striped bass, white bass, and sunshine bass (individually or in total), of which no more than six may exceed 24 inches in total length

• 15 Chain pickerel

• 50 panfish (for example: bluegill, speckled perch, shellcracker, spotted sunfish, warmouth and redfin pickerel individually or in total)

• 2 Butterfly peacock bass, only one of which may be longer than 17 inches in total length

• 0 Speckled peacock bass. Immediately release unharmed all speckled peacock bass

*Total possession limit for the above fish is two days' bag limit.*

## Commercial Licenses
### (excluding issuing fees)

| | |
|---|---|
| Resident Commercial . . . .$ | 25.00 |
| Resident Freshwater Fish Dealer . . . . . . . . . . . . . . .$ | 40.00 |
| Non-Resident Commercial Fishing . . . . . . . . . . . . . .$ | 100.00 |
| Non-Resident Retail Fish Dealer . . . . . . . . . . . . . . .$ | 100.00 |
| Non-Resident Wholesale Fish Dealer . . . . . . . . . . .$ | 100.00 |
| Non-Resident Fish Buyer .$ | 50.00 |

Resident Commercial fishing license stamps are issued by the county tax collector; all other commercial fishing licenses are issued only by the Florida Fish and Wildlife Conservation Commission.

## FLORIDA RECORD FRESHWATER FISH CATCHES
### (As of October 1998)

| Species | Weight | Place | Year |
|---|---|---|---|
| Bass, largemouth | 17 lb. 4½ oz. | Polk County | 1986 |
| Bass, largemouth | 20 lb. 2 oz. | Pasco County | 1923* |
| Bass, redeye | 7 lb. 13¼ oz. | Apalachicola River | 1989 |
| Bass, spotted | 3 lb. 12 oz. | Apalachicola River | 1985 |
| Bass, striped | 42 lb. 4 oz. | Apalachicola River | 1993 |
| Bass, sunshine | 16 lb. 5 oz. | Lake Seminole | 1985 |
| Bass, Suwannee | 3 lb. 14¼ oz. | Suwannee River | 1985 |
| Bass, white | 4 lb. 11 oz. | Apalachicola River | 1982 |
| Bass, butterfly peacock | 9 lb. ¼ oz. | Miami-Dade County | 1993 |
| Black crappie | 3 lb. 8 oz. | Lake Talquin | 1992 |
| Bluegill | 2 lb. 15¼ oz. | Washington County | 1989 |
| Bowfin | 19 lb. | Lake Kissimmee | 1984 |
| Bullhead, brown | 5 lb. 11 oz. | Duval County | 1995 |
| Carp | 40 lb. 9 oz. | Apalachicola River | 1981* |
| Catfish, blue | 61 lb. 8 oz. | Escambia County | 1996 |
| Catfish, channel | 44 lb. 8 oz. | Lake County | 1985 |
| Catfish, flathead | 43 lb. 8 oz. | Apalachicola River | 1997 |
| Catfish, flathead | 57 lb. 8 oz. | Hillsborough River | 1975* |
| Catfish, white | 18 lb. 13 oz. | Withlacoochee River | 1991 |
| Flier | 1 lb. 4 oz. | Lake Iamonia | 1992 |
| Gar, alligator | 123 lb. | Choctawhatchee River | 1995 |
| Gar, Florida | 7 lb. | Oklawaha River | 1988 |
| Gar, longnose | 41 lb. | Sumter County | 1985 |
| Oscar | 2 lb. 5¼ oz. | Lake Okeechobee | 1994 |
| Pickerel, chain | 5 lb. 12 oz. | Holmes County | 1995 |

| Pickerel, chain | 8 lb. | Gadsden County | 1971* |
|---|---|---|---|
| Pickerel, redfin | 1 lb. 1 oz. | Bradford County | 1993 |
| Shad, American | 5 lb. 3 oz. | St. Johns River | 1990/92 |
| Sunfish, redbreast | 2 lb. 1¼ oz. | Suwannee River | 1988 |
| Sunfish, redear | 4 lb. 13¾ oz. | Jackson County | 1986 |
| Sunfish, spotted | 0 lb. 13¼ oz. | Suwannee River | 1984 |
| Warmouth | 2 lb. 7 oz. | Okaloosa County | 1985 |

*Not certified

## SALTWATER FISHING FEES AND REGULATIONS

Florida residents, non-residents, and recreational divers must have a saltwater fishing license to take fish in saltwater unless covered by one of the following exemptions:

—Any individual under 16 years of age;

—Any Florida resident fishing in saltwater from land or from a structure fixed to the land;

—Any individual fishing from a vessel issued a Vessel Saltwater Fishing License;

—Fishing aboard a vessel that has a valid saltwater products license;

—Any person 65 years of age or older who holds a valid Florida driver's license or Florida voter registration card;

—Any Florida resident who is a member of the Armed Forces while home on leave for 30 days or less, with valid orders in his or her possession;

—Any individual who has been accepted by the Florida Department of Health and Rehabilitation Services for developmental services;

—Any individual fishing from a licensed fishing pier;

—A Florida resident who is certified as totally and permanently disabled is entitled, without charge, to a permanent saltwater fishing license.

### License Costs, annual (excluding issuing fee)

| | |
|---|---|
| Resident annual license | $ 12.00 |
| Resident 10-Day | $ 10.00 |
| Non-Resident annual license | $ 30.00 |
| Non-Resident 7-Day | $ 15.00 |

| | |
|---|---|
| Charter boat owner (11 or more customers) | $ 800.00 |
| Charter boat owner (3 to 10 customers) | $ 400.00 |
| Charter boat owner (2 customers or less) | $ 200.00 |

The state now issues lifetime and five-year saltwater fishing licenses. For details, see freshwater license fees above.

In addition to the saltwater fishing license, any person required to have the license who takes or possesses snook or crawfish must have a snook or crawfish stamp affixed to the license. Each stamp costs $2.

A line of demarcation between salt and fresh water has been established in the rivers, streams, and bayous of the coastal regions. If planning to fish in these areas, inquire locally for the point beyond which a freshwater fishing license is required.

Florida's state waters consist of all waters within nine nautical miles of the shoreline in the Gulf of Mexico and three nautical miles of the shoreline in the Atlantic Ocean. For fisheries purposes, the federal waters are the waters 200 miles seaward of state waters.

Saltwater food fish not used must be returned to the water alive. No size limits on saltwater fish are stated with the exceptions of those listed below. Not permitted to be taken, injured, or killed are marine turtles, porpoise, manta rays, manatees, or coral. In addition, it is illegal to spearfish in Pennekamp Coral Reef State Park, Collier County, that part of Monroe County from Long Key north to the Miami-Dade County line, and in the immediate area of all public bathing beaches, commercial or public fishing piers, bridge catwalks, and jetties. It also is illegal to spearfish in fresh water or for freshwater fish in brackish water.

### Minimum Legal Lengths, Bag Limits

(Note—All fish measured from tip of nose to rear center of tail. Sizes and bag limits subject to change; check most current regulations. The following also apply only to coastal waters within three nautical miles of the east coast, and nine nautical miles of the west coast.)

| Species | Size Limit | Bag Limit |
|---|---|---|
| Amberjack | 28" | Three |
| Black drum | 14-24" | Five |
| Sea bass | 8" | None |
| Bluefish | 12" | Ten |
| Bonefish | 18" | One |
| Cobia | 33" | Two |
| Dolphin | None | Ten |
| Flounder | 11" | None |
| Grouper | 20" | Six |
| King mackerel | 12" | Two |
| Spanish mackerel | 12" | Ten |
| Black mullet | None | Fifty |
| Pompano | 10" | None |
| Redfish | 18-27" | One |
| Snapper | 13" | Two |
| Snook | 24-34" | Two |
| Sea trout | 14-24" | Ten |
| Tarpon | None | Two |

Although most of Florida's saltwater fish occur throughout the state's long coastline, fishing for any particular species may be better in one area than in another. Following is a brief listing of species often encountered in each area:

**Northeast Atlantic Coast**—Surf casting for redfish, blues, drum. Inside bays and inlets for trout, redfish, drum, bluefish, and tarpon.

**Central East Coast**—Trout; redfish in the surf and inshore; drum, tripletail, jack crevalle. Lower areas for sailfish and snook.

**Lower East Coast**—Sailfishing entire area but particularly off Stuart and Palm Beach. In Gulf Stream, sailfish, marlin, tuna, mako shark, dolphin. Along shoreline, snook, tarpon, blues, trout, and mackerel during runs.

**The Keys**—Upper Keys produce trout, redfish, snapper, and noted for bonefish. Area also good for permit, tarpon, grouper, amberjack, barracuda, and wahoo.

**Northwest Gulf Coast**—Red snapper, flounder, cobia, trout, blue runner, and grouper.

**Upper Gulf Coast**—Trout, redfish, flounder, grouper, tarpon in summer; mangrove snapper in fall; offshore runs of cobia, kingfish, and mackerel in spring.

**Middle Gulf Coast**—Tarpon from the Homosassa River to Boca Grande, grouper and jack offshore, and snook, cobia, trout, kingfish, mackerel.

**Lower Gulf Coast**—Tarpon, snook, redfish, and pompano; mackerel during runs.

## FLORIDA RECORD SALTWATER FISH CATCHES
### (All tackle—As of October 1998)

| Species | Weight | Place | Year |
|---|---|---|---|
| Amberjack | 142 lb. | Islamorada | 1979 |
| Barjack | 4 lb. 2 oz. | Key West | 1984 |
| Barracuda | 67 lb. | Islamorada | 1949 |
| Bass, black sea | 5 lb. 1 oz. | Panama City | 1956 |
| Bass, striped | 33 lb. 2 oz. | Tallahassee | 1989 |
| Bluefish | 22 lb. 2 oz. | Jensen Beach | 1973 |
| Blue runner | 8 lb. 5 oz. | Pensacola | 1995 |
| Bonefish | 15 lb. 6 oz. | Islamorada | 1977 |
| Catfish, gafftopsail | 8 lb. 12 oz. | Stuart | 1991 |
| Catfish, hardhead | 3 lb. 5 oz. | Sebastian | 1993 |

Cobia . . . . . . . . . . . . . . .128 lb. 12 oz. . . . . . . . . . . . .Pensacola . . . . .1995
Croaker . . . . . . . . . . . . . . .3 lb. 12 oz. . . . . . . . . . . . .Pensacola . . . . .1992
Dolphin . . . . . . . . . . . . . .77 lb. 12 oz. . . . . . . . . . . . .Fort Pierce . . . . .1985
Drum, black . . . . . . . . . . . . . . .93 lb. . . . . . .Fernandina Beach . . . . .1957
Drum, red . . . . . . . . . . . . .51 lb. 12 oz. . . . . . . . . . . . . .Cocoa . . . . .1996
Flounder . . . . . . . . . . . . .20 lb. 9 oz. . . . . . . . . .Nassau County . . . . .1983
Grouper, gag . . . . . . . . . . . .71 lb. 3 oz. . . . . . . . . . . . . .Destin . . . . .1991
Grouper, Nassau . . . . . . . . . .3 lb. 4 oz. . . . . . . . . . . .Key Largo . . . . .1984
Grouper, red . . . . . . . . . . . .39 lb. 8 oz. . . . . . . . . .Port Canaveral . . . .1991
Grouper, Warsaw . . . . . . .436 lb. 12 oz. . . . . . . . . . . . . . .Destin . . . . .1985
Grouper, yellowfin . . . . . . . .34 lb. 6 oz. . . . . . . . . . . .Key Largo . . . . .1988
Grunts, margates . . . . . . . .12 lb. 12 oz. . . . . . . . . . . . . .Ft. Pierce . . . . .1994
Hind, speckled . . . . . . . . . .42 lb. 6 oz. . . . . . . . . . . . . .Destin . . . .1987
Hogfish . . . . . . . . . . . . . . .19 lb. 8 oz. . . . . . .Daytona Beach . . . .1962
Jack, Crevalle . . . . . . . . . . . . . .57 lb. . . . . . . . . . . . . . .Jupiter . . . . .1993
Jack, horse-eye . . . . . . . . . .24 lb. 8 oz. . . . . . . . . . . . . . .Miami . . . . .1982
Jewfish . . . . . . . . . . . . . . . . .680 lb. . . . . . .Fernandina Beach . . . . .1961
Ladyfish . . . . . . . . . . . . . .4 lb. 10 oz. . . . . . . . . . . . . . . .Jupiter . . . . .1992
Mackerel, cero . . . . . . . . . .15 lb. 8 oz. . . . . . . . . . . . .Key West . . . . .1984
Mackerel, king . . . . . . . . . . . . . .90 lb. . . . . . . . . . . . .Key West . . . . .1976
Mackerel, Spanish . . . . . . . . . . . .12 lb. . . . . . . . . . . . .Fort Pierce . . . . .1984
Marlin, blue . . . . . . . . . . . .980 lb. 8 oz. . . . . . . . . . . . . . .Destin . . . . .1985
Marlin, white . . . . . . . . . . . . . .161 lb. . . . . . . . . . .Miami Beach . . . . .1938
Permit . . . . . . . . . . . . . . . .53 lb. 4 oz. . . . . . . . . . . .Lake Worth . . . . .1994
Pompano, African . . . . . . . .50 lb. 8 oz. . . . . . . . . .Daytona Beach . . . .1990
Pompano, Florida . . . . . . . . .8 lb. 1 oz. . . . . . . . . .Flagler Beach . . . . .1984
Runner, rainbow . . . . . . . . . . . . .17 lb. . . . . . . . . . . .Key West . . . . .1987
Sailfish, Atlantic . . . . . . . .116 lb. 10 oz. . . . . . . . . . .Boca Raton . . . . .1996
Scamp . . . . . . . . . . . . . . . .24 lb. 4 oz. . . . . . . . . .Port Canaveral . . . . .1991
Seatrout, spotted . . . . . . . . .17 lb. 7 oz. . . . . . . . . . . . . .Ft. Pierce . . . . .1995
Shark, blacktip . . . . . . . . . . . . . .152 lb. . . . . . . . . . . . .Sebastian . . . . .1987
Shark, bull . . . . . . . . . . . . . . .517 lb. . . . . .Panama City Beach . . . .1981
Shark, dusky . . . . . . . . . . . . . .764 lb. . . . . . . . . . .Longboat Key . . . . .1982
Shark, hammerhead . . . . . . . . . .991 lb. . . . . . . . . . . . . .Sarasota . . . . .1982
Shark, lemon . . . . . . . . . . . . . . .397 lb. . . . . . . . . . . . .Dunedin . . . . .1977
Shark, mako . . . . . . . . . . .911 lb. 12 oz. . . . . . . . . . . .Palm Beach . . . . .1962
Shark, spinner . . . . . . . . . . . . . .190 lb. . . . . . . . . . .Flagler Beach . . . . .1986
Shark, thresher . . . . . . .544 lb. 8 oz. . . . . . . . . . . . . .Destin . . . . .1984
Shark, tiger . . . . . . . . . . . . .1,065 lb. . . . . . . . . . . . .Pensacola . . . . .1981
Shark, white . . . . . . . . . . . . . .686 lb. . . . . . . . . . . .Key West . . . . .1988
Sheepshead . . . . . . . . . . . . .15 lb. 2 oz. . . . . . . . . . . .Homosassa . . . . .1981
Snapper, cubera . . . . . . . . . . . . .116 lb. . . . . . . . . . . .Clearwater . . . . .1979
Snapper, gray . . . . . . . . . . . . . . .17 lb. . . . . . .Port Canaveral . . . . .1992
Snapper, lane . . . . . . . . . . . .6 lb. 6 oz. . . . . . . . . . . . .Pensacola . . . . .1991
Snapper, mutton . . . . . . . . .28 lb. 5 oz. . . . . . . . . . .John's Pass . . . .1993
Snapper, red . . . . . . . . . . .46 lb. 8 oz. . . . . . . . . . . . . .Destin . . . . .1985
Snapper, yellowtail . . . . . . . . .8 lb. 9 oz. . . . . . . . . . .Fort Myers . . . . .1996
Snook . . . . . . . . . . . . . . . . .44 lb. 3 oz. . . . . . . . . . . .Fort Myers . . . . .1984
Spearfish, longnose . . . . . . .61 lb. 8 oz. . . . . . . . . . . .Islamorada . . . . .1981
Swordfish . . . . . . . . . . . . .612 lb. 12 oz. . . . . . . . . . . .Key Largo . . . . .1978
Tarpon . . . . . . . . . . . . . . . . . . .243 lb. . . . . . . . . . . .Key West . . . . .1975
Triggerfish, gray . . . . . . . . .8 lb. 9 oz. . . . . . . . . . . . .Pensacola . . . . .1995
Tripletail . . . . . . . . . . . . . . . .32 lb. . . . . . .Apalachicola Bay . . . . .1988

Tuna, bigeye . . . . . . . . . . . . . . .167 lb.  . . . . . . . . . .Miami Beach . . . . .1957
Tuna, blackfin  . . . . . . . . . . .42 lb. 8 oz.  . . . . . . . . . . . . .Duck Key . . . . .1995
Tuna, skipjack  . . . . . . . . . . .31 lb. 8 oz.  . . . . . . . . . .Miami Beach . . . . .1949
Tuna, yellowfin . . . . . . . . . . . . .230 lb. . . . . . . . . . . . . .Key West . . . . .1993
Tunny, little  . . . . . . . . . . . . . . .27 lb. . . . . . . . . . . . . .Key Largo . . . . .1976
Wahoo . . . . . . . . . . . . . . . . . . .139 lb. . . . . . . . . . . . .Marathon . . . . .1960
Weakfish . . . . . . . . . . . . . . . . . .10 lb. . . . . . . . . .Port Canaveral . . . .1987

## INJURED WILDLIFE

Any encountered injured wildlife, especially large species such as manatees, should be reported to the Florida Fish and Wildlife Conservation Commission. In some instances, for seabirds, raptors (hawks, owls, eagles), or small mammals, the local Animal Control office or Humane Society can direct you to an animal rehabilitation site. It is not advisable to attempt home nursing for two reasons: the success rate is about nil and state law prohibits possessing wildlife.

## FLORIDA SHARK ATTACKS

Most shark attacks in the United States occur in Florida.

| Year | Fatal | Non-fatal |
|------|-------|-----------|
| 1990 | 0 | 9 |
| 1991 | 0 | 12 |
| 1992 | 0 | 12 |
| 1993 | 0 | 8 |
| 1994 | 0 | 23 |
| 1995 | 0 | 31 |
| 1996 | 0 | 13 |
| 1997 | 0 | 25 |
| 1998 | 1 | 18 |

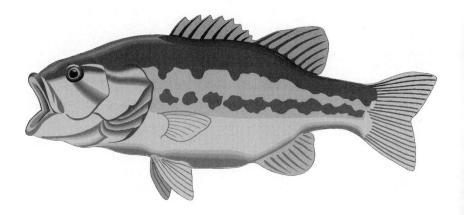

# WATERWAYS AND BOATING

## INTRACOASTAL WATERWAY

Florida, with more coastline than any state except Alaska, and with hundreds of navigable rivers and lakes, offers unlimited opportunities for sailing, pleasure cruising, canoeing, and exploring. Among the most widely traveled and enjoyable water highways is the state's Intracoastal Waterway. It is in three parcels—the Atlantic section, the Okeechobee section, and the West Coast section. The trio makes up the Intracoastal Waterway of Florida, which extends from Jacksonville in northeast Florida, down the east coast, across the southern peninsula to the west coast, and northward to Tarpon Springs.

### Atlantic Intracoastal Waterway

Construction of the Intracoastal Waterway of Florida was the outgrowth of a desire to connect the chain of rivers, lakes, and lagoons along Florida's east coast into a continuous waterway. The original construction was done by the Florida East Coast Canal Company under a state statute that provided for grants of land to railroad and canal companies.

Actual construction began in 1881 on a channel that was to be five feet deep and 50 feet wide, extending from Jacksonville to Miami. The work was completed in 1912, but the channel dimensions were never attained in full, and it was seldom maintained. Tolls were charged, but operation was not profitable, and in 1923 the canal went into receivership.

Prodding from the chambers of commerce along the east coast prompted the Legislature in 1927 to create the Florida Inland Navigation District, a special taxing district consisting of 11 east coast counties from Duval to Miami-Dade. It soon became part of a more widely proposed federal project by the Corps of Engineers so that the Florida section actually was constructed and is maintained by the U.S. Army Corps of Engineers District in Jacksonville, in cooperation with the Florida Inland Navigation District.

The original Florida east coast waterway today is part of the Atlantic Intracoastal Waterway, a continuous and connected system of sheltered inland channels for commercial barges and pleasure boats that actually extends 1,391 miles between Trenton, New Jersey, on the Delaware River, to Miami. The channels are between 10 and 12 feet deep, and have a bottom width of 90 feet or more.

Florida's Atlantic Intracoastal Waterway starts at Fernandina Beach and follows coastal rivers and lagoons through the resorts of Jacksonville Beach, St. Augustine, Daytona Beach, and close to the Kennedy Space Center at Cape Canaveral. It then continues through the resort cities of Cocoa, Melbourne, Vero Beach, Fort Pierce, Jensen Beach, West Palm Beach, Fort Lauderdale, and many other Gold Coast cities, ending at Biscayne Bay between Miami Beach and Miami.

The Atlantic waterway has a channel of 12-foot depth at low water south to Fort Pierce, and thence a 10-foot depth south to Miami.

From Fernandina Beach to Miami the waterway is generally protected from strong winds and rough water, with the exceptions of Mosquito Lagoon, Indian River, and Lake Worth, where conditions can become quite choppy. Fixed bridges over the entire Intracoastal Waterway in Florida generally provide a minimum vertical clearance of 65 feet at mean high water, and horizontal clearance of 90 feet between fenders. Several exceptions exist in the Miami area, and boaters are urged to obtain a summary of bridge clearance data from the Florida Inland Navigation District. In addition, there are many lift-type bridges all along the ICW that have to be opened for captains of larger boats to clear. It is recommended that boaters use a reliable cruising guide to find out what times these spans are opened.

## Okeechobee Intracoastal Waterway

The Okeechobee section extends from Stuart on the east coast to Fort Myers on the west coast, and was opened in 1937. It covers more than 150 miles and is the state's only cross state waterway connecting the Atlantic Ocean with the Gulf of Mexico.

The Okeechobee waterway is made up of three areas, each different—the first 38 miles from the east are in the St. Lucie Canal, the center area is actually Lake Okeechobee, and the third area is made up of the Caloosahatchee Canal and River that leads into the Gulf.

The route from Stuart is well protected and feeds into Lake Okeechobee through a system of locks. On entering the lake, a boater has two routes to choose from. They have the direct route option of crossing unprotected Lake Okeechobee, the second largest body of freshwater in the U.S., or the partially protected "Rim Route" that hugs the huge lake's southern shore. The direct route is 22 nautical miles (approximately 40 statute miles) and the Rim Route about 8 or 9 nautical miles longer. Both arrive at Moore Haven, a city on the lake's western edge.

Depths on Lake Okeechobee and its connecting canals can vary substantially from those shown on charts, depending on rainfall. Charted depths are based on a "normal" low water level of 12.5 feet above sea level. In a wet year the lake may be three or four feet deeper than the chart shows, and in dry spells it can be as much as two feet shallower than the chart figure. Current available depths are posted at every lock.

For the neophyte boater, the Okeechobee Intracoastal Waterway is an ideal cruise, presenting no navigation problems. The entire distance of 150 miles consists simply of hopping through canals and rivers. And there is little chance of getting into trouble because a boater is never more than a short distance from a highway or village. On-shore services and accommodations are everywhere, including motels, restaurants, marinas, and camps. Those choosing to "anchor off" have a good many sheltered coves and anchorages in which to drop the hook.

The waterway has five locks and more than 20 bridges. Passing through the locks is quite simple. Each lock can be reached by telephone, if a boater wishes information about the route, depths, clearances, and general conditions.

No currents must be contended with along the Okeechobee Intracoastal Waterway. Tides at both Stuart and Fort Myers are only one foot and therefore create no problem.

## West Coast Intracoastal Waterway

Marine interests along the west coast petitioned Congress in 1934 for an inland waterway adjacent to the Gulf of Mexico. In 1939, after a study, the Corps of Engineers recommended such a waterway from the Caloosahatchee River in Lee County to the Anclote River in Pinellas County. The project was put on hold during World War II, but in 1945 Congress enacted legislation calling for a nine-foot channel, 100 feet wide, and approximately 100 miles long.

The channel was to run through six counties, thereby necessitating formation of the West Coast Inland Navigation District in 1947. Represented were the counties of Lee, Charlotte, Sarasota, Manatee, Hillsborough, and Pinellas.

In the mid-1950s, the district began acquiring thousands of acres of right-of-way and spoil areas necessary for the project. The first dredging began in 1960, from the Caloosahatchee River northward toward Boca Grande. In 1961 another dredge worked south from the Anclote River toward Tampa Bay. Another dredge in 1962 dug south from Tampa Bay toward Venice, and two years later dredging started from Boca Grande toward Venice. The complex Venice overland cut was commenced in 1965 and finished three years later, linking the previously dug sections of channel and in effect completing the 150-mile waterway.

Since the project was authorized, additional channels have been incorporated, including the Venice Inlet, Cats Point Channel connecting Gulfport to the waterway, and the Sunshine Skyway Channel connecting lower Tampa Bay with Boca Ciega Bay. Total cost of the West Coast Intracoastal Waterway was more than $10 million.

From the Caloosahatchee River the waterway winds northward to the Anclote River west of Tarpon Springs in a bending course, utilizing dug channels, natural bays and passes, harbors and sounds—frequently challenging the navigational skills of a boater. The waterway is nine feet deep and 100 feet wide, except in the Cats Point Channel that links Gulfport with the waterway; there the depth is six feet and the width 80 feet.

The west coast waterway is generally protected from high winds and rough water, with the exceptions of open waters of San Carlos Bay, Sarasota Bay, Tampa Bay, Clearwater Harbor, and St. Joseph Sound. Passes should be entered on a rising tide and the best time is during mid-day, when the sun is high and the bright light shows up shoal areas and shallow waters.

Some of the most beautiful and unspoiled coastlands in Florida are found along the west coast waterway. It is an ecological wonderland. Side trip possibilities are endless, including trips to Sanibel and Captiva islands for shell hunting. Boats also can cruise up the numerous wide rivers in the region, such as the Peace, the Manatee, the Hillsborough, and the Myakka.

**The Missing Link**

No inland route along the coast has been dredged for the Intracoastal Waterway from the Anclote River at Tarpon Springs to the Panhandle region. The section often is referred to as "the missing link" in the waterway. Construction of this section has been authorized by Congress but has not yet begun. Boats traveling this route have the option of hugging the unpopulated shoreline northward or taking a more direct route by angling across the open Gulf of Mexico. The waterway resumes on the northern Gulf shore between St. Mark's Light and Carrabelle. The distance from Tarpon Springs to St. Mark's Light is 145 miles and is not recommended for novice boaters or captains of smaller craft.

## MAJOR CANALS

Miami Canal . . . . . . . 81 miles long
Caloosahatchee River
   (Lake Okeechobee to
   Gulf of Mexico . . . . .69 miles long
North New River
   Canal . . . . . . . . . . .65 miles long
Hillsboro Canal . . . . . 52 miles long
West Palm Beach
   Canal . . . . . . . . . . .42 miles long
St. Lucie
   (Lake Okeechobee
   to Atlantic Ocean) . .40 miles long

## LIGHTHOUSES

Thirty-two operating lighthouses rim the Florida coastline. Keeping them functioning is the responsibility of the U.S. Coast Guard. Lighthouses in the Panhandle are maintained by the Coast Guard station in New Orleans; those on the peninsula and the Keys by the Miami station. The traditional lighthouse, with its keeper living on the site and regularly polishing the lamps, disappeared in the 1960s. Today, lighthouses are turned on and off by photocells and electric timers.

| Name | General Location | Height (feet) Above Water |
|------|------------------|---------------------------|
| Alligator Reef | Florida Keys | 136 |
| Amelia Island | Fernandina Beach | 107 |
| American Shoal | Lower Florida Keys | 109 |
| Boca Grande Rear | Gasparilla Island | 105 |
| Cape Canaveral | Cape Canaveral | 137 |
| Cape Florida | Key Biscayne | 95 |
| Cape San Blas | Port St. Joe | 101 |
| Cape St. George | Off Apalachicola | 72 |
| Carysfort Reef | Upper Florida Keys | 100 |
| Cosgrove Shoal | Florida Keys | 49 |
| Crooked River | Carrabelle | 115 |
| Dry Tortugas | Florida Keys | 151 |
| Egmont Key | Off Tampa Bay | 85 |
| Fowey Rocks | Upper Florida Keys | 110 |
| Hillsboro Inlet | Deerfield Beach | 136 |
| Jupiter Inlet | Jupiter | 146 |
| Key West | Lower Florida Keys | 91 |
| Molasses Reef | Florida Keys | 45 |
| Pacific Reef | Florida Keys | 44 |
| Pensacola | Pensacola | 191 |
| Ponce de Leon Inlet | New Smyrna Beach | 159 |
| Port Boca Grande | Gasparilla Island | 41 |
| Pulaski Shoal | Florida Keys | 49 |
| Rebecca Shoal | Florida Keys | 66 |
| Sand Key | Lower Florida Keys | 109 |
| Sanibel Island | Off Fort Myers | 98 |
| Smith Shoal | Florida Keys | 47 |
| Sombrero Key | Upper Florida Keys | 142 |
| St. Augustine | St. Augustine | 161 |
| St. Johns | Jacksonville | 83 |
| St. Marks | St. Marks | 82 |
| Tennessee Reef | Florida Keys | 49 |

## BOATING FEES AND REGULATIONS

All vessels operated on Florida waters must be registered and/or numbered in Florida except:

—vessels used exclusively on private lakes or ponds

—vessels owned by the federal government

—vessels used exclusively as life boats

—non-motor-powered vessels

—vessels with a current number from another state or from another country temporarily using Florida waters (less than 90 consecutive days).

—vessels newly purchased in Florida (less than 30 days).

In addition, all vessels except those documented vessels and non-motor-powered boats less than 16 feet in length must be titled in Florida.

Boat titles and registrations are made at county tax collector offices. Applicants must provide proof of ownership. Registration must be renewed each year in the birth month of the owner.

Annual registration fees are:

Class A-1 (less than 12 feet) ............................. $ 6.75
Class A-2 (12 feet to less than 16 feet) .................... $ 13.75
Class 1 (16 feet to less than 26 feet) ...................... $ 21.75
Class 2 (26 feet to less than 40 feet) ...................... $ 53.75
Class 3 (40 feet to less than 65 feet) ...................... $ 85.75
Class 4 (65 feet to less than 110 feet) .................... $101.75
Class 5 (110 feet and over) ............................. $125.75

Some counties impose an additional fee.

Upon receipt and approval of registration, the owner is issued a certificate of number and a validation decal. The certificate must be on board whenever the boat is used and the decal must be properly displayed on the bow.

Fee for titling a vessel is $5.25. There is an additional $1 fee to record each existing lien and an additional $4.00 fee for titling a vessel previously registered out of state. The owner must show proof of payment of sales tax for the vessel, motor, and trailer.

### Documented Boats

Florida law requires titling of undocumented vessels, but owners of larger boats can document their vessels with the U.S. Coast Guard. A marine document is proof of ownership and is recognized internationally. A person owning a documented boat for use in Florida still must register it in Florida. Documented vessels must display the validation decal on the windshield or port side window.

### Hull ID Number

All boats built since 1972 must have a hull identification number permanently attached to the transom on the starboard side above the waterline. A later regulation, in 1984, requires the number also be permanently attached in a second, unexposed location. Owners of homemade boats should contact the Florida Fish and Wildlife Conservation Commission for a hull number. The number is similar to the serial number on a car.

### Law Enforcement on Florida Waters

Because Florida has a fatality accident rate of 16 persons per 100,000 boats, which is three times the national average, the state closely monitors the use of alcohol by boaters.

By operating on Florida waterways, a person is deemed to have given consent to be tested for alcohol if arrested for operating under the influence. Penalties for operating a vessel under the influence of alcohol or drugs include fines of up to $2,500.00, imprisonment of up to one year, non-paid public service work, and mandatory substance abuse counseling.

Sentencing is mandatory; the "suspended sentence" is a thing of the past for impaired boat operators. If a drunken operator kills another person, the penalty jumps to 15 years in prison and a fine of up to $10,000.00. Florida has a chemical test law for boat operators. Refusal to submit to a breath or urine test can incur a fine of $500.00. If an operator causes death or serious injury to someone, police may use reasonable force to require the operator to submit to a blood test.

## ADDITIONAL BOATING REGULATIONS

Florida maintains boating regulations that are in addition to federal rules and requirements. Among them:

### Age Restrictions

—Persons less than 14 years of age shall not operate a Personal Watercraft.

—No person born after September 30, 1980, may operate a vessel powered by a motor of 10 horsepower or greater unless he or she has in their possession a photographic identification and a boater safety identification card issued for successful completion of an approved boating safety course. This law will be progressively phased in until October 1, 2001, when all persons 21 years of age or younger will be subject to this law.

### Personal Flotation Devices

Every child under 6 years of age must wear a USCG approved PFD on a vessel less than 26' while the vessel is underway. PWC operators and passengers must wear an approved Type I, II, III, or VPFD. Required PFDs must be readily accessible.

### Speed Limits and Reckless Operation

No vessel can be operated within Florida in a reckless or negligent manner, including excessive speed in regulated or congested areas, operating in a manner that may cause an accident, operating in a swimming area with bathers present, towing water skiers where obstructions exist or a fall might cause them to be injured, bow riding or riding on the gunwale or transom where no seating is provided, or endangering life or property. Boats may not tow water skiers, aquaplanes or similar devices without a wide-angle rearview mirror or an observer on board, and may not tow in darkness. Boaters must be aware of and obey manatee protection restrictions.

### Accident Reporting

Any accident involving death, disappearance, or personal injury, or damage greater than $500.00 must be reported. A "boating accident" includes, but is not limited to, capsizing, collision, foundering, flooding, fire, explosion, and the disappearance of a vessel other than by theft. Accidents must be reported immediately to the nearest office of the Florida Fish and Wildlife Conservation Commission office or the Florida Marine Patrol.

### RED TIDE

Few natural phenomena are so disastrous to Florida's waters, coasts, fishing, and tourist industry, and so unpleasant to its residents, as what is known as Red Tide. It has been around for hundreds, perhaps thousands, of years, all over the world. A 1996 outbreak was the worst ever recorded in Florida waters.

Red Tide is the popular name given a peculiar discoloration of seawater caused by microscopic organisms. Usually these discolorations are observed along coasts where they are frequently accompanied by the widespread death of fish and other marine animals.

Scientists at a Miami laboratory found that the color and slimy consistency of the water during Red Tide is partly due to the presence of what then was an undescribed microscopic form of life. It has been given the name *Gymnodinium brevis,* shortened into the slang description of Jim Brevis. It is one-thousandth of an inch across and travels about the water by means of two whip-like threads, one trailing behind it and one running around its middle.

A single-celled creature with both animal and plant characteristics, it is present in seawater off the west coast of Florida in quantities of less than 1,000 to the quart. In this concentration it appears to be harmless. During periods of Red Tide, however, it has increased its numbers to 60 million and higher to the quart. In this concentration it is violently poisonous to fish and marine mammals.

Odorless, colorless gases irritating a person's eyes, nose, and throat often occur in conjunction with outbreaks of Red Tide. Scientists have learned these irritant gases are given off when samples of Red Tide water are heated or violently shaken.

Because Jim Brevis behaves somewhat like a plant, it requires fertilizer for growth. Normally the most important of these in the ocean are phosphates. With a normal phosphate level, the one-cell creature remains in a normal balance in the ocean. It is when some additional nutrients appear in the water that the creature seems to multiply. What these nutrients are remains open to study. More than a dozen theories regarding the cause of Red Tide outbreaks have been offered by scientists. To date, all are just theories. Among them are:

**A.** Swollen rivers or streams that, for unknown reasons, carry an unusually heavy burden of fertilizer-like minerals fertilize coastal areas of the sea and thus cause the one-cell creature to reproduce at rapid rates.

**B.** Fertilizers moved down rivers are used by microscopic plants and are converted into more complicated compounds that are essential for the growth of the one-cell creatures.

**C.** Fresh water contains some substances necessary for Jim Brevis growth, and the more saline water of the Gulf has certain other materials that are needed. Where and when the fresh and salt water mix in proper proportions, Jim Brevis blooms.

**D.** In deep water there is insufficient sunlight to allow growth of Jim Brevis, but this deep water is usually rich in fertilizer or nutrients. When these materials are brought to the surface and light by some force, Jim Brevis takes advantage of the extra food supply to reproduce.

**E.** At certain times it is natural for these one-cell creatures to begin an extremely rapid reproduction.

**F.** Some plant or animal may develop in small numbers over a wide area, then be concentrated into a small area by wind and water currents. As these concentrated masses die their decomposing bodies become fertilizer for Jim Brevis.

**G.** Rocky bases under coastal areas contain underground channels through which water can flow. Fresh water carrying dissolved nutrients obtained from the land flows under the beaches and shorelines out as far as several miles at sea before escaping into saltwater. Jim Brevis blooms on these irregular excesses of nutrients.

**H.** Outcrops of phosphate rock on the sea floor provide for intermittent release of nutrients under varying conditions of water current, salinity, and turbulence.

## CROSS-FLORIDA BARGE CANAL

The saga of the Cross-Florida Barge Canal began early in the 19th Century when, in 1818, Secretary of War John Calhoun "directed some partial examination near the headwaters of the St. Mary's River and the Suwannee River with the view to inland communication between the Atlantic and Gulf."

Between 1825 and 1923 the subject became an almost annual debate in Congress. Pro arguments dwelt on protecting wartime commerce and avoiding attacks by pirates. In 1825 the annual losses due to wrecks in the

## CROSS-FLORIDA BARGE CANAL

Florida Keys and shoals was about $500,000, a sum considered "almost sufficient" to build a canal across the peninsula. At that time, however, the recommended route united "the waters of the St. Johns River with those of the river Suwannee requiring a canal of not more than 20 miles in length."

In 1829 Congress decided to ascertain "the most eligible route for a canal." Use of the Oklawaha River north of Ocala was prominently mentioned. But surveyors recommended dismissal of the idea because of impractability.

Surveys and debate did not cease, however, and finally in the 1930s, construction was started as Depression-work. A Florida water conservation committee promptly filed a brief against the proposed canal and in 1936 work was halted. Some 4,000 acres of land had been cleared, 12 million cubic yards of dirt moved, and $5.4 million expended.

Then, in 1942, Congress authorized a lock-type, high-level canal across north-central Florida. It was assigned to the Corps of Engineers, but no money was appropriated. When World War II ended, the corps did design a ship canal but no work was done.

Presidential candidate John Kennedy in 1960 saw the canal as a popular issue in Florida and endorsed the idea. A study by the Corps of Engineers stated that the canal would show a profit of 17 cents on each dollar it cost. Congress was impressed and in 1963 voted a million-dollar construction appropriation. Work began in 1964 with President Johnson detonating an explosive charge near Palatka.

For five years the protests of conservationists were isolated and ineffective. Then, aroused by what has been termed the "rape of the Oklawaha," organized groups of university professors and ecologists began to make themselves heard. The canal became a major issue in the 1970 election campaigns.

To appease the conservationists, President Nixon stopped work on the canal. Some 300 acres of wildlife habitat already had been written off by conservationists as the result of earlier work, but they urged authorities to draw down the 13,000-acre Rodman Reservoir to save an estimated 700 acres of trees inundated when the basin was flooded in 1969.

The federal government and a federal judge supported the draw-down but a Jacksonville judge issued an injunction preventing it. More years of legal maneuvering followed. In 1974 Federal Judge Harvey Johnsen ruled that President Nixon had no authority to stop canal work and that only Congress had the power.

But in 1976 the state cabinet voted 6-1 to ask Congress to abandon the project. It further asked Congress to restore the Oklawaha River and to use the already completed portion of the canal for public recreation. (The 110-mile-long canal, between Jacksonville and Yankeetown, was to be 12 feet deep and 150 feet wide. Completed were three of five navigational locks, three dams, and four of 11 planned bridges.)

In 1986, Congress deauthorized the canal, and cut off any more construction funds. It also agreed to buy, for $32 million, the canal right-of-way lands through Duval, Marion, Putnam, Citrus, Clay, and Levy counties that the state had purchased.

Florida balked at the suggested reimbursement, however, contending the land now was worth closer to $100 million. State officials also worried that signing over the right-of-way to the federal government risked the project being revived some day. Instead, Florida political leaders and conservationists asked to keep title to the vast right-of-way and use it for parks and nature trails. They also beseeched the Corps of Engineers to tear down the locks and dams and return the Oklawaha River to its original state.

Finally, in November 1990, nearly 20 years after President Nixon halted canal construction, President Bush signed legislation that officially killed the project and turned the route over to the state. It gave Florida control of the 110-mile-long waterway under the condition that it be preserved as a "greenway" for conservation and recreation.

Two months later, in January 1991, Florida governor Lawton Chiles and the Cabinet approved a resolution signaling the demise of the canal and the beginning of plans to convert 77,000 acres of canal land into a huge state park.

When deauthorized in 1986, the project had used up $70 million, destroyed 4,000 acres of hardwood forests, and done irreparable damage to the Oklawaha River.

## MAJOR BRIDGES

| Bridge | Spans | Length (Feet) | Vertical Clearance (Feet) | Date |
|---|---|---|---|---|
| Seven-Mile | Money Key Channel | 35,716 | 28 | 1938 |
| Sunshine Skyway | Tampa Bay | 21,640 | 175 | 1987 |
| Buckman | St. Johns River | 16,300 | 65 | 1969 |
| Howard Frankland | Tampa Bay (old span) | 15,893 | 43 | 1958 |
| | (new span) | 15,893 | 49 | 1989 |
| Pensacola Bay | Pensacola Bay | 15,640 | 50 | 1960 |
| Gandy | Tampa Bay | | | |
| | (Recreation span) | 13,781 | 43 | 1956 |
| | (old span) | 14,784 | 43 | 1975 |
| | (new span) | 13,886 | 43 | 1997 |
| Escambia | Escambia Bay | 13,577 | 50 | 1970 |
| Napoleon Broward | St. Johns River | 10,646 | 175 | 1989 |
| John Mathews | St. Johns River | 7,375 | 149 | 1953 |
| New Shands | St. Johns River | 6,662 | 45 | 1961 |
| Bahia Honda | Bahia Honda Channel | 5,356 | 55 | 1938 |
| Caloosahatchee | Caloosahatchee River | 4,966 | 55 | 1962 |
| Arthur Sollee | Intracoastal Canal | 4,594 | 65 | 1988 |
| Acosta | St. Johns River | 3,740 | 57 | 1922 |
| Fuller Warren | St. Johns River | 3,667 | 37 | 1954 |
| Hathaway | West Bay | 3,358 | 50 | 1960 |
| Courtney Campbell | Tampa Bay | 3,274 | 45 | 1974 |
| Blackwater Bay | Blackwater Bay | 2,931 | 45 | 1968 |
| Dunn's Creek | U.S. 1 | 2,699 | — | 1987 |
| St. Johns | St. Johns River | 2,655 | 45 | 1961 |
| Navarre | Santa Rosa Sound | 2,640 | 50 | 1960 |
| Isaiah Hart | St. Johns River | 2,504 | 30 | 1968 |
| Manatee | Manatee River | 2,225 | 40 | 1957 |
| East MacArthur | Biscayne Bay | 2,155 | 35 | 1958 |
| Julia Tuttle Causeway | Biscayne Bay | 2,150 | 64 | 1959 |

## MAJOR BRIDGES (continued)

| Bridge | Spans | Length (Feet) | Vertical Clearance (Feet) | Date |
|---|---|---|---|---|
| West MacArthur | Intracoastal Canal | 2,114 | 35 | 1961 |
| Main Street | St. Johns River | 1,900 | 38 | 1941 |
| Trout River (I-95) | Trout River | 1,835 | 30 | 1959 |
| Apalachicola River | Apalachicola River | 1,636 | 35 | 1959 |
| Trout River (U.S. 17) | Trout River | 1,458 | 30 | 1958 |
| 36th Street | Biscayne Bay | 1,138 | 41 | 1959 |
| Trout River | I-295 | 1,105 | — | 1976 |
| East Las Olas | Intracoastal Canal | 1,095 | 33 | 1958 |

### The Sunshine Skyway

One of Florida's most spectacular bridges, the Sunshine Skyway, opened in May 1987 across the mouth of Tampa Bay, connecting Pinellas County with the northern end of Manatee County. The center of the span is in Hillsborough County.

It took five years to build and cost $244 million. The new bridge replaced the original Skyway, a twin-span structure, half of which was built in 1954 and the other span in 1971. One of those spans collapsed in May 1980 when struck by a freighter. The tragedy caused 35 deaths when a Greyhound bus and several passenger cars dropped 150 feet into Tampa Bay.

The new bridge has a main span of 1,200 feet, compared with 864 feet for the old Skyway. Total length of the new bridge is 4.1 miles. The twin cable towers are 432 feet tall and the roadway is 192 feet above the water at its peak. Designed by engineer Jean Muller, the new Sunshine Skyway is a superstructure of hollow concrete segments strung together with steel cables attached to two tall pylons. It will survive winds of 135 mph, although wind tunnel tests have shown it could withstand winds as high as 236 mph.

Muller's Skyway won a 1988 Presidential Award for Design Excellence and was declared by the award jurors "a work of art."

### CANOE TRAILS

The Florida Canoe Trail system was established by the state to offer the public a way to discover and explore the state's unique environment. The system currently consists of 38 canoe trails, totaling 1,150 miles of scenic waterways.

A canoe trail is a publicly owned stream, often flowing through private property. In most cases the riverbanks are privately owned and not open to public use so canoeists are required not to trespass, abuse, or litter the banks and shorelines of a canoe trail. Being public waters, the canoe trails are open to many kinds of users, including motorboaters.

Following are brief descriptions of the 38 trails (in geographic order):

**1. PERDIDO RIVER.** Forming the border between Florida and Alabama, the Perdido River gently curves past woodlands of pine, cypress, and juniper. Several small ponds or sloughs, hidden along the banks, provide additional canoeing opportunities.

**2. COLDWATER RIVER.** This Panhandle river features crystal clear water and white sand bottoms. Dotted along the banks are sandbars perfect for camping or picnicking. Like other west Florida streams, the current of this creek can be faster than many peninsular Florida rivers.

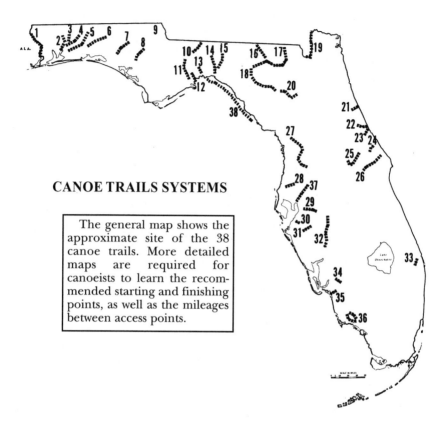

## CANOE TRAILS SYSTEMS

The general map shows the approximate site of the 38 canoe trails. More detailed maps are required for canoeists to learn the recommended starting and finishing points, as well as the mileages between access points.

**3. SWEETWATER/JUNIPER CREEKS.** Sweetwater Creek is narrow and swift with winding curves, but after it joins Juniper Creek the curves become gentler and the creek widens. Spring runs trickle into this clear stream. The water level fluctuates rapidly after heavy rains.

**4. BLACKWATER RIVER.** The dark, tannin-stained waters of the Blackwater contrast with the pure white sandbars found along its bends. Flowing through the western highlands, this beautiful trail is lined with cedar, maple, and cypress. This fast flowing river trail ends at Blackwater River State Park.

**5. YELLOW RIVER.** The upper portion of the Yellow River is a fast flowing stream draining the western highlands and Florida's highest elevation. Hardwood forests and high sandy banks frame the river. Downstream the river deepens and slows as it passes through cypress and gum swamps. Part of the trail borders Eglin Air Force Base.

**6. SHOAL RIVER.** A nature lover's dream, the Shoal River threads its way through northwest Florida wilderness. This narrow river passes by sandy hills and broad sandbars. The surrounding forest is a mixture of maple, birch, oak, gum, and cypress.

**7. HOLMES CREEK.** In contrast with other streams of west Florida, Holmes Creek slowly winds its way past high sandy banks and through lush swamplands. Many low-hanging branches and sharp twisting bends add a bit of challenge to canoeists.

**8. ECONFINA CREEK.** Experienced canoeists will find this virtually unspoiled stream a technical paddling challenge. It flows through scenic river swamps, hammocks, and pine flatwoods. The springs that feed this swift-flowing stream have cut deep canyons in the limestone.

**9. CHIPOLA RIVER.** Beginning at Florida Caverns State Park, this trail passes through 50 miles of river swamps and hardwood forests. High limestone bluffs and caves are accessible from the river. Some rapids, including "Look and Tremble Falls," challenge even experienced canoeists.

**10. OCHLOCKONEE RIVER (UPPER).** Beginning near the Georgia line, the narrow portion of the Ochlockonee twists around cypress knees and blowdowns toward Lake Talquin. Low water requires some portaging.

**11. OCHLOCKONEE RIVER (LOWER).** More than 50 miles of this trail wind through the Apalachicola National Forest, past high pine bluffs and dense hardwoods. Near the Ochlockonee River State Park, the end of the trail, the river widens and motor boats are common. Releases from Jackson Bluff Dam vary the river level.

**12. SOPCHOPPY RIVER.** This dark-colored river twists and bends its way around cypress knees as it swiftly courses through the Apalachicola National Forest. At low water levels, the trip requires many pullovers and some wading.

**13. WAKULLA RIVER.** The four-mile trail on this beautiful cypress-lined river makes an unhurried half-day trip. The slow current makes a round-trip easy. Wildlife is abundant along the river.

**14. WACISSA RIVER.** The sparkling waters of the narrow, swift Wacissa twist and turn through the Aucilla Wildlife Management Area. The entrance to the lower section of the trail is obscured by aquatic plants and over-hanging willow trees.

**15. AUCILLA RIVER.** This coffee-colored river is recommended for experienced canoeists. Rapids and manmade dams along the trail can be a challenge, and they become more numerous and hazardous during low water.

**16. WITHLACOOCHEE RIVER (NORTH).** Flowing through swamplands and past sandy beaches and limestone outcrops, the trail contains several shoal areas. The trail ends at Suwannee River State Park.

**17. SUWANNEE RIVER (UPPER).** The Suwannee River flows through areas of pristine river swamp and along wide sandy banks. There are numerous access points offering a choice of one-day excursions. Even experienced canoeists are recommended to portage "Big Shoals" rapids. The Stephen Foster State Folk Culture Center is accessible from the trail, and the Suwannee River State Park marks the trail's end.

**18. SUWANNEE RIVER (LOWER).** Continuing from Suwannee River State Park, the lower section of the Suwannee River also contains numerous shoals during low water. Portage may be necessary. Abundant wildlife and beautiful scenery make this a popular trail.

**19. ST. MARY'S RIVER.** The many snow-white sandbars along this river make camping easy and enjoyable. Forming the state border, the St. Mary's gently curves through the wilderness of north Florida and south Georgia.

**20. SANTA FE RIVER.** This trail begins just below River Rise State Preserve where the Santa Fe returns to the surface after a three-mile-long underground journey. The lazy current and gentle curves makes the Santa Fe a good beginner's canoe trail. There are some small shoals during low water, but they are generally passable.

**21. PELLICER CREEK.** This four-mile trail makes an easy half-day canoe trip.

**22. BULOW CREEK.** The Bulow Creek trail loops upstream from Bulow Plantation Ruins State Historic Site, then returns to the trailhead before continuing on to the Intracoastal Waterway where it ends. The creek flows through grassy coastal marshes characteristic of the Atlantic coast.

**23. TOMOKA RIVER.** This 130-mile trail loops upstream from the trailhead where the narrow river threads its way among cypress trees. Moving downstream, the river widens as it flows through open coastal marsh and then into Tomoka State Park.

**24. SPRUCE CREEK.** This east-central Florida trail passes through several habitats including dense hardwood forests and coastal saltwater marsh. Two loops, a five-mile round trip upstream and a nine-mile round trip downstream, make up this trail. Both loops begin and end at Moody Bridge.

**25. WEKIVA RIVER/ROCK SPRINGS RUNS.** Rock Springs Run forms the border between Wekiva Springs State Park and Rocks Springs Run State Preserve. The run meets the Wekiva River at the park. The tannin-stained waters of the Wekiva River twist through pine and hardwood uplands and dense swamplands, and pass through the Lower Wekiva River State Preserve before flowing into the St. Johns River.

**26. ECONLOCKHATCHEE RIVER.** Generally untouched by development, the "Econ," as it is known to locals, winds past white sandy beaches and through oak-palm hammocks. The beginning is narrow, shallow, and cypress-lined. Downstream, the river broadens and deepens, and the curves become gentler.

**27. WITHLACOOCHEE RIVER (SOUTH).** Flowing out of the Green Swamp in west-central Florida, the Withlachoochee River trail twists and winds through lush cypress swamps, hardwood and pine forests, and scattered residential areas. Birds and other wildlife abound along the 83-mile trail.

**28. PITHLACHASCOTEE RIVER.** This short trail is recommended for canoeists with some experience. The Pithlachascotee has tight curves in the narrow upper segment that demand technical paddling skills. It widens to long straight stretches on the lower section.

**29. ALAFIA RIVER.** Within an hour's drive of Tampa, the Alafia meanders under a spreading canopy of pine, cypress, and cedar trees. The river flows swiftly over a limestone bed that exposes shoals in low water.

**30. LITTLE MANATEE RIVER.** The short trail on this pristine river winds through a variety of habitats including sand pine scrub, willow marsh, and hardwood forests on its way to the take-out at Little Manatee State Recreation Area. It makes a good half-day trip.

**31. UPPER MANATEE RIVER.** Subtropical vegetation lines the banks of this gently winding trail. It is an easy half-day trip. Water levels and flow vary with releases from Lake Manatee Dam.

**32. PEACE RIVER.** As the name implies, this ideal canoe trail offers a peaceful meandering trip away from civilization. The river originates in the Green Swamp and is alternately bordered by sand bluffs, grassy areas, and dense forests. The opportunities for nature observation, especially birding, are abundant.

**33. LOXAHATCHEE RIVER.** This beautiful eight-mile trail winds through a cypress swamp lush with ferns and orchids. Within Jonathan Dickinson State Park, the river twists through mangrove swamps. A variety of wildlife species make their homes along the banks.

**34. HICKEY CREEK.** An easy half-day trip, Hickey Creek trail flows through subtropical hammocks. The trail ends at the locks on the Caloosahatchee River.

**35. ESTERO RIVER.** This trail offers an easy, one-day adventure from Koreshan State Historic Site among mangrove islands and coves. When the trail opens into Estero Bay, canoeists can select a variety of routes to explore the mangrove islands before returning upstream.

**36. BLACKWATER RIVER/ROYAL PALM HAMMOCK.** This 13-mile loop trail through Collier-Seminole State Park is a good trail for beginning canoeists. The tidal creeks and mangrove wilderness areas are quiet and pristine.

**37. HILLSBOROUGH RIVER.** This 32-mile tannin-laden course starts in the wilderness and ends in the city. Its upper stage, from Crystal Springs to the Hillsborough River State Park, with rapids, portage, and numerous blind branches, is not for the inexperienced. But the remainder is an easy, scenic meander through transitioning landscape.

**38. HISTORIC BIG BEND PADDLING TRAIL.** Florida's first "outside" course runs in the Gulf of Mexico from the St. Marks River lighthouse to the Suwannee River along the largely undeveloped Big Bend coast. Although navigable by canoe and modern sea kayaks, as well, NOAA and Coast Guard charts are recommended.

## WATER MANAGEMENT DISTRICTS

Five water management districts covering the entire state are at the forefront of agencies assigned to preserve the state's natural resources.

Created in 1972, their mission is to preserve, conserve, and provide for public use of the state's waterways. They pursue that mission by regulation of waterways, by land acquisitions, by promoting public awareness of waterways, by assuring that the

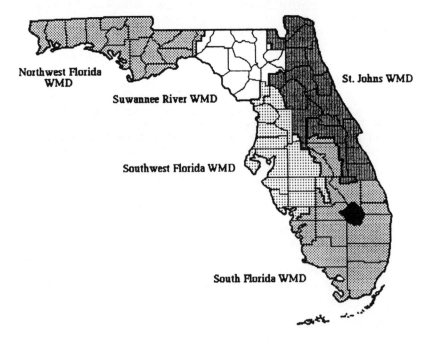

Northwest Florida WMD

St. Johns WMD

Suwannee River WMD

Southwest Florida WMD

South Florida WMD

public's need for water is met, by setting standards to reduce flood damage, by regulating location and construction of wells and septic tanks, and by controlling withdrawal or diversion of water from rivers.

The districts obtain most of their revenue from property taxes and a percentage of the state's documentary stamp tax. Much of the money goes for purchase of frontage along the state's rivers.

The frontage assures continued quality of the waterways, and provides scores of recreational parks for the public. For example, the Suwannee River Water Management District has purchased thousands of acres along the Suwannee so that today the public is the largest landowner along the famous river.

The map on the previous page shows the counties served by each of the five water management districts.

## TOPS IN POOLS

Florida leads the nation in the popularity of swimming pools. The state has 89.4 pools per 1,000 people. Arizona is the U.S. runner-up with 73.7 pools, followed, surprisingly, by three northeastern states, Connecticut with 58, New Jersey with 53.1 and New Hampshire with 50.2.

## DANGEROUS CRAFT

Personal watercraft accounted for 34 percent of all boating accidents in Florida, according to the National Park service.

## WRECK

The remains of a 1764 shipwreck off St. Augustine were discovered (in January 1999)—the British sloop *Industry,* the oldest wreck thus far found off the nation's oldest city. Evidence of the site was discovered in 1998 in state-approved dives. In a well-documented incident, the ship ran onto a sand bar 325 yards off the city while carrying cannon, cannonballs, ammunition, money, and tools to the new British outpost. Relics will be displayed at the St. Augustine Lighthouse Museum. The wreck, however, was vandalized and two historic cannons were stolen from the site.

## LOVE BOATS

Miami operates the world's largest cruise port, hosting two-thirds of the world's cruise-ship passengers.

# MOTORING

## DRIVER'S LICENSING

A person is required to obtain a Florida driver's license if that person has children enrolled in the state's public schools, or is registered to vote, or has filed for homestead exemption, or accepts employment in the state, or has lived in Florida more than six consecutive months. Anyone moving to Florida with a valid driver's license from another state must get a Florida license within 30 days of becoming a Florida resident.

The following persons may drive in Florida without having a Florida license if they have a valid license from another state or country:

—Any non-resident who is at least 16 years old

—Persons employed by the U.S. government driving a government vehicle on official business

—A non-resident working for a firm on contract with the U.S. government

—A non-resident attending college in Florida

—Persons who drive only vehicles such as farm tractors or road machines

—A licensed driver who lives in another state and travels regularly into Florida

—Non-resident migrant farm workers, providing they have a valid driver's license from their home state

—Members of armed forces stationed in Florida

### Restricted Driver's License

A person learning to drive must obtain a restricted operator's license, or learner's license, even when learning in the company of an adult licensed driver. Applicants for a restricted license must be at least 15 years old; must pass a vision, road signs, and road rules test; must have the signature of one parent on a consent form if under age 18; must show proof of a traffic law and substance abuse education course or a license from another jurisdiction; and must produce two official forms of identification.

A restricted license permits driving only during daytime hours until six months prior to 16th birthday, at which time night driving with such a license is permitted. Accompanying a restricted license driver must be a licensed driver at least 21 years of age, seated in the passenger side of the front seat.

Sixteen-year-olds may have a full license but may not drive between 11:00 P.M. and 6:00 A.M. without a licensed 21-year-old driver accompanying them, unless driving to or from work. Seventeen-year-old drivers are similarly restricted from 1:00 A.M. to 5:00 A.M.

Under 18-year-olds can lose their driving privileges for fewer violation points than adult drivers, and for a growing list of school-elated infractions, including unexcused absences.

All drivers under the age of 21 can have licenses suspended immediately for six months for any infraction involving alcohol at a .02 level.

The license does not permit the learner to operate a motorcycle with more than 150 cubic centimeter displacement until the 16th birthday.

### Restrictions Entered on Licenses

Various restrictions may be printed on a person's driver's license. They include:

—Motorcycle only, meaning the person has passed the tests only for motorcycle licensing

—Corrective lenses, meaning the person cannot pass the vision test without glasses or contact lenses

—Outside mirror (left side), when a person cannot hear an ordinary horn or is blind in one eye

—Steering wheel knob or power steering, when a person does not have full use of both hands or has only one hand

—Mechanical turn indicator, when a person has lost the use of either arm

—Daylight only, when a person has difficulty seeing at night and an eye doctor recommends no night driving

—Automatic transmission, when a person, because of physical condition, requires an automatic transmission to pass the driving test

—Business purposes, when the person is licensed to drive only to and from work, to a job, or for educational, church, or medical purposes

—Employment purposes, when a person is licensed to drive only to and from work for job training

## Test Requirements and Fees

Applicants for an original Florida license, including those persons holding valid out-of-state licenses, must take a test that covers vision, road signs, and road rules. The applicant must provide the vehicle, which will be inspected to make sure it is safe and in good working order.

Following the test the driver examiner may or may not approve the application. If the applicant is not approved, the test may be taken again at another time.

Appointments for taking the driver's test are urged, but not required, at all 146 driver's license offices. Days and hours of each office vary.

### Fees

| | |
|---|---|
| Initial License Fee for first Florida license | $ 20.00 |
| License Renewal | $ 15.00 |
| Restricted License | $ 20.00 |
| Commercial License | $ 50.00 |
| License Valid only in Florida | $ 15.00 |
| Duplicate License (if original lost or stolen) | $ 10.00 |
| Replacement License (stolen, with police report) | free |
| Replacement License (must turn in incorrect license) | $ 10.00 |
| Delinquent Fee (for renewals if license expired less than 12 months before renewal application) | $ 1.00 |
| Identification Card* | $ 3.00 |
| Duplicate ID Card (if original lost or stolen) | $ 2.50 |
| Motorcycle Endorsement (for licenses that required applicant pass written cycle test and on-cycle test) | $ 5.00 |
| Service Fee after license had been revoked | $ 50.00 |
| Service Fee after license had been suspended | $ 25.00 |
| Service Fee after financial responsibility suspension | $ 15.00-500.00 |
| Service Charge to clear a suspension | $ 25.00 |

Some driver's license services delivered at tax collector offices carry an additional $5.25 fee.

*A person who does not have a driver's license but needs an identification card may obtain one at a driver's license office. Requirements are the applicant be 12 years of age or older, present a Social Security number, and have two items of identification. The card includes a color photo, name, sex, race, address, date of birth, and physical description. It is valid for four years.*

## License Renewal

A driver's license is valid for four or six years. Applicants who have a conviction-free record for the previous three years can obtain a six-year license, and must pass a required examination. A four-year renewal is available by mail.

Notice that a license will soon expire is mailed to each driver 30 days before the birthday expiration date. Licenses must be renewed on or before a person's birthday.

## Persons Ineligible for Licenses

A Florida license is not issued to a person whose license is under suspension or revocation in any state, who is addicted to drugs or alcohol, who cannot drive because of mental or physical problems, or who is under the legal age for licensing.

A license can be suspended in Florida if the driver:

—Makes a fraudulent driver license application

—Is unable to drive safely

—Allows license to be used for illegal purposes

—Has license ordered suspended by court

—Refuses to take an alcohol or drug test if ordered to

—Misuses a restricted license

—Earns a certain number of traffic offenses points

—Fails to pay fine after breaking traffic law

A license can be revoked for up to six months if a driver is found guilty or motor vehicle records show:

—Driving under influence of alcohol or drugs

—A felony in which a motor vehicle is used

—Not stopping to help when the vehicle is in an accident and causes injury

—Lying about ownership or operation of vehicle

—Three cases of reckless driving in one year

—An immoral act in which a motor vehicle is used

—Three major offenses or 15 point-receiving offenses within five years

—A felony for drug possession

—Vision worse than standard minimum

A driver's license will be revoked for a minimum three years when the motorist, because of reckless driving, kills someone, or when the motorist kills someone because of driving under the influence of alcohol or drugs or other controlled substances.

And a lifetime revocation can occur if a motorist is convicted in a manslaughter case involving a vehicle and also accumulates four convictions of driving under the influence.

A person found guilty of driving after a license has been suspended or revoked can be jailed.

## Point System

The state assesses points against drivers for various violations. Points can lead to suspension of a license.

| Violation | Points |
|---|---|
| Leaving scene of accident resulting in property damage of more than $50 | 6 |
| Unlawful speed resulting in an accident | 6 |
| Reckless driving | 4 |
| Any moving violation resulting in an accident | 4 |
| Passing a stopped school bus | 4 |
| Unlawful speed, 16 mph or more over posted limit | 4 |
| Unlawful speed, 15 mph or less over posted limit | 3 |
| All other moving violations | 3 |
| Improper equipment on vehicle | 2 |

A license will be suspended 30 days if the driver accumulates 12 points in a 12-month period. Accumulating 18 points within 18 months draws a 90-day suspension. A total of 24 points within 36 months is punished by a one-year suspension.

## Driving Under the Influence

The unlawful blood alcohol content level in Florida is .08 or higher. Penalties include:

• **First conviction**—a minimum 180 days license revocation, minimum $250 fine, possible imprisonment up to six months plus a year's probation and 50 hours of community service, and attendance in substance abuse course.

• **Second conviction**—a minimum five years license revocation (if offense within five years of first conviction), minimum $500 fine, minimum 10 days in jail (if offense within three years of first conviction).

• **Third conviction**—a minimum 10 years license revocation (if offense within 10 years of first conviction), minimum $1,000 fine, minimum 30 days in jail (if offense within five years of first conviction).

It is illegal for motorists to drink alcoholic beverages while they drive, and possession of an open alcohol container in a moving vehicle is punishable by a fine.

Fines and imprisonment are higher if blood alcohol level is .20 or higher, or if a minor is in the vehicle.

**Implied Consent Law**

By driving in Florida, a motorist stopped for possible driving under the influence has agreed to take, if asked, a blood test, urine test, or breath test. To refuse means to risk a driver's license being suspended for one year.

In driving under the influence cases involving death or injury, a driver can be required to take a blood test. If a driver is unconscious or in no condition to refuse the blood test, samples of the motorist's blood may be withdrawn.

### VEHICLE INSURANCE

Florida has two motor vehicle insurance laws—Financial Responsibility law and the No-Fault law.

The Financial Responsibility law requires owners and operators of motor vehicles to be financially responsible for damages or injuries they may cause to others in an accident. Coverage required is $10,000 Bodily Injury Liability, $20,000 Bodily Injury Liability to two or more persons, and $10,000 Property Damage Liability. To have an accident without this coverage can result in suspension of driver's license and tags for up to three years.

The No-Fault law requires anyone who owns or has a registered motor vehicle to carry $10,000 Personal Injury Protection (PIP) and $10,000 Property Damage Liability (PDL). No one can buy a tag and registration for a car without this insurance. Failure to carry No-Fault can result in suspension of both driver's license and tags for up to three years.

### VEHICLE INSPECTIONS

Florida's vehicle inspections ended in 1981 after 13 years. But because of air pollution concerns, the state has mandated that six urban counties conduct auto emissions inspections every two years. The counties are Hillsborough, Pinellas, Miami-Dade, Broward, Palm Beach, and Duval. New cars are exempt from testing.

### SEAT BELTS

Driver and front seat passengers are required by Florida law to wear seat belts. Violation is punishable by a $20 fine. Children, including teen-agers, riding in the back seat are required to have the appropriate restraints.

### LITTERING

People who throw trash from their vehicles onto public streets or highways are subject to a fine up to $500 or a jail term up to 60 days.

### BICYCLES AND MOPEDS

Bicycle riders have rights and responsibilities, just as motor vehicle operators, and do receive tickets for traffic violations. Children's safety helmets are required. Moped riders must hold a valid driver's license but no motorcycle endorsement is required.

---

### DEADLY DRIVING

Tampa Bay had the second highest rate of traffic fatalities among the nation's metropolitan areas of more than a million people in 1997. It registered 17.6 traffic deaths per 100,000 population, second only to Kansas City. Miami ranked seventh, with a fatality rate of 16.16. Ironically, both areas have improved their records. Orlando led the nation in pedestrian deaths.

## LICENSE TAG RATES*

| Classification | Pounds | Rates |
|---|---|---|
| Automobile, private use | through 2,499 | $26.60 |
| Automobile, private use | 2,500-3,499 | $34.60 |
| Automobile, private use | 3,500 up | $44.60 |
| Fifth wheel travel trailer up to 35 ft | | $23.10 |
| Fifth wheel travel trailer over 35 ft | | $30.10 |
| Travel trailers over 35 feet | | $36.10 |
| Camp trailer (folded walls) | | $18.10 |
| Chassis Mount camper | through 4,499 | $28.10 |
| Chassis Mount camper | 4,500 up | $43.10 |
| Motor home, self-propelled through 4,499 | | $28.10 |
| Motor home, self-propelled 4,500 up | | $43.10 |
| Motorcycles over 5 brake hp | | $20.60 |
| Motorcycles not over 5 brake hp | | $20.60 |
| Moped | | $15.60 |
| Motorized bicycles | | $13.10 |
| Antiques (passenger cars or trucks) | | $16.10 |

| Classification | Pounds | Rates |
|---|---|---|
| Trucks, private and commercial | through 1,999 | $23.10 |
| Trucks, private and commercial | 2,000 to 3,000 | $23.10 |
| Trucks, private and commercial | 3,001 to 5,000 | $41.10 |

| Classification | Length | Rate |
|---|---|---|
| Mobile homes | up to 35 ft | $24.10 |
| Mobile homes | 35 to 40 ft | $29.10 |
| Mobile homes | 40 to 45 ft | $34.10 |
| Mobile homes | 45 to 50 ft | $39.10 |
| Mobile homes | 50 to 55 ft | $44.10 |
| Mobile homes | 55 to 60 ft | $49.10 |
| Mobile homes | 60 to 65 ft | $54.10 |
| Mobile homes | over 65 ft | $84.10 |

*Effective July 1, 1991, the legislature added a $2.00 surcharge, and another $2.00 for future replacement of metal tags, to selected rates in the above chart. A new metal tag carries a $10.00 surcharge.*

### Specialty Tags

In 1987 the state began selling a special license tag that honored the crew of the ill-fated *Challenger* spacecraft. Motorists wishing to buy the tag in lieu of a regular vehicle tag were asked to pay an additional fee, which was used to build a memorial for the astronauts killed in the tragedy.

Sales were so successful that every year thereafter the state has offered more specialty license tags, so that by 1994 there were approximately 55 available.

Not all were issued after 1987; some, such as those for veterans and horseless carriages, have been available for decades. Most of these older specialty tags carry no added fee. But with the *Challenger* tag and the numerous other recent specialty tags, revenue from the added fee is passed on to the group or institution honored on the tag.

Below is a list of major specialty tags now being offered. Figures are as of April 1999. The fee listed is, of course, in addition to the cost of a regular tag, per year for five years.

| Type | Special Fee | Cumulative Issued |
|---|---|---|
| *Challenger* | $25 | 655,633 |
| Manatee | $20 | 432,157 |
| Panther | $25 | 332,107 |
| Univ. of Florida | $25 | 183,459 |
| Florida State Univ. | $25 | 158,637 |
| Florida Salutes Veterans | $15 | 72,014 |
| Univ. of Miami | $25 | 70,098 |
| U.S. Olympics | $15 | 66,529 |
| Support Education | $15 | 55,777 |
| Florida Arts | $20 | 55,670 |
| Invest in Children | $20 | 43,389 |
| Indian River Lagoon | $15 | 38,269 |
| Florida A&M Univ | $25 | 34,679 |
| Sea Turtles | $17.50 | 20,794 |
| Univ. of Central Florida | $25 | 18,922 |
| Large Mouth Bass | $25 | 18,600 |
| U.S. Special Olympics | $15 | 15,915 |
| Univ. of South Florida | $25 | 14,614 |
| Agriculture | $20 | 10,194 |
| Police Athletic League | $20 | 6,525 |
| Florida International Univ. | $25 | 6,276 |
| Univ. of West Florida | $25 | 5,267 |
| Florida Atlantic Univ. | $25 | 4,974 |
| Univ. of North Florida | $25 | 4,758 |
| Bethune-Cookman College | $25 | 4,462 |
| Boy Scouts | $20 | 2,089 |
| Girl Scouts | $20 | 1,374 |
| Florida Gulf Coast Univ. | $25 | 206 |

Florida also issues specialty tags for fans of the state's professional sports teams with revenues going not to the teams but to the state's Professional Sports Development Trust and to the Florida Sports Foundation.

| Type | Special Fee | Cumulative Issued |
|---|---|---|
| Miami Dolphins | $25 | 25,305 |
| Jacksonville Jaguars | $25 | 17,390 |
| Orlando Magic | $25 | 15,879 |
| Florida Panthers | $25 | 9,361 |
| Tampa Bay Buccaneers | $25 | 8,659 |
| Miami Heat | $25 | 5,010 |
| Tampa Bay Lightning | $25 | 4,720 |
| Florida Marlins | $25 | 4,289 |
| Tampa Bay Devil Rays | $25 | 2,474 |
| Orlando Predators | $25 | 759 |
| Tampa Bay Storm | $25 | 486 |

In 1998, for the fourth year in a row, the most popular specialty tag in the state was the Manatee license plate. The 10 most popular specialty license plates in Florida based on numbers sold in 1998 were:

1. Manatee
2. Panther
3. *Challenger*
4. University of Florida
5. Florida State University
6. Education
7. Florida Arts
8. Invest in Children
9. Indian River Lagoon
10. U.S. Olympics

Approximately 842,000 vehicles have specialty tags assigned to them, eight percent of the total vehicles eligible to purchase special tags.

New specialty auto tags available in 1999 include Florida Sheriffs Youth Ranch, Conserve Wildlife, Keep Kids Drug Free, Barry University, Protect the Wild Dolphin, and the Everglades River of Grass. New specialty tags available in 2000 include U.S. Marine Corps., Choose Life, Share the Road, Florida Wildflower, Tampa Bay Estuary, and Florida Memorial College.

Florida also issues specialty tags for vehicles or drivers meeting specific criteria. Special vehicle tags include those for Horseless Carriages, Street Rods, and Collector Cars. Eligible drivers may purchase tags identifying them as Congressional Medal of Honor recipients, National Guardsmen, members of U.S. Reserve armed forces, ex-prisoners of war, paralyzed veterans, disabled veterans, disabled wheelchair veterans, the wheelchair-bound, Seminole or Miccosukee Indians, amateur radio operators, Purple Heart recipients and their widows, or Pearl Harbor survivors. These tags involve only a nominal fee. More than 80,000 Florida vehicles carry such specialty tags.

Additional fees are collected annually. Florida license plates, including specialty tags, have a five-year lifetime and are updated by decals. The state gives a specialty tag five years to attract 10,000 vehicles. If it does not, it is dropped from the list.

## TRAFFIC STATISTICS

| Year | Licensed Drivers | Registered Vehicles | Mileage (Millions) | Accidents | Deaths | Mileage Death Rate* |
|------|------|------|------|------|------|------|
| 1960 | 2,710,665 | 2,717,121 | 21,171 | 124,630 | 1,245 | 5.9 |
| 1965 | 3,358,747 | 3,460,096 | 27,737 | 169,408 | 1,665 | 6.0 |
| 1970 | 4,143,442 | 4,730,034 | 39,992 | 238,740 | 2,170 | 5.4 |
| 1975 | 6,320,822 | 6,995,683 | 61,715 | 283,086 | 2,040 | 3.3 |
| 1980 | 7,809,423 | 7,797,375 | 75,281 | 201,385 | 2,879 | 3.8 |
| 1985 | 9,630,975 | 10,827,693 | 87,000 | 216,596 | 2,870 | 3.3 |
| 1987 | 10,246,063 | 11,738,273 | 92,865 | 215,886 | 2,891 | 3.1 |
| 1988 | 10,648,019 | 11,997,948 | 105,030 | 256,543 | 3,152 | 3.0 |
| 1989 | 11,109,288 | 12,276,272 | 108,876 | 252,439 | 3,033 | 2.8 |
| 1990 | 11,612,402 | 12,465,790 | 109,997 | 216,245 | 2,951 | 2.7 |
| 1991 | 12,170,821 | 11,184,146** | 113,484 | 195,312 | 2,523 | 2.2 |
| 1992 | 11,440,126** | 11,205,320 | NA | 169,233 | 2,271 | NA |
| 1993 | 11,767,409 | 11,159,938 | 119,768 | 199,039 | 2,719 | 2.3 |
| 1994 | 11,992,578 | 11,393,982 | 120,929 | 206,183 | 2,722 | 2.3 |
| 1995 | 12,019,156 | 12,062,731 | 127,800 | 228,589 | 2,847 | 2.2 |
| 1996 | 12,343,598 | 12,003,929 | 129,637 | 241,377 | 2,847 | 2.2 |
| 1997 | 12,691,835 | 12,170,375 | 133,276 | 240,639 | 2,811 | 2.1 |

*Per million miles
**Decrease represents change in accounting procedures
NA: Not available.

## WORST INTERSECTIONS

The ten most dangerous intersections in Florida, based on number of accidents in 1998 are:

1. Sunset Point Road and U.S. 19, Clearwater
2. Highways 434 and 436, Altamonte Springs
3. Highways 50 and 436, Orlando
4. Flamingo Road and Pines Boulevard, Pembroke Pines
5. Dale Mabry Highway and Waters Avenue, Tampa

6. Pines Boulevard and University Drive, Pembroke Pines
7. Goldenrod Road and University Boulevard, Orlando
8. Beach Boulevard and St. John's Bluff Road, Jacksonville
9. Curlew Road and U.S. 19, Palm Harbor
10. Drew Street and U.S. 19, Clearwater.

The Sunset Point Road and U.S. 19 intersection in Clearwater, with 211 accidents, is the eighth most dangerous intersection in the United States.

## AMTRAK STATIONS

Passenger train service is available in Florida through the following Amtrak stations:

| | | |
|---|---|---|
| Chipley | Kissimmee | Sanford |
| Crestview | Lake City | Sebring |
| Dade City | Lakeland | Tallahassee |
| Deerfield Beach | Madison | Tampa |
| DeLand | Miami | Waldo |
| Delray Beach | Ocala | West Palm Beach |
| Fort Lauderdale | Okeechobee | Wildwood |
| Hollywood | Palatka | Winter Haven |
| Jacksonville | Pensacola | Winter Park |

## INTERSTATE HIGHWAY SYSTEM

Four main interstate routes traverse Florida. The longest is Interstate 75, extending from the Georgia line south through Lake City and Ocala, into the Tampa Bay area, and southward adjacent to Bradenton, Sarasota, Venice, Fort Myers, and Naples. From Naples, an eastward route, designated I-75 but known as Alligator Alley, crosses the lower peninsula to connect with the east coast in Broward County. Various spurs such as I-275 lead off I-75, acting as a beltway into the nearby cities of Tampa and St. Petersburg and across the Sunshine Skyway.

Interstate 10 is a 362-mile highway between Jacksonville on the east coast and the Alabama state line near Pensacola. The route is a nearly straight line across northern Florida.

Running the depth of the state along the east coast is Interstate 95, a heavily traveled corridor taking the traveler from Jacksonville all the way to Miami, a drive of 347 miles. Numerous spurs exit traffic to the dozens of metropolitan areas fronting on the Atlantic Ocean.

The state's fourth major artery is Interstate 4, a 132-mile segment cutting across the mid-peninsula and connecting the Tampa Bay area with the east coast area of Daytona Beach, after passing through Orlando.

## FLORIDA TURNPIKE

Started in 1953, the Florida Turnpike, also known as the Ronald Reagan Parkway, is a 356-mile trip from its northern entrance at Wildwood, just south of Ocala, to Miami and on through its 47-mile extention to Homestead. It was built in different stages over a period of 11 years, being finished in 1964.

Prior to the turnpike, most travelers through central Florida used U.S. 27. Today, the turnpike handles the bulk of traffic leading from the central Florida area of Ocala to Orlando and east coast destinations farther south.

The turnpike consists of 65 interchanges where tollbooths issue tickets and collect fares. Fares are charged according to the number of axles on a vehicle. Class 2 fares below, indicating two axles, refers to passenger cars. Vehicles with more axles, such as trucks, pay higher fares.

The chart shows tolls starting at the Wildwood interchange, the northernmost entrance to the turnpike. The distance from Wildwood to Miami on the turnpike is 309 miles. Another 47 miles of turnpike, called the Homestead Extension, continues from Miami to Homestead.

| Interchange | Class 2 Fare | Miles |
|---|---|---|
| Wildwood | $ — | — |
| Leesburg | $ 1.00 | .19 |
| Orlando (East/West) | $ 2.00 | .39 |
| Orlando (I-4) | $ 2.50 | .45 |
| Kissimmee/St. Cloud | $ 4.00 | .60 |
| Fort Pierce | $ 8.50 | .152 |
| Port St. Lucie | $ 9.10 | .162 |
| Stuart. | $ 9.60 | .171 |
| Jupiter | $ 10.70 | .188 |
| Palm Beach Gardens | $ 11.10 | .195 |
| West Palm Beach | $ 11.60 | .205 |
| Lake Worth | $ 12.20 | .211 |
| Boca Raton | $ 12.90 | .234 |
| Pompano Beach | $ 13.15 | .244 |
| Fort Lauderdale | $ 13.65 | .255 |
| Hollywood | $ 13.90 | .260 |
| North Miami | $ 14.40 | .309 |

*The toll collection switches to coin boxes in Miami, and the total additional toll to Homestead is $3.00.*

**Emergency Call Boxes**

Motorists traveling Florida's interstates have available to them emergency call boxes placed every mile along the roadways in some areas. They communicate with the nearest Florida Highway Patrol station.

A motorist needing help can stop at a box, open the door, and press one of the three buttons inside. One signals the need for a tow truck, a second for police, and a third for medical help. The signal is transmitted by microwave to the patrol station. Help then is dispatched to the numbered box.

The boxes are installed along sections of Interstates 10 and 75 in north Florida, on I-75 between Sarasota and Naples, on I-95 from Nassau to Martin counties, along Alligator Alley between Naples and the Fort Lauderdale area, on I-4 in Volusia County, and along the 306-miles of the Florida Turnpike.

In many areas, well posted, the highway patrol can also be contacted via cellular phone by dialing *FHP.

---

### OUCH

Truck drivers suffer the most workplace injuries in Florida based on lost workdays, but more construction workers die on the job, according to the Florida Department of Labor and Employment Security.

In 1998, 85 construction workers were killed while working compared with 59 truck drivers. Transportation accidents took the heaviest toll on working Floridians, followed by assaults and violent acts. A total of 384 people died on the job. Fifty-nine were killed in falls, 30 were electrocuted, and 7 died in fires or explosions.

Truck drivers had injuries involving nearly one-third more lost workdays than the runners-up, non-construction laborers and hospital workers.

Supervisors and proprietors in sales had the third largest death toll, with 21, while 15 farm workers died on the job. Law enforcement lost 13.

Sprains and strains were the most frequent injuries, accounting for more than half of all workplace injuries. Most injuries were caused by contact with objects and equipment, followed by overexertion.

# AIRPORTS

## Passenger Enplanements at Commercial Airports
### 1998

| | |
|---|---:|
| Miami International | 34,533,268 |
| Orlando International | 27,305,149 |
| Tampa International | 13,370,630 |
| Fort Lauderdale International | 12,277,411 |
| Palm Beach International | 5,820,869 |
| Southwest Florida International (Ft. Myers) | 4,447,865 |
| Jacksonville International | 4,300,000 |
| Sarasota/Manatee Regional | 1,631,214 |
| Pensacola Regional | 1,159,368 |
| Orlando Sanford International | 1,034,584 |
| Tallahassee Regional | 956,390 |
| St. Petersburg/Clearwater International | 883,086 |
| Daytona Beach Regional | 781,501 |
| Melbourne Regional | 574,579 |
| Okaloosa Regional | 550,377 |
| Key West International | 545,766 |
| Gainesville Regional | 358,044 |
| Panama City/Bay County Regional | 342,965 |
| Naples Municipal | 118,982 |
| Marathon | 71,778 |
| **Grand Total** | **110,029,242** |

## PUBLIC AIRPORTS

| Airport and Associated City | Distance and Direction from City | Airport and Associated City | Distance and Direction from City |
|---|---|---|---|
| **Airglades** Clewiston | 6 W | **Bob Lee Airport** DeLand | 5 N |
| **Albert Whitted Municipal** St. Petersburg | 1 E | **Bob Sikes Airport** Crestview | 3 NE |
| **Ames Field** Trenton | 3 W | **Bob White Airport** Zellwood | 1 W |
| **Apalachicola Municipal** Apalachicola | 2 W | **Boca Raton** Boca Raton | 2 NW |
| **Arcadia Municipal** Arcadia | 2 SE | **Brown's SPB\*** Winter Haven | 3 NW |
| **Arthur Dunn Airport** Titusville | 2 NW | **Buchan Airport** Englewood | 2 N |
| **Avon Park Municipal** Avon Park | 1 SW | **Calhoun County** Blountstown | 2 E |
| **Bartow Municipal** Bartow | 4 NE | **Chalk's SPB\*** Miami | 1 E |
| **Belle Glade** Belle Glade | 1 NE | **Charlotte County** Punta Gorda | 3 E |
| **Biscayne SPB\*** Miami | 6 NNE | **Circle T Ranch** Indiantown | 3 NE |
| | | **Clearwater Executive** Clearwater | 2 NE |
| | | **Clewiston Municipal** Clewiston | 1 S |

| | | | | |
|---|---|---|---|---|
| **Coastal Airport** | 12 NW | | **Inverness** | 2 SE |
| Pensacola | | | Inverness | |
| **Costin Airport** | 2 S | | **Jacksonville International** | 10 N |
| Port St. Joe | | | Jacksonville | |
| **Craig Field** | 9 E | | **Kay Larkin Airport** | 3 W |
| Jacksonville | | | Palatka | |
| **Cross City** | 1 E | | **Keystone Airpark** | 5 N |
| Cross City | | | Keystone Heights | |
| **Crystal River-Homosassa** | 3 SE | | **Key West International** | SE |
| Crystal River | | | Key West | |
| **Daytona Beach Regional** | 3 SE | | **Kissimmee Municipal** | 2 W |
| Daytona Beach | | | Kissimmee | |
| **DeFuniak Springs Municipal** | 2 W | | **La Belle Municipal** | 1 S |
| DeFuniak Springs | | | La Belle | |
| **DeLand Municipal** | 3 NE | | **Lake City Municipal** | 3 E |
| DeLand | | | Lake City | |
| **Destin** | 1 E | | **Lakeland Municipal** | 5 SW |
| Destin | | | Lakeland | |
| **Dunnellon Municipal** | 5 E | | **Lake Wales Municipal** | 2 W |
| Dunnellon | | | Lake Wales | |
| **Everglades** | 1 SW | | **Leesburg Municipal** | 4 E |
| Everglades | | | Leesburg | |
| **Ferguson Airport** | 8 SW | | **Madison County** | 2 NW |
| Pensacola | | | Lee | |
| **Fernandina Beach Municipal** | 4 S | | **Marathon Airport** | E |
| Fernandina Beach | | | Marathon | |
| **Flagler County** | 3 E | | **Marco Island Airport** | 10 NE |
| Bunnel | | | Marco Island | |
| **Flying Ten Airport** | 10 W | | **Marianna Municipal** | 5 NE |
| Gainesville | | | Marianna | |
| **Fort Lauderdale Executive** | 6 N | | **Massey Ranch Airport** | 3 S |
| Fort Lauderdale | | | New Smyrna Beach | |
| **Fort Lauderdale-Hollywood Intl.** | 4 SW | | **Melbourne Regional** | 2 NW |
| Fort Lauderdale | | | Melbourne | |
| **Fort Meade Airport** | 1 E | | **Merritt Island** | 25 E |
| Fort Meade | | | Cocoa | |
| **Fort Walton Beach Airport** | 2 E | | **Miami International** | 9 NW |
| Fort Walton Beach/Navarre | | | Miami | |
| **Gainesville Regional** | 4 NE | | **Mid-Florida** | 3 E |
| Gainesville | | | Eustis | |
| **George T. Lewis** | 1 W | | **Milton Field** | 3 E |
| Cedar Key | | | Milton | |
| **Herlong Field** | 9 SW | | **Naples** | 2 NE |
| Jacksonville | | | Naples | |
| **Hernando County Airpark** | 7 SW | | **New Hibiscus Airpark** | 9 W |
| Brooksville | | | Vero Beach | |
| **Hilliard Airpark** | 1 E | | **New Smyrna Beach Municipal** | 3 NW |
| Hilliard | | | New Smyrna Beach | |
| **Homestead General Aviation** | 5 NW | | **North Perry** | 6 W |
| Homestead | | | Hollywood | |
| **Immokalee** | 1 NE | | **Ocala Municipal** | 2 W |
| Immokalee | | | Ocala | |

| | | | |
|---|---|---|---|
| **Okeechobee County** | 3 NW | **St. George Island** | 8 SE |
| Okeechobee | | Apalachicola | |
| **Opa-Locka 1** | 1 N | **St. Lucie County International** | 3 NW |
| Miami | | Fort Pierce | |
| **Opa-Locka West** | 14 NW | **St. Pete-Clearwater Intl.** | 9 N |
| Miami | | St. Petersburg | |
| **Orlando Country Airport** | 4 NE | **Sanford Municipal** | 3 SE |
| Plymouth-Apopka | | Sanford | |
| **Orlando Executive Airport** | 3 E | **Sarasota-Bradenton** | 3 N |
| Orlando | | Sarasota | |
| **Orlando International** | 7 SE | **Sebastian Municipal** | 1 W |
| Orlando | | Sebastian | |
| **Orlando West** | 8 W | **Sebring Airport & Ind. Park** | 7 SE |
| Orlando | | Sebring | |
| **Ormond Beach Municipal** | 3 NW | **Shell Creek Airpark** | 8 NE |
| Ormond Beach | | Punta Gorda | |
| **Page Field** | 4 S | **South Lakeland Airport** | 4 W |
| Fort Myers | | Mulberry | |
| **Palm Beach County Glades** | 3 W | **Southwest Florida Regional** | 8 SE |
| Pahokee | | Fort Myers | |
| **Palm Beach County Park** | 5 SW | **Space Center Executive** | 6 S |
| West Palm Beach | | Titusville | |
| **Palm Beach International** | 3 W | **Suwannee County** | 2 W |
| West Palm Beach | | Live Oak | |
| **Panama City-Bay County** | 4 NW | **Tallahassee Commercial** | 7 NW |
| Panama City | | Tallahassee | |
| **Pensacola Regional** | 3 NE | **Tallahassee Municipal** | 5 SW |
| Pensacola | | Tallahassee | |
| **Perry-Foley** | 3 S | **Tamiami** | 15 SW |
| Perry | | Miami | |
| **Peter O. Knight** | 2 S | **Tampa International** | 8 W |
| Tampa | | Tampa | |
| **Pierson Municipal** | 1 N | **Tampa Executive Airport** | 20 NW |
| Pierson | | Odessa | |
| **Pilot Country Airport** | 15 S | **Thompson Field** | 2 W |
| Brooksville | | Carrabelle | |
| **Plant City Municipal** | 5 W | **Tri-County** | 7 NE |
| Plant City | | Bonifay | |
| **Pompano Beach** | 1 NE | **Umatilla Municipal** | 1 E |
| Pompano Beach | | Umatilla | |
| **Quincy Municipal** | 2 NE | **Valkaria Field** | 1 W |
| Quincy | | Valkaria | |
| **River Ranch** | 22 E | **Vandenberg** | 7 E |
| Lake Wales | | Tampa | |
| **Rockledge Airpark** | 1 S | **Venice Municipal** | 1 N |
| Rockledge | | Venice | |
| **Rudy's Gliderport** | 8 SW | **Vero Beach Municipal** | 1 NW |
| High Springs | | Vero Beach | |
| **St. Augustine Airport & SPB*** | 5 N | **Wakulla County** | 3 S |
| St. Augustine | | Panacea | |
| **St. Cloud Airpark** | 1 S | **Watson Island Heliport**** | 1 E |
| St. Cloud | | Miami | |

| | | | |
|---|---|---|---|
| **Wauchula Municipal** | 5 SW | **Witham Field** | 1 SE |
| Wauchula | | Stuart | |
| **West Pasco Airport** | 7 S | **Zephyrhills Municipal** | 1 SE |
| New Port Richey | | Zephyrhills | |
| **Williston Municipal** | 2 SW | | |
| Williston | | *SPB—sea plane base* | |
| **Winter Haven Municipal** | 3 NW | ***also dirigible landing base* | |
| Winter Haven | | | |

## ORGAN DONATIONS

Florida allows motorists to indicate on their driver's license or identification card that they wish to donate organs or tissues after their death.

## SAVE OUR COAST PROGRAM

Launched in 1981, the Save Our Coast program's objective is to purchase coastal lands, primarily beaches, for use as public recreation or conservation areas. The Department of Natural Resources sells bonds for land acquisition. The first property purchased under the Save Our Coast program was a 208-acre Okaloosa County tract with a mile of Gulf beach frontage. More than $13 million was spent to purchase the property, now named the Burney Henderson State Recreation Area.

# TOURISM

Florida drew 48 million tourists in 1998, a record for the $41-billion annual industry. The prospect is for the trend to continue. Although Canadian visitors to the state were down dramatically, to 1.7 million compared with 2.1 million the year before, officials were heartened by a national travel survey that found that more Americans plan to vacation in Florida during 2000 and 2001 than anywhere else. It also found that 37 percent of those planning vacations list Florida as their destination.

Tourism is Florida's number one industry, and it directly employs 820,000 Floridians. The state has more than 4,650 hotels and motels with 340,000 rooms. They have an average occupancy rate of 73 percent and an average daily room rate of $82.75.

Despite the heralded popularity of Central Florida's attraction zone, most Florida visitors make the Miami-Ft. Lauderdale area their destination. The Orlando area, however, is close behind, followed by Tampa Bay, the Panhandle, the Space Coast (including Daytona Beach), the Jacksonville-St. Augustine area, and the Ft. Myers-Naples area.

## AGES OF VISITORS

| | Air | | Auto | |
|---|---|---|---|---|
| **Age Group** | **Males** | **Females** | **Males** | **Females** |
| **Up to 6 years** | .4% | .4.3% | .5.3% | .6.3% |
| **7 to 17** | .8% | .8.4% | 10.9% | .11.2% |
| **18 to 25** | .6.6% | .7.6% | .5.8% | .6.2% |
| **26 to 35** | 17.2% | 17.8% | 10.9% | .11.4% |
| **36 to 45** | 22.8% | 20.1% | 14.8% | .15.1% |
| **46 to 55** | 18% | 16.5% | 14.5% | .14.3% |
| **56 to 65** | 14% | 14.8% | 17.9% | .19.1% |
| **66 or over** | .9.6% | 10.6% | .20% | .16.4% |

## MARITAL STATUS OF VISITORS

| | Air | Auto | | Air | Auto |
|---|---|---|---|---|---|
| Married | .67.8% | .82.5% | Widowed | .5.9% | .3.1% |
| Single | .22.3% | .12.3% | Other | .3.8% | .2.1% |

## INCOME OF VISITORS

| | Air | Auto | | Air | Auto |
|---|---|---|---|---|---|
| $0,000-9,999 | .2.4% | .2.8% | $70,000-79,999 | .8.3% | .6.1% |
| $10,000-19,999 | .4.2% | .7% | $80,000-89,999 | .7.3% | .3.9% |
| $20,000-29,999 | .8.4% | .14.5% | $90,000-99,999 | .5.7% | .2.1% |
| $30,000-39,999 | 11.5% | .19% | $100,000-$124,999 | .7.4% | .2.1% |
| $40,000-49,999 | 11.3% | .15.7% | $125,000-$149,999 | .3.9% | .1.4% |
| $50,000-59,999 | 11.8% | .14.4% | $150,000 and above | .8.8% | .2% |
| $60,000-69,999 | .8.8% | .8.4% | | | |

*(Note: Not all percentages total 100 percent because surveys were multiple choice and some visitors checked more than one answer in a category.)*

## VISITORS' EDUCATIONAL LEVELS

|                          | Air    | Auto   |
|--------------------------|--------|--------|
| K-11th grade             | 1%     | 1%     |
| High school graduate     | 1.9%   | 5.9%   |
| Some college             | 19.1%  | 33.7%  |
| College graduate         | 18.9%  | 24.2%  |
| Post-graduate work       | 33.3%  | 24.1%  |
| Advanced degree          | 9.1%   | 3.7%   |
| Currently enrolled       | 15.7%  | 7%     |
| Vocational-Technical     | 1%     | 1%     |
| Other                    | 1.7%   | 1.3%   |

## TOP TEN PLACES OF ORIGIN

| Air            |       | Auto           |       |
|----------------|-------|----------------|-------|
| New York       | 12.5% | Georgia        | 15.7% |
| California     | 6.2%  | Ohio           | 5.7%  |
| New Jersey     | 5.9%  | North Carolina | 5.3%  |
| Ohio           | 5.7%  | Michigan       | 4.9%  |
| Texas          | 5.7%  | New York       | 4.9%  |
| Pennsylvania   | 5.5%  | Alabama        | 4.6%  |
| Illinois       | 5.3%  | Tennessee      | 4.5%  |
| Massachusetts  | 4.4%  | Texas          | 4.5%  |
| Georgia        | 4.1%  | South Carolina | 4.3%  |
| Michigan       | 4.1%  | Pennsylvania   | 4.1%  |

## TEN MOST VISITED ATTRACTIONS

| Air                |       | Auto                 |       |
|--------------------|-------|----------------------|-------|
| EPCOT Center       | 14.5% | Walt Disney World    | 12.9% |
| Walt Disney World  | 14.2% | EPCOT Center         | 12.6% |
| Disney-MGM Studios | 11.5% | Disney-MGM Studios   | 12%   |
| Universal Studios  | 8.1%  | Universal Studios    | 7.9%  |
| Sea World          | 4.4%  | Sea World            | 6.1%  |
| Parks/Preserves    | 4.3%  | Busch Gardens        | 4.3%  |
| Busch Gardens      | 4%    | Spaceport USA        | 2.9%  |
| Spaceport USA      | 2.4%  | Parks/Preserves      | 2.8%  |
| Typhoon Lagoon     | 2.2%  | Cypress Gardens      | 2.3%  |
| Lake Buena Vista   | 1.9%  | Church Street Station| 1.7%  |

*EPCOT Center and Disney MGM studios are part of the Walt Disney World complex but are counted separately because they have their own admission.

## TEN MOST VISITED COUNTIES

| Air          |       | Auto          |       |
|--------------|-------|---------------|-------|
| Miami-Dade   | 15.5% | Orange        | 18.6% |
| Broward      | 11%   | Bay           | 11.4% |
| Orange       | 9.4%  | Volusia       | 9.7%  |
| Palm Beach   | 9.4%  | Okaloosa      | 6%    |
| Pinellas     | 4.9%  | Duval         | 4.8%  |
| Hillsborough | 4.3%  | Brevard       | 4.3%  |
| Bay          | 4.2%  | Pinellas      | 4%    |
| Brevard      | 4.1%  | Hillsborough  | 3.6%  |
| Lee          | 4.1%  | Broward       | 3.5%  |
| Sarasota     | 3.8%  | Osceola       | 3.5%  |

## PRIMARY PURPOSE OF VISIT

| | Air | Auto |
|---|---|---|
| Vacation | 36.2% | 59.2% |
| Business | 29.6% | 10% |
| Visit Friends/Relatives | 28.6% | 27.8% |
| Convention | 2.4% | 7% |
| Cruise | 1.6% | 5% |
| Other | .8% | 8% |
| Honeymoon | 7% | 5% |

## ACTIVITIES ENJOYED

| | Air | Auto |
|---|---|---|
| Shopping/Restaurants | 16.8% | 20.6% |
| Rest/Relaxation | 16.8% | 16.2% |
| Beaches | 15% | 13.1% |
| Climate | 12.2% | 12.5% |
| Attractions/Cruises | 7.7% | 7.1% |
| Pool activities | 6.9% | 8.7% |
| Historical sites | 4.1% | — |
| Fishing | 3.9% | — |
| Golf | 3.4% | 3.4% |
| Dancing/Night life | 2.6% | 4% |
| Boating | — | 2.3% |
| Water sports | — | 2.1% |

## LODGING PREFERENCES (In Order)

| | Air | Auto |
|---|---|---|
| Hotel or Motel | 47.8% | 38.7% |
| Friends/Relatives | 37.1% | 33.5% |
| Condo/Apt/Home (own) | 7.8% | 9.3% |
| Condo/Apt/Home (rent) | 4.1% | 9.2% |
| Campground/RV Park | 4% | 2.1% |
| Timeshare units | 1.1% | 5.7% |
| Other | 1.6% | 1.4% |

## EXPENDITURE AVERAGES

| | Air | Auto |
|---|---|---|
| Transportation | 10.70% | 73% |
| Gasoline | 2% | 3.78% |
| Food (Grocery) | 5.91% | 6.48% |
| Food (Restaurant) | 22.41% | 10.97% |
| Lodging | 30.89% | 18.49% |
| Entertainment | 9.55% | 6.71% |
| Gifts | 8.18% | 3.47% |
| Other | 7.08% | 2.82% |

## FAVORITE WITH FOREIGNERS

Florida was the number one vacation destination of international visitors in 1998. More than 5.3 million tourists from overseas visited the state during the year, drawn, they said, by its sand, sun, and fun. The state was most popular with residents of the United Kingdom.

## 1998 TOP INTERNATIONAL VISITORS

1. Canada
2. Caribbean nations
3. United Kingdom
4. Brazil
5. Germany
6. Argentina
7. Venezuela
8. France
9. Italy
10. Japan

## WHERE FLORIDA GOES

More than 16 percent of Florida households reported taking a vacation in 1997, and more than half left the state when they did. The most popular destinations out of state were Georgia, followed by North Carolina, New York, and California.

The Caribbean was the favorite of Floridians leaving the country, followed by Europe and Canada.

For those staying in the state, Orlando was the overwhelming favorite of Floridians, with more than one-third of all intrastate tourists heading there. Tampa and Daytona Beach were the runner-up destinations, although more than 14 percent of residents traveling within the state went "elsewhere."

## PLANT SAVERS

Joining 18 other major gardens in the U.S. in preserving nearly 3,000 species of plants near extinction are two Florida gardens, Bok Tower Gardens at Lake Wales and Fairchild Tropical Gardens at Miami. Fewer than 20 percent of these plants now receive any kind of protection, and fewer than 10 percent have been cultivated.

## SPENDING MORE

Foreign tourists visited California in greater numbers but spent more money in Florida in 1995, according to latest U.S. Department of Commerce statistics. Although 9.4 million international tourists visiting California that year, spending $11.1 billion, Florida's 7.2 million international tourists in 1995 spent $11.6 billion.

# MAJOR ATTRACTIONS

Most major attractions are members of the Florida Attractions Association, an organization committed to providing fair admission, courtesy, cleanliness, ethical operation, and quality exhibits and entertainment. They are

**A World of Orchids** at Kissimmee presents gardens of exquisite flowering orchids.

**Adventure Island** is Tampa Bay's only recreational water park and is home to a championship volleyball complex, adjacent to Busch Gardens in Tampa.

**Adventure Landing/Shipwreck Island Waterpark** on Jacksonville Beach includes Florida's only uphill water coaster.

**Ah-Tha-Thi-Ki Museum** at Fort Lauderdale features the history and culture of Florida's Seminole Indians.

**Alhambra Dinner Theater,** one of Jacksonville's oldest attractions, offers professional Broadway musicals with dinner.

**American Police Hall of Fame** in Miami exhibits crime and law enforcement memorabilia.

**Babcock Wilderness Adventures** at Punta Gorda offers swamp-buggy rides through Florida's hinterlands.

**Billie Swamp Safari** offers swamp-buggy eco-tours deep in the Everglades, midway between Ft. Lauderdale and Naples off I-75.

**Bok Tower Gardens** at Lake Wales is a serene landscaped garden from which rises a tower offering carillon music.

**Broadway Palm Dinner Theater** offers professional plays and musicals in Fort Myers.

**Buccaneer Bay** is Florida's only natural spring water park, at Weeki Wachee.

**Busch Gardens** at Tampa is a 300-acre period Africa theme park with the world's largest inverted roller-coaster.

**Butterfly World** at Coconut Creek is a tropical rain forest with botanical gardens and thousands of exotic butterflies.

**Captiva Cruises** tour the barrier and out islands off Fort Myers.

**Caribbean Gardens** in Naples is a 52-acre botanical and zoological preserve.

**Chinatown-Splendid China** at Kissimmee is a dining, shopping, and entertainment oriented taste of China.

**Church Street Station** in Orlando is a historic downtown entertainment center and food emporium.

**Clearwater Marine Aquarium** allows visitors to view the rehabilitation and long-term care of dolphins and other sea creatures.

**Conch Tour Train** offers close-up views of historic Key West.

**Coral Castle** in Homestead was singlehandedly built over 30 years.

**Cypress Gardens** near Winter Haven offers water ski shows, its famous gardens, and its Butterfly Conservatory.

**Edison/Ford Winter Estates** in Fort Myers feature tours of the neighboring homes and work areas of the two famous innovators and inventors.

**Ernest Hemingway Home and Museum** in Key West displays the long-term inspiration for the author.

*Europa Seakruz* sails day and evening with dinner and entertainment from Madeira Beach. Sister ships sail from Fort Myers and Miami Beach.

**Everglades Alligator Farm** near Homestead is Florida's oldest alligator farm and features airboat rides into the wilderness.

**Everglades Wonder Gardens** at Bonita Springs provides a glimpse of the past featuring numerous exotic animals.

**Fairchild Tropical Gardens** at Miami is an 83-acre botanical garden of palms, cycads, and colorful tropical plants.

*First Lady of Jacksonville* cruises the historic St. John's River while serving lunch, and dinner with dancing.

**Flamingo Gardens** in Fort Lauderdale is a tram tour, or a walk through native hammocks and the Wray Botanical Gardens.

**Florida Aquarium,** Florida's newest, in Tampa, explores Florida's water story from its underground sources to the open sea.

**Florida Boat Tours** at Everglades City has professional guides lead guests through the Everglades via air boat.

**Florida International Museum** in St. Petersburg hosts splendid international exhibits of the world's art treasures.

**Fred Bear Museum** in Gainesville displays the lore of archery and bowhunting through the ages.

**Fury Catamarans** at Key West offers snorkeling and sailing around the Florida Keys.

**Gatorland** in Orlando is home to thousands of alligators, crocodiles, and wildlife birds.

**Green Meadows Farm** near Kissimmee provides a closeup look at a working farm, with numerous animals to feed and pet.

**Historical Museum of Southern Florida** in Miami offers a tour through south Florida's past at one of the largest private regional history museums in North America.

**Homosassa Springs State Wildlife Park** allows visitors to walk underwater in the natural spring and meet friendly manatees.

**Hubbard's Marina Cruises** takes visitors on deep-sea fishing trips daily into the Gulf of Mexico from John's Pass Village on Madeira Beach.

*Jungle Queen Riverboat* at Fort Lauderdale provides a barbecue and dinner cruise up New River.

**Kennedy Space Center** offers tours of the space launch facility and tells the story of the U.S. space effort in three Imax theaters.

**Key West Aquarium** provides individual and guided tours.

**King Henry's Feast** in Orlando features continuous family entertainment including a five-course dinner at a country estate.

**Lightner Museum** in St. Augustine is the legacy of one man's collection of antiques and mechanical musical instruments.

**Lion Country Safari** at West Palm Beach is a 500-acre drive-through wildlife preserve, North America's original "cageless zoo."

**Lowry Park Zoo** in Tampa includes mammals, birds, and reptiles, many on the endangered list.

**Mai-Kai Polynesian Dinner** in Fort Lauderdale offers dinner and the spectacular "Islander Revue."

**Marineland Ocean Resort** in Marineland is the world's original marine attraction featuring dolphin and other water-themed shows.

**Medieval Times** in Kissimmee entertains with a feast, jousting, and sword fighting in an 11th-century castle.

**Miami Metrozoo** represents the finest in zoo design, providing visitors scenes of exotic animals in natural habitats.

**Miami Museum of Science & Space Transit Planetarium** explore the wonders of science and nature with hands-on activities.

**Miami Seaquarium** includes whale, dolphin, and shark feedings.

**Miami Youth Museum** offers a fun experience for children of all ages with kid-sized interactive exhibits.

**Miccosukee Indian Village** near Miami shows how the Miccosukee tribe lived and still exists in the heart of Florida's Everglades.

**Monkey Jungle** in Miami hosts a colony of wild monkeys in a tropical setting.

**Morikami Museum and Japanese Gardens** in Delray Beach provides a taste of Japan in a 200-acre park.

**MOSI—the Museum of Science & Industry** in Tampa features hands-on exhibits and IMAX film presentations.

**Museum of Science and History of Jacksonville** examines, among other things, the history of man in northeast Florida.

**Naples Trolley Tours** offers a nostalgic trolley ride through the city, with reboarding privileges throughout.

**National Museum of Naval Aviation** in Pensacola focuses on naval aviation past and present.

**Oldest Store Museum** in St. Augustine exhibits a collection of 100,000 items from the past.

**Parrot Jungle and Gardens** in Miami displays more than a thousand birds including colorful, performing macaws.

**Potter's Wax Museum** in St. Augustine features 150 figures.

**Ringling Museum of Art** at Sarasota covers a 68-acre estate that includes the official state art museum, the circus museum, the Ringling home, and the Asolo Theatre.

**Ripley's Believe It or Not! Museum** in Orlando displays the world's most unusual collection of oddities, curiosities, and art objects collected by the famous traveler.

**St. Augustine Alligator Farm** exhibits include all 23 species of crocodiles found around the world.

**St. Augustine Scenic Cruise** is a conducted tour of the St. Augustine waterfront and Matanzas Bay.

**St. Augustine's Ripley's Believe It or Not! Museum** is the original featuring one-of-a-kind exhibits.

**St. Augustine Trains** present a seven-mile tour of the nation's oldest city.

**Salvadore Dali Museum** in downtown St. Petersburg is home to the world's most comprehensive collection of the works of the late Spanish surrealist.

**Sawgrass Recreation Park** at Fort Lauderdale has tours via airboat, an alligator and reptile exhibit, and an 18th-century Indian village.

**Sea World of Florida** in Orlando is a spectacle of shows and exhibits featuring killer whales, dolphins, penguins, sharks, seals, polar bears, and other creatures of the sea.

**Silver Springs** at Ocala is a 350-acre nature theme park famous for its glass-bottom boats.

**Spanish Quarter Museum** in St. Augustine is a living history museum in a restored colonial building.

**Teddy Bear Museum** in Naples features more than 3,000 versions in a mecca for collectors.

**Theater of the Sea** at Islamorada features native fish and marine life in close encounters with visitors.

**Universal Studios Florida** at Orlando is a spacious motion picture and television lot and entertainment center.

**U.S. Astronaut Hall of Fame** in Titusville showcases America's first astronauts through their historic missions.

**Viscaya** in Miami is a 70-room Italian Renaissance-style palace set in 10 acres of formal gardens along Biscayne Bay.

**Walt Disney World Resort** at Orlando is the nation's leading vacation destination with 28,000 acres featuring four theme parks—the Magic Kingdom, EPCOT Center, Disney-MGM Studios, and Typhoon Lagoon.

**Weeki Wachee Springs** at Weeki Wachee features daily live underwater productions featuring the "living mermaids."

**Weeks Air Museum** in Miami displays antique engines and propellers along with a collection of 35 aircraft from World War I and II.

**Wet 'n Wild** in Orlando is the nation's best-attended recreational water park.

**Zorayda Castle** in St. Augustine is a reproduction of the Alhambra, Spain's most famous castle.

# ——————— TREASURE HUNTING ———————

Experts estimate that between 1,200 and 1,800 ships ranging from 16th century galleons to World War II vessels have been sunk or wrecked off Florida during the past 450 years. Of these, more than 100 went down in the Florida Straits and another 175 along the Atlantic coast in the 17th and 18th centuries, many of them carrying gold and silver from the New World to the Old.

Scores of them are still there, and buried in their hulls is the treasure that brought them to the New World in the first place. Often-precise Spanish bookkeeping records listed the exact treasure on board. Those records also include the dates and causes, usually hurricanes, of a ship's foundering.

Some marine archaeologists maintain files listing many of the wrecks, the dates, the contents of their cargoes, how far offshore the wrecks lie, the water depth, type of sea bed, and any other known information, as well as whether salvage attempts have been made. Among known wrecks are

—Ten galleons of Spain's silver armada of 1715 carrying gold, silver, precious gems, and rare Chinese porcelain are thought to lie scattered off an area between Fort Pierce and Sebastian Inlet.

—The *San Pedro* and some 20 other ships that were part of a 1733 fleet that was hit by a hurricane while sailing up the Florida Keys.

—Seven or so French wrecks carrying gold and silver that sunk somewhere off New Smyrna on the Atlantic coast.

—Wrecks among the shoals off the Gulf coast from Cape San Blas to Cape St. George to Lighthouse Point in the Apalachicola area of the Panhandle.

—Wrecks in the Florida Keys off Cape Sable on Florida's southwestern coast and at many spots along the east coast.

Many other rumored treasure sites lie within Florida's boundaries. There are supposed spots around Shell Creek near Punta Gorda at which the Spanish buccaneer Baldazar buried treasure. One pioneer claimed a treasure map handed down to him by descendants of the pirate Gasparilla in 1909 indicates a treasure lies near the mouth of Alligator Creek in south Charlotte County. He claimed to have found one of the several treasures indicated on the map, but it was hijacked from him.

Nine pirate treasure chests supposedly dropped off Caladesi Island were the object of an intense search by some Lakeland men in 1934. They located one large, rectangular, barnacle-covered object, but attempts to raise it were thwarted by the 1935 Labor Day hurricane. The fierce storm washed away their equipment and sand again covered the chest—if it was indeed one.

In 1959, a salvage team raised 18 tons of relics from one of 40 Spanish galleons wrecked July 13, 1733. The find included a chest of gold coins, kegs of silver bars, and historical items.

In 1962, pieces of what may have been an old Spanish galleon or English pirate ship were found by workers driving pilings for a motel near Panama City. Among the articles uncovered was an 800-pound cannon cast before 1756.

Digging at Placida in 1964 unearthed 32 pieces of eight. Mint marks indicated the coins came from Peru around 1696. And in 1965 two young men reported finding thousands of dollars in U.S. gold coins on the ocean floor off Fort Pierce. It is thought these coins were payrolls for the U.S. troops fighting in either the Seminole or Civil wars.

One of the most successful of the professional hunts was conducted in 1964 by the Real Eight Corporation.

Searching south of Cape Canaveral, where a Spanish flotilla wrecked in 1715 with an estimated booty of $14 million or more, Real Eight brought up Spanish gold and silver valued at $1.6 million, plus another $50,000 in artifacts. Continuing its digging, the corporation reportedly brought up another $1 million and by 1969 its find was estimated nearer to $5 million. Of course, values placed on such recoveries often cannot be verified and treasure hunters are apt to undervalue or overvalue their finds based on present or future motives.

Ironically, one of the single most valuable recoveries made by Real Eight was not rescued from the deep water. A gold necklace, worth more than $50,000, was found on the beach near the search site following a 1962 storm.

Around the same time, members of another professional treasure hunting company, Treasure Salvors, studied charts and manifests in the Spanish archives in an attempt to locate the 28 treasure-laden ships of Spain's Terra Firma fleet, which sailed out of Havana, Cuba, Sept. 5, 1622. Less than 24 hours out of port, the fleet was hit by a ferocious storm as it moved through the Straits of Florida. Eight vessels sank, among them the *Nuestra Senora de Atocha* and her sister ship, *La Margarita*. Both were recorded to have been carrying tremendous treasures.

Their research finished, Treasure Salvors began diving about 40 miles southwest of Key West in the Marquesas Islands. The first silver bar they found matched in weight, fineness, and registration number, a bar listed on the *Atocha's* manifest. Within nine days, divers recovered two other 60-pound silver bars, 711 silver coins, guns and cannonballs, religious jewelry, and pottery. The *Atocha* yielded millions of dollars' worth of the ship's reported 40-ton treasure.

It is known the Spanish tried to recover the *Atocha* treasure immediately after the ships sunk, and may have found much of the gold and silver. But they were unable to work the site very long, for another storm arose during the recovery effort and destroyed their site marker. For more than 350 years treasure hunters had been trying to pinpoint the site. None succeeded—until Treasure Salvors.

The *Atocha* recovery has been expensive. Although the value of the salvage finds have been estimated at $40 million, the company spent more than $7 million on the effort. In addition, the company president's son and daughter-in-law were killed when an excavation boat capsized at the wreck site in 1975.

Nevertheless, encouraged by the *Atocha* discovery, the firm concentrated on finding the sister ship, *La Margarita,* and its treasure. In February 1980 it began the search after a thorough study of centuries-old manifests. Five months later, in July, it again reported success. An estimated $12 million in treasure, including a gold chain 11 feet long, was brought to the surface in one week. The company rates its finding of *La Margarita* to be the single richest shipwreck salvaged in modern times.

By 1985, Treasure Salvors had recovered more than $100 million in gold, silver, and artifacts. The company's president, Mel Fisher, estimated another $250 million remains on the sea floor. In 1987, Fisher sold his company to four Atlanta men for $7 million.

Divers in the Florida Keys have made a business of guiding eager would-be treasure hunters to the sites of galleons sunk in the Florida Straits, but professionals offer little encouragement. The amateur's chance of finding anything of value is almost nil—first, because the Spanish sent recovery teams to reclaim much of the lost treasures shortly after they sank and, second, because most professional divers have already thoroughly searched the area. If they spotted an unexploited wreck they would not lead others to it.

One expert believes that as much Spanish gold and silver was dropped in Florida by soldiers and sailors marching overland after losing their vessels as remains in the waters. After researching the subject in 1950, the then-attorney general of Florida estimated that some $165 million is still buried beneath Florida's sands, $30 million of it originally the property of pirate Jose Gaspar.

Underwater treasure finds continue. In July 1987, the *Nuestra Senora de la Maravilla,* a Spanish galleon sunk in 1659, was located. The ship had set off for Spain from Mexico in 1656 with treasure. It stopped in Cuba and when underway again, collided with another ship in fog near the Bahamas. Among the finds from the ship are gold chains, silver coins, cannons, and emeralds—one weighing 100 carats.

A Tampa company in 1990 announced it had found a 17th-century Spanish shipwreck in deep water off southwest Florida near the Dry Tortugas. Gold bars, silver coins, navigational tools, clay jars, and other artifacts recovered were independently appraised to have a value of $4.8 million.

Not so successful was an Alachua County company that began digging in 1989 along the shores of the Suwannee River near Fowlers Bluff for gold reportedly buried at the site by pirates. Three chests were believed to have been buried on the river banks in the 1820s, and a map pinpointing the chests was reportedly once in the possession of an area resident, Emmit Baird. Eyewitnesses recorded that in 1897 Baird recovered one of the chests. He never admitted it, and the map disappeared after his death years later. In the 1920s an attempt was made to recover the remaining two chests; witnesses say one of the chests was brought up but a rope broke and it plunged back into the watery hole. Since then several more attempts have been made to recover the chests, including a three-month-long dig in 1989 by the Alachua company. But after building a cofferdam and going down 30 feet, workers gave up when water kept flooding the excavation.

# ARTS AND CULTURE

## MUSEUMS AND ART CENTERS
### (Members of the Florida Association of Museums)

**Anna Maria**
Anna Maria Island Historical Museum

**Apalachicola**
Apalachicola Maritime Museum
John Gorrie State Museum

**Auburndale**
Florida Citrus Showcase

**Barberville**
Pioneer Settlement for the Creative Arts

**Bartow**
Polk County Historical Museum

**Belleair**
Florida Gulf Coast Art Center

**Boca Raton**
Boca Raton Historical Society Museum and Gift Shop
Boca Raton Museum of Art
Children's Museum of Boca Raton
Children's Science Explorium
International Museum of Cartoon Art
Ritter Art Gallery
University Galleries, Florida Atlantic University

**Bokeelia**
Useppa Island Historical Museum

**Bowling Green**
Paynes Creek State Historic Site

**Boynton Beach**
Boynton Cultural Centre

**Bradenton**
DeSoto National Memorial
Manatee Village Historical Park
Powel Crosley Museum of the Entrepreneur
South Florida Museum, Bishop Planetarium & Parker Manatee Aquarium

**Bristol**
Torreya State Park/Gregory House

**Brooksville**
Heritage Museum

**Bunnell**
Bulow Plantation Ruins State Historic Site

**Bushnell**
Dade Battlefield St. Historic Site

**Cantonment**
Roy L. Hyatt Environmental Center

**Cape Coral**
Cape Coral Historical Museum
The Children's Science Center

**Cedar Key**
Cedar Key Historical Museum
Cedar Key State Museum

**Chokoloskee**
Historic Smallwood Store

**Christmas**
Fort Christmas Museum

**Clearwater**
Clearwater Marine Aquarium
Moccasin Lake Nature Park
Professional Beach Volleyball Hall of Fame

**Clewiston**
Ah-Tha-Thi-Ki Museum
Clewiston Museum

**Cocoa**
Astronaut Memorial Planetarium and Observatory
Brevard Museum of History and Natural Science
Florida Solar Energy Center (University of Central Florida)

**Coconut Creek**
Pompano Beach Historical Society Museum

**Coconut Grove**
Barnacle State Historic Site

**Coral Gables**
Florida Museum of Hispanic and Latin American Art
Lowe Art Museum

**Coral Springs**
Coral Springs Museum of Art

**Crystal River**
Crystal River State Archeological Site
Marine Science Station

**Dade City**
Pioneer Florida Museum

**Dania**
Graves Museum of Archaeology and Natural History
Hollywood Art Museum

**Davie**
Broward Community College Gallery
Buehler Planetarium, Broward Community College
Flamingo Gardens
Young at Art Children's Museum

**Daytona Beach**
Halifax Historical Museum/ Archives
Museum of Arts and Sciences
Southeast Museum of Photography
The Art League of Daytona Beach

**Deerfield Beach**
1920 Old School House
Butler House (1923)
Pioneer House (Kester Cottage) 1930s
South Florida Railway Museum

**DeLand**
African American Museum of the Arts
DeLand House Museum/West Volusia Historical Society
DeLand Museum of Art
Duncan Art Gallery, Stetson Department of Art
Gillespie Museum of Minerals

**Delray Beach**
Cason Cottage Museum
Cornell Archives Room
Cornell Museum of Art and History
Morikami Museum & Japanese Gardens

**Destin**
Destin Fishing Museum

**Dunedin**
Dunedin Fine Art Center
Dunedin Historical Society Museum

**Eatonville**
Zora Neale Horston Roof Garden Museum

**Eglin Air Force Base**
Air Force Armament Museum

**Ellenton**
Gamble Plantation State Historic Site

**Estero**
Koreshan State Historic and Mound Key State Archaeological Site

**Eustis**
Eustis Historical Museum & Preservation Society, Inc.

**Everglades City**
Museum of the Everglades

**Fernandina Beach**
Amelia Island Museum of History
Fort Clinch State Park

**Fort Lauderdale**
Bonnet House
Fort Lauderdale Historical Museum
International Swimming Hall of Fame
Museum of Art
Museum of Discovery & Science
Old Dillard Museum
Seminole Tribal Museum
Stranahan House
Terramar Visitors Center

**Fort Myers**
Burroughs House
Calusa Nature Center & Planetarium
Edison and Ford Winter Estates
Edison Community College Gallery of Fine Art
Fort Myers Historical Museum
Imaginarium Hands-On Museum and Aquarium
Railroad Museum of South Florida

**Fort Pierce**
Harbor Branch Oceanographic Museum
Heathcote Botanical Gardens
St. Lucie County Historical Museum
UDT-Seal Museum

**Fort Walton Beach**
Camp Walton Schoolhouse Museum
FOCUS Center Science Museum
Fort Walton Beach Art Museum
Indian Temple Mound Museum

**Gainesville**
EXPO, The Children's Museum of Gainesville

Florida Museum of Natural History
Harn Museum of Art
Kanapaha Botanical Gardens
Matheson Historical Center
Morningside Nature Center
Santa Fe Community College Teaching Zoo
Santa Fe Gallery, Santa Fe Community College
Thomas Center Galleries
University of Florida University Galleries

**Gulf Breeze**
Gulf Islands National Seashore (Fort Pickens Area)

**Gulfport**
Gulfport Historical Museum

**Hawthorne**
Marjorie Kinnan Rawlings State Historic Site

**Hobe Sound**
Trapper Nelson Interpretive Site at Jonathan Dickinson State Park

**Hollywood**
Art and Culture Center of Hollywood

**Homeland**
Homeland Heritage Park

**Homestead**
Historic Homestead Town Hall Museum

**Homosassa Springs**
Homosassa Springs State Wildlife Park

**Inverness**
Museum of Citrus County History—1912 Citrus Courthouse Nat. Register
Museum of Citrus County History—Coastal Heritage—Old City Hall

**Islamorada**
Matheson House Lignumvitae Key State Botanical Site

**Jacksonville**
Cummer Museum of Art & Gardens
Florida Community College Kent Campus Museum/Gallery
Jacksonville Maritime Museum Society, Inc.
Jacksonville Museum of Contemporary Art

Jacksonville Zoological Gardens
Karpeles Manuscript Library
Kingsley Plantation Timucuan Preserve, NPS
Museum of Science and History
Museum of Southern History
Sojourner Truth Library Museum
Timucuan Ecological and Historic Preserve/Ft Caroline Nat'l Memorial
Tree Hill Jacksonville's Nature Center

**Juno Beach**
Marinelife Center of Juno Beach

**Jupiter**
Florida History Center & Museum
Jupiter Inlet Light, DuBois Home

**Key Biscayne**
Cape Florida Lighthouse Bill Baggs State Recreation Area

**Key Largo**
John Pennekamp Coral Reef State Park

**Key West**
Audubon House and Gardens
Donkey Milk House, c. 1866 Historic Home
East Martello Gallery and Museum
Fort Zachary Taylor State Historic Site
Historic House Museum
Lighthouse Museum
Mel Fisher Maritime Museum
The Oldest House

**Kissimmee**
Osceola Center for the Arts
Osceola County Historical Museum and Pioneer Enrichment Center
Osceola County Pioneer Center

**Lake City**
Columbia County Historical Museum
Florida Sports Hall of Fame

**Lake Monroe**
Central Florida Zoological Park

**Lake Wales**
Bok Tower Gardens
Lake Wales Museum and Cultural Center (The Depot)

**Lake Worth**
Museum of Polo and Hall of Fame
Museum of the City of Lake Worth
Museum of Contemporary Art

**Lakeland**
Explorations V Children's Museum
Mobile Museum of Polk County
Polk Museum of Art
Internal Sport Aviation Museum

**Largo**
Heritage Village

**Live Oak**
Suwannee County Historical Museum

**Longboat Key**
Longboat Key Art Center

**Madison**
North Florida Community College Art Gallery

**Maitland**
Holocaust Memorial Resource and Education Center
Maitland Art Center
Maitland Historical Society and Museums
Zora Neale Hurston National Museum of Fine Arts

**Marathon**
Tropical Crane Point Hammock

**Mayport**
Marine Science Education Center

**Melbourne**
Brevard Museum of Art and Science, Inc.
Florida Institute of Technology Botanical Gardens
Liberty Bell Memorial Museum

**Melbourne Beach**
McLarty Treasure Museum

**Miami**
American Police Museum and Hall of Fame
Bay of Pigs Museum
Black Heritage Museum
Claire-Mendel Gallery of Art
Coral Gables Merrick House
Cuban Museum of the Americas
Fairchild Tropical Garden
Gallery North, Miami-Dade Community College, North Campus
Gold Coast Railroad
Historical Museum of Southern Florida
Holocaust Documentation and Education Center Inc.

International Fine Arts College
Historical Costume Museum
Miami Art Museum
Miami Children's Museum
Miami Fire Museum, Inc.
Miami Metrozoo
Miami Museum of Science and Space Transit Planetarium
Miami Youth Museum
Miami-Dade Community College Kendall Campus Art Gallery
Miami-Dade Community College, Wolfson Galleries
The Art Museum at Florida International University
Vizcaya Museum and Gardens
Weeks Air Museum

**Miami Beach**
Art Center/South Florida
Bass Museum of Art
The Wolfsonian, Florida International University
Ziff Jewish Museum of Florida: Home of Mosaic

**Miami Lakes**
Jay I. Kislak Foundation, Inc.

**Micanopy**
Micanopy Historical Society Museum

**Mount Dora**
Antique Boat Museum
Mount Dora Center for the Arts
Royellou Museum

**Mulberry**
Mulberry Phosphate Museum

**Naples**
Collier County Museum
Conservancy Museum of Natural History
Philharmonic Center for the Arts-Gallery
Teddy Bear Museum of Naples

**New Port Richey**
West Pasco Historical Society Museum and Library

**New Smyrna Beach**
Atlantic Center for the Arts

**Niceville**
Arts Center Galleries, Okaloosa-Walton Community College

**North Miami**
Museum of Contemporary Art in Miami

**North Miami Beach**
Ancient Spanish Monastery of St. Bernard De Clairvaux Cloisters

**North Palm Beach**
Florida Power & Light Historical Museum
William T. Kirby Nature Center/John D. MacArthur Beach State Park

**Ocala**
Appleton Museum of Art
Discovery Science Center
Don Garlits Museum of Drag Racing
Silver River Museum and Environmental Education Center

**Oldsmar**
Oldsmar Center

**Olustee**
Olustee Battlefield Historic Site

**Orange City**
Children's Museum/Discovery Center

**Orlando**
Harry P. Leu Gardens
Kennedy Space Center Visitor Complex
Museum of the Seminole Tribe
Orange County Historical Museum
Orlando Museum of Art
Orlando Science Center
Pine Castle Folk Art Center
University of Central Florida Art Gallery
Valencia Community College East Campus Art Galleries

**Ormond Beach**
Fred Dana Marsh Museum Tomoka State Park
Ormond Memorial Art Museum & Gardens

**Osprey**
Historic Spanish Point

**Palatka**
Putnam Historic Museum
Ravine State Gardens

**Palm Beach**
Henry Morrison Flagler Museum
Hibel Museum of Art
Palm Beach Maritime Museum
Society of the Four Arts

**Palm Coast**
Florida Agricultural Museum

**Panama City**
Gulf Coast Community College Art Gallery
John Hargrove Motor Car Museum
Junior Museum of Bay County
Visual Arts Center of Northwest Florida

**Panama City Beach**
Museum of Man in the Sea

**Parrish**
Florida Gulf Coast Railroad Museum

**Patrick AFB**
Air Force Space and Missile Museum

**Pensacola**
Historic Pensacola Village and T.T. Wentworth, Jr. State Museum
National Museum of Naval Aviation
Pensacola Historical Museum
Pensacola Junior College Visual Arts Gallery
Pensacola Museum of Art
University of West Florida Art Gallery

**Perry**
Forest Capital State Museum

**Plant City**
Pioneer Heritage Museum

**Plantation**
Plantation Historical Museum

**Point Washington**
Eden State Gardens

**Pompano Beach**
International Game Fish Assn Museum

**Ponce Inlet**
Ponce De Leon Inlet Lighthouse

**Port St. Joe**
Constitution Convention State Museum

**Punta Gorda**
Florida Adventure Museum

**Safety Harbor**
Safety Harbor Museum of Regional History

**St. Augustine**
Castillo de San Marcos and Ft. Matanzas National Monuments
Lightner Museum

Museum of Weapons and Early American History
    Oldest House Museum
    Pena-Peck House
    St. Augustine Lighthouse & Museum
    St. Photios Greek Orthodox National Shrine
    Spanish Quarter Museum
    World of Golf Hall of Fame
**St. James City**
    Museum of the Islands
**St. Marks**
    San Marcos de Apalache State Historic Site
**St. Petersburg**
    Boyd Hill Nature Center
    Florida International Museum
    Great Explorations - The Hands On Museum
    Leepa-Rattner Museum and Art Education Center
    Museum of Fine Arts
    Pier Aquarium, Inc.
    Ransom Art Center at Eckerd College
    St. Petersburg Museum of History
    Salvador Dali Museum
    Science Center of Pinellas County
    Florida Holocaust Museum
**Sanford**
    Sanford Museum
    Museum of Seminole County History
    School Board of Seminole County Student Museum
**Sanibel**
    Bailey-Matthews Shell Museum
**Sarasota**
    Crowley Museum and Nature Center
    Gulf Coast Wonder and Imagination Zone
    Marie Selby Botanical Gardens
    Mote Marine Aquarium
    Ringling Museum of Art
    Sarasota Visual Arts Center
    Selby Gallery Ringling School of Art & Design
**Sebring**
    Children's Museum of the Highlands
    Highlands Hammock State Park
    Museum of Florida's Art and Culture
**Silver Springs**

Marion County Museum of History
**Starke**
    Camp Blanding Museum
**Stuart**
    Elliott Museum
    Gilbert's Bar House of Refuge
    Hutchinson Island Coastal Science Center
    Maritime and Yachting Museum of the Treasure Coast
    Stuart Heritage Museum
**Tallahassee**
    Alfred B. Maclay State Gardens
    Black Archives at Union Bank
    Black Archives Research Center & Museum
    Foster-Tanner Fine Arts Gallery
    Knott House Museum
    Lake Jackson Mounds State Archaeological Site
    LeMoyne Art Museum
    Museum of Art/Tallahassee
    Museum of Fine Arts Florida State University
    Museum of Florida History
    Odyssey Science Center
    Riley House Museum of African American History and Culture
    Tallahassee Museum of History & Natural Science
**Tampa**
    Children's Museum of Tampa
    Cracker Country Florida State Fairgrounds
    Florida Aquarium
    Henry B. Plant Museum
    Hillsborough County Historical Commission Museum and Library
    Lowry Park Zoological Garden
    MOSI (Museum of Science & Industry)
    Tampa Bay History Center
    Tampa Museum of Art
    Tampa Police Museum
    Univ. of Tampa Lee Scarfone Gallery
    USF Contemporary Art Museum
    Ybor City State Museum
**Tarpon Springs**
    Tarpon Springs Cultural Center Museum
**Tavares**
    Lake County Historical Museum

**Tequesta**
Lighthouse Gallery & School of Art
**Thonotosassa**
Hillsborough River State Park at Fort Foster
**Titusville**
Astronaut Hall of Fame U. S. Space Camp
Valiant Air Command Aviation Museum
**Valparaiso**
Heritage Museum (Valparaiso)
**Venice**
Venice Art Center
**Vero Beach**
Center for the Arts
Indian River Citrus Museum
McKee Botanical Garden
**West Palm Beach**
Ann Norton Sculpture Garden
Armory Art Center
Bink Glisson Historical Museum and Yesteryear Village
Imagination Station
Mounts Botanical Garden
Norton Museum of Art
Palm Beach Zoo at Dreher Park
South Florida Science Museum
**White Springs**
Stephen Foster State Folk Culture Center
**Winter Haven**
Polk Community College Art Gallery
Water Ski Hall of Fame
**Winter Park**
Cornell Fine Arts Museum
Morse Museum of American Art
Winter Park Historical Association and Museum
**Note:** The Cayman Island National Museum at Grand Cayman also is a member of the Florida Association.

## SYMPHONY ORCHESTRAS
**(Chamber, Pops, Youth, Community College, University)**

Alachua County Youth Orchestra (Gainesville)
Atlantic Classical Orchestra (Stuart)
The Bach Festival Chamber Orchestra (Winter Park)

Brevard Symphony Orchestra (Melbourne)
Brevard Symphony Youth Orchestra (Melbourne)
Broward Community College Youth Symphony (Pompano Beach)
Broward Symphony Orchestra (Fort Lauderdale)
Central Florida Symphony (Ocala)
Charlotte Chamber Music Society (Punta Gorda)
Concert Association of Greater Miami (Miami Beach)
Daytona Beach Symphony Society (Daytona Beach)
Emil Maestre Music Association (St. Augustine)
Florida Orchestra (Tampa)
Florida Philharmonic Orchestra (Fort Lauderdale)
Florida Space Coast Philharmonic (Cocoa)
Florida State University Symphony (Tallahassee)
Florida Symphony Pops (Boca Raton)
Florida Symphony Youth Orchestra (Winter Park)
Florida West Coast Symphony Orchestra (Sarasota)
Florida West Coast Symphony Youth Orchestra (Sarasota)
Gainesville Chamber Orchestra (Gainesville)
Greater Miami Youth Symphony (Miami)
Greater Palm Beach Symphony (Palm Beach)
Greater Pensacola Symphony Orchestra (Pensacola)
Imperial Symphony Orchestra (Lakeland)
Jacksonville Symphony Association (Jacksonville)
The Naples Philharmonic (Naples)
New World Symphony (Miami)
Northwest Florida Symphony Orchestra (Niceville)
Ocala Festival Orchestra (Ocala)
Okaloosa Symphony Orchestra (Fort Walton Beach)
Org. Sinfonica Nacional de Guatemala (Miami)
Palm Beach Pops (Palm Beach)

Palm Beach Symphonette (Palm Beach)

Pinellas Youth Symphony (St. Petersburg)

Royal Symphonic Pops Orchestra of Florida (Miami Beach)

Sarasota-Manatee Community Orchestra (Longboat Key)

South Florida Youth Symphony (Miami)

Southwest Florida Symphony (Fort Myers)

St. Johns River City Band (Jacksonville)

The Tallahassee Symphony (Tallahassee)

Tampa Bay Chamber Orchestra (Tampa)

Tampa Bay Community Symphony (St. Petersburg)

Tampa Bay Symphony (Seminole)

Tampa Bay Youth Orchestras (Tampa)

Treasure Coast Symphony (Fort Pierce)

Venice Symphony (Venice)

## ARTISTS HALL OF FAME

The Florida Artists' Hall of Fame was created by the 1986 Legislature to honor individuals who have made significant contributions to the arts in Florida. The Hall of Fame is permanently installed on the Plaza level of the Capitol in Tallahassee, with additional information about each member displayed on the 22nd floor.

Members to date are writers Marjorie Kinnan Rawlings, Ernest Hemingway, John D. MacDonald, and Marjory Stoneman Douglas; circus magnate John Ringling; patrons Ralph Hubbard Norton and former Secretary of State George Firestone; playwrights George Abbott and Tennessee Williams; folklorist Zora Neale Hurston; visual artists A. E. ("Bean") Backus, Duane Hanson, Robert Rauschenberg, Jerry N. Uelsmann, Hiram D. Williams, and Martin Johnson Heade; actor Burt Reynolds; musicians Ray Charles and Ellen Taaffee Zwilich; songwriter Will McLean; choreographer and dancer Edward Villela; photographer Clyde Butcher; and troubadour Gamble Rogers.

---

### Post Office Murals

During the Great Depression the U.S. Department of Treasury commissioned artists to paint murals in all post office buildings erected during the 1930s. In all, 1,118 were done under this program, but few remain. Twelve in Florida have survived.

They are in post offices (and other government buildings that served as post offices in the 1930s) in the cities of West Palm Beach, Miami, Fort Pierce, Miami Beach, Palm Beach, Sebring, Lake Wales, Madison, Milton, Tallahassee, DeFuniak Springs, and Jasper. Others at the Starke and Perry post offices no longer exist.

A hanging in the Lake Worth post office was commissioned under a different federal program during the 1930s.

All the murals depict facets of Florida history or life. Some of them measure up to 10 by 14 feet.

The most famous murals are in the West Palm Beach post office and commemorate "The Barefoot Mailman." Enshrined in legend by having one of their number presumably fall prey to an alligator, the "barefoot" mailmen walked the mail along the beach from Palm Beach to Miami and back in the late 1880s and represented a communications revolution. The three-day trip cut seven weeks from the time it took to send a letter from Miami to New York.

Artists were paid an average of $700.00 to paint the giant canvases.

*(continue on next page)*

Today the Florida Department of State continues to hire artists for works in new state public buildings. The program requires that half a percent of the cost of a new public building be set aside to buy art from Florida artists for display in and around the buildings.

## CULTURAL CALENDAR

Specific dates for the following may be obtained from area chambers of commerce.

**January**
Bok Tower Gardens' Camellia Celebration, Lake Wales
Key West Literary Seminar, Key West
Art Deco Weekend, Miami Beach
Los Olas Art Fair, Ft. Lauderdale
Art Expo Craft Show, Key West
Stephen Foster Day, White Springs

**February**
Bach Festival, Winter Park
Bok Tower Azalea Celebration, Lake Wales
Miami International Film Festival, Miami
Black Heritage Festival, New Smyrna Beach
National Art Festival, Naples
Greek Festival, Melbourne
Old Hyde Park Village Art Festival, Tampa

**March**
Blue Grass Festival, Kissimmee
Italian Renaissance Festival, Miami
Rediscover San Luis, Tallahassee
Seminole Indian Days, Cokoloskee
Gasparilla Sidewalk Art Festival, Tampa
SPIFFS International Folk Fair, St. Petersburg
Manatee Heritage Week , Bradenton
Indigenous People's Cultural Festival, Lakeland
Antiquarian Book Fair, St. Petersburg
Winter Park Art Festival, Winter Park

**April**
Blues Festival, Jacksonville
Festival of States, St. Petersburg
Bookfest of the Palm Beaches, West Palm Beach
Jazz Festival, Pensacola

**May**
Old Spanish Trail Festival, Crestview
Spring Craft Fair, Miami
Florida Folk Fesival, White Springs
Music Festival, Sarasota

**June**
Billy Bowlegs Festival, Fort Walton Beach
International Food & Music Festival, Cocoa
Gospel Jubilee, Live Oak
Lincolnville Music Festival, St. Augustine

**July**
Beethoven by the Beach, Ft. Lauderdale
Florida International Festival, Daytona Beach
Hemingway Days, Key West
Ybor City Summer Arts & Crafts Festival, Tampa

**August**
Atlantic Shakespeare Festival, St. Augustine
SummerFest, Vero Beach
Obon Festival, Delray Beach

**September**
Springfield Jazz & Heritage Festival, Jacksonville
Pioneer Florida Day Festival, Dade City
Osceola Art Festival, Kissimmee

**October**
Jazz Festival, Clearwater
Seminole Indian and Florida Pioneer Festival, Cocoa
Riverwalk Fall Art Show, Ft. Lauderdale
Octoberfest Music Festival, Brooksville

**November**
  Riverwalk   Blues   Fest,   Ft.
Lauderdale
  Great    Gulf    Coast    Arts
Festival, Pensacola
  Jazz    Festival    of    South
Walton, Seaside
  Halifax Art Festival, Daytona Beach
  French Film Festival, Sarasota

Fall Festival of the Arts, DeLand
International Folk Festival, Eustis

**December**
  Native American Indian Festival,
Melbourne
  Festival of Lights, Fanning Springs
  Selby Gardens Holiday Celebration,
Sarasota

## AUDITORIUMS AND ARENAS

| City | Name | Seating |
|---|---|---|
| Boca Raton | University City Auditorium | 2,395 |
| Bradenton | Municipal Auditorium | 1,600 |
| Clearwater | Ruth Eckerd Hall | 2,182 |
| Coconut Creek | Omni Auditorium | 1,960 |
| Coral Springs | City Centre Theater | 1,534 |
| Davie | Davie Arena | 7,500 |
| Daytona Beach | Ocean Center | 9,496 |
| | Municipal Stadium | 10,000 |
| | Peabody Auditorium | 2,552 |
| DeLand | Municipal Stadium | 6,000 |
| Eustis | Lake County Expo Hall | 2,440 |
| Fort Lauderdale | Omni Auditorium | 2,007 |
| | Amaturo Theater | 595 |
| | Bailey Hall | 1,197 |
| | Parker Playhouse | 1,200 |
| | War Memorial Auditorium | 2,110 |
| | Broward Performing Arts Center | 2,700 |
| Fort Myers | Lee Civic Center | 9,000 |
| | Exhibition Hall | 1,233 |
| | Harborside Convention Center | 3,134 |
| | Performing Arts Hall | 1,765 |
| Fort Pierce | St. Lucie County Civic Center | 4,000 |
| Gainesville | O'Connell Center | 12,000 |
| | Performing Arts Center | 1,823 |
| Jacksonville | Veterans Memorial Coliseum | 10,276 |
| | Civic Auditorium | 3,809 |
| | Flag Pavilion | 2,000 |
| | Convention Center | 7,000 |
| | Florida Theatre Performing Arts | 1,978 |
| Key Biscayne | Tennis Center at Crandon Park | 14,000 |
| Kissimmee | Tupperware Center Theater | 2,000 |
| Lakeland | Civic Center Theater | 2,282 |
| | George Jenkins Arena | 10,000 |
| Melbourne | Brevard Performing Arts Center | 1,193 |
| | Melbourne Auditorium Theater | 1,400 |
| Miami | Knight International Center | 5,174 |
| | County Auditorium-Theater | 2,498 |
| | Coconut Grove Exhibition Hall | 10,600 |
| | Bayfront Park Auditorium | 19,000 |

|                  |                                    |        |
|------------------|------------------------------------|-------:|
|                  | Expo Center                        | 5,000  |
|                  | Municipal Auditorium               | 10,400 |
|                  | Metrozoo Amphitheater              | 1,500  |
|                  | Gusman Performing Arts Center      | 1,739  |
|                  | Marine Stadium                     | 6,500  |
|                  | Miami Arena                        | 16,640 |
| Miami Beach      | Convention Center                  | 12,000 |
|                  | Jackie Gleason Theater             | 2,716  |
| Naples           | Philharmonic Center                | 1,221  |
| Orlando          | Orange County Civic Center         | 11,072 |
|                  | Expo Centre                        | 1,300  |
|                  | Bob Carr Performing Arts Center    | 2,518  |
|                  | Univ. of Central Fla. Arena        | 5,500  |
|                  | Centroplex-Arena                   | 15,500 |
| Palmetto         | Manatee Civic Center               | 4,000  |
| Panama City      | Marina Civic Center                | 2,900  |
| Pensacola        | Civic Center                       | 10,268 |
|                  | Bayfront Auditorium                | 2,574  |
|                  | Saenger Theater                    | 1,778  |
|                  | Univ. of West Fla. Main Theater    | 450    |
| Punta Gorda      | Charlotte County Memorial          | 1,416  |
| Rockledge        | Brevard County Fair Stadium        | 8,000  |
| St. Petersburg   | Bayfront Center Arena              | 8,140  |
|                  | Bayfront Center Mahaffey Theater   | 2,000  |
|                  | Tropicana Field                    | 50,000 |
| Sarasota         | Asolo Center for Performing Arts   | 503    |
|                  | Civic Center Exhibition Hall       | 1,200  |
|                  | Opera House                        | 1,033  |
|                  | Van Wezel Performing Arts Hall     | 1,761  |
| Sunrise          | Sunrise Music Theater              | 4,088  |
|                  | National Car Rental Center         | 19,452 |
| Tallahassee      | Civic Center                       | 14,000 |
|                  | Fla. A&M Gaither Athletic Center   | 3,500  |
|                  | Florida State Conference Center    | 1,100  |
| Tampa            | Univ. of South Florida Sun Dome    | 11,063 |
|                  | Florida State Fair and Expo Center | 12,000 |
|                  | Florida State Fair Music Hall      | 4,500  |
|                  | Performing Arts Center             | 3,600  |
|                  | Convention Center                  | 11,100 |
|                  | Ice Palace                         | 19,510 |
| West Palm Beach  | WPB Auditorium                     | 2,119  |
|                  | Kravis Center for Performing Arts  | 2,200  |
|                  | WPB Municipal Arena                | 7,056  |

## MISS FLORIDA WINNERS
### (Miss America Contest)

The annual Miss Florida pageant dates back to the 1930s when it was held at Miami Beach and sponsored by the Miami Beach Jaycees. In later years the pageant, sponsored by the Florida Jaycees, was held in Orlando in 1947, in Marineland in 1948, and in Jacksonville from 1949 to 1953. In 1954 and 1955, sponsorship was taken over by the Florida Citrus Exposition and the pageant held in Winter Haven. Sarasota became the pageant site in 1956, where it remained through 1968, first under the sponsorship of Sunshine Springs and Gardens and then by the Sarasota County Chamber of Commerce. Since 1969, it has been staged in Orlando and sponsored by the Miss Florida Pageant of Orlando.

Following are the pageant winners and the city, county, or university they represented in the competition. Miss Florida 1992 went on to win the 1993 Miss America Pageant.

1935—Elizabeth Hull, Plant City
1936—Not held
1937—Not held
1938—Mary Joyce Walsh, Miami
1939—Rose Marie Magrill, Miami
1940—Not held
1941—Mitzi Strother, Miami
1942—Eileen Irma Knapp, Miami
1943—Muriel Elizabeth Smith, Miami
1944—Virginia Warlen, Miami
1945—Virginia Freeland, Miami
1946—Jacquelyn Jennings, Miami
1947—Eula Ann McGehee, St. Petersburg
1948—Rosemary Carpenter, Miami
1949—Shirley Ann Rhodes, Tampa
1950—Janet Ruth Crockett, St. Petersburg
1951—Mary Godwin, Gainesville
1952—Marcia Crane, Orlando
1953—Marjorie Simmons, Tampa
1954—Ann Gloria Daniel, Dade City
1955—Sandra Wirth, Miami
1956—Sally Fisher, Miami
1957—Dorothy Steiner, Boca Raton
1958—Dianne Tauscheer, Orlando
1959—Nancy Rae Purvis, Manatee County
1960—Kathy Magda, Fort Lauderdale
1961—Sherry Grimes, Sarasota
1962—Gloria Brody, Jacksonville
1963—Flora Jo Chandonnet, Miami
1964—Priscilla Schnarr, Hollywood
1965—Carol Blum, Fort Lauderdale
1966—Diane Colston, Sarasota (resigned, title filled by runner-up Christine Torgeson, Manatee County)
1967—Dawn Cashwell, Pensacola
1968—Linda Fitts, Panama City
1969—Lynee Edea Topping, Marco
1970—Lisa Louise Donovan, Sarasota
1971—Barbara Jo Ivey, Winter Park

1972—Suzanne Charles, Miami
1973—Ellen Meade, Manatee County
1974—Delta Burke, Orlando
1975—Ann Schmalzried, Univ. of Florida
1976—Nancy Stafford, Fort Lauderdale
1977—Cathy LaBelle, Tampa
1978—Caroline Cline, Tampa (resigned, title filled by runner-up Wendy Sue Cheatham, Lee County)
1979—Marti Sue Phillips, Manatee County
1980—Caroline Dungan, Manatee County
1981—Dean Herman, Jacksonville
1982—Deanne Pitman, Sanford
1983—Kimberly Boyce, Manatee County
1984—Lisa Valdez, Manatee County
1985—Monica Farrell, Jacksonville
1986—Molly Pesce, Forrest City
1987—Jennifer Anne Sauder, Homestead
1988—Melissa Aggeles, Manatee County
1989—Sandra Frick, Coral Springs
1990—Dana Dalton, Orlando
1991—Mary Ann Olson, Manatee County
1992—Leanza Cornett, Jacksonville
1993—Nicole Padgett, Fort Myers
1994—Magan Elizabeth Welch, De Land
1995—Kristen Alicia Beall Ludecke, Eustis
1996—Jamie Bolding, Mount Dora
1997—Christy Neuman, Jacksonville
1998—Lissette Gonzales, Miami
1999—Kelli Meierhenry, Orlando

## STATE OF THE ARTS

Florida has more than 300 museums and galleries, 80 dance companies, 250 theater companies, and a score of symphony orchestras. In all, the arts organizations in the state employ more than 35,000.

## ADULTHOOD

In 1973 Florida lowered the legal age from 21 to 18. As a result, 18-year-olds now are permitted to apply for jobs as policemen and firemen, drive city buses, and be notary publics and bondsmen; they can also gamble, purchase a shotgun or rifle, enter into contracts, obtain credit, purchase automobiles, and get married. An 18-year-old also can vote, be called for jury duty, run for city or county office, and be sued. A person still must be 21 years old, however, to purchase a handgun and to run for the legislature. Drinking age in Florida also is 21.

## COMMON-LAW MARRIAGES

The legitimacy of new common-law marriages was abolished in Florida in 1968. Only those live-in arrangements or common-law marriages that began prior to 1968 are recognized and require a divorce to end.

## MAIDEN NAME

Florida does not require a married woman to take her husband's name. A court in 1976 stated that although it is general custom for a woman to change her name upon marriage, law does not compel her to. Early records show husband and wife often were known by different names, according to the court. Mere recitation of marriage vows, stated the court, does not legally change a woman's name.

# AGRICULTURE

Next to tourism, agriculture is Florida's primary economic resource. Each year, Florida is often the nation's top producer of citrus, sugarcane, tomatoes, foliage, honey, and strawberries. Other Florida commodities often in the top 10 nationally are eggs, peanuts, beef cattle, tobacco, potatoes, and broilers. Florida produces all of the nation's commercially grown limes and mangos.

## CITRUS INDUSTRY

The citrus tree is a native of the Orient, from which it was carried by man ever westward, to India, to the Mediterranean, and then across the Atlantic Ocean. It is believed to have been first brought to the Americas by Columbus. He brought citrus seeds that were planted on the island of Haiti.

The first seeds planted on the mainlands of the Americas were brought by the expedition of Juan de Grijalva when he landed in Central America in mid-July 1518. Exact date of the citrus tree's introduction into Florida is not known, but from a statement made by Pedro Menendez, dated April 2, 1579, it appears citrus fruits were growing in abundance around St. Augustine at that time. Early settlers in Florida some two centuries later found wild citrus trees scattered over the state. One of the oldest cultivated groves planted in Florida is thought to be the Don Phillipe grove in Pinellas County, planted some time between 1803 and 1820. It is believed that Duncan grapefruit originated in this grove. The site now is Phillipe Park near Safety Harbor.

Citrus production in Florida had soared to an all-time high of more than five million boxes when the Great Freeze of 1894-95 almost totally wiped out the citrus industry. It was not until 1909-10 that this level was again reached. Since that time the volume steadily increased and by the mid-1940s Florida was producing more than half the nation's citrus fruit supply.

Florida surpassed all other states in bearing citrus acreage in 1932-33 with 265,400 acres, which accounted for 46 percent of the U.S. total bearing acreage. As the decade of the 1970s began, Florida's dominance of the nation's citrus production became even more apparent and in 1980-81 the Sunshine State was producing 61.9 percent of the nation's supply.

Severe freezes in 1983 and 1985 seriously hurt Florida's citrus industry. The effects showed up in a 15 percent reduction in the number of citrus farms to 8,121 in 1987, from 9,588 in 1982. Groves also were severely harmed in 1984 and 1985 when many growers were ordered to burn their trees because of an outbreak of citrus canker disease. Some large growers, economically hurt by the dual scourges, did not replant. Others, to avoid the freezes of north and central Florida, have replanted farther south in counties such as Hendry, Lee, and Collier. Despite the decade's adversities, Florida in the 1989-90 season produced 62.7 percent of the nation's citrus.

After the tree-killing freezes in the 1980s, growers replaced groves in central Florida with younger trees and planted more trees in south Florida, to take advantage of its warmer climate. With no comparable freezes so far in the 1990s, production is at a record high. In the 1997-98 season, Florida produced more than 76 percent of the nation's citrus.

### Major Citrus Varieties

**AVON LEMON** is a most popular lemon of all around use. It is of good quality in fresh fruit form, and of superior quality for processing.

**DANCY TANGERINE** is the smallest and best known of the Mandarin tangerine group. It has high color, and peels and sections smoothly. Used for out-of-hand eating, fruit cups, salads, and concentrates, the Dancy is in season from November to March.

**DUNCAN GRAPEFRUIT** is considered superior in flavor to other grapefruits. It is generally large with a thick, pale yellow skin, contains some seeds, and its flesh is white. With a season from September to May, the Duncan is used for halves, sections, juice, fruit cups, salads, and concentrates.

**HAMLIN ORANGE** is an early season orange, maturing between October and December. It is medium size, oval shaped, has a slightly thin skin and few seeds, and is used primarily as fresh fruit. It is also excellent for juice and concentrate.

**KEY LIME** is grown principally in the Florida Keys and along the Gulf coast. It is a seedy, small-sized fruit colored light green to yellow and ripens year around. Use is limited mainly to Key Lime pies, a south Florida specialty.

**KUMQUAT** is a small, orange-like fruit three-quarters to an inch in size with a spicy sweet rind and tart flesh. It is used widely for decorative purposes, but is often eaten whole, and used in marmalade, jellies, and candies.

**MARSH SEEDLESS GRAPEFRUIT** is a medium to large fruit, usually flattened at each end. Its skin is thin, smooth, and yellow. The flesh is white and nearly seedless. Used for halves, juice, sections, fruit cups, salads, and concentrates, it ripens between October and June.

**MEYER LEMON** is rated the best looking of the lemon family. Not a true lemon, it is a hybrid of orange and grapefruit, has an oval grapefruit shape, and a slight grapefruit flavor with an orange texture. The skin is smooth and thin, with an orange tinge and a high juice content. The Meyer is popular with home gardeners because of its showiness and dependability.

**PERSIAN LIME** is larger than the Key lime. It is oval-shaped, seedless, has a smooth, dark green skin and pale green pulp, and yields abundant acid juice of excellent flavor. It accounts for most of the state's lime production. It also is called the Tahiti lime.

**TANGELO** is a tangerine-grapefruit hybrid. It resembles an orange in appearance and a tangerine in flavor. Its skin is generally thin and either smooth or slightly bumpy. It is best for fresh fruit or out-of-hand eating.

**TEMPLE ORANGE** is a mid-season hybrid of sweet orange and tangerine, placing it in the tangor family. It peels easily and is generally regarded as an excellent eating orange, but it also is used for concentrates, juice, salads, and fruit cups.

**THOMPSON PINK GRAPEFRUIT** is a mutation of Marsh seedless and has a similar taste. Used for halves, sections, fruit cups, and salads, it is in season October to May.

**VALENCIA ORANGE,** the "juice orange," is the most widely planted orange in the world. Medium to large size, the Valencia matures late, from February to June, but may be kept on the tree several months during which it grows sweeter. The Valencia accounts for roughly half of the Florida orange crop. It is difficult to peel and section, and best used for concentrates, juice, sections, fruit cups, and salads.

**WASHINGTON NAVEL ORANGE** is an early season orange known as an eating orange because it peels and sections easily, and is generally seedless. It is characterized by a distinctive "navel" on the blossom end.

### Citrus Acreage by County, 1998

| County | Acres |
| --- | --- |
| Brevard | 10,715 |
| Charlotte | 21,522 |
| Collier | 35,655 |
| De Soto | 67,192 |
| Glades | 10,776 |
| Hardee | 52,340 |

| | | | |
|---|---|---|---|
| Hendry | .100,124 | Osceola | .15,535 |
| Highlands | .75,909 | Palm Beach | .10,617 |
| Hillsborough | .27,428 | Pasco | .11,360 |
| Indian River | .64,138 | Polk | .102,457 |
| Lake | .20,864 | St. Lucie | .103,894 |
| Lee | .11,871 | Sarasota | .2,332 |
| Manatee | .23,807 | Seminole | .1,411 |
| Martin | .46,439 | Volusia | .1,477 |
| Miami-Dade | .2,792 | All others | .175 |
| Okeechobee | .12,244 | **State Total** | **.845,260** |
| Orange | .9,188 | | |

### Citrus Acreage by Year, 1966-1996

| Census Year | Oranges | Grapefruit | Specialty Fruit | Total Acres |
|---|---|---|---|---|
| 1966 | 673,086 | 103,224 | 81,772 | 858,082 |
| 1968 | 713,400 | 119,883 | 97,966 | 931,249 |
| 1970 | 715,806 | 124,050 | 101,615 | 941,471 |
| 1972 | 659,418 | 124,142 | 94,459 | 878,019 |
| 1974 | 642,431 | 130,326 | 91,341 | 864,098 |
| 1976 | 628,567 | 137,909 | 85,893 | 852,369 |
| 1978 | 616,020 | 136,342 | 78,873 | 831,235 |
| 1980 | 627,174 | 139,994 | 78,165 | 845,283 |
| 1982 | 636,864 | 139,939 | 71,053 | 847,856 |
| 1984 | 573,991 | 134,680 | 52,694 | 761,365 |
| 1986 | 466,252 | 117,845 | 40,395 | 624,492 |
| 1988 | 536,737 | 119,606 | 41,586 | 697,929 |
| 1990 | 564,809 | 125,300 | 42,658 | 732,767 |
| 1992 | 608,636 | 135,166 | 47,488 | 791,290 |
| 1994 | 653,370 | 146,915 | 54,407 | 854,692 |
| 1996 | 656,598 | 144,416 | 56,847 | 857,861 |

## FLORIDA ORANGE PRODUCTION
### (in millions of boxes)

| | |
|---|---|
| 1997-98 | 244 |
| 1996-97 | 215.5 |
| 1995-96 | 203.2 |
| 1994-95 | 205.5 |
| 1993-94 | 174.4 |
| 1992-93 | 186.6 |
| 1991-92 | 139.8 |
| 1990-91 | 151.6 |
| 1989-90 | 110.2 |
| 1988-89 | 146.6 |

## WHEN TO PICK FLORIDA CITRUS

In the land of backyard fruit trees, fruit often rots on the trees not from disinterest but from confusion about when it should be picked.

**Grapefruit:** Grapefruit: white and pink, can be picked when it appears ripe anytime except July and August.

**Red Navel Oranges:** October, November, and December.

**Ambersweet Oranges:** September through January.

**Hamlin Oranges:** October, November, and December.

**Navel Oranges:** October through January.

**Pineapple Oranges:** October through February.

**Valencia Oranges (the juice orange):** February through June.

**Temple Oranges:** January, February, and March.

**Sunburst and Fallglow Tangerines:** October, November, and December.

**Robinson Tangerines:** September, October, and November.

**Royal Lee Tangerines:** November and December.

**Dancy Tangerines:** December and January.

**Honey Tangerines:** January through April.

**Nova Tangelos:** October and November.

**Orlando Tangelos:** November, December, and January.

**Mineola Tangelos:** January and February.

## SELECTED FRUIT SPECIES

Besides a variety of citrus, Florida offers a delicious selection of other fruits not common to most of the U.S. Among them are:

**AVOCADO** was a dinner treat for the explorer Cortez when he feasted with Montezuma II in the early 1500s. Indians in Central America have eaten avocados for centuries, but the fruit first came to this country in 1833 when Henry Perrine brought some trees from Mexico and planted them just south of Miami. By 1880 the fruit was being grown commercially. The avocado matures at different times in different sites in Florida, but is most plentiful between January and July. Those trees that bear well usually come from a seedling to which good varieties have been grafted. Avocados are loaded with calories, a tiny piece of just four ounces containing nearly 300 calories. And, except for the ripe olive, an avocado has more oil than any other fruit. It also contains much protein, but little sugar. Avocados come round, oval, and elongated. Growers divide them into three "races"—the thin-skinned Mexican, the West Indian (Florida's commercial crop), and the hardy Guatemalan fruit.

**BANANAS** are not grown commercially in Florida to any extent. The varieties often seen in the state, usually in backyards, are the Lady Finger or Hart, which bears a small fruit four to six inches long weighing about two ounces; the Cavendish of Chinese origin, a dwarf-type tree that grows to about five to seven feet in height; and the Horse or Hog banana, often grown as an ornamental planting. It takes 12 to 18 months for a banana plant to bear fruit. A medium-sized banana has about 90 calories.

**BARBADOS CHERRY** is a soft, juicy fruit that grows to about one inch in diameter, is deep red in color, and usually sprouts in clusters of two or three. The plants are dense and spreading and can grow as tall as 12 feet when not trimmed. In south Florida the tiny cherry flowers, usually pale pink or rose, blossom in April; the fruit begins to ripen in early May. Barbados cherries can be tart or sweet, and are quite perishable. The cherries have a higher acid content than other fruits; just one berry provides a daily ration of Vitamin C.

**CALAMONDIN** is a relative of the citrus and looks like a tiny orange or tangerine. Because the fruit is so sour it often is used as a substitute for limes or lemons. The calamondin tree is relatively small but bears volumes of fruit, each usually less than an inch in diameter. Florida newcomers often confuse the kumquat with the calamondin because both are used mainly as ornamental trees. The calamondin tree blossoms most of the summer, with the green fruit turning to a ripening orange color in fall. The fruit is ready for picking in winter.

**CARAMBOLA**, an exotic-looking fruit from Asia, is quite tropical and easily killed by freezing temperatures. The egg-shaped, slightly translucent fruit is yellow and has a shiny, waxy look when ripe. The flesh is crisp and juicy and may be sweet or acid. The carambola can be eaten fresh or used in drinks or to make jelly. It is not grown commercially, and is relatively rare, even in backyards.

**CARISSA,** seen mainly as a hedge, actually produces a dark fruit that matures in the summer and grows to two inches in diameter. The skin is thin and the juice white and fairly gummy. With the seeds removed, carissa is used in salads and sauces or can be eaten off the bush. Carissa makes a tight hedge because its shrubs have strong, two-pointed thorns. Its small white flower is wonderfully fragrant.

**CEYLON GOOSEBERRY** is an attractive shrub that can be grown farther north in Florida than most tropical trees, and its fruit is excellent for salads, jellies, and preserves. The plants are easy to grow. Its fruit is round, about an inch in diameter, and turns to maroon-purple when ripe. The berry's flesh is acidic and juicy with soft, flat seeds.

**CITRON** is a tree that looks much like an overgrown lemon tree. The fruit's skin is quite thick and resembles a lemon. It is often preserved and used in candies or cakes. Citron pulp has only a tiny amount of juice.

**COCONUTS,** grown on trees primarily in south Florida, have been fighting a losing battle with blight for more than two decades. To the shopper, the best coconuts are heavy, with milk sloshing around inside. Without milk, the coconut is spoiled. Moldy eyes also are undesirable. Caution is advised in eating coconuts off trees in Florida because many of the trees, to save them from blight, are being injected with antibiotics and insecticides.

**CUSTARD APPLE** has never been popular for the dinner table, but deserves mention because it is grown so abundantly in south Florida. The fruit also is called the Jamaica Apple or Bullock's Heart. Almost smooth on the surface and reddish brown when ripe, the fruit grows to weigh a pound when mature. It tapers from a rather flat top side, where it is attached to the twig, to more of a point at the bottom. It is sometimes mistaken for the Cherimoya, well known in Cuba. The custard apple fruit has little dietary significance; its flavor may seem quite insipid and sweet.

**FIG** is a small brownish to yellow fruit grown in many backyards. From June until September, when a fig tree begins to shed leaves, its fruit is plentiful. Ripe figs are quite soft and perishable and when overripe give off a fermented smell. The fruit needs no flavoring and is best eaten when freshly picked. Beware, however, for figs are slightly laxative. The trees like warm weather best, but will grow in protected areas farther north.

**GRAPES** are grown in most areas of the state, regardless of the soil, the temperature, or the rainfall. In recent years they have been the basis for a growing wine industry in the state. Numerous varieties are grown. Muscadine hybrids are popular in central Florida. The Scuppernong, an old favorite, gives forth a bronze fruit with delicious, musky-flavored juice and pulp. Many growers rate its flavor unexcelled. The wild grape is usually black with thick skin and heavy flesh but little juice, and makes a popular wild grape jelly.

**GUAVA** trees are small and spreading, appearing more like shrubs. Believed to have come from Peru, guava trees are related to the custard apple, but there the comparison ends, for unlike custard apple, the guava is desired and served in many ways. The flavor is unforgettable—musky but sweet and, when ripe, quite aromatic. Guava fruit varies from one to four inches in diameter, its flesh ranging from white to pink to light red. The fruit is used as a paste, marmalade, or sauce and can be eaten directly off the tree. Vitamin C content is high.

**JACKFRUIT** is quite large, often weighing from 10 to 40 pounds. Because the tree itself grows large, it is often used as an ornamental. Jackfruit is ripe in south Florida in July and August. The fruit is oblong and many grow to two feet in length.

Its skin is rough to the touch. Inside, the flesh is soft, juicy, and yellow when ripe, and can be eaten fresh or preserved. The seeds are sometimes roasted and eaten.

**JAMBOLAN PLUM** ripens from May through July, its deep purple-maroon fruit making a delicious jelly. Its tartness demands plenty of sugar. The fruit is slightly curved and grows to about one inch in length.

**LOQUAT** is a garden-gate variety tree that reaches 20 feet in height. Its thick foliage springs white, fragrant flowers. Sometimes the tree is grown for the flower rather than the fruit. Loquat fruit is round or oval and one to three inches long. It is pale orange to yellow with large seeds. The rather acidic flavor reminds one of a cherry. Its skin is thin, the flesh firm and somewhat meaty. The fruit ripens early in the winter, but a second flowering may occur in spring. Loquats, like kumquats, can be preserved whole or can be made into jams and preserves.

**LYCHEE NUT** has an origin buried in antiquity. Even its name is spelled several different ways. In any case, a lychee nut, resembling a strawberry in its fresh form, is a taste treat. Some say its flavor is like a grape, others liken it to a raisin. The outside of the lychee nut is rough and scale-like, but peels easily. Lychee trees grow to 40 feet or more in height, with dense, shiny leaves.

**MACADAMIA NUTS,** also called the Queensland Nut, is grown in modest numbers in Florida. The tree often reaches 30 feet in height and produces shiny green leaves that look like holly. The fruit is a round brown seed that contains the edible white kernel or nut.

**MANGO** is the apple of the tropics and one of the world's finest fruits. It is an import from Asia that bears fruit from May to October. The tree itself grows quite large, with attractive green, leathery leaves. Mangos may weigh up to four pounds. They can be apple-shaped, round or oblong, and the color may be green, yellow, or a subdued red. Some say mangos have the scent of turpentine, and some mangos do, but the Haden, the most popular variety, does not. Mangos can be peeled and sliced, or eaten like peaches. For first-timers, however, caution is advised—some people break out in a rash after touching or eating this rich fruit.

**MONSTERA DELICIOSA** is a vine-like shrub, also called Ceriman, and has huge split leaves with aerial roots. Its flower looks like a calla lily and an ear of corn combined. From summer to early fall, at least a year after blooming, the fruit turns to soft pulp. The scaly peel comes off easily, and the fruit has a delicate pineapple-banana smell and taste. But beware, for the pulp can burn the mouth with its crystals.

**PAPAYAS** are a football-shaped fruit, green or yellow in color, and emit a pungent smell that is welcomed by some and rejected by others. Papaya's skin is smooth and thin; its fruit can be cubed, chilled and sweetened, or left unsweetened and eaten like a melon. Papaya has an enzyme called papain that breaks down protein; it is used to tenderize meats and is believed to aid digestion. The fruit mixes well in salads and, when green, makes an excellent pie. The juice is used in face creams, teas, and syrups. Do not confuse papayas with paw paws, which are grown in colder climates.

**PECANS** are a sizable commercial crop in Florida, mostly grown in north Florida. The nuts mature in the fall and are in much demand during the holiday season.

**PINEAPPLE** plantations used to be plentiful in the Keys generations ago, and today some remain in the Miami and Fort Pierce areas. Short-stemmed, the plants grow to only two or three feet in height. Leaves are long, thin, and sharp-pointed with rough edges. Purplish flowers grow separately at the plant's top but together near its base, where they form the fruit.

**PERSIMMON** comes in both a native variety common in Florida and also in a cultivated Japanese variety. The Japanese type is about three inches long, longer than the native variety, has a yellow skin that turns reddish as it ripens, and is best eaten fresh.

**POMEGRANATE** is found throughout Florida, grows on bushes 15 to 20 feet high, and produces a fruit the size of an orange. Its smooth leather skin is yellow or red. Inside, several "cells" contain small grains of juicy red pulp, but it is the sweet seeds that are generally eaten. It is used for drinks, jellies, and marmalades.

**SAPODILLA** is a handsome evergreen tree that yields a white latex from which chicle, the base of chewing gum, is made. The fruit grows to about four inches in diameter with a harsh, brown skin. When ripe, it can be used as a dessert fruit.

**SAPOTE** is not a well-known tree because it grows only in the southern sector of Florida, and because its fruit yield is sparse. The fruit ripens in May, is yellowish, grows up to four inches in diameter, is shaped like a top, has a thin skin, a soft flesh, and can be sweet or bitter. It can be eaten fresh, and is used in ices and jellies.

**SEA GRAPE** is used more as an ornamental shrub than as a fruit-bearer. It provides attractive foliage and does furnish purple grape-like clusters of fruit. It is most commonly used to make jelly, or juice for fruit punch.

**SOURSOP** is a small tree with leathery, shiny leaves that is grown as a "dooryard" tree in south Florida. The large, heart-shaped fruit weighs up to four pounds. The fruit flesh is aromatic but has a cottony texture. Soursop sherbet is delicious.

**STRAWBERRY,** a major Florida crop, is grown mostly in the central part of the state, primarily near Plant City. Harvesting begins as early as January if the weather has been warm, but March is the major month for harvest. Newspapers in the area often run classified ads inviting residents to come to the fields and pick their own berries at a bargain rate. One innovation in recent years is the black plastic planting strip through which baby plants are pulled, thereby keeping the berries free of sand and ground rot to increase the yield.

**SURINAM CHERRY** plants make excellent hedges, growing from three feet upward. Leaves are reddish when small, then turn green as they grow larger. A white flower means a cherry soon will form. The main crop comes in spring, its fruit ribbed and bright red. The flesh is juicy and soft, and has an unusual resin-like odor, which is unpleasant to some. Cherries can be eaten off the plant or used in salads, jellies, and sherbets.

**TAMARIND** is used as a shade tree in south Florida but bears a fruit pod about six inches long. When young, the pod is green and acidic; it is used at this stage for seasoning of fish and meats. Inside the outer brown shell a mature pod contains the pulp from which tamarindade is made.

---

### Varieties of Watermelon

Watermelon lovers have an increasing variety of the fruit from which to choose in Florida, the nation's leading producer of watermelons. And new types come out almost annually as researchers strive to create a sweeter, more disease-resistant melon with fewer seeds.

Years ago the biggest seller was the Cannonball. But it was too susceptible to various field wilt diseases, prompting researchers to search for a more

*(continued on next page)*

hardy yet equally popular replacement. After years of crossbreeding, they came up with the now familiar Charleston Gray. Developed in 1954 in South Carolina, the Charleston Gray has wilt-resistant qualities as well as excellent flavor.

A Kansas grower, noting the Charleston Gray's popularity, began experimenting with the melon, crossing it with other types of existing melons. The result was that in 1963 another winner was introduced, the Crimson Sweet.

That same year University of Florida researcher J. M. Crall borrowed from the Charleston Gray's qualities to create still a third popular seller today, the Jubilee.

Currently, the Charleston Gray, Crimson Sweet, and Jubilee account for about 75 percent of all retail sales. Experts believe the Crimson Sweet and Jubilee sell so well partly because they are both striped and people expect watermelons to be striped. The Charleston Gray has no stripes but makes up for this shortcoming by satisfying another consumer prejudice about watermelons: size. It is an oblong, unusually large melon that persuades shoppers that it offers a lot for the money.

A watermelon similar in size and shape to the popular Charleston Gray called the Charlee is showing up on fruit stands. It is the result of matings of the Charleston Gray with such lesser-known varieties as the Calhoun Gray and the Smokylee.

Also a newcomer is a spinoff of the popular Jubilee, called the Jubilee II. On the fruit stand it is hard to differentiate from the original Jubilee, but watermelon experts say the Jubilee II has better texture, a sweeter flavor, and a more attractive interior color.

Today's smaller American families, averaging two adults and one child, are creating a demand for smaller watermelons. This trend is being met by "icebox melons." Among the earliest of this smaller type is the Georgia-born Sugar Baby, and the New Hampshire Midget. So far, both have had limited sales. The Midget suffers from a rind so thin that pickers must wear soft gloves or risk puncturing the fruit. As for the Sugar Baby, its problem is it fast loses its quality and flavor between harvesting and marketing.

In 1986 Florida growers got their own icebox melons when Crall developed the Minilee and Mickeylee. Each weighs an average of seven to nine pounds, compared to the larger variety of melons that often tip the scales at 20 pounds or more. Neither the Minilee nor the Mickeylee is striped, but both are rated to be internally more red than other melons, and have smaller and fewer seeds.

Researchers have been flirting with a watermelon variety that has the sweetness and flavor of the best sellers but none of the seeds. In recent years a "Seedless Watermelon" has appeared on shelves, but it has had few takers. The industry refers to this seedless variety as Tri-X 313 and Tri-X 317, both tracing back to an experimental grower in Indiana. Samplers say the seedless offers excellent quality but at a high price.

Floridians moving from other regions of the country also may be familiar with numerous other varieties that are seldom seen in the Sunshine State, namely the Allsweet, Peacock, Yellow Flesh, Graybelle, Early Canada, Dixielee, and the Petite Sweet.

These varieties still may have their supporters, but Florida watermelons continue to dominate the national market. The state produces about 30 percent of all watermelons consumed in the U.S.

*(continued on next page)*

*(continued from previous page)*

Florida growers also are quick to point out that the state's watermelons are a nutritious food. A 10-inch slice about one-inch thick is only 152 calories but supplies 77 percent of the daily recommended Vitamin C, 35 percent of the daily recommended Vitamin B-6, 26 percent of the daily requirement of thiamine, and 560 milligrams of potassium.

## PRINCIPAL VEGETABLES BY PRODUCING AREAS

### 1. West

**Escambia County:** Potatoes
**Holmes, Jackson, Washington counties:** Butter beans, field peas, watermelons.
**Gadsden County:** Pole beans, squash, sweet corn, tomatoes.

### 2. North

**Starke, Brooker, Lake Butler areas:** Lima beans, snap beans, cucumbers, green peppers, squash, strawberries.
**Hastings area:** Cabbage, potatoes.
**Gainesville, Alachua area:** Bush beans, cucumbers, peppers, potatoes, squash.
**Island Grove, Hawthorne areas:** Cucumbers, peppers, sweet corn, squash, watermelons.

### 3. North Central

**Oxford, Pedro areas:** Tomatoes, watermelons.
**Sanford, Oviedo, Zellwood areas:** Cabbage, carrots, celery, sweet corn, cucumbers, escarole, greens, lettuce, peppers, radishes, spinach.
**Webster area:** Cucumbers, eggplant, peppers.

### 4. West Central

**Plant City, Balms areas:** Bush and pole beans, lima beans, cabbage, cucumbers, eggplant, field peas, greens, squash, strawberries, watermelons.
**Palmetto, Ruskin areas:** Cabbage, cauliflower, potatoes, strawberries, tomatoes, watermelons.
**Sarasota area:** Cabbage, celery, sweet corn, escarole, lettuce, radishes.
**Wauchula area:** Cucumbers, eggplant, peppers, tomatoes, watermelons.

### 5. East Central

**Fort Pierce area:** Tomatoes, watermelons.

### 6. Southwest

**Fort Myers, Immokalee areas:** Sweet corn, cucumbers, eggplant, peppers, potatoes, squash, tomatoes, watermelons.

### 7. Everglades

Bush beans, cabbage, celery, Chinese cabbage, sweet corn, escarole, greens, lettuce, potatoes, radishes.

### 8. Southeast

**Martin County:** Cabbage, potatoes, tomatoes, watermelons.
**Pompano Beach area:** Bush beans, lima beans, sweet corn, cucumbers, eggplant, peppers, squash, tomatoes.
**Homestead area:** Bush and pole beans, cabbage, sweet corn, cucumbers, potatoes, squash, strawberries, tomatoes.

## HOME VEGETABLE PLANTING GUIDE

| Vegetable | North | Central | South |
|---|---|---|---|
| Beans, Snap | Mar-Apr, Aug-Sep | Feb-Mar | Sep-Mar |
| Beans, Pole | Mar-May | Feb-Apr | Jan-Feb September |
| Beans, Lima | Mar-Apr | Mar-May | Sep-Mar |
| Beets | Sep-Mar | Oct-Mar | Oct-Feb |
| Broccoli | Aug-Sep *Nov-Feb | Aug-Sep *Nov-Feb | Sep-Oct *Dec-Jan |

| Cabbage | Aug-Sep | Aug-Sep | Sep-Oct |
| | *Nov-Feb | *Nov-Feb | *Dec-Jan |
| Cabbage, Chinese | Oct-Feb | Oct-Feb | Nov-Jan |
| Carrots | Sep-Mar | Oct-Mar | Oct-Feb |
| Chard | Sep-Mar | Oct-Apr | Oct-Apr |
| Collards | Aug-Feb | Sep-Feb | Sep-Jan |
| Corn, sweet | Mar-Apr | Feb-Mar | Jan-Mar |
| Cowpeas | Mar-May | Mar-May | Feb-May |
| Eggplant | *March | *March | *Sep-Feb |
| Endive | Sep-Feb | Sep-Feb | Sep-Jan |
| Lettuce | Sep-Oct | Sep-Feb | Sep-Feb |
| | Feb-Mar | | |
| Melon | Mar-Apr | Feb-Mar | Feb-Mar |
| Okra | Mar-June | Mar-Aug | Feb-Oct |
| Onions, green | *Aug-Apr | *Aug-Mar | *Sep-Mar |
| Peas | Jan-Mar | Sep-Feb | Sep-Feb |
| Pepper | *March | *Feb | *Oct-Feb |
| Radish | Oct-Mar | Oct-Mar | Oct-Mar |
| Spinach | Oct-Feb | Oct-Feb | Nov-Jan |
| Squash | Mar-Apr | Aug-Sep | Sep-Mar |
| | September | Feb-Mar | |
| Tomato | *Mar-Apr August | *Jan-Feb *Aug-Sep | *Aug-Mar |
| Turnip | Aug-May | Sep-Feb | Oct-Feb |

*Transplants or sets*

## RECORD-SIZED VEGETABLES
### (Records kept by Institute
### of Food and Agricultural Sciences)

| Vegetable (variety) | Size | County |
|---|---|---|
| Bean, lima (pod) | — ft 9 in. | St. Lucie |
| Beet (unknown) | .5 lb. | Duval |
| Boniata (unknown) | 12 lb. 10 oz. | Seminole |
| Broccoli (Southern Comet) | 5 lb. 4 oz. | Suwannee |
| Cabbage (unknown) | 19 lb. 7 oz. | Suwannee |
| Calabaza (unknown) | 36 lb. 8 oz. | Seminole |
| Cantaloupe (N.C. giant) | 29 lb. 8 oz. | Levy |
| Carrot (Chantenay) | 3 lb. 1 oz. | Pinellas |
| Cassava | 8 lb. 14 oz. | Highlands |
| Cauliflower (Snow Crown) | 15 lb. 6 oz. | Alachua |
| Chicory (Magdeburg) | 1 lb. 3 oz. | Alachua |
| Collard (unknown) | 13 ft. 3 in. | Leon |
| Corn, sweet (ear) | 1 lb. 15 oz. | Suwannee |
| Cucumber (weight) | 4 lb. 8 oz. | Suwannee |
| Cucumber (length) | 2 ft. 3 in. | Suwannee |
| Eggplant (Fla. Market) | 4 lb. 8 oz. | Palm Beach |
| Garlic | 1 lb. 8 oz. | St. Johns |
| Honeydew | 5 lb. 2 oz. | Escambia |
| Jicama (unknown) | 21 lb. 8 oz. | Palm Beach |
| Kohlrabi (Giganti) | 19 lb. 8 oz. | Duval |
| Melon, winter | 50 lb. | Palm Beach |
| Mustard | 7 lb. 5 oz. | Suwannee |
| Okra plant (La. Velvet) | — lb. 8 oz. | Suwannee |
| Okra stalk (length) | 19 ft. 11 in. | Flagler |

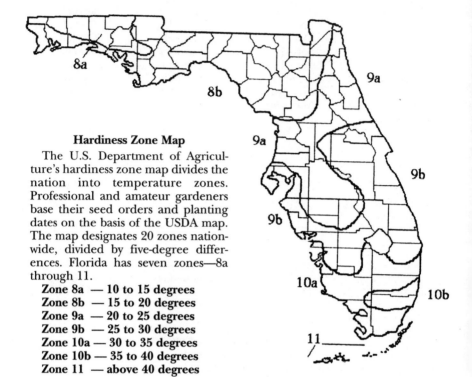

**Hardiness Zone Map**

The U.S. Department of Agriculture's hardiness zone map divides the nation into temperature zones. Professional and amateur gardeners base their seed orders and planting dates on the basis of the USDA map. The map designates 20 zones nationwide, divided by five-degree differences. Florida has seven zones—8a through 11.

Zone 8a — 10 to 15 degrees
Zone 8b — 15 to 20 degrees
Zone 9a — 20 to 25 degrees
Zone 9b — 25 to 30 degrees
Zone 10a — 30 to 35 degrees
Zone 10b — 35 to 40 degrees
Zone 11 — above 40 degrees

| | | |
|---|---|---|
| Onion (Grano) | 3 lb. 11 oz. | Manatee |
| Pepper (experimental) | 1 lb. 1 oz. | Palm Beach |
| Potato (Frito Lay 92) | 2 lb. 13 oz. | St. Johns |
| Potato (sweet) | 30 lb. 2 oz. | Seminole |
| Pumpkin (Atlantic giant) | 242 lb. | Suwannee |
| Radish, summer (red summer) | 3 lb. 12 oz. | Palm Beach |
| Radish, winter (unknown) | 25 lb. | Hillsborough |
| Radish, daikon | 23 lb. 5 oz. | Alachua |
| Rutabaga (unknown) | 22 lb. | Lake |
| Squash,banana | 39 lb. | Lake |
| Squash, butternut | 23 lb. 12 oz. | Santa Rosa |
| Squash, Hubbard | 131 lb. 12 oz. | Santa Rosa |
| Squash, scal | 2 lb. 1 oz. | Alachua |
| Squash, spaghetti | 25 lb. 14 oz. | St. Johns |
| Squash, summer | 4 lb. 1 oz. | Suwannee |
| Squash, zucchini | 10 lb. 8 oz. | Gilchrist |
| Taro | — lb. 8 oz. | Palm Beach |
| Tomato (Delicious) | 3 lb. | Orange/Marion |
| Turnip (Shogoin) | 18 lb. 4 oz. | Union |
| Watermelon (Carolina cross) | 205 lb. | Levy |
| Winter Melon | 50 lb. | Palm Beach |
| Yam (True) | 12 lb.15 oz. | Palm Beach |

## FERN CAPITAL

The leatherleaf fern is possibly the most important cut foliage crop in Florida. The ferns and leafy greens are used in floral arrangements, and no state produces more cut foliage. The industry of 600 growers is centered in Volusia County, primarily around the town of Pierson, but it has spread to nearby Lake, Orange, and Putnam counties.

The plumosa fern was introduced into Volusia County in the late 1800s by a Massachusetts man named Pierson who had raised it in hothouses up north. He found that his indoor crop thrived outdoors in Florida. The plumosa fern was the exclusive fern crop in the area until the mid-1940s, when growers began to experiment with the leatherleaf fern. Today, leatherleaf accounts for approximately 95 percent of sales.

Leatherleaf and plumosa ferns are not to be confused with ferns such as Boston and maidenhair, which are used as potted plants or hanging baskets. Volusia County's products are used mostly as background material by florists.

Florida fern production has no defined peak season, the crop being grown and harvested year round. Harvesting is done by hand, and each field can be cut weekly with an average yield of 18 cases of cut, bunched ferns per acre. Because the plant is regenerative, each planting can last several years or more.

## ADD FERTILIZER

Sandy Florida soils are poor and the wise gardener uses fertilizers. Organic fertilizers supply steady but slow nutrients. Commercial fertilizers are also available and provide a quicker boost of nitrogen, phosphorous, and potassium. In addition, gardens and landscapes need periodic applications of iron, zinc, magnesium, manganese, copper, and boron. Experts say a common problem, particularly with citrus trees, is a lack of iron.

## AGRICULTURAL INSPECTION STATIONS

Florida has established 21 agricultural inspection stations along its many roads leading into and out of the state to help fight and control diseases and pests in vegetables and fruits. The inspection stations make an unbroken chain on every paved road across the Suwannee and St. Mary's rivers in north Florida. They are intended to make it impossible for a trucker or motorist to bring agricultural products into Florida, or to take them out, without the products being inspected. Numerous unpaved roads lead to both rivers that must be crossed when leaving the state, but none of the unpaved roads has a crossing bridge. The state, in concert with federal agricultural officials, in 1934 began building the Florida inspections stations to prevent inferior fruit, mainly citrus, from leaving the state for northern markets. All trucks and trailers are required to stop at the stations, which are open every hour of every day.

## FLORIDA AGRICULTURE HALL OF FAME

In 1980 a Hall of Fame was established to recognize those individuals who have contributed to the agricultural industry of Florida. Nominees are submitted by their peers. Inductees have been:

**1981:** Edwin H. Finlayson—farmer and county agent
Thomas G. Lee—dairyman

Nathan Mayo—state Commissioner of Agriculture
Henry O. Partin—cattleman
Hoyle Pounds—inventor
Egbert N. Reasoner—horticulturist
**1982:** Irlo O. Bronson—cattleman
Gilbert A. Tucker—cattleman
J. Francis Cooper—agricultural writer, broadcaster
Louis E. Larson—dairyman
Pliny W. Reasoner—horticulturist
Don A. Storms, Sr.—educator
**1983:** Willard M. Fifield—researcher, educator
Robert G. Pitman, Jr.—agricultural tax expert
Herman J. Reitz—scientist, administrator, author
James N. Watson—county agent, county fair co-founder
**1984:** Raymond B. Becker—researcher
John M. Fox—researcher
**1985:** Alan J. Norden—researcher
**1986:** John Duda—farm and packing house machinery developer
Andrew Duda, Jr.—marketing specialist
**1987:** Louis G. MacDowell—researcher
Edwin L. Moore—researcher
Cedric D. Atkins—researcher
Lena S. Hughes—researcher
B. Edmund David, Jr.—cattle breeder, trade promoter
**1988:** Ben Hill Griffin, Jr.—cattleman, processor
Anthony T. Rossi—inventor, citrus grower, marketer
J. O Pearce, Jr.—cattle and livestock leader
James S. Wershow—educator, agricultural tax expert
**1989:** Paul B. Dickman—inventor, grower
John B. Boy, Sr.—sugar cane industry leader
Ruth S. Wedgworth—agricultural innovator
**1990:** Peter S. Harlee—tomato industry leader
Charles P. Lykes—cattleman, meatpacking executive
Donald L. Wakeman—educator
**1991:** Robert H. Harms—poultry nutrition researcher
Raymond P. Oglesby—plant scientist
Carl G. Rose—Thoroughbred horse breeder
E. T. York, Jr.—educator
**1992:** Doyle Carlton, Jr.—cattleman
Tony J. Cunha, Jr.—educator
Julian B. Lane—dairyman
Joseph O'Farrell, Sr.—Thoroughbred horse racing breeder
**1993:** Curtis Peterson—nurseryman, landscape architect
Edgar Price, Jr.—citrus executive
Edward J. Campbell—agricultural innovator, conservationist
Vance Vogel—tomato grower
**1994:** Julia Morton—botanist
Marshall Watkins—extension service director
Karl Albritton—citrus leader
William Loften—educator
John Mortensen—vegetable breeder
**1995:** Elton L. Hinton—educator
J. Wayne Reitz—educator

Latimer H. Turner—cattleman
George H. Wedgeworth—vegetable and sugar producer
**1996:** Neal Plamer ("Pal") Brooks—tropical fruit grower
Snead Young Mathews Davis—cattle rancher
Henry Gatrell—swine rancher
Barnette E. ("Barney") Greene, Jr.—cattle rancher, citrus grower
Wayne Mixon, Governor—farmer
**1997:** William ("Bill") H. Krome—tropical fruit grower
J. R. ("Jack") Sprat—agriculture pioneer
Raymon F. Tucker—horse breeder, cattle rancher
Robert ("Bob") Billingsley Whisenant—agriculture pioneer
Stephen M. Yoder—farmer and rancher
**1998:** Miles Edward Groover—4H and minority development
Maxie D. Love, Jr.—farm finance
Elliott L. Maguire—forestry
Mabel Claprood Simmons—ornamental horticulture
Edna Pearce Lockett—cattle rancher, business and government leader
**1999:** Alto Lee Adams, Jr.—cattle rancher, environmentalist
Bert J. Harris, Jr.—legislator
Ken F. Jorgensen—farmer
Copeland Newbern—educator
John Powell Wallace—poultry farmer

---

### CATTLE COUNTRY

Floridians are aware their state is the fourth most populated in the nation, but few know that it also is the biggest cattle state east of the Mississippi River. Second only to the citrus and agricultural industry, ranching in Florida involves nearly 2 million cattle and 2,000 cowboys.

The state's largest cattle operation is the 300,000-acre Deseret Ranch, which spreads out over both Osceola and Brevard counties. It is owned by the Mormon church in Salt Lake City.

But large, privately owned spreads of pasture and rangeland are prevalent throughout the hinterland of central and south Florida. Places like Arcadia, Fort Meade, Kissimmee, Yeehaw Junction, and Okeechobee still are known to many residents as cow towns. In all, some 5 million acres of the state are devoted to raising cattle. Registered cattle brands in Florida number nearly 3,000.

The state's rangeland is largely grass and marshes, hammocks and brush. Thus, the acreage is best worked by cowboys on horseback, not by ranch-hands in four-wheel-drive vehicles as is done today in much of the West.

Historians say Florida got its start in cattle from the Spanish settlers, who brought with them a breed that today is called the Florida Cracker. For 400 years this scrawny but tough animal was the only breed that could survive the heat, bugs, and parasites of subtropical Florida.

Cousins to the Texas Longhorn, Florida Cracker cattle are now nearly extinct. But some ranchers, with the aid of the Florida Department of Agriculture and the Florida Cracker Cattle Association, are determined to revive the breed in large numbers.

Florida Crackers usually are small and lean. They come in every color and pattern, and sport long, threatening horns. Their supporters say the timing is excellent to revive the breed because Florida Crackers produce a lean type of beef, a desirable quality in today's fat-conscious society.

*(continued on next page)*

*(continued from previous page)*

Most credited with saving the state's cattle industry, however, is an imported breed, the Brahma. Brought from India via Texas, Brahmas have proven most resistant to Florida's heat and disease. Since their introduction, they have been crossed with the Angus to produce the Brangus, with the Charolais to produce the Charbrays, and with the Herefords to produce the Brafords, all of which flourish on Florida's tough rangeland.

Because Florida lacks feed grain production, state ranchers sell and ship about three-quarters of a million calves each fall to western states such as Colorado, Texas, Oklahoma, and Arizona.

Rustling was, and still is, a problem in Florida. The Florida Department of Law Enforcement uses four undercover agents to chase down cattle thieves.

## MAJOR FOOD FESTIVALS

Specific dates for the following are available from area chambers of commerce.

### January

Epiphany Glendi (Tarpon Springs)
Kumquat Festival (Dade City)
Florida Citrus Festival (Winter Haven)
Upper Keys Seafood Festival (Islamorada)

### February

Seafood Festival (Everglades City)
Strawberry Festival (Plant City)
Palm Beach Seafood Festival (West Palm Beach)
Grant Seafood Festival (Melbourne)
Lions Club Shrimp Festival (Estero)
Italian Feast & Festival (Venice)

### March

Catfish Festival (Crescent City)
Chowder Cook-Off (Cocoa Beach)
Strawberry Festival (Plant City)
Chili Cookoff (Lake Wales)

### April

Ribfest & Hot Air Balloon Rally (Melbourne)
Seafood Festival (Fort Lauderdale)
Seafood Festival (Fort Walton Beach)
Crawfish Festival (Jacksonville Beach)
Shrimp Festival (Fernandina Beach)
Wild Beast Festival (Trenton)

### May

Crawfish Fiesta (Pensacola)
Taste of the Everglades (Everglades City)
Zellwood Corn Festival (Zellwood)

### June

Blueberry Festival (Palatka)
Watermelon Festival (Monticello)

### July

A Taste of Soul Festival (Orlando)

### August

Possum Festival (Wausau)
Crawfish Festival (Jacksonville)

### September

Labor Day Fish Fry (Punta Gorda)
Lobster Festival (Pensacola)
Scallop Day Festival (Port St. Joe)
Grape Festival (Melrose)

### October

Seafood Festival (Destin)
Taste of Florida (Tampa)
Indian Summer Seafood Festival (Panama City Beach)
Seafood Festival (Mayport)
Mullet Festival (Oak Hill)
Boggy Bayou Mullet Festival (Niceville)

### November

Seafood Festival (Apalachicola)
Florida Tastefest (Jacksonville)
Country Fried Festival (Jacksonville)
Seafood & Arts Festival (Ruskin)
Seafood Festival (Inglis-Yankeetown)

## EXOTIC PEST PLANTS

Twenty-seven percent of the state's plants are intruders, referred to as exotic species. Only Hawaii has a higher percentage. It is a cause of concern among state biologists. They see signs that the plant newcomers, breeding indiscriminately, are choking out the state's natives, estimated to number 3,448 species.

Native plants are part of a biological chain. If the chain is interrupted by exotic species, it affects every other insect, bird, or mammal that depends on the native plants.

Trying to stave off the introduction into Florida of new exotic species, and curtail those that already are entrenched, state officials are forbidding nurseries and growers to sell some exotic species familiar to Floridians. Among them are Brazilian pepper, punk trees, Australian pines, and the Chinese tallow tree. Biologists see such species as pollutants, and harmful to the state's ecology as hazardous wastes.

Some exotics were brought into Florida years ago to alleviate ecological problems. For example, the Australian pine and kudzu were planted to prevent soil erosion. The punk tree, formally known as the melaleuca, was imported to soak up water from the Everglades and thus make that region suitable for development.

Two exotic pest plant lists exist. One is the Department of Environmental Protection's list of prohibited aquatic weeds. The other list is a compilation by the Exotic Pest Plant Council; it contains more than 400 exotic plant species that either now threaten Florida's ecology or that will cause problems if left unchecked.

Some species on the council's list will surprise homeowners. One is schefflera. It is not a problem in northern Florida, but in south Florida it has proliferated so wildly that it is crowding out such native plants as oaks, saw palmetto, and scrub rosemary. Plant experts say that in the south schefflera is shading and thus killing out the native plants, ruining the region's natural ecosystem.

Seven of the most troublesome exotic plant species are

1.) Melaleuca, sometimes called the punk tree or cajeput. It grows 80 to 100 feet tall, its trunk is layered with papery bark, and the tree's leaves have a medicinal odor. The tree flowers in summer and fall with white bottlebrush blooms. Brought to Florida in the early 1900s to dry up wetlands, the tree is considered a destroyer of natural habitat. One acre of melaleuca consumes 2,100 gallons of water per hour.

2.) Catclaw Mimosa, brought into Florida in 1953 from Central America. A shrub, it grows up to 10 feet tall. It has stems for fern-type fans composed of smaller leaflets. Blooms are fluffy pink balls. Also a threat to the state's wetlands, this plant obstructs water flow while increasing flooding and sedimentation. A mature plant is capable of producing 40,000 seeds.

3.) Australian pine, planted in Florida in the late 1800s to prevent soil erosion in coastal areas. It grows best in sandy soil and salty open areas. It can soar to 115 feet. Not a true pine, the tree's branches are covered by thin needles of dark green. Its small cones are round and prickly. The tree uproots easily in high winds because its roots are so shallow. Almost nothing grows under this tree because it sheds needles laced with a chemical that kills native species. *(continued on next page)*

*(continued from previous page)*

4.) Brazilian pepper, which reportedly came into Florida around Punta Gorda in the 1920s from Brazil. It reaches up to 40 feet, and bears small white flowers in early fall that are followed by hundreds of round berries. Birds eat the berries, spreading hundreds of seedlings. The tree's rapid growth often chokes out native plants.

5.) The Chinese tallow tree, sometimes called the popcorn tree. It originated in China and grows up to 30 feet tall. Its leaves have sharp, prickly edges. An attractive tree, it has been used to beautify highways and public areas in north Florida, but can grow anywhere in Florida. The tree has the potential of becoming the melaleuca of north Florida.

6.) Hydrilla, an aquatic plant from Africa, was discovered in Florida in 1960 in both a Miami canal on the east coast and in the Crystal River on the West Coast. Hydrilla has long, thin stems segmented into three- or five-leafed whorls and it grows at the rate of one inch a day. It thrives in more than 50,000 acres of Florida lakes and waterways, and is hard on the state's fish population. Since 1980, Florida has spent more than $50 million to control this plant and in the same period it is estimated to have caused an adverse economic impact of a quarter-billion dollars.

7.) Kudzu, a supervine. Each shoot grows as much as 12 inches a day. It was introduced into the South by the U.S. government in the 1930s as a means of preventing soil erosion. In less than two decades, this species covered a half-million acres of farmland. It shades and crowds out native species. Asians use kudzu as food, a medicine to treat colds and diarrhea, a sobering agent, and to make a superb, acid-free paper, but to Americans it is a nuisance plant that is a place where, says a Southern folktale, naughty children are tossed to quickly disappear.

Other major exotic plants that state officials prefer would go away are: the Bishopwood tree, woman's tongue, earleaf acacia, Cuban laurel, lofty fig, banyan tree, air potato, climbing fern, cork tree, downy rose myrtle, Japanese honeysuckle, jasmine, Java plum, lather leaf, lead tree, Murray red gum, rose apple, shoebutton ardisia, strawberry guava, and tree hibiscus.

Aquatic weeds fouling Florida's water, and listed as prohibited, are alligator weed, African elodea, ambulia, Eurasian watermilfoil, exotic bur-reed, hippo grass, hygro, tropical pickerelweed, water-aloe, water chestnut, water fern, water lily, and water spinach.

---

## ORANGE CROP

Florida orange production in 1999 fell 24 percent from 1998. Hot, dry weather early in the season was blamed. Growers harvested an estimated 185.7 million 90-pound boxes for the season ending in the spring, compared with a record 244-million the year before. Florida produces 90 percent of the orange juice consumed in the U.S.

---

## CHICKENS LIVE FREE

Escaped and otherwise wild chickens are protected in the city of Key West.

# POPULATION

## ESTABLISHING LEGAL RESIDENCY

To become a resident of Florida, a person must establish a home or a permanent dwelling place and demonstrate intent to make Florida the place of permanent legal residence. No fixed waiting period is required for a person to become a resident, but newcomers are urged to show their intent by filing a sworn statement with the clerk of circuit court in the county where the new home is situated. A small charge is made for recording the affidavit.

No residency requirements are necessary for employment with state or county government agencies, but preference may be given to Florida residents.

Once a resident, the Floridian is entitled to property tax exemptions of $25,000 on the assessed value of the homestead.

To vote in Florida, a person must be 18 years of age or older, a citizen of the U.S., and a permanent resident of Florida and of the county in which the resident wishes to vote. One must register to vote, of course, with the county supervisor of elections.

Jurors are selected from lists of Florida driver's license holders who are U.S. citizens.

Pupils in kindergarten through 12th grade whose parents or guardians are non-residents may be charged a tuition fee at the time the pupil is enrolled. Fees may be waived for certain categories such as military personnel. To qualify for in-state tuition fees at a state public university or community college, the student (or parent or guardian, if the student is a dependent) must have resided in Florida for 12 consecutive months prior to enrollment.

To obtain a divorce in Florida, one of the parties in the marriage must live in Florida for six months before filing the petition.

All candidates for public office must be U.S. citizens and registered voters in Florida. Candidates for governor, lieutenant governor, and the cabinet must be at least 30 years of age and have been a Florida resident the preceding seven years. A candidate for the state legislature must be at least 21 years old and live in the district he or she wishes to represent. Candidates for local offices must be residents of their appropriate districts.

To operate a motor vehicle in Florida, new residents are required to obtain a Florida driver's license within 30 days, and register their motor vehicles within 10 days of accepting gainful employment, entering children in public schools, registering to vote, or filing for homestead exemption. Full-time non-resident college students and non-resident military personnel on active duty in Florida are exempt from this requirement.

For a resident statewide non-commercial fishing license, an applicant must have resided for six continuous months in Florida, or filed a domicile certificate with the county clerk.

Establishing legal residence in Florida does not automatically make a person from another country a citizen of the U.S. A foreign national, although having become a legal Florida resident, still must become a U.S. citizen to vote, serve on a jury, or hold elective office. Floridians without U.S. citizenship wishing to obtain it should seek information from the U.S. Immigration and Naturalization Service in Miami.

## POPULATION OF THE STATE:
### EARLIEST CENSUS TO 1990

| | | | |
|---|---|---|---|
| 1830 | 34,730 | 1920 | 968,470 |
| 1840 | 54,477 | 1930 | 1,468,211 |
| 1850 | 87,445 | 1940 | 1,897,414 |
| 1860 | 140,424 | 1950 | 2,771,305 |
| 1870 | 187,748 | 1960 | 4,951,580 |
| 1880 | 196,493 | 1970 | 6,791,418 |
| 1890 | 391,422 | 1980 | 9,739,992 |
| 1900 | 528,542 | 1990 | 12,937,926 |
| 1910 | 752,619 | | |

## COUNTY POPULATIONS AND DENSITIES
### (1990 Census)

| County | 1980 | 1990 | Persons Per Square Mile |
|---|---|---|---|
| Alachua | 151,369 | 181,596 | 188.9 |
| Baker | 15,289 | 18,486 | 31.4 |
| Bay | 97,740 | 126,994 | 147.5 |
| Bradford | 20,023 | 22,515 | 73.8 |
| Brevard | 272,959 | 398,978 | 304.6 |
| Broward | 1,018,257 | 1,255,488 | 1,029.1 |
| Calhoun | 9,294 | 11,011 | 19.4 |
| Charlotte | 58,460 | 110,975 | 133.4 |
| Citrus | 54,703 | 93,515 | 141.5 |
| Clay | 67,052 | 105,986 | 164.6 |
| Collier | 85,971 | 152,099 | 71.8 |
| Columbia | 35,399 | 42,613 | 54.0 |
| De Soto | 19,039 | 23,865 | 33.1 |
| Dixie | 7,751 | 10,585 | 14.9 |
| Duval | 571,003 | 672,971 | 801.1 |
| Escambia | 233,794 | 262,798 | 344.9 |
| Flagler | 10,913 | 28,701 | 56.9 |
| Franklin | 7,661 | 8,967 | 15.9 |
| Gadsden | 41,674 | 41,105 | 78.6 |
| Gilchrist | 5,767 | 9,667 | 27.8 |
| Glades | 5,992 | 7,591 | 8.5 |
| Gulf | 10,658 | 11,504 | 19.9 |
| Hamilton | 8,761 | 10,930 | 21.2 |
| Hardee | 20,357 | 19,499 | 30.9 |
| Hendry | 18,599 | 25,773 | 21.7 |
| Hernando | 44,469 | 101,115 | 199.0 |
| Highlands | 47,526 | 68,432 | 61.2 |
| Hillsborough | 646,939 | 834,054 | 785.4 |
| Holmes | 14,723 | 15,778 | 32.6 |
| Indian River | 59,896 | 90,208 | 164.3 |
| Jackson | 39,154 | 41,375 | 44.1 |
| Jefferson | 10,703 | 11,296 | 18.5 |
| Lafayette | 4,035 | 5,578 | 10.0 |
| Lake | 104,870 | 152,104 | 130.8 |
| Lee | 205,266 | 335,113 | 333.4 |
| Leon | 148,655 | 192,493 | 276.6 |

Levy . . . . . . . . . . . . . . .19,870 . . . . . . . . . .25,923 . . . . . . . . . . . . . . . .22.8
Liberty . . . . . . . . . . . . .4,260 . . . . . . . . . . .5,569 . . . . . . . . . . . . . . . .6.6
Madison . . . . . . . . . . . .14,894 . . . . . . . . . .16,569 . . . . . . . . . . . . . . . .23.4
Manatee . . . . . . . . . . .148,445 . . . . . . . . .211,707 . . . . . . . . . . . . . . .274.2
Marion . . . . . . . . . . . .122,488 . . . . . . . . .194,833 . . . . . . . . . . . . . . .117.9
Martin . . . . . . . . . . . . .64,014 . . . . . . . . .100,900 . . . . . . . . . . . . . . .173.4
Miami-Dade . . . . . .1,625,509 . . . . . . .1,937,094 . . . . . . . . . . . . . .918.5
Monroe . . . . . . . . . . .63,188 . . . . . . . . .78,024 . . . . . . . . . . . . . . .55.0
Nassau . . . . . . . . . . . .32,894 . . . . . . . . .43,941 . . . . . . . . . . . . . . .65.5
Okaloosa . . . . . . . . .109,920 . . . . . . . .143,776 . . . . . . . . . . . . . . .144.1
Okeechobee . . . . . . .20,264 . . . . . . . . .29,627 . . . . . . . . . . . . . . .38.0
Orange . . . . . . . . . .470,867 . . . . . . . .677,491 . . . . . . . . . . . . . . .675.5
Osceola . . . . . . . . . . .49,287 . . . . . . . .107,728 . . . . . . . . . . . . . . .73.4
Palm Beach . . . . . . .576,754 . . . . . . . .863,518 . . . . . . . . . . . . . . .335.1
Pasco . . . . . . . . . . . .193,661 . . . . . . . .281,131 . . . . . . . . . . . . . . .364.2
Pinellas . . . . . . . . . .728,531 . . . . . . . .851,659 . . . . . . . . . . . . . .2,756.2
Polk . . . . . . . . . . . . .321,652 . . . . . . . .405,382 . . . . . . . . . . . . . . .198.1
Putnam . . . . . . . . . . .50,549 . . . . . . . . .65,070 . . . . . . . . . . . . . . .74.0
St. Johns . . . . . . . . . .51,303 . . . . . . . . .83,829 . . . . . . . . . . . . . . .127.0
St. Lucie . . . . . . . . . .87,182 . . . . . . . .150,171 . . . . . . . . . . . . . . .240.1
Santa Rosa . . . . . . . . .55,988 . . . . . . . . .81,608 . . . . . . . . . . . . . . .70.8
Sarasota . . . . . . . . . .202,251 . . . . . . . .277,776 . . . . . . . . . . . . . . .493.4
Seminole . . . . . . . . .179,752 . . . . . . . .287,529 . . . . . . . . . . . . . . .816.9
Sumter . . . . . . . . . . . .24,272 . . . . . . . . .31,577 . . . . . . . . . . . . . . .55.0
Suwannee . . . . . . . . .22,287 . . . . . . . . .26,780 . . . . . . . . . . . . . . .39.0
Taylor . . . . . . . . . . . .16,532 . . . . . . . . .17,111 . . . . . . . . . . . . . . .16.3
Union . . . . . . . . . . . .10,166 . . . . . . . . .10,252 . . . . . . . . . . . . . . .41.8
Volusia . . . . . . . . . . .258,762 . . . . . . . .370,712 . . . . . . . . . . . . . . .307.1
Wakulla . . . . . . . . . . .10,887 . . . . . . . . .14,202 . . . . . . . . . . . . . . .22.4
Walton . . . . . . . . . . . .21,300 . . . . . . . . .27,760 . . . . . . . . . . . . . . .24.5
Washington . . . . . . . .14,509 . . . . . . . . .16,919 . . . . . . . . . . . . . . .27.7

In 1998 population estimates, Pinellas County continued to have the highest population density, with 2,842 per square mile, and Liberty County continued as the least densely populated, with 8 persons per square mile.

## POPULATION OF CITIES
### (1990 Census)

| Incorporated Places | Counties | 1980 | 1990 |
|---|---|---|---|
| Alachua | Alachua | 3,866 | 4,529 |
| Alford | Jackson | 548 | 472 |
| Altamonte Springs | Seminole | 21,499 | 34,879 |
| Altha | Calhoun | 478 | 497 |
| Anna Maria | Manatee | 1,537 | 1,744 |
| Apalachicola | Franklin | 2,565 | 2,602 |
| Apopka | Orange | 6,019 | 13,512 |
| Arcadia | De Soto | 6,002 | 6,488 |
| Archer | Alachua | 1,230 | 1,372 |
| Astatula | Lake | 755 | 981 |
| Atlantic Beach | Duval | 1,471 | 1,636 |
| Atlantis | Palm Beach | 1,325 | 1,653 |

| | | | |
|---|---|---|---|
| Auburndale | Polk | 6,501 | 8,858 |
| Avon Park | Highlands | 8,026 | 8,042 |
| | | | |
| Baldwin | Duval | 1,526 | 1,450 |
| Bal Harbor | Miami-Dade | 2,973 | 3,045 |
| Bartow | Polk | 14,780 | 14,716 |
| Bascom | Jackson | 134 | 90 |
| Bay Harbor Islands | Miami-Dade | 4,869 | 4,703 |
| Bell | Gilchrist | 227 | 267 |
| Belleair | Pinellas | 3,673 | 3,968 |
| Belleair Beach | Pinellas | 1,643 | 2,070 |
| Belleair Bluffs | Pinellas | 2,522 | 2,128 |
| Belleair Shore | Pinellas | 80 | 60 |
| Belle Glade | Palm Beach | 16,535 | 16,177 |
| Belle Isle | Orange | 2,848 | 5,272 |
| Belleview | Marion | 1,913 | 2,666 |
| Beverly Beach | Flagler | 217 | 312 |
| Biscayne Park | Miami-Dade | 3,088 | 3,068 |
| Blountstown | Calhoun | 2,632 | 2,404 |
| Boca Raton | Palm Beach | 49,446 | 61,492 |
| Bonifay | Holmes | 2,534 | 2,612 |
| Bowling Green | Hardee | 2,310 | 1,836 |
| Boynton Beach | Palm Beach | 35,624 | 46,194 |
| Bradenton | Manatee | 30,227 | 43,779 |
| Bradenton Beach | Manatee | 1,603 | 1,657 |
| Branford | Suwannee | 622 | 670 |
| Briny Breezes | Palm Beach | 387 | 400 |
| Bristol | Liberty | 1,044 | 937 |
| Bronson | Levy | 853 | 875 |
| Brooker | Bradford | 429 | 312 |
| Brooksville | Hernando | 5,582 | 7,440 |
| Bunnell | Flagler | 1,816 | 1,873 |
| Bushnell | Sumter | 983 | 1,998 |
| | | | |
| Callahan | Nassau | 869 | 946 |
| Callaway | Bay | 7,486 | 12,253 |
| Campbellton | Jackson | 336 | 202 |
| Cape Canaveral | Brevard | 5,733 | 8,014 |
| Cape Coral | Lee | 32,103 | 74,991 |
| Carrabelle | Franklin | 1,304 | 1,200 |
| Caryville | Washington | 633 | 631 |
| Casselberry | Seminole | 15,037 | 18,911 |
| Cedar Grove | Bay | 1,104 | 1,479 |
| Cedar Key | Levy | 700 | 668 |
| Center Hill | Sumter | 751 | 735 |
| Century | Escambia | 2,394 | 1,989 |
| Chattahoochee | Gadsden | 5,332 | 4,382 |
| Chiefland | Levy | 1,986 | 1,917 |
| Chipley | Washington | 3,330 | 3,866 |
| Cinco Bayou | Okaloosa | 202 | 322 |
| Clearwater | Pinellas | 86,212 | 98,784 |
| Clermont | Lake | 5,461 | 6,910 |
| Clewiston | Hendry | 5,219 | 6,085 |

| | | | |
|---|---|---|---|
| Cloud Lake | Palm Beach | 160 | 121 |
| Cocoa | Brevard | 16,096 | 17,722 |
| Cocoa Beach | Brevard | 10,926 | 12,123 |
| Coconut Creek | Broward | 8,174 | 17,485 |
| Coleman | Sumter | 1,022 | 857 |
| Cooper City | Broward | 10,140 | 20,791 |
| Coral Gables | Miami-Dade | 43,241 | 40,091 |
| Coral Springs | Broward | 37,349 | 79,443 |
| Cottondale | Jackson | 1,056 | 900 |
| Crescent City | Putnam | 1,722 | 1,859 |
| Crestview | Okaloosa | 7,617 | 9,886 |
| Cross City | Dixie | 2,154 | 2,041 |
| Crystal River | Citrus | 2,873 | 4,044 |
| | | | |
| Dade City | Pasco | 5,234 | 5,633 |
| Dania | Broward | 11,796 | 13,024 |
| Davenport | Polk | 1,509 | 1,529 |
| Davie | Broward | 29,278 | 47,217 |
| Daytona Beach | Volusia | 54,553 | 61,921 |
| Daytona Beach Shores | Volusia | 1,324 | 2,335 |
| Deerfield Beach | Broward | 39,193 | 46,325 |
| De Funiak Springs | Walton | 5,563 | 5,120 |
| DeLand | Volusia | 15,571 | 16,491 |
| Delray Beach | Palm Beach | 34,475 | 47,181 |
| Destin | Okaloosa | 3,913 | 8,080 |
| Dundee | Polk | 2,227 | 2,335 |
| Dunedin | Pinellas | 30,203 | 34,012 |
| Dunnellon | Marion | 1,427 | 1,624 |
| | | | |
| Eagle Lake | Polk | 1,678 | 1,758 |
| Eatonville | Orange | 2,185 | 2,170 |
| Ebro | Washington | 233 | 255 |
| Edgewater | Volusia | 6,726 | 15,337 |
| Edgewood | Orange | 1,034 | 1,062 |
| El Portal | Miami-Dade | 2,055 | 2,457 |
| Esto | Holmes | 304 | 253 |
| Eustis | Lake | 9,453 | 12,967 |
| Everglades | Collier | 524 | 321 |
| | | | |
| Fanning Springs | Gilchrist/Levy | 314 | 493 |
| Fellsmere | Indian River | 1,161 | 2,179 |
| Fernandina Beach | Nassau | 7,259 | 8,765 |
| Flagler Beach | Flagler | 2,208 | 3,820 |
| Florida City | Miami-Dade | 6,174 | 5,806 |
| Fort Lauderdale | Broward | 153,279 | 149,377 |
| Fort Meade | Polk | 5,546 | 4,976 |
| Fort Myers | Lee | 37,454 | 45,206 |
| Fort Pierce | St. Lucie | 33,802 | 36,830 |
| Fort Walton Beach | Okaloosa | 20,829 | 21,471 |
| Fort White | Columbia | 386 | 268 |
| Freeport | Walton | 669 | 843 |
| Frostproof | Polk | 2,995 | 2,808 |
| Fruitland Park | Lake | 2,259 | 2,754 |

| | | | |
|---|---|---|---|
| Gainesville | Alachua | 81,371 | 84,770 |
| Glen Ridge | Palm Beach | 235 | 207 |
| Glen St. Mary | Baker | 462 | 480 |
| Golden Beach | Miami-Dade | 612 | 774 |
| Golf | Palm Beach | 110 | 234 |
| Golfview | Palm Beach | 210 | 153 |
| Graceville | Jackson | 2,918 | 2,675 |
| Grand Ridge | Jackson | 591 | 536 |
| Greenacres City | Palm Beach | 8,777 | 18,683 |
| Green Cove Springs | Clay | 4,154 | 4,497 |
| Greensboro | Jackson | 562 | 586 |
| Greenville | Madison | 1,096 | 950 |
| Greenwood | Jackson | 577 | 474 |
| Gretna | Gadsden | 1,557 | 1,981 |
| Groveland | Lake | 1,992 | 2,300 |
| Gulf Breeze | Santa Rosa | 5,478 | 5,530 |
| Gulfport | Pinellas | 11,180 | 11,727 |
| Gulf Stream | Palm Beach | 475 | 690 |
| | | | |
| Haines City | Polk | 10,799 | 11,683 |
| Hallandale | Broward/Miami-Dade | 36,517 | 30,996 |
| Hampton | Bradford | 466 | 296 |
| Hastings | St. Johns | 636 | 595 |
| Havana | Gadsden | 2,782 | 1,654 |
| Haverhill | Palm Beach | 1,249 | 1,058 |
| Hawthorne | Alachua | 1,303 | 1,305 |
| Hialeah | Miami-Dade | 145,254 | 188,004 |
| Hialeah Gardens | Miami-Dade | 2,700 | 7,713 |
| Highland Beach | Palm Beach | 2,030 | 3,209 |
| Highland Park | Polk | 184 | 155 |
| High Springs | Alachua | 2,491 | 3,144 |
| Hillcrest Heights | Polk | 177 | 221 |
| Hilliard | Nassau | 1,869 | 1,751 |
| Hillsboro Beach | Broward | 1,554 | 1,748 |
| Holly Hill | Volusia | 9,953 | 11,141 |
| Hollywood | Broward | 121,323 | 121,697 |
| Holmes Beach | Manatee | 4,018 | 4,810 |
| Homestead | Miami-Dade | 20,668 | 26,866 |
| Horseshoe Beach | Dixie | 304 | 252 |
| Howey-in-the-Hills | Lake | 626 | 724 |
| Hypoluxo | Palm Beach | 573 | 830 |
| | | | |
| Indialantic | Brevard | 2,883 | 2,844 |
| Indian Creek | Miami-Dade | 103 | 44 |
| Indian Harbour Beach | Brevard | 5,967 | 6,933 |
| Indian River Shores | Indian River | 1,254 | 2,278 |
| Indian Rocks Beach | Pinellas | 3,717 | 3,963 |
| Indian Shores | Pinellas | 984 | 1,405 |
| Inglis | Levy | 1,173 | 1,241 |
| Interlachen | Putnam | 848 | 1,160 |
| Inverness | Citrus | 4,095 | 5,797 |
| Islandia | Miami-Dade | 12 | 13 |

| Jacksonville | Duval | 540,920 | 672,971 |
|---|---|---|---|
| Jacksonville Beach | Duval | 15,462 | 17,839 |
| Jacob City | Jackson | 224 | 261 |
| Jasper | Hamilton | 2,093 | 2,099 |
| Jay | Santa Rosa | 633 | 666 |
| Jennings | Hamilton | 749 | 712 |
| Juno Beach | Palm Beach | 1,142 | 2,121 |
| Jupiter | Palm Beach | 9,868 | 24,986 |
| JupiterInlet Colony | Palm Beach | 378 | 405 |
| Jupiter Island | Martin | 364 | 549 |
| | | | |
| Kenneth City | Pinellas | 4,344 | 4,462 |
| Key Colony Beach | Monroe | 977 | 977 |
| Keystone Heights | Clay | 1,056 | 1,315 |
| Key West | Monroe | 24,382 | 24,832 |
| Kissimmee | Osceola | 15,487 | 30,050 |
| | | | |
| La Belle | Hendry | 2,287 | 2,703 |
| La Crosse | Alachua | 170 | 122 |
| Lady Lake | Lake | 1,193 | 8,071 |
| Lake Alfred | Polk | 3,163 | 3,622 |
| Lake Butler | Union | 1,830 | 2,116 |
| Lake City | Columbia | 9,257 | 10,005 |
| Lake Clarke Shores | Palm Beach | 3,174 | 3,364 |
| Lake Hamilton | Polk | 1,552 | 1,128 |
| Lake Helen | Volusia | 2,047 | 2,344 |
| Lakeland | Polk | 54,422 | 70,576 |
| Lake Mary | Seminole | 2,853 | 5,929 |
| Lake Park | Palm Beach | 6,909 | 6,704 |
| Lake Placid | Highlands | 963 | 1,158 |
| Lake Wales | Polk | 8,466 | 9,670 |
| Lake Worth | Palm Beach | 270,482 | 8,564 |
| Lantana | Palm Beach | 8,048 | 8,392 |
| Largo | Pinellas | 58,180 | 65,674 |
| Lauderdale-by-the-Sea | Broward | 2,639 | 2,990 |
| Lauderdale Lakes | Broward | 25,426 | 27,341 |
| Lauderhill | Broward | 37,271 | 49,708 |
| Laurel Hill | Okaloosa | 610 | 543 |
| Lawtey | Bradford | 692 | 676 |
| Layton | Monroe | 88 | 183 |
| Lazy Lake | Broward | 31 | 33 |
| Lee | Madison | 297 | 306 |
| Leesburg | Lake | 13,191 | 14,903 |
| Lighthouse Point | Broward | 11,488 | 10,378 |
| Live Oak | Suwannee | 6,732 | 6,332 |
| Longboat Key | Manatee/Sarasota | 4,843 | 5,937 |
| Longwood | Seminole | 10,029 | 13,316 |
| Lynn Haven | Bay | 6,239 | 9,298 |
| | | | |
| Macclenny | Baker | 3,851 | 3,966 |
| McIntosh | Marion | 404 | 411 |
| Madeira Beach | Pinellas | 4,520 | 4,225 |

| | | | |
|---|---|---|---|
| Madison | Madison | 3,487 | 3,345 |
| Maitland | Orange | 8,763 | 9,110 |
| Malibar | Brevard | 1,118 | 1,977 |
| Malone | Jackson | 897 | 765 |
| Manalapan | Palm Beach | 329 | 312 |
| Mangonia Park | Palm Beach | 1,419 | 1,453 |
| Margate | Broward | 35,891 | 42,985 |
| Marianna | Jackson | 7,006 | 6,292 |
| Marineland | Flagler/St. Johns | 31 | 21 |
| Mary Esther | Okaloosa | 3,530 | 4,139 |
| Mascotte | Lake | 1,112 | 1,761 |
| Mayo | Lafayette | 891 | 917 |
| Medley | Miami-Dade | 537 | 663 |
| Melbourne | Brevard | 46,536 | 59,646 |
| Melbourne Beach | Brevard | 2,713 | 3,021 |
| Melbourne Village | Brevard | 1,004 | 591 |
| Mexico Beach | Bay | 632 | 992 |
| Miami | Miami-Dade | 346,681 | 358,548 |
| Miami Beach | Miami-Dade | 96,298 | 92,639 |
| Miami Shores | Miami-Dade | 9,244 | 10,084 |
| Miami Springs | Miami-Dade | 12,350 | 13,268 |
| Micanopy | Alachua | 737 | 612 |
| Midway | Gadsden | 1,385 | 852 |
| Milton | Santa Rosa | 7,206 | 7,216 |
| Minneola | Lake | 851 | 1,515 |
| Miramar | Broward | 32,813 | 40,663 |
| Monticello | Jefferson | 2,994 | 2,573 |
| Montverde | Lake | 397 | 890 |
| Moore Haven | Glades | 1,250 | 1,432 |
| Mount Dora | Lake | 5,883 | 7,196 |
| Mulberry | Polk | 2,932 | 2,988 |
| | | | |
| Naples | Collier | 17,581 | 19,505 |
| Neptune Beach | Duval | 5,248 | 6,816 |
| Newberry | Alachua | 1,826 | 1,644 |
| New Port Richey | Pasco | 11,448 | 14,044 |
| New Smyrna Beach | Volusia | 13,557 | 16,543 |
| Niceville | Okaloosa | 8,624 | 10,507 |
| Noma | Holmes | 113 | 207 |
| North Bay Village | Miami-Dade | 4,920 | 5,383 |
| North Lauderdale | Broward | 18,661 | 26,506 |
| North Miami | Miami-Dade | 42,566 | 49,998 |
| North Miami Beach | Miami-Dade | 36,553 | 35,359 |
| North Palm Beach | Palm Beach | 11,344 | 11,343 |
| North Port | Sarasota | 6,205 | 11,973 |
| North Redington Beach | Pinellas | 1,156 | 1,135 |
| | | | |
| Oak Hill | Volusia | 938 | 917 |
| Oakland | Orange | 658 | 700 |
| Oakland Park | Broward | 22,944 | 26,326 |
| Ocala | Marion | 37,170 | 42,045 |
| Ocean Breeze Park | Martin | 466 | 519 |

| | | | |
|---|---|---|---|
| Ocean Ridge | Palm Beach | 1,355 | 1,570 |
| Ocoee | Orange | 7,803 | 12,778 |
| Okeechobee | Okeechobee | 4,225 | 4,943 |
| Oldsmar | Pinellas | 2,626 | 8,361 |
| Opa-locka | Miami-Dade | 14,460 | 15,283 |
| Orange City | Volusia | 2,909 | 5,347 |
| Orange Park | Clay | 8,766 | 9,488 |
| Orchid | Indian River | 23 | 10 |
| Orlando | Orange | 128,291 | 164,693 |
| Ormond Beach | Volusia | 21,438 | 29,721 |
| Otter Creek | Levy | 167 | 136 |
| Oviedo | Seminole | 3,074 | 11,114 |
| | | | |
| Pahokee | Palm Beach | 6,346 | 6,822 |
| Palatka | Putnam | 10,175 | 10,201 |
| Palm Bay | Brevard | 18,560 | 62,632 |
| Palm Beach | Palm Beach | 9,729 | 9,814 |
| Palm Beach Gardens | Palm Beach | 14,407 | 22,965 |
| Palm Beach Shores | Palm Beach | 1,232 | 1,040 |
| Palmetto | Manatee | 8,637 | 9,268 |
| Palm Shores | Brevard | 77 | 210 |
| Palm Springs | Palm Beach | 8,166 | 9,763 |
| Panama City | Bay | 33,346 | 34,378 |
| Panama City Beach | Bay | 2,148 | 4,051 |
| Parker | Bay | 4,298 | 4,598 |
| Parkland | Broward | 545 | 3,558 |
| Paxton | Walton | 659 | 600 |
| Pembroke Park | Broward | 5,306 | 4,933 |
| Pembroke Pines | Broward | 35,862 | 65,452 |
| Penney Farms | Clay | 630 | 609 |
| Pensacola | Escambia | 57,619 | 58,165 |
| Perry | Taylor | 825 | 7,151 |
| Pierson | Volusia | 1,085 | 2,988 |
| Pinellas Park | Pinellas | 32,811 | 43,426 |
| Plantation | Broward | 48,653 | 66,692 |
| Plant City | Hillsborough | 17,064 | 22,754 |
| Polk City | Polk | 576 | 1,439 |
| Pomona Park | Putnam | 791 | 663 |
| Pompano Beach | Broward | 63,063 | 72,411 |
| Ponce de Leon | Holmes | 454 | 406 |
| Ponce Inlet | Volusia | 1,003 | 1,704 |
| Port Orange | Volusia | 18,756 | 35,317 |
| Port Richey | Pasco | 2,165 | 2,523 |
| Port St. Joe | Gulf | 4,027 | 4,044 |
| Port St. Lucie | St. Lucie | 14,690 | 55,866 |
| Punta Gorda | Charlotte | 6,797 | 10,747 |
| | | | |
| Quincy | Gadsden | 8,591 | 7,444 |
| | | | |
| Raiford | Union | 259 | 198 |
| Reddick | Marion | 657 | 554 |
| Redington Beach | Pinellas | 1,708 | 1,626 |
| Redington Shores | Pinellas | 2,142 | 2,366 |

| | | | |
|---|---|---|---|
| Riviera Beach | Palm Beach | 26,489 | 27,639 |
| Rockledge | Brevard | 11,877 | 16,023 |
| Royal Palm Beach | Palm Beach | 3,423 | 14,589 |
| | | | |
| Safety Harbor | Pinellas | 6,461 | 15,124 |
| St. Augustine | St. Johns | 11,985 | 11,692 |
| St. Augustine Beach | St. Johns | 1,289 | 3,657 |
| St. Cloud | Osceola | 7,840 | 12,453 |
| St. Leo | Pasco | 917 | 1,009 |
| St. Lucie | St. Lucie | 593 | 584 |
| St. Marks | Wakulla | 286 | 307 |
| St. Petersburg | Pinellas | 238,767 | 238,629 |
| St. Pete Beach | Pinellas | 9,354 | 9,200 |
| San Antonio | Pasco | 529 | 776 |
| Sanford | Seminole | 23,176 | 32,387 |
| Sanibel | Lee | 3,363 | 5,468 |
| Sarasota | Sarasota | 48,868 | 50,961 |
| Satellite Beach | Brevard | 9,163 | 9,889 |
| Sea Ranch Lakes | Broward | 584 | 619 |
| Sebastian | Indian River | 2,861 | 10,205 |
| Sebring | Highlands | 8,736 | 8,900 |
| Seminole | Pinellas | 6,419 | 9,251 |
| Sewall's Point | Martin | 1,187 | 1,588 |
| Shalimar | Okaloosa | 390 | 341 |
| Sneads | Jackson | 1,690 | 1,746 |
| Sopchoppy | Wakulla | 444 | 367 |
| South Bay | Palm Beach | 3,886 | 3,558 |
| South Daytona | Volusia | 11,252 | 12,482 |
| South Miami | Miami-Dade | 10,895 | 10,404 |
| South Palm Beach | Palm Beach | 1,304 | 1,480 |
| South Pasadena | Pinellas | 4,188 | 5,644 |
| Springfield | Bay | 7,504 | 8,715 |
| Starke | Bradford | 5,306 | 5,226 |
| Stuart | Martin | 9,467 | 11,936 |
| Sunrise | Broward | 39,681 | 64,407 |
| Surfside | Miami-Dade | 3,763 | 4,108 |
| Sweetwater | Miami-Dade | 8,067 | 13,909 |
| | | | |
| Tallahassee | Leon | 106,179 | 124,773 |
| Tamarac | Broward | 29,376 | 44,822 |
| Tampa | Hillsborough | 271,578 | 280,015 |
| Tarpon Springs | Pinellas | 13,251 | 17,906 |
| Tavares | Lake | 4,984 | 7,383 |
| Temple Terrace | Hillsborough | 11,278 | 16,444 |
| Tequesta | Palm Beach | 3,685 | 4,499 |
| Titusville | Brevard | 31,910 | 39,394 |
| Treasure Island | Pinellas | 6,316 | 7,266 |
| Trenton | Gilchrist | 1,131 | 1,287 |
| | | | |
| Umatilla | Lake | 1,872 | 2,350 |
| | | | |
| Valparaiso | Okaloosa | 6,142 | 4,672 |
| Venice | Sarasota | 12,424 | 16,922 |

| | | | |
|---|---|---|---|
| Vernon | Washington | 885 | 778 |
| Vero Beach | Indian River | 16,176 | 17,350 |
| Virginia Gardens | Miami-Dade | 2,098 | 2,212 |
| Waldo | Alachua | 993 | 1,017 |
| Wauchula | Hardee | 3,296 | 3,253 |
| Wausau | Washington | 347 | 313 |
| Webster | Sumter | 856 | 746 |
| Weeki Wachee | Hernando | 8 | 53 |
| Welaka | Putnam | 492 | 533 |
| West Melbourne | Brevard | 5,078 | 8,399 |
| West Miami | Miami-Dade | 6,076 | 5,727 |
| West Palm Beach | Palm Beach | 63,305 | 67,643 |
| Westville | Holmes | 343 | 257 |
| Wewahitchka | Gulf | 1,742 | 1,779 |
| White Springs | Hamilton | 781 | 704 |
| Wildwood | Sumter | 2,665 | 3,421 |
| Williston | Levy | 2,240 | 2,179 |
| Wilton Manors | Broward | 12,742 | 11,804 |
| Windermere | Orange | 1,302 | 1,371 |
| Winter Garden | Orange | 6,789 | 9,745 |
| Winter Haven | Polk | 21,119 | 24,725 |
| Winter Park | Orange | 22,339 | 22,242 |
| Winter Springs | Seminole | 10,475 | 22,151 |
| Worthington Springs | Union | 220 | 178 |
| Yankeetown | Levy | 600 | 635 |
| Zephyrhills | Pasco | 6,137 | 8,220 |
| Zolfo Springs | Hardee | 1,495 | 1,219 |

---

## POPULATION HIGHLIGHTS

Nine of the nation's fastest growing metropolitan areas were in Florida, according to the 1990 census. They were the areas of Ocala, Bradenton, Fort Myers, Naples, Daytona Beach, Orlando, Melbourne, Fort Pierce, and West Palm Beach.

Between 1980 and 1990, Hispanic populations in the Miami/Fort Lauderdale area increased 70.9 percent to 1,061,846; in the Tampa/St. Petersburg area 73.5 percent to 139,248; in the Orlando area 271.2 percent to 96,418; in the West Palm Beach/Boca Raton/Delray Beach area 133.7 percent to 66,613, and in Jacksonville 16.2 percent to 181,265.

More than half the population of Miami-Dade County, 56 percent, was of Hispanic heritage. Florida's population continued to grow older. In 1980 the state's median age was 34.7; in 1990 it rose to 36.4.

The Native American population of the state nearly doubled from 1980 to 1990, from 19,257 to 36,335. Accounting for the increase has been an influx of Indians from different tribes into the state seeking economic opportunities. The state's two resident Indian tribes–Seminoles and Miccosukees–showed little population increase; Seminoles numbered about 2,000, and Miccosukees about 400.

The largest concentration of Finns outside of Finland was the Lake Worth/Lantana area, in which 17,000 Finns lived the year around.

*(continued on next page)*

(continued from previous page)

About 20 percent of the state's then 12.9 million people lived in north Florida, while the remaining 80 percent were divided equally between central and south Florida.

Florida rose from the 20th largest state in 1950, with fewer residents than Kentucky, to the fourth largest in 1990, with nearly four times as many residents as Kentucky.

The fastest growing county between 1980 and 1990 was Flagler, which nearly tripled its population.

More New Yorkers lived in south Florida than any other group. They have represented as much as 18.5 percent of the population in Palm Beach, Broward, and Miami-Dade counties.

University of Florida population researchers predict the state's population will continue to grow steadily but at a slower rate during the next three decades, reaching 19 million by the year 2020.

Florida's population center, which drifted steadily southward for 150 years, is beginning to drift northward. The population center of the state is in central Polk County about four miles east of the town of Homeland.

Each day Florida grows by 600 new residents, despite the fact that an estimated 800 people a day leave the state.

## ANDREW'S LASTING IMPACT

Hurricane Andrew, which tore through South Florida in August 1992, continues to have far-reaching effects on the region's population and housing. More than half of Miami-Dade County's homes were destroyed. More than 90 percent of the housing units in its southern reaches were damaged. More than 250,000 people had to leave their homes, with more than half of those moving in with relatives or friends. While the county's population was about the same in 1994 as it was before the storm hit, it was an estimated 40,000 to 50,000 smaller than it would have been if the hurricane had not occurred, given the growth in previous years.

## NOT SO OLD

Florida was not the "oldest" state in the Union in 1997, according to the U.S. Census Bureau, but it was close. West Virginia was the oldest, with the median age of its citizens at 38.1 years. Florida was the next oldest, at 38.0 years. Utah was the "youngest" state, with a median age of 26.9 years. It was the only state with most of its citizens under the age of 30.

## NORTHERN FLORIDIANS

North Florida has the highest percentage of native Floridians, and its residents express the highest satisfaction with living in Florida. Seventy-one percent of non-native Floridians consider themselves Floridians, and 84 percent told a Leadership Florida survey in 1999 that they plan on remaining in the state. Eighty-five percent of immigrants from Cuba told surveyors they consider themselves Floridians. Nearly 25 percent of respondents were born in Florida, a statistically equal sample came originally from the northeastern U.S., 23 percent from the Midwest or other U.S. states outside the South. Nearly 15 percent came from other Southern states and 12.6 percent were foreign born. Recently arrived retirees were the least likely to consider themselves Floridians and had the least satisfaction with living in the state.

# VITAL STATISTICS

## LEADING CAUSES OF RESIDENT DEATHS
### (Per 100,000 population)

| Age Group | Cause of Death | Rank | Deaths | 1998 Rates |
|---|---|---|---|---|
| Less than One | ALL CAUSES | — | 1,415 | 728.8 |
| | Perinatal conditions | 1 | 685 | 352.8 |
| | Congenital anomalies | 2 | 264 | 136 |
| | Sudden Infant Death | 3 | 118 | 60.8 |
| | Accidents | 4 | 57 | 29.4 |
| | Heart disease | 5 | 37 | 19.1 |
| 1 to 4 | ALL CAUSES | — | 304 | 39.9 |
| | Accidents | 1 | 151 | 19.8 |
| | Homicide & legal intervention | 2 | 25 | 3.3 |
| | Congenital anomalies | 3 | 24 | 3.1 |
| | Cancer | 4 | 16 | 2.1 |
| | Heart Disease | 5 | 9 | 1.2 |
| 5 to 14 | ALL CAUSES | — | 427 | 22.2 |
| | Accidents | 1 | 176 | 9.2 |
| | Cancer | 2 | 57 | 3 |
| | Heart Disease | 3 | 32 | 1.7 |
| | Homicide & legal intervention | 4 | 27 | 1.4 |
| | Congenital anomalies | 5 | 23 | 1.2 |
| 15 to 24 | ALL CAUSES | — | 1,521 | 84.3 |
| | Accidents | 1 | 707 | 39.2 |
| | Homicide & legal intervention | 2 | 225 | 12.5 |
| | Suicide | 3 | 199 | 11 |
| | Cancer | 4 | 81 | 4.5 |
| | Heart Disease | 5 | 40 | 2.2 |
| 25 to 34 | ALL CAUSES | — | 2,586 | 130.1 |
| | Accidents | 1 | 714 | 35.9 |
| | HIV | 2 | 318 | 16.02 |
| | Suicide | 3 | 303 | 15.2 |
| | Homicide & legal intervention | 4 | 275 | 13.8 |
| | Cancer | 5 | 261 | 13.1 |
| 35 to 44 | ALL CAUSES | — | 5,597 | 246.2 |
| | Cancer | 1 | 1,013 | 44.6 |
| | Accidents | 2 | 988 | 43.5 |
| | Heart disease | 3 | 725 | 31.9 |
| | HIV | 4 | 638 | 28.1 |
| | Suicide | 5 | 462 | 20.3 |
| 45 to 54 | ALL CAUSES | — | 8,743 | 456.2 |
| | Cancer | 1 | 2,740 | 143 |
| | Heart disease | 2 | 1,835 | 95.7 |
| | Accidents | 3 | 671 | 35 |
| | Chronic liver disease & cirrhosis | 4 | 386 | 20.1 |
| | Suicide | 5 | 367 | 19.1 |
| 55 to 64 | ALL CAUSES | — | 14,318 | 995.3 |
| | Cancer | 1 | 5,451 | 378.9 |
| | Heart disease | 2 | 3,818 | 265.4 |

| | | | | |
|---|---|---|---|---|
| | Chronic Obstructive Pulmonary Disease | .3 | .656 | .45.6 |
| | Stroke | .4 | .576 | .40 |
| | Diabetes | .5 | .510 | .35.5 |
| 65 to 74 | ALL CAUSES | — | .30,834 | .2,136.9 |
| | Cancer | .1 | .10,895 | .755 |
| | Heart disease | .2 | .9,039 | .626.4 |
| | Chronic Obstructive Pulmonary Disease | .3 | .2,114 | .146.5 |
| | Stroke | .4 | .1,512 | .104.8 |
| | Diabetes | .5 | .1,069 | .74.1 |
| 75 up | ALL CAUSES | — | .91,355 | .6,881 |
| | Heart disease | .1 | .33,009 | .2,636.9 |
| | Cancer | .2 | .17,267 | .1,300.6 |
| | Stroke | .3 | .7,363 | .554.6 |
| | Chronic Obstructive Pulmonary Disease | .4 | .5,106 | .384.6 |
| | Pneumonia & influenza | .5 | .3,102 | .233.6 |

## LIFE EXPECTANCY

A person born in Florida in 1998 could expect to live 77.5 years, the same as in 1997. Floridians' life expectancy exceeds that of the U.S. as a whole, as it has for more than 30 years.

Life expectancy increased for men, but decreased for women. The life expectancy of nonwhite females declined to 75.0 years in 1998. It stood at 75.9 in 1993.

White Florida females born in 1998 have a life expectancy of 81.5 years, the highest of any group, but down from 81.6 the year before. White males could expect to live 75.3 years, up from 75.2 in 1997. Nonwhite males continued to have the shortest life expectancy at 68.4 years, but that was an increase over the year before and more than a full year longer than the life expectancy registered in 1993.

## BIRTHS

In 1995, live births to Florida residents dropped to 188,535, the lowest of the decade. But births have rebounded since and bounced upward again in 1998 to 195,564, an increase of 1.7 percent over 1997.

Florida's birth rate remained at 13.0 per 1,000 population, the lowest rate since reliable birth statistics were established in the state with the 1920 census. Florida's birth rate has lagged behind the national rate throughout the century. The 1998 U.S. rate was 14.7 per 1,000 population. The state's birth rate climbed throughout the 1980s and stood at 15.1 in 1990.

The birth rate among whites continued at 11.5, the lowest on record. The birthrate among nonwhites was 20.9 per 1,000, an increase over 1997's 20.7.

The percentage of births to mothers under the age of 18 again decreased in 1998 but the percentage of births for nonwhite mothers was still twice the percentage of white mothers. Of live births to unwed mothers, 20.2 percent were to women 18 years and younger. Births to mothers 18 or younger accounted for 8.8 percent of the total. Births to mothers age 35 and over accounted for 13.3 percent of all births. Of mothers aged 15 to 19 years, 22.2 percent had one or more previous live births.

More than one in three births, 36.6 percent, was to an unwed mother. For nonwhites, nearly two of every three live births, or 62.3 percent, were to unwed mothers. The rate among white mothers was 27.9 percent.

Of the resident live births in 1998, 8.1 percent of births involved a birth-weight of less than 2,500 grams (5 lbs., 8.2 oz.) while 1.6 percent had a birthweight of less than 1,500 grams (3 lbs., 4.9 oz.). At the other end of the scale, 9 percent of resident live births had birthweights of 4,000 grams (8 lbs., 13.1 oz.) or more. Ninety-nine percent of all births occurred in hospitals in 1998 and 88.1 percent of those hospital births were attended by a physician, with 82 percent of all mothers receiving prenatal care in the first trimester. More births occurred in December than in any other month.

## DEATHS

Florida resident deaths increased to a record high of 157,160 in 1998, an increase of 2.2 percent from 1997.

Heart disease continued to be the leading cause of death followed, as it has been, by cancer, stroke, pulmonary disease, and accidents. Heart disease caused nearly one in every three deaths in the state.

Cancer was the cause in almost one in every four deaths. Respiratory cancer was the most pervasive cause of cancer death for all except nonwhite females, who died instead from cancer of the digestive organs and peritoneum.

Accidents were the leading cause of death among the population between the ages of 1 through 34, accounting for more than a third, 36.1 percent, of all deaths in that age group.

There were 332 fewer deaths associated with the HIV virus in 1998 than in 1997, a 17.7 percent decrease, but it remained the fourth leading cause of death among nonwhites. The death rate among nonwhite males was greater than the rate for white males and females and nonwhite females combined. HIV was the second leading cause of death in persons 25 through 34, accounting for 12.3 percent of total deaths, down from 16.6 percent in 1997.

The homicide death rate for nonwhite males dropped, but the rate remained more than 1.5 times the combined rate for white males, white females, and nonwhite females.

Including homicide, major external causes of death (accident, suicide, and legal intervention) accounted for 5.8 percent of deaths in the state during 1998.

Pneumonia and influenza, and diabetes were the sixth and seventh most frequent causes of death.

Both the number and the rate of neonatal (under 28 days) deaths decreased slightly in 1998. The number increased one percent for whites, but decreased 0.2 percent for nonwhites. However, the nonwhite neonatal death rate, at 7.5, was almost twice the white rate, 3.8. Overall the neonatal death rate was 4.8 per 1,000 live births, less than half the rate in 1980. There was an overall increase in infant (under one year) deaths. It rose from a record low of 7.1 deaths per 1,000 births in 1997 to 7.2 in 1998, above the national U.S. rate. However, the infant mortality rate has dropped 25 percent since 1990 and is less than half the rate of 1980. The infant mortality rate for nonwhites, at 11.4, is nearly double the rate for whites, 5.8. Of the total deaths occurring in the first year of life, 65.9 percent were less than 28 days old with 37.8 percent occurring among those less than one day old. Both the number and the ratio of fetal (20 or more weeks gestation) deaths decreased in 1998, up 0.2 percent among whites, but down 1 percent among nonwhites. Of fetal deaths, 18.4 percent occurred to mothers residing in Miami-Dade County and about one in ten occurred to a mother who was aged 18 or younger.

## ACCIDENTS

A total of 9,176 persons died in 1998 due to accidents. The largest number, 2,929, died in motor vehicle accidents. The second greatest killer was falls, accounting for 832 deaths, followed by poisonings, 655; drowning, 393; suffocation, 265; fire-related, 126; and medicosurgical, 80.

Other fatal accidents, in order, include: electric current, 48; air and space transport, 42; struck by object, 40; machinery, 35; cataclysms 34; water transport (except drowning), 26; railway, 25; firearms, 22; excessive heat, 19; cutting and piercing instruments, 10; explosives, 10; lightning, 9; hunger/thirst/exposure/neglect, 8; venomous animals and plants, 6; injury caused by animals (other than venomous), 5; excessive cold, 3; and air pressure, 2.

## DISPOSAL OF REMAINS

After its two-decade rise in popularity, cremation passed the incidence of burial for those who died in Florida in 1997. Of the 159,354 recorded deaths, 40.1 percent resulted in burial, while 43.2 percent were cremations. Removal of remains from the state continued to decline, to 16.0. Burial accounted for 74.6 percent of all nonwhite dispositions, as compared to only 35.9 percent for whites. Cremations were more prevalent among whites, accounting for 46.6 percent, as compared with only 15.3 percent for nonwhites. Whites also accounted for more removals out of state, 16.8 percent, than nonwhites, 9.3 percent. January recorded the highest number of deaths.

## MARRIAGES AND DISSOLUTIONS

The marriage rate decreased to 9.4 from 10.7 per thousand in 1997, but remained well above the U.S. rate. Meanwhile, the dissolution rate, including annulments, also decreased in 1998 to a rate of 5.3 per 1,000, continuing the decline trend of the decade, but still higher than the U.S. average. Because many of Florida's dissolutions are granted to persons who establish residency in the state specifically for this purpose, the state has a dissolution rate more than 30 percent higher than the U.S. rate.

The number of marriages in 1998 decreased to 141,344 from the previous year's record high of 158,783. Dissolutions increased to 80,466.

May was the most popular month in 1998 to be married, while July was the month in which the most dissolutions of marriage were granted.

## MARRIAGE LICENSES

Marriage license applications can be taken out in the clerk of circuit court's office in any county, regardless of where the parties live in Florida. Minimum legal age is 18 for both males and females. If the parties are not of legal age, both parents, if living, or a legal guardian, must sign their consent to the marriage. The license has no expiration date. The marriage may take place in any county, but the license must be returned within 10 days after the marriage to the county which issued it for there to be an official record of the union.

However, prospective newlyweds who are Floridians are required to take a 4-hour marriage course or wait three days for a license. Those who opt for the three-day waiting period will pay a high price, $88.50, for a marriage license. Those taking the course may obtain a marriage license for $56.00. The courses are given by churches and other non-profit organizations. Non-residents do not have to meet the requirements. The law requiring either counseling or a cooling off period also mandates that Florida high school students take a course on marriage, although that curriculum may be included in another course.

## FLORIDA: A NICE PLACE TO LIVE

Florida is first choice among Americans polled as the place they'd like to live other than their current state of residence. Arizona, California, Colorado, Tennessee, North Carolina, and Hawaii were the runner-ups in that order, according to a 1997 Louis Harris poll.

# CRIME

## CRIMES AND RATES

Florida's Department of Law Enforcement has compiled crime statistics from county and municipal law enforcement agencies since 1930. The latest available figures cover 1998, a period in which both the overall crime rate and violent crime rate declined again. Arrests increased significantly, but the arrest of juvenile offenders declined.

Crimes are indexed in seven categories: violent crimes of murder, forcible sex offenses, robbery, and aggravated assault; and non-violent crimes of burglary, larceny, and motor vehicle theft.

Police agencies have placed renewed emphasis on domestic violence, an area that accounted for an alarming increase of crime in this decade. In 1998, such crimes declined by more than 2 percent.

### 1998

Crime Volume
Violent . . . . . . . . . . . . . . . . . . . . . . . . . . . . . . . . . . . . . . . . . . . 139,673
Non-Violent . . . . . . . . . . . . . . . . . . . . . . . . . . . . . . . . . . . . . . 885,427
TOTAL . . . . . . . . . . . . . . . . . . . . . . . . . . . . . . . . . . . . . . . . . 1,025,100
Property Values
Total Stolen: . . . . . . . . . . . . . . . . . . . . . . . . . . . . . . . . . . . $1,677,734,624
TOTAL RECOVERED: . . . . . . . . . . . . . . . . . . . . . . . . . . . . . . $627,943,306
Arrests
Adult. . . . . . . . . . . . . . . . . . . . . . . . . . . . . . . . . . . . . . . . . . . . . 748,503
Juvenile. . . . . . . . . . . . . . . . . . . . . . . . . . . . . . . . . . . . . . . . . . . 131,688
TOTAL. . . . . . . . . . . . . . . . . . . . . . . . . . . . . . . . . . . . . . . . . . 880,191

| Offense Totals | 1997 | 1998 | Percentage Change |
|---|---|---|---|
| **Murder** | **1,014** | **966** | **-4.7** |
| Firearm | 634 | 589 | -7.1 |
| Knife | 129 | 115 | -10.9 |
| Barehanded | 87 | 86 | -1.1 |
| Other | 164 | 176 | 7.3 |
| **Forcible sex offenses** | **13,224** | **12,702** | **-3.9** |
| Rape | 7,672 | 7,393 | -3.6 |
| Sodomy | 1,680 | 1,561 | -7.1 |
| Fondling | 3,872 | 3,748 | -3.2 |
| **Robbery** | **40,703** | **36,130** | **-11.2** |
| Firearm | 15,707 | 13,937 | -11.3 |
| Knife | 2,695 | 2,500 | -7.2 |
| Barehanded | 17,946 | 15,655 | -12.8 |
| Other | 4,355 | 4,038 | -7.3 |
| **Aggravated Assault** | **95,860** | **89,875** | **-6.2** |
| Firearm | 18,436 | 16,825 | -8.7 |
| Knife | 18,541 | 17,696 | -4.6 |
| Barehanded | 12,542 | 11,609 | -7.4 |
| Other | 46,341 | 43,745 | -5.6 |
| **Burglary** | **214,894** | **202,559** | **-5.7** |
| Forced Entry | 143,602 | 134,822 | -6.1 |
| No Forced Entry | 54,949 | 53,269 | -3.1 |
| Attempted Entry | 16,343 | 14,468 | -11.5 |

**Larceny.** . . . . . . . . . . . . . . . . **599,190** . . . . . . . **578,774** . . . . . . . . . . . . . **-3.4**
   Pocket Picking . . . . . . . . . . . . . 5,495 . . . . . . . . . 5,889 . . . . . . . . . . . . . 7.2
   Purse Snatching . . . . . . . . . . . 2,367 . . . . . . . . . 2,092 . . . . . . . . . . . . -11.6
   Shoplifting . . . . . . . . . . . . . . . 90,903 . . . . . . . . 84,190 . . . . . . . . . . . . . -7.4
   From Motor Vehicle. . . . . . . 136,891 . . . . . . . 133,563 . . . . . . . . . . . . . -2.4
   Motor Vehicle Parts . . . . . . . . 91,906 . . . . . . . 92,169 . . . . . . . . . . . . . .03
   Bicycles. . . . . . . . . . . . . . . . . 35,744 . . . . . . . . 28,835 . . . . . . . . . . . . -19.3
   From Buildings . . . . . . . . . . . 45,977 . . . . . . . . 47,280 . . . . . . . . . . . . . 2.8
   From Vending Machines. . . . . 3,201 . . . . . . . . . 3,871. . . . . . . . . . . . . 20.9
   All Other . . . . . . . . . . . . . . . 186,706 . . . . . . . 180,885 . . . . . . . . . . . . . -3.1
**Auto Theft** . . . . . . . . . . . . . . **108,872** . . . . . . . **104,094** . . . . . . . . . . . . . **-4.4**

**TOTAL** . . . . . . . . . . . . . . . **1,073,757** . . . . . **1,025,100** . . . . . . . . . . . . . **-4.5**

## CRIME TRENDS

| Year | Total Crimes | Percentage Change | Violent Crimes | Percentage Change | Non-Violent Crimes | Percentage Change |
|------|------|------|------|------|------|------|
| 1992 | 1,112,746. | -1.5. | 161,137 | 1.87. | 951,609 | -2.05 |
| 1993 | 1,116,567 | 0.34. | 161,789 | 0.4. | 954,778 | 0.33 |
| 1994 | 1,130,875 | 1.28. | 157,835 | -2.44. | 973,040 | 1.91 |
| 1995 | 1,078,619. | -4.62. | 150,208. | -4.83. | 928,411 | -4.59 |
| 1996 | 1,079,642 | 0.09. | 151,369 | 0.76. | 928,273 | -0.01 |
| 1997 | 1,073,757. | -0.5. | 150,801. | -0.5. | 922,956 | -0.6 |
| 1998 | 1,025,100. | -4.5. | 139,673. | -7.4. | 885,427 | -4.1 |

### Domestic Violence

| Primary Offense | 1997 | 1998 | Percentage Change |
|------|------|------|------|
| Murder | 161 | 190. | 18 |
| Manslaughter | 9 | 22 | 144.4 |
| Rape | 1,365 | 1,440 | 5.5 |
| Sodomy | 460 | 411. | -10.7 |
| Fondling | 932 | 955 | 2.5 |
| Aggrav. Assault | 26,561 | 25,162. | -5.3 |
| Aggrav. Stalking. | 298 | 247. | -17.3 |
| Simple Assault | 101,305 | 99,428. | -1.9 |
| Threat/Intimid. | 4,681 | 4,817 | 2.9 |
| Simple Stalking | 610 | 673 | 10.3 |
| **TOTAL** | **136,382** | **133,345** | **-2.2** |

### Domestic Violence
### Victim's Relationship to Offender

| | 1997 | 1998 |
|------|------|------|
| Spouse | 42,602 | 40,007 |
| Parent | 10,507 | 10,592 |
| Child | 9,979 | 9,672 |
| Sibling | 9,360 | 9,384 |
| Other Family | 8,233 | 8,214 |
| Cohabitant. | 44,326 | 42,685 |
| Other. | 11,375 | 12,791 |

## Value of Stolen Property—1998

| Type | Stolen Value | Recovered Value |
|------|-------------|-----------------|
| Currency, Notes, etc. | $92,260,400 | $2,989,532 |
| Jewelry, Prec. Metals | $158,244,003 | $10,669,191 |
| Clothing, Furs | $34,552,351 | $4,447,401 |
| Motor Vehicles | $850,681,998 | $546,567,792 |
| Office Equipment | $86,021,979 | $4,113,787 |
| TVs, Stereos, etc. | $70,723,892 | $3,782,930 |
| Firearms | $7,512,728 | $800,906 |
| Household Goods | $24,417,214 | $1,628,667 |
| Consumable Goods | $18,846,256 | $1,598,253 |
| Livestock | $921,514 | $119,840 |
| Miscellaneous | $333,552,289 | $51,224,747 |
| **TOTALS** | **$1,677,734,624** | **$627,943,306** |

## Vehicle Recovery

| | 1997 | 1998 |
|------|------|------|
| Stolen and Recovered Locally | 44,625 | 45,606 |
| Stolen Locally and Recovered by Other Jurisdictions | 24,972 | 26,293 |
| Stolen in Other Jurisdictions and Recovered Locally | 30,887 | 29,509 |

## Arson—1998

| Structure | Inhabited | Abandoned | Attempted |
|-----------|-----------|-----------|-----------|
| Single Residence | 884 | 117 | 74 |
| Other Residence | 303 | 24 | 19 |
| Storage | 39 | 17 | 3 |
| Ind./Manufacturing | 18 | 3 | 1 |
| Commercial | 237 | 30 | 15 |
| Community/Public | 175 | 13 | 10 |
| All Other Structures | 78 | 22 | 10 |
| Motor Vehicles | 592 | 229 | 38 |
| Other Mobile | 29 | 8 | 3 |
| Other | 619 | 159 | 19 |
| **TOTAL** | **2,974** | **622** | **1,927** |

### Juvenile Arrests/ Cases Received—1997

| | |
|------|------|
| Murder | 97 |
| Attempted Murder | 148 |
| Sexual Battery | 896 |
| Other Felony Sex Offenses | 801 |
| Armed Robbery | 1,311 |
| Other Robbery | 1,999 |
| Aggrav. Assault, Battery | 8,721 |
| Arson | 564 |
| Burglary | 18,206 |
| Auto Theft | 5,401 |
| Grand Larceny | 4,289 |
| Dealing, Stolen Property | 394 |
| Concealed Firearm | 693 |
| Forgery | 452 |
| Non-Marijuana Felony Drug | 4,670 |
| Felony Marijuana | 1,258 |
| Escape | 965 |
| Resisting Arrest, Violent | 539 |
| Shoot/Throw Deadly Missile | 1,067 |
| Felony Traffic | 68 |
| Other Felonies | 6,295 |
| Misdemeanors | 90,589 |
| **OFFENSE TOTAL** | **149,423** |

### Adult Arrests—1997

| | |
|------|------|
| Murder | 853 |
| Rape | 2,328 |

| | |
|---|---|
| Robbery. . . . . . . . . . . . . . . . . . 6,441 | Possess Opium/Cocaine . . . . . 26,716 |
| Aggravated Assault . . . . . . . . . 33,522 | Possess Marijuana . . . . . . . . . . 17,628 |
| Burglary. . . . . . . . . . . . . . . . . 15,338 | Possess Syn. Drugs . . . . . . . . . . . . . 1 |
| Larceny . . . . . . . . . . . . . . . . . . 44,785 | Possess Other Drugs . . . . . . . . . 7,888 |
| Motor Vehicle Theft . . . . . . . . . 6,376 | Bookmaking. . . . . . . . . . . . . . . . . 40 |
| Manslaughter. . . . . . . . . . . . . . . 146 | Lottery/Number Violations. . . . . . 33 |
| Other Assaults. . . . . . . . . . . . . 44,801 | Other Gambling . . . . . . . . . . . . 231 |
| Arson . . . . . . . . . . . . . . . . . . . . . 337 | Family Offenses. . . . . . . . . . . . . 3,059 |
| Forgery/Counterfeiting . . . . . . 3,962 | DUI . . . . . . . . . . . . . . . . . . . . . 32,961 |
| Fraud. . . . . . . . . . . . . . . . . . . 17,105 | Liquor Laws . . . . . . . . . . . . . . . . 147 |
| Embezzlement . . . . . . . . . . . . . . . 14 | Drunkenness . . . . . . . . . . . . . . . 2,928 |
| Stolen Property . . . . . . . . . . . . 2,617 | Disorderly Conduct. . . . . . . . . . 5,264 |
| Vandalism . . . . . . . . . . . . . . . . 1,860 | Curfew/Loitering . . . . . . . . . . . 1,696 |
| Weapons Violations. . . . . . . . . . 6,923 | All Other Offenses . . . . . . . . 109,622 |
| Prostitution/Commercialized | |
| Sex . . . . . . . . . . . . . . . . . . . . 4,216 | **TOTAL . . . . . . . . . . . . . . . 418,898** |
| Other Sex Offenses. . . . . . . . . . 2,635 | |
| Sale Opium/Cocaine . . . . . . . 12,179 | Still to be Processed . . . . . . . 118,244 |
| Sale Marijuana . . . . . . . . . . . . . 2,674 | In the first six months of 1998, |
| Sale Synthetic Narcotics . . . . . . . . . 5 | crime fell another 3.8 percent from |
| Sale Other Dangerous Drugs . . 1,567 | the same period the year before. |

## FDLE CRIME LABORATORIES

A growing percentage of drug detection is being processed through the FDLE's six regional crime laboratories. Most laboratory work includes chemical analysis, document investigations, firearm tests, latent fingerprint tests, and crime scene analyses.

Florida Department of Law Enforcement Crime Laboratories are located in the following cities:

| Location | Counties Served |
|---|---|
| Pensacola | Escambia, Santa Rosa, Jackson, Okaloosa, Walton, Holmes, Washington, Bay |
| Jacksonville | Alachua, Baker, Bradford, Clay, Duval, Nassau, St. Johns, Putnam, Gilchrist, Union, Flagler, Levy |
| Orlando | Volusia, Marion, Lake, Seminole, Orange, Brevard, Osceola, Indian River, St. Lucie, Okeechobee, Martin, Palm Beach, Broward, Miami-Dade |
| Tallahassee | Gadsden, Liberty, Calhoun, Gulf, Franklin, Wakulla, Jefferson, Taylor, Suwannee, Madison, Lafayette, Hamilton, Columbia, Leon, Dixie |
| Tampa | Citrus, Hardee, Hernando, Highlands, Polk, Hillsborough, Manatee, Pasco, Pinellas, Sarasota, Sumter |
| Fort Myers | De Soto, Charlotte, Glades, Lee, Hendry, Collier, Monroe |

## CORRECTIONAL INSTITUTIONS

| Facility | City | Max. Inmate Capacity | Inmates (July 1998) |
|---|---|---|---|
| Apalachee Correctional. . . . . . | Sneads . . . . . . . . . . . | 1,535 . . . . . . . . . . . . | 1,468 |
| Avon Park Correctional. . . . . . | Avon Park . . . . . . . . | 1,188 . . . . . . . . . . . . | 1,199 |
| Baker Correctional . . . . . . . . . | Olustee . . . . . . . . . . | 1,267 . . . . . . . . . . . | 882 |

| | | | |
|---|---|---|---|
| Bay Correctional** | Panama City | 750 | 680 |
| Brevard Correctional | Sharpes | 1,024 | 1,233 |
| Broward Correctional* | Pembroke Pines | 540 | 533 |
| Calhoun Correctional | Blountstown | 1,325 | 1,248 |
| Central Fla. Recp. Ctr | Orlando | 2,251 | 2,032 |
| Century | Century | 1,381 | 1,347 |
| Charlotte Correctional | Punta Gorda | 996 | 954 |
| Columbia | Lake City | 1,382 | 1,324 |
| Cross City Correctional | Cross City | 1,071 | 896 |
| Dade Correctional | Florida City | 793 | 1,112 |
| De Soto Correctional | Arcadia | 1,154 | 1,195 |
| Everglades Correctional | Miami | 1,448 | 1,534 |
| Florida Correctional* | Lowell | 1,215 | 766 |
| Florida State Prison | Starke | 1,497 | 1,383 |
| Gadsden Correctional* ** | Quincy | 768 | 797 |
| Gainesville Correctional** | Gainesville | 380 | 346 |
| Glades Correctional | Belle Glade | 812 | 942 |
| Gulf Correctional | Wewahitchka | 1,686 | 1,147 |
| Hamilton Correctional | Jasper | 1,491 | 1,536 |
| Hardee Correctional | Bowling Green | 1,404 | 1,490 |
| Hendry Correctional | Immokalee | 1,247 | 983 |
| Hernando Correction | Brooksville | 459 | 353 |
| Hillsborough Correctional | Riverview | 275 | 290 |
| Holmes Correctional | Bonifay | 1,327 | 1,198 |
| Indian River Correctional | Vero Beach | 204 | 357 |
| Jackson Correctional | Malone | 1,381 | 1,414 |
| Jefferson Correctional* | Monticello | 910 | 889 |
| Lake Correctional | Clermont | 872 | 932 |
| Lake City Correctional | Lake City | 350 | 340 |
| Lancaster Correctional | Trenton | 779 | 855 |
| Lawtey Correctional | Lawtey | 732 | 626 |
| Liberty Correctional | Bristol | 1,340 | 1,334 |
| Madison Correctional | Madison | 1,341 | 1,186 |
| Marion Correctional | Lowell | 1,241 | 1,360 |
| Martin Correctional | Indiantown | 1,438 | 1,350 |
| Mayo Correctional | Mayo | 949 | 829 |
| Moore Haven Correctional** | Moore Haven | 750 | 698 |
| New River Correctional | Raiford | 1,672 | 1,616 |
| North Fla. Recp. Ctr | Lake Butler | 2,307 | 2,231 |
| Okaloosa Correctional | Crestview | 991 | 1,031 |
| Okeechobee Correctional | Okeechobee | 1,023 | 1,277 |
| Polk Correctional | Polk City | 1,251 | 1,050 |
| Putnam Correctional | East Palatka | 396 | 419 |
| Quincey Correctional | Quincey | 391 | 345 |
| River Junction Correctional | Chattahoochee | 725 | 425 |
| Santa Rosa Correctional | Milton | 512 | 817 |
| South Bay Correctional** | South Bay | 1,318 | 1,225 |
| South Fla. Recp. Ctr | Miami | 1,959 | 1,531 |
| Sumter Correctional | Bushnell | 1,726 | 1,666 |
| Taylor Correctional | Perry | 1,061 | 1,143 |
| Tomoka Correctional | Daytona Beach | 1,253 | 1,167 |
| Union Correctional | Raiford | 1,492 | 1,710 |
| Walton Correctional | DeFuniak Springs | 1,345 | 1,299 |

Washington Correctional ..... Vernon .......... 1,061 ........... 1,130
Zephyrhills Correctional ...... Zephyrhills. ........ 651 ............ 327
*Women's institution
**Privately operated facility

Florida law allows correctional facilities to operate at 150 percent of capacity. Although statistically some prisons appear overcrowded, most operate auxiliary facilities with sliding capacities.

In addition to those in such facilities, more than 2,000 inmates are in vocational camps, hospitals, community correction centers (work release), and drug treatment facilities. An additional 142,911 were under community control at the end of June 1997.

There were 380 prisoners on Death Row.

## INCARCERATION BY OFFENSE— 1998

| Offense | Number of Inmates (as of July 1998) |
|---|---|
| Homicide, first degree | 4,992 |
| Homicide, second degree | 4,020 |
| Homicide, third degree | 109 |
| Homicide, other | 47 |
| Manslaughter | 742 |
| DUI, manslaughter | 458 |
| DUI, cause injury | 162 |
| DUI, no injury | 244 |
| Leaving scene | 128 |
| Sexual battery, capital | 2,349 |
| Sexual battery, life | 1,260 |
| Sexual battery, 1st degree | 865 |
| Sexual battry, 2nd degree | 531 |
| Sexual battery, other | 198 |
| Lewd, lascivious | 1,934 |
| Robbery, armed | 7,033 |
| Robbery, unarmed | 3,120 |
| Home invasion, robbery | 151 |
| Home invasion, other | 1 |
| Carjacking | 338 |
| Aggravated assault | 731 |
| Aggravated battery | 2,856 |
| Assault and battery on officer | 957 |
| Battery, other | 85 |
| Aggravated stalking | 95 |
| Resisting arrest, violence | 357 |
| Kidnapping | 1,437 |
| Arson | 367 |
| Child abuse | 239 |
| Other violent offenses | 115 |
| Burglary, structure | 2,407 |
| Burglary, dwelling | 5,760 |
| Burglary, armed | 2,030 |
| Burglary, assault | 1,639 |
| Burglary, other | 83 |
| Grand theft | 1,032 |
| Grant theft, auto | 974 |
| Stolen property | 1,760 |
| Forgery, uttering, counterfeiting | 446 |
| Worthless checks | 106 |
| Fraud | 274 |
| Other theft | 226 |
| Drugs, trafficking | 2,286 |
| Drugs, possession | 1,964 |
| Drugs, other | 6,215 |
| Escape | 877 |
| Weapon, discharging | 316 |
| Weapon, illegal possession | 1,478 |
| Racketeering | 151 |
| Traffic, other | 122 |
| Pollution, hazardous materials | 3 |
| Other offenses | 188 |
| N/A | 22 |

**TOTAL .................. 66,280**

## PRISONER PROFILE—1998

The majority of inmates in Florida prisons in July 1998 were 34 years old or younger (largest segment being between 30 and 34 years of age). Of the more than 66,000 inmates, 62,768 were men. White males numbered 26,731, while black males totaled 34,778. Among the 3,512 women inmates, 1,891 were black.

Inmates from Miami-Dade County made up the largest contingent, with 9,213, almost 14 percent of the prison population. For 49.8 percent of the prison population, it is their first stay in a state correctional facility. A majority of inmates were sentenced to less than ten years; 1.7 percent, or 1,116, were sentenced to more than 50 years, while life sentences or death sentences have been imposed on 11.1 percent of the population, or 7,355 inmates. Habitual offenders numbered 10,381, or 16 percent of the inmate population.

Nearly 55 percent of the prison population was considered to be in excellent health, but 1.5 percent were seriously ill.

Although most prisoners claim to have a high school education, less than 13 percent do, and state assessment tests indicate that nearly 17 percent are functionally illiterate; 48 percent function with basic literacy skills.

## A DEATH SENTENCE'S LONG JOURNEY THROUGH THE COURTS

The time between the day a murderer is caught and the day he or she is executed can be years, sometimes more than a decade. Appeals, new trials, new hearings, court reviews, and clemency pleadings—all grind slowly through the judicial system.

• **Step One**—Trial. If guilty and sentenced to death, the case moves to . . .

• **Step Two**—Automatic review by the Florida Supreme Court. If that court upholds the sentence, defense attorneys move to . . .

• **Step Three**—An appeal to the U.S. Supreme Court which, if it refuses to reconsider the case, may prod the case on to . . .

• **Step Four**—A hearing before the cabinet acting in its role as clemency board, which if denied, moves the case to . . .

• **Step Five**—the first death warrant signed by the governor, which prompts defense attorneys to . . .

• **Step Six**—Petition the Florida Supreme Court a second time with briefs stating new evidence is available, which if denied, takes lawyers back to . . .

• **Step Seven**—The trial court, which is advised the defendant did not get a fair first trial or that new evidence is now available, and if the trial court adheres to its original decision, the defense lawyers move to . . .

• **Step Eight**—the Florida Supreme Court a third time and if that court refuses to stay the execution, defense attorneys file to . . .

• **Step Nine**—the Federal District Court, which is told the defendant deserves a stay of execution or that the sentence is unfair and if the Federal District Court refuses to change the sentence, defense lawyers move to . . .

• **Step Ten**—the U.S. Eleventh Court of Appeals in Atlanta with an appeal to stop the execution and if that court is not swayed, the defense moves to . . .

• **Step Eleven**—a final appeal to the U.S. Supreme Court, which if unmoved, leaves only one last walk . . . to execution.

## DEATH ROW

Florida began using the electric chair for execution in 1924. Prior to then, hanging was in order, usually carried out at the jail or prison where the inmate was confined. The 1923 Legislature specified the chair would henceforth be used, and it provided for a permanent death chamber at the main state prison near Starke.

From 1924 until 1964, at which time executions were temporarily halted over court battles relating to capital punishment, Florida electrocuted 196 persons. The oldest was 59, the youngest three were all 16. Two-thirds of the total were black.

On Sept. 12, 1977, when Gov. Reubin Askew signed the first death penalty since 1964, there were 89 persons on Florida's death row–53 white men, 35 black men, and 1 white woman. In July 1998, there were 367 persons on death row—219 white men, 127 black men, 17 other men, 2 white women, 1 black women, and 1 other woman.

By January 1999, the total number of executions in Florida since the reinstatement of the death penalty in 1977 numbered 43.

The executioner, always known as "John Doe," is hired from applicants for the job. His identity is never made known, and in the death house he wears a mask and is screened from the view of witnesses and victims. He has only one job in the prison system—flipping the switch at the nod of the prison superintendent. For this he is paid $150 per execution.

The death chamber itself is an austere room, 12 by 15 feet, housing only a massive oak chair bolted down upon a rubber mat for double insulation. Behind the chair are two telephones. One is for the institution, the other is for the governor in event of an eleventh-hour stay order.

The source of power for the chair is a diesel generator capable of producing 3,000 volts and 20 amperes. A transformer behind the chair turns that into 40,000 watts, enough to shoot the body temperature of the inmate up to 150 degrees. In fact, it usually is necessary for prison officials removing the body from the chair to wait a few minutes for the body to cool down.

The prisoner, when seated in the chair, faces a glass partition behind which is a small room accommodating 22 seats. The state requires 12 official witnesses. These are handpicked by the warden. The remaining 10 seats are for news reporters.

The execution procedure calls for the warden, when the warrant for the execution is delivered to the prison, to go to the inmate's cell and read the death order. Setting the date and time is the warden's responsibility. After the reading, the inmate is immediately transferred to one of six cells on the bottom floor of the death row wing. Here the inmate is closer to the small room holding the chair. Some officials have noted it is 13 steps from the closest cell to the chair. Once in the new cell, the prisoner is guarded around the clock.

Minutes prior to execution time, the prisoner is taken to the "prep room" at the end of the corridor. The head and right leg are shaved for the electrical attachments, the head soaked with salty water to assure good contact by the electrodes. Clothes for the prisoner are made in the prison factory—a white shirt and dark trousers. When in the chair, the inmate has a rubber hood placed over his head.

Less than four minutes after the prisoner enters the death chamber it is all over. The body is slipped into a dark coat, ready for burial. If the inmate has no family or means to have a private funeral, the state takes care of the finale with burial in a prison cemetery in Union County.

## SHERIFFS

| County | Sheriff |
|---|---|
| Alachua | Stephen M. Oelrich |
| Baker | Joey Dobson |
| Bay | Guy Tunnell |
| Bradford | Bob Milner |
| Brevard | Phil Williams |
| Broward | Ken Jenne |
| Calhoun | W. G. ("Buddy") Smith |
| Charlotte | Richard Worrh |
| Citrus | Jeff Dawsy |
| Clay | Scott Lancaster |
| Collier | Don Hunter |
| Columbia | Frank Owens |
| De Soto | Vernon Keen |
| Dixie | Dewey Hatcher |
| Duval | Nat Glover |
| Escambia | Jim Lowman |
| Flagler | Robert McCarthy |
| Franklin | Bruce Varnes |
| Gadsden | W. A. Woodham |
| Gilchrist | David Turner |
| Glades | James ("Jim") Rider |
| Gulf | Frank McKeithen |

Hamilton . . . . . . . . . . . . Harrell Reid
Hardee . . . . . . . . . J. Loran Cogburn
Hendry . . . . . . . . . . . . . . Ronnie Lee
Hernando. . . . . . . . . Tom Mylander
Highlands . . . . . . . . Howard Godwin
Hillsborough . . . . . . . Cal Henderson
Holmes . . . . . . . . . . . . . Dennis Lee
Indian River. . . . . . . . Gary Wheeler
Jackson. . . . . . . . . . John P. McDaniel
Jefferson. . . . . . Kenneth Fortune, Sr.
Lafayette . . . . . . . . . . Dwayne Walker
Lake . . . . . . . . . . . George Knupp, Jr.
Lee. . . . . . . . . . . . . . John McDougall
Leon . . . . . . . . . . . . . Larry Campbell
Levy . . . . . . . . . . . . . . . . . Ted Glass
Liberty . . . . . . . . . . . . . . J. L. Bailey
Madison . . . . . . . . . . . . Joe C. Peavy
Manatee . . . . . . . . . . . Charlie Wells
Marion . . . . . . Horace ("Ed") Dean
Martin . . . . . . . . Robert L. Crowder
Miami-Dade. . . . . . . Carlos Alvarez*
Monroe . . . . . . . . . Richard D. Roth
Nassau . . . . . . . W. R. ("Ray") Geiger
Okaloosa. . . . . . . Charles W. Morris
Okeechobee . . . . . . . . Edward Miller
Orange . . . . . . . . . . . . . Kevin Beary
Osceola. . . . . C. W. ("Charlie") Croft
Palm Beach . . . . . . Robert Neumann
Pasco . . . . . . . . . . . . . . Lee Cannon
Pinellas. . . . . . . . . . . . Everett Rice
Polk . . . . . . . . . . Lawrence Crow, Jr.
Putnam . . . . . . . . . . Taylor Douglas
St. Johns . . . . . . . . . . . . Neil Perry
St. Lucie . . . . . . . . . Bobby Knowles
Santa Rosa . . . . . . . . . . . Jerry Brown
Sarasota . . . . . . . . . Geoffrey Monge
Seminole . . . . . . . . Donald Eslinger
Sumter. . . . . . . . William O. ("Bill")
Farmer, Jr.
Suwannee. . . . . . . . . Alton K. ("Al")
Williams
Taylor. . . . L. E. ("Bummy") Williams
Union . . . . . . . . . . Jerry Whitehead
Volusia. . . . . . . . . . . . . . Bob Vogel
Wakulla. . . . . . . . . . David F. Harvey
Walton . . . . . . . Quinn A. McMillan
Washington . . . . . . . . . . . Fred Peel
*appointed, director, Miami-Dade Police Dept

## YOUTH RANCHES

The Florida Sheriffs Youth Ranches
began when two sheriffs traveled to

Texas to bring back two teenage
armed robbery suspects and learned
of a ranch established for needy and
neglected boys. They brought the
idea home with them and soon their
colleagues in the Florida Sheriffs
Association joined them in a private
effort to help kids, one that today is
recognized as one of the nation's
finest residential child-care programs.

When the sheriffs sought to buy
land on the Suwannee River to establish such a ranch, a Live Oak civic
club and a local business leader combined to donate 140 acres to the project. The sheriffs took out bank loans
to purchase 410 additional acres.
They were down to $2,000.00 when
word of the project finally went public
beyond Live Oak, and donations
began pouring in, enabling the sheriffs to build their first ranch cottage in
time for staff and the first residents to
arrive in 1959.

Today, there are five Youth
Ranches, including Girls Villa, two
camps, and numerous other child-
care programs serving the children of
Florida. They are still sponsored by
the Florida Sheriffs Association and
still funded by private donations.

## NOTABLE UNSOLVED
## FLORIDA CRIMES

Florida has had its share of
unsolved murders and disappear-
ances. Some have received national
attention, while others are notorious
only to Floridians. Following are some
of the most talked-about to this day.

**1915**—Trenton physician Henry
Owens is gunned down and dragged
through town streets by an angry
mob. Only motive ever considered
was that Owens, separated from his
wife, was romancing another woman.
No arrests were ever made.

**1957**—Wealthy Parrish grocer
Gettis Lee and his wife disappear.
Muriel Lee's body is found two days
later in a ditch along a rural road near
Parrish. Her husband's skeleton is not
discovered until 1963, in a scrub field

also near town. A possible link to illegal gambling was rumored.

**1959**—University of Florida student Chandler Steffens is murdered while on break in his Sarasota home. He had been bound, slashed, and his face covered in an adhesive mask. More than 400 persons were questioned and 48 given polygraph tests, but the murderer was never found.

**1959**—Ranch hand Clifford Walker, his wife, and two children are found shot to death in their Christmas-decorated Osprey home. No motive or leads have been uncovered. The case earned national attention when mentioned by writer Truman Capote in his best-selling classic, *In Cold Blood*.

**1966**—Nancy Leichner, 21, and Pamela Nater, 20, vanish while walking near Alexander Springs in the Ocala National Forest. The women left their campsite without their purses, shoes, and other belongings. Investigators found the day's park sign-in sheet had been torn out. Despite 10 days of searching, the two women never were found.

**1966**—Nationally renowned computer expert Robert Sims, 42, his wife, and 12-year-old daughter are shot to death in their Tallahassee home. No motive was established, although police reported finding "enough evidence to fill five file drawers."

**1969**—The body of a woman age 25 to 35 is found neatly stuffed inside a steamer trunk left under a tree in south St. Petersburg. A heavy, blunt instrument appears to have caused a wound on her forehead, but her death is listed as due to strangulation. Fingerprint and dental charts have not identified her.

**1976**—Bones identified as those of 21-year-old Douglas Sumner of Tampa are found by hunters in rural Dixie County. An investigation reveals Sumner was padlocked to a pine tree during the previous year and left to starve. Objects at the scene included a Bible, a wallet, keys, a belt, clothing fragments, and the novel *A Man Called Peter*. Theories about Sumner's slow death ranged from suicide to a religious ritual to drug-related.

**1980**—Tampa pediatrician Juan Dumois, his two sons, and an unrelated man are killed by a gunman at a Holmes Beach boat ramp. Police theorize the kills may have been the work of a psychopath. Witnesses reported the gunman ran to a waiting getaway car.

**1991**—A series of home invasions leaves a couple in Port Charlotte shot to death and a man and three of his stepchildren (ages 9, 11, and 13) shot to death in North Port. One child, 8, is shot but survives. No suspects have been charged despite a $10,000 reward.

**1993**—Jennifer Renee Odom, a 13-year-old Pasco County student, disappears after getting off her school bus approximately 150 yards from her front door. Her body was found six days later in another county. Her schoolbooks, backpack, clarinet, and purse, with her when she disappeared, have never been found, nor has her killer or killers.

**1997**—Four years after the slaying and disappearance of Jennifer Renee Odom, another girl from the same Pasco area, 12-year-old Sharra Ferger, was found in a field brutally murdered. A neighbor was arrested but cleared by DNA evidence.

**1997**—Sabrina Aisenberg was kidnapped from her crib in her parents' upscale Brandon home by an abductor who passed through unlocked doors in the pre-dawn hours without disturbing the family dog. A nationwide search has produced no clues toward the infant's fate. Her well-respected parents declined to cooperate with police after they found themselves prime suspects. In 1999, her parents were indicted by a federal grand jury and charged, not with murder or kidnapping, but with conspiracy and lying to a grand jury.

## TOP TEN PLACES TO HAVE YOUR CAR STOLEN

Florida ranked second only to California in auto theft in 1997, according to the Florida Department of Law Enforcement. The year saw 108,872 vehicles stolen, an increase of 4.92 percent.

The top ten places to have our car stolen in Florida were:

| County | 1997 Auto Thefts | Percent Change from 1996 |
|---|---|---|
| 1. Miami-Dade | 33,968 | +4.92 |
| 2. Broward | 16,005 | +3.44 |
| 3. Palm Beach | 8,770 | +14.48 |
| 4. Hillsborough | 7,921 | (-21.03) |
| 5. Orange | 7,032 | +8.79 |
| 6. Duval | 5,561 | +13.72 |
| 7. Polk | 4,991 | +45.81 |
| 8. Pinellas | 3,352 | (-0.69) |
| 9. Lee | 2,749 | +11.79 |
| 10. Volusia | 1,913 | +18.97 |

The dramatic decline in auto thefts in Hillsborough County was attributed to vastly increased enforcement measures, which evidently drove car thieves to neighboring Polk County, which experienced the state's largest percentage increase.

## CRIME RATE

Tampa had the 5th highest crime rate in the nation, according to the 1998 FBI crime report, edging past Miami. St. Louis, Missouri, had the highest crime rate, with 149.5 incidents per 100,000 population. Tampa's rate was 121.9, while Miami, ranking 6th, had a crime rate of 120.5. Tallahassee ranked 22nd, St. Petersburg, 33rd, Hollywood, 56th, Hialeah, 61st, Jacksonville, 68th, Clearwater, 83rd, and Pembrooke Pines, 171st. Coral Springs rounded out Florida cities among the FBI's top 200 at 178th, with a crime rate of 39.1.

## EVERYDAY NOISE BANNED

Martin County has banned every sound from its quiet streets. An ordinance caps noise levels for homes at 60 decibels, businesses at 65 decibels and the maximum noise level on industrial or agricultural sites at 70 decibels. Nighttime levels are lower still. Violation carries a $500.00. A normal speaking voice is in the range of 60 decibels.

# MEDIA

## DAILY NEWSPAPERS
### (More than 250,000 circulation)

**Fort Lauderdale
Sun-Sentinel**
200 E. Las Olas Boulevard
Fort Lauderdale 33301
**Miami Herald**
One Herald Plaza
Miami 33132

**Orlando Sentinel**
633 N. Orange Avenue
Orlando 32801
**St. Petersburg Times**
490 First Ave. S.
St. Petersburg 33701

**Tampa Tribune**
202 S. Parker Street
Tampa 33606

### (100,000-250,000 circulation)

**Daytona Beach News-
Journal**
901 Sixth Street
Daytona Beach 32017
**Florida Times-Union**
One Riverside Avenue
Jacksonville 32202

**Florida Today**
One Gannett Plaza
Melbourne 32940
**Fort Myers News-Press**
2442 Martin Luther
King Blvd.
Fort Myers 33901

**Sarasota Herald-
Tribune**
801 S. Tamiami Trail
Sarasota 34236
**Palm Beach Post**
2751 S. Dixie Highway
West Palm Beach 33405

### (50,000-100,000 circulation)

**Diario Las Americas**
2900 NW 39th Street
Miami 33142
**El Miami Herald**
3191 Coral Way
Miami 33145

**Gainesville Sun**
2700 SW 13th Street
Gainesville 32608
**Lakeland Ledger**
401 S. Missouri Avenue
Lakeland 33801

**Pensacola News Journal**
One News Journal Plaza
Pensacola 32501
**Tallahassee Democrat**
277 N. Magnolia Drive
Tallahassee 32301

### (10,000-50,000 circulation)

**Boca Raton News**
33 SE Third Street
Boca Raton 33432
**Bradenton Herald**
102 Manatee Avenue W.
Bradenton 34205
**Charlotte Sun Herald**
23170 Harborview Road
Charlotte Harbor 33980
**Citrus County Chronicle**
1624 N. Meadowcrest
Boulevard
Crystal River 34429
**Fort Pierce Tribune**
600 Edwards Road
Fort Pierce 34982
**Hernando Today**
15299 Cortez Blvd.
Brooksville 34613
**Highlands Today**
231 U.S. 27 North
Sebring 33870

**Leesburg Daily
Commercial**
212 E. Main Street
Leesburg 32749
**Naples Daily News**
1075 Central Avenue
Naples 33940
**Northwest Florida Daily
News**
200 Racetrack Road
Fort Walton Beach
32549
**Ocala Star Banner**
2121 SW 19th Road
Ocala 34474
**Palatka Daily News**
1825 St. Johns Ave.
Palatka 32177
**Panama City News-
Herald**
501 W. 11th Street
Panama City 32401

**St. Augustine Record**
158 Cordova Street
St. Augustine 32084
**Stuart News**
1939 S. Federal
Highway
Stuart 34994
**Vero Beach Press-
Journal**
1801 U.S. 1
Vero Beach 32960
**Volusian**
111 S. Alabama Ave.
DeLand 32721
**Winter Haven News
Chief**
650 Sixth Street SW
Winter Haven 33880

## (Under 10,000 circulation)

**Cape Coral Daily Breeze**
2510 Del Prado Boulevard
Cape Coral 33904
**Clay Today**
1564 Kingsley Avenue
Orange Park 32073
**Daily Okeechobee News**
107 SW 17th Street
Okeechobee 34974
**DeLand Sun News**
111 S. Alabama Avenue
DeLand 32721

**Jackson County Floridan**
4403 Constitution Lane
Marianna 32448
**Jacksonville Financial News & Daily Record**
10 N. Newnan St.
Jacksonville 32202
**Key West Citizen**
3420 North Side Drive
Key West 33040
**Lake City Reporter**
126 E. Duval Street
Lake City 32055

**New Smyrna Beach Observer**
823 S. Dixie Freeway
New Smyrna Beach 32168
**Palm Beach Daily News**
265 Royal Poinciana Way
Palm Beach 33480
**Sanford Herald**
300 N. French Avenue
Sanford 32771

## WEEKLY NEWSPAPERS
### (Paid Circulation Publications)

| City | Newspaper |
|---|---|
| Apalachicola | Apalachicola Times |
| Apopka | Apopka Chief |
| Arcadia | The Arcadian |
| | De Soto County Times |
| Auburndale | Auburndale Star |
| | Sun-Times of Canada |
| Avon Park | Avon Park News Sun |
| Bartow | Polk County Democrat |
| Belle Glade | Sun |
| Belleview | Voice of South Marion |
| Blountstown | County Record |
| Boca Grande | Gasparilla Gazette |
| | Boca Beacon |
| Bonifay | Holmes County Advertiser |
| | Holmes County Times |
| Branford | Branford News |
| Bristol | Free Press |
| | Calhoun-Liberty Journal |
| Bronson | Levy County Journal |
| Bunnell | Flagler/Palm Coast News Tribune |
| Bushnell | Sumter County Times |
| Callahan | Nassau County Record |
| Captiva | Current |
| Carrabelle | Carrabelle Times |
| Cedar Key | Cedar Key Beacon |

| City | Newspaper |
|---|---|
| Chattahoochee | Twin City News |
| Chiefland | Chiefland Citizen |
| Chipley | Washington County News |
| | Washington County Post |
| Clermont | South Lake Press |
| Clewiston | Clewiston News |
| Crawfordville | Wakulla News |
| Crescent City | Courier Journal |
| Crestview | News Leader |
| Cross City | Dixie County Advocate |
| Dade City | Pasco News |
| Daytona Beach | Daytona Times |
| DeBary | Southwest Volusia Reporter |
| DeFuniak Springs | Herald |
| Deerfield Beach | Beacon |
| Destin | Destin Log |
| Dunnellon | Riverland News |
| Eastpoint | Chronicle |
| Eustis | Eustis News |
| Everglades City | Everglades Echo |
| Fern Park | Heritage Florida Jewish News |
| Fernandina Beach | News-Leader |
| Fort Lauderdale | Westside Gazette |
| | El Herald deBroward |

|  |  |
|---|---|
|  | South Florida |
|  | Business Journal |
| **Fort Meade** | Fort Meade Leader |
| **Fort Myers** | La Semana |
| **Fort Pierce** | Chronicle |
| **Frostproof** | Frostproof News |
| **Gainesville** | Record |
| **Graceville** | Graceville News |
| **Green Cove** |  |
| **Springs** | Clay County Informer |
| **Gulf Breeze** | Sentinel |
|  | Santa Rosa Sun |
| **Haines City** | Haines City Herald |
| **Hallandale** | Hallandale Digest |
| **Havana** | Havana Herald |
| **Hialeah** | La Vox Calle |
|  | El Sol de Hialeah |
| **High Springs** | High Springs Herald |
| **Hollywood** | Community News |
| **Homestead** | South Dade News |
|  | Leader |
| **Jacksonville** | Mandarin News |
|  | Jacksonville Advocate |
|  | El Heraldo Latino |
|  | Business Journal |
| **Jacksonville** |  |
| **Beach** | Ponte Verde Recorder |
|  | The Beaches Leader |
| **Jasper** | Jasper News |
| **Jupiter** | Courier |
| **Key Biscayne** | Islander News |
| **Keystone** |  |
| **Heights** | Lake Region Monitor |
| **Kissimmee/** |  |
| **St. Cloud** | News-Gazette |
| **Lake Butler** | Union County Times |
| **Lake Placid** | Lake Placid Journal |
| **Lake Wales** | Lake Wales News |
|  | Highlander |
| **Lake Worth** | Herald and Coastal |
|  | Observer |
| **Lakeland** | Polk County Banner |
| **Live Oak** | Suwannee Democrat |
| **MacClenny** | Baker County Press |
|  | Baker County |
|  | Standard |
| **Madison** | Madison Enterprise- |
|  | Recorder |
|  | Madison County |
|  | Carrier |
| **Marathon** | Florida Keys |
|  | Keynoter |

|  |  |
|---|---|
| **Marco Island** | Marco Island Eagle |
| **Mayo** | Mayo Free Press |
| **Merritt Island** | Press |
| **Miami** | El Nevo Patria |
|  | Miami Times |
|  | La Voz |
|  | Today |
|  | Miami Courier |
| **Milton** | Santa Rosa Press |
|  | Gazette |
| **Monticello** | Monticello News |
| **Moore Haven** | Glades County |
|  | Democrat |
| **Mount Dora** | Mount Dora Topic |
| **Mulberry** | Mulberry Press |
| **Naples** | Everglades Echo |
| **Niceville** | The Bay Beacon |
| **North Port** | North Port Sun |
|  | Herald |
| **Orange City** | Southwest Volusia |
|  | Reporter |
| **Orlando** | Florida Catholic |
|  | Orlando Times |
|  | La Semana |
|  | Florida Sun Review |
|  | Orlando Business |
|  | Journal |
| **Oviedo** | Voice |
| **Panama City** | Voice |
| **Pensacola** | Escambia Sun Press |
|  | New American Press |
|  | Pensacola Voice |
| **Pensacola** |  |
| **Beach** | Island |
| **Perry** | Perry Taco Times |
|  | Perry News-Herald |
| **Pinellas Park** | News |
| **Plant City** | The Courier |
| **Polk City** | Press |
| **Port St. Joe** | The Star |
| **Punta Gorda** | Punta Gorda Herald |
| **Quincy** | Gadsden County |
|  | Times |
| **Rockledge** | Reporter |
| **St. Petersburg** | Weekly Challenger |
| **Sanibel/** |  |
| **Captiva** | Island Reporter |
|  | The Islander |
| **Sarasota** | Sarasota Bulletin |
|  | Pelican Press |
| **Sebastian** | Sun |
| **Sebring** | News-Sun |

| Starke | Bradford County Telegraph | Umatilla | North Lake Outpost |
| Tallahassee | Capital Outlook | Venice | Venice Gondolier |
| Tampa | Free Press | Wauchula | The Herald-Advocate |
| | La Gaceta | West Palm Beach | Palm Beach Gazette |
| | Florida Sentinel Bulletin | Wewahitchka | Gulf County Breeze |
| | Tampa Bay Business Journal | Williston | Williston Sun/ Suwannee Valley News |
| Tavares | Citizen | | The Pioneer |
| Tavernier | Reporter | Winter Garden | West Orange Times |
| Trenton | Gilchrist County Journal | Winter Park | Observer |
| | | Zephyrhills | Zephyrhills News |

## NEWSPAPER HALL OF FAME

The Florida Press Association in 1989 created the Florida Newspaper Hall of Fame, whose members' pictures and biographies are on display at the Florida Press Center in Tallahassee. Members are:

Herbert Davidson, editor of the *Daytona Beach News-Journal* for 34 years.

Loyal Frisbie, editor of the *Polk County Democrat* in Bartow for 25 years.

John Paul Jones, Jr., newspaper reporter and editor, and journalism professor at University of Florida.

John S. Knight, publisher of the *Miami Herald* and builder of the Knight-Ridder newspaper chain.

Eugene I. Matthews, publisher of the *Bradford County Telegraph* in Starke.

Hugh B. McCallum, publisher of the *Daily Florida Union* in Jacksonville in the 1880s.

John H. Perry, Jr., president and chairman of Perry Publications, Inc.

Nelson Poynter, editor and publisher of the *St. Petersburg Times* and founder of Poynter Institute for Media Studies.

Martin Anderson, former *Orlando Sentinel* owner.

Barbara Frye, reporter for United Press International.

James L. Knight of Knight-Ridder Newspapers.

Rae O. Weimer, dean at University of Florida.

David Lawrence, Sr., political columnist.

Fred Pettijohn, editor at *Fort Lauderdale News/Sun-Sentinel.*

Malcolm Johnson, editorial editor of *Tallahassee Democrat.*

James A. Clendinen, *Tampa Tribune* editorial writer.

Charles H. Jones, *Florida Times-Union* publisher.

Robert Gore, owner and publisher of the *Fort Lauderdale Daily News.*

Robert Hudson, 37 years with the *Titusville Star-Advocate.*

James H. Jesse, publisher of the *Punta Gorda Herald,* the *Boca Raton News, Cocoa Today,* and *Pensacola News Journal.*

Ernest F. Lyons, editor with the *Stuart News.*

Virgil ("Red") Newton, managing editor of the *Tampa Tribune.*

William Straub, editor of the *St. Petersburg Times.*

Beryl Bowden, publisher of the *Clewiston News.*

Al Neuharth, President and Chairman, Gannett Newspapers.

Eugene Patterson, editor and publisher of the *St. Petersburg Times.*

John Schumann, founder of the *Vero Beach Press-Journal.*

## TELEVISION STATIONS

| City | Call Letters | Channel | Network |
|------|-------------|---------|---------|
| Bonita Springs | WZVN | 26 | ABC |
|  | WSFP | 30 | PBS |
| Boca Raton | WPPB | 63 | Ind. |
| Boynton Beach | WXEL | 42 | PBS |
| Bradenton | WXPX | 66 | PAX |
| Cape Coral | WFTX | 36 | Fox |
| Clearwater | WCLF | 22 | Ind. |
| Clermont | WKCF | 18 | WB |
| Cocoa | WTGL | 52 | Ind. |
|  | WBCC | 68 | Edu. |
| Daytona Beach | WESH | 2 | NBC |
| Fort Myers | WBBH | 20 | NBC |
|  | WINK | 11 | CBS |
|  | WEVU | 7 | UPN |
|  | WGCU | 30 | PBS |
| Fort Lauderdale | WSCV | 51 | Ind. |
|  | WSFP | 30 | PBS |
| Fort Pierce | WTVX | 34 | Ind. |
|  | WTCE | 21 | Ind. |
| Fort Walton Beach | WAWD | 58 | Ind. |
|  | WFGX | 35 | Ind. |
|  | WPAN | 53 | Ind. |
| Gainesville | WCJB | 20 | ABC |
|  | WUFT | 5 | PBS |
| Hialeah | WSCV | 51 | Telemundo |
| High Springs | WGFL | 53 | Ind. |
| Hollywood | WYHS | 69 | Ind. |
| Inverness | WGOX | 64 | Ind. |
| Jacksonville | WAWS | 30 | PAX |
|  | WJWB | 17 | WB |
|  | WJXT | 4 | CBS |
|  | WTEV | 47 | UPN |
|  | WTLV | 12 | NBC |
|  | WJCT | 7 | PBS |
|  | WJEB | 59 | Ind. |
| Lakeland | WMOR | 32 | Ind. |
| Melbourne | WRSF | 43 | Ind. |
|  | WOPX | 56 | PAX |
| Miami | WLRN | 17 | Edu. |
|  | WCIX | 6 | CBS |
|  | WPBT | 2 | PBS |
|  | WPLG | 10 | ABC |
|  | WSVN | 7 | Fox |
|  | WTVJ | 4 | NBC |
|  | WBFS | 33 | UPN |
|  | WPXM | 35 | PAX |
|  | WDZL | 39 | WB |
|  | WLTV | 23 | Univision |
| Naples | WNPL | 46 | Ind. |

| | | | |
|---|---|---|---|
| New Smyrna Beach | WCEU | 15 | PBS |
| Ocala | WOGX | 51 | Fox |
| Orlando | WKMG | 6 | CBS |
| | WFTV | 9 | ABC |
| | WMFE | 24 | PBS |
| | WNTO | 26 | Ind. |
| | WOFL | 35 | Fox |
| | WACX | 55 | Ind. |
| | WRBW | 65 | UPN |
| | WVEN | 63 | Univision |
| Palm Beach | WFGC | 61 | Ind. |
| Panama City | WJHG | 7 | NBC |
| | WMBB | 13 | ABC |
| | WFSG | 56 | PBS |
| | WPXG | 28 | Fox |
| Pensacola | WEAR | 3 | ABC |
| | WJTC | 44 | Ind. |
| | WSRE | 23 | PBS |
| St. Petersburg | WTOG | 44 | UPN |
| | WTSP | 10 | CBS |
| | WTTA | 38 | WB |
| Sarasota | WWSB | 40 | ABC |
| Tallahassee | WTWC | 40 | NBC |
| | WFSU | 11 | PBS |
| | WTXL | 27 | ABC |
| | WCTV | 6 | CBS |
| | WTLH | 49 | Fox |
| Tampa | WFTS | 28 | ABC |
| | WTVT | 13 | Fox |
| | WFLA | 8 | NBC |
| | WEDU | 3 | PBS |
| | WUSF | 16 | Edu. |
| | WBHS | 50 | USA |
| | WRMD | 57 | Telemundo |
| | WVEA | 61 | Univision |
| Tequesta | WPBF | 25 | ABC |
| Venice | WBSV | 62 | Ind. |
| West Palm Beach | WFLX | 29 | Fox |
| | WPEC | 12 | CBS |
| | WPTV | 5 | NBC |
| | WXEL | 42 | PBS |
| | WPXP | 67 | PAX |

# WOMEN'S HALL OF FAME

| Inducted | Hall of Fame Member |
| --- | --- |

**1982:**

Mary McLeod Bethune—educator, civil rights leader (1875-1955)

Helene S. Coleman—civic leader (1925- )

Elaine Gordon—legislator (1931- )

Wilhelmina Celeste Goehring Harvey—first woman mayor of Key West (1912- )

Paula Mae Milton—educator, dramatist (1939-1980)

Barbara Jo Palmer—athletic director (1948- )

**1984:**

Roxcy O'Neal Bolton—feminist leader (1926- )

Barbara Landstreet Frye—journalist (1922-1982)

Lena B. Smithers Hughes—citrus scientist (1910-1987)

Zora Neale Hurston—author (1901-1960)

Sybil Collins Mobley—educator (1925- )

Helen Lennehan Muir—journalist, author (1911- )

Gladys Pumariega Soler—pediatrician (1930-1993)

Julia DeForest Sturtevant Tuttle—Miami pioneer (1848-1898)

**1986:**

Annie Ackerman—political leader (1914-1989)

Rosemary Barkett—judge (1939- )

Gwendolyn Sawyer Cherry—legislator (1923-1979)

Dorothy Dodd—journalist, author, state librarian (1902-1994)

Marjory Stoneman Douglas—journalist, author (1890-1998)

Elsie Jones Hare—educator (1903-1985)

Elizabeth McCullough Johnson—first women state senator (1909-1973)

Frances Bartlett Kinne—educator, college president, Jacksonville University (1917- )

Arva Jeane Moore Parks—author (1939- )

Marjorie Kinnan Rawlings—author (1896-1953)

Florence Barbara Seibert—biochemist (1898-1991)

Marilyn K. Smith—volunteer (1936-1985)

Eartha Mary Magdalene White—educator, publisher (1876-1974)

**1992:**

Jacqueline Cochran—aviator (1910?-1980)

Carrie P. Meek—member of Congress (1926- )

Ruth Bryan Owen—member of Congress (1885-1954)

**1993:**

Betty Skelton Frankman—aviator, auto racer (1926- )

Paulina Pedroso—Cuban independence leader (1845-1925)

Janet Reno—U.S. Attorney General (1938- )

**1994:**

Nikki Beare—feminist (1928- )

Betty Mae Tiger Jumper—Seminole Chief (1923- )

Gladys D. Milton—midwife (1924- )

**1995:**      Evelyn Stocking Crosslin—physician (1919-1991)
            JoAnn Hardin Morgan—engineer (1940-  )
            Sarah ("Aunt Frances") Brooks Pryor—postmaster (1877-1972)

**1996:**      Marjorie Harris Carr—environmentalist (1915-1997)
            Betty Castor—Commission of Education (1941-  )
            Ivy Julia Cromartie Stranahan—Seminole mentor (1881-1971)

**1997:**      Alicia Baro—political leader (1918-  )
            Carita Doggett Corse—author, historian, feminist (1891-1978)
            M. Athalie Range—Secretary of Community Affairs (1916-  )

**1998:**      Helen Gordon Davis—legislator (1926-  )
            Mattie Belle Davis—judge (1910-  )
            Christine Fulwylie-Bankston—poet (1916-1998)

# LIBRARIES

## DOCUMENT LIBRARIES

State documents are distributed to the following depository libraries and are available to Florida citizens for use either in the libraries or on interlibrary loan:

**Boca Raton**
Florida Atlantic University Library
**Cocoa**
Cocoa Public Library
**Coral Gables**
University of Miami Library
**Daytona Beach**
Volusia County Library Center
**DeLand**
Stetson University Library
**Fort Lauderdale**
Broward County Division of
Libraries
**Fort Myers**
Lee County Library System
**Gainesville**
University of Florida Library
**Jacksonville**
Jacksonville Public Library
Jacksonville University Swisher
Library
University of North Florida Library
**Miami**
Florida International University
Library
Miami-Dade Public Library
**North Miami**
Florida International University
Library, Bay Vista Campus
**Ocala**
Ocala Public Library
**Orlando**
Orange County Library
University of Central Florida
Library
**Panama City**
Northwest Regional Library System
**Pensacola**
University of West Florida Library
**St. Petersburg**
St. Petersburg Public Library
**Tallahassee**
Florida State University Strozier
Library
State Library of Florida

**Tampa**
Tampa-Hillsborough
County Libraries
University of South Florida Library
**West Palm Beach**
West Palm Beach Public Library

U.S. documents are distributed to the following depository libraries:
**Boca Raton**
Florida Atlantic University Library
**Casselberry**
Seminole County Public Library
**Clearwater**
Clearwater Public Library
**Coral Gables**
University of Miami Richter Library
**Daytona Beach**
Volusia County Public Library
**DeLand**
Stetson University DuPont-Ball
Library
**Fort Lauderdale**
Broward County Library
Nova University Law Library
**Fort Pierce**
Indian River Community College
Library
**Gainesville**
University of Florida Law Library
University of Florida Libraries
**Jacksonville**
Haydon Burns Public Library
Jacksonville University Swisher
Library
University of North Florida
Carpenter Library
**Key West**
Florida Keys Community College
Library
**Lakeland**
Lakeland Public Library
**Leesburg**
Lake-Sumter Community College
Library

**Melbourne**
Florida Institute of Technology
Library
**Miami**
Florida International Library
Miami-Dade Public Library
St. Thomas University Library
**North Miami**
Florida International University
Library
**Orlando**
University of Central Florida
Library
**Palatka**
St. Johns River Community College
Library
**Panama City**
Bay County Public Library
**Pensacola**
University of West Florida Library

**Port Charlotte**
Charlotte-Glades Public Libraries
**St. Petersburg**
St. Petersburg Public Library
Stetson University Law Library
**Sarasota**
Selby Public Library
**Tallahassee**
Florida A&M University Library
Florida State University Law Library
Florida State University Strozier
Library
Florida Supreme Court Library
State Library of Florida
**Tampa**
Tampa-Hillsborough Public Library
University of South Florida Library
University of Tampa Kelce Library
**Winter Park**
Rollins College Olin Library

## FREE LIBRARY SERVICE

Available to Florida residents through the Florida State Library at
Tallahassee is a statewide Inter-Library Loan service. The service permits residents to borrow almost any book in the state library by mail. A person seeking
a specific book may go to the local library and fill out a small form that is sent
to Tallahassee; if the state library cannot fill the request from its stacks it will
send the request via a computer network to the major libraries around the
state. If they cannot fill the request, it may be sent on a national computer to
libraries and universities throughout the country. When the book is found it is
sent to the local library for pickup. The service is free.

## HIGH TECH JOBS

Florida ranked sixth among the states in the number of high-tech jobs in
1999, according to the American Electronics Association, but its high-tech
workers earn substantially less than the national average.

# EDUCATION

Public education in Florida began in 1822 when the region became a territory. At that time every sixteenth section of land in each township was reserved for primary schools. In practice, however, the only actual teaching was done at a few Spanish missions.

Until 1845 the only true public schools in the territory were in Franklin and Monroe counties. The few who were educated attended private academies. With statehood, interest in a public school system grew, and in 1851 counties were authorized to levy taxes for the support of common schools, up to $4 per child. The legislature also provided that if income from a permanent state school fund did not reach at least $2 per child, other state funds could be used to make up the difference.

Each Florida county is a unified school district. Schools are financed by county ad valorum taxes. The state supplements those revenues with direct funding to each county based on a formula designed to insure equitable funding for every school district regardless of its location, economy, or the property tax base available to support it.

## ADMISSION REQUIREMENTS

All children who have attained the age of 6 or who will have attained that age by Feb. 1 of any school year, or who are between the ages of 6 and 16, are required to attend school regularly during the entire school term.

Any child who has attained the age of 6 on or before Sept. 1 of the school year and who has been enrolled in a public school, or has satisfactorily completed the requirements for kindergarten in a nonpublic school from which the district school board accepts transfer of academic credit, shall be enrolled.

Children who have attained the age of 5 on or before Sept. 1 of the school year shall be eligible for admission to public kindergartens during the school year. Kindergarten is a mandatory grade.

A child who attained the age of 16 during the school year shall not be required to attend school beyond his birthday.

A legal birth certificate or other authentic proof of a child's age, as required by law, must be submitted prior to a student's initial entry into kindergarten.

For other than the first grade, a transcript or last report card is required. In general, the opening of the school year occurs in the first week of September and ends the last week in May, with 180 school days on the calendar.

All public schools are directed and controlled at the county level by a county school board. The chief officer is the superintendent of schools, who may be elected or appointed. Textbooks are provided free. School bus service is available to all rural and suburban pupils residing two miles or more from school. Some variation may occur in some of the larger cities where city bus service is operating. A pupil whose parents or guardian are nonresidents must pay a tuition fee at enrollment. No fee is charged if the parent or guardian is in military service, a migratory agricultural worker, or a federal civilian employee where the federal government provides an educational subsidy.

## CITY AND COUNTY

According to 1997 population estimates, 49.3 percent (7.3 million) of Floridians live in incorporated cities, while 50.7 percent (7.4 million) reside "in the counties."

## PUBLIC SCHOOL ENROLLMENT
### Pre-kindergarten–Grade 12
### (As of Fall 1998)

| County | Pupils |
|---|---|
| Alachua | 29,462 |
| Baker | 4,624 |
| Bay | 25,881 |
| Bradford | 3,961 |
| Brevard | 68,476 |
| Broward | 232,900 |
| Calhoun | 2,241 |
| Charlotte | 16,242 |
| Citrus | 14,479 |
| Clay | 27,422 |
| Collier | 31,222 |
| Columbia | 9,497 |
| DeSoto | 4,594 |
| Dixie | 2,361 |
| Duval | 128,081 |
| Escambia | 45,696 |
| Flagler | 6,044 |
| Franklin | 1,448 |
| Gadsden | 7,710 |
| Gilchrist | 2,577 |
| Glades | 1,147 |
| Gulf | 2,397 |
| Hamilton | 2,279 |
| Hardee | 5,155 |
| Hendry | 7,533 |
| Hernando | 16,355 |
| Highlands | 11,361 |
| Hillsborough | 160,264 |
| Holmes | 3,721 |
| Indian River | 14,598 |
| Jackson | 7,812 |
| Jefferson | 1,953 |
| Lafayette | 1,050 |
| Lake | 27,994 |
| Lee | 54,382 |
| Leon | 31,241 |
| Levy | 6,199 |
| Liberty | 1,275 |
| Madison | 3,501 |
| Manatee | 34,148 |
| Marion | 37,900 |
| Martin | 16,052 |
| Miami-Dade | 363,361 |
| Monroe | 9,510 |
| Nassau | 10,366 |
| Okaloosa | 30,551 |
| Okeechobee | 6,553 |
| Orange | 138,747 |
| Osceola | 30,246 |
| Palm Beach | 146,162 |
| Pasco | 45,743 |
| Pinellas | 110,870 |
| Polk | 76,837 |
| Putnam | 13,063 |
| St. Johns | 18,740 |
| St. Lucie | 28,561 |
| Santa Rosa | 22,062 |
| Sarasota | 34,190 |
| Seminole | 57,973 |
| Sumter | 5,802 |
| Suwannee | 5,853 |
| Taylor | 3,596 |
| Union | 2,332 |
| Volusia | 59,892 |
| Wakulla | 4,722 |
| Walton | 5,757 |
| Washington | 3,431 |
| University Laboratory Schools | 3,839 |
| **TOTAL** | **2,351,975** |

### PRIVATE SCHOOLS

More than 11 percent of Florida's schoolchildren, 270,554 in grades K12 for the 1998-99 school year, attend nonpublic schools. These schools are required to meet public health and safety standards and attendance requirements but the state generally has declined to codify or apply additional strictures on them. The state recognizes the standards of various nonpublic school accrediting agencies and it can and does provide special services to children in non-public schools when appropriate.

There are private schools open in every county save four. Miami-Dade County has the largest private school enrollment, at 49,885.

Most of the state's private schools are not expected to participate in its revolutionary new voucher system because of the additional regulations the program carries.

## HOMESCHOOLING

The "homeschooling" education movement is developing in Florida, and in 1998 involved 25,930 students. There are homeschoolers in every Florida county, with Broward having the largest homeschooled population, at 2,337.

As with private schools, the state regulates education at home only lightly. Parents must register their children with their local school district, may not teach the children of others, must maintain records and materials, and must provide the district with an annual evaluation of their children's progress, although they have a wide variety of options on how to do that.

Local school districts in turn must provide homeschoolers with special needs with special services, and some districts are providing homeschoolers with extra curricula opportunities, including varsity sports. School districts do not give diplomas to homeschoolers, but the state will provide a homeschooler with a General Equivalency Diploma (GED) to those who qualify for and seek it.

## STATE UNIVERSITY SYSTEM

Florida's university system was established in 1905 when the legislature passed the Buckman Act, which consolidated the state's various post-high school institutions into three institutions under a Board of Control. After consolidation, the system consisted of the University of the State of Florida in Gainesville, the Florida A&M University in Tallahassee, and the Florida State College for Women in Tallahassee.

As the state's population grew, urban areas started to compete for degree granting institutions. By 1963, the University of South Florida in Tampa was operating. In addition, Florida Atlantic University in Boca Raton was on the drawing board and two more institutions, one in Pensacola and one in Orlando, were authorized.

To coordinate the growing system, the legislature created the Board of Regents as the single governing body of the state-supported universities. Today, the system consists of ten universities placed throughout the state.

### University of Florida

UF is a residential, land-grant institution and the oldest and largest of the state's public universities. It has a comprehensive range of teaching and research programs at the graduate and undergraduate levels. The school, in Gainesville, was established in 1853. Campus size is 1,948 acres. Median age of students is 21, with about 8 percent from out of state.

### Florida State University

FSU is a comprehensive, graduate-research university offering undergraduate, graduate, advanced graduate, and professional programs of study. It is in Tallahassee, the state capital, providing interaction with government agencies. Established in 1857, FSU campus size is 1,088 acres. Median student age is 22, with about 10 percent of the enrollment from out of state.

### University of South Florida

USF is a metropolitan, four-year undergraduate and graduate university in Tampa with a branch in St. Petersburg. It also operates prestigious New College in Sarasota. The main Tampa campus is 1,902 acres. Student median age is 23; 9 percent of students come from out of state.

### Florida A&M University

FAMU was founded in 1887 as a land-grant university in Tallahassee. It was created to provide post-secondary education for the state's black citizens. The university is principally undergraduate with the largest proportion of students enrolled at the lower levels, although numerous degrees are offered at the graduate level. Housed on a 419-acre campus, FAMU student median age is 21. Sixteen percent are not Florida residents.

## University of West Florida

UWF, situated in Pensacola on 1,000 acres, began classes in 1963. Among programs of emphasis are Coastal Zone Studies, Public Administration, Biology, and Finance. It grants both undergraduate and graduate degrees. Student median age is 26. About 5 percent of the enrollment is from out of state.

## Florida Atlantic University

FAU was founded in 1962 as an upper division and graduate university. In 1984 it enrolled its first freshman class, and the school now offers a wide variety of programs at all levels. In Boca Raton, FAU is placed on 886 acres. Median student age is 26, with 8 percent enrollment from out of state.

## University of Central Florida

UCF, in Orlando, is an urban, research-oriented university emphasizing undergraduate and graduate teaching, basic and applied research, and public service. Development of the Orlando area has contributed significantly to UCF's growth. Established in 1963, the campus covers 1,277 acres. Student median age is 23, with 5 percent of students from out of state.

## Florida International University

FIU, in Miami, was chartered in 1965 and opened in 1972 as an upper division and beginning graduate institution. The main campus is on 539 acres, but full degree programs are available on two campuses in Greater Miami, and at two academic centers in the Fort Lauderdale area. Age of students averages between 20 and 24. Nearly 11 percent of students are from out of state.

## University of North Florida

UNF opened in Jacksonville in 1972 as an upper division school but now offers full programs at both undergraduate and graduate levels. Median student age is 28, with only 3 percent of enrollment coming from out of state.

## Florida Gulf Coast University

Florida's newest and tenth state university, four-year Florida Gulf Coast University, at Fort Myers, welcomed its first students in the fall of 1997. It is already noted nationally for its "no tenure" policy and its advocacy of distance learning.

## STATE UNIVERSITY SYSTEM ENROLLMENT

### (1998-99)

| | |
|---|---|
| Florida A&M University, Tallahassee | 8,986 |
| Florida Atlantic University, Boca Raton | 8,026 |
| Florida Gulf Coast University, Fort Myers | 1,872 |
| Florida International University, North Miami | 14,328 |
| Florida State University, Tallahassee | 24,069 |
| University of Central Florida, Orlando | 15,660 |
| University of Florida, Gainesville | 35,700 |
| University of North Florida, Jacksonville | 5,971 |
| University of South Florida, Tampa | 17,528 |
| University of West Florida, Pensacola | 4,356 |
| **Total University System Enrollment** | **136,496** |

The state university system does not have a standard tuition. Tuition, fees, and other costs vary from one university to another and, at multi-campus universities, from one campus to another.

## AVERAGE UNIVERSITY TUITIONS AND FEES (1998-99)
### Per Credit Hour Per Semester

**State Resident Students**

Undergraduates............................................... $ 67.17
Graduate Students............................................ $143.90

**Out-of-State Students**

Undergraduates............................................... $274.69
Graduate Students............................................ $502.45

## UNIVERSITY FEES PER YEAR
## FOR MEDICAL PROGRAMS (1997-98)

**(Medical)**

State Resident Students..................................... $10,451.96
Out-of-State Students ...................................... $28,103.00

**(Dentistry)**

State Resident Students..................................... $ 9,183.66
Out-of-State Students ...................................... $24,532.38

**(Veterinary)**

State Resident Students..................................... $ 7,836.28
Out-of-State Students ...................................... $20,729.22

## LAW SCHOOL TUITIONS
### Per Credit Hour Per Semester

State Resident Students..................................... $163.02
Out-of-State Students....................................... $538.76

## BOARD OF REGENTS

Jon C. Moyle, Jupiter
Steve Uhlfelder, Tallahassee
Thomas F. Petway, III, Chairman, Jacksonville
Elizabeth G. Lindsay, Sarasota
Welcom H. Watson, Fort Lauderdale
Tom Gallagher, Education Commissioner, Tallahassee
Charlton B. Daniel, Jr., Gainesville
James F. Heekin, Jr., Altamonte Springs
J. Collier Merrill, Pensacola
Adolfo Henriques, Miami
Gwendolyn F. McLin, Okahumpka
Dennis M. Ross, Seminole
Philip D. Lewis, West Palm Beach
Student Regent: Ashley B. Moody, Gainesville

## STATE COMMUNITY COLLEGE SYSTEM

Florida's community colleges make up a public two-year college program dating back to 1947 with the creation of Palm Beach Junior College. But the system did not take on statewide significance until 1955 when the legislature established the Community College Council, which set up a master plan for public community colleges throughout Florida. Each college was to be within commuting distance of potential students.

Today, 28 community colleges serve all of Florida, offering associate degrees, the first two years of a baccalaureate degree, vocational education, and adult continuing education. To meet the commuting requirement, many have multiple campuses. Listed are main campus sites. The most current enrollment figures available for each college are for 1998, and follow.

## COMMUNITY COLLEGES

| College | City | Enrollment |
|---|---|---|
| Brevard | Cocoa | 4,488 |
| Broward | Fort Lauderdale | 12,878 |
| Central Florida | Ocala | 2,231 |
| Chipola | Marianna | 1,371 |
| Daytona Beach | Daytona Beach | 4,310 |
| Edison | Fort Myers | 4,327 |
| Florida | Jacksonville | 17,760 |
| Florida Keys | Key West | 785 |
| Gulf Coast | Panama City | 3,439 |
| Hillsborough | Tampa | 8,761 |
| Indian River | Fort Pierce | 8,500 |

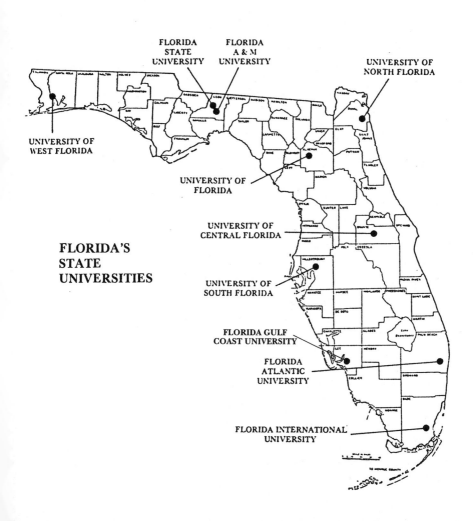

FLORIDA STATE UNIVERSITY

FLORIDA A & M UNIVERSITY

UNIVERSITY OF NORTH FLORIDA

UNIVERSITY OF WEST FLORIDA

UNIVERSITY OF FLORIDA

UNIVERSITY OF CENTRAL FLORIDA

**FLORIDA'S STATE UNIVERSITIES**

UNIVERSITY OF SOUTH FLORIDA

FLORIDA GULF COAST UNIVERSITY

FLORIDA ATLANTIC UNIVERSITY

FLORIDA INTERNATIONAL UNIVERSITY

| | | |
|---|---|---|
| Lake City | Lake City | 1,863 |
| Lake-Sumter | Leesburg | 1,045 |
| Manatee | Bradenton | 4,875 |
| Miami-Dade | Miami | 30,628 |
| North Florida | Madison | 817 |
| Okaloosa-Walton | Niceville | 3,437 |
| Palm Beach | Lake Worth | 8,364 |
| Pasco-Hernando | Dade City | 2,554 |
| Pensacola | Pensacola | 6,825 |
| Polk | Winter Haven | 2,754 |
| St. Johns | Palatka | 2,009 |
| St. Petersburg | St. Petersburg | 9,455 |
| Santa Fe | Gainesville | 7,306 |
| Seminole | Sanford | 6,388 |
| South Florida | Avon Park | 2,320 |
| Tallahassee | Tallahassee | 5,140 |
| Valencia | Orlando/Kissimmee | 12,674 |
| **TOTAL** | | **177,304** |

## PRIVATE COLLEGES AND UNIVERSITIES

Florida's private upper-level schools far outnumber those in the state university system, but many have small enrollments or only part-time enrollments, and are specialized, teaching art or Bible studies and other theological subjects. Some are large and prestigious institutions, however, and the following list is of those institutions accredited by the Southern Association of Colleges and Schools.

Barry University, Miami Shores
Bethune-Cookman College, Daytona Beach
Clearwater Christian College, Clearwater
College of Boca Raton, Boca Raton
Eckerd College, St. Petersburg
Edward Waters College, Jacksonville
Embry-Riddle Aeronautical University, Daytona Beach
Flagler College, St. Augustine
Florida Baptist Bible Theological College, Graceville
Florida College, Temple Terrace
Florida Institute of Technology, Melbourne
Florida Memorial College, Miami
Florida Southern College, Lakeland
Fort Lauderdale College, Fort Lauderdale
International Fine Arts College, Miami
ITT Technical Institute, Tampa
Jacksonville University, Jacksonville
Jones College, Jacksonville

Keiser College of Technology, Fort Lauderdale
Lynn University, Boca Raton
Miami Christian College, Miami
New England Institute of Technology, West Palm Beach
Nova University, Fort Lauderdale
Orlando College, Orlando
Palm Beach Atlantic College, West Palm Beach
Prospect Hall College, Hollywood
Ringling School of Art and Design, Sarasota
Rollins College, Winter Park
Saint John Vianney College Seminary, Miami
St. Leo University, St. Leo
Saint Thomas University, Miami
St. Vincent de Paul Seminary, Boynton Beach
Sarasota County Technical Institute, Sarasota
Southeastern Academy, Kissimmee
Southeastern College Assemblies of God, Lakeland

Southeastern University of Health
   Sciences, N. Miami Beach
Stetson University, DeLand
Stetson College of Law, St.
   Petersburg
Tampa College, Tampa
Trinity College of Florida, Holiday

University of Miami, Coral Gables
University of Sarasota, Sarasota
University of Tampa, Tampa
Walden University, Naples
Warner Southern College, Lake
   Wales
Webber College, Babson Park

## SCHOOLS RATE A GOOD

A recent poll revealed that only 4.5 percent of the Floridians surveyed thought state schools were doing an excellent job. More than 37 percent responded with a "fair" rating of public schools, while 25.6 percent said the state's public schools were "good."

## HIGH SCHOOL MASCOTS/NICKNAMES

*Eagles* is Florida's most popular high school nickname, with 40 schools opting for the bird as their mascot. Ten other schools use variations on the Eagle theme. *Panthers* is the second most popular, with 29, followed by *Tigers* (23), and *Bulldogs* (22). *Lions* and *Wildcats* terrorize opponents on behalf of 19 schools each.

Several schools enjoy unusual nicknames, including the Tarpon Springs *Spongers,* the Laurel Hill *Hoboes,* the Lakeland *Dreadnoughts,* the Miami Beach *Hi-Tides,* and the Miami *Stingarees.*

But perhaps the most distinctive nickname belongs to Fort Lauderdale High School. There, the *Flying L's* where dubbed thus in 1917 by a sportswriter and the name stuck. Its other distinction is that it is the only Florida High School nickname not chosen by contest or by a committee.

# BANKS

## HISTORY OF BANKING IN FLORIDA

The development of commerce and banking in Florida often is at odds with the popular history of the state as perceived both then and now.

The history of Florida banking began with what today would be called a private/public partnership. That deal forged in 1565 was made personally between Philip II of Spain and St. Augustine founder Pedro Menendez de Aviles. Under its terms, Menendez would conquer Florida and establish a colony all at his own expense. In return, Menendez received a large land grant and an exclusive on maritime trade. It was a proprietary arrangement, not dissimilar to other Spanish colonial empire systems and those used by other European nations.

But after nine relatively successful years, Menendez died. His influence was such that Spain was left to either abandon the Florida project or convert it to being a directly controlled military outpost, the option the crown exercised for strategic reasons. Florida languished for nearly two centuries, introducing only one item of eventual benefit: citrus.

Florida became English in 1763, a spoil of the Seven Years' War, and private enterprise made its first appearance since Menendez. English trading companies, based in Georgia, began operations in Florida. Most important among them was Panton, Leslie and Co., which worked diligently to increase Florida trade, most involving its customer, the Indians. Under British administration, shipping rose dramatically, as did exports. Indigo was Florida's first cash crop with exports rising from 3 tons in 1770 to more than 60 tons just 12 years later. Citrus exports went from 21 barrels in 1764 to 65,000 barrels in 1776.

The Spanish returned in 1783 but not all the British left. Panton, Leslie and Co. remained, encouraged to do so by the Spanish administration primarily because of its position relative to the Indians.

Most of the major Southeastern tribes included Florida in their trading markets and while they had other priorities, they were noted for their business acumen and innovation including the hiring of commercial managers to run their enterprises, a practice that continues today. Their relationship with the Panton firm also was modern: the company served as banker and factor for the tribes. The hand-in-glove relationship between the Panton partners and the Creek, Cherokee, Choctaw, and Chickasaw nations, as well as the breakaway Seminoles, was a major factor in the decision to break the barrier they represented with Andrew Jackson's march into Florida.

John Forbes and Co., the successor to the Panton firm, provided what early nineteenth-century banking services were available to the fewer than 15,000 residents of the new U.S. territory. In the first year as military governor, Jackson wrote to then Secretary of State John Quincy Adams requesting a branch of the Bank of the United States for Pensacola. Nothing happened, however, and private banking such as it was continued. With a quickly growing population, the need for a consistent medium of exchange (something Florida had never experienced), and broader access to credit became apparent. Although fought for several years by civilian governor William Duval who feared Florida falling victim to the "bank frenzie" rampant in the states, the territory chartered its first bank, the Bank of Florida at Tallahassee, in 1828 with a capitalization of a half-million dollars. It, too, was a private/public partnership with half its directors chosen from investors, the other half appointed by the governor and the legislative council. It became the depository for state funds. The Bank of West Florida at Marianna was chartered in 1829, followed by the Bank of St. Augustine and the Bank of Pensacola two years later. The competition arrived in 1832 with the chartering of the Central Bank of Tallahassee with $1 million in authorized capital.

Banking in Florida during its territorial period was a typical mixture of politics and economics, battered by the Indian wars. A great benefit of territorial banking was the issuance of species that traded at par and was accepted in all channels of internal trade. But that ended with the panic of 1837 and the suspension of specie throughout the United States. As local money became valueless, Floridians came to depend on bank bills of exchange, most issued by Georgia institutions. All of the territorial banks eventually closed.

The St. Joseph Constitution put severe restrictions on banking and the first years of statehood saw the return of private banking, primarily through agents from out of state institutions. Economic conditions improved with statehood and in 1853, the legislature, now representing more than 100,000 residents, began chartering banks again, but only a half dozen operating banks prior to the outbreak of the War Between the States. In January 1861, Florida seceded from the Union and the following month joined in the formation of the Confederacy.

From the start of the Civil War, however, Florida was broke. Tax collections were negligible. The state issued war bonds and sold federal lands it had seized. Florida banks made loans to the state and "railroad notes" filled the currency gap when silver coinage became too scarce for everyday transactions. When Confederate currency entered Florida, residents hoarded Florida notes and bills, issued by the state, but soon both declined in value. The economy also suffered from the federal blockade although many subsequent leading Florida families earned their fortunes and their reputations as blockade-runners. Inflation caused by scarcity further weakened the medium of exchange. Even the state dabbled in what would today be called the "black market" to bring in revenue. Florida's primary task in the war was to serve as a gateway for goods and as the Confederacy's breadbasket. By the end of the war, it could do neither and most Floridians were bankrupt.

Private banking returned after the war with more than a half dozen domestic operations a decade after the war. The economy began to recover rather quickly during Reconstruction with Northern capital entering the state for legitimate investment and with a vast upswing in something the state would soon get used to: immigration from other states.

Reconstruction established the Freedmen's Bank under federal regulation with branches in Tallahassee and Jacksonville opening in 1866. Corruption took its toll, however, and the Florida bank was closed in 1874, paying 62 cents on the dollar to its depositors.

The National Bank Act, passed to bring order out of chaos during the Civil War, came to Florida in 1874 with the chartering of the First National Bank of Florida at Jacksonville in 1874. It thrived without competition until 1880 and beyond but went into receivership in 1903 when its phosphate investments collapsed. The year 1886 was a banner one for the opening of national banks, and all flourished for a while but of the group that came into being, only one survives in a straight line from that time, now part of an interstate holding company.

Although banks opened and closed regularly at the end of the nineteenth century and the beginning of the twentieth, by comparison to banking in the rest of the nation, Florida's compared favorably, ebbing and flowing with booms and panics and adjusting to the establishment of the Federal Reserve System.

But in 1925 came disaster, the bust of the Florida boom. Rampant real estate and other business speculation was reflected at Florida banks. That year there were 271 banks in Florida. Deposits were $875 million, up from $180 million just three years before, and rising at a rate of $32 million a month.

Then the bottom fell out, real estate values crashed, and banks began to fail at a rate of more than one a month. The state was further buffeted by the economic impact of horrific hurricanes in 1926 and 1928. Finally, the stock market crashed in 1929 and the rest of the nation joined Florida in the Great Depression. By 1934, the number of state banks fell to 105 and deposits from their 1920s peak of $269.1 million to just $38.5 million. National banks survived the federal bank holiday of 1933 and only one went into receivership.

Modern banking in Florida matches that of the rest of the nation, except that it has had to contend with ever expanding growth, fueled primarily by its vast increase in population.

## FLORIDA'S SHRINKING HOLDINGS

Bank "merger-mania" has hurt Florida more than any other state. Florida has lost 20 percent of its banking assets to out-of-state banks since 1992, an estimated $30 billion. It has gone from 6th to 13th among the country's banking centers as ranked by states in less than a decade. Most of Florida's losses went into gains for North Carolina and Alabama.

## OUT-OF-STATE BANKS OPERATING IN FLORIDA
### Ranked by their Total National Assets—1998

| Bank | Assets | Headquarters |
|---|---|---|
| 1. Bank of America* | $617 billion | Charlotte, North Carolina |
| 2. First Union | $237 billion | Charlotte, North Carolina |
| 3. SunTrust | $93 billion | Atlanta, Georgia |
| 4. Wachovia | $64 billion | Winston-Salem, North Carolina |
| 5. AmSouth | $41 billion | Birmingham, Alabama |
| 6. SouthTrust | $38 billion | Birmingham, Alabama |
| 7. Regions | $37 billion | Birmingham, Alabama |
| 8. Union Planters | $32 billion | Memphis, Tennessee |
| 9. Huntington | $28 billion | Columbus, Ohio |
| 10. Compass | $17.3 billion | Birmingham, Alabama |
| 11. Colonial | $10.5 billion | Montgomery, Alabama |

*doing business as NationsBank

## URBAN AREAS

The 1990 federal census listed Florida as having 27 urban areas. The largest was the Miami/Hialeah area, with 1,914,860 residents. It was followed by Tampa/St. Petersburg/Clearwater, with a population of 1,708,710; Fort Lauderdale/Hollywood/Pompano Beach, with 1,238,134; and Orlando, with 887,116.

## FLORIDA TOP 20 BANKS—1997
### (Ranked by Total Assets)

| Bank | City | Total Assets (in thousands) |
|---|---|---|
| 1. NationsBank | Jacksonville | $232,397,000* |
| 2. Barnett Bank NA. | Jacksonville | 42,828,483* |
| 3. SunTrust Bank, Cen. Fla | Orlando | 7,867,203 |
| 4. SunTrust Bank, S. Fla | Fort Lauderdale | 4,477,617 |
| 5. SunTrust Bank, Miami. | Miami | 3,540,470 |
| 6. North Trust Bank Miami NA. | Miami | 2,559,392 |
| 7. SunTrust Bank Tampa Bay | Tampa. | 2,505,699 |
| 8. Union Planters Bank of Miami | Miami | 2,156,360 |
| 9. Sun Bank Gulf Coast. | Sarasota | 1,913,350 |
| 10. Republic Bank | St. Petersburg. | 1,550,789 |
| 11. Republic Nat. Bank | Coral Gables. | 1,510,434 |
| 12. SunTrust Bank, SW Fla. | Fort Myers | 1,373,710 |
| 13. SunTrust Bank, Nature Cst. | Brooksville | 1,350,739 |
| 14. Hamilton Bank. | Miami | 1,339,969 |
| 15. City National Bank of Fla | Miami | 1,214,977 |
| 16. Suntrust Bank E. Cent. Fl. | Daytona Beach | 1,072,705 |
| 17. SunTrust Bank, N. Fl. | Jacksonville. | 1,043,081 |
| 18. Suntrust Bank Mid-Fla. | Winter Haven | 968,450 |
| 19. Republic Sec. Bank. | W. Palm Beach | 948,291 |
| 20. 1st Nat. Bank, Treasure Coast | Stuart. | 940,921 |

*In 1998-99, NationsBank entered in a merger takeover of Florida's Barnett Bank and California's Bank of America.

## FLORIDA TOP 20 FEDERAL CREDIT UNIONS—1997
### (Ranked by Total Assets)

| Credit Union | City | Total Assets (in rounded thousands) |
|---|---|---|
| 1. Suncoast Schools | Tampa | $1,783,200 |
| 2. Jax Navy | Jacksonville | 1,355,400 |
| 3. Eastern Financial | Miami Springs | 1,049,000 |
| 4. GTE | Tampa | 645,400 |
| 5. Space Coast | Melbourne | 606,400 |
| 6. Eglin. | Ft. Walton Beach | 549,300 |
| 7. MacDill. | Tampa | 511,100 |
| 8. Fairwinds | Orlando | 494,900 |
| 9. Tyndall | Panama City | 425,900 |
| 10. Tropical | Miami | 408,400 |
| 11. Central Florida Educators | Orlando | 390,900 |
| 12. IBM Southeast. | Boca Raton. | 355,200 |
| 13. Miami-Dade County Schools | Miami | 347,000 |
| 14. Pen Air | Pensacola | 317,400 |
| 15. Education Community | Jacksonville. | 315,300 |
| 16. MidFlorida Schools | Lakeland | 277,100 |
| 17. Publix Employees | Lakeland | 258,600 |
| 18. Your Campus. | Gainesville | 256,600 |
| 19. Florida Telco | Jacksonville. | 240,000 |
| 20. Florida Aircraft | W. Palm Beach | 214,000 |

# UTILITIES

## PUBLIC SERVICE COMMISSION

Regulation of utilities companies is the responsibility of the Public Service Commission. The commission was established by the legislature in 1887 as the Florida Railroad Commission. At that time, its primary purpose was regulating railroads. But regulatory authority was added over the years to include telephone companies (in 1911) and electric utilities (in 1951). Today, the commission, renamed in 1965, also regulates the water and sewer and natural gas industries.

All five commission members are appointed by the governor to four-year terms. Present commissioners are Susan Clark, J. Terry Deason, Julia Johnson, E. Leon Jacobs, and Joe A. Garcia (Chairman).

### TELEPHONE COMPANIES
### 1999

| Name/Headquarters | Number of Exchanges | Access Lines |
|---|---|---|
| **ALLTEL Florida** | | |
| Live Oak | .27 | .82,719 |
| **Bell South Telecommunications** | | |
| Miami | .102 | .6,481,986 |
| **GT Com** | | |
| Florala, Alabama | .2 | .2,440 |
| **Frontier Communications Company of the South** | | |
| Atmore, Alabama | .2 | .4,266 |
| **GT Com Telephone Company** | | |
| Port St. Joe | .13 | .33,702 |
| **GTE Florida** | | |
| Tampa | .24 | .2,368,938 |
| **GT Com** | | |
| Perry | .2 | .10,273 |
| **ITS** | | |
| Indiantown | .1 | .3,573 |
| **Northeast Florida Telephone Company** | | |
| MacClenny | .2 | .8,592 |
| **Quincy Telephone Company** | | |
| Quincy | .3 | .13,270 |
| **Sprint Florida (Centel)** | | |
| Tallahassee | .35 | .428,816 |
| **Sprint Florida (United)** | | |
| Altamonte Springs | .69 | .1,619,226 |
| **Vista-United Telecommunications** | | |
| Lake Buena Vista | .2 | .15,236 |
| **TOTAL** | .284 | .11,073,001 |

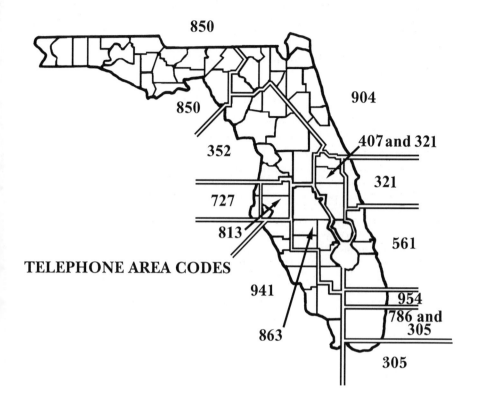

**850**

**850**

**352**

**727**

**813**

**941**

**863**

**904**

**407 and 321**

**321**

**561**

**954**

**786 and 305**

**305**

**TELEPHONE AREA CODES**

### Thirteen Telephone Area Codes

Florida got its 12th and 13th area codes in 1999 and gave Brevard County, home of Kennedy Space Center, the one it always wanted: 3-2-1.

The new 321 area code also will be overlaid in central Florida on the existing 407 area code, including Orlando, requiring that metropolitan area to go to ten-digit dialing between local area codes, just as Miami and Tampa Bay do.

The other new area code is 863, split off from 941. The new area includes Polk Country and runs south through the inland counties to, and including, Hendry County.

The state's area codes are:

**305:** Old numbers in Miami-Dade County and the Keys portion of Monroe County;

**321:** Brevard County and new numbers in the metropolitan Orlando area;

**352:** West Central Florida, including Gainesville and a portion of Pasco County;

**407:** Old numbers in the metropolitan Orlando area and all numbers in Brevard County;

**561:** the southeast Atlantic Coast;

**727:** Pinellas County and a portion of Pasco County;

**786:** New numbers in Miami-Dade County;

**813:** Hillsborough County and a portion of Pasco County;

**850:** The Florida Panhandle, including Pensacola and Tallahassee;
**863:** Inland south central Florida, including Lakeland;
**904:** North Florida, including Jacksonville;

**941:** The Southwest Florida Gulf Coast, including Sarasota, Ft. Myers, and mainland Monroe County, and;

**954:** Ft. Lauderdale's Broward County.

## ELECTRIC UTILITIES

The state is served by three types of electric utilities. They are rural cooperatives, investor-owned, and municipal utilities.

### Rural Electric Cooperatives

Florida's 16 electric rural distribution cooperatives serve power to more than one million residents. Other utilities, the municipal and investor-owned, also serve within the cooperative areas but their services are either to towns or cities or along major highways. By far, the majority of land area in the state is served by the 16 cooperatives. That vast area requires 46,000 miles of electric lines for cooperatives to serve roughly 10 percent of the state's population. By contrast, to service the other 90 percent, municipal and investor-owned utilities have strung 70,000 miles of lines. Florida's first electric cooperative was organized in 1936. At that time, only 7.8 percent of Florida farms had electricity. Today, more than 99 percent of rural residents receive power.

The cooperatives, and the counties or parts of counties they serve, are:

| Cooperative | Headquarters | Counties Serviced |
|---|---|---|
| Tri-County | Madison | Jefferson, Madison, Taylor |
| Escambia River | Jay | Escambia, Santa Rosa |
| Choctawhatchee | DeFuniak Springs | Santa Rosa, Walton, Holmes, Okaloosa |
| Gulf Coast | Wewahitchka | Washington, Gulf, Calhoun, Bay |
| Suwannee Valley | Live Oak | Hamilton, Columbia, Suwannee, Lafayette |
| Okefenokee | Nahunta,Ga. | Nassau, Duval, Baker |
| West Florida | Graceville | Washington, Holmes, Calhoun, Jackson |
| Talquin | Quincy | Gadsden, Leon, Liberty, Wakulla, Franklin |
| Central Florida | Chiefland | Dixie, Gilchrist, Levy, Alachua |
| Sumter | Sumterville | Marion, Sumter, Levy, Hernando, Citrus, Pasco, Lake |
| Clay | Keystone Heights | Duval, Clay, Levy, Putnam, Columbia, Baker, Bradford, Union, Alachua, Volusia, Lake, Marion |

Withlacoochee ........Dade City ................Citrus, Hernando,
                                              Hillsborough, Pasco,
                                              Pinellas, Polk
Peace River ..........Wauchula ................Hardee, De Soto,
                                              Polk, Indian River,
                                              Manatee, Highlands,
                                              Sarasota, Brevard,
                                              Hillsborough,
                                              Osceola
Lee County ..........North Fort Myers ..........Lee, Charlotte,
                                              Collier, Hendry
Glades ..............Moore Haven .............Glades, Highlands,
                                              Okeechobee,
                                              Hendry
Florida Keys .........Tavernier ................Monroe

## COOPERATIVE UTILITIES
## TYPICAL ELECTRICAL BILL COMPARISONS
### Residential Service (January 1999)

| Cooperative | Minimum Bill or Customer Charge | KWH 500 | KWH 1000 |
|---|---|---|---|
| Central Florida | $ 8.50 | $44.25 | $80.00 |
| Choctawhatchee | $12.32 | $42.46 | $72.60 |
| Clay | $ 9.00 | $38.65 | $68.30 |
| Escambia River | $ 7.00 | $41.40 | $75.80 |
| Florida Keys | $ 7.00 | $41.23 | $75.46 |
| Glades | $10.50 | $49.50 | $88.50 |
| Gulf Coast | $10.00 | $42.40 | $74.80 |
| Lee County | $ 5.00 | $42.30 | $79.60 |
| Okefenokee | $10.00 | $45.50 | $81.00 |
| Peace River | $10.50 | $50.75 | $91.00 |
| Sumter | $ 8.25 | $44.00 | $79.75 |
| Suwannee Valley | $ 8.73 | $47.73 | $86.73 |
| Talquin | $ 8.00 | $43.50 | $79.00 |
| Tri-County | $10.00 | $51.46 | $92.93 |
| West Florida | $ 8.00 | $42.46 | $76.92 |
| Withlachoochee | $ 9.75 | $44.87 | $79.98 |

*Above figures exclude local taxes. December 1998 Fuel and Purchased Power Costs are included.*

## HOUSING PRICES UP

Buying a home in Florida got more expensive during 1998, in some areas dramatically so. Median price of a home in Panama City rose to $100,000, a 37 percent increase over 1997. The price rose 32 percent in Naples (to $184,100), 19 percent at Fort Myers ($101,900), 16 percent in the Sarasota/Bradenton area ($124,500), and 10 percent at Fort Walton Beach ($109,300). Home prices declined 4 percent at Ocala (to $60,800), 2 percent at Gainesville ($95,300), and 1 percent in the Space Coast area ($82,200). The median price of a Florida home rose 5 percent to $97,900.

## INVESTOR-OWNED UTILITIES
## TYPICAL ELECTRIC BILL COMPARISONS
### Residential Service
### (January 1999)

| Utility | Minimum Bill or Customer Charge | KWH 500 | 1000 |
|---|---|---|---|
| Florida Power & Light Company | $5.65 | $38.76 | $74.36 |
| Florida Power Corp.* | $8.85 | $46.22 | $83.58 |
| Gulf Power Company | $8.07 | $34.95 | $61.83 |
| Tampa Electric Company | $8.50 | $43.26 | $78.02 |
| Florida Public Utilities Company | | | |
| Marianna Division | $8.30 | $35.26 | $62.21 |
| Fernandina Beach Division | $7.00 | $31.20 | $55.39 |

*Above figures exclude local taxes, but include 1.5 percent gross receipt tax. October 1998-December 1998 Fuel Rates are included.*
*\*Purchased in 1999 by Carolina Power and Light of Raliegh, North Carolina.*

## MUNICIPAL UTILITIES
## TYPICAL ELECTRIC BILL COMPARISONS
### Residential Service
### (January 1999)

| Municipal Utilities | Minimum Bill or Customer Charge | KWH 500 | 1000 |
|---|---|---|---|
| Alachua | $ 8.00 | $49.90 | $91.80 |
| Bartow | $ 6.60 | $48.69 | $90.78 |
| Blountstown | $ 3.50 | $40.02 | $76.54 |
| Bushnell | $ 6.75 | $43.95 | $81.15 |
| Chattahoochee | $ 4.50 | $40.94 | $77.37 |
| Clewiston | $ 6.50 | $40.40 | $74.30 |
| Fort Meade | $12.96 | $51.42 | $89.88 |
| Fort Pierce | $ 5.35 | $44.48 | $83.60 |
| Gainesville | $ 4.90 | $38.38 | $73.00 |
| Green Cove Springs | $ 6.00 | $43.46 | $80.92 |
| Havana | $ 6.00 | $49.99 | $93.98 |
| Homestead | $ 5.50 | $44.30 | $83.09 |
| Jacksonville | $ 5.50 | $36.83 | $68.15 |
| Jacksonville Beach | $ 4.50 | $41.90 | $79.30 |
| Key West | $ 4.76 | $47.51 | $90.26 |
| Kissimmee | $ 3.90 | $36.81 | $69.71 |
| Lake Worth | $ 2.78 | $40.96 | $79.14 |
| Lakeland | $ 3.94 | $40.02 | $76.10 |
| Leesburg | $ 5.00 | $40.98 | $76.95 |
| Moore Haven | $ 8.50 | $45.55 | $82.60 |
| Mount Dora | $ 4.94 | $45.14 | $85.34 |
| New Smyrna Beach | $ 5.65 | $40.24 | $74.82 |
| Newberry | $ 7.50 | $47.20 | $86.89 |
| Ocala | $ 7.00 | $42.47 | $77.94 |
| Orlando | $ 6.00 | $41.74 | $77.47 |
| Quincy | $ 2.40 | $40.23 | $78.06 |
| Reedy Creek | $ 2.85 | $40.61 | $78.36 |
| St. Cloud | $ 6.48 | $45.07 | $83.66 |

| Municipal Utilities | Minimum Bill or Customer Charge | KWH | |
|---|---|---|---|
| | | 500 | 1000 |
| Starke | $ 6.45 | $43.70 | $80.95 |
| Tallahassee | $ 4.94 | $45.84 | $86.74 |
| Vero Beach | $ 7.00 | $44.10 | $81.20 |
| Wauchula | $ 8.62 | $44.48 | $80.33 |
| Williston | $ 6.00 | $49.42 | $92.84 |

*Above figures exclude local taxes. December 1998 Fuel and Purchased Power Costs are included.*

## INVESTOR-OWNED NATURAL GAS UTILITIES
## TYPICAL GAS BILL COMPARISONS
### Residential Service (January 1998)

| Utility | Minimum Bill or Customer Charge | Therms | |
|---|---|---|---|
| | | 40 | 100 |
| Chesapeake Utilities Corp. | $7.00 | $44.24 | $100.09 |
| City Gas Co. of Florida | $7.00 | $42.93 | $ 96.83 |
| Florida Public Utilities | $8.00 | $32.80 | $ 70.01 |
| Indiantown Gas Co. | $5.00 | $22.86 | $ 49.66 |
| Peoples Gas System Inc. | $7.00 | $38.96 | $ 86.91 |
| Peoples Gas System (Western Division) | $7.00 | $41.73 | $ 93.83 |
| St. Joe Natural Gas Co. | $5.00 | $40.16 | $ 92.89 |
| Sebring Gas System Inc. | $7.00 | $35.09 | $ 77.22 |
| South Florida Natural Gas Co. | $7.00 | $40.77 | $ 91.43 |

## NUCLEAR PLANTS IN FLORIDA

Florida has five nuclear power plants that provide about 17 percent of the state's electricity. The Crystal River plant is owned by Florida Power Corp. of St. Petersburg. The other four plants are owned by Florida Power & Light Co. of Miami.

| Plant Name | Location | Year Service Began |
|---|---|---|
| Turkey Point 3 | Miami-Dade County | 1972 |
| Turkey Point 4 | Miami-Dade County | 1973 |
| St. Lucie 1 | St. Lucie County | 1976 |
| St. Lucie 2 | St. Lucie County | 1983 |
| Crystal River | Citrus County | 1977 |

# GOVERNMENT

Florida has two United States senators and 23 representatives in Congress. Following are the current Florida members in Congress.

## U.S. SENATORS

### Connie Mack (R)

Born—Philadelphia, Pa., Oct. 29, 1940
Education—BA degree, University of Florida
Prior occupation—banker
Elected to U.S. House 1982; to U.S. Senate 1988
Address—902 Hart Building, Washington, DC 20510
Phone—(202) 224-5274

### Bob Graham (D)

Born—Coral Gables, Fla., Nov. 9, 1936
Education—BS degree, University of Florida; Harvard University Law School
Prior occupation—governor of Florida
Elected in 1986
Address—241 Dirksen Building, Washington, DC 20510
Phone—(202) 224-3041

## U.S. REPRESENTATIVES

### 1st District
### Joe Scarborough (R)

Born—Atlanta, Ga., April 9, 1963
Education—JD degree, University of Florida
Prior occupation—attorney
Elected in 1994
Address—1523 Longworth Building, Washington, DC 20515
Phone—(202) 225-5235
District Office: Pensacola

### 2nd District
### F. Allen Boyd (D)

Born—Valdosta, Ga., June 6, 1945
Education—BS degree, Florida State University
Prior occupation—farmer
Military service—U.S. Army
Elected in 1996
Address—1237 Longworth Building, Washington, DC 20515
Phone—(202) 225-4452
District Offices: Tallahassee, Panama City

### 3rd District
### Corrine Browne (D)

Born—Jacksonville, Fla., Nov. 11, 1946
Education—BS degree, Florida A&M University; EdS degree, University of Florida
Prior occupation—educator

Elected in 1982
Address—1610 Longworth Building, Washington, DC 20515
Phone-(202) 225-0123
District Offices: Jacksonville, Gainesville, Daytona Beach

### 4th District
### Tillie Fowler (R)

Born—Milledgeville, Ga., Dec. 23, 1942
Education—AB degree, Emory University; JD degree, Emory University Law School
Prior occupation—attorney
Elected in 1992
Address—413 Cannon Building, Washington, DC 20515
Phone—(202) 225-2501
District Offices: Daytona Beach, DeLand, Jacksonville

### 5th District
### Karen L. Thurman (D)

Born—Rapid City, S.D., Jan. 12, 1951
Education—AA degree, Sante Fe Community College; BA degree, University of Florida
Prior occupation—teacher
Elected in 1992
Address—130 Cannon Building, Washington, DC 20515
Phone—(202) 225-1002

District Offices: Gainesville, Inverness, New Port Richey

### 6th District
### Clifford B. Stearns (R)

Born—Washington, D.C., April 16, 1941
Education—BS degree, George Washington University
Prior occupation—motel management
Military service—U.S. Air Force
Elected in 1988
Address—2352 Rayburn Building, Washington, DC 20515
Phone—(202) 225-5744
District Offices: Orange Park, Leesburg, Ocala

### 7th District
### John L. Mica (R)

Born—Binghamton, N.Y., Jan. 27, 1943
Education—AA degree, Miami-Dade Community College; BA degree, University of Florida
Prior occupation—businessman
Military service—U.S. Air Force
Elected in 1992
Address—336 Cannon Building, Washington, DC 20515
Phone—(202) 225-4035
District Offices: Deltona, Fern Park, Port Orange

### 8th District
### Bill McCollum (R)

Born—Brooksville, Fla., July 12, 1944
Education—BA and JD degrees, University of Florida
Prior occupation—attorney
Military service—U.S. Navy
Elected in 1992
Address—2266 Rayburn Building, Washington, DC 20515
Phone—(202) 225-2176
District Office: Orlando

### 9th District
### Michael Bilirakis (R)

Born—Tarpon Springs, Fla., July 16, 1930
Education—BS degree, Univ. of Pittsburgh; JD degree, Univ. of Florida

Prior occupation—attorney
Military service—U.S. Air Force
Elected in 1982
Address—2240 Rayburn Building, Washington, DC 20515
Phone—(202) 225-5755
District Offices: Clearwater, Land O'Lakes

### 10th District
### C. W. ("Bill") Young (R)

Born—Harmarville, Pa., Dec. 16, 1930
Education—Pinellas County public schools
Prior occupation—insurance executive
Military service—National Guard
Elected in 1992
Address—2407 Rayburn Building, Washington, DC 20515
Phone—(202) 225-5961
District Office: Indian Rocks Beach

### 11th District
### James O. Davis (D)

Born—Tampa, Fla., Oct. 11, 1957
Education—JD degree, University of Florida
Prior occupation—attorney
Elected in 1996
Address—327 Cannon Building, Washington, DC 20515
Phone—(202) 225-3376
District Office: Tampa

### 12th District
### Charles T. Canady (R)

Born—Lakeland, Fla., June 22, 1954
Education—BA degree, Haverford College; JD degree, Yale Law School
Prior occupation—attorney
Elected in 1992
Address—1222 Longworth Building, Washington, DC 20515
Phone—(202) 225-1252
District Office: Lakeland

### 13th District
### Dan Miller (R)

Born—Highland Park, Mich., May 30, 1942
Education—BA degree, Yale University; MBA degree, Emory University; PhD degree, Louisiana State University

Prior occupation—businessman
Elected in 1992
Address—117 Cannon Building,
Washington, DC 20515
Phone—(202) 225-5015
District Offices: Bradenton, Sarasota

### 14th District
### Porter J. Goss (R)

Born—Waterbury, Conn., Nov. 26,
1938
Education—BA degree, Yale
University
Prior occupation—CIA officer;
businessman
Elected in 1988
Address—108 Cannon Building,
Washington, DC 20515
Phone—(202) 225-2536
District Offices: Fort Myers, Naples,
Punta Gorda

### 15th District
### Dave Weldon (R)

Born—Amityrille, N.Y., Aug. 31, 1953
Education—MD degree, State U. of
N.Y.—Buffalo
Prior occupation—physician
Elected in 1994
Address—216 Cannon Building,
Washington, DC 20515
Phone—(202) 225-3026
District Office: Palm Bay

### 16th District
### Mark Foley (R)

Born—Newton, Mass., Sept. 8, 1954
Education—Palm Beach Junior
College
Prior occupation—businessman
Elected in 1994
Address—506 Rayburn Building,
Washington, DC 20515
Phone—(202) 225-7931
District Office: West Palm Beach

### 17th District
### Carrie Meek (D)

Born—Tallahassee, Fla., April 29, 1926
Education—BS degree, Florida A&M
University; MS degree, University
of Michigan; Florida Atlantic
University

Prior occupation—professor;
administrator
Elected in 1992
Address—404 Cannon Building,
Washington, DC 20515
Phone—(202) 225-4506
District Office: N. Miami Beach

### 18th District
### Ileana Ros-Lehtinen (R)

Born—Havana, Cuba, July 15, 1952
Education—BS and MS degrees, Fla.
International Univ.
Prior occupation—teacher; principal
Elected in 1988
Address—2440 Rayburn Building,
Washington, DC 20515
Phone—(202) 225-3931
District Office: Miami

### 19th District
### Robert Wexler (D)

Born—Queens, N.Y., Jan. 2, 1961
Education—BS degree, University of
Florida; JD degree, George
Washington University
Prior occupation—attorney
Elected in 1996
Address—1609 Longworth Building,
Washington, DC 20515
Phone—(202) 225-3001
District Office: Boca Raton

### 20th District
### Peter Deutsch (D)

Born—Bronx, N.Y., April 1, 1957
Education—BA degree, Swarthmore
College; JD degree, Yale University
Prior occupation—attorney; non-
profit executive
Elected in 1992
Address—204 Cannon Building,
Washington, DC 20515
Phone—(202) 225-7931
District Offices: Big Pine Key, Key
Largo, Key West, Pembroke Pines

### 21st District
### Lincoln Diaz-Balart (R)

Born—Havana, Cuba, Aug. 13, 1954
Education—BA degree, University of
South Florida; JD degree, Case
Western Reserve University

Prior occupation—attorney
Elected in 1992
Address—431 Cannon Building,
Washington, DC 20515
Phone—(202) 225-4211
District Office: Miami

## 22nd District
## Clay Shaw (R)

Born—Miami, Fla., April 19, 1939
Education—BS degree, Stetson U.;
MBA degree, U. of Alabama; JD
degree, Stetson Law School
Prior occupation—businessman;
attorney
Elected in 1980
Address—2267 Rayburn Building,
Washington, DC 20515

Phone—(202) 225-3026
District Offices: Fort Lauderdale,
West Palm Beach

## 23rd District
## Alcee L. Hastings (D)

Born—Altamonte Springs, Fla., Sept.
5, 1936
Education—BA degree, Fisk
University; JD degree, Florida A&M
University College of Law
Prior occupation—attorney
Elected in 1992
Address—1039 Longworth Building,
Washington, DC 20515
Phone—(202) 225-1313
District Offices: Fort Lauderdale,
West Palm Beach

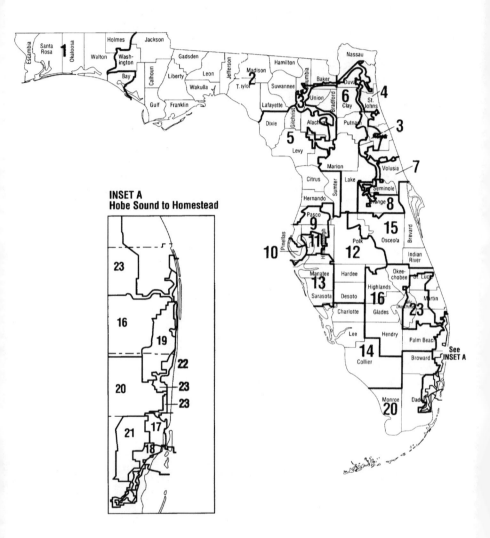

## CONGRESSIONAL
## DISTRICTS

The 23 Congressional Districts awarded Florida are single-member districts and aligned according to population as of 1990 by the Florida legislature. All congressmen are elected to two-year terms.

## STATE CONSTITUTION

Acquisition of Florida by the U.S. from Spain in 1819 ended a 300-year period during which Florida was an international pawn among nations striving for control of the Gulf of Mexico and Atlantic sea-lanes. Under U.S. rule the territory developed rapidly, and by 1837 its legislative council authorized an election to determine popular opinion on statehood. The idea was approved and the historic Constitutional Convention of 1838 was called to meet in St. Joseph.

Major features of the document limited the vote to white males over 21 years of age who were enrolled in the state militia, and the decision to elect, by popular vote, 17 senators and 41 representatives, with the governor the only state executive officer to be elected by the people.

Congress admitted Florida to the Union in 1845. To keep a balance between slave and free states, Iowa, a free state, was admitted at the same time as Florida, a slave state.

In 1861, Florida seceded from the Union, the third southern state to do so after the outbreak of the War Between the States. When the war ended, President Andrew Johnson set up a provisional government in Florida. Its appointed governor, William Marvin, called for a constitutional convention in 1865. The 1865 constitution promptly annulled the state's secession ordinance but contained provisions that still harbored discrimination against Negroes. As a result, Congress refused to seat the Florida congressional delegation and re-instituted military rule in Florida and several other southern states whose constitutions were not acceptable.

To free the state from such rule, Floridians called another constitutional convention for 1868. This constitution, sometimes referred to as the Carpetbagger's Constitution, extended voting privileges to all males 21 and older, including Negroes. This proviso, along with others more acceptable to politicians in Washington, earned Congressional approval; Florida was once again in the Union and had its civil government restored.

By the mid-1880s, economic and political factional disputes developed within the state and another constitution, the 1885 Constitution, was drafted and enacted. It represented a compromise between the necessities of the times and the political philosophy of the Old South. But, with most of the state's population in the northern counties, the document was conceived primarily with the problems of the north Florida agricultural area in mind.

Amended over the years, the 1885 Constitution got its last thorough revision in 1968. This revision was brought about in part by Florida's tremendous urban growth in middle and south Florida following World War II, making necessary reapportionment of the state legislature. The 1968 Constitution requires that reapportionment take place after each 10-year federal census, it allows the governor to succeed himself if he has not served more than six years, and it keeps the state's unique elected cabinet system. The state continues to operate under this revised 1885 Constitution.

## PREAMBLE

We, the people of the State of Florida, being grateful to Almighty God for our constitutional liberty, in order to secure its benefits, perfect our government, ensure domestic tranquility, maintain public order, and guarantee equal civil and political rights to all, do ordain and establish this constitution.

## ARTICLE I
## DECLARATION OF RIGHTS

SECTION 1. **Political power**—All political power is inherent in the people. The enunciation herein of certain rights shall not be construed to deny or impair others retained by the people.

SECTION 2. **Basic rights**—All natural persons are equal before the law and have inalienable rights, among which are the right to enjoy and defend life and liberty, to pursue happiness, to be rewarded for industry, and to acquire, possess and protect property; except that the ownership, inheritance, disposition and possession of real property by aliens ineligible for citizenship may be regulated or prohibited by law. No person shall be deprived of any right because of race, religion or physical handicap.

SECTION 3. **Religious freedom**—There shall be no law respecting the establishment of religion or prohibiting or penalizing the free exercise thereof. Religious freedom shall not justify practices inconsistent with public morals, peace or safety. No revenue of the state or any political subdivision or agency thereof shall ever be taken from the public treasury directly or indirectly in aid of any church, sect, or religious denomination or in aid of any sectarian institution.

SECTION 4. **Freedom of speech and press**—Every person may speak, write and publish his sentiments on all subjects but shall be responsible for the abuse of that right. No law shall be passed to restrain or abridge the liberty of speech or of the press. In all criminal prosecution and civil actions for defamation the truth may be given in evidence. If the matter charged as defamatory is true and was published with good motives, the party shall be acquitted or exonerated.

SECTION 5. **Right to assemble**—The people shall have the right peaceably to assemble, to instruct their representatives, and to petition for redress of grievances.

SECTION 6. **Right to work**—The right of persons to work shall not be denied or abridged on account of membership or non-membership in any labor union or labor organization. The right of employees, by and through a labor organization, to bargain collectively shall not be denied or abridged. Public employees shall not have the right to strike.

SECTION 7. **Military power**—The military shall be subordinate to the civil.

SECTION 8. **Right to bear arms**—The right of the people to keep and bear arms in defense of themselves and of the lawful authority of the state shall not be infringed, except that the manner of bearing arms may be regulated by law.

SECTION 9. **Due process**—No person shall be deprived of life, liberty or property without due process of law, or be twice put in jeopardy for the same offense, or be compelled in any criminal matter to be a witness against himself.

SECTION 10. **Prohibited law**—No bill of attainder, ex post facto law or law impairing the obligation of contracts shall be passed.

SECTION 11. **Imprisonment for debt**—No person shall be imprisoned for debt, except in cases of fraud.

SECTION 12. **Searches and seizure**—The right of the people to be secure in their persons, houses, papers and effects against unreasonable searches and seizures, and against the unreasonable interception of private communications by any means, shall not be violated. No warrant shall be issued except upon probable cause, supported by affidavit, particularly describing the place or places to be searched, the person or persons, thing or things to be seized, the communication to be intercepted, and the nature of evidence to be obtained. Articles or information obtained in violation of this right shall not be admissible in evidence.

SECTION 13. **Habeas corpus**—The writ of habeas corpus shall be grantable of right, freely and without cost. It shall be returnable without delay, and shall never be suspended unless, in case of rebellion or invasion, suspension is essential to the public safety.

SECTION 14. **Bail**—Until adjudged guilty, every person charged with a crime or violation of municipal or county ordinance shall be entitled to release on reasonable bail with sufficient surety unless charged with a capital offense punishable by life imprisonment and the proof of guilt is evident or the presumption is great.

SECTION 15. **Prosecution for crime; offenses committed by children**—(a) No person shall be tried for capital crime without presentment or indictment by a grand jury, or for other felony without such presentment, or indictment or an information under oath filed by the prosecuting officer of the court, except persons on active duty in the militia when tried by courts martial; (b) When authorized by law, a child as therein defined may be charged with a violation of law as an act of delinquency instead of crime and tried without a jury or other requirements applicable to criminal cases. Any child so charged shall, upon demand made as provided by law before a trial in a juvenile proceeding, be tried in an appropriate court as an adult. A child found delinquent shall be disciplined as provided by law.

SECTION 16. **Rights of accused**—In all criminal prosecutions the accused shall, upon demand, be informed of the nature and cause of the accusation against him, and shall be furnished a copy of the charges, and shall have the right to have compulsory process for witnesses, to confront at trial adverse witnesses, to be heard in person, by counsel or both, and to have a speedy and public trial by impartial jury in the county where

the crime was committed. If the county is not known, the indictment or information may change venue in two or more counties conjunctively and proof that the crime was committed in that area shall be sufficient; but before pleading the accused may elect in which of those counties he will be tried. Venue for prosecution of crimes committed beyond the boundaries of the state shall be fixed by law.

SECTION 17. **Excessive punishments**—Excessive fines, cruel or unusual punishment, attainder, forfeiture of estate, indefinite imprisonment, and unreasonable detention of witnesses are forbidden.

SECTION 18. **Administrative penalties**—No administrative agency shall impose a sentence of imprisonment, nor shall it impose any other penalty except as provided by law.

SECTION 19. **Costs**—No person charged with crime shall be compelled to pay costs before a judgment of conviction has become final.

SECTION 20. **Treason**—Treason against the state shall consist only in levying war against it, adhering to its enemies, or giving them aid and comfort, and no person shall be convicted of treason except on the testimony of two witnesses to the same overt act or on confession in open court.

SECTION 21. **Access to courts**—The courts shall be open to every person for redress of any injury, and justice shall be administered without sale, denial or delay.

SECTION 22. **Trial by jury**—The right of trial by jury shall be secure to all and remain inviolate. The qualifications and the number of jurors, not fewer than six, shall be fixed by law.

SECTION 23. **Right of privacy**—Every natural person has the right to be let alone and free from governmental intrusion into his private life except as otherwise provided herein. This section shall not be construed to limit the public's right of access to public records and meetings as provided by law.

## STATE GOVERNMENT

The state constitution declares that the powers of state government be divided into three separate and relatively independent branches—executive, legislative, and judicial. It is basically the same governmental system found at the national level and in all 50 states. But the application of this basic system is in some ways unique in Florida.

## EXECUTIVE BRANCH

This branch is charged with administration and enforcement of the state's laws. Part of the state's deviation from executive branches of other states is in Florida's cabinet system. Florida's constitution states that in addition to a governor and lieutenant governor "there shall be a cabinet composed of a secretary of state, an attorney general, a comptroller, a treasurer, a commissioner of agriculture, and a commissioner of education." The constitution not only declares that each of the cabinet members has basic powers and duties, but each also "shall exercise such powers and perform such duties as may be prescribed by law." That declaration, in effect, gives the cabinet officers powers equal to the governor.

At monthly meetings of the governor and cabinet, for example, the officials meet as equals on most matters. When the cabinet votes on an issue, each cabinet member, and the governor, has one vote. Sometimes, the governor, who is assigned "supreme executive powers" by the constitution, is outvoted by the other six cabinet members. One of the few times the governor cannot be outvoted is in the granting of pardons.

This method of operation violates a basic rule of government, that is, giving an elected official the authority to perform his or her duties and then holding that official fully responsible for such performance. Under the cabinet system, the governor is held responsible but does not have the authority nor the means to fulfill that responsibility. Nevertheless, Florida's system has operated successfully. At least, voters have not seen fit to change the system, although they have been asked to several times.

The governor and cabinet members are elected in even numbered years, between presidential elections. That was not always so. Before 1965, state officials were elected in the same year as presidents. But, when Floridians voted Republican in the national elections of 1952, 1956, and 1960, state Democrats feared that a landslide Republican presidential vote could ride Republicans into state offices. So they chose to change the year of election for state officials, thus divorcing campaigns of state officeholders from those surrounding the national election.

Term of office for the governor and cabinet officers is four years. Before the 1968 constitutional revision, the governor could serve but one term; now a governor may serve two terms in succession. Cabinet officers may be reelected for any number of years.

Voters in 1998 amended Florida's constitution to weaken the Cabinet system, making the Secretary of State and Commissioner of Education gubernatorial appointments and removing their cabinet status. They also voted to combine the offices of Comptroller and Treasurer /Insurance Commissioner into one position. The change will take effect in 2003, leaving the Cabinet made up of the Governor, the Commissioner of Agriculture, the Attorney General, and a chief financial officer.

## THE GOVERNOR

The governor is responsible for the day-to-day operations of the state and is its chief law enforcement officer. Heads of those departments for which the governor is responsible are appointed by the governor. The governor also appoints heads of those departments that are under both the governor and cabinet, but at least three of the other cabinet members must agree to the appointment. The governor also appoints individual members of many regulatory boards and commissions.

By executive order, the governor may suspend from office any state or county elected official who is not subject to impeachment. Grounds for such suspension include malfeasance, misfeasance, neglect of duty, drunkenness, incompetence, permanent inability to perform duties, and commission of a felony. The governor cannot suspend the lieutenant governor, cabinet members, nor judges of the supreme court, appeals courts, or circuit courts; they can be removed only by impeachment by the legislature.

The governor also has authority to fill vacancies in county or state elected offices that may occur between elections.

## LIEUTENANT GOVERNOR

The 1968 revision of the constitution authorized the new position of lieutenant governor. Duties were left to the discretion of the governor and legislature, with the only constitutional chore being to assume the office of governor should the office become vacant due to death, impeachment trial, incapacity, absence, or resignation.

The lieutenant governor is elected on the same ticket as the governor; they run as a team.

## DEPARTMENTS DIRECTLY UNDER GOVERNOR'S CONTROL

Departments that are the direct responsibility of the governor include:

**DEPARTMENT OF BUSINESS AND PROFESSIONAL REGULATION:** Licenses, examines, and investigates complaints that have to do with establishing qualifications and skills for various occupations such as barbers, accountants, landscape architects, engineers, osteopaths, chiropractors, watchmakers, and so on. It is financed not by taxes but by fees charged for testing and licenses.

**DEPARTMENT OF CHILDREN AND FAMILY SERVICES:** Handles child abuse investigations, economic assistance programs, and mental health and substance abuse counseling. Created Jan. 1, 1997, from the dismantled Department of Health and Rehabilitative Services.

**DEPARTMENT OF ELDER AFFAIRS:** Oversees the needs of and provides services to the state's older population.

**DEPARTMENT OF ENVIRONMENTAL PROTECTION:** Regulates and monitors the state's environment, concerning itself with prevention of air, water, and land pollution, and enforcing adopted rules and regulations.

**DEPARTMENT OF HEALTH:** Heads the state's public health efforts and regulates the health-care profession. Established Jan. 1, 1997 by the legislature.

**DEPARTMENT OF TRANSPORTATION:** Concerns itself with the state's primary roads, interstate highway system, secondary road network, mass transportation, licensing of airports, and the operation of toll roads.

**CITRUS COMMISSION:** Establishes grading criteria and standards for all types of citrus fruits, as well as researching new uses for citrus and conducting advertising campaigns promoting Florida's production. Funded by taxes and levies on growers.

**DEPARTMENT OF LABOR AND EMPLOYMENT SECURITY:** Charged with labor and employment security of employees in Florida, and operates unemployment offices.

**DEPARTMENT OF MANAGEMENT SERVICES:** Administers the state employees merit system, prepares a state budget, and drafts long-range comprehensive plans for development of the state.

**DEPARTMENT OF CORRECTIONS:** Responsible for the rehabilitation of adult and youthful law offenders, and operates and oversees prisons.

**DEPARTMENT OF COMMUNITY AFFAIRS:** Serves as a liaison between local, state, and federal governmental units in connection with public housing, planning grants, and civil defense.

**DEPARTMENT OF LOTTERY:** Conducts and manages the state lottery games.

## DEPARTMENTS UNDER BOTH GOVERNOR AND CABINET

**DEPARTMENT OF LAW ENFORCEMENT:** Leads the state government's war on crime. Department agents may investigate reports and complaints of wrongdoing in all sectors, including suspected law-breaking charges against appointed or elected officials.

**DEPARTMENT OF SAFETY AND MOTOR VEHICLES:** Enforces the state's traffic laws, tests drivers and issues licenses, and oversees sale of vehicle tags.

**DEPARTMENT OF REVENUE:** Administers and enforces state laws that produce revenue for the state. It collects funds from all sources and turns them over to the state treasurer for deposit.

**OFFICE OF EXECUTIVE CLEMENCY:** Made up of cabinet officers, it has the authority to grant pardons. Before a pardon is granted, however, the governor must cast an affirmative vote.

**BOARD OF ADMINISTRATION:** This board, composed of the governor, the state treasurer, and the comptroller, administers debt service for county road and bridge bonds, and county or state school bonds. It must approve bonds of all state agencies before issuance.

**DEPARTMENT OF VETERANS AFFAIRS:** Focuses exclusively on the needs of Florida's nearly two million veterans.

## DEPARTMENTS DIRECTLY UNDER CABINET CONTROL

**DEPARTMENT OF STATE:** Headed by the secretary of state, and responsible for elections throughout the state, for maintaining an archives of state documents and actions, and for issuing charters to corporations.

**DEPARTMENT OF LEGAL AFFAIRS:** Headed by the attorney general, this department serves as legal advisor to state officials, and issues legal opinions upon request from public officials.

**DEPARTMENT OF BANKING AND FINANCE:** Headed by the comptrol-

ler, it keeps records of all state revenues collected and disbursed, publishes annual reports on the financial status of each county, and supervises banks and other financial institutions.

**DEPARTMENT OF INSURANCE:** Headed by the state treasurer, this department is the custodian of all state funds. It also licenses insurance companies wishing to do business in the state. The treasurer, as state fire marshal, also is charged with investigating suspicious fires.

**DEPARTMENT OF AGRICULTURE:** Headed by the commissioner of agriculture, it provides state services to agricultural interests in Florida. It also operates the state's farmers markets and inspects weighing and measuring devices such as gasoline pumps and market scales.

**DEPARTMENT OF EDUCATION:** Headed by the commissioner of education, this department allocates state educational funds to local school boards, and is charged with overseeing matters in the state's primary and secondary public schools and in its community colleges. A board of regents with the department is responsible for the rules and operation of the ten state universities.

## INDEPENDENT DEPARTMENTS

**MILITARY DEPARTMENT:** Heading this department, which is authorized to provide a state militia, is the state adjutant general. But the governor is the commander-in-chief of all state military forces while not in federal service, and appoints officers in the state's national guard.

**PUBLIC SERVICE COMMISSION:** This commission crosses the traditional lines that separate the executive, legislative, and judicial branches of state government. The commission has control of rates and services provided by transportation businesses and privately owned utilities and telephone companies operating in Florida. It has subpoena powers and can levy fines. Members of the five-person commission are appointed by the governor.

**PROBATION AND PAROLE COMMISSION:** Determines which prisoners in the state's penal system shall be paroled, fixes the conditions of parole, and supervises the parole. It also supervises persons placed on probation by courts.

**FISH AND WILDLIFE CONSERVATION COMMISSION:** Responsible for establishing and enforcing rules and regulations governing hunting and freshwater fishing in the state.

## THE CABINET

**Governor**
**Jeb Bush (R)**
Born—Midland, Tex., Feb. 11, 1953
Education—BA, University of Texas
Prior occupation—businessman
Elected in 1998
Term ends—January 2003

**Lieutenant Governor\***
**Frank Brogan (R)**
Born—Lafayette, Ind., Sept. 6, 1953
Education—BA, Univ. of Connecticut; MA, Florida Atlantic Univ.
Prior occupation—Commissioner of Education
Elected in 1998

Term ends—January 2003
**Attorney General**
**Bob Butterworth (D)**
Born—Passaic, N.J., Aug. 20, 1942
Education—BS degree, Univ. of Florida; JD degree, Univ. of Miami
Prior occupation—attorney
Elected in 1986
Term ends—January 2003

**Commissioner of Agriculture**
**Bob Crawford (D)**
Born—Bartow, Fla., Jan. 26, 1948
Education—University of Miami
Prior occupation—real estate, citrus
Elected in 1990
Term ends—January 2003

**Comptroller**
**Bob Milligan (R)**
Born—Teaneck, N.J., Dec. 27, 1932
Education—BA degree, U.S. Naval
Academy; MA degree, University of
Rochester
Prior occupation—military
Military service—U.S. Marine Corps
Elected in 1994
Term ends—January 2003
**Commissioner of Education**
**Tom Gallagher (R)**
Born—Wilmington, Del., Feb. 3,
1944
Education—University of Miami
Prior occupation—businessman, for-
mer Treasurer/Insurance
Commission
Military service—U.S. Army
Elected in 1998
Term ends—January 2003

**Treasurer and Insurance Commissioner**
**Bill Nelson (D)**
Born—Miami, Fla., Sept. 29, 1942
Education—BA degree, Yale
University; LLD degree, University
of Virginia
Prior occupation—attorney, con-
gressman, astronaut
Elected in 1994
Term ends—January 2003
**Secretary of State**
**Katherine Harris (R)**
Born—Key West, Fla., April 5, 1957
Education—BA, Agnew Scott; MPA,
Harvard
Prior occupation—state senator, real
estate
Elected in 1998
Term ends—January 2003
*\*Member of the Cabinet only when serv-
ing as Acting Governor.*

## GOVERNORS OF FLORIDA

**Provisional/Military**
Andrew Jackson—1821-22

**Territorial**
William DuVal—1822-34
John H. Eaton—1834-35
Richard K. Call—1835-40
Robert R. Reid—1840-41
Richard K. Call—1841-44
John Branch—1844-45

**State**
William D. Moseley—1845-49
Thomas Brown—1849-53
James E. Broome—1853-57
Madison S. Perry—1857-61
John Milton—1861-65
A. K. Allison—1865\*
William Marvin—1865\*
David S. Walker—1865-68
Harrison Reed—1868-72
Ossian B. Hart—1873-74 (Died in
office)
Marcellus L. Stearns—1874-77
George F. Drew—1877-81
William D. Bloxham—1881-85
Edward A. Perry—1885-89

Francis P. Fleming—1889-93
Henry L. Mitchell—1893-97
William D. Bloxham—1897-1901
W. S. Jennings—1901-05
Napoleon B. Broward—1905-09
Albert W. Gilchrist—1909-13
Park Trammell—1913-17
Sidney J. Catts—1917-21
Cary A. Hardee—1921-25
John W. Martin—1925-29
Doyle E. Carlton—1929-33
David Scholtz—1933-37
Fred P. Cone—1937-41
Spessard L. Holland—1941-45
Millard F. Caldwell—1945-49
Fuller Warren—1949-53
Dan T. McCarty—1953 (Died in
office)
Charley E. Johns—1953-55\*
LeRoy Collins—1955-61
Farris Bryant—1961-65
Haydon Burns—1965-67\*\*
Claude Kirk, Jr.—1967-71
Reubin Askew—1971-79
Robert Graham—1979-87
Wayne Mixson—1987
Bob Martinez—1987-91
Lawton Chiles—1991-98 (Died in office)

Buddy MacKay—1998-99*
Jeb Bush—1999-
*Not elected governor but served in the position by appointment, in most cases

*because of death of elected governor.*
***Burns in 1965 served only two years as the election cycle was ordered changed.*

## SHORTEST TERM

The shortest term as governor was the three-day tenure of Wayne Mixson from Jan. 3 to Jan. 6, 1987. As lieutenant governor under Governor Graham, Mixson was sworn in as governor when Graham, newly elected to the U.S. Senate, had to be in Washington, D.C., three days before his gubernatorial term expired. With the newly elected Governor Martinez not scheduled to be sworn in until Jan. 6, Mixson became governor for three days.

## LEGISLATIVE BRANCH

The Florida Legislature consists of two bodies, the state senate and the house of representatives. Legislation on any subject may be introduced into either house. Regular sessions of the legislature are each year, for 60 days, beginning in February. Special sessions, for 20 days, may be called by the governor.

The senate and house exercise tremendous influence on the daily lives of Florida residents. They do so both through enacting state laws and through passing laws applying to specific cities, counties, or regions. Because of its control over the affairs of cities and counties, plus its control over the appointments of the governor, and its investigative and budgetary control over all phases of state government and state agencies, the legislature is considered by many to be the most powerful of the three branches of state government.

## SENATORS AND HOUSE MEMBERS AND DISTRICTS

### SENATE

The senate has 40 members, each elected to a four-year term. One-half the senate is elected every two years, providing for staggered terms. Representation is based on population. In 1990 the state's estimated population was 12.9 million, meaning each senator represents an area of approximately 350,000 residents. Because population is the key factor in designating various senate districts, some senators find themselves representing only one county or part of one, while others may represent several counties.

### HOUSE OF REPRESENTATIVES

House representation also is based solely on population. The house has 120 members, or one for approximately every 100,000 residents. All members are elected every two years, during general elections held in even-numbered years. As is true in the senate, the house has some members who represent only a portion of a county, others representing an entire county or more.

### STATE SENATE DISTRICTS
### (Counties Within Districts)

1. Holmes, Washington. Portions of Bay, Escambia, Okaloosa, Santa Rosa, and Walton.
2. Portions of Alachua, Clay, Duval, Putnam, and St. Johns.
3. Calhoun, Franklin, Gadsden, Gulf, Jackson, Liberty, and Wakulla. Portions of Bay, Jefferson, Leon, and Madison.
4. Baker, Dixie, Gilchrist, Hamilton, Lafayette, Nassau, and Taylor. Portions of Alachua, Bradford, Citrus, Columbia, Jefferson, Leon, Levy, Madison, Marion, Suwannee, and Union.
5. Portions of Alachua, Bradford,

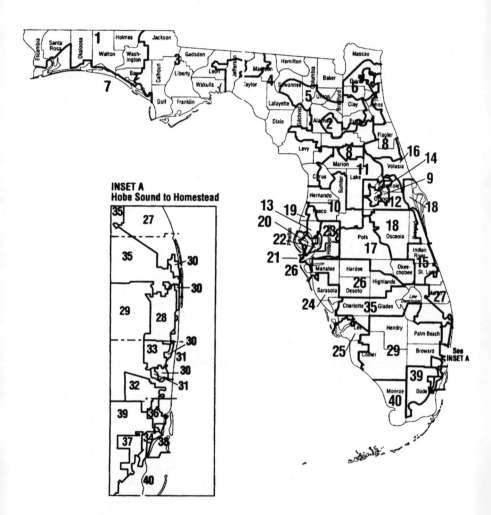

INSET A
Hobe Sound to Homestead

## SENATE DISTRICTS

The Florida Senate consists of 40
members elected for four-year terms.
All odd-numbered Senate seats are
elected at one time; the even-numbered seats another time. Boundary
lines for the districts were drawn by
the legislature, based on the 1990
census.

Clay, Columbia, Levy, Marion, Putnam, Suwannee, and Union.

6. Portions of Clay, Duval, and St. Johns.
7. Portions of Bay, Escambia, Okaloosa, Santa Rosa, and Walton.
8. Flagler. Portions of Duval, Marion, St. Johns, and Volusia.
9. Portions of Orange and Seminole.
10. Hernando. Portions of Pasco, Polk, and Sumter.
11. Lake. Portions of Citrus, Marion, Seminole, and Sumter.
12. Portions of Orange, Osceola, Seminole, and Volusia.
13. Portions of Hillsborough and Pasco.
14. Portions of Orange and Seminole.
15. Portions of Brevard, Indian River, and St. Lucie.
16. Portions of Volusia.
17. Portions of Highlands, Hillsborough, Okeechobee, and Polk.
18. Portions of Brevard and Osceola.
19. Portions of Pasco and Pinellas.
20. Portions of Hillsborough and Pinellas.
21. Portions of Hillsborough, Manatee, and Pinellas.
22. Portion of Pinellas.
23. Portion of Hillsborough.
24. Portions of Charlotte, Lee, and Sarasota.
25. Portions of Collier and Lee.
26. De Soto and Hardee. Portions of Highlands, Hillsborough, Manatee, and Sarasota.
27. Portions of Indian River, Martin, Palm Beach, and St. Lucie.
28. Portions of Broward and Palm Beach.
29. Hendry. Portions of Broward, Collier, and Palm Beach.
30. Portions of Broward and Palm Beach.
31. Portions of Broward and Palm Beach.
32. Portions of Broward and Miami-Dade.
33. Portion of Broward.
34. Portion of Miami-Dade.
35. Glades. Portions of Charlotte, Lee, Martin, Okeechobee, and Palm Beach.
36. Portion of Miami-Dade.
37. Portion of Miami-Dade.
38. Portion of Miami-Dade.
39. Portion of Miami-Dade.
40. Monroe. Portions of Miami-Dade

## HOUSE DISTRICTS
### (Counties Within Districts)

1. Portions of Escambia, Okaloosa, and Santa Rosa.
2. Portion of Escambia.
3. Portion of Escambia.
4. Portions of Escambia, Okaloosa, and Santa Rosa.
5. Holmes and Washington. Portions of Okaloosa and Walton.
6. Portion of Bay.
7. Calhoun, Gulf, Jackson, and Liberty. Portions of Bay, Gadsden, Leon, and Walton.
8. Portions of Gadsden and Leon.
9. Portion of Leon.
10. Franklin, Jefferson, Levy, Taylor, and Wakulla. Portions of Alachua, Dixie, Gilchrist, Leon, and Marion.
11. Columbia, Hamilton, Lafayette, Madison, and Suwanee. Portions of Dixie and Gilchrist.
12. Baker, Bradford, Nassau, and Union. Portions of Duval.
13. Portions of Clay and Duval.
14. Portion of Duval.
15. Portion of Duval.
16. Portion of Duval.
17. Portion of Duval.
18. Portions of Duval and St. Johns.
19. Portions of Clay, Duval, and St. Johns.
20. Portions of Clay, Flagler, St. Johns, and Volusia.
21. Putnam. Portions of Clay and Marion.
22. Portions of Alachua and Marion.

23. Portions of Alachua and Marion.
24. Portion of Marion.
25. Portions of Lake, Marion, Seminole, and Volusia.
26. Portions of Flagler, Lake, and Volusia.
27. Portion of Volusia.
28. Portion of Volusia.
29. Portion of Brevard.
30. Portion of Brevard.
31. Portion of Brevard.
32. Portions of Brevard, Indian River, and Orange.
33. Portions of Orange, Seminole, and Volusia.
34. Portions of Orange and Seminole.
35. Portions of Orange and Seminole.
36. Portion of Orange.
37. Portions of Orange and Seminole.
38. Portions of Lake and Orange.
39. Portion of Orange.
40. Portion of Orange.
41. Portions of Lake, Orange, and Osceola.
42. Portions of Lake, Marion, and Sumter.
43. Citrus. Portions of Hernando and Marion.
44. Portions of Hernando, Lake, Pasco, Polk, and Sumter.
45. Portions of Hernando and Pasco.
46. Portion of Pasco.
47. Portions of Hillsborough and Pinellas.
48. Portions of Hillsborough and Pinellas.
49. Portion of Pinellas.
50. Portion of Pinellas.
51. Portion of Pinellas.
52. Portion of Pinellas.
53. Portion of Pinellas.
54. Portion of Pinellas.
55. Portions of Manatee and Pinellas.
56. Portion of Hillsborough.
57. Portion of Hillsborough.
58. Portion of Hillsborough.
59. Portion of Hillsborough.
60. Portion of Hillsborough.
61. Portions of Hillsborough and Pasco.
62. Portion of Hillsborough.
63. Portion of Polk.
64. Portion of Polk.
65. Portion of Polk.
66. Portions of Hillsborough and Polk.
67. Portions of Hillsborough, Manatee, and Sarasota.
68. Portion of Manatee.
69. Portion of Sarasota.
70. Portion of Sarasota.
71. Portions of Charlotte and Sarasota.
72. De Soto and Hardee. Portions of Charlotte and Lee.
73. Portion of Lee.
74. Portions of Charlotte, Lee, and Sarasota.
75. Portions of Collier and Lee.
76. Portion of Collier.
77. Glades and Hendry. Portions of Collier and Highlands.
78. Portions of Highlands, Martin, Okeechobee, Palm Beach, and St. Lucie.
79. Portions of Okeechobee and Osceola.
80. Portions of Indian River and St. Lucie.
81. Portions of Martin and St. Lucie.
82. Portions of Martin and Palm Beach.
83. Portion of Palm Beach.
84. Portion of Palm Beach.
85. Portion of Palm Beach.
86. Portion of Palm Beach.
87. Portion of Palm Beach.
88. Portion of Palm Beach.
89. Portion of Palm Beach.
90. Portion of Broward.
91. Portions of Broward and Palm Beach.
92. Portion of Broward.
93. Portion of Broward.
94. Portion of Broward.
95. Portion of Broward.
96. Portion of Broward.
97. Portion of Broward.
98. Portion of Broward.

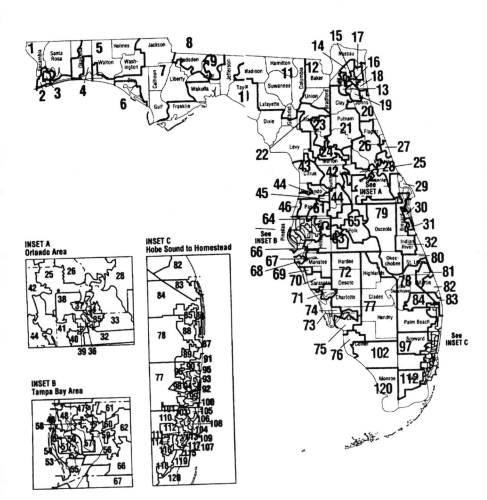

## HOUSE DISTRICTS

The Florida House of Representatives consists of 120 seats. All members serve two-year terms. Boundary lines for the districts were drawn by the legislature, based on the 1990 census.

| | |
|---|---|
| 99. Portion of Broward. | 109. Portion of Miami-Dade. |
| 100. Portion of Broward. | 110. Portion of Miami-Dade. |
| 101. Portions of Broward and Miami-Dade. | 111. Portion of Miami-Dade. |
| | 112. Portion of Miami-Dade. |
| 102. Portions of Collier and Miami-Dade. | 113. Portion of Miami-Dade. |
| | 114. Portion of Miami-Dade. |
| 103. Portion of Miami-Dade. | 115. Portion of Miami-Dade. |
| 104. Portion of Miami-Dade. | 116. Portion of Miami-Dade. |
| 105. Portion of Miami-Dade. | 117. Portion of Miami-Dade. |
| 106. Portion of Miami-Dade. | 118. Portion of Miami-Dade. |
| 107. Portion of Miami-Dade. | 119. Portion of Miami-Dade. |
| 108. Portion of Miami-Dade. | 120. Monroe. Portion of Miami-Dade. |

## LEGISLATORS

### STATE SENATORS

Bronson, Charlie—Indian Harbour Beach
District 18—(R)

Brown-Waite, Ginny—Brooksville
District 10—(R)

Burt, Locke—Ormond Beach
District 16—(R)

Campbell, Walter—Tamarac
District 33—(D)

Carlton, Lisa—Osprey
District 24—(R)

Casas, Roberto—Hialeah
District 39—(R)

Childers, W. D.—Pensacola
District 1—(D)

Clary, Charlie—Fort Walton Beach
District 7—(R)

Cowin, Anna—Leesburg
District 11—(R)

Dantzler, Rick—Winter Haven
District 17—(D)

Dawson, M. Mandy—Ft. Lauderdale
District 30—(D)

Diaz-Balart, Lincoln—Miami
District 37—(R)

Dyer, Buddy—Orlando
District 14—(D)

Forman, Howard C.—Hollywood
District 32—(D)

Geller, Steve—Fort Lauderdale
District 29—(D)

Grant, John—Tampa
District 13—(R)

Gutman, Alberto—Miami
District 34—(R)

Hargrett, James ("Jim"), Jr.—Tampa
District 21—(D)

Holzendorf, Betty—Jacksonville
District 2—(D)

Horne, Jim—Jacksonville
District 6—(R)

Jennings, Toni—Orlando
District 9—(R)

Jones, Daryl—Miami
District 40—(D)

King, Jim—Jacksonville
District 8—(R)

Kirkpatrick, George—Gainesville
District 5—(D)

Klein, Ron—Boca Raton
District 28—(D)

Kurth, Patsy Ann—Palm Bay
District 15—(D)

Latvala, Jack—Palm Harbor
District 19—(R)

Lee, Tom—Plant City
District 23—(R)

McKay, John—Bradenton
District 26—(R)

Meek, Kendrick—Miami
District 36—(D)

Mitchell, Richard—Jasper
District 4—(D)

Myers, William G.—Stuart
District 27—(R)

Rossin, Tom—West Palm Beach
District 35—(D)

Saunders, Burt—Naples
District 25—(R)

Scott, James A.—Fort Lauderdale
District 31—(R)

Sebesta, James—Tampa
District 20—(R)

Silver, Ronald—North Miami Beach
District 38—(D)

Sullivan, Donald—Seminole

District 22—(R)
Thomas, Pat—Tallahassee
District 3—(D)
Webster, Daniel—Winter Gardens
District 12—(R)

## STATE REPRESENTATIVES

Albright, George—Ocala
District 24—(R)
Andrews, William F.—Delray Beach
District 87—(R)
Argenziano, Nancy—Lecanto
District 43—(R)
Arnall, Joseph—Jacksonville Beach
District 18—(R)
Bainter, Stan—Eustis
District 25—(R)
Ball, Randy—Mims
District 29—(R)
Barreiro, Gustavo A., Jr.—Miami
District 107—(R)
Bense, Allan George—Panama City
District 6—(R)
Betancourt, Annie—Miami
District 116—(D)
Bilirakis, Gus Michael—Tarpon
Springs
District 48—(R)
Bitner, David—Punta Gorda
District 71—(R)
Bloom, Elaine—Miami Beach
District 106—(D)
Boyd, Janegale—Monticello
District 10—(D)
Bradley, Rudolph—St. Petersburg
District 55—(R)
Bronson, Irlo, Jr.—Kissimmee
District 79—(D)
Brooks, Bob—Winter Park
District 35—(R)
Brown, Shirley—Sarasota
District 69—(D)
Bullard, Larcenia—Miami
District 118—(D)
Bush, James, III—Miami
District 109—(D)
Byrd, Johnnie B., Jr.—Plant City
District 62—(R)
Casey, Bob—Gainesville
District 22—(R)
Chestnut, Cynthia—Gainesville
District 23—(D)

Constantine, Lee—Altamonte Springs
District 37—(R)
Cosgrove, John F.—Miami
District 119—(D)
Couch, Marvin—Oviedo
District 33—(R)
Crady, George—Yulee
District 12—(D)
Crist, Victor—Temple Terrace
District 60—(R)
Crow, Larry—Palm Harbor
District 49—(R)
Dawson- White, Muriel—Ft.
Lauderdale
District 93—(D)
Detert, Nancy C.—Orlando
District 70—(R)
Diaz De La Portilla, Alex—Miami
District 115—(R)
Dockery, Paula—Lakeland
District 64—(R)
Edwards, Lori—Auburndale
District 65—(D)
Eggelletion, Josephus—Lauderdale
Lakes
District 94—(D)
Farcas, Frank—St. Petersburg
District 52—(R)
Fasano, Mike—New Port Richey
District 45—(R)
Feren, Steven—Plantation
District 98—(D)
Flanagan, Mark—Bradenton
District 68—(R)
Florentino, Heather—New Port
Richey
District 46— (R)
Frankel, Lois—West Palm Beach
District 85—(D)
Fuller, James—Jacksonville
District 16—(R)
Futch, Howard—Indialantic
District 30—(R)
Garcia, Rodolfo, Jr.—Hialeah
District 110—(R)
Gay, Greg—Cape Coral
District 74—(R)
Geller, Steven—Hallandale
District 101—(D)
Goode, Harry, Jr.—Melbourne
District 31—(R)
Greene, Addie—West Palm Beach
District 84—(D)

Hafner, Lars—St. Petersburg
District 53—(D)
Harrington, Lindsay—Punta Gorda
District 72—(R)
Hart, Chris—Tampa
District 57—(R)
Healey, Edward—West Palm Beach
District 86—(D)
Henriques, Bob—Tampa
District 58—(D)
Heyman, Sally A.—North Miami
Beach
District 105—(D)
Hill, Anthony—Jacksonville
District 14—(D)
Jacobs, Suzanne—Delray Beach
District 88—(D)
Jones, Dennis—Seminole
District 54—(R)
Kelly, Everett A.—Tavares
District 42—(R)
Kilmer, Bev—Marianna
District 7—(R)
King, James E., Jr.—Jacksonville
District 17—(R)
Klein, Ron—Boca Raton
District 89—(D)
Kosmas, Suzanne—New Smyrna Beach
District 28—(D)
Kyle, Bruce—Fort Myers
District 73—(R)
Lacasa, Carlos—Miami
District 117—(R)
Laurent, John—Bartow
District 66—(R)
Lawson, Alfred, Jr.—Tallahassee
District 8—(D)
Lippman, Frederick—Hollywood
District 100—(D)
Littlefield, Ken—Dade City
District 61—(R)
Livingston, Ralph—Fort Myers
District 75—(R)
Logan, Willie—Opa-Locka
District 103—(D)
Lynn, Evelyn—Ormond Beach
District 27—(R)
Mackenzie, Anne—Fort Lauderdale
District 99—(D)
Maygarden, Jerry L.—Pensacola
District 2—(R)
Melvin, Jerry—Fort Walton Beach
District 4—(R)

Merchant, Sharon—North Palm
Beach
District 83—(R)
Miller, Jeff—Milton
District 1—(R)
Miller, Lesley, Jr.—Tampa
District 59—(D)
Minton, O. R., Jr.—Fort Pierce
District 78—(D)
Morroni, John—Clearwater
District 50—(R)
Morse, Luis—Miami
District 113—(R)
Murman, Sandra L.—Tampa
District 56—(R)
Ogles, Mark—Bradenton
District 67—(R)
Patterson, Pat—DeLand
District 26—(R)
Peaden, Durell—Crestview
District 5—(R)
Posey, Bill—Rockledge
District 32—(R)
Pruitt, Ken—Port St. Lucie
District 81—(R)
Putnam, Adam H.—Lakeland
District 63—(R)
Rayson, John—Pompano Beach
District 90—(D)
Reddick, Alzo—Orlando
District 39—(D)
Ritchie, DeeDee—Pensacola
District 3—(D)
Ritter, Stacy Joy—Coral Springs
District 96—(D)
Roberts-Burke, Beryl—Miami
District 108—(D)
Rodriguez-Chomat, Jorge—Miami
District 114—(R)
Rojas, Luis—Hialeah Gardens
District 102—(R)
Sanderson, Debby—Fort Lauderdale
District 91—(R)
Saunders, Burt—Naples
District 76—(R)
Sembler, Charles—Vero Beach
District 80—(R)
Sindler, Robert—Apopka
District 38—(D)
Smith, Kelley—Palatka
District 21—(D)
Sorenson, Ken—Key West
District 120—(R)

Spratt, Joe—Coral Springs
District 77—(D)
Stabins, Jeff—Spring Hill
District 44—(R)
Stafford, Tracy—Fort Lauderdale
District 92—(D)
Stansel, Dwight—Lake City
District 11—(D)
Starks, Bob—Casselberry
District 34—(R)
Sublette, Bill—Orlando
District 40—(R)
Thrasher, John—Orange Park
District 19—(R)
Tobin, Jack—Coconut Creek
District 95—(D)
Trovillion, Allen—Winter Park
District 36—(R)
Turnbull, Marjorie R.—Tallahassee
District 9—(D)
Valdes, Carlos—Miami
District 111—(R)
Villalobos, J. Alex—Miami
District 112—(R)
Wallace, Rob—Tampa
District 47—(R)
Warner, Tom—Stuart
District 82—(R)
Wasserman-Schultz, Debbie—Davie
District 97—(D)
Waters, Leslie—Pinellas Park
District 51—(R)
Webster, Daniel—Ocoee
District 41—(R)
Wiles, F. Douglas—St. Augustine
District 20—(D)
Wilson, Frederica S.—Miami
District 104—(D)
Wise, Stephen—Jacksonville
District 13—(R)
Vacant—Jacksonville
District 15

## HOW LAWS ARE MADE

All state laws must be enacted by the legislature, and each law is restricted to a single subject plus such details that are connected with that subject. A bill may originate in either the house or senate.

To be introduced by a house mem-ber, a bill must be prepared in proper form and delivered to the clerk of the house. The clerk assigns it a number, and it is then read on the house floor by its title only. After the title reading, it is referred by the house speaker to the appropriate committee for discussion.

The committee studies the bill, hearing witnesses for or against it. If the committee votes to recommend the bill not be passed, it will not be considered by the full house. (A two-thirds vote of the house, however, can bring the measure to the house floor.) If the committee recommends passage of the bill, the bill is placed on the house calendar for a second reading.

At this reading house members may vote their approval of the bill, in which case it is revised (engrossed) with amendments, if any, that house members want included. The bill is then placed on the house calendar for a third and final reading, during which it often is debated before the final vote on its fate.

Should the house vote for passage, the bill is sent to the senate where it undergoes the same treatment, that is, first reading, committee hearing, second reading, engrossment, third reading, and final vote.

Often the house and senate versions of the same bill will differ as a result of amendments and changes made after a committee hearing or floor debate. When this occurs, the differences in the bill are settled in a special conference committee whose members come from both the house and senate. Once the differences are ironed out, the final version is sent back to both the house and senate where it is again voted on for final passage.

Bills that pass both the house and senate are called "acts," and they are sent on to the governor for signature. The governor has three choices—sign the act and make it law, hold it for seven days and permit it to become law without signature, or veto it.

Vetoed "acts" are returned to the

legislature where both the house and senate can override the governor's veto. To override, each body must again pass the bill or "act" by a two-thirds majority.

## JUDICIAL BRANCH

Florida's judicial branch of state government consists of a series of courts with differing levels of authority and jurisdictions. Judicial power is vested in a Supreme Court, District Courts of Appeal, circuit courts, and county courts.

### Supreme Court

This highest of state courts consists of seven members. Each is appointed by the governor, but must submit to a statewide merit retention vote in the general election that occurs after the justice has served at least 12 months. The election provides a six-year term. Justices then select one of their number to be chief justice for a two-year term. Five justices constitute a quorum, but before decisions are reached, four members must concur, regardless of the number present.

The Supreme Court hears appeals directly from trial courts in criminal cases when the death penalty has been imposed; in civil cases when the trial court's decision passes on the validity of a state or federal law, a treaty, or on a provision of the state or federal constitutions, or in cases concerning the validity of revenue or general obligations bonds. All other appeals must be processed through a District Court of Appeals.

### District Court of Appeals

The state is divided into five appellate districts, each with a court of appeals. Each court has 9 to 13 judges elected to six-year staggered terms. Four judges may constitute a quorum but a majority of the total court members is required for it to reach a decision. The appeals courts have jurisdiction of all appeals not directly appealable to the Supreme Court or a circuit court. An appeals court also may issue writs of mandamus, certiorari, prohibition, quo warranto, and habeas corpus.

### Circuit Court

This court is the state's highest trial court, and the one with the most general jurisdiction. The state is divided into 20 judicial circuits, and circuit judges are elected to six-year terms. In each circuit the judges choose from among them a chief judge who is responsible for administrative supervision of the circuit and county courts in each circuit.

Circuit courts have exclusive original jurisdiction in all actions of law not vested in county courts. That includes all civil actions involving amounts in excess of $2,500. Circuit courts also cover proceedings relating to settlement of estates; competency and involuntary hospitalization; all cases in equity including all cases relating to juveniles except certain traffic cases; all cases involving legality of tax assessments or tolls; actions of ejectment; actions involving titles or boundaries or rights of possession of real property; all felonies or misdemeanors arising out of same circumstances as a felony; and jurisdiction over all appeals from county courts.

### County Court

At least one county court judge is specified for each county, and is elected to a four-year term. Vested in county courts is jurisdiction over all misdemeanor cases that the circuit court does not have authority to try, all violations of municipal ordinances, and all civil actions in which the amount involved is less than $2,500.

### SUPREME COURT JUSTICES
(Six-year Terms)

Leander J. Shaw . . (To January 2003)
Harry Lee
Arnstead  . . . . . . .(To January 2003)
Charles T. Wells  . .(To January 2003)
Peggy Ann
Quince . . . . . . . . .(To January 2005)
Major B. Harding  (To January 2005)
R. Fred Lewis . . . .(To January 2005)
Barbara Joan
Pariente  . . . . . . . .(To January 2005)

## DISTRICT COURTS OF APPEALS

**First Appellate District, Counties:** Escambia, Okaloosa, Santa Rosa, Walton, Franklin, Gadsden, Jefferson, Leon, Liberty, Wakulla, Columbia, Dixie, Hamilton, Lafayette, Madison, Suwannee, Taylor, Clay, Duval, Nassau, Alachua, Baker, Bradford, Gilchrist, Levy, Union, Bay, Calhoun, Gulf, Holmes, Jackson, and Washington.

**Second Appellate District, Counties:** Pasco, Pinellas, Hardee, Highlands, Polk, De Soto, Manatee, Sarasota, Hillsborough, Charlotte, Collier, Glades, Hendry, and Lee.

**Third Appellate District, Counties:** Miami-Dade and Monroe.

**Fourth Appellate District, Counties:** Palm Beach, Broward, Indian River, Martin, Okeechobee, and St. Lucie.

**Fifth Appellate District, Counties:** Citrus, Hernando, Lake, Marion, Sumter, Flagler, Putnam, St. Johns, Volusia, Orange, Osceola, Brevard, and Seminole.

## JUDICIAL CIRCUITS

**First:** Escambia, Okaloosa, Santa Rosa, and Walton counties.

**Second:** Franklin, Gadsden, Jefferson, Leon, Liberty, and Wakulla counties.

**Third:** Columbia, Dixie, Hamilton, Lafayette, Madison, Suwannee, and Taylor counties.

**Fourth:** Clay, Duval, and Nassau counties.

**Fifth:** Citrus, Hernando, Lake, Marion, and Sumter counties.

**Sixth:** Pasco and Pinellas counties.

**Seventh:** Flagler, Putnam, St. Johns, and Volusia counties.

**Eighth:** Alachua, Baker, Bradford, Gilchrist, Levy, and Union counties.

**Ninth:** Orange and Osceola counties.

**Tenth:** Hardee, Highlands, and Polk counties.

**Eleventh:** Miami-Dade County

**Twelfth:** De Soto, Manatee, and Sarasota counties.

**Thirteenth:** Hillsborough County.

**Fourteenth:** Bay, Calhoun, Gulf, Holmes, Jackson, and Washington counties.

**Fifteenth:** Palm Beach County.

**Sixteenth:** Monroe County.

**Seventeenth:** Broward County.

**Eighteenth:** Brevard and Seminole counties.

**Nineteenth:** Indian River, Martin, Okeechobee, and St. Lucie counties.

**Twentieth:** Charlotte, Collier, Glades, Hendry, and Lee counties.

## STATE AGENCIES

**Administration, Board of**
1801 Hermitage Boulevard
Tallahassee 32317

**Agriculture and Consumer Services, Department of**
The Capitol
Tallahassee 32399

**Attorney General**
The Capitol
Tallahassee 32399

**Auditor General**
111 W. Madison Street
Tallahassee 32302

**Banking & Finance, Department of**
101 E. Gaines Street
Tallahassee 32399

**Bar Examiners, Board of**
1891 Elder Court
Tallahassee 32399

**Business and Professional Regulation, Department of**
1940 N. Monroe Street
Tallahassee 32399

**Children and Family Services, Department of**
2639 North Monroe Street
Tallahassee 32399

**Citrus, Department of**
1115 E. Memorial Boulevard
Lakeland 33801

**Community Affairs, Department of**
2555 Shumard Boulevard
Tallahassee 32399

**Comptroller (see Banking)**

**Corrections, Department of**
2601 Blair Stone Road
Tallahassee 32399

**Education, Department of**
325 W. Gaines Street
Tallahassee 32399

**Elder Affairs, Department of**
The Capitol
Tallahassee 32399

Environmental Protection,
Department of
2600 Blair Stone Road
Tallahassee 32399
Ethics Commission
The Capitol
Tallahassee 32302
Executive Clemency, Office of
2822 Remington Green
Circle, #101
Tallahassee 32308
Fire Marshal (see Insurance)
Fish and Wildlife Conservation
Commission
620 S. Median Street
Tallahassee 32399
Governor
The Capitol
Tallahassee 32399
Health, Department of
2020 Capital Circle SE
Tallahassee 32399
Highway Safety and Motor Vehicles,
Department of
Neil Kirkman Building
Tallahassee 32399
Insurance, Department of
The Capitol
Tallahassee 32399
Juvenile Justice, Department of
2737 Centerview Drive
Tallahassee 32399
Labor and Employment Security,
Department of
Hartman Building
Tallahassee 32399
Law Enforcement, Department of
P.O. Box 1489
Tallahassee 32302

Legal Affairs, Department of
The Capitol
Tallahassee 32399
Lottery, Department of
250 Marriott Drive
Tallahassee 32301
Management Services,
Department of
4050 Esplanade Way
Tallahassee 32399
Military Affairs, Department of
State Arsenal
St. Augustine 32085
Parole Commission
1309 Winewood Boulevard
Tallahassee 32399
Prosecution Coordination Office
The Capitol
Tallahassee 32399
Public Counsel, Office of
111 West Madison Street
Tallahassee 32399
Public Service Commission
2540 Shumard Oak Boulevard
Tallahassee 32399
Revenue, Department of
Carlton Building
Tallahassee 32399
State, Department of
The Capitol
Tallahassee 32399
Transportation, Department of
Haydon Burns Building
Tallahassee 32399
Veterans Affairs, Department of
P.O. Box 1437
St. Petersburg 33731

## STATE SYMBOLS

### STATE TREE

Designated by the 1953 Legislature, the Sabal Palm (Sabal Palmetto) possesses a majesty that sets it apart from other trees. It is tolerant of a wide variety of soil types and grows throughout the state. The Sabal Palm played an important part in the early history of Florida, providing both food and shelter for the settlers. The young buds were eaten, the trunks were cut into logs for the walls of forts and homes, and leaves made weather-resistant roof thatching.

### POET LAUREATE

Edmund Skellings of Dania was appointed Florida's poet laureate in 1980.

### STATE THEATER

The 1965 Legislature established the Asolo Theater, in the Ringling

Museum complex at Sarasota, as the official "State Theater of Florida." Three other theaters in Florida are designated state theaters—the Hippodrome in Gainesville, the Caldwell Theatre Co. in Boca Raton, and the Coconut Grove Playhouse in Miami.

## STATE ART MUSEUM

Sarasota's John and Mabel Ringling Museum of Art was designated by the 1980 Legislature as Florida's official art museum.

## STATE NICKNAME

The state nickname, "Sunshine State," was adopted by the 1970 Legislature.

## STATE SONG

A legend has arisen surrounding composer Stephen Foster's famous song, "Old Folks at Home." The story goes that Foster needed the name of a river containing two syllables. He looked at a map of the southern part of the United States and his eyes fell on a Florida river, the "Suwannee," which had three syllables. He shortened it to "Swanee" and used it in the song, "Old Folks at Home," which was adopted as Florida's official song by the 1935 Legislature.

## STATE GEM AND STATE STONE

The 1970 Legislature named the moonstone as Florida's state gem on the occasion of the second moon landing, which originated from Cape Canaveral. In 1979, the Legislature added the agatized coral as the state stone.

## STATE SHELL

In 1969, the horse conch or giant band shell, known for its vibrant pinkish-orange coloring, was selected the state shell.

## STATE REPTILE

The alligator was named state reptile by the 1987 Legislature.

## STATE MARINE MAMMALS

The manatee, or sea cow, was chosen the state marine mammal by the 1975 Legislature. At the same time, the Legislature designated the dolphin as the state saltwater mammal.

## STATE BIRD

The 1927 Legislature chose the mockingbird to be the official state bird. A year-round Florida resident, this gray songster is an expert imitator of other birds' call notes. Its Latin name means "mimic of many tongues."

## STATE BUTTERFLY

The 1996 Legislature designated the Zebra Longwing as the state butterfly.

## STATE FLAG

The present state flag, which features the state seal garnished with diagonal red bars, was proposed in a constitutional amendment by the 1889 Legislature. Voters in 1900 approved the amendment and the existing state flag was officially adopted.

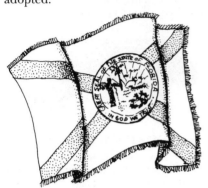

## STATE BEVERAGE

The 1967 Legislature declared "the juice obtained from mature oranges of the species citrus sinensus and hybrids is hereby adopted as the official beverage of the State of Florida."

## STATE LITTER CONTROL

The litter control symbol and official litter control trademark of the Florida Federation of Garden Clubs—"Glenn Glitter"—was adopted by the 1978 Legislature as the Florida litter control symbol.

## STATE ANIMAL

The Florida panther, a cousin of the mountain lion and an endangered species, was named state animal by the 1982 Legislature.

## STATE FISH

Two fish were adopted by the 1975 Legislature to be the official fish symbols for the state—the largemouth bass as the freshwater fish, and the Atlantic sailfish as the saltwater. No other state has two state fish.

## STATE FLOWER

As a tribute to the role of citrus in the state's economy, the 1909 Legislature proclaimed the orange blossom as the state flower.

## STATE WILDFLOWER

The coreopsis, a tall, yellow flower found in every county, was designated the state wildflower by the 1991 Legislature. The coreopsis is a periennial wildflower resembling the black-eyed Susan. It has a long blooming season and reseeds itself. The flower is a food source for seed-eating birds, and is neither toxic nor invasive.

## STATE SOIL

Mayakka Fine Sand, a deep sandy soil that covers 800,000 acres southward from St. Augustine on the east coast and Cedar Key on the west coast, was named the state's official soil by the 1989 Legislature.

## FLAGS OVER FLORIDA

The flags of five nations have flown over Florida: Spain, France, Great Britain, the United States, and the Confederate States of America.

Some historians say Florida's first state flag was designed by the "governor first elected," William D. Moseley, and flew for the first, and last, time at his inaugural ceremonies on June 25, 1845. It had five horizontal bars in blue, orange, red, white, and green, with the printed legend "Let Us Alone." It was never officially adopted as the state flag.

Prior to the War Between the States, various unofficial "secession" flags were being flown throughout the state, but at the 1868 Constitutional Convention an official state flag

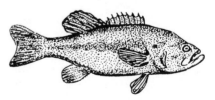

finally was designed. It bore the state's seal on a field of white.

The design was altered in 1900 when the state's voters okayed the addition of diagonal red bars. A minor change occurred in 1966 when voters voted to change the flag's dimensions so it would conform to the flag industry's rectangular standard.

## STATE SEAL

Before becoming a state, Florida, as a territory, had a seal. It was described as follows: "An American eagle with outspread wings, resting on a bed of clouds, occupies the center of a circular field. In the right talon of the eagle are three arrows, in the left an olive branch. Above the eagle is a semi-circle of 13 stars. Around the outer circle is the legend, 'The Territory of Florida.' The diameter of the seal is two inches."

When the territorial constitution of 1838 was adopted, seven years prior to Florida joining the Union, the framers stated the seal designed for the territory shall become the official seal for Florida when it becomes a state " . . . with such devices as the governor first elected may direct . . ."

It turned out the first-elected governor, William D. Moseley, did indeed have some "devices" for the seal that he wished to direct and he ordered a new seal. It was to be the first Great Seal of the State of Florida. Delivered to the secretary of state in December 1846, a year after statehood, it was ordered to replace the territory seal.

Records do not indicate who designed the new seal, nor is there a description of it. But from impressions on early official documents, it has been described as follows:

"An outline map of Florida occupies the top and right of a circular field. On an island in the lower left are one large and three small palm trees and an oak tree, under which sits a female figure with one hand outstretched to the Gulf of Mexico and the other holding a pike upon which rests a liberty cap. About her are casks and boxes and a variety of flowering shrubs. On the water are four ships— a three-masted square-rigger under full sail, another under jibs and topsails, a schooner, and a fishing shack. The legend around the outer rim is 'State of Florida—In God is Our Trust.' The diameter of the seal is two and three-fourths inches."

Gov. Moseley's seal was used during the War Between the States. And the 1865 constitution, which had the effect of taking Florida out of the Confederacy following the war, stated, "The state seal last heretofore used shall continue to be the Great Seal of the State." But in the 1868 constitution, which readmitted Florida to the Union, state officials ordered the legislature to "adopt a seal for the state, and such a seal shall be the size of the American silver dollar, but said seal shall not again be changed after its adoption by the legislature."

*Present Seal*

*1868 Seal*

Following these orders, the 1868 Legislature adopted a joint resolution that was approved by Gov. Harrison Reed that year. The resolution stated: "That a seal the size of the American silver dollar having in the center thereof a view of the sun's rays over a highland in the distance, a cocoa tree, a steamboat on water, and an Indian female scattering flowers in the foreground, encircled by the words, 'Great Seal of the State of Florida: In God We Trust,' be and the same is hereby adopted as the Great Seal of the State of Florida."

The 1885 constitution, under which the state operated until 1968, retained that seal. In the 1968 constitution revision, the design of the seal was formally made the legislature's responsibility. It since has chosen not to redesign it, but merely to refine it (in 1985), as shown on the previous page.

## STATE TAXES

Florida is prohibited by its constitution from levying a personal income tax. The state also has no inheritance tax. Among its major taxes are those listed below.

### Ad Valorem Tax

Statutes provide for the annual assessment and collection of ad valorem taxes on real and personal property. These taxes are assessed and collected at the county level as revenue for counties, municipalities, school districts, and special taxing districts.

Each year the county property appraiser is to determine the "just value" of all real property in the county as of Jan. 1. Factors determining "just value" include present cash value, use, location, quantity and size, cost or replacement value, and condition. On the basis of "just value," less exemptions and immunities, the tax due is computed by applying the millage rates established by the taxing authorities in that county. Counties are required to provide property owners with a TRIM (Truth in Millage) notice, which details past, present, and proposed taxation based on assessments.

The tax bill is mailed to the taxpayer usually no later than Nov. 1 and payment must be made to the tax collector by March 31 of the following year. Discounts are allowed for early payment. Payment on an installment plan is also usually offered.

### Homestead and Personal Exemptions

The state's constitution provides a series of exemptions from taxation on an owner-occupied home, condominium, or cooperative apartment.

Every person who has legal or equitable title to real property in the state and who resides thereon, and in good faith makes it his or her permanent home, is eligible for $25,000.00 homestead exemption. Applicants must reside on their property on January 1 of the current taxable year and apply for the exemption by March 1. Annual renewal of the exemption is automatic unless the status of the property changes.

An extra $500.00 exemption may be claimed by widows and by widowers, by non-veteran homeowners totally and permanently disabled, and by veteran homeowners with a 10 percent or greater disability if that disability is military service-connected.

Certain others are eligible for complete exemption from property taxes. They include quadriplegics; totally and permanently disabled veterans; totally disabled persons confined to a wheelchair; totally and permanently disabled persons who are blind, or who are partially blind but cannot meet an income test; and paraplegics and hemiplegics if their total household income does not exceed $14,500.00 annually.

SALES TAX BRACKETS EFFECTIVE
02/01/88 ON ALL 6% TAXABLE TRANSACTIONS
(FLORIDA DEPT. OF REVENUE)

| Amount of Sale | Tax | Amount of Sale | Tax | Amount of Sale | Tax | Amount of Sale | Tax |
|---|---|---|---|---|---|---|---|
| .10- .16 | .01 | 5.10- 5.16 | .31 | 10.10- 10.16 | .61 | 15.10- 15.16 | .91 |
| .17- .33 | .02 | 5.17- 5.33 | .32 | 10.17- 10.33 | .62 | 15.17- 15.33 | .92 |
| .34- .50 | .03 | 5.34- 5.50 | .33 | 10.34- 10.50 | .63 | 15.34- 15.50 | .93- |
| .51- .66 | .04 | 5.51- 5.66 | .34 | 10.51- 10.66 | .64 | 15.51- 15.66 | .94 |
| .67- .83 | .05 | 5.67- 5.83 | .35 | 10.67- 10.83 | .65 | 15.67- 15.83 | .95 |
| .84- 1.09 | .06 | 5.84- 6.09 | .36 | 10.84- 11.09 | .66 | 15.84- 16.09 | .96 |
| 1.10- 1.16 | .07 | 6.10- 6.16 | .37 | 11.10- 11.16 | .67 | 16.10- 16.16 | .97 |
| 1.17- 1.33 | .08 | 6.17- 6.33 | .38 | 11.17- 11.33 | .68 | 16.17- 16.33 | .98 |
| 1.34- 1.50 | .09 | 6.34- 6.50 | .39 | 11.34- 11.50 | .69 | 16.34- 16.50 | .99 |
| 1.51- 1.66 | .10 | 6.51- 6.66 | .40 | 11.51- 11.66 | .70 | 16.51- 16.66 | 1.00 |
| 1.67- 1.83 | .11 | 6.67- 6.83 | .41 | 11.67- 11.83 | .71 | 16.67- 16.83 | 1.01 |
| 1.84- 2.09 | .12 | 6.84- 7.09 | .42 | 11.84- 12.09 | .72 | 16.84- 17.09 | 1.02 |
| 2.10- 2.16 | .13 | 7.10- 7.16 | .43 | 12.10- 12.16 | .73 | 17.10- 17.16 | 1.03 |
| 2.17- 2.33 | .14 | 7.17- 7.33 | .44 | 12.17- 12.33 | .74 | 17.17- 17.33 | 1.04 |
| 2.34- 2.50 | .15 | 7.34- 7.50 | .45 | 12.34- 12.50 | .75 | 17.34- 17.50 | 1.05 |
| 2.51- 2.66 | .16 | 7.51- 7.66 | .46 | 12.51- 12.66 | .76 | 17.51- 17.66 | 1.06 |
| 2.67- 2.83 | .17 | 7.67- 7.83 | .47 | 12.67- 12.83 | .77 | 17.67- 17.83 | 1.07 |
| 2.84- 3.09 | .18 | 7.84- 8.09 | .48 | 12.84- 13.09 | .78 | 17.84- 18.09 | 1.08 |
| 3.10- 3.16 | .19 | 8.10- 8.16 | .49 | 13.10- 13.16 | .79 | 18.10- 18.16 | 1.09 |
| 3.17- 3.33 | .20 | 8.17- 8.33 | .50 | 13.17- 13.33 | .80 | 18.17- 18.33 | 1.10 |
| 3.34- 3.50 | .21 | 8.34- 8.50 | .51 | 13.34- 13.50 | .81 | 18.34- 18.50 | 1.11 |
| 3.51- 3.66 | .22 | 8.51- 8.66 | .52 | 13.51- 13.66 | .82 | 18.51- 18.66 | 1.12 |
| 3.67- 3.83 | .23 | 8.67- 8.83 | .53 | 13.67- 13.83 | .83 | 18.67- 18.83 | 1.13 |
| 3.84- 4.09 | .24 | 8.84- 9.09 | .54 | 13.84- 14.09 | .84 | 18.84- 19.09 | 1.14 |
| 4.10- 4.16 | .25 | 9.10- 9.16 | .55 | 14.10- 14.16 | .85 | 19.10- 19.16 | 1.15 |
| 4.17- 4.33 | .26 | 9.17- 9.33 | .56 | 14.17- 14.33 | .86 | 19.17- 19.33 | 1.16 |
| 4.34- 4.50 | .27 | 9.34- 9.50 | .57 | 14.34- 14.50 | .87 | 19.34- 19.50 | 1.17 |
| 4.51- 4.66 | .28 | 9.51- 9.66 | .58 | 14.51- 14.66 | .88 | 19.51- 19.66 | 1.18 |
| 4.67- 4.83 | .29 | 9.67- 9.83 | .59 | 14.67- 14.83 | .89 | 19.67- 19.83 | 1.19 |
| 4.84- 5.09 | .30 | 9.84- 10.09 | .60 | 14.84- 15.09 | .90 | 19.84- 20.09 | 1.20 |

## Beverage Tax

| Type of Beverage | Alcohol by Volume | Excise Tax Per Gallon |
|---|---|---|
| Beer | —— | $ .48 |
| Wine | less than 17.2% | $2.25 |
| Wine | 17.2% or more | $3.00 |
| Sparkling Wine | all | $3.50 |
| Wine Coolers | all | $2.25 |
| Liquor | under 17.2% | $2.25 |
| Liquor | 17.2% to 55.7% | $6.50 |
| Liquor | 55.7% or more | $9.53 |

## Cigarette Tax

Cigarettes of common size are taxed at 33.9 cents a package. For larger sizes and non-standard packs, the rate is 42.4 cents a package. All non-cigarettes tobacco products other than cigars are taxed at the rate of 25 percent of the wholesale sales price.

## Citrus Tax

A tax of 35 cents per box is imposed on grapefruit, 29 cents on oranges, and 35 cents on all other varieties. For processed fruit the tax is 35 cents a box on grapefruit, 16.5 cents on oranges, and 16.5 cents on all other varieties. Revenues are used to promote Florida citrus products. The tax is paid by growers and processors.

## Documentary Stamp Tax

On promissory notes, mortgages, trust deeds, security agreements, and other written promises to pay money, the tax imposed is 35 cents per $100; on documents that convey an interest in realty, the tax imposed is 70 cents per $100.

## Drivers' Licenses

(A schedule of fees is listed in the Motoring section.)

## Estate Taxes

Florida has no inheritance tax; however, any estate with a gross value of $600,000 or more must file a federal estate tax return. If the estate also has Florida property, it must file a copy of the federal estate tax return with Florida and pay any Florida estate tax due.

## Hunting and Fishing Licenses

(A schedule of licenses for various types of hunting and fishing, for residents and nonresidents, is in the Hunting and Fishing section.)

## Intangible Tax

Stocks, bonds, notes, and the like are taxed at 2 mills annually, mortgages at 2 mills at time of recording.

A 2-mill tax is also imposed on obligations secured by liens on Florida realty. Each taxpayer and spouse is granted a $20,000 exemption annually.

## Local Option Tax

**Transit Surtax:** Eligible counties may impose, if approved by referendum, a 1 percent sales surtax on a transit system's transactions.

**Convention Development:** Eligible counties may impose a 1 to 3 percent tax on transient rentals.

**Gasoline:** Any county may levy up to six cents per gallon upon majority vote of the county commission. An additional one cent per gallon may be imposed upon approval in a countywide referendum.

**Tourist Development:** A county, upon referendum approval, may impose a 1 to 5 percent tax on rental charges in the county. In addition, the county may charge another 1 percent tourist impact tax on referendum approval.

## Motorboat Licenses

(Cost of licenses for varying size boats is in the Boating section.)

## Motor Fuel Tax

The tax rates on gasoline include 18.4 cents federal, 12.1 cents state, 9.5 cents county, and 2 cents state pollution tax. Each county, subject to a referendum, may levy a tax of 1 cent on motor fuel, special fuel, and alternative fuels.

## Motor Vehicle Licenses

(Rates differ for all types and weights of vehicles. See Motoring section for specific rates.)

## Pari-Mutuel Tax

Tax on the handle (total amount) for a regular season of racing is as follows: horse racing, 3.3 percent of handle; jai-alai, 7.1 percent of handle; and greyhounds, 7.6 percent of handle. In addition, the state imposes a $100 license fee per horserace, $80 per jai-alai game, and $80 per greyhound race. An admissions tax of 15 percent also is charged patrons at pari-mutuel facilities.

**Sales Tax**

The greatest amount of state revenue is derived from a 6 percent tax on retail sales. Some counties have voted an additional sales tax of up to 1 percent.

**Corporate Income Tax**

A tax based on net income is imposed on all domestic and foreign corporations, associations, financial institutions, and other artificial entities. Individuals, partnerships, estates, and private trusts are not subject to the tax.

## COUNTY TAX COMPARISON

The following chart ranks Florida counties highest to lowest by average millage rates assessed. Millage is the rate at which property is taxed for ad valorem purposes. One mill equals $1 of tax per $1,000 of assessed property value.

The columns at right indicate taxable property values within each county and rank of county according to revenue. Homeowners receive a $25,000 "homestead" exemption.

| Rank | County | Average Millage | Taxable Property Value (thousands) | Rank by Revenue |
|---|---|---|---|---|
| 1 | Baker | 23.2464 | 185,018 | (59) |
| 2 | Sarasota | 23.0540 | 15,879,017 | (10) |
| 3 | Alachua | 22.4314 | 3,564,471 | (30) |
| 4 | Hendry | 22.2900 | 883,252 | (40) |
| 5 | Duval | 22.0448 | 17,318,517 | (8) |
| 6 | Wakulla | 21.3140 | 232,622 | (56) |
| 7 | Hardee | 20.8800 | 474,187 | (46) |
| 8 | Union | 20.6704 | 70,839 | (66) |
| 9 | Columbia | 20.4204 | 637,971 | (42) |
| 10 | Gilchrist | 20.2434 | 151,146 | (63) |
| 11 | Pasco | 20.2240 | 6,265,816 | (18) |
| 12 | Sumter | 20.0890 | 453,359 | (47) |
| 13 | Dixie | 20.0124 | 158,707 | (61) |
| 14 | St. Lucie | 20.0098 | 5,882,862 | (19) |
| 15 | Hamilton | 19.7604 | 206,315 | (57) |
| 16 | Lafayette | 19.7434 | 79,087 | (65) |
| 17 | Leon | 19.5510 | 5,328,947 | (21) |
| 18 | Glades | 19.3380 | 284,741 | (53) |
| 19 | Gadsden | 19.2960 | 412,704 | (49) |
| 20 | Hernando | 19.1730 | 3,038,351 | (31) |
| 21 | Okeechobee | 19.1367 | 707,224 | (41) |
| 22 | Suwannee | 18.9864 | 378,443 | (50) |
| 23 | Broward | 18.8401 | 48,036,889 | (3) |
| 24 | Jefferson | 18.7884 | 164,864 | (60) |
| 25 | Escambia | 18.7580 | 4,339,301 | (27) |
| 26 | Putnam | 18.6860 | 1,226,884 | (39) |
| 27 | Miami-Dade | 18.5930 | 67,803,042 | (1) |
| 28 | Hillsborough | 18.4572 | 21,474,535 | (6) |
| 29 | Levy | 18.3590 | 591,035 | (43) |
| 30 | Pinellas | 18.2297 | 21,474,535 | (5) |
| 31 | Citrus | 18.0600 | 2,887,865 | (32) |
| 32 | Manatee | 17.8804 | 7,914,378 | (15) |
| 33 | De Soto | 17.8550 | 543,646 | (44) |
| 34 | Clay | 17.8426 | 2,564,500 | (33) |

| 35 | Liberty | 17.8220 | 58,351 | (67) |
| 36 | Highlands | 17.7480 | 1,979,732 | (36) |
| 37 | Madison | 17.7334 | 200,515 | (58) |
| 38 | St. Johns | 17.7280 | 4,336,130 | (28) |
| 39 | Washington | 17.6710 | 238,978 | (55) |
| 40 | Volusia | 17.5810 | 11,267,736 | (12) |
| 41 | Taylor | 17.5594 | 353,843 | (51) |
| 42 | Polk | 17.3060 | 8,759,180 | (14) |
| 43 | Bradford | 17.0220 | 281,906 | (54) |
| 44 | Flagler | 16.8500 | 2,040,714 | (35) |
| 45 | Calhoun | 16.7090 | 133,720 | (64) |
| 46 | Franklin | 16.5420 | 436,490 | (48) |
| 47 | Palm Beach | 16.4997 | 50,329,078 | (2) |
| 48 | Nassau | 16.4891 | 1,532,838 | (38) |
| 49 | Walton | 16.2720 | 1,768,503 | (37) |
| 50 | Seminole | 16.1962 | 10,033,515 | (13) |
| 51 | Osceola | 16.1275 | 4,863,673 | (23) |
| 52 | Santa Rosa | 16.0210 | 2,373,507 | (34) |
| 53 | Gulf | 15.8870 | 321,713 | (52) |
| 54 | Indian River | 15.7458 | 5,313,363 | (21) |
| 55 | Martin | 15.6000 | 6,965,860 | (16) |
| 56 | Jackson | 15.5690 | 499,631 | (45) |
| 57 | Bay | 15.1800 | 3,599,983 | (29) |
| 58 | Marion | 15.1480 | 4,694,574 | (24) |
| 59 | Holmes | 15.0210 | 155,755 | (62) |
| 60 | Lake | 14.9890 | 4,423,650 | (26) |
| 61 | Brevard | 14.9865 | 12,372,735 | (11) |
| 62 | Lee | 14.7843 | 19,085,834 | (7) |
| 63 | Orange | 14.6639 | 29,701,996 | (4) |
| 64 | Charlotte | 14.1785 | 5,654,146 | (20) |
| 65 | Monroe | 13.1640 | 6,853,531 | (17) |
| 66 | Okaloosa | 13.1640 | 4,486,337 | (25) |
| 67 | Collier | 12.5895 | 16,038,210 | (9) |

## FINANCE

Florida is but one of the states required by its constitution to operate on a balanced budget, allowing deficits only within the confines of long-term bonded indebtedness.

The state's greatest source of revenue is its 6 percent sales tax collected on the sale of all goods except unprepared foods, prescription medicines, and some services. But a tax based solely on consumer spending leaves the state budget very much at the mercy of the general economy.

However, since that has always been the case, the government, with the aid of the Florida Economic Consensus Estimating Conference, has learned not only to live with the situation but to live within it. If that panel sees that on-going revenues are insufficient to cover appropriated state spending, such spending is curbed into balance until projected revenues indicate it can resume. The conference has predicted slower growth for Florida in 2000, but still slightly better than for the U.S. as a whole.

Florida does not have an income tax, as it is specifically banned by the state constitution. Florida has numerous other taxes and fees but many are required by law to fund specific purposes.

Florida's finances are operated through "funds." The state's major funds are the General Fund, used for most normal government functions; the Special Revenue Funds (there are several), which handle revenues that are legally restricted to expenditures for specific purposes; Capital Projects Funds, Debt Service Funds, and Fiduciary Funds, in which the state acts as trustee or agent for both governmental and private organizations.

Florida government also operates Enterprise Funds, of which the largest is the Florida Lottery. As "Enterprise" implies, these are funds that function as would private sector businesses. State-owned and operated enterprises netted $1.1 billion in fiscal year 1998.

In all, Florida operates 170 component units. These are legally separate units for which the state is financially accountable, including joint ventures, non-profit organizations, and public-private partnerships. Primarily dealing with education, their financial operations are part of the public record. They are all on the books primarily to keep the state budget from being misleading or incomplete in the eyes of officials, legislators, or the public.

Ad valorem taxes are reserved to the counties, which also get a share of the sales tax and have the option of adding up to an additional one percent within their confines. The counties are also the major recipients in the state's spending, primarily through their school systems.

Generally, health and social service spending makes for the largest state expenditure by function. It accounted for 35 percent of the state's budget in fiscal 1998. Education spending took up 27 percent, while the operation of the government itself declined to 11 percent. Capital outlays increased to account for 8 percent of the budget, public safety declined to 7 percent, and other costs incurred by government took 12 percent.

Taxes again accounted for 61 percent of the state's governmental revenues in 1998. Fees and similar

charges increased slightly to 7 percent, while licenses and permits remained at 3 percent. "Other" income accounted for 4 percent. After taxes, the second largest revenue generator was grants and donations, which provided 25 percent of the state's operating revenues.

Florida's state government spending for FY98 increased to $33.4 billion. But its income for the period was $35.8 billion, providing the state with "surplus revenues" again.

The governmental fund, the General Fund, has a balance of $9.2 billion, an increase of $2 billion over Fiscal Year 1997. Unreserved funs equaled $6.08 billion at the end of the fiscal year, a $1.13 billion increase over the previous year.

One of the most remarkable aspects of Florida's finances is the Working Capital Fund, where some surplus revenues go. The fund is so obscure that even legislators and leaders have to be reminded in official documents of the fund's popular nickname: the Rainy Day Fund. So beyond non-partisan as to be ecumenical, the Rainy Day Fund is reserved for genuine crisis. (There is a similar fund just for hurricanes that contained $2.2 billion at the beginning of FY99.) The Rainy Day Fund has not been used to kite a budget or to cover a deficit. The state also holds a wide variety of reserves for anticipated expenses.

Surplus, reserve, and trust revenues don't remain idle. The State Treasurer invests the money of the state, counties, and other units in certificates of deposit in Florida banks, direct obligations of the U.S. Treasury, commercial paper and banker's acceptances, medium-term corporate notes, and commingled and mutual funds. At the end of FY98, Florida had more than $14 billion working.

Entering fiscal 1999, Florida maintained a high bond rating from Moody's Investor Services (Aa2), Standard and Poor's Corp. (AA+), and Fitch IBAC, Inc. (AA). Outstanding general obligation bonds at June 30, 1997, totaled $13.7 billion. Most were issued to finance capital outlay for educational projects of local school districts, community colleges, and state universities. Some went for infrastructure and environmental projects. Most Florida bonds reach maturity in the second decade of the new century.

The state does not count as assets those it considers priceless and irreplaceable, such as its vast collections of everything from art to artifacts.

As of mid-1998, Florida had pension assets of $83.8.8 billion, funding 91.25 percent of its obligation.

Florida self-insures its general liability, its real capital assets, its employee health care and its medical professional exposure with commercial insurance backup. Florida operates hospitals and medical centers through its universities including medical, dental, and veterinary schools. As of July 1998, it had a total exposure of $675.2 million.

### FY98 FLORIDA REVENUES
#### (in thousands)

| | |
|---|---:|
| Taxes | $21,895,836 |
| Licenses and permits | 908,028 |
| Fees and charges | 2,582,493 |
| Grants and donations | 8,933,147 |
| Investment earnings | 589,347 |
| Fines, forfeitures, judgments | 338,908 |
| Flexible benefits contributions | 56,505 |
| Refunds | 537,394 |
| Other | 7,860 |
| **TOTAL** | **$35,849,518** |

### FY98 SPENDING
#### (in thousands)

| | |
|---|---:|
| Economic opportunities, agriculture & employment | $922,992 |
| Public safety | 2,477,335 |
| Education | 9,034,923 |
| Health & social concerns | 11,778,321 |
| Housing & community development | 168,915 |
| Natural resources & environmental management | 614,329 |
| Recreation & culture | 150,813 |
| Transportation | 871,040 |
| Gov't. direction & support | 3,754,842 |
| Capital outlay | 2,694,903 |
| Debt service | 904,607 |
| **TOTAL** | **$33,373,020** |

### TAX REVENUES BY SOURCE
#### (in thousands)

| | 1997 | 1998 |
|---|---:|---:|
| Sales tax | $12,113,145 | $13,349,272 |
| Motor fuel tax | 1,438,264 | 1,518,286 |
| Corporate income tax | 1,358,387 | 1,395,566 |
| Intangible personal property tax | 980,914 | 1,164,297 |
| Documentary stamp tax | 864,216 | 1,005,378 |

| | | |
|---|---|---|
| Unemployment compensation tax | | 573,381 |
| Alcoholic beverage tax | 553,919 | 566,277 |
| Gross receipts utility tax | 585,466 | 638,077 |
| Cigarette tax | 431,221 | 444,838 |
| Estate tax | 568,875 | 563,665 |
| Insurance premium tax | 417,775 | 426,511 |
| Hospital public assistance tax | 253,725 | 272,722 |
| Workers Compensation special disability tax | 85,807 | 207,609 |
| Pollutant tax | 213,843 | 215,992 |
| Pari-mutuel wagering tax | 64,835 | 63,526 |
| Citrus excise tax | 68,379 | 65,026 |
| Solid materials severance tax | 64,680 | 61,269 |
| Aviation fuel tax | 55,766 | 16,623 |
| Utility regulatory tax | 27,173 | 27,898 |
| Smokeless tobacco tax | 19,287 | 21,001 |
| Oil & gas production tax | 10,472 | 6,539 |
| Other | 1,175 | 1,365 |
| **TOTAL** | **$20,177,324** | **$22,605,110** |

## LOW TAX

Sixteen counties in Florida collect the 6 percent state sales tax without an additional local option added to it. The counties are: Alachua, Brevard, Broward, Citrus, Collier, Franklin, Hernando, Lee, Marion, Orange, Palm Beach, Pasco, Polk, Putnam, St. Johns, and Volusia.

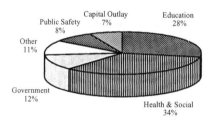

**Expenditures by Function - 1997**

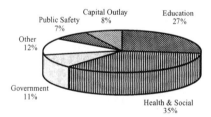

**Expenditures by Function - 1998**

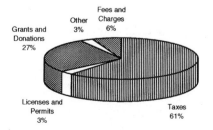

**Revenue Sources - 1997**

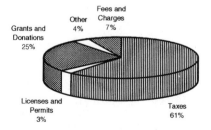

**Revenue Sources - 1998**

## CITY GOVERNMENT

Cities or municipalities are "creatures of the legislature," explains the Supreme Court. It refers to the fact that the constitution states, "Municipalities may be established or abolished . . . their charters amended" by the legislature. The legislature has the power by "general or specific law" to control the operation of a city, to abolish it, to change its charter, to incorporate in it any restrictions it desires, even to enact a law concerning a city.

Use of this power is, of course, tempered by a city's voter control over their members of the legislature at election time.

There are two ways to establish a municipality in Florida. One is for the legislature to grant a specific charter under state law, usually a special law applying to only one city. The other method is for freeholders (property owners) in an area to establish a city under a general charter, as provided for under a general law of the state.

The first method calls for the legislature, after having advertised its intention of passing a law to create a city, or after having provided for a referendum among affected citizens, to pass a law giving the new city its charter. Most such laws encompass a referendum seeking approval of residents affected.

The second method permits "freeholders and registered voters of any hamlet, village or town not less than 1,000 in number . . . to establish for themselves a municipal government." In most cases, cities are established in Florida by the first, rather than the second, method. That is because the incorporation requirements under the second method are cumbersome.

Florida has many communities that have features of a city but not the legal status of one. Some of these "cities" even boast populations greater than established municipalities. Usually, residents of these large communities prefer to remain unincorporated for tax purposes. To live in an incorporated area or city means to be subject to additional taxes, that is, a city resident must pay not only county and school board taxes but also the city's taxes.

Increasingly, residents of unincorporated areas rely heavily on the county government for services often afforded by a city government, and a growing number of counties levy additional taxes on residents of areas that receive city-type services.

Three types of municipal government are prevalent in Florida—council/manager, council/mayor, and the commission.

Most popular is the council/manager type, particularly in larger cities. Day-to-day operation of the government is assigned to the full-time city manager, who is appointed by the elected council members. He or she does not make policy, but implements it as it comes from the council. The manager often is a professional, someone trained and educated in municipal government operations. A council/manager type may have a mayor, but his or her duties often are limited to presiding at meetings and representing the city at ceremonial functions. He or she does not have any more power, or a greater vote, than any council member. The mayor's selection often is made by the council members, and the position often is rotated among the members.

In the council/mayor type of government, the mayor is the chief administrative officer. Elected separately from the council, he or she is responsible only to the voters. Under this form the mayor usually has veto powers over the council, but his or her veto can be overridden.

The commission type is generally found in smaller cities. Commission members are elected by voters and not only set city policy but administer it as well. One commissioner may be responsible for roads, another for parks, and so on. Charters of most cities incorporate features from all three types of government.

## LIVING WILL

Under Florida law, adults have the right to make certain decisions concerning medical treatment and to have that right and their wishes respected if they are too ill to make such decisions themselves at the time, codified as a Living Will.

Persons have the right, under certain conditions, to decide whether to accept or reject medical treatment, including whether to continue medical treatment and/or other procedures that would prolong their lives artificially. A Living Will contains a person's personal directions about life-prolonging treatment in the case of serious illness that could cause death.

A person may also designate another person, or surrogate, who may make decisions for them if he or she becomes mentally or physically unable to do so. This surrogate may function on the ill person's behalf for a brief time, or longer for a life threatening or a non-life threatening illness. Clear limits may be put on what a surrogate may do.

The 1999 legislature strengthened the law by adding "end-stage" condition to the situations that would trigger the provisions of a living will and specified feeding and hydration as "life prolonging procedures" that a living will could prevent.

## LEGAL HOLIDAYS

The following holidays, provided by Florida statutes, are observed as paid-holidays by state agencies:

New Year's Day—January 1
Martin Luther King, Jr.'s birthday—third Monday in January
Memorial Day—observed last Monday in May
Independence Day—July 4
Labor Day—observed on first Monday in September
Veterans Day—November 11
Thanksgiving—observed the Friday after Thanksgiving Day
Christmas—December 25

(If any of these holidays fall on Saturday, the preceding Friday is observed as the holiday. If any fall on Sunday, the following Monday is observed as the holiday.)

Florida statutes also prescribe other "legal" holidays, days that institutions and individuals may or may not choose to observe. They are:

Robert E. Lee's birthday—January 19
Lincoln's birthday—February 12
Susan B. Anthony's birthday—February 15
Washington's birthday (Presidents' Day)—observed third Monday in February
Good Friday
Confederate Memorial Day—April 26
Jefferson Davis' birthday—June 3
Flag Day—June 14
Columbus Day—second Monday in October
General Elections Day—first Tuesday after first Monday in November

## POPULATION CENTER

Florida's center of population—the point from which an equal number of people live east, west, north, and south—is shifting northward. In 1989, the center was reported to be in central Polk County near the town of Homeland. For years, the center had been moving south. In 1950 it was just east of Zephyrhills along the Pasco-Polk county line; in 1960 it slid 25 miles southeast of the 1950 center, in a spot just west of Haines City in Polk County. By 1970 the population center had moved another 16 miles southwest to an area just south of Lake Garfield in Polk County. And between 1970 and 1980 the center, although moving only six miles but again to the south, was pegged at Lake Buffum in Polk County. The 1989 shift of the center northward is the first time in the state's history that the movement was not toward the south. Demographic experts believe the population's northward movement is due to lack of room for expansion in Miami-Dade, Broward, and Palm Beach counties on the southeast coast and a growing flight of residents from congested metropolitan areas.

---

## TRADE

Florida ranked 8th among the states in 1998 in exports to other nations, according to the U.S. Department of Commerce. That year it exported $24.4 billion in goods.

### FLORIDA'S TOP EXPORT DESTINATIONS

1. Brazil
2. Venezuela
3. Columbia
4. Argentina
5. Dominican Republic
6. Honduras
7. Costa Rica
8. Chile
9. Guatemala
10. Peru

### FLORIDA'S TOP SOURCES OF IMPORTS

1. Japan
2. Dominican Republic
3. Brazil
4. Germany
5. Honduras
6. Costa Rica
7. Columbia
8. Mexico
9. Guatemala
10. France

### FLORIDA'S TOP EXPORT PRODUCTS

1. Machinery
2. Electrical machinery
3. Passenger Vehicles
4. Optical, medical instruments
5. Woven apparel
6. Fertilizer
7. Aircraft, spacecraft
8. Knit apparel
9. Plastics
10 Pharmaceutical products

### FLORIDA'S TOP IMPORTED PRODUCTS

1. Passenger vehicles
2. Woven apparel
3. Knit apparel
4. Machinery
5. Electrical machinery
6. Aircraft, spacecraft
7. Fish, Seafood
8. Mineral fuel, oil, etc.
9. Precious stones, metals
10. Organic chemicals

# ELECTIONS

## VOTER REGULATIONS

Any U.S. citizen who is at least 18 years old, or who will turn 18 before an election and who is a permanent Florida resident and resides in the county where he or she wishes to register, is eligible to vote in Florida.

If any questions arise at registration time regarding the person's eligibility, the supervisor of elections may require proof of qualification.

Persons not entitled to vote are those not registered, those judged mentally incompetent, and those convicted of a felony who have not had their civil rights restored.

### ELECTIONS 2000

Presidential Preference
Primary . . . . . . . . . . .March 14
First Primary . . . . . . .September 5
Second Primary . . . . .October 3
General Election . . . .November 7

In addition, some Florida cities will hold municipal elections in the spring of 2000.

### VOTING TERMS

"Primary election" means the election preceding the general election, and held to select a party nominee. The first primary is a nomination or elimination election; the second primary, often called the "runoff primary," is sometimes necessary when no candidates in the first primary receive a majority of the votes cast so that the two top vote-getters must vie again for their party's nomination.

"General election" means an election held on the first Tuesday after the first Monday in November in the even-numbered years for the purpose of elective offices and voting on constitutional amendments.

"Elector" is synonymous with the word voter.

A "freeholder" is a person who owns taxable property in the state.

"Absentee voter" is a voter who votes by absentee ballot prior to election day for one or more of the following reasons:

(a) Is unable to go to the polls without another's assistance, usually due to physical disability.

(b) Is a voting inspector, poll worker, or is serving in a capacity requiring assignment at a different precinct on voting day than the precinct in which the person is registered to vote.

(c) Cannot attend the polls on election day for reasons of religion.

(d) Has changed residency to another county after the registration books are closed.

(e) Will not be in the county where registered on election day.

A person who moves out of the county in which he or she is registered into another Florida county, after registration books are closed, is permitted to vote by absentee ballot in the old county in national and state races.

A person moving to another state after registration books are closed is permitted to vote by absentee ballot in Florida for national races if the person's new state deems he or she is not yet eligible there as a voter.

*Present Seal*

*1868 Seal*

## REGISTERED VOTERS
### (As of July 1999)

| County | Republican | Democrat | Minor | None | Total |
|---|---|---|---|---|---|
| Alachua | 28,590 | 56,657 | 1,581 | 13,235 | 100,063 |
| Baker | 1,235 | 9,522 | 64 | 273 | 11,094 |
| Bay | 30,641 | 42,793 | 3,307 | 8,670 | 85,411 |
| Bradford | 2,533 | 9,415 | 40 | 863 | 12,851 |
| Brevard | 131,684 | 110,582 | 6,698 | 36,118 | 285,082 |
| Broward | 257,988 | 430,556 | 1,052 | 135,852 | 825,448 |
| Calhoun | 551 | 5,751 | 45 | 146 | 6,493 |
| Charlotte | 44,843 | 30,892 | 1,976 | 12,802 | 90,513 |
| Citrus | 30,566 | 32,243 | 1,534 | 11,251 | 75,594 |
| Clay | 43,084 | 23,021 | 1,059 | 9,714 | 76,878 |
| Collier | 67,031 | 28,147 | 2,530 | 17,436 | 115,144 |
| Columbia | 7,963 | 19,595 | 535 | 2,187 | 30,280 |
| Desoto | 3,521 | 9,718 | 530 | 958 | 14,727 |
| Dixie | 945 | 8,729 | 175 | 175 | 10,024 |
| Duval | 151,631 | 217,918 | 10,590 | 44,899 | 425,038 |
| Escambia | 67,068 | 80,782 | 3,647 | 16,291 | 167,788 |
| Flagler | 12,385 | 11,881 | 528 | 4,314 | 29,108 |
| Franklin | 862 | 5,862 | 32 | 302 | 7,058 |
| Gadsden | 2,340 | 20,780 | 193 | 815 | 24,128 |
| Gilchrist | 1,545 | 5,635 | 71 | 513 | 7,764 |
| Glades | 1,209 | 4,112 | 162 | 228 | 5,711 |
| Gulf | 1,518 | 7,726 | 61 | 358 | 9,663 |
| Hamilton | 600 | 5,892 | 56 | 142 | 6,690 |
| Hardee | 2,075 | 7,515 | 101 | 462 | 10,153 |
| Hendry | 4,140 | 9,846 | 236 | 1,218 | 15,440 |
| Hernando | 41,412 | 38,602 | 1,357 | 14,336 | 95,707 |
| Highlands | 23,776 | 23,177 | 1,422 | 5,408 | 53,783 |
| Hillsborough | 169,626 | 209,902 | 9,215 | 68,371 | 457,114 |
| Holmes | 973 | 8,127 | 47 | 254 | 9,401 |
| Indian River | 37,443 | 21,648 | 1,539 | 7,879 | 68,509 |
| Jackson | 4,037 | 19,813 | 187 | 969 | 25,006 |
| Jefferson | 1,076 | 5,826 | 89 | 236 | 7,227 |
| Lafayette | 230 | 3,522 | 0 | 79 | 3,831 |
| Lake | 58,885 | 42,904 | 2,426 | 13,680 | 117,895 |
| Lee | 120,041 | 79,175 | 4,479 | 37,459 | 241,154 |
| Leon | 35,896 | 78,692 | 2,334 | 12,694 | 129,616 |
| Levy | 3,907 | 11,246 | 354 | 801 | 16,308 |
| Liberty | 148 | 3,275 | 4 | 43 | 3,470 |
| Madison | 1,150 | 8,126 | 88 | 168 | 9,532 |
| Manatee | 75,256 | 55,271 | 554 | 25,484 | 156,565 |
| Marion | 57,350 | 58,069 | 4,384 | 15,005 | 134,808 |
| Martin | 46,319 | 22,201 | 2,203 | 10,804 | 81,527 |
| Miami-Dade | 318,777 | 389,654 | 1,871 | 131,111 | 841,413 |
| Monroe | 18,677 | 19,767 | 1,781 | 8,026 | 48,251 |
| Nassau | 12,257 | 16,174 | 622 | 2,348 | 31,401 |
| Okaloosa | 58,172 | 30,675 | 555 | 14,771 | 104,173 |
| Okeechobee | 6,025 | 14,785 | 293 | 1,484 | 22,587 |
| Orange | 153,009 | 149,159 | 7,833 | 52,685 | 362,686 |
| Oseceola | 30,100 | 34,857 | 3,396 | 13,749 | 82,102 |
| Palm Beach | 226,395 | 281,208 | 14,532 | 100,294 | 622,429 |

| | | | | |
|---|---|---|---|---|
| Pasco | 89,822 | 89,865 | 511 | 38,671 | 218,869 |
| Pinellas | 245,838 | 217,168 | 17,331 | 95,025 | 575,362 |
| Polk | 96,887 | 118,533 | 3,417 | 28,920 | 247,757 |
| Putnam | 9,661 | 25,309 | 1,042 | 2,815 | 38,827 |
| Santa Rosa | 33,415 | 26,804 | 1,513 | 6,623 | 68,355 |
| Sarasota | 110,566 | 63,273 | 3,346 | 29,666 | 206,851 |
| Seminole | 93,820 | 63,893 | 3,722 | 28,522 | 189,957 |
| St. Johns | 40,505 | 29,635 | 1,759 | 11,005 | 82,904 |
| St. Lucie | 53,936 | 57,791 | 5,461 | 19,151 | 136,339 |
| Sumter | 9,729 | 13,518 | 467 | 3,009 | 26,723 |
| Suwanee | 3,996 | 14,246 | 1,140 | 455 | 19,837 |
| Taylor | 1,530 | 10,070 | 134 | 302 | 12,036 |
| Union | 583 | 5,287 | 31 | 142 | 6,043 |
| Volusia | 99,974 | 114,657 | 5,400 | 37,064 | 257,095 |
| Wakulla | 2,139 | 9,473 | 130 | 527 | 12,269 |
| Walton | 8,677 | 15,273 | 494 | 2,443 | 26,887 |
| Washington | 2,219 | 10,547 | 210 | 539 | 13,515 |

**TOTALS: ... 3,300,782 .. 3,706,767 ... 144,476 ... 1,162,239 ... 8,314,264**

There are 11 minor parties recognized by the state: the American Party, the Conservative Party, Florida Socialist Workers, the Green Party, the Independence Party of Florida, the Independent Party, Libertarian Party, Natural Law Party, Reform Party, Reform Silly Party, and United States Taxpayers. Most registered voters who consider themselves "Independents" are actually registered as "Not Affiliated." Florida moves from Closed to Open primary elections in 2000.

## MAJOR ELECTIVE OFFICES

| Office | Term | Salary | Requirements |
|---|---|---|---|
| **U.S. Senate** | Six years | $136,600 | Must be at least 30 years old, a U.S. citizen for nine years, and a Florida resident. |
| **U.S. House** | Two years | $136,600 | Must be at least 25 years old, a U.S. citizen for seven years, and a Florida resident. |
| **Governor** | Four years | $110,961 | Must be at least 30 years old and a Florida resident for seven years. |
| **Lt. Governor** | Four years | $106,296 | Must be at least 30 years old and a Florida resident for seven years. |
| **State Cabinet** | Four years | $106,870 | Must be at least 30 years old and a Florida resident for seven years. |
| **Attorney General** | — | — | Must be a member of the Florida Bar for five years. |
| **Public Service Commissioner** | Four years | $105,987 | May not hold any interest in a railroad or utility. |
| **Florida Supreme** | | | |

| | | | |
|---|---|---|---|
| **Court Justice** | Six years | $141,131 | Must be a member of the Florida Bar for 10 years. |
| **District Court of Appeals Judge** | Six years | $123,583 | Must be a member of the Florida Bar for 10 years. |
| **Circuit Court Judge** | Six years | $110,111 | Must be a member of the Florida Bar for 10 years. |
| **State Senate** | Four years | $25,668 | Must be at least 21 years old and a state resident for two years. |
| **State House of Representatives** | Two years | $25,668 | Must be at least 21 years old and a state resident for two years. |
| **County Commissioner** | Four years | * | Must be a resident of the district at least six months. |
| **School Board** | Four years | * | Must be a resident of the district at least six months. |
| **Tax Collector** | Four years | * | Must be a registered voter. |
| **Tax Assessor** | Four years | * | Must be a registered voter. |
| **Supervisor of Elections** | Four years | * | Must be a registered voter. |
| **County Judge** | Four years | * | Must be a member the of Florida Bar. |
| **State Attorney** | Four years | ** | Must be a member of the Florida Bar for five years. |
| **Clerk of Court** | Four years | * | Must be a registered voter. |
| **Sheriff** | Four years | * | Must be a registered voter. |
| **Superintendent of Schools** | Four years | * | Must be a registered voter.*** |

*Determined in part by population of district.
**Determined in part by population of Judicial Circuit.
***Does not apply to appointed superintendents.

### STATE PRESIDENTIAL VOTE, 1848 TO PRESENT
#### (Major Party Popular Vote in Florida)

**1848:** Zachary Taylor (Whig) . . . . .4,117
Lewis Cass (Dem.) . . . . . . . .3,083
**1852:** Franklin Pierce (Dem.) . . . .4,318
Winfield Scott (Whig) . . . . .2,875
**1856:** James Buchanan (Dem.) . . .6,358
Millard Fillmore (American) 4,833
**1860:** John C. Breckinridge (Dem.)8,155
John Bell
(Constitutional Union) . . . .4,731
Stephen A. Douglas
(Ind. Dem.) . . . . . . . . . . . . .221
**1864:** (No election)

**1868:** Republican electors
chosen by Legislature
**1872:** Ulysses S. Grant (Rep.) . . .17,765
Horace Greeley (Dem.) . . .15,428
**1876:** Rutherford B. Hayes (Rep.)23,849
Samuel J. Tilden (Dem.) . .22,923
**1880:** Winfield S. Hancock (Dem.)27,925
James A. Garfield (Rep.) . .23,686
**1884:** Grover Cleveland (Dem.) .31,766
James G. Blaine (Rep.) . . .28,031
**1888:** Grover Cleveland (Dem.) .39,561
Benjamin Harrison (Rep.) .26,659

**1892:** Grover Cleveland (Dem.) .30,143
James Weaver (People's) . . .4,843
**1896:** William J. Bryan (Dem.) . .30,683
William McKinley (Rep.) . .11,288
William J. Bryan (People's) .2,053
John M. Palmer
(National Dem.) . . . . . . . . .1,778
**1900:** William J. Bryan (Dem.) . .28,625
William McKinley (Rep.) . . .7,314
William J. Bryan (People's) .1,070
John G. Woolley
(Prohibition) . . . . . . . . . . .2,234
**1904:** Alton B. Parker (Dem.) . . .27,046
Theodore Roosevelt (Rep.) .8,314
Thomas E. Watson (People's)1,605
Eugene Debs (Socialist) . . . .2,337
**1908:** William J. Bryan (Dem.) . .31,104
William H. Taft (Rep.) . . . .10,654
Eugene Debs (Socialist) . . . .3,747
Eugene Chafin (Prohibition)1,356
**1912:** Woodrow Wilson (Dem.) . .36,417
William H. Taft (Rep.) . . . . .4,279
Eugene Debs (Socialist) . . . .4,806
Eugene Chafin (Prohibition)1,854
Theodore Roosevelt
(Progressive) . . . . . . . . . . .4,535
**1916:** Woodrow Wilson (Dem.) . .55,984
Charles Evans Hughes
(Rep.) . . . . . . . . . . . . . . . .14,611
A. L. Benson (Socialist) . . . .7,814
J. Frank Hanly (Prohibition) 4,855
**1920:** James M. Cox (Dem.) . . . .90,515
Warren G. Harding (Rep.) 44,853
Warren G. Harding
(Rep. White) . . . . . . . . . .10,118
Eugene Debs (Socialist) . . . .5,189
Aaron Sherman (Prohibition)5,124
**1924:** John W. Davis (Dem.) . . . .62,083
Calvin Coolidge (Rep.) . . .30,633
Herman Faris (Prohibition) 5,498
Robert M. La Follette
(Progressive) . . . . . . . . . . .8,625
Gilbert Nations (American) .2,315
**1928:** Herbert Hoover (Rep.) . .144,168
Alfred E. Smith (Dem.) . .101,764
Norman Thomas (Socialist) .4,036
William Foster (Communist) 3,704
**1932:** Franklin D. Roosevelt
(Dem.) . . . . . . . . . . . . . .206,307
Herbert Hoover (Rep.) . . .69,170

**1936:** Franklin D. Roosevelt
(Dem.) . . . . . . . . . . . . . .249,117
Alfred Landon (Rep.) . . . .78,248
**1940:** Franklin D. Roosevelt
(Dem.) . . . . . . . . . . . . . .359,334
Wendell Willkie (Rep.) . .126,158
**1944:** Franklin D. Roosevelt
(Dem.) . . . . . . . . . . . . . .339,377
Thomas E. Dewey (Rep.) .143,215
**1948:** Harry S. Truman (Dem.) .281,988
Thomas E. Dewey (Rep.) .194,280
Strom Thurmond
(States Rights) . . . . . . . . .89,750
Henry A. Wallace
(Progressive) . . . . . . . . . .11,620
**1952:** Dwight D. Eisenhower
(Rep.) . . . . . . . . . . . . . . .544,036
Adlai E. Stevenson (Dem.)444,036
**1956:** Dwight D. Eisenhower
(Rep.) . . . . . . . . . . . . . . .643,849
Adlai E. Stevenson (Dem.)480,371
**1960:** Richard M. Nixon (Rep.) .795,476
John F. Kennedy (Dem.) .748,700
**1964:** Lyndon B. Johnson (Dem.)948,540
Barry M. Goldwater (Rep.)905,941
**1968:** Richard M. Nixon (Rep.) .886,804
Hubert H. Humphrey
(Dem.) . . . . . . . . . . . . . .676,794
George C. Wallace
(Am. Ind.) . . . . . . . . . . .624,207
**1972:** Richard M. Nixon (Rep.)1,857,759
George S. McGovern
(Dem.) . . . . . . . . . . . . . .718,117
**1976:** Jimmy Carter (Dem.) . .1,636,000
Gerald R. Ford (Rep.) . .1,469,531
**1980:** Ronald Reagan (Rep.) .2,046,951
Jimmy Carter (Dem.) . .1,419,475
**1984:** Ronald Reagan (Rep.) .2,730,350
Walter F. Mondale
(Dem.) . . . . . . . . . . . . .1,448,816
**1988:** George Bush (Rep.) . . .2,618,885
Michael S. Dukakis
(Dem.) . . . . . . . . . . . . .1,656,701
**1992:** George Bush (Rep.) . . .2,137,752
Bill Clinton (Dem.) . . . .2,051,845
H. Ross Perot (Ind.) . . .1,041,607
**1996:** Bill Clinton (Dem.) . . . .2,545,968
Bob Dole (Rep.) . . . . . .2,243,324
H. Ross Perot (Ref.) . . . . .483,776

## RECENT GENERAL ELECTION RESULTS
### 1998 General Election

### U.S. Senate

Bob Graham (Dem.) .................................2,429,702
Charlie Crist (Rep.) ...............................1,456,192

### U.S. House of Representatives

**Dist. 1:** Joe Scarborough (Rep.) ..........................140,031
Tom Wells (Write-in) ................................45
**Dist. 2:** F. Allen Boyd (Dem.) ...........................138,401
Timothy W. Stein (Write-in) ........................2,812
**Dist. 3:** Corrine Brown (Dem.) ............................66,362
Bill Randall (Rep.) ................................53,074
**Dist. 4:** Tillie Fowler (Rep.) ..........................Unopposed
**Dist. 5:** Karen Thurman (Dem.) ...........................131,995
Jack Gargan (Ref.) .................................67,133
**Dist. 6:** Clifford B. Stearns (Rep.) ....................Unopposed
**Dist. 7:** John Mica (Rep.) ...............................Unopposed
**Dist. 8:** Bill McCollum (Rep.) ...........................104,146
Al Krulick (Dem.) ..................................54,187
**Dist. 9:** Michael Bilirakis (Rep.) ......................Unopposed
**Dist. 10:** C. W. ("Bill") Young (Rep.) ..................Unopposed
**Dist. 11:** James O. Davis (Dem.) ...........................85,167
Joe Chillura (Rep.) ................................46,107
**Dist. 12:** Charles T. Canady (Rep.) .....................Unopposed
**Dist. 13:** Dan Miller (Rep.) ............................Unopposed
**Dist. 14:** Porter J. Goss (Rep.) ........................Unopposed
**Dist. 15:** Dave Weldon (Rep.) .............................129,232
David R. Golding (Dem.) ............................75,129
**Dist. 16:** Mark Foley (Rep.) ............................Unopposed
**Dist. 17:** Carrie Meek (Dem.) ...........................Unopposed
**Dist. 18:** Ileana Ros-Lehtinen (Rep.) ...................Unopposed
**Dist. 19:** Robert Wexler (Dem.) .........................Unopposed
**Dist. 20:** Peter Deutsch (Dem.) .........................Unopposed
**Dist. 21:** Lincoln Diaz-Balart (Rep.) .....................84,017
Patrick Cusack (Dem.) ..............................28,378
**Dist. 22:** Clay Shaw (Rep.) .............................Unopposed
**Dist. 23:** Alcee L. Hastings (Dem.) .....................Unopposed

### State Cabinet

#### Secretary of State

Katherine Harris (Rep.) ...........................2,056,811
Karen Gievers (Dem.) ..............................1,775,188

#### Attorney General

Bob Butterworth (Dem.) ............................2,296,228
Dave Bludworth (Rep.) .............................1,554,811

#### Comptroller

Bob Milligan (Rep.) ...............................2,281,651
Newall Daughtrey (Dem.) ...........................1,485,668

#### Treasurer/Insurance Commissioner

Bill Nelson (Dem.) ................................2,189,740
Tim Ireland (Rep.) ................................1,680,043

**Commissioner of Education**
Tom Gallagher (Rep.) .................................2,176,200
Peter Wallace (Dem.) .................................1,676,502

**Commissioner of Agriculture**
Bob Crawford (Dem.) .................................2,344,878
Rich Faircloth (Rep.) .................................1,445,771

### President and Vice President
### (1996—By County)

| County | Clinton Gore (Dem.) | Dole Kemp (Rep.) | Perot Choate (Ref.) |
|---|---|---|---|
| Alachua | 40,144 | 25,303 | 8,072 |
| Baker | 2,273 | 3,684 | 10 |
| Bay | 17,020 | 28,290 | 5,922 |
| Bradford | 3,356 | 4,038 | 819 |
| Brevard | 80,416 | 87,980 | 25,249 |
| Broward | 320,736 | 142,834 | 38,964 |
| Calhoun | 1,794 | 1,717 | 630 |
| Charlotte | 27,121 | 27,836 | 7,783 |
| Citrus | 22,042 | 20,114 | 7,244 |
| Clay | 13,246 | 30,332 | 3,281 |
| Collier | 23,182 | 42,590 | 6,320 |
| Columbia | 6,691 | 7,588 | 1,970 |
| De Soto | 3,219 | 3,272 | 965 |
| Dixie | 1,731 | 1,398 | 652 |
| Duval | 112,258 | 126,857 | 13,844 |
| Escambia | 37,768 | 60,839 | 8,587 |
| Flagler | 9,583 | 8,232 | 2,185 |
| Franklin | 2,095 | 1,563 | 878 |
| Gadsden | 9,405 | 3,813 | 938 |
| Gilchrist | 1,985 | 1,939 | 841 |
| Glades | 1,530 | 1,361 | 521 |
| Gulf | 2,480 | 2,424 | 1,054 |
| Hamilton | 1,734 | 1,518 | 406 |
| Hardee | 2,417 | 2,926 | 851 |
| Hendry | 3,882 | 3,855 | 1,135 |
| Hernando | 28,520 | 22,039 | 7,272 |
| Highlands | 14,244 | 15,608 | 3,739 |
| Hillsborough | 144,223 | 136,621 | 25,154 |
| Holmes | 2,310 | 3,248 | 1,208 |
| Indian River | 16,373 | 22,709 | 4,635 |
| Jackson | 6,665 | 7,187 | 1,602 |
| Jefferson | 2,543 | 1,851 | 393 |
| Lafayette | 829 | 1,166 | 316 |
| Lake | 29,750 | 35,089 | 8,813 |
| Lee | 65,692 | 80,882 | 18,389 |
| Leon | 50,058 | 33,914 | 6,672 |
| Levy | 4,938 | 4,299 | 1,774 |
| Liberty | 868 | 913 | 376 |
| Madison | 2,791 | 2,195 | 578 |
| Manatee | 41,835 | 44,059 | 10,360 |
| Marion | 37,033 | 41,397 | 11,340 |
| Martin | 20,851 | 28,516 | 5,005 |
| Miami-Dade | 317,378 | 209,634 | 24,722 |
| Monroe | 15,218 | 12,021 | 4,817 |
| Nassau | 7,276 | 12,134 | 1,657 |
| Okaloosa | 16,434 | 40,631 | 5,432 |
| Okeechobee | 4,824 | 3,415 | 1,666 |
| Orange | 105,513 | 106,026 | 18,191 |
| Osceola | 21,870 | 18,335 | 6,091 |
| Palm Beach | 230,621 | 133,762 | 30,739 |
| Pasco | 66,472 | 48,346 | 18,011 |
| Pinellas | 184,728 | 152,125 | 36,990 |
| Polk | 66,735 | 67,943 | 14,991 |
| Putnam | 12,008 | 9,781 | 3,272 |
| Santa Rosa | 10,923 | 26,244 | 4,957 |
| Sarasota | 63,648 | 69,198 | 14,939 |
| Seminole | 45,051 | 59,778 | 9,357 |
| St. Johns | 16,713 | 27,311 | 4,205 |
| St. Lucie | 36,168 | 28,892 | 8,482 |
| Sumter | 7,014 | 5,960 | 2,375 |
| Suwannee | 4,479 | 5,742 | 1,874 |
| Taylor | 3,583 | 3,188 | 1,140 |
| Union | 1,388 | 1,636 | 425 |
| Volusia | 78,905 | 63,067 | 17,319 |
| Wakulla | 3,054 | 2,931 | 1,091 |
| Walton | 5,341 | 7,706 | 2,342 |
| Washington | 2,992 | 3,552 | 1,287 |
| **TOTAL** | **2,545,967** | **2,243,354** | **483,119** |

The Libertarian Party ticket of Browne/Jorgensen was on the ballot in Florida and received a total of 23,312 votes. Four qualified write-in candidates, those registered with the state, received a total of 4,547 votes, of which 4,096 went to the Green Party ticket of Nader/Souto.

## GUBERNATORIAL VOTE, 1845 to PRESENT
### (Election Results)

**1845:** William D. Mosely (Dem.) .3,292
Richard K. Call (Whig) . . .2,679

**1848:** Thomas Brown (Whig) . . .3,801
William Bailey (Dem.) . . . .3,354

**1852:** James E. Broome (Dem.) . .4,628
George T. Ward (Whig) . . .4,336

**1856:** Madison S. Perry (Dem.) . .6,214
David S. Walker
(American) . . . . . . . . . . .5,894

**1860:** John Milton (Dem.) . . . . . .6,994
Edward Hopkins
(ConstitutionalUnion) . . .5,284

**1865:** David S. Walker
Conservative Dem.—no
opposition) . . . . . . . . . . .5,873

**1868:** Harrison Reed (Rep.) . . .14,421
George W. Scott (Dem.) . .7,731
Samuel Walker
(Radical Rep.) . . . . . . . .2,251

**1872:** Ossian B. Hart (Rep.) . . .17,603
William D. Bloxham
(Dem.) . . . . . . . . . . . . .16,004

**1876:** George F. Drew (Dem.) . .24,179
Marcellus L. Stearns
(Rep.) . . . . . . . . . . . . .23,984

**1880:** William D. Bloxham
(Dem.) . . . . . . . . . . . . .28,378
Simon D. Conover (Rep.) 23,297

**1884:** Edward A. Perry (Dem.) .32,087
Frank W. Pope (Rep.) . . .27,845

**1888:** Francis P. Fleming (Dem.) 40,255
V. J. Shipman (Rep.) . . . .26,485

**1892:** Henry L. Mitchell (Dem.) 32,064
Alonzo P. Baskin
(People's) . . . . . . . . . . .8,309
N. J. Hawley (Prohibition) . .297

**1896:** William D. Bloxham
(Dem.) . . . . . . . . . . . . .27,172
Edward R. Gunby Rep.) . . .8,290
William A. Weeks
(People's) . . . . . . . . . . .5,270

**1900:** William S. Jennings
(Dem.) . . . . . . . . . . . . .29,251
Matthew B. MacFarlane
(Rep.) . . . . . . . . . . . . .6,238
A. M. Morton (People's) . . .631

**1904:** Napoleon B. Broward
(Dem.) . . . . . . . . . . . . .28,971
Matthew B. MacFarlane
(Rep.) . . . . . . . . . . . . .6,357
W. R. Healey . . . . . . . . . . .1,270

**1908:** Albert W. Gilchrist
(Dem.) . . . . . . . . . . . . .33,036
John M. Cheney (Rep.) . . .6,453
A. J. Pettigrew (Socialist) . .2,427

**1912:** Park Trammel (Dem.) . . .38,977
Thomas W. Cox (Socialist) 3,647
William R. O'Neal (Rep.) .2,646
William C. Hodges
(Progressive) . . . . . . . . . .2,314
J. W. Bingham
(Prohibition) . . . . . . . . . .1,061

**1916:** Sidney J. Catts (Dem.) . . .39,546
William V. Knott (Dem.) .30,343
George W. Allen (Rep.) . .10,333
C. C. Allen (Socialist) . . . .2,470
Noel A. Mitchell . . . . . . . . . .193

**1920:** Gary A. Hardee (Dem.) .103,407
George E. Gay (Rep.) . . .23,788
W. L. VanDuzer
(Rep. White) . . . . . . . . . .2,654
F. C. Whitaker (Socialist) . .2,823

**1924:** John W. Martin (Dem.) . .84,181
William R. O'Neal (Rep.) 17,499

**1928:** Doyle E. Carlton (Dem.) 148,455
W. J. Howey (Rep.) . . . .95,018

**1932:** Dave Sholtz (Dem.) . . . .186,270
W. J. Howey (Rep.) . . . .93,353

**1936:** Fred P. Cone (Dem.) . . .253,638
E. E. Callaway (Rep.) . . . .59,832

**1940:** Spessard Holland (Dem.—no
opposition) . . . . . . . .334,152

**1944:** Millard F. Caldwell
(Dem.) . . . . . . . . . . . . .361,007
Bert L. Acker (Rep.) . . . .96,321

**1948:** Fuller Warren (Dem.) . .381,459
Bert L. Acker (Rep.) . . . .76,153

**1952:** Dan McCarty (Dem.) . . .624,463
Harry S. Swan (Rep.) . . .210,009

**1954:** LeRoy Collins (Dem.) . .287,769
J. Tom Watson (Rep.) . . .69,852

| | | | | |
|---|---|---|---|---|
| **1956:** | LeRoy Collins (Dem.) . .747,753 | | | Jerry Thomas (Rep.) . . .709,438 |
| | William A. Washburne | | **1978:** | Robert Graham |
| | (Rep.) . . . . . . . . . . . . .266,980 | | | (Dem.) . . . . . . . . . .1,406,580 |
| **1960:** | Farris Bryant (Dem.) . . .849,407 | | | Jack Eckerd (Rep.) . . .1,123,888 |
| | George C. Petersen | | **1982:** | Robert Graham |
| | (Rep.) . . . . . . . . . . . . .569,936 | | | (Dem.) . . . . . . . . . .1,739,553 |
| **1964:** | Haydon Burns (Dem.) . .933,554 | | | L. A. Bafalis (Rep.) . . . .949,023 |
| | Charles Holley (Rep.) . .686,297 | | **1986:** | Bob Martinez (Rep.) . .1,847,525 |
| **1966:** | Claude Kirk (Rep.) . . . .821,190 | | | Steve Pajcic (Dem.) . . .1,538,620 |
| | Robert King High | | **1990:** | Lawton Chiles (Dem.) .1,995,206 |
| | (Dem.) . . . . . . . . . . . .668,233 | | | Bob Martinez (Rep.) . .1,535,068 |
| **1970:** | Reubin Askew (Dem.) . .984,305 | | **1994:** | Lawton Chiles (Dem.) .2,135,008 |
| | Claude Kirk (Rep.) . . . .746,243 | | | Jeb Bush (Rep.) . . . . . .2,071,068 |
| **1974:** | Reubin Askew (Dem.) .1,118,954 | | **1998:** | Jeb Bush (Rep.) . . . . . .2,186,283 |
| | | | | Buddy MacKay(Dem.) .1,771,269 |

## 1998 PROPOSED CONSTITUTIONAL AMENDMENT VOTES

The proposed Amendments to the Florida Constitution, the first four proposed by the Legislature, the next nine proposed by the Constitutional Revision Commission, and how they fared on the November 1998 ballot.

1. Allows tax exemptions for historic property even if owner is not engaged in restoring it. **YES:** 1,967,251 **NO:** 1,643,181

2. Writes the death penalty into the Constitution, allows any method of execution not banned by the U.S. Constitution, requires Florida courts to apply U.S. Supreme Court standards for "cruel and unusual." **YES:** 2,670,859 **NO:** 1,000,818

3. Allows cities and counties, but not school boards, to grant an extra $25,000 homestead exemption to homeowners over 65 with no more than $20,000 in household income. **YES:** 2,550,907 **NO:** 1,178,791

4. Allows deeds, mortgages, and other documents to be recorded at branch offices outside the county seat. **YES:** 2,536,357 **NO:** 886,494

5. Enables state to continue to sell bonds to raise money to buy environmental lands, merges the Game and Fresh Water Fish Commission and the Marine Fisheries Commission, and codifies state policy to conserve and protect natural resources. **YES:** 2,626,000 **NO:** 1,005,949

6. Directs the state to provide an "efficient, safe, secure and high quality system of education," and makes that "a paramount duty of the state." **YES:** 2,619,326 **NO:** 1,067,476

7. Shifts more of the costs of Florida's court system from the counties to the state, and allows for more appointed judgeships. **YES:** 2,025,284 **NO:** 1,533,320

8. Shrinks the Cabinet from six independent officers to three: attorney general, agriculture commissioner, and chief fiscal officer, allows for the appointment of a state board of education (currently the Cabinet) which would appoint the Commissioner of Education, one of the Cabinet offices eliminated. **YES:** 1,946,965 **NO:** 1,559,188

9. Equality guaranteed to all natural persons would specifically include females and adds national origin to the list of circumstances protected from discrimination. **YES:** 2,412,219 **NO:** 1,228,542

10. Allows local governments to give property owners tax breaks for conservation purposes, and allows state to exempt cities and special districts from taxes on private property used for public purposes. **YES:** 1,751,337 **NO:** 1,763,654

11. Requires public campaign financing for statewide elections, eases process for minor parties to be on the ballot, opens primary elections to all voters, and makes all school board elections non-partisan. **YES:** 2,235,887 **NO:** 1,220,840

12. Allows counties to increase statewide three-day waiting period for handgun purchases and extends regulation to gun shows. **YES:** 2,650,297 **NO:** 1,031,046

13. Retains Taxation and Budget Reform Commission but restricts it to meet every 20 rather than every 10 years, and other "housekeeping" provisions. **YES:** 1,866,433 **NO:** 1,527,497

## FIRST AND SECOND

Beth Johnson was the first woman elected to the Florida Senate. The second woman elected to the Florida Senate was Beth Johnson. The original was from Orlando, the second from Cocoa.

## URBAN AREAS

The 1990 federal census listed Florida as having 27 urban areas. The largest was the Miami/Hialeah area, with 1,914,860 residents. It was followed by Tampa/St. Petersburg/Clearwater, with a population of 1,708,710; Fort Lauderdale/Hollywood/Pompano Beach, with 1,238,134; and Orlando, with 887,116.

## ISLANDS

Florida has the second highest number of islands among the states, with Alaska having the most. Florida's number of islands of 10 acre size or greater is estimated to be 4,510.

# FOREIGN CONSULS

Many countries maintain one or more Foreign Consular Offices in Florida. Below is a list of those countries and the cities where offices are situated. (For specific addresses and phone numbers call directory assistance for those cities.)

Antigua & Barbuda—Miami
Argentina—Miami, Orlando
Austria—Miami
Bahamas—Miami
Barbados—Coral Gables
Belgium—Miami
Belize—Miami
Bolivia—Miami
Brazil—Miami
Canada—Miami
Chile—Miami
Colombia—Coral Gables
Costa Rica—Miami, Clearwater
Cyprus—Ponte Verde Beach
Czech Republic—Fort Lauderdale
Denmark—Miami, Jacksonville, Tampa
Dominican Republic—Miami, Jacksonville
Ecuador—Miami
El Salvador—Miami
Equatorial Guinea—Miami Springs
Finland—Miami, West Palm Beach
France—Miami, Orlando
Germany—Miami, Jacksonville, Cape Coral
Great Britain—Miami, Orlando
Guatemala—Fort Lauderdale, Coral Gables
Guinea—Jacksonville
Guyana—Fort Lauderdale
Haiti—Miami
Honduras—Coral Gables, Tampa
Hungary—Coral Gables
Iceland—Hollywood, Tallahassee
Ireland—Fort Lauderdale
Israel—Miami

Italy—Jacksonville, Miami, Longwood, Sarasota, Pensacola
Jamaica—Miami
Japan—Miami
Korea—Miami
Luxembourg—Miami
Mali—Fort Lauderdale
Malta—Pompano Beach
Mexico—Miami, Orlando
Miccosuckee Nation*—Miami
Monaco—Delray Beach
Netherlands—Jacksonville, Miami, Orlando
Nicaragua—Miami
Norway—Miami, Jacksonville, Pensacola, Tampa
Panama—Miami
Paraguay—Miami
Peru—Miami, Tampa
Poland—Miami
Portugal—Coral Gables
São Tomé & Principe—Miami
Senegal—Miami
Spain—Coral Gables
Surinam—Miami
Sweden—Fort Lauderdale, Clearwater, Jacksonville
Switzerland—Miami
Thailand—Coral Gables
Togo—Miami
Trinidad & Tobago—Miami
Tunisia—Miami
Turkey—Miami
Uruguay—Coral Gables
Venezuela—Miami
*Recognized by the State of Florida.

## COASTAL MANAGEMENT

Passed by the state legislature in 1978, the Coastal Management Act is designed to protect, maintain, and develop coastal resources. The entire state is designated as a "coastal zone" falling under the jurisdiction of several state agencies charged with reconciling the impact of development on the environment. Instrumental in decisions is an advisory committee comprised of citizens from government, industry, and environmental concerns, all appointed by the governor.

# MILITARY

During World War II Florida was one of the major training areas of the nation, particularly for the training of pilots. Municipal airports in every part of the state were taken over by the Army Air Corps, predecessor of the present U.S. Air Force. Men from around the nation and foreign countries made their temporary homes in Florida while instructors taught them to fly fighters, bombers, and other types of aircraft.

Gen. Jimmy Doolittle and his flight crews received special training in launching B-25s from the decks of an aircraft carrier at what is now part of Eglin Air Force Base near Fort Walton Beach. After completing their training, they flew their planes to the nation's West Coast, loaded them aboard the carrier, and in April 1942 conducted the first air raid on Tokyo. A monument to this event is situated along U.S. 90 between Crestview and DeFuniak Springs, just north of Eglin.

The state also was an important site for naval bases during the war. With the state's vast coastline on both the Atlantic Ocean and the Gulf of Mexico, Florida's ports were strategically located in the Navy's fight against German U-Boats.

Many of the jungle fighters of the U.S. Army were trained in the semi-tropical regions of Florida before they went into battle in the South Pacific. The state's shores and beaches were the scene of many soldiers' and marines' first taste of amphibious training.

## INSTALLATIONS

Florida has major military installations throughout the state. Bases play a vital role in local economies by providing substantial payrolls for large numbers of people who, in turn, buy local goods and services. Each base also allocates a percentage of its procurement activity to small or disadvantaged businesses. Counties impacted by the military receive additional federal education funds. Bases in the state include:

| | |
|---|---|
| Air National Guard, 125th Fighter Group | Jacksonville |
| Cape Canaveral Air Station | Cape Canaveral |
| Cecil Field Naval Air Station | Jacksonville |
| Coast Guard Air Station | St. Petersburg |
| Coast Guard Air Station | Miami |
| Eglin Air Force Base | Valparaiso |
| Homestead Air Force Reserve Base | Homestead |
| Key West Naval Air Station | Key West |
| MacDill Air Force Base | Tampa |
| Mayport Naval Station (near Jacksonville) | Mayport |
| National Guard Adjutant General | St. Augustine |
| National Guard Maintenance Office | Camp Blanding |
| Panama City Naval Coastal Systems Center | Panama City |
| Patrick Air Force Base | Cocoa Beach |
| Pensacola Naval Training Center | Pensacola |
| Tyndall Air Force Base | Panama City |
| Whiting Field Naval Air Station | Milton |

## MEDAL OF HONOR WINNERS
(place of residence in parentheses)

**Army-Air Force**

Bennett, Emory L., Pfc. (Cocoa)*

Bowen, Hammett L., Jr., S/Sgt. (Jacksonville)*

Cutinha Nicholas J., Spec. 4 (Fernandina Beach)*

Femoyer, Robert E., 2nd Lt. (Jackson)*

McGuire, Thomas B., Jr., Maj. (MacDill Field)

Mills, James H., Pvt. (Fort Meade)

Nininger, Alexander R., Jr., 2nd Lt. (Fort Lauderdale)*

Sims, Clitford C., S/Sgt (Port St. Joe)*

Varnum, Charles A., Capt. (Pensacola)

**Navy/Marine Corps**

Carter, Bruce W., Pfc. (Jacksonville)*

Corry, William M., Lt. Comdr. (Quincy)*

Jenkins, Robert H., Pfc. (Interlachen)*

Lassen, Clyde E., Lt. (Fort Myers)

Lopez, Baldomero, 1st Lt. (Tampa)*

McCampbell, David, Comdr. (Pensacola)

McTureous, Robert M., Jr., Pvt. (Altoona)*

Ormsbee, Francis E., Jr., CMM* (Pensacola)

Smedley, Larry E., Cpl. (Orlando)*

*Posthumous award*

## NATIONAL CEMETERIES

Florida has four national cemeteries. One, **Bay Pines National Cemetery** at St. Petersburg, is filled. A second is **Barrancas National Cemetery** in Pensacola, and a third is **Florida National Cemetery** in St. Augustine. The fourth, the **Withlacoochee National Cemetery,** in Bushnell near the Sumter Correctional Institution, completed its $65 million first building phase in May 1988. It currently has 125 acres available for burial, with an additional 275 acres to be developed in the future. Adequate burial space for 180,000 persons will be afforded at the new cemetery.

---

### THE C.S.S. *FLORIDA*

Damage done by Confederate cruisers to U.S. merchant marine commerce during the Civil War is estimated at more than $15 million. The C.S.S. *Florida* was one of the most successful Confederate cruisers. During two years of operation she is credited with destroying more than $4 million worth of shipping commerce, including the burning of 46 enemy vessels. Built in England, the C.S.S. *Florida* put to sea in 1862. She weighed 700 tons, had a length of 192 feet, a beam of just over 27 feet, and a maximum cruising speed of 12 knots. In November 1864, after Federal capture, the C.S.S. *Florida* collided with a U.S. Army vessel and sank off the Virginia coast.

---

### CIVIL WAR BLOCKADE

In order to cut off the delivery of useful goods to the South during the Civil War, President Abraham Lincoln established a shipping blockade that surrounded the entire Florida peninsula westward to the Mexican border. Steamships continued to run the blockade, but success favored a long, low, swift silhouette and a shallow draft. Smokeless coal was the fuel of choice.

# SPACE EXPLORATION

## CAPE CANAVERAL —SPACE CENTER

Midway between Jacksonville and Miami, on Florida's east coast, the National Aeronautics and Space Administration operates the huge Spaceport. The sprawling launch installation, with its gargantuan engineering creations that send off manned and unmanned space flights, contrasts sharply with the surrounding natural setting and early history of this area.

Cape Canaveral on the Atlantic Ocean buffers Merritt Island to its west, which lies between the cape and the mainland. The area is a rich deposit for archaeologists, who have uncovered traces of human activity on the island predating the Christian era. They have found burial mounds and refuse piles left by Indians, and relics from Spanish and French forays into the area during 16th-century explorations. Some experts believe the Kennedy Space Center built on Merritt Island rests over sites where Western civilization first came to the New World.

Today, astronauts train and lift off into space within the view of duck hunters and fishermen along the adjacent Banana River. Much of the area, in fact, despite its technological development, still remains in a natural state as a national wildlife refuge.

The cape and Merritt Island were chosen for the U.S. space program shortly after World War II. In the program's early years, Redstone and Jupiter rockets were launched from the cape from blockhouses protecting 50-man firing teams from the unexpected. Launch crews of the later 1950s multiplied many times into an organization that, at its peak in September 1968, employed 26,500 administrators, engineers, and technicians. This upsurge in activity occurred during the manned flights of Mercury, Gemini, and Apollo missions.

In 1960, seven years after exploratory rockets began lifting off the cape and manned flights were being readied, the space agency began expanding its modest land holdings on the cape and Merritt Island. In 1962 it bought 84,000 upland acres and leased from the state of Florida another 56,000 submerged acres, most of which lie within Mosquito Lagoon. The cost of the expansion was $72 million.

Today, the southern boundary of the space center runs east/west along the Barge Canal that connects Port Canaveral with the Banana and Indian rivers, and parallels the southern tip of Cape Canaveral. From that point the tract extends northward some 30 miles, almost as far as New Smyrna Beach. The spread is bounded on the east by the Atlantic Ocean, and on the west by the Indian River.

From the beginning, NASA, the National Aeronautic and Space Administation, has maintained a good neighbor policy and left unchanged some vital features of Merritt Island's ecology and economy. The agency, in the course of its acquisitions, took over 3,300 acres containing 185,000 citrus trees; the groves were then leased to the former owner so he could care for and harvest the fruit. Beekeepers were paid by NASA to maintain hives for pollination of the citrus groves. NASA also fenced off three private burial grounds containing 19 graves on its newly acquired property and permits relatives to visit them as they wish.

Meanwhile, wildlife continues to inhabit the area, apparently oblivious or inured to rocket blastoffs, the daily presence of thousands of space workers, and heavy vehicular traffic. Raccoons, bobcats, alligators, and wild pigs still roam the scrub palmetto on Merritt Island. And the Audubon Society still conducts, successfully, an annual bird census in the area, usually identifying more than 200 species.

On the cape, across the Banana River from Merritt Island, a rocket museum marks the site from which, on Jan. 31, 1958, the U.S. launched its first Earth satellite, *Explorer I,* and from which the first U.S. astronaut, Alan Shepard, was sent into suborbital flight on May 5, 1961.

The name of the cape—Canaveral—dates back for centuries. It was renamed Cape Kennedy upon the death of President John F. Kennedy, but in 1973 its original name was restored. The facilities on the cape remain known as the Kennedy Space Center.

## MANNED LAUNCHES
### PROJECT MERCURY RECORD

| Spacecraft | Date | Astronauts | Highlights |
|---|---|---|---|
| *Freedom 7* | May 5,1961 | Alan Shepard | Suborbital |
| *Liberty Bell 7* | July 21, 1961 | Virgil Grissom | Suborbital |
| *Friendship 7* | Feb. 20, 1962 | John Glenn | 3 orbits |
| *Aurora 7* | May 24, 1962 | Scott Carpenter | 3 orbits |
| *Sigma 7* | Oct. 3,1962 | Walter Schirra | 6 orbits |
| *Faith 7* | May 15, 1963 | Gordon Cooper | 22 orbits |

### PROJECT GEMINI RECORD

| Spacecraft | Date | Astronauts | Highlights |
|---|---|---|---|
| *Gemini 3* | May 23,1965 | Virgil Grissom<br>John Young | 3 orbits |
| *Gemini 4* | June 3, 1965 | James McDivitt<br>Edward White | 62 orbits/<br>spacewalk |
| *Gemini 5* | Aug. 21,1965 | Gordon Cooper<br>Charles Conrad | 120 orbits |
| *Gemini 7* | Dec. 4, 1965 | Frank Borman<br>James Lovell | 206 orbits |
| *Gemini 6* | Dec. 15,1965 | Walter Schirra<br>Thomas Stafford | 163 orbits |
| *Gemini 8* | Mar. 16, 1966 | Neil Armstrong<br>David Scott | Docking in space |
| *Gemini 9* | June 3, 1966 | Thomas Stafford<br>Eugene Cernan | Rendezvous<br>spacewalk |
| *Gemini 10* | July 18,1966 | John Young<br>Michael Collins | Rendezvous<br>spacewalk |
| *Gemini 11* | Sept. 12, 1966 | Charles Conrad<br>Richard Gordon | Docking |
| *Gemini 12* | Nov. 11,1966 | James Lovell<br>Edwin Aldrin | Spacewalks |

### PROJECT APOLLO RECORD

| Spacecraft | Date | Astronauts | Highlights |
|---|---|---|---|
| *Apollo 7* | Oct. 11, 1968 | Walter Schirra<br>Donn Eisele<br>Walter Cunningham | 163 orbits |
| *Apollo 8* | Dec. 21, 1968 | Frank Borman<br>James Lovell<br>William Anders | Voyage<br>around moon |
| *Apollo 9* | Mar. 3, 1969 | James McDivitt.<br>Russell Schweickart<br>David Scott | 151 orbits |
| *Apollo 10* | May 18, 1969 | Thomas Stafford<br>Eugene Cernan<br>John Young | Descent to<br>9 miles of<br>moon surface |

| | | | |
|---|---|---|---|
| *Apollo 11* . . . . . . . July 16, 1969 | . . . . Neil Armstrong | . . . . . . . Landing on |
| | Edwin Aldrin | moon |
| | Michael Collins | |
| *Apollo 12* . . . . . . Nov. 14, 1969 | . . . . Charles Conrad | . . . . . Second moon |
| | Alan Bean | landing |
| | Richard Gordon | |
| *Apollo 13* . . . . . . . Apr. 13, 1970 | . . . . . . . James Lovell | . . . . . Aborted after |
| | John Schwigert | 87 hours |
| | Fred Haise | |
| *Apollo 14* . . . . . . Jan. 30, 1971 | . . . . . . Alan Shepard | . . . . . . Lunar rocks |
| | Edgar Mitchell | collected |
| | Stuart Roosa | |
| *Apollo 15* . . . . . . . July 26, 1971 | . . . . . . . David Scott | . . . . . . . . Geological |
| | James Irwin | probe on |
| | Alfred Worden | moon |
| *Apollo 16* . . . . . . Apr. 16, 1972 | . . . . . . . John Young | . . . . . . . . Fifth lunar |
| | Thomas Mattingly | moon probe |
| | Charles Duke | |
| *Apollo 17* . . . . . . Dec. 7, 1972. | . . . . Eugene Cernan | . . . . . . . . Geological |
| | Harrison Schmidt | probe on |
| | Ronald Evans | moon |

## SKYLAB PROGRAM RECORD

| | | | |
|---|---|---|---|
| *Skylab* . . . . . . . . May 14, 1973. | . . . . . . . Unmanned | . . . . . . . Launch of a |
| | | space station |
| *Skylab I* . . . . . . . May 26, 1973. | . . . . . Charles Conrad | . . . . . . . Shakedown |
| | Joseph Kerwin | cruise |
| | Paul Weitz | |
| *Skylab II* . . . . . . . July 28, 1973 | . . . . . . . . Alan Bean | . . . . . 80,000 photos |
| | Owen Garriott | taken |
| | Jack Lousma | |
| *Skylab III* . . . . . . Nov. 16, 1973 | . . . . . . . Gerald Carr | . . . . . . . . . . . 85 day |
| | Edward Gibson | mission |
| | William Pogue | |

## APOLLO FINALE

| | | | |
|---|---|---|---|
| *Apollo-Soyuz* | | |
| Linkup . . . . . . . . July 16, 1975 | . . . . Thomas Stafford | . . . . . . . . . . . Linkup |
| | Vance Brand | with |
| | Donald Slayton | Soviet |
| | | spacecraft |

## Space Shuttle Flight Program

On April 12, 1981, shuttle flights into space with reusable spacecraft were inaugurated. Launched from Cape Canaveral, these craft are sent into orbit with regularity, carrying large crews that conduct experiments and launch both military and commerical satellites. Flights were halted temporarily in early 1986 when the spacecraft *Challenger* exploded after liftoff on Jan. 28, killing the seven astronauts aboard. Shuttle flights resumed in 1988.

## ASTRONAUTS MEMORIAL

In January 1987, NASA and directors of the Astronauts Memorial Foundation agreed on a six-acre tract on which to build a monument to fallen astronauts. It is situated near the Visitors Center at Spaceport USA and features a 50-foot wide by 40-foot high mirror-finished granite surface that tracks the sky and names the astronauts who perished in the space program.

**Killed While Training**

1964—Theodore Freeman
1966—Charles Bassett
　　　Elliot See
1967—Clifton Williams
1991—Manley Lenier Carter

**Killed in Fire Aboard *Apollo I***

Jan. 27, 1967

Roger B. Chaffee
Virgil I. Grissom
Edward H. White

**Killed in Shuttle *Challenger* Explosion**

Jan. 28, 1986
Greg Jarvis
Christa McAuliffe
Ron McNair
Ellison Onizuka
Judy Resnick
Dick Scobee
Mike Smith

## FIRST COMMERCIAL FLIGHT

The world's first regularly scheduled airline was inaugurated by Tony Jannus and his Benoist plane on January 1, 1914, when he flew across Tampa Bay from St. Petersburg to Tampa.

## HIGHEST LAND

Florida's highest sections are (1) from Orlando south to Sebring, with elevations varying from less than 40 feet above sea level to 325 feet at the summit of Iron Mountain near Lake Wales, and (2) an area near DeFuniak Springs in the northwest with an elevation of 345 feet at Lakewood.

# SPORTS

## FLORIDA SPORTS HALL OF FAME

The Florida Sports Hall of Fame was founded in 1958 by the Florida Sports Writers Association. Each year sports writers elect new inductees. As the major criteria for election, the inductees must have been born or lived in Florida, or achieved the majority of their sports fame in the state. Site of the Hall of Fame is Lake City. Those enshrined and the sport they excelled in are as follows:

Bobby Allison, auto racing
Ottis Anderson, football
Don Aranow, ocean racing
Red Barber, announcer
Rick Barry, basketball
Deane Beman, golf
Patty Berg, golf
Fred Biletnikoff, football
Otis Boggs, announcer
Wade Boggs, baseball
Tommy Bolt, golf
Julius Boros, golf
Nick Bouniconti, football
Bobby Bowden, football
Pat Bradley, golf
Scott Brantley, football
Lew Burdette, baseball
Norm Carlson, administration
Steve Carlton, baseball
Joanne Carner, golf
Jimmy Carnes, track
Don Carter, bowling
Gary Carter, baseball
Rick Casares, football
Charles Casey, football
Tracy Caulkins, swimming
Wes Chandler, football
Dean Chenoweth, boat racing
Eugene ("Torchy") Clark, basketball
Jerry Collins, greyhound racing
Chris Collinsworth, football
Pete Cooper, golf
Jim Courier, tennis
Dave Cowens, basketball
Gene Cox, football
Larry Csonka, football
Hugh Culverhouse, football
Fran Curci, football
Andre Dawson, baseball
Jim Dooley, football
Herb Dudley, softball
Angelo Dundee, boxing
Hugh Durham, basketball
James Everett, Sr., football

Chris Evert, tennis
Rex Farrior, football
Forrest Ferguson, football
Don Fleming, football
Ray Floyd, golf
Edward Flynn, boxing
Bill France, auto racing
Betty Frankman, auto racing
Don Fraser, baseball
Shirley Fry, tennis
Rowdy Gaines, swimming
Jake Gaither, football
Willie Galimore, football
Don Garlits, drag racing
Steve Garvey, baseball
Ben Geraghty, baseball
Althea Gibson, tennis
Artis Gilmore, basketball
Lafayette Golden, administration
Curt Gowdy, baseball broadcasting
Ray Graves, football
Peter Gregg, auto racing
Bob Griese, football
Andy Gustafson, football
Nicole Haislett, swimming
Jack Harding, administration
Doris Hart, tennis
Bill Hartack, horse racing
Bob Hayes, football
Hurley Haywood, auto racing
Ted Hendricks, football
Nash Higgins, track/football
Nancy Hogshead, swimming
Dick Howser, baseball
Marcelino Huerta, football
Wayne Huizenga, pro sports team owner
Fred Hutchinson, baseball
Julian Jackson, boxing
Davey Johnson, baseball
Jimmy Johnson, football
Deacon Jones, football
Joe Justice, baseball, golf
Jim Kelly, football
Nick Kotys, football

Al Lang, baseball
Floyd Lay, administration
Bernie Little, hydroplanes
Larry Little, football
Henry "Pop" Lloyd, baseball
Al Lopez, baseball
Greg Louganis, diving
Bob Masterson, football
Walter Mayberry, football
Dick Mayer, golf
Jack McClairen, basketball
Jack McDowell, football
Tom McEwen, sports writer
Bill McGrotha, sports writer
Tom McRae, baseball
George Mira, football
Nat Moore, football
Perry Moss, football
Gardnar Mulloy, tennis
Bob Murphy, golf
Needles, horse racing
Jack Nelson, swimming
Jack Nicklaus, golf
Tom Nugent, baseball
Stephen C. O'Connell, boxing
George Olsen, Gator Bowl
John ("Buck") O'Neil, baseball
Charlie Owens, golf
Richard Pace, administration
Arnold Palmer, golf
John Pennell, track and field
Newton Perry, swimming
Bill Peterson, football
Lou Piniella, baseball
Dick Pope, Jr., water skiing
Dick Pope, Sr., water skiing
Edwin Pope, sportswriter
John Powell, baseball
Paul Quinn, coach
Tim Raines, baseball
Jim Rathmann, auto racing
Rick Rhoden, baseball
Dot Richardson, softball

Bobby Riggs, tennis
Ken Riley, football
Joe Robbie, administration
Fireball Roberts, auto racing
Robin Roberts, baseball
Chi Chi Rodriguez, golf
Tony Romeo, football
Al Rosen, baseball
Lyn St. James, auto racing
Doug Sanders, golf
Gene Sarazen, golf
Herb Score, baseball
Earnie Seiler, Orange Bowl
Ron Sellers, football
Lee Roy Selmon, football
Rip Sewell, baseball
Frank Shorter, running
Don Shula, football
Hal Smeltzly, baseball
Emmitt Smith, football
Freddie Solomon, football
Steve Spurrier, football
George Steinbrenner, baseball
Pat Summerall, announcer
Don Sutton, baseball
Charlie Tate, football
Zack Taylor, baseball
Vinny Testaverde, football
Gen. James Van Fleet, football
Don Veller, football
Dale Van Sickel, football
Dick Vitale, basketball
Don Wallen, basketball
Paul Waner, baseball
Charlie Ward, football
Paul Warfield, football
Casey Weldon, football
Glenn Wilkes, basketball
Ted Williams, baseball
Early Wynn, baseball
Garo Yepremian, football
Jack Youngblood, football
Babe Zaharias, track/golf

## MAJOR STADIUMS AND ARENAS

| Name | City | Seating |
|---|---|---|
| Bragg Stadium | Tallahassee | 25,500 |
| Citrus Bowl | Orlando | 70,217 |
| Doak S. Campbell | Tallahassee | 80,500 |
| Florida Field | Gainesville | 83,000 |
| Ice Palace | Tampa | 19,510 |
| Alltell Stadium | Jacksonville | 82,000 |
| Pro Player Stadium | Miami | 75,192 |

Miami Arena . . . . . . . . . . . . . . . . . . Miami . . . . . . . . . . . . . . . . . . .16,640
Orange Bowl . . . . . . . . . . . . . . . . Miami . . . . . . . . . . . . . . . . . . .72,319
Orlando Arena . . . . . . . . . . . . . . Orlando . . . . . . . . . . . . . . . .15,500
O'Connell Center . . . . . . . . . . . . . Gainesville . . . . . . . . . . . . . .12,500
Sun Dome . . . . . . . . . . . . . . . . . . . Tampa . . . . . . . . . . . . . . . . .10,895
Tropicana Field . . . . . . . . . . . . . . . St. Petersburg . . . . . . . . . . . . .50,000
Raymond James Stadium. . . . . . . . . Tampa . . . . . . . . . . . . . . . . .65,000

## FOOTBALL BOWLS
### Orange Bowl, Miami

1933—Miami (Fla.) 7, Manhattan 0
1934—Duquesne 33, Miami (Fla.) 7
1935—Bucknell 26, Miami (Fla.) 0
1936—Catholic U. 20, Mississippi 19
1937—Duquesne 13, Miss. State 12
1938—Auburn 6, Michigan State 0
1939—Tennessee 17, Oklahoma 0
1940—Georgia Tech 21, Missouri 7
1941—Miss. State 14, Georgetown 7
1942—Georgia 40, TCU 26
1943—Alabama 37, Boston College 21
1944—LSU 19, Texas A&M 14
1945—Tulsa 26, Georgia Tech 12
1946—Miami (Fla.) 13, Holy Cross 6
1947—Rice 8, Tennessee 0
1948—Georgia Tech 20, Kansas 14
1949—Texas 41, Georgia 28
1950—Santa Clara 21, Kentucky 13
1951—Clemson 15, Miami (Fla.) 14
1952—Georgia Tech 17, Baylor 14
1953—Alabama 61, Syracuse 6
1954—Oklahoma 7, Maryland 0
1955—Duke 34, Nebraska 7
1956—Oklahoma 20, Maryland 6
1957—Colorado 27, Clemson 21
1958—Oklahoma 48, Duke 21
1959—Oklahoma 21, Syracuse 6
1960—Georgia 14, Missouri 0
1961—Missouri 21, Navy 14
1962—LSU 25, Colorado 7
1963—Alabama 17, Oklahoma 0
1964—Nebraska 13, Auburn 7
1965—Texas 21, Alabama 17
1966—Alabama 39, Nebraska 28
1967—Florida 27, Georgia Tech 12
1968—Oklahoma 26, Tennessee 24
1969—Penn State 15, Kansas 14
1970—Penn State 10, Missouri 3
1971—Nebraska 17, LSU 12
1972—Nebraska 38, Alabama 6
1973—Nebraska 40, Notre Dame 6
1974—Penn State 16, LSU 9
1975—Notre Dame 13, Alabama 11

1976—Oklahoma 14, Michigan 6
1977—Ohio State 27, Colorado 10
1978—Arkansas 31, Oklahoma 6
1979—Oklahoma 31, Nebraska 24
1980—Oklahoma 24, Florida State 7
1981—Oklahoma 18, Florida State 17
1982—Clemson 22, Nebraska 15
1983—Nebraska 21, LSU 20
1984—Miami (Fla.) 31, Nebraska 30
1985—Washington 28, Oklahoma 17
1986—Oklahoma 25, Penn State 10
1987—Oklahoma 42, Arkansas 8
1988—Miami (Fla.) 20, Oklahoma 14
1989—Miami (Fla.) 23, Nebraska 3
1990—Colorado 10, Notre Dame 9
1991—Notre Dame 21, Colorado 6
1992—Miami (Fla.) 22, Nebraska 0
1993—Florida State 27, Nebraska 14
1994—Florida State 18, Nebraska 16
1995—Nebraska 24, Miami (Fla.) 17
1996—Florida State 31, Notre
      Dame 26
1996—(Dec.) Nebraska 41, Va. Tech 21
1998—Nebraska 42, Tennessee 17
1999—Florida 31, Syracuse 10

### Citrus Bowl, Orlando

1947—Catawba 31, Maryville College 6
1948—Catawba 7, Marshall College 0
1949—Murray State 21, Sul Ross 21
1950—St. Vincent 7, Emory & Henry 6
1951—Morris Harvey 35, Emory &
      Henry 14
1952—Stetson U. 35, Arkansas St. 20
1953—E. Texas St. 33, Tennessee
      Tech 0
1954—E. Texas St. 7, Arkansas St. 7
1955—Omaha 7, East Kentucky 6
1956—Juniata College 6, Missouri Valley 6
1957—W. Texas St. 20, Miss. Southern 13
1958—E. Texas St. 10, Miss. Southern 9
1959—E. Texas St. 26, Missouri Valley 7
1960—Mid. Tenn. St. 21, Presbyterian 12
1961—Lamar Tech 21, Middle Tenn. 14
1962—Houston 47, Miami (Ohio) 28
1963—W. Kentucky St. 27, USCG 0

1964—E. Carolina 14, Massachusetts 13
1965—E. Carolina 31, Maine 0
1966—Morgan State 14, Westchester St. 6
1967—Tennessee-Martin 25,
    Westchester St. 8
1968—Richmond 49, Ohio U. 42
1969—Toledo 56, Davidson 33
1970—Toledo 40, William & Mary 12
1971—Toledo 28, Richmond 3
1972—Tampa 21, Kent State 18
1973—Miami (Ohio) 16, Florida 7
1974—Miami (Ohio) 21, Georgia 10
1975—Miami (Ohio) 20, So. Carolina 7
1976—Oklahoma St. 49, Brigham
    Young U. 21
1977—Florida State 40, Texas Tech 17
1978—No. Carolina St. 30, Texas Tech 17
1979—LSU 34, Wake Forest 10
1980—Florida 35, Maryland 20
1981—Missouri 19, So. Miss. 17
1982—Auburn 33, Boston College 26
1983—Tennessee 30, Maryland 23
1984—Florida State 17, Georgia 17
1985—Ohio State 10, BYU 7
1986—(Dec.) Auburn 16, USC 7
1988—(Jan.) Clemson 35, Penn State 10
1989—Clemson 13, Oklahoma 6
1990—Illinois 31, Virginia 21
1991—Georgia Tech 45, Nebraska 21
1992—California 37, Clemson 13
1993—Georgia 21, Ohio State 14
1994—Penn State 31, Tennessee 13
1995—Alabama 24, Ohio State 17
1996—Tennessee 20, Ohio State 14
1997—Tennessee 48, Northwestern 28
1998—Florida 21, Penn State 6
1999—Michigan 45, Arkansas 31

**Gator Bowl, Jacksonville**

1946—Wake Forest 26, So. Carolina 14
1947—Oklahoma 34, No. Carolina St. 13
1948—Maryland 20, Georgia 20
1949—Clemson 24, Missouri 23
1950—Maryland 20, Missouri 7
1951—Wyoming 20, Wash. & Lee 7
1952—Miami (Fla.) 14, Clemson 0
1953—Florida 14, Tulsa 13
1954—Texas Tech 35, Auburn 13
1955—Auburn 33, Baylor 13
1956—Vanderbilt 25, Auburn 13
1957—Georgia Tech 21, Pittsburgh 14
1958—Tennessee 3, Texas A&M 0
1959—Mississippi 7, Florida 3
1960—Arkansas 14, Georgia Tech 7

1961—Florida 13, Baylor 12
1962—Penn State 30, Georgia Tech 15
1963—Florida 17, Penn State 7
1964—No. Carolina 36, Air Force 0
1965—Florida St. 36, Oklahoma 19
1966—Georgia Tech 31, Texas Tech 21
1967—Tennessee 18, Syracuse 12
1968—Penn State 17, Florida State 17
1969—Missouri 35, Alabama 10
1970—Florida 14, Tennessee 13
1971—Auburn 35, Mississippi 28
1972—Georgia 7, No. Carolina 3
1973—Auburn 24, Colorado 3
1973—(Dec.) Texas Tech 28,
    Tennessee 19
1974—Auburn 27, Texas 3
1975—Maryland 13, Florida 0
1976—Notre Dame 20, Penn State 9
1977—Pittsburgh 34, Clemson 3
1978—Clemson 17, Ohio State 15
1979—No. Carolina 17, Michigan 15
1980—Pittsburgh 37, So. Carolina 9
1981—No. Carolina St. 31, Arkansas 27
1982—Florida St. 31, W. Virginia 12
1983—Florida 14, Iowa 8
1984—Oklahoma St. 21, So. Carolina 14
1985—Florida St. 34, Oklahoma St. 23
1986—Clemson 27, Stanford 21
1987—LSU 30, So. Carolina 13
1989—(Jan.) Georgia 34, Michigan St. 27
1989—(Dec.) Clemson 27, West Virginia 7
1991—(Jan.) Michigan 36, Mississippi 3
1991—(Dec.) Oklahoma 48, Virginia 14
1993—Florida 27, No. Carolina St. 10
1994—Alabama 24, No. Carolina 10
1995—Syracuse 41, Clemson 0
1997—(Jan.)North Carolina 20, West
    Virginia 13
1998—North Carolina 42, Virginia
    Tech 3
1999—Georgia Tech 35, Notre Dame 28

**Outback Bowl, Tampa**

1986—(Dec.) Boston College 27,
    Georgia 24
1988—(Jan.) Michigan 28, Alabama 24
1989—Syracuse 23, LSU 10
1990—Clemson 30, Illinois 0
1991—Auburn 31, Ohio State 14
1992—Syracuse 24, Ohio State 17
1993—Tennessee 38, Boston College 23
1994—Michigan 42, No. Carolina St. 7
1995—Wisconsin 34, Duke 20
1996—Penn State 43, Auburn 14

1997—Alabama 17, Michigan 14
1998—Georgia 33, Wisconsin 6
1999—Penn State 26, Kentucky 14

### Sunshine Classic, Miami (Carquest Bowl)

1990—(Dec.) Florida State 24, Penn State 17
1991—Alabama 30, Colorado 25
1993—(Jan.) Stanford 24, Penn State 3
1994—(Jan.) Boston College 31, Virginia 13
1995—So. Carolina 24, West Virginia 21
1995—(Dec.) N. Carolina 20, Arkansas 10
1996—Miami (Fla.) 31, Virginia 21
1997—Georgia Tech 35, West Virginia 30

### (Micron P.C. Bowl)

1998—(Dec.) Miami (Fla.) 46, N. Carolina St. 23

### Super Bowls Played in Florida

1968 (Miami)—Green Bay Packers 33 Oakland Raiders 14
1969 (Miami)—New York Jets 16 Baltimore Colts 7
1971 (Miami)—Baltimore Colts 16 Dallas Cowboys 13
1976 (Miami)—Pittsburgh Steelers 21 Dallas Cowboys 17
1979 (Miami)—Pittsburgh Steelers 35 Dallas Cowboys 31
1984 (Tampa)—Los Angeles Raiders 38 Washington Redskins 9
1989 (Miami)—San Francisco 49ers 20 Cincinnati Bengals 16
1991 (Tampa)—New York Giants 20 Buffalo Bills 19
1995 (Miami)—San Francisco 49ers 49 San Diego 26
1999 (Miami)—Denver Broncos 34 Atlanta Falcons 19

### GRAPEFRUIT LEAGUE

Florida's climate has made it a favorite spring training site for major league baseball teams. Following is a compilation of places and years that teams have trained in the Sunshine State:

**Avon Park**
1927-29:      Cardinals

**Bradenton**
1923-24:      Cardinals

| | |
|---|---|
| 1925-27: | Phillies |
| 1928-29: | Red Sox |
| 1930-36: | Cardinals |
| 1938-40: | Braves |
| 1948-62: | Braves |
| 1963-68: | Athletics |
| 1969- : | Pirates |

**Clearwater**

| | |
|---|---|
| 1923-32: | Dodgers |
| 1936-40: | Dodgers |
| 1942: | Indians |
| 1946: | Indians |
| 1947- : | Phillies |

**Cocoa**

| | |
|---|---|
| 1964-83: | Astros |

**Daytona Beach**

| | |
|---|---|
| 1937: | Cardinals |
| 1942: | Dodgers |
| 1946: | Dodgers |
| 1955: | Orioles |
| 1973-81: | Expos |

**DeLand**

| | |
|---|---|
| 1942: | Browns |

**Dunedin**

| | |
|---|---|
| 1977- : | Blue Jays |

**Fort Lauderdale**

| | |
|---|---|
| 1946-47: | Yankees |
| 1962-95: | Yankees |
| 1997: | Orioles |

**Fort Myers**

| | |
|---|---|
| 1925-36: | Athletics |
| 1940-41: | Indians |
| 1955-68: | Pirates |
| 1969-86: | Royals |
| 1992- : | Twins |
| 1993- : | Red Sox |

**Fort Pierce**

| | |
|---|---|
| 1954: | Pirates |

**Gainesville**

| | |
|---|---|
| 1919: | Giants |
| 1921: | Phillies |

**Haines City**

| | |
|---|---|
| 1988- : | Royals |

**Homestead**

| | |
|---|---|
| 1993-94: | Indians |

**Jacksonville**

| | |
|---|---|
| 1918: | Pirates, Athletics |
| 1919-20: | Dodgers, Yankees |
| 1922: | Dodgers |

**Jupiter**
| | |
|---|---|
| 1988- : | Cardinals, Expos |

**Kissimmee**
| | |
|---|---|
| 1983- : | Astros |
| 1998- : | Braves |

**Lakeland**
| | |
|---|---|
| 1923-27: | Indians |
| 1934-42: | Tigers |
| 1946- : | Tigers |

**Leesburg**
| | |
|---|---|
| 1922-24: | Phillies |

**Melbourne**
| | |
|---|---|
| 1994- : | Marlins |

**Miami**
| | |
|---|---|
| 1918: | Braves |
| 1920: | Reds |
| 1933: | Dodgers |
| 1941-42: | Giants |
| 1946: | Giants |
| 1947: | Browns |
| 1959-90: | Orioles |

**Miami Beach**
| | |
|---|---|
| 1934-35: | Giants |
| 1940-42: | Phillies |
| 1946: | Phillies |
| 1947: | Pirates |

**Orlando**
| | |
|---|---|
| 1923-30: | Reds |
| 1934-35: | Dodgers |
| 1936-42: | Senators |
| 1946-60: | Senators |
| 1961-91: | Twins |
| 1998- : | Braves |

**Pensacola**
| | |
|---|---|
| 1930-31: | Red Sox |
| 1936: | Giants |

**Plant City**
| | |
|---|---|
| 1988-97: | Reds |

**Pompano Beach**
| | |
|---|---|
| 1961-86: | Senators/Rangers |

**Port Charlotte**
| | |
|---|---|
| 1987- : | Rangers |

**Port St. Lucie**
| | |
|---|---|
| 1988- : | Mets |

**St. Petersburg**
| | |
|---|---|
| 1918: | Phillies |
| 1922-24: | Braves |
| 1925-37: | Braves, Yankees |
| 1938-42: | Cardinals, Yankees |
| 1946-50: | Cardinals, Yankees* |
| 1951: | Cardinals, Giants* |
| 1952-61: | Cardinals, Yankees |
| 1962-87: | Mets |
| 1962-97: | Cardinals |
| 1994-96: | Orioles |
| 1998- : | Devil Rays |

**Sanford**
| | |
|---|---|
| 1942: | Braves |
| 1951: | Giants |

**Sarasota**
| | |
|---|---|
| 1924-27: | Giants |
| 1933-42: | Red Sox |
| 1946-58: | Red Sox |
| 1960-97: | White Sox |
| 1991-93: | Orioles |
| 1998- : | Reds |

**Tampa**
| | |
|---|---|
| 1919: | Red Sox |
| 1920-29: | Senators |
| 1930: | Tigers |
| 1931-42: | Reds |
| 1946-53: | Reds |
| 1954-59: | Reds, White Sox |
| 1960-87: | Reds |
| 1996- : | Yankees |

**Tarpon Springs**
| | |
|---|---|
| 1925-27: | Browns |

**Vero Beach**
| | |
|---|---|
| 1949- : | Dodgers* |

**West Palm Beach**
| | |
|---|---|
| 1928-36: | Browns |
| 1946-62: | Athletics |
| 1962-68: | Braves |
| 1969-72: | Braves, Expos |
| 1973-97: | Braves |
| 1981-97: | Expos |

**Winter Haven**
| | |
|---|---|
| 1924: | White Sox |
| 1928-37: | Phillies |
| 1940: | Giants |
| 1966-93: | Red Sox |
| 1993- : | Indians |

*Indicates split training sites by a team or teams during one or several years.*

## SPRING TRAINING SITES

| City | Major League Team | Stadium | Seating |
|------|-------------------|---------|---------|
| Bradenton | Pirates | McKechnie Field | 5,000 |
| Port Charlotte | Rangers | Charlotte Co. Stadium | 6,000 |
| Clearwater | Phillies | Jack Russell Stadium | 4,700 |
| Dunedin | Blue Jays | Dunedin Stadium | 3,450 |
| Fort Lauderdale | Orioles | Fort Lauderdale Stadium | 7,500 |
| Fort Myers | Twins | Hammond Stadium | 7,500 |
| | Red Sox | City of Palms Park | 6,690 |
| Haines City | Royals | Baseball City Stadium | 7,000 |
| Jupiter | Cardinals, Expos | Roger Dean Stadium | 7,500 |
| Kissimmee | Astros | Osceola County Stadium | 5,000 |
| | Braves | Disney's Wide World of Sports | 7,500 |
| Lakeland | Tigers | Joker Marchant Stadium | 7,000 |
| Melbourne | Marlins | Space Coast Stadium | 7,500 |
| Orlando | Braves | Disney's Wide World of Sports | 7,500 |
| Port St. Lucie | Mets | Thomas White Stadium | 7,300 |
| St. Petersburg | Devil Rays | Al Lang Field | 7,000 |
| Sarasota | Reds | Ed Smith Stadium | 7,500 |
| Tampa | Yankees | Legends Field | 10,387 |
| Vero Beach | Dodgers | Holman Stadium | 6,500 |
| West Palm Beach | Expos | Municipal Stadium | 5,000 |
| Winter Haven | Indians | Chain O'Lakes Park | 4,500 |

## FLORIDA STATE LEAGUE
### (Class A)

| City | Major League Team Affiliation |
|------|-------------------------------|
| Brevard | Marlins |
| Clearwater | Phillies |
| Daytona | Cubs |
| Dunedin | Blue Jays |
| Fort Myers | Twins |
| Kissimmee | Astros |
| Lakeland | Tigers |
| Port Charlotte | Rangers |
| Port St. Lucie | Mets |
| Sarasota | Reds |
| St. Petersburg | Devil Rays |
| Tampa | Yankees |
| Vero Beach | Dodgers |
| West Palm Beach | Expos |
| Winter Haven | Red Sox |

(Florida has two teams in the Class AA Southern League. They are the Jacksonville Suns [Tigers] and the Orlando Rays [Devil Rays].

## COLLEGE FOOTBALL TEAMS

**University of Florida,** Gainesville
Nickname: Gators
Coach: Steve Spurrier
Colors: Orange and Blue
Conference: SEC

**University of Miami,** Coral Gables
Nickname: Hurricanes
Coach: Dennis Erickson
Colors: Green and White
Conference: Big East

**Florida State University,** Tallahassee
Nickname: Seminoles
Coach: Bobby Bowden
Colors: Garnet and Gold
Conference: ACC

**Florida A&M,** Tallahassee
Nickname: Rattlers
Coach: Billy Joe
Colors: Orange and Green
Conference: Mid-Eastern

**University of Central Florida,** Orlando
Nickname: Knights
Coach: Mike Kruczek
Colors: Black and Gold
Conference: Independent

**Bethune-Cookman,** Daytona Beach
Nickname: Wildcats

Coach: Alvin Wyatt
Colors: Maroon and Gold
Conference: Mid-Eastern

**University of South Florida,** Tampa
Nickname: Bulls
Coach: Jim Leavitt
Colors: Green and Gold
Conference: Independent

**Jacksonville University,** Jacksonville
Nickname: Dolphins
Coach: Steve Gilbert
Colors: Green and White
Conference: Independent

Both Florida Atlantic University and Florida International University will field Varsity football teams in 2001.

## PROFESSIONAL FOOTBALL TEAMS

**Jacksonville Jaguars,** Jacksonville
Coach: Tom Coughlan
Colors: Teal and Black
Conference: American (Central Division)

**Miami Dolphins,** Miami
Coach: Jimmy Johnson
Colors: Aqua and Orange
Conference: American (Eastern Division)

**Tampa Bay Buccaneers,** Tampa/St. Petersburg
Coach: Tony Dungy
Colors: Red and Pewter
Conference: National (Central Division)

## NATIONAL BASKETBALL ASSOCIATION TEAMS

**Miami Heat**
Coach: Pat Riley
Colors: Orange and Black
Conference: Eastern (Atlantic Division)

**Orlando Magic**
Coach: Chuck Daly
Colors: Blue, Silver, and Black
Conference: Western (Midwest Division)

## OTHER PROFESSIONAL TEAMS

The American League Tampa Bay Devil Rays and the National League Florida Marlins are the state's two major league baseball teams. The National Hockey League is represented by two teams, the Tampa Bay Lightning in Tampa and the Florida Panthers in Miami. The Orlando Solar Bears play in the International Hockey League. Arena Football has become a popular sport for Florida fans who support three major teams, the Tampa Bay Storm, the Orlando Predators, and the Florida Bobcats. Professional soccer, widely popular in the state during the 1970s, returned to the state with the Major Soccer League's Tampa Bay Mutiny in 1996, joined by the Miami Fusion in 1998. Women's professional sports are represented by the Orlando Miracle basketball team and the Tampa Bay Firestix softball team.

## GOLF

Several states claim to have more golf courses than any other state, but the clear leader of year-round facilities is Florida with 1,170 private, semiprivate, and public courses operating every day with more under construction. Florida alone has more golf courses than any nation on earth. Private courses reserve play for their members and guests and such courses are fully subscribed, booked from dawn until dusk with no tee times available for the general player. Semiprivate clubs either have some open times available for non-member players, or as a matter of policy reserve open times specifically for the open golfer. Public courses are available to all. However, in winter, spring and fall, reservations are required. At the height of summer, midday tee times are often available but reservations are required for dawn departures. "Twilight golf", summer play beginning late in the afternoon but lasting until the last light of Daylight Saving Time (and peninsula Florida is at the western end of the time zone) is popular enough to usually require reservations. Many of Florida's urban areas also offer "executive play" on shorter —and quicker—"Par-3" courses.

## SKIN DIVING

Opportunities in Florida for skin diving are unlimited, thanks to the state's long coastline and its thousands of lakes, rivers, and springs.

Best months for diving along the coastline are May through September when waters tend to be warm and visibility at its best. An exception is the Florida Keys, where diving is excellent the year round.

Most divers prefer the winter months for inland diving. Cold weather destroys algae and the decrease in area rainfall means a lower water table, thus noticeably clearer water.

Recompression chamber sites, sometimes required in diving accident emergencies, are available at:

Naval Ship Research and Development Lab, Panama City

Naval Aerospace Medical Testing, Pensacola

University of Miami (School of Marine Sciences), Miami

Shands Teaching Hospital, Univ. of Florida, Gainesville

Bay Memorial Hospital, Panama City

## SKYDIVING

Florida is the world center of Skydiving with no less than five different venues in the state laying claim to being the sport's international capital. DeLand, Zephyrhills, Sebastian, Lake Wales, and Titusville all purport to be the capital of the increasingly popular international sport. Together, the five centers host more than a half million jumps annually, drawing competitors, including military teams, for training and for major competitions, usually held in and around major holidays. Other Florida skydiving venues, catering more to recreational skydivers, account for another 100,000 jumps a year. Because of the activity, 80 percent of the world's skydiving equipment is manufactured in Florida, primarily at Zephyrhills and DeLand. The sport is so active in those cities that both host retail stores for participants.

## SUNSHINE STATE GAMES

The State of Florida established the Sunshine State Games in 1980 to both foster physical fitness and to develop athletes in the Olympic and Pan-American sports. Although it was the second such event in the nation, its success spurred other states to establish similar games.

The key to its success was believed to be its inaugural policy of allying the Florida games with the Olympic movement, thereby giving each of its events the sanctions required to be taken seriously.

The inaugural games were held in Gainesville but through the years it has become a moveable sports feast with the state's cities bidding annually to host them.

In less than a decade, there was more to bid on. The Sunshine States Games had become the largest multi-sport event in the world, so large that they had to be broken into several Games events to accommodate both the number of athletes and the cities' ability to host them. Still, most sports must require entry via qualifying round competitions to achieve a place in the Games event. The ceremonial "Sunshine State Games," featuring many of the Games' original core sports, are still held annually in July, and are still the primary prize for the state's major cities. Events spun off from the summer contests over the years have allowed the state's smaller cities to participate in the Games' success.

In addition to the Games events, The Games' organization also holds regional sports festivals throughout the state and operates a full season of highly competitive Senior Games culminating in a state championship. The Sunshine State Games are open to Floridians who are members of each sports's U.S. Olympic Committee-sponsored National Governing Bodies which also make the rules. Residency rules are loose, including students and military personnel. A Florida address is the rule for the Senior contest. Foreign athletes who are residents and seek to compete in the Games must belong to their nation's National Governing Body and, if required by the sport, carry an international "license" to compete.

The Sunshine State Games are administered by the Florida Sports Foundation, a quasi-government agency that also promotes professional sports in the state.

## HORSES

### The Thoroughbreds

The Thoroughbred horse industry in Florida goes back to a single man, breeder Carl Rose, who recognized the state's valuable climate and limestone soil in 1917 but waited until the late 1930s to actually launch his 500-acre farm, Rosemere.

But it was not until 1956 that Florida's Thoroughbred industry— today the nation's third largest— began to soar. It was that year that a once-sickly Florida colt named Needles became the state's first Kentucky Derby and Belmont Stakes winner. Needles was also named national champion that same year, an honor that, combined with his Derby win, placed him in the company of just two other U.S. racehorse legends: Count Fleet and Citation.

A mere two years later, new Thoroughbred farms were sprouting up in Ocala—from four in 1956 to 28 by 1958. That same year, Carry Back was foaled at Ocala Stud and in 1961 became Florida's second Kentucky Derby winner, with a Preakness win for good measure. In 1978, Florida had its first Triple Crown winner, Affirmed.

Although in a slump through most of the decade, the state's

Thoroughbred remains a billion dollar business.

## FLORIDA'S RACING CHAMPIONS
### Kentucky Derby Winners

| | |
|---|---|
| Needles | 1956 |
| Carry Back | 1961 |
| Foolish Pleasure | 1975 |
| Affirmed | 1978 |
| Unbridled | 1990 |
| Silver Charm | 1997 |

### Preakness Stakes Winners

| | |
|---|---|
| Carry Back | 1961 |
| Affirmed | 1978 |
| Codex | 1980 |
| Aloma's Ruler | 1982 |
| Gate Dancer | 1984 |
| Silver Charm | 1997 |

### Belmont Stakes Winners

| | |
|---|---|
| Needles | 1956 |
| Hail to All | 1965 |
| High Echelon | 1970 |
| Affirmed | 1978 |
| Conquistador Cielo | 1982 |

## FLORIDA-BRED NATIONAL CHAMPIONS

| Year | Horse | Championship Won |
|---|---|---|
| 1955 | Needles | 2-year-old colt |
| 1956 | Needles | 3-year-old colt |
| 1959 | My Dear Girl | 2-year-old filly |
| 1961 | Carry Back | 3-year-old colt |
| 1965 | Roman Brother* | Handicap horse |
| 1968 | Top Knight | 2-year-old colt |
| 1968 | Dr. Fager* | Sprinter |
| 1968 | Dr. Fager* | Handicap horse |
| 1968 | Dr. Fager* | Grass horse |
| 1968 | Process Shot | 2-year-old filly |
| 1969 | Ta Wee | Sprinter |
| 1970 | Office Queen | 3-year-old filly |
| 1970 | Forward Gal | 2-year-old filly |
| 1972 | Susan's Girl | 3-year-old filly |
| 1973 | Desert Vixen | 3-year-old filly |
| 1973 | Shecky Green | Sprinter |
| 1973 | Susan's Girl | Handicap mare |
| 1974 | Foolish Pleasure | 2-year-old colt |
| 1974 | Desert Vixen | Handicap mare |
| 1975 | Honest Pleasure | 2-year-old colt |
| 1975 | Dearly Precious | 2-year-old filly |
| 1977 | Affirmed* | 2-year-old colt |
| 1978 | Affirmed* | 3-year-old colt |

| 1978 | It's In the Air . . . .2-year-old filly |
| 1978 | Mac Diarmida . . . . .Grass horse |
| 1978 | Dr. Patches . . . . . . . . . .Sprinter |
| 1981 | Wayward Lass . . . .3-year-old filly |
| 1982 | Conquistador Cielo*3-year-old colt |
| 1982 | Gold Beauty . . . . . . . . .Sprinter |
| 1984 | Eillo . . . . . . . . . . . . . . .Sprinter |
| 1985 | Tasso . . . . . . . . . .2-year-old colt |
| 1985 | Cozzene . . . . . . . . . . . .Turf colt |
| 1985 | Precisionist . . . . . . . . . .Sprinter |
| 1986 | Brave Raj . . . . . . .2-year-old filly |
| 1986 | Smile . . . . . . . . . . . . . .Sprinter |
| 1990 | Unbridled . . . . . .3-year-old colt |
| 1990 | Meadow Star . . . .2-year-old filly |
| 1990 | Itsallgreektome . . . . .Turf horse |
| 1992 | Gilded Time . . . .2-year-old Colt |
| 1993 | Hollywood Wildcat 3-year-old Filly |
| 1994 | Cherokee Run . . . . . . . .Sprinter |
| 1994 | Holy Bull* . . . . .3-year-old Colt |
| 1995 | Not Surprising . . . . . . .Sprinter |
| 1996 | Jewel Princess . . . .Older Female |
| 1996 | Skip Away . . . . . . . .Older Male |
| 1997 | Skip Away . . . . . . . .Older Male |
| 1997 | Silver Charm . . . .3-year-old colt |

*Horse of the Year*

## SHOW JUMPING

Florida annually welcomes thousands of riders who participate in a two-month-long series of equestrian competitions in West Palm Beach and Tampa. The state's balmy winter weather and luxurious equestrian facilities appeal particularly to devotees of the Olympic sport of show jumping. Dozens of top Olympic riders from around the world compete to qualify for upcoming international contests.

The sport of show jumping involves riders who must pilot their mounts around an obstacle course. The horse and rider team completing the course in the fastest time with fewest downed obstacles is the winner.

## RACETRACKS AND JAI-ALAI FRONTONS

Pari-mutuel wagering takes place at the state's racetracks and jai-alai frontons. None is open the year round but, instead, each is granted a number of days and dates it may operate. In most cases, the number of days is between 40 and 130. Because dates change annually, it is best to check with each site to learn when the specific track or fronton is open (names of the cities are in parentheses). Pari-mutual facilities have begun offering low-stakes poker rooms and some remain open to offer satellite wagering on events at other facilities.

### Horse Tracks

Tropical Park (Calder-Miami)
Tampa Bay Downs (Oldsmar)
Gulfstream Park (Hallandale)
Hialeah Park (Hialeah)
Calder Race Course (Miami)

### Harness Tracks

Pompano Park (Pompano Beach)

### Quarter Horse Racing

Classic Mile Park (Ocala)

### Jai Alai Frontons

Jai Alai Palace (Dania)
Miami Jai Alai (Miami)
Palm Beach Jai Alai (West Palm Beach)
Fort Pierce Jai Alai (Fort Pierce)
Orlando Jai Alai (Orlando)
Ocala Jai Alai (Ocala)

### Greyhound Tracks

Tampa Kennel Club (Tampa)
Jacksonville Kennel Club (Jacksonville)
St. Johns County Greyhound (St. Johns)
Bonita Kennel Club (Bonita Springs)
Hollywood Kennel Club (Hollywood)
Sanford-Orlando Kennel Club (Longwood)
Palm Beach Kennel Club (West Palm Beach)
St. Petersburg Kennel Club (St. Petersburg)
Orange Park Kennel Club (Jacksonville)
Biscayne Kennel Club (Miami Shores)
Daytona Beach Kennel Club (Daytona Beach)
Pensacola Greyhound Racing (Pensacola)

Seminole Racing (Casselberry)
Sarasota Kennel Club (Sarasota)
Sports Palace (Melbourne)
Washington County Kennel Club
   (Ebro)
Jefferson County Kennel Club
   (Monticello)
Flagler Kennel Club (Miami)

## BETTING INFORMATION

Pari-mutuel wagering in Florida covers horses, dogs, and jai alai, but all tracks and frontons may not offer all the types of wagering reported below.

**Daily Double:** A wager combining choices in the first and second events on the program. A person must select the winner of both events to win.

**Perfecta:** A wager combining two choices in the same event. Choices must finish in the exact order the wager was made.

**Trifecta:** Choices must finish first, second, and third in the exact order picked and as listed on the ticket.

**Perfecta Wheel:** "Wheel the three to win," for instance, involves tickets on 3-1, 3-2, 3-4, 3-5, 3-6; and so on; "wheel the three to place" provides tickets on 1-3, 2-3, 4-3, 5-3, 6-3, and so on.

**Trifecta Wheel:** "Wheel the three to win" provides one ticket covering all possible combinations with the three on top. It is also possible to "wheel the three to place" or "wheel the three to show"—in a Trifecta Wheel. Your choices must finish in the exact position that they are wheeled (either first, second, or third) as indicated on the ticket.

**Boxing:** Calls for combining three or more choices to cover all possible combinations. To box 10 choices, for example, requires 120 box tickets making 720 combinations. Of course, the more choices boxed the more the wager.

## MAJOR ANNUAL SPORTING EVENTS

Specific dates for the events below will vary from year to year, but may be obtained by contacting the chamber of commerce in the appropriate area (cities are in parentheses).

### January

Orange Bowl (Miami)
Citrus Bowl (Orlando)
Gator Bowl (Jacksonville)
Miniature Harness Racing
   (Ocala)
SCCA Winter Nationals Road Race
   (Palm Beach Gardens)
Celebrity Golf Classic (New Port
   Richey)
Walt Disney World Marathon
   (Orlando)
Hall of Fame Bowl (Tampa)
Polo Challenge Cup (West Palm
   Beach)
Health South LPGA Classic
   (Orlando)
Office Depot LPGA Golf (West
   Palm Beach)
Doral-Ryder PGA Golf (Miami)
Super Bowl XXXV (Tampa, 2001)

### February

Goody's 300 (Daytona Beach)
Daytona 500 (Daytona Beach)
Gasparilla Distance Classic
   (Tampa)
Silver Spurs Rodeo (Kissimmee)
GTE Classic Senior PGA Golf
   (Tampa)
Winter Equestrian Festival (Palm
   Beach)
National Offshore Sail Races (St.
   Petersburg)
Yankee Yacht Race (Key West)

### March

McDonald's America Cup
   Gymnastics (Orlando)
President's Cup Regatta (Tampa)
Gatornationals drag racing
   (Gainesville)
12 Hours of Sebring (Sebring)
Honda Classic PGA Golf (Coral
   Springs)
BayHill Invitational PGA Golf
   (Orlando)
Players Championship PGA Golf
   (Ponte Verde Beach)
Winter Equestrian Festival
   (Tampa)

## April

PGA Senior Championship (Palm Beach Gardens)

Tampa Bay Triathlon (St Petersburg)

Orange Cup Regatta (Lakeland)

Gulf Coast Offshore Power Boat Races (Panama City Beach)

Title Holder LPGA Championship (Daytona Beach)

Easter Boogie skydiving (Zephyrhills)

## May

Tarpon Rodeo (Sanibel Island)

Clearwater to Key West Yacht Race (Key West)

Great Dock Canoe Race (Naples)

## June

Miracle Strip Open Spearfishing Tournament (Panama City Beach)

Summerfest Canoe Race (Fort Myers)

Ladies Billfish Tournament (Panama City Beach)

Southernmost Seminole Golf Tournament (Key West)

## July

Sunshine State Games (Tampa)

Silver Spurs Rodeo (Kissimmee)

Destin Shark Fishing Tournament (Destin)

Central Florida Soap Box Derby (Sanford)

Florida State Water Ski Championships (Mulberry)

Pepsi 400 (Daytona Beach)

## August

King Mackerel Tournament (Destin)

Fishathon (St. Petersburg)

Canterbury Dressage Horse Show (Newberry)

Greater Jacksonville Offshore Grand Prix (Jacksonville Beach)

## September

World Series of Softball (Daytona Beach)

DeLand Fireman's Association River Raft Race (DeLand)

Men's ASA Slow Pitch National Tournament (Altamonte Springs)

## October

Weeki Wachee River Raft Regatta (Weeki Wachee)

Dixie Sailing Regatta (Sanford)

NSRA Southeast Street Rod Nationals (Tampa)

Disney-Oldsmobile PGA Classic (Orlando)

## November

Nature Coast Amateur Golf Tournament (Ridge Manor)

Florida-Georgia Football Game (Jacksonville)

Kahlua Club International Yacht Races (Clearwater)

## December

Gator Bowl Junior Tennis Championships (Newberry)

Ted Keller International Diving Meet (Fort Lauderdale)

Great Florida Shootout (Kissimmee)

Carquest Bowl (Miami)

JC Penney PGA/LPGA Classic (Palm Harbor)

---

### NEW RECORD

If you can't break an old record, establish a new one. Swimming booster Ron Collins set one such record when he swam up Tampa Bay. He accomplished the 24-mile feat in 9 hours and 52 minutes, in April 1997. The course, longer than an English Channel swim, ran from the Blackthorn Memorial at the Sunshine Skyway Bridge to a bay landmark, Rocky Point.

# LOTTERY

Florida's lottery has consistently ranked as one of the nation's richest since it began January 12, 1988. Its first week, the lottery sold 95 million $1.00 tickets, a national record.

During its first year, 1988 to 1989, Florida lottery ticket sales were $1.6 million. In its second year, sales topped $2 billion, and third year sales reached $2.19 billion. In 1991-92, sales rose to $2.3 billion. For 1992-93, sales topped $2.174 billion and 1993-94 saw sales of $2.297 billion. Sales in 1994-95 matched the record at $2.3 billion. 1995-96 showed sales slackening somewhat to $2.06 billion, but they rebounded in 1996-97 to 2.16 billion. Sales in 1997-98 were $2.1 billion. An $86.04 million jackpot on March 20, 1993, was the third highest ever for the state's five-year-old lottery and sixth largest in the U.S.

But in 1999, it was radically changed. David Griffin, Gov. Jeb Bush's appointee as Lottery secretary, in October switched the once-a-week pick-6 Lotto drawing featuring a $6 million estimated prize to a twice-a-week game with an estimated $3 million prize in the hope that it would vastly increase the number of "rollovers," games no one won, thus escalating the amount of the prize once it was won. The prize is determined by the number of $1.00 tickets sold until someone hits the jackpot.

To virtually insure more rollovers, Griffin added four more numbers to the mix (50, 51, 52, and 53), increasing the odds against winning from 13.9 million to one to nearly 23 million to one. At the same time, Griffin restored big money payoffs for runners-up, those with five, four, and three numbers correct in the drawing. Those prizes had been cut drastically during Gov. Lawton Chiles's administration.

Distribution of lottery funds is according to a formula that requires that 50 percent of all money in the jackpot goes to pay winning tickets, 38 percent goes to enhance education, 5.5 percent goes to retailers who sell the tickets, and the remaining 6.5 percent goes to lottery administration. Since its inception through mid-May 1997, lottery sales stood at $19.846 billion and the lottery had created 473 millionaires.

The largest grand prize won in the Lotto game its first year was $55 million, a record North American lottery jackpot at that time. It's largest prize to date was $106.5 million paid to six winners in 1990; 1999 saw a $69.8 million prize, the fifth largest in the lottery's history and the largest prize in four years.

Prizes of $599.00 or less are paid by Lotto retailers. Prizes over that amount, except the grand prize, are paid in full, less the required federal tax withholding, at any of the state's lottery offices. Grand prize winners are paid in 20 equal annual installments, again less federal tax withholding. The payout is inheritable. In 1999, the lottery began offering winners the option of taking a reduced lump-sum payout, reduced because the 20-year payout is based on an annuity.

Besides Lotto, the state lottery offers many ongoing scratch-off card games. To keep up interest in the games, the Department of Lottery often discontinues old games and begins new ones several times a year. Three-, four-, and five-number drawing games are offered daily with smaller payoffs than the large Lotto. The state joined the multi-state "Powerball" program in 1998 but withdrew before actually participating. It added its own 4+1 Mega-Ball game in 1999.

Not surprisingly, most lottery winners have come from the state's most populous areas, with most winning tickets being sold in Miami, followed by Jacksonville, Tampa, Orlando, Fort Lauderdale, and St. Petersburg.

Florida does not tax lottery winnings, but the Internal Revenue Service requires lottery administrators withhold 20 percent of all lottery prizes over $5,000 won by U.S. citizens.

Florida's lottery was approved in a 1986 statewide referendum when voters, by a two-to-one margin, asked that the Florida constitution's ban on lotteries be removed.

**Top Florida Lottery Prizes**

| Jackpot | Date | Winners |
|---|---|---|
| $106.5 million | September 1990 | 6 |
| 89.78 million | October 1990 | 6 |
| 86.04 million | March 1993 | 3 |
| 81.20 million | April 1995 | 5 |
| 69.80 million | February 1999 | 5 |
| 58.48 million | December 1997 | 2 |
| 58.39 million | April 1990 | 5 |
| 55.16 million | September 1988 | 1 |
| 47.56 million | February 1992 | 5 |

## HOW-TO FOR LOTTERY WINNERS

A Florida Lottery Department pamphlet advises Lotto winners about getting financial advice, dealing with the press, and paying taxes. Among the words of wisdom: "Consider using professional financial and legal advisors." And when talking to the media, "try to relax, be friendly, and enjoy the experience." The booklet also suggests changing your telephone number.

# COUNTY MAPS

# ALACHUA COUNTY

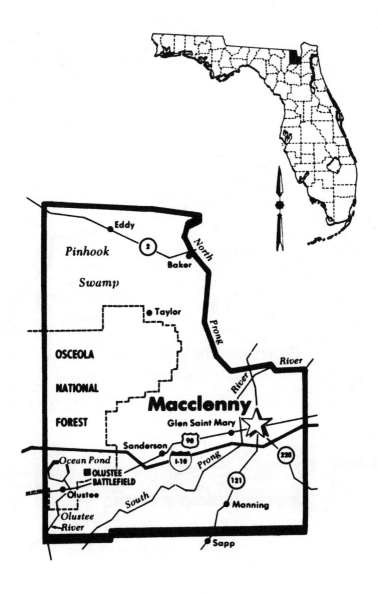

# BAKER COUNTY

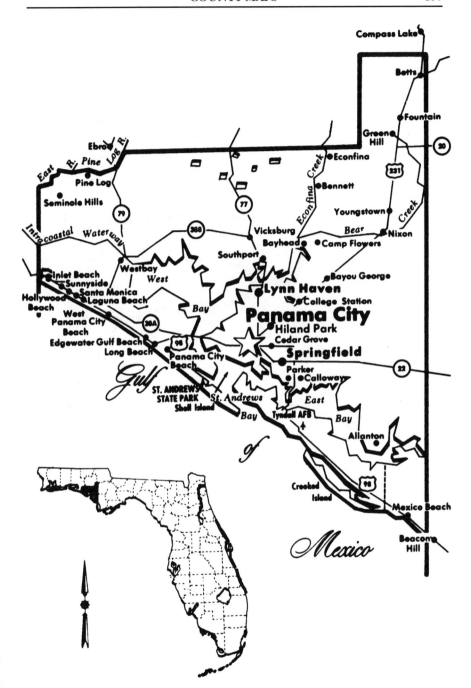

**BAY COUNTY**

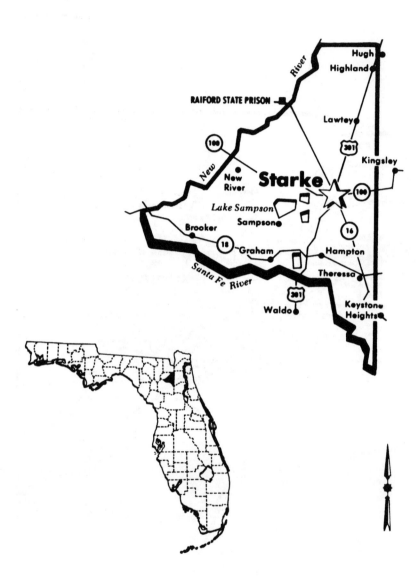

# BRADFORD COUNTY

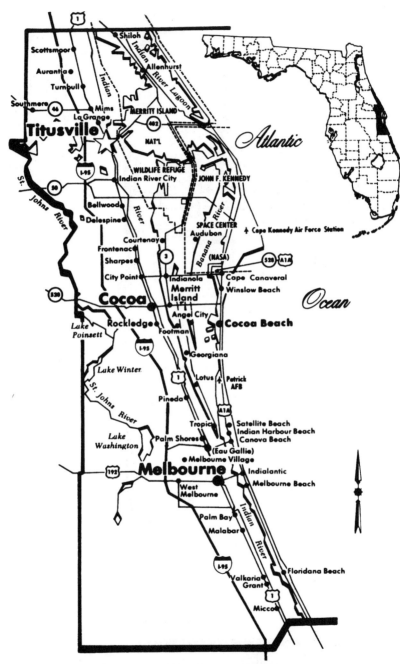

# BREVARD COUNTY

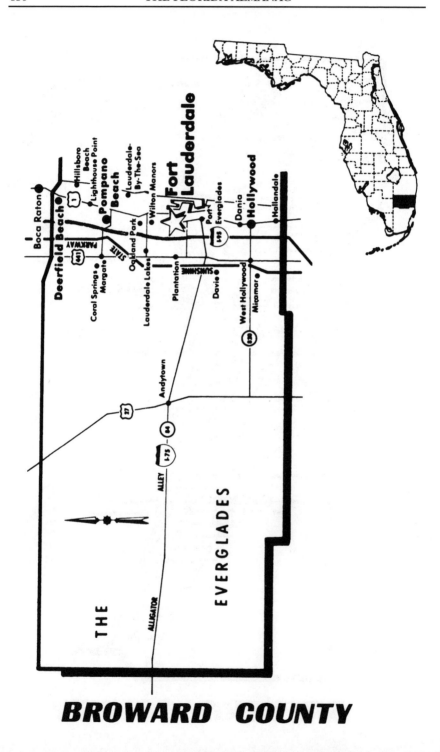

**BROWARD COUNTY**

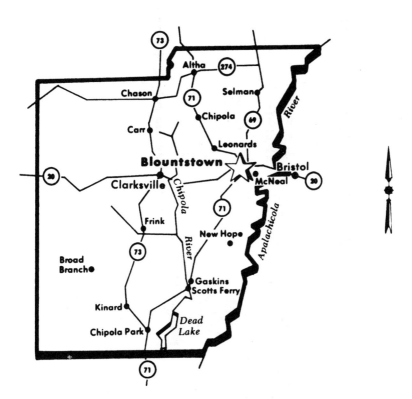

# CALHOUN COUNTY

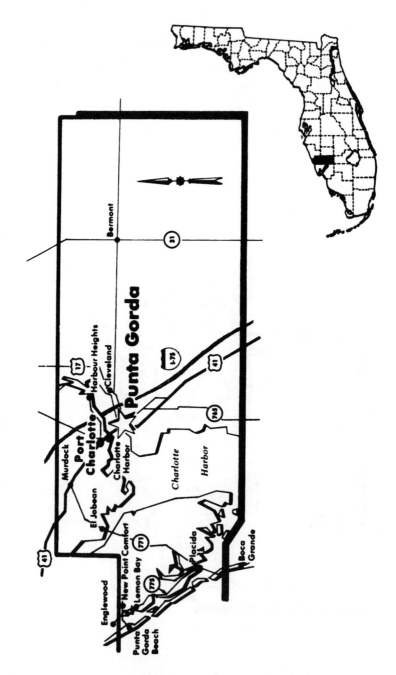

# CHARLOTTE COUNTY

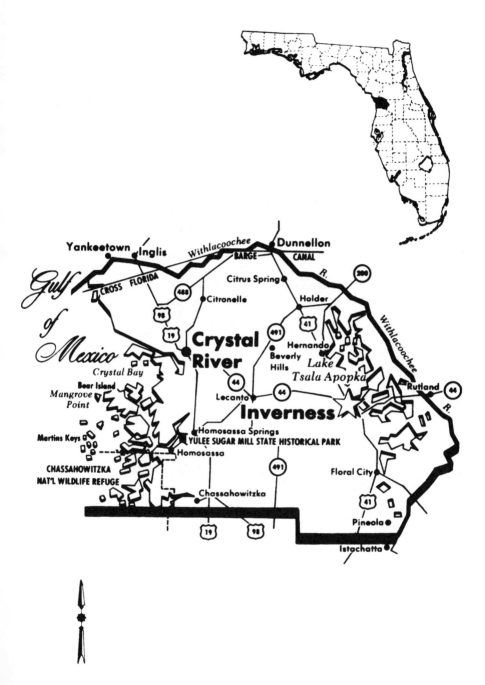

# CITRUS COUNTY

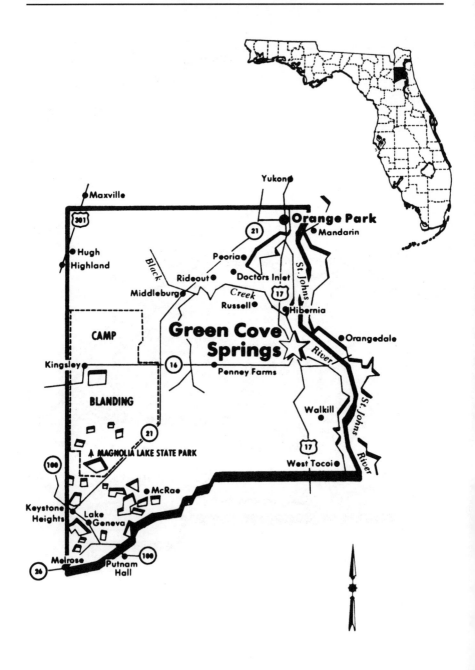

**CLAY COUNTY**

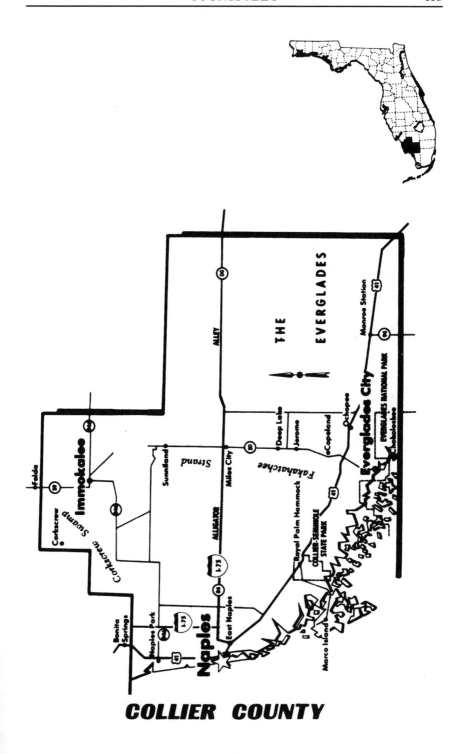

**COLLIER COUNTY**

# COLUMBIA COUNTY

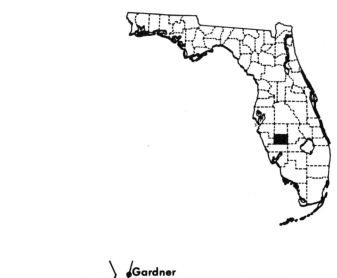

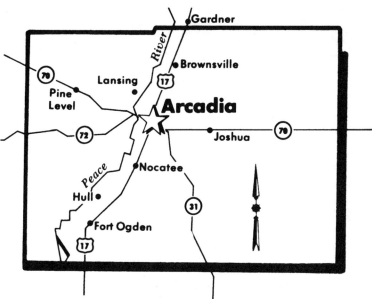

# DE SOTO COUNTY

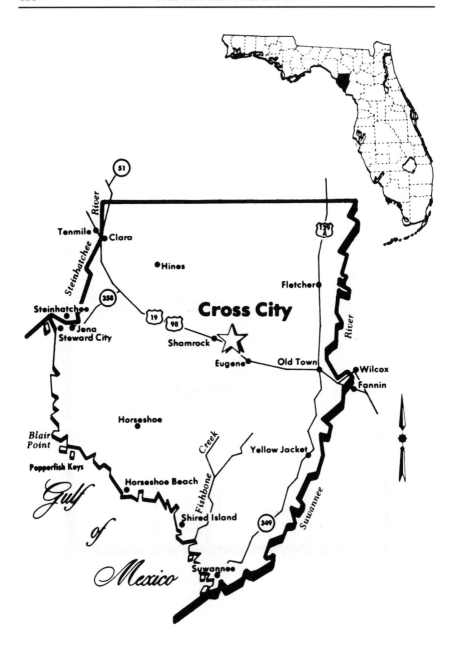

# DIXIE COUNTY

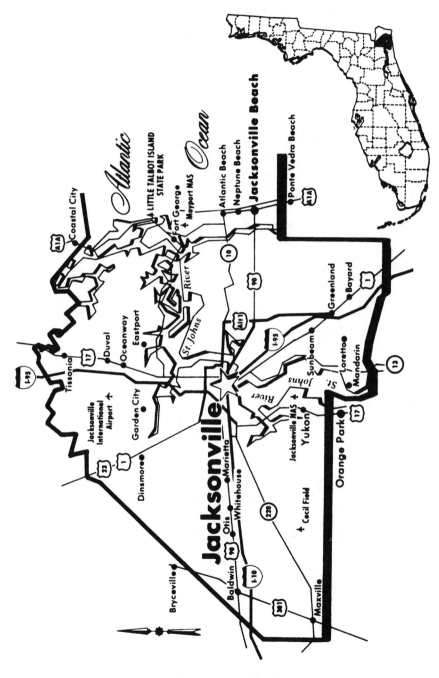

**DUVAL COUNTY**

# ESCAMBIA COUNTY

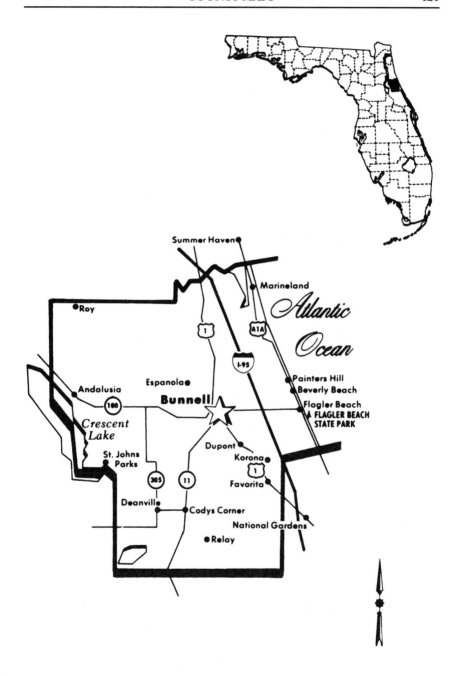

# FLAGLER COUNTY

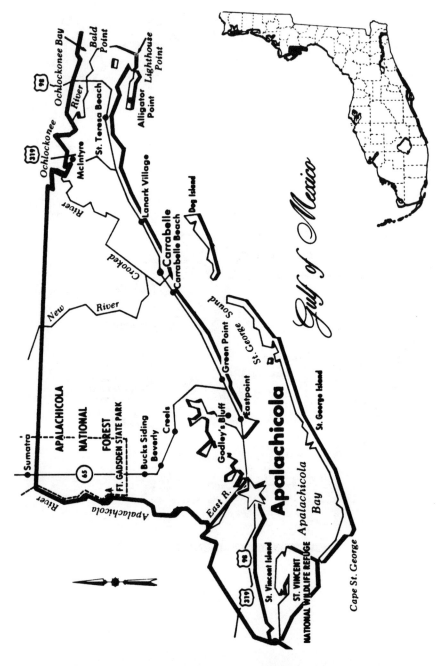

# FRANKLIN COUNTY

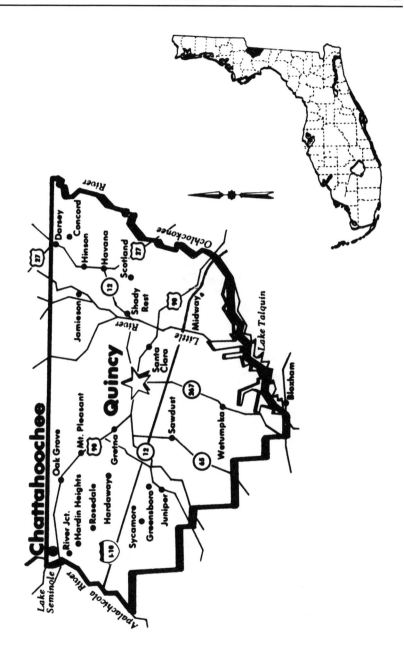

# GADSDEN COUNTY

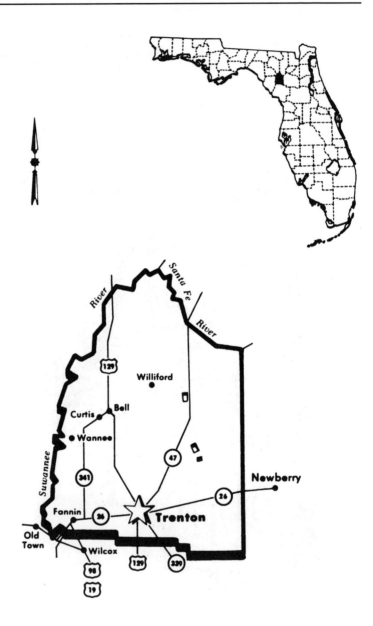

# *GILCHRIST COUNTY*

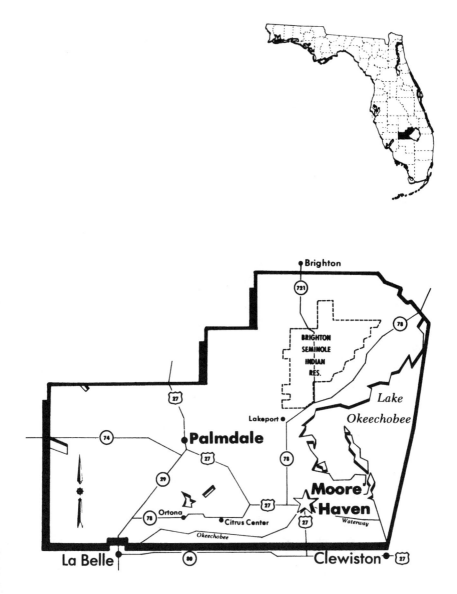

# GLADES COUNTY

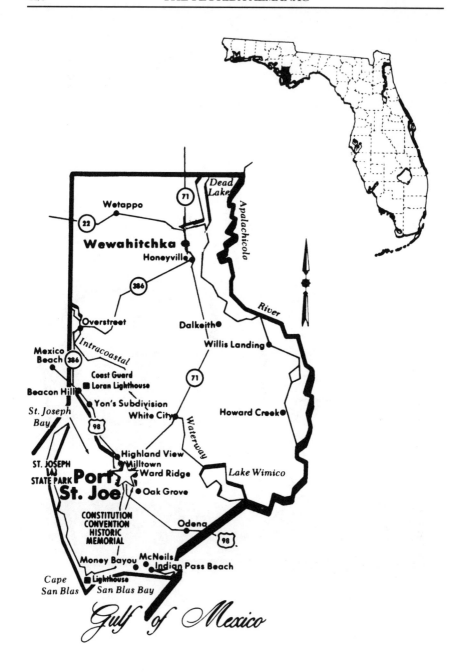

# GULF COUNTY

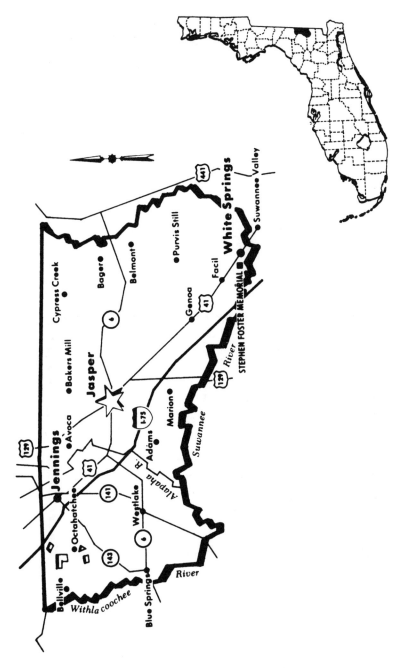

# HAMILTON COUNTY

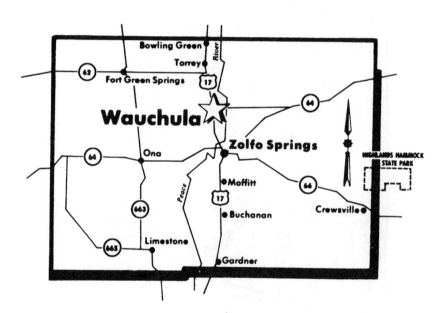

# HARDEE COUNTY

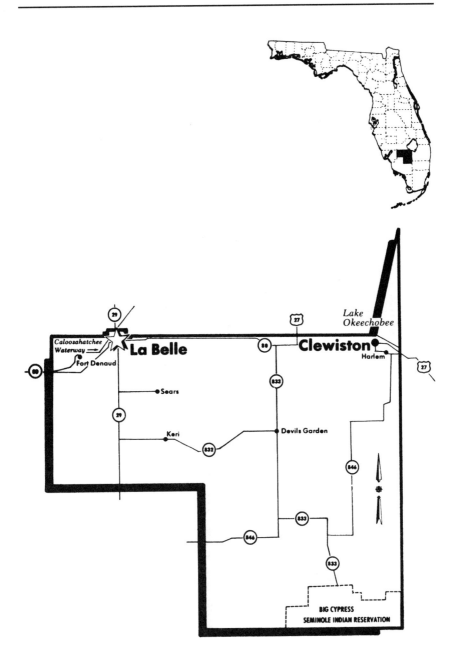

# HENDRY COUNTY

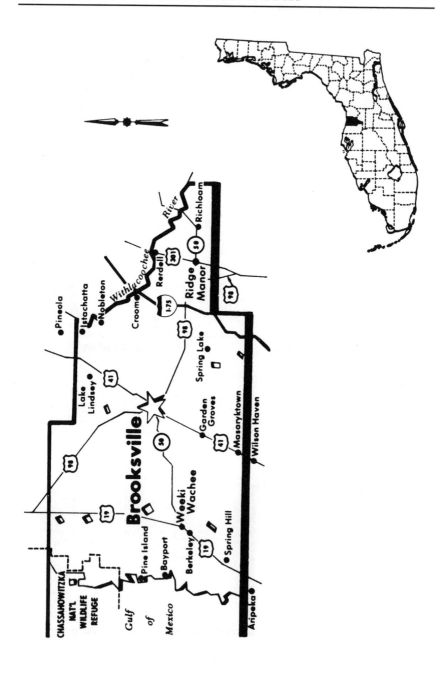

# HERNANDO COUNTY

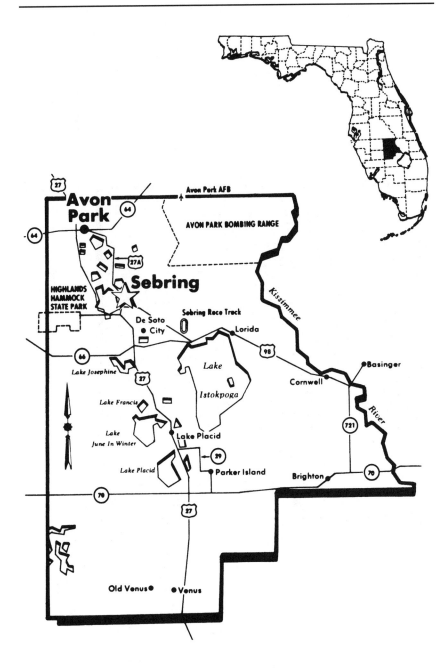

# HIGHLANDS COUNTY

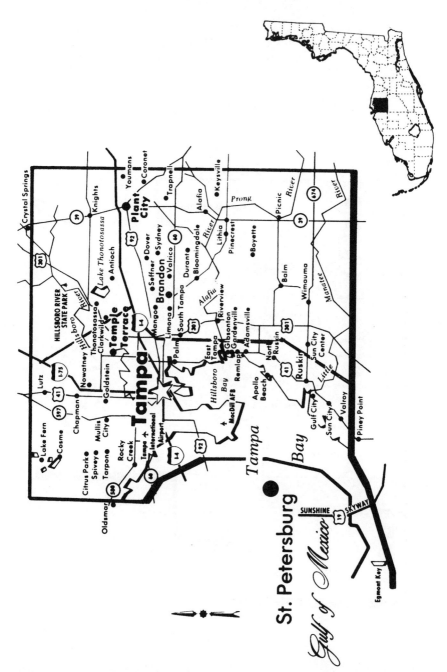

# HILLSBOROUGH COUNTY

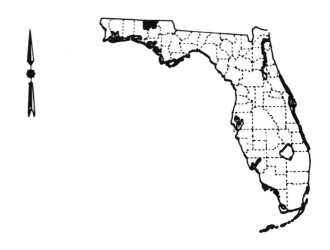

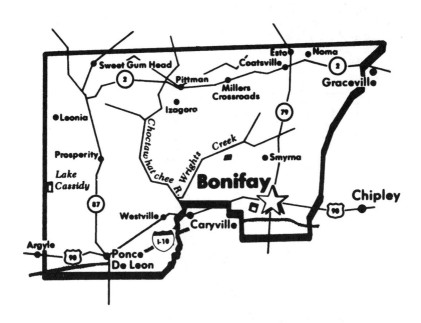

# HOLMES COUNTY

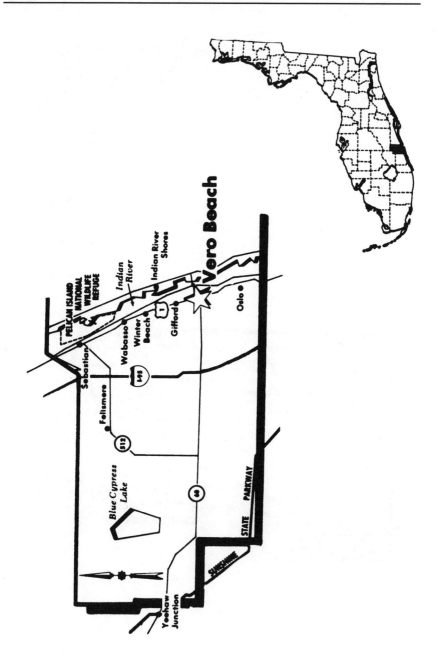

# INDIAN RIVER COUNTY

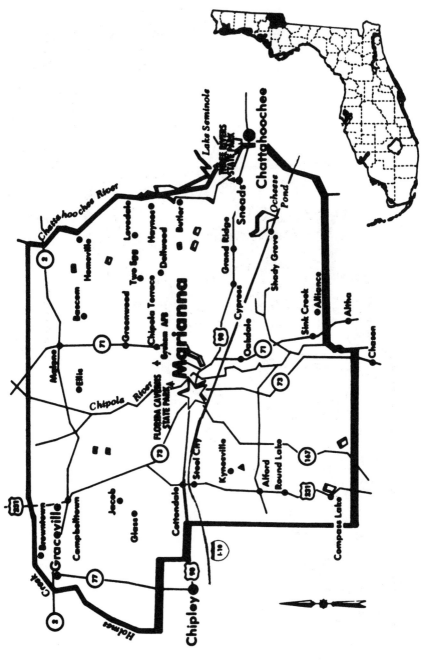

# JACKSON COUNTY

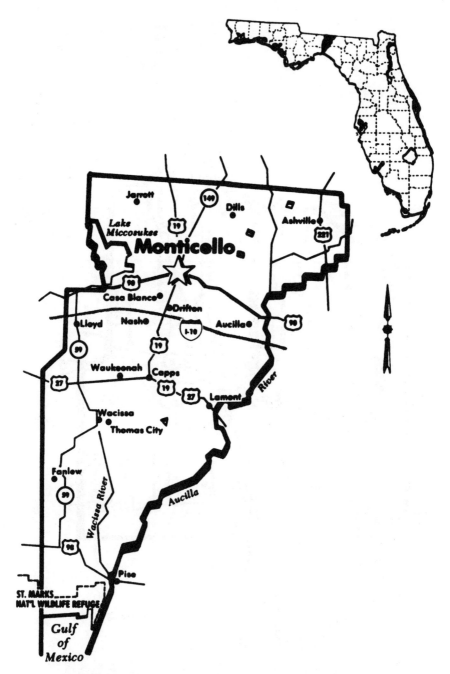

Jarrott

Dills

Ashville
221

Lake
Miccosukee

**Monticello**

Casa Blanca

Drifton

Lloyd

Nash

Aucilla

I-10

Waukeenah

Capps

Wacissa

Lamont

River

Thomas City

Fanlew

Aucilla

Wacissa River

Piso

ST. MARKS
NAT'L WILDLIFE REFUGE

Gulf
of
Mexico

# JEFFERSON COUNTY

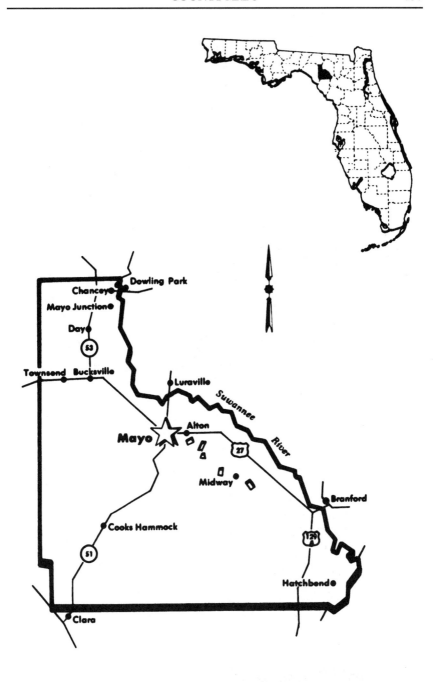

# LAFAYETTE COUNTY

# LAKE COUNTY

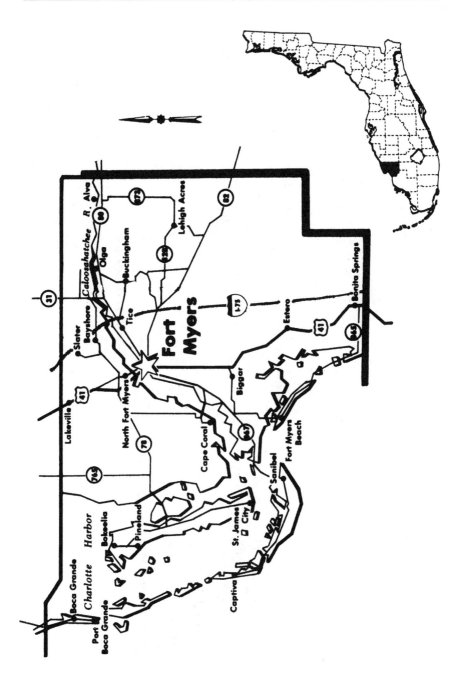

# LEE COUNTY

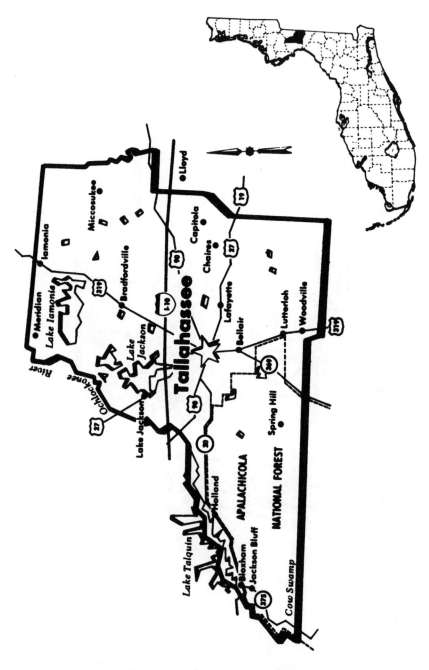

# LEON COUNTY

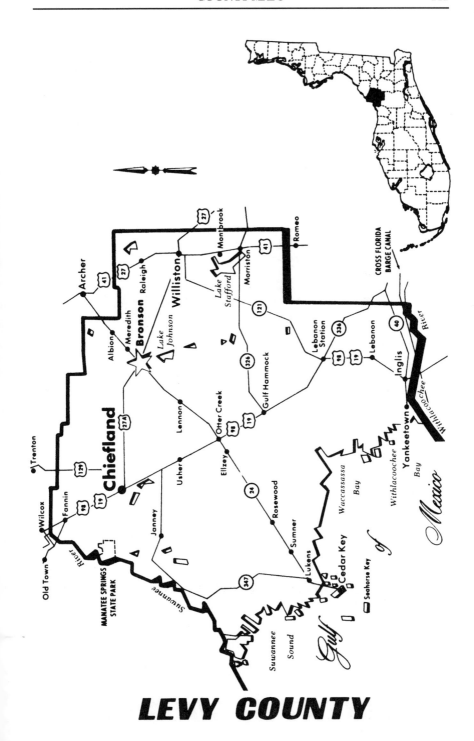

# LEVY COUNTY

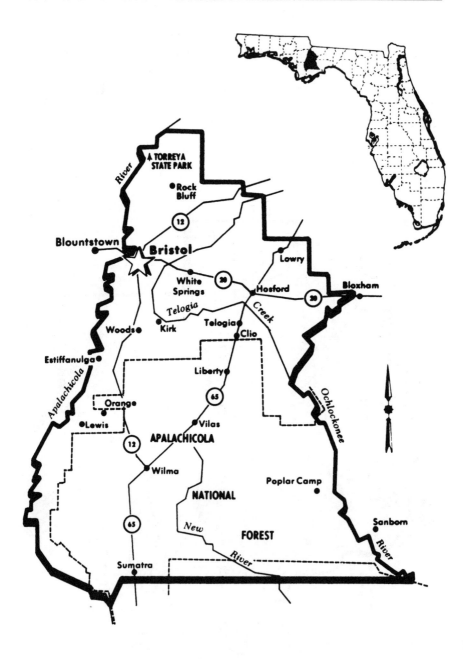

# LIBERTY COUNTY

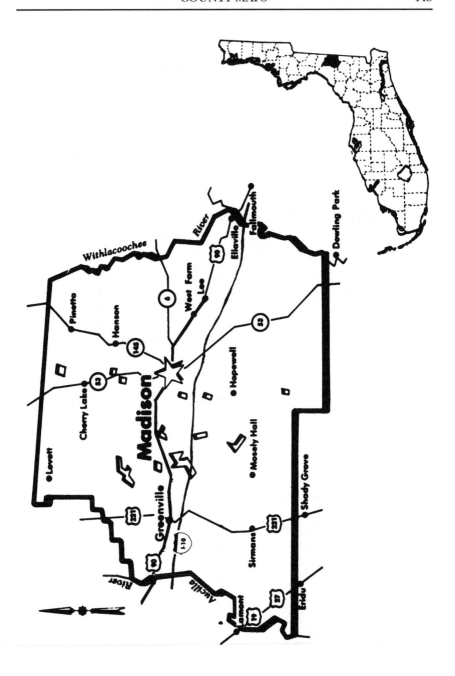

# MADISON COUNTY

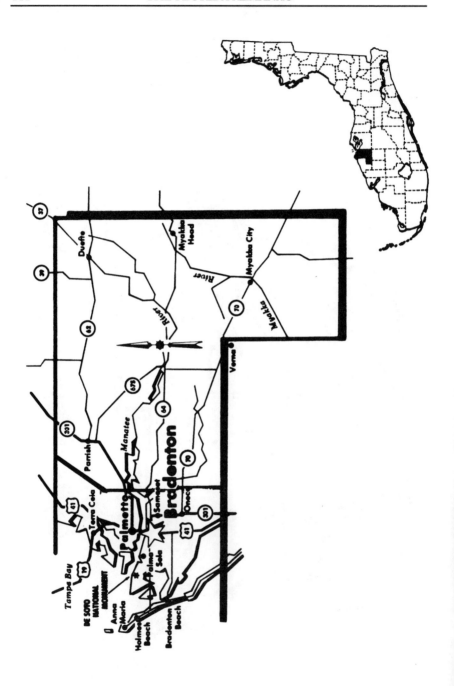

# MANATEE COUNTY

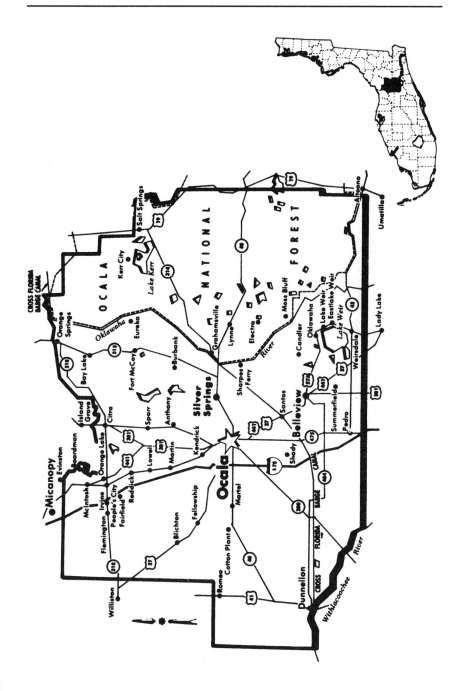

# MARION COUNTY

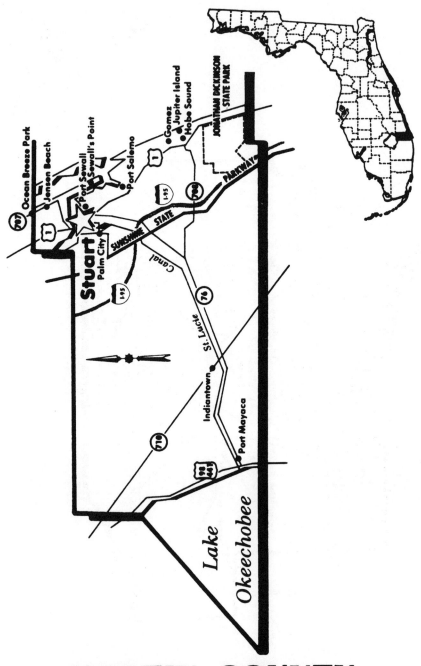

# MARTIN COUNTY

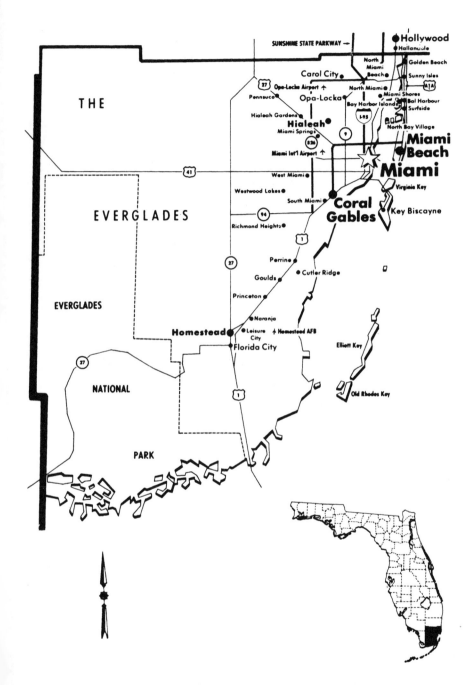

**MIAMI-DADE COUNTY**

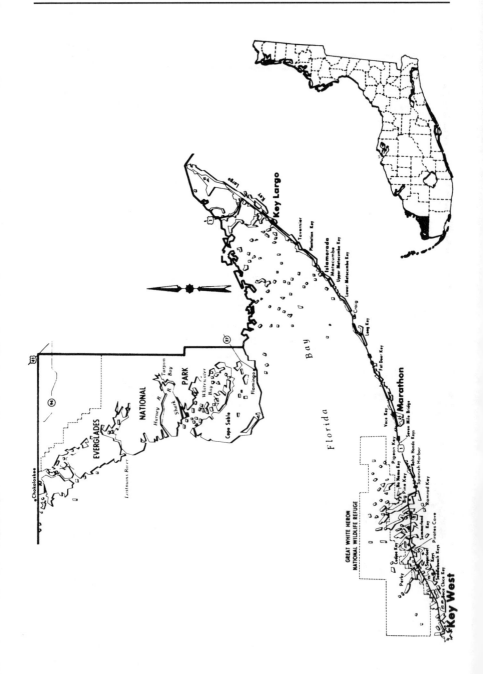

# MONROE COUNTY

# NASSAU COUNTY

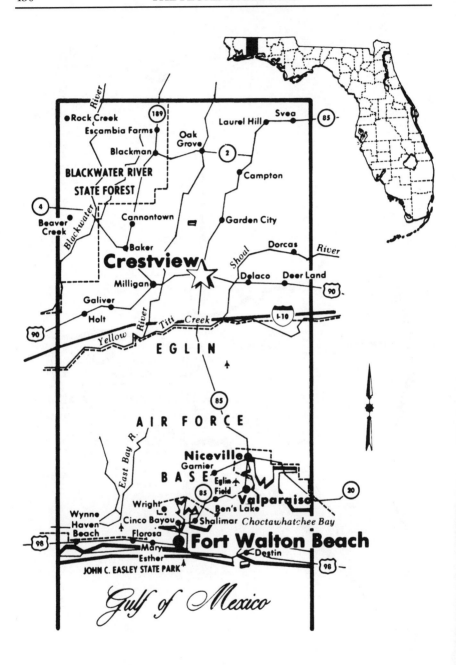

# OKALOOSA COUNTY

# OKEECHOBEE COUNTY

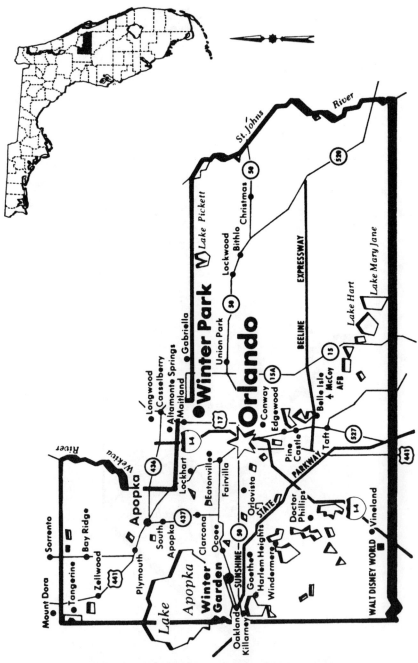

# ORANGE COUNTY

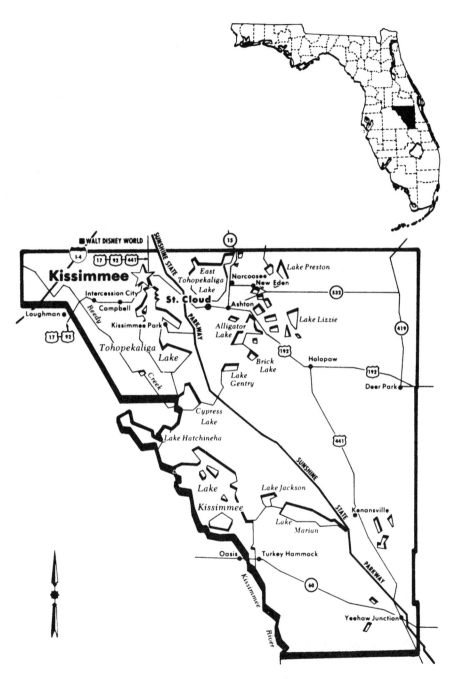

# OSCEOLA COUNTY

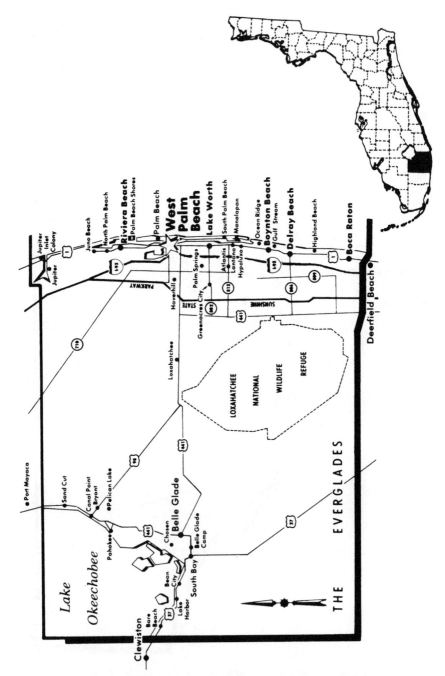

**PALM BEACH COUNTY**

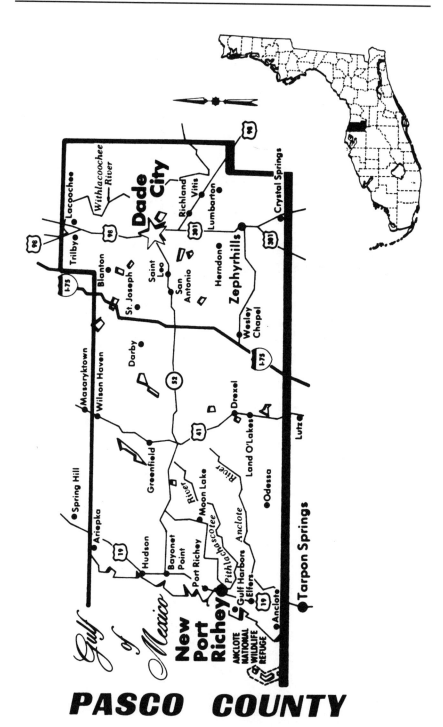

**PASCO COUNTY**

*Gulf*

Tarpon Springs

*Lake Turpon*

Crystal Beach

Ozona          Palm Harbor
                    Curlew

                    Oldsmar

*of*

Dunedin

Clearwater          Coachmane          Safety Harbor
                                        Dellwood
                              Bayview

Belleair Beach
                    Belleair
Belleair          Bluffs     Largo          High Point     St. Petersburg-Clearwater
Belleair Shore                                              International Airport

                    Walsingham          Ulmerton

Indian Rocks Beach

Indian Rocks Beach
South Shore          Seminole          Pinellas          *Tampa*
                                        Park
Redington Shores                        Kenneth City
North Redington Beach
Redington Beach          Bay Pines
Madeira Beach

                                        St. Petersburg
Treasure Island
                                        *Bay*
*Mexico*
                    South Pasadena
St. Petersburg Beach          Gulfport

                    Tierra Verde          SUNSHINE

                                          SKYWAY

Mullet Key
FT. DE SOTO PARK

# PINELLAS COUNTY

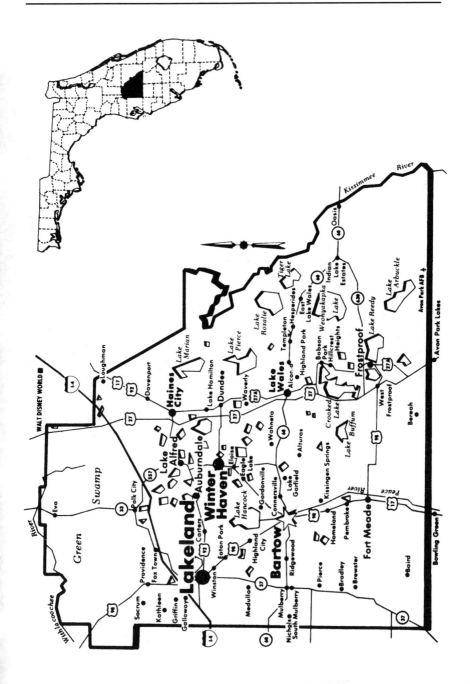

# POLK COUNTY

# PUTNAM COUNTY

Jacksonville Beach

Ponte Vedra Beach

Ponte Vedra

A1A

Palm Valley

Intracoastal

*Tolomato River*

Durbin

Switzerland
Sampson Church

South Ponte Vedra Beach

*St. Johns*

*River*

I-95

1

Waterway

*Atlantic*

Orangedale

*Ocean*

16

16

Tocoi Jct.

Picolata

Bakersville

**St. Augustine**

Vilano Beach

CASTILLO DE SAN MARCOS NAT'L MON.

13

College
Park

ANASTASIA STATE PARK

St. Augustine Beach

*St. Johns*

Riverdale

Vermont Heights

Moultrie

*Matanzas River*

1

Elkton

207

Dupont Center

FRANK BUTLER STATE PARK

Crescent Beach

*River*

Spuds

206

Hastings

I-95

FT. MATANZAS NAT'L MON.

Summer Haven

FAVER-DYKES STATE PARK

Yelvington

A1A

# ST. JOHNS COUNTY

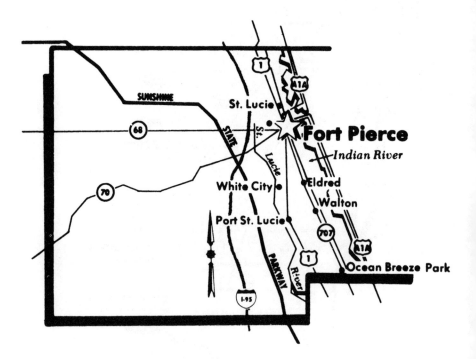

# ST. LUCIE COUNTY

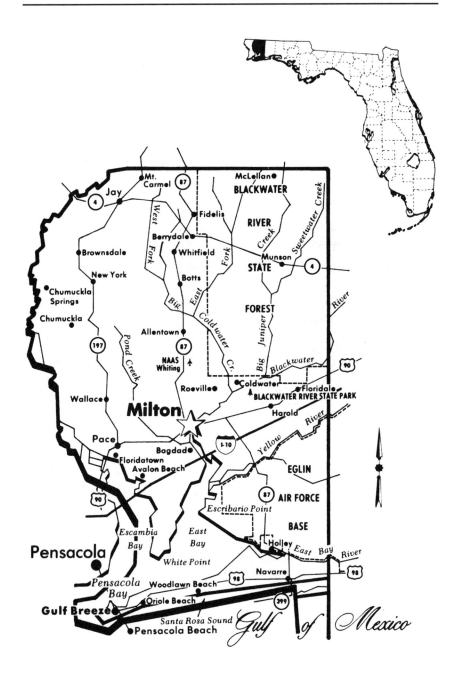

# SANTA ROSA COUNTY

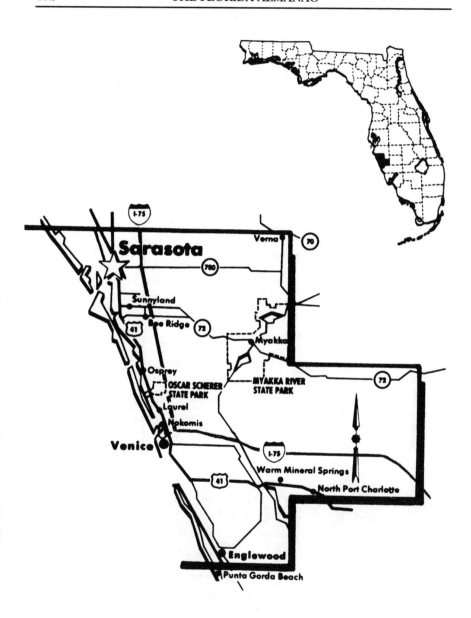

# SARASOTA COUNTY

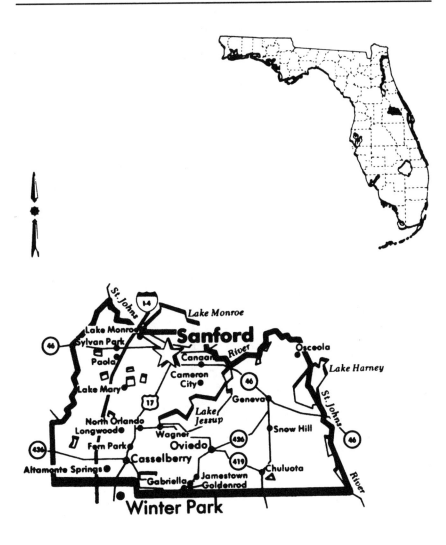

# SEMINOLE COUNTY

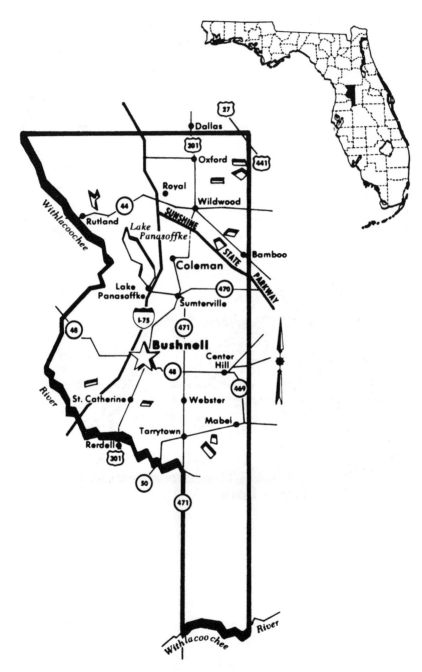

# SUMTER COUNTY

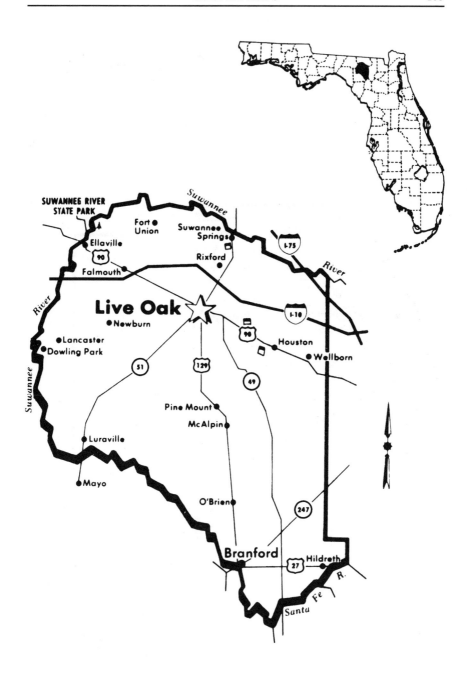

# SUWANNEE COUNTY

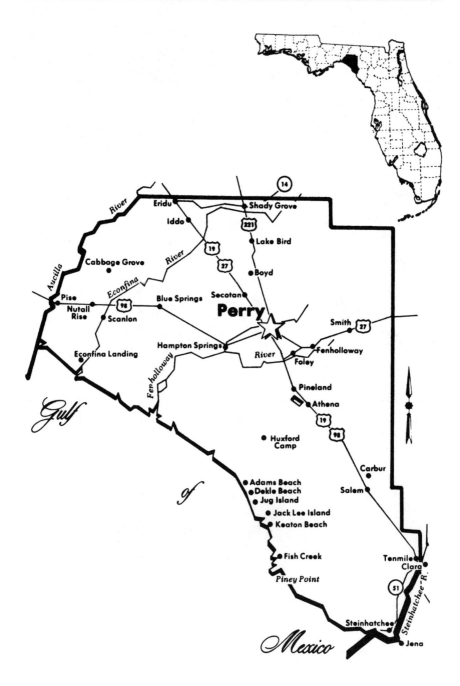

# TAYLOR COUNTY

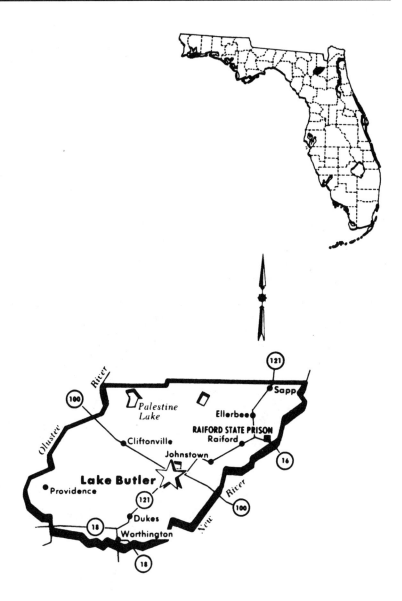

# UNION COUNTY

# VOLUSIA COUNTY

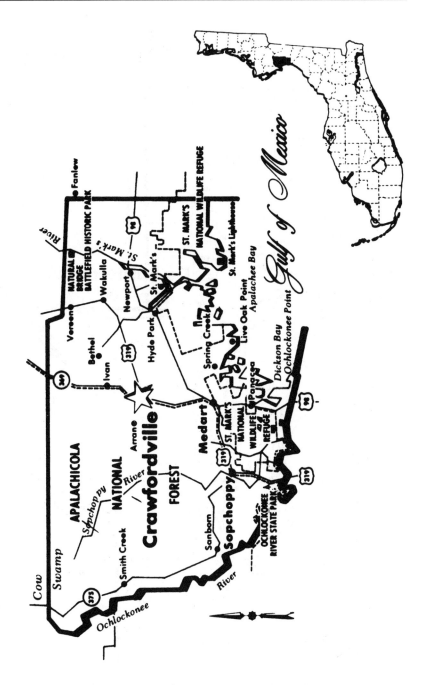

# WAKULLA COUNTY

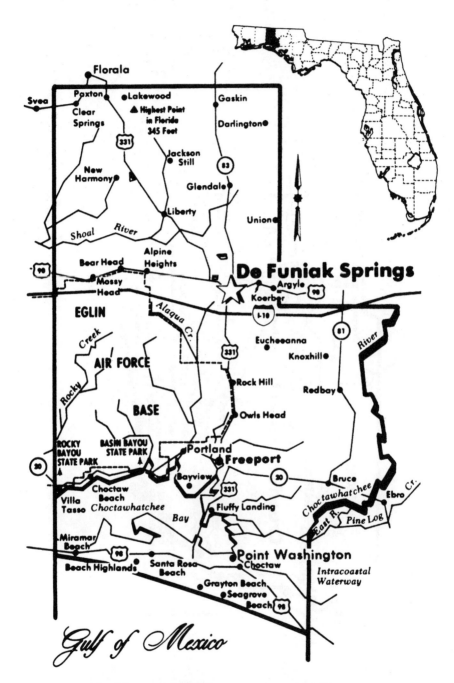

## WALTON COUNTY

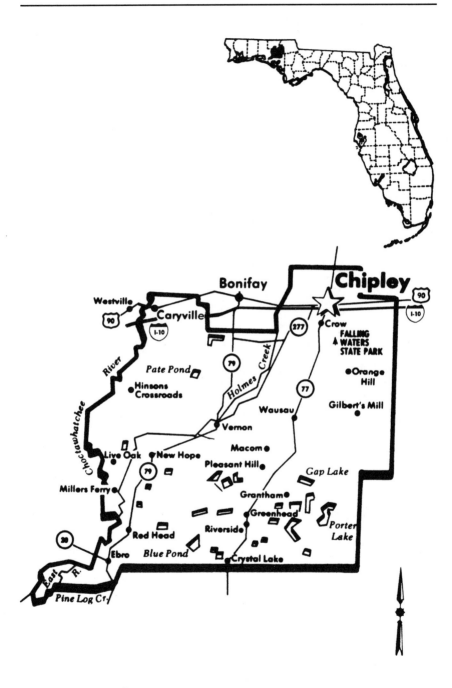

# WASHINGTON COUNTY

# ─────── TOLL-FREE NUMBERS ───────

Following are toll-free phone numbers established by various agencies or private organizations to assist Floridians. Dial 1-800 before the listed numbers.

| | |
|---|---|
| Abuse Hotline | 962-2873 |
| AIDS Hotline | 342-2437 |
| Automobile complaints (Lemon Law) | 321-5366 |
| Banking complaints (Comptroller) | 848-3792 |
| Blind services | 342-1828 |
| Child abuse | 342-9152 |
| Child support collection | 622-5437 |
| Consumer information | 435-7352 |
| Department of Insurance, consumer service | 342-2762 |
| Disability, comprehensive information | dial toll free: 1-888-838-2253 |
| Discrimination in housing and employment | 342-8170 |
| Domestic Abuse | 500-1119 |
| Elder Helpline (service information) | 963-5337 |

Fish and Wildlife Conservation Commission, Wildlife Alert Emergency:

| | |
|---|---|
| Northwest | 342-1676 |
| Northeast | 342-8105 |
| Central | 342-9620 |
| Southern | 282-8002 |
| Everglades | 432-2046 |

| | |
|---|---|
| Fishing Licenses (to order) | dial toll free: 1-888-347-4356 |
| Food Stamp fraud | 342-9274 |
| Hazardous/toxic materials information | 367-4378 |
| Health Cost Containment and Complaints | dial toll-free: 1-888-419-3456 |
| Hunting Licenses (to order) | dial toll free: 1-888-486-8356 |
| Internal Revenue Service | 829-1040 |
| Internal Revenue Service (hearing impaired) | 829-4059 |
| Livestock Theft Hotline | 342-5869 |
| Marine Patrol | 342-5367 |
| Medicare claims and information | 333-7586 |
| Missing and Exploited Children, National | 843-5678 |
| Oil and chemical spills, terrorism (national number) | 424-8802 |
| Poison Control Center | 282-3171 |
| Professional regulation complaints | 342-7940 |
| Public Service Commission | 342-3552 |
| Radon Gas Hotline | 543-8279 |
| Social Security | 772-1213 |
| Sport Fishing information | 275-3474 |
| State Bar association legal information | 342-8011 |
| Unemployment fraud | 342-9909 |
| Veterans (to report fraud and waste) | 488-8244 |
| Veterans Affairs | 827-1000 |
| Workers compensation claims | 342-1741 |

---

## SNAKEBIT

Venomous snakes bit 1,579 people in Florida in 1998, with more than half the attacks coming from rattlesnakes. Only two people died from the bites.

# ZIP CODES

| | | | | | |
|---|---|---|---|---|---|
| 32615 | Alachua | 34601 | Brooksville | 33441 | Deerfield Beach |
| 32420 | Alford | 33439 | Bryant | 32433 | DeFuniak Springs |
| 32346 | Alligator Point | 32009 | Bryceville | 32724 | DeLand |
| 32714 | Altamonte Springs | 32110 | Bunnell | 32130 | DeLeon Springs |
| 32421 | Altha | 33513 | Bushnell | 33444 | Delray Beach |
| 32702 | Altoona | 32011 | Callahan | 32738 | Deltona |
| 33820 | Alturas | 32426 | Campbellton | 32541 | Destin |
| 33920 | Alva | 33438 | Canal Point | 32030 | Doctors Inlet |
| 32034 | Amelia Island | 32111 | Candler | 33527 | Dover |
| 34216 | Anna Maria | 32533 | Cantonment | 33834 | Duette |
| 32617 | Anthony | 32920 | Cape Canaveral | 33838 | Dundee |
| 32320 | Apalachicola | 33907 | Cape Coral | 34698 | Dunedin |
| 33572 | Apollo Beach | 33924 | Captiva | 34432 | Dunnellon |
| 32712 | Apopka | 32322 | Carrabelle | 33530 | Durant |
| 34266 | Arcadia | 32427 | Caryville | 33839 | Eagle Lake |
| 32618 | Archer | 32706 | Cassadaga | 32631 | Earleton |
| 32422 | Argyle | 32707 | Casselberry | 32133 | East Lake Weir |
| 34679 | Aripeka | 32625 | Cedar Key | 32131 | East Palatka |
| 34705 | Astatula | 33514 | Center Hill | 32328 | Eastpoint |
| 32102 | Astor | 32535 | Century | 33030 | East Rockland Key |
| 32233 | Atlantic Beach | 32324 | Chattahoochee | 33840 | Eaton Park |
| 33823 | Auburndale | 32626 | Chiefland | 32751 | Eatonville |
| 33825 | Avon Park | 32428 | Chipley | 32437 | Ebro |
| 33827 | Babson Park | 34138 | Chokoloskee | 32149 | Edgar |
| 32530 | Bagdad | 32709 | Christmas | 32132 | Edgewater |
| 32531 | Baker | 32766 | Chuluota | 32542 | Eglin AFB |
| 33503 | Balm | 32113 | Citra | 34680 | Elfers |
| 32105 | Barberville | 32710 | Clarcona | 33927 | El Jobean |
| 33830 | Bartow | 32430 | Clarksville | 32033 | Elkton |
| 32423 | Bascom | 33765 | Clearwater | 34222 | Ellenton |
| 33744 | Bay Pines | 33767 | Clearwater Beach | 34295 | Englewood |
| 32619 | Bell | 34711 | Clermont | 33928 | Estero |
| 33786 | Belleair Beach | 33440 | Clewiston | 32726 | Eustis |
| 34420 | Belleview | 32922 | Cocoa | 34139 | Everglades City |
| 33430 | Belle Glade | 32931 | Cocoa Beach | 32633 | Evinston |
| 34461 | Beverly Hills | 33521 | Coleman | 32634 | Fairfield |
| 33040 | Big Coppitt Key | 34137 | Copeland | 33854 | Fedhaven |
| 33043 | Big Pine Key | 34215 | Cortez | 33930 | Felda |
| 33042 | Big Torch Key | 32431 | Cottondale | 32948 | Fellsmer |
| 32244 | Blountstown | 32327 | Crawfordville | 32034 | Fernandina Beach |
| 33921 | Boca Grande | 32112 | Crescent City | 34729 | Ferndale |
| 33431 | Boca Raton | 32536 | Crestview | 32136 | Flagler Beach |
| 33922 | Bokeelia | 32628 | Cross City | 32140 | Florahome |
| 32425 | Bonifay | 32640 | Cross Creek | 34436 | Floral City |
| 34135 | Bonita Springs | 34681 | Crystal Beach | 32307 | Florida A&M |
| 32007 | Bostwick | 34429 | Crystal River | 32306 | Florida State |
| 33834 | Bowling Green | 32524 | Crystal Springs | | University |
| 33436 | Boynton Beach | 33042 | Cudjoe Key | 33310 | Fort Lauderdale |
| 34206 | Bradenton | 32432 | Cypress | 32134 | Fort McCoy |
| 34217 | Bradenton Beach | 33884 | Cypress Gardens | 33841 | Fort Meade |
| 33835 | Bradley | 33525 | Dade City | 33907 | Fort Myers |
| 33511 | Brandon | 33004 | Dania | 33931 | Fort Myers Beach |
| 32008 | Branford | 33837 | Davenport | 34267 | Fort Ogden |
| 32321 | Bristol | 32013 | Day | 34981 | Fort Pierce |
| 32621 | Bronson | 32114 | Daytona Beach | 32548 | Fort Walton Beach |
| 32622 | Brooker | 32713 | De Bary | 32038 | Fort White |

| | | | | | | |
|---|---|---|---|---|---|
| 34755 | Minneola | 32177 | Palatka | 33956 | St. James City |
| 32577 | Molino | 32901 | Palm Bay | 33574 | St. Leo |
| 32344 | Monticello | 33480 | Palm Beach | 32355 | St. Marks |
| 34756 | Montverde | 33408 | Palm Beach | 33730 | St. Petersburg |
| 33471 | Moore Haven | | Gardens | 32358 | St. Teresa |
| 32668 | Morriston | 34990 | Palm City | 32356 | Salem |
| 32434 | Mossy Head | 32135 | Palm Coast | 32134 | Salt Springs |
| 32757 | Mount Dora | 33944 | Palmdale | 33576 | San Antonio |
| 32352 | Mount Pleasant | 34220 | Palmetto | 32087 | Sanderson |
| 32776 | Mount Plymouth | 34683 | Palm Harbor | 32771 | Sanford |
| 33860 | Mulberry | 32346 | Panacea | 33957 | Sanibel |
| 33938 | Murdock | 32401 | Panama City | 32187 | San Mateo |
| 34251 | Myakka City | 32407 | Panama City | 32615 | Santa Fe |
| 33856 | Nalcrest | | Beach | 32459 | Santa Rosa Beach |
| 34102 | Naples | 34219 | Parrish | 34230 | Sarasota |
| 32266 | Neptune Beach | 32925 | Patrick AFB | 32937 | Satellite Beach |
| 32669 | Newberry | 32538 | Paxton | 32189 | Satsuma |
| 34653 | New Port Richey | 32079 | Penney Farms | 32775 | Scottsmoor |
| 32168 | New Smyrna | 32501 | Pensacola | 32958 | Sebastian |
| | Beach | 32347 | Perry | 33870 | Sebring |
| 32578 | Niceville | 32180 | Pierson | 33584 | Seffner |
| 33863 | Nichols | 33945 | Pineland | 33770 | Seminole |
| 34661 | Nobleton | 33781 | Pinellas Park | 32190 | Seville |
| 34268 | Nocatee | 32350 | Pinetta | 32357 | Shady Grove |
| 34275 | Nokomis | 33946 | Placida | 32579 | Shalimar |
| 34252 | Noma | 33566 | Plant City | 32959 | Sharpes |
| 33408 | North Palm Beach | 32768 | Plymouth | 34489 | Silver Springs |
| 34292 | North Port | 32454 | Point Washington | 32460 | Sneads |
| 32759 | Oak Hill | 33868 | Polk City | 32358 | Sopchoppy |
| 34760 | Oakland | 32181 | Pomona Park | 32776 | Sorrento |
| 32071 | O'Brien | 33060 | Pompano Beach | 33493 | South Bay |
| 34478 | Ocala | 32455 | Ponce de Leon | 33082 | South Florida |
| 33037 | Ocean Reef | 32082 | Ponte Vedra Beach | 32409 | Southport |
| 34141 | Ochopee | 33952 | Port Charlotte | 32192 | Sparr |
| 32183 | Ocklawaha | 32129 | Port Orange | 34601 | Spring Hill |
| 34761 | Ocoee | 34668 | Port Richey | 32091 | Starke |
| 33556 | Odessa | 32456 | Port St. Joe | 32359 | Steinhatchee |
| 34762 | Okahumpka | 34981 | Port St. Lucie | 33040 | Stock Island |
| 34972 | Okeechobee | 34992 | Port Salerno | 34994 | Stuart |
| 34677 | Oldsmar | 33950 | Punta Gorda | 33044 | Sugarloaf |
| 32680 | Old Town | 32185 | Putnam Hall | 32335 | Sumatra |
| 32072 | Olustee | 32351 | Quincy | 34492 | Summerfield |
| 33865 | Ona | 32083 | Raiford | 33042 | Summerland Key |
| 34264 | Oneco | 33042 | Ramrod Key | 33585 | Sumterville |
| 33054 | Opa-Locka | 32686 | Reddick | 33586 | Sun City |
| 32763 | Orange City | 33523 | Ridge Manor | 33573 | Sun City Center |
| 32681 | Orange Lake | 33597 | Ridge Manor | 32428 | Sunny Hills |
| 32073 | Orange Park | | Estates | 32461 | Sunnyside |
| 32182 | Orange Springs | 33569 | Riverview | 32692 | Suwannee |
| 32862 | Orlando | 33867 | River Ranch | 33587 | Sydney |
| 32174 | Ormond Beach | 32955 | Rockledge | 32301 | Tallahassee |
| 34229 | Osprey | 32957 | Roseland | 34270 | Tallevast |
| 32764 | Osteen | 33947 | Rotonda West | 33601 | Tampa |
| 32683 | Otter Creek | 34221 | Rubonia | 32777 | Tangerine |
| 32765 | Oviedo | 33570 | Ruskin | 34689 | Tarpon Springs |
| 34484 | Oxford | 34695 | Safety Harbor | 32778 | Tavares |
| 34660 | Ozona | 32084 | St. Augustine | 33070 | Tavernier |
| 33476 | Pahokee | 34769 | St. Cloud | 32360 | Telogia |
| 32767 | Paisley | 32328 | St. George Island | 33617 | Temple Terrace |

| | | | | | |
|---|---|---|---|---|---|
| 34250 | Terra Ceia | 32305 | Wakulla Springs | 33598 | Wimauma |
| 32159 | The Villages | 32694 | Waldo | 34786 | Windermere |
| 33592 | Thonotosassa | 32568 | Walnut Hill | 32971 | Winter Beach |
| 32780 | Titusville | 33873 | Wauchula | 34787 | Winter Garden |
| 32693 | Trenton | 32463 | Wausau | 33880 | Winter Haven |
| 33593 | Trilby | 33877 | Waverly | 32789 | Winter Park |
| 32784 | Umatilla | 33597 | Webster | 32707 | Winter Springs |
| 33124 | University of | 32195 | Weirsdale | 32362 | Woodville |
| | Miami | 32193 | Welaka | 32697 | Worthington |
| 32580 | Valparaiso | 32094 | Wellborn | | Springs |
| 33594 | Valrico | 33416 | West Palm Beach | 34797 | Yalaha |
| 34285 | Venice | 33327 | Weston | 34498 | Yankeetown |
| 33960 | Venus | 32464 | Westville | 32466 | Youngstown |
| 32462 | Vernon | 32465 | Wewahitchka | 32097 | Yulee |
| 32960 | Vero Beach | 32096 | White Springs | 32798 | Zellwood |
| 32970 | Wabbaso | 34785 | Wildwood | 33540 | Zephyrhills |
| 32361 | Wacissa | 32696 | Williston | 33890 | Zolfo Springs |

## STORM SURGE RISKS

Florida's Division of Emergency Management estimates that about 25 percent of the state's population resides in areas that would be seriously affected by a Category 3 or stronger hurricane storm surge. Regions of the central-southern Gulf Coast south of St. Petersburg are considered to be at the most risk because some 90 percent of residents live on land that would be submerged by swollen tides.

## MILES OF FRESH WATER

Florida has 3 million acres of freshwater lakes and 12,000 miles of streams and rivers. From those waters over 250 different species of freshwater fishes have been collected.

## GATOR ATTACKS

There have been 249 documented alligator attacks on humans in the past 50 years resulting in nine deaths.

# MILEAGES

| | BARTOW | BELLE GLADE | BOYNTON BEACH | BRADENTON | CLEARWATER | COCOA | CORAL GABLES | DAYTONA BEACH | FORT LAUDERDALE | FORT MYERS | FORT PIERCE | FORT WALTON BEACH | GAINESVILLE | HIALEAH | HOLLYWOOD | JACKSONVILLE | KEY WEST |
|---|---|---|---|---|---|---|---|---|---|---|---|---|---|---|---|---|---|
| Apalachicola | 312 | 449 | 480 | 324 | 287 | 342 | 518 | 293 | 507 | 407 | 411 | 122 | 196 | 512 | 510 | 234 | 662 |
| Arcadia | 50 | 104 | 139 | 53 | 94 | | 174 | 161 | 162 | 46 | 100 | 465 | 183 | 168 | 166 | 241 | 317 |
| Bartow | | 140 | 171 | 64 | 61 | 94 | 208 | 113 | 198 | 96 | 108 | 415 | 133 | 203 | 201 | 184 | 353 |
| Bradenton | 64 | 157 | 192 | | 41 | 164 | 222 | 172 | 215 | 83 | 153 | 427 | 168 | 221 | 219 | 236 | 358 |
| Brooksville | 64 | 204 | 234 | 85 | 55 | 111 | 276 | 110 | 262 | 160 | 173 | 351 | 85 | 267 | 265 | 151 | 417 |
| Bushnell | 60 | 200 | 226 | 94 | 76 | 95 | 271 | 89 | 261 | 159 | 164 | 354 | 78 | 263 | 265 | 140 | 412 |
| Clearwater | 61 | 198 | 230 | 41 | | 152 | 263 | 160 | 256 | 124 | 170 | 390 | 132 | 261 | 259 | 195 | 399 |
| Crestview | 413 | 547 | 577 | 422 | 385 | 440 | 616 | 387 | 605 | 505 | 508 | 33 | 294 | 610 | 608 | 318 | 760 |
| Cross City | 162 | 299 | 330 | 174 | 137 | 192 | 368 | 148 | 357 | 257 | 261 | 255 | 51 | 362 | 360 | 111 | 512 |
| Dade City | 42 | 181 | 211 | 72 | 60 | 107 | 250 | 109 | 239 | 138 | 150 | 373 | 100 | 245 | 243 | 161 | 394 |
| DeFuniak Springs | 382 | 519 | 549 | 394 | 357 | 412 | 588 | 359 | 577 | 477 | 480 | 47 | 265 | 582 | 580 | 290 | 732 |
| DeLand | 94 | 192 | 209 | 153 | 141 | 71 | 269 | 23 | 239 | 188 | 140 | 386 | 98 | 263 | 246 | 100 | 413 |
| Fort Lauderdale | 198 | 67 | 30 | 215 | 256 | 167 | 31 | 232 | | 139 | 98 | 610 | 321 | 27 | 8 | 323 | 183 |
| Fort Myers | 96 | 81 | 132 | 83 | 124 | 193 | 139 | 208 | 139 | | 126 | 510 | 229 | 145 | 143 | 287 | 275 |
| Fort Pierce | 108 | 72 | 69 | 153 | 170 | 69 | 130 | 134 | 98 | 126 | | 515 | 225 | 125 | 106 | 220 | 281 |
| Gainesville | 133 | 263 | 293 | 168 | 132 | 156 | 332 | 97 | 321 | 229 | 225 | 301 | | 326 | 324 | 71 | 476 |
| Jacksonville | 184 | 292 | 293 | 236 | 195 | 156 | 354 | 91 | 323 | 287 | 220 | 327 | 71 | 350 | 331 | | 505 |
| Jasper | 204 | 334 | 362 | 232 | 195 | 224 | 402 | 160 | 392 | 304 | 293 | 247 | 74 | 397 | 395 | 89 | 547 |
| Key West | 353 | 222 | 212 | 358 | 399 | 350 | 156 | 416 | 183 | 275 | 281 | 765 | 476 | 161 | 175 | 505 | |
| Kissimmee | 46 | 140 | 167 | 110 | 97 | 50 | 217 | 71 | 197 | 141 | 102 | 415 | 126 | 212 | 205 | 152 | 361 |
| Lake City | 175 | 305 | 332 | 205 | 169 | 194 | 374 | 129 | 361 | 273 | 263 | 267 | 46 | 368 | 366 | 60 | 518 |
| Live Oak | 195 | 325 | 355 | 215 | 179 | 217 | 393 | 152 | 383 | 291 | 286 | 244 | 65 | 388 | 386 | 84 | 537 |
| Madison | 224 | 354 | 384 | 240 | 204 | 246 | 423 | 182 | 412 | 320 | 315 | 217 | 94 | 417 | 415 | 111 | 567 |
| Marianna | 326 | 463 | 493 | 338 | 301 | 356 | 531 | 303 | 521 | 421 | 424 | 103 | 209 | 526 | 524 | 234 | 675 |
| Miami | 211 | 80 | 54 | 229 | 270 | 192 | 7 | 257 | 24 | 146 | 123 | 626 | 334 | 8 | 17 | 347 | 158 |
| Moore Haven | 104 | 35 | 85 | 122 | 163 | 144 | 104 | 197 | 93 | 55 | 76 | 516 | 228 | 99 | 97 | 278 | 248 |
| Naples | 132 | 117 | 164 | 119 | 160 | 232 | 103 | 248 | 134 | 36 | 162 | 549 | 268 | 109 | 126 | 325 | 236 |
| Ocala | 97 | 226 | 253 | 134 | 103 | 119 | 295 | 80 | 284 | 193 | 185 | 326 | 37 | 289 | 291 | 99 | 438 |
| Okeechobee | 94 | 48 | 75 | 117 | 153 | 105 | 126 | 163 | 105 | 90 | 36 | 505 | 217 | 120 | 113 | 244 | 270 |
| Orlando | 59 | 157 | 184 | 121 | 106 | 47 | 234 | 55 | 214 | 154 | 116 | 398 | 109 | 229 | 222 | 133 | 378 |
| Palatka | 142 | 249 | 256 | 188 | 157 | 118 | 316 | 53 | 285 | 234 | 187 | 343 | 44 | 312 | 293 | 53 | 468 |
| Panama City | 353 | 490 | 520 | 364 | 328 | 382 | 558 | 334 | 548 | 448 | 451 | 66 | 237 | 553 | 551 | 265 | 702 |
| Pensacola | 459 | 592 | 623 | 467 | 433 | 485 | 661 | 436 | 650 | 550 | 554 | 40 | 339 | 655 | 653 | 368 | 805 |
| Perry | 208 | 344 | 375 | 219 | 183 | 237 | 413 | 188 | 402 | 302 | 306 | 210 | 91 | 408 | 406 | 130 | 557 |
| Punta Gorda | 75 | 105 | 155 | 59 | 100 | 169 | 163 | 187 | 163 | 24 | 126 | 486 | 208 | 168 | 166 | 267 | 299 |
| St. Augustine | 157 | 254 | 256 | 216 | 185 | 118 | 316 | 53 | 285 | 251 | 187 | 363 | 72 | 312 | 293 | 38 | 468 |
| Sarasota | 76 | 154 | 189 | 12 | 52 | 176 | 211 | 184 | 211 | 71 | 150 | 438 | 180 | 216 | 214 | 248 | 344 |
| Sebring | 48 | 94 | 123 | 79 | 109 | 124 | 162 | 140 | 152 | 86 | 85 | 460 | 171 | 157 | 155 | 221 | 304 |
| Tallahassee | 260 | 397 | 427 | 271 | 235 | 289 | 465 | 237 | 455 | 355 | 358 | 159 | 143 | 460 | 458 | 168 | 606 |
| Tampa | 39 | 178 | 209 | 40 | 20 | 130 | 247 | 138 | 237 | 123 | 148 | 394 | 130 | 242 | 241 | 196 | 391 |
| Titusville | 99 | 160 | 157 | 158 | 146 | 19 | 217 | 46 | 186 | 194 | 88 | 431 | 142 | 213 | 194 | 135 | 369 |
| Vero Beach | 94 | 87 | 83 | 155 | 153 | 55 | 144 | 120 | 113 | 141 | 14 | 499 | 210 | 140 | 121 | 210 | 295 |
| West Palm Beach | 158 | 40 | 10 | 181 | 217 | 127 | 71 | 192 | 40 | 121 | 59 | 569 | 278 | 70 | 48 | 279 | 223 |

| | LAKELAND | LEESBURG | MIAMI | MIAMI BEACH | OCALA | ORLANDO | PANAMA CITY | PENSACOLA | PLANT CITY | POMPANO BEACH | ST. AUGUSTINE | ST. PETERSBURG | SARASOTA | TALLAHASSEE | TAMPA | WEST PALM BEACH | WINTER HAVEN |
|---|---|---|---|---|---|---|---|---|---|---|---|---|---|---|---|---|---|
| Apalachicola | 299 | 254 | 520 | 522 | 223 | 295 | 60 | 168 | 295 | 500 | 263 | 301 | 335 | 76 | 291 | 469 | 312 |
| Arcadia | 62 | 121 | 176 | 180 | 147 | 107 | 402 | 505 | 73 | 160 | 205 | 79 | 80 | 309 | 89 | 129 | 60 |
| Bartow | 13 | 73 | 211 | 216 | 97 | 59 | 353 | 458 | 23 | 192 | 157 | 59 | 76 | 260 | 39 | 158 | 12 |
| Bradenton | 66 | 115 | 229 | 233 | 134 | 121 | 364 | 467 | 56 | 213 | 216 | 26 | 12 | 271 | 40 | 181 | 76 |
| Brooksville | 52 | 43 | 275 | 282 | 53 | 65 | 288 | 391 | 47 | 255 | 135 | 63 | 97 | 195 | 45 | 224 | 69 |
| Bushnell | 47 | 22 | 271 | 277 | 41 | 49 | 292 | 394 | 46 | 251 | 123 | 78 | 105 | 199 | 60 | 220 | 62 |
| Clearwater | 54 | 97 | 270 | 274 | 103 | 106 | 328 | 433 | 44 | 250 | 185 | 21 | 52 | 235 | 20 | 217 | 67 |
| Crestview | 397 | 352 | 618 | 619 | 321 | 393 | 86 | 53 | 393 | 598 | 352 | 403 | 436 | 150 | 389 | 567 | 410 |
| Cross City | 150 | 105 | 371 | 372 | 73 | 145 | 189 | 295 | 145 | 350 | 123 | 151 | 186 | 96 | 142 | 320 | 162 |
| Dade City | 29 | 43 | 253 | 257 | 63 | 61 | 311 | 413 | 25 | 232 | 145 | 57 | 83 | 218 | 38 | 201 | 44 |
| DeFuniak Springs | 369 | 324 | 590 | 591 | 293 | 365 | 67 | 81 | 365 | 570 | 324 | 371 | 405 | 122 | 361 | 539 | 382 |
| DeLand | 89 | 45 | 263 | 268 | 61 | 35 | 324 | 427 | 98 | 230 | 63 | 138 | 165 | 231 | 119 | 199 | 82 |
| Fort Lauderdale | 210 | 253 | 24 | 29 | 284 | 214 | 548 | 650 | 221 | 9 | 285 | 241 | 211 | 455 | 237 | 40 | 198 |
| Fort Myers | 109 | 167 | 146 | 151 | 193 | 154 | 448 | 550 | 119 | 152 | 251 | 109 | 71 | 355 | 123 | 121 | 106 |
| Fort Pierce | 121 | 157 | 123 | 128 | 185 | 116 | 451 | 554 | 132 | 90 | 187 | 167 | 150 | 358 | 148 | 59 | 108 |
| Gainesville | 121 | 68 | 334 | 336 | 37 | 109 | 237 | 339 | 124 | 314 | 72 | 145 | 180 | 143 | 130 | 278 | 126 |
| Jacksonville | 181 | 128 | 347 | 348 | 99 | 133 | 265 | 368 | 186 | 314 | 38 | 217 | 248 | 168 | 196 | 279 | 181 |
| Jasper | 191 | 139 | 405 | 406 | 108 | 180 | 182 | 287 | 194 | 383 | 124 | 211 | 243 | 85 | 196 | 352 | 203 |
| Key West | 365 | 407 | 158 | 164 | 438 | 378 | 702 | 805 | 376 | 191 | 468 | 381 | 344 | 606 | 391 | 223 | 353 |
| Kissimmee | 45 | 59 | 220 | 224 | 89 | 17 | 353 | 455 | 56 | 188 | 115 | 94 | 121 | 257 | 78 | 155 | 34 |
| Lake City | 162 | 110 | 376 | 378 | 79 | 151 | 204 | 310 | 165 | 353 | 94 | 185 | 217 | 108 | 167 | 321 | 174 |
| Live Oak | 182 | 130 | 396 | 397 | 99 | 171 | 181 | 284 | 187 | 376 | 117 | 195 | 227 | 85 | 183 | 345 | 188 |
| Madison | 216 | 159 | 425 | 426 | 128 | 200 | 152 | 255 | 212 | 405 | 146 | 220 | 252 | 55 | 208 | 374 | 224 |
| Marianna | 313 | 268 | 534 | 535 | 237 | 309 | 53 | 137 | 309 | 514 | 268 | 317 | 349 | 66 | 305 | 483 | 326 |
| Miami | 224 | 266 | | 5 | 297 | 237 | 561 | 663 | 234 | 33 | 310 | 255 | 217 | 468 | 251 | 67 | 212 |
| Moore Haven | 117 | 159 | 107 | 111 | 191 | 143 | 454 | 557 | 128 | 106 | 240 | 148 | 119 | 361 | 143 | 77 | 105 |
| Naples | 145 | 202 | 110 | 115 | 229 | 194 | 483 | 589 | 155 | 143 | 292 | 146 | 107 | 391 | 159 | 160 | 144 |
| Ocala | 84 | 31 | 297 | 299 | | 72 | 264 | 366 | 87 | 277 | 82 | 116 | 146 | 171 | 98 | 242 | 92 |
| Okeechobee | 107 | 148 | 129 | 130 | 180 | 108 | 443 | 546 | 117 | 96 | 206 | 145 | 114 | 348 | 133 | 65 | 94 |
| Orlando | 54 | 42 | 237 | 242 | 72 | | 336 | 438 | 63 | 205 | 98 | 104 | 130 | 243 | 84 | 171 | 47 |
| Palatka | 130 | 78 | 310 | 314 | 54 | 92 | 281 | 387 | 139 | 276 | 28 | 173 | 200 | 184 | 152 | 245 | 127 |
| Panama City | 340 | 295 | 561 | 562 | 264 | 336 | | 107 | 336 | 541 | 298 | 344 | 376 | 97 | 332 | 507 | 353 |
| Pensacola | 442 | 397 | 663 | 665 | 366 | 438 | 107 | | 442 | 643 | 404 | 448 | 481 | 199 | 434 | 609 | 455 |
| Perry | 195 | 150 | 416 | 417 | 118 | 191 | 145 | 248 | 191 | 396 | 158 | 196 | 231 | 52 | 187 | 365 | 208 |
| Punta Gorda | 88 | 146 | 169 | 175 | 172 | 133 | 424 | 526 | 99 | 176 | 230 | 85 | 48 | 331 | 99 | 145 | 87 |
| St. Augustine | 152 | 106 | 310 | 314 | 82 | 98 | 298 | 404 | 168 | 277 | | 198 | 230 | 201 | 180 | 243 | 145 |
| Sarasota | 78 | 126 | 217 | 223 | 146 | 130 | 376 | 481 | 68 | 210 | 230 | 39 | | 283 | 51 | 179 | 88 |
| Sebring | 63 | 102 | 165 | 169 | 134 | 86 | 397 | 500 | 74 | 144 | 183 | 106 | 92 | 304 | 90 | 113 | 51 |
| Tallahassee | 247 | 202 | 468 | 469 | 171 | 243 | 97 | 199 | 243 | 448 | 201 | 248 | 283 | | 239 | 412 | 260 |
| Tampa | 33 | 81 | 251 | 255 | 98 | 84 | 332 | 434 | 22 | 230 | 180 | 19 | 51 | 239 | | 199 | 49 |
| Titusville | 94 | 75 | 211 | 215 | 105 | 41 | 369 | 471 | 103 | 177 | 99 | 143 | 170 | 276 | 124 | 146 | 87 |
| Vero Beach | 107 | 143 | 137 | 142 | 173 | 101 | 437 | 542 | 117 | 104 | 173 | 153 | 165 | 343 | 133 | 73 | 84 |
| West Palm Beach | 173 | 216 | 67 | 71 | 242 | 171 | 507 | 609 | 184 | 31 | 243 | 208 | 179 | 412 | 199 | | 158 |

# SELECTED BOOKS

As the state's population grows, so do the number of books written about Florida. The editors have selected the following titles as a guide to assist readers who want to learn more about the state.

## Archaeology/Geology

Brown, Robin C.: *Florida's Fossils, a Guide to Location, Identification and Enjoyment.*

Hoffmeister, John E.: *Land from the Sea: the Geologic Story of South Florida.*

Rouse, Irving: *A Survey of Indian River Archaeology, Florida.*

## Architecture

Curl, Donald: *Mizner's Florida: American Resort Architecture.*

DeWire, Elinor: *Guide to Florida's Lighthouses.*

Dunlop, Beth: *Florida's Vanishing Architecture.*

Frisbie, Louise K.: *Florida's Fabled Inns.*

Kaufelt, Lynn M.: *Key West Writers and Their Houses.*

Stewart, Laura and Susanne Hupp: *Florida Historic Homes.*

Warnke, James R.: *Balustrades and Gingerbread: Key West's Handcrafted Homes and Buildings.*

## Autobiography/Biography

Acton, Patricia N.: *Invasion of Privacy: The Cross Creek Trial of Marjorie Kinnan Rawlings.*

Bigelow, Gordon E.: *Frontier Eden: The Literary Career of Marjorie Kinnan Rawlings.*

Doherty, Herbert J., Jr.: *Richard Keith Call: Southern Unionist.*

Douglas, Marjory Stoneman: *Voice of the River.*

Glassman, Steve and Kathryn Seidel: *Zora in Florida.*

Griffith, Leon O.: *Ed Ball: Confusion to the Enemy.*

Hartley, William and Ellen: *Osceola.*

Johnston, Alva: *The Legendary Mizners.*

Martin, Sidney W.: *Florida's Flagler.*

McLendon, James: *Papa Hemingway in Key West.*

Shofner, Jerrel H.: Daniel Ladd: *Merchant Prince of Frontier Florida.*

## Fiction Set in Florida

Frank, Pat: *Alas, Babylon.*

Hall, James W.: *Under Cover of Daylight; Mean High Tide.*

Hemingway, Ernest: *To Have and Have Not.*

Hirschfeld, Burt: *Key West.*

Hurston, Zora Neale: *Their Eyes Were Watching God.*

Kantor, MacKinlay: *The Noise of Their Wings.*

MacDonald, John D.: *Condominium.*

Pratt, Theodore: *The Barefoot Mailman.*

Rawlings, Marjorie Kinnan: *The Yearling; Cross Creek; South Moon Under; Golden Apples.*

Smith, Patrick D.: *A Land Remembered.*

Wilder, Robert: *Flamingo Road.*

## Folklore

Morris, Alton C.: *Folksongs of Florida.*

Reaver, J. Russell: *Florida Folktales.*

## Government

Morris, Allen: *The Florida Handbook* (published biennially since 1947).

## Guides

*AAA TourBook Florida.*

Bardon, Doris and Murray Laurie: *Museums & More.*

Birnbaum, Steve: *Walt Disney World: The Official Guide.*

*Fodor's Florida.*

Hiller, Herbert L.: *Guide to the Small and Historic Lodgings of Florida.*

Insight Guides: *Florida.*

Kosoy, Ted: *Kosoy's Travel Guide to Florida and the South.*

Marth, Del and Martha J.: *The Rivers of Florida*.

O'Brien, Dawn and Becky Matkov: *Florida's Historic Restaurants*.

O'Reilly, John: *Boater's Guide to the Upper Florida Keys*.

Stachowicz, Jim: *Diver's Guide to Florida and the Florida Keys*.

Toner, Mike and Pat: *Florida by Paddle and Pack*.

*Woodall's Florida Campground Directory*.

Young, Claiborne S.: *Cruising Guide to Eastern Florida; Cruising Guide to Western Florida; Cruising Guide to the Northern Gulf Coast*.

## History

Bartram, William: *Travels of William Bartram* (edited by Mark Van Doren).

Bickel, Karl: *The Mangrove Coast*.

Bloodworth, Bertha E. and Alton C. Morris: *Places in the Sun: The History and Romance of Florida Place-Names*.

Burnett, Gene: *Florida's Past*.

Carson, Ruby Leach and Charlton W. Tebeau: *Florida: From Indian Trail to Space Age*.

Covington, James W.: *The Seminoles of Florida*.

Davis, William Watson: *The Civil War and Reconstruction in Florida*.

Douglas, Marjory Stoneman: *Florida: The Long Frontier*.

Dunn, Hampton: *Yesterday's Tampa; Yesterday's Clearwater, Wish You Were Here*.

Foster, Charles C.: *Conchtown USA*.

Frisbie, Louise K.: *Yesterday's Polk County*.

Fuller, Walter: *This Was Florida's Boom*.

Gannon, Michael: *The Cross in the Sand; The New History of Florida*. Ed.

Godown, Marion and Alberta Rawchuck: *Yesterday's Fort Myers*.

Hahn, John H.: *Apalachee: The Land Between the Rivers*.

Kleinberg, Howard: *The Florida Hurricane & Disaster 1992 & 1926*.

Lanier, Sidney: Florida: *Its Scenery, Climate and History*.

Lyon, Eugene: *The Search for the Atocha*.

Mahon, John K.: *The Second Seminole War*.

Marth, Del: *Yesterday's Sarasota; Once Upon a Time, a History of St. Petersburg*.

Morris, Allen: *Florida Place Names*.

Nolan, David: *Fifty Feet in Paradise*.

Owsley, Frank L., Jr.: *The C.S.S. Florida*.

Paisley, Clifton: *The Red Hills of Florida*.

Patrick, Rembert W.: *Florida Under Five Flags*.

Richardson, Joseph M.: *The Negro in the Reconstruction of Florida*.

Schell, Rolfe F.: *History of Fort Myers Beach*.

Schofield, Arthur C.: *Yesterday's Bradenton*.

Smiley, Nixon: *Yesterday's Florida; Yesterday's Miami*.

Stowe, Harriet Beecher: *Palmetto Leaves*.

Tebeau, Charlton: *A History of Florida*.

Wickman, Patricia: *Osceola's Legacy*.

Windhorn, Stan and Wright Langley: *Yesterday's Key West*.

Wright, J. Leitch, Jr.: *Florida in the American Revolution*.

## Lifestyles

Bothwell, Dick: *BUM (Brighten Up Monday) Stories*.

Clark, Janie: *Seniorcise*.

Keane, Gerald B.: *Florida Law*.

Key West Women's Club: *Key West Cookbook*.

Marth, Martha J.: *Florida Horse Owner's Field Guide; Florida Dog Owner's Guide*.

McGarry, Betty: *Practical Guide to Florida Retirement*.

Phillips, Elwood: *Florida Retirees' Handbook*.

Pohl, William and John Ames: *Speaking of Florida*.

## Nature/Environment

Alvarez, Kenneth C.: *Twilight of the Panther*.

Bansemer, Roger: *Southern Shores*.

Bell, Ritchie C. and Taylor, Bryan J.: *Florida Wild Flowers and Roadside Plants.*

Campbell, George: *An Illustrated Guide to Some Poisonous Plants and Animals of Florida.*

Carr, Archie: *The Everglades.*

Craighead, F. C.: *Orchids and Other Air Plants of the Everglades National Park.*

De Freitas, Stan: *Complete Guide to Florida Gardening.*

Douglas, Marjory Stoneman: *The Everglades: River of Grass.*

Fernald, Edward A. and Donald J. Patton: *Water Resources Atlas of Florida.*

Fichter, George S.: *Birds of Florida.*

Fleming, Glenn; Pierre Genelle; and Robert W. Long: *Wild Flowers of Florida.*

Fletcher, Leslie: *Florida's Fantastic Fauna and Flora.*

*Florida's Sandy Beaches, an Access Guide.*

Koukoulis, Andrew: *Poisonous Snakes of Florida.*

Lakela, Olaga and Robert W. Long: *Ferns of Florida.*

Luer, Carlyle A.: *The Native Orchids of Florida.*

McMullen, James P.: *The Cry of the Panther.*

Mesouf, Hank and June Cleo: *Florida: Polluted Paradise.*

Morton, Julia: *Plants Poisonous to People in Florida and Other Warm Areas.*

Rogers, David and Constance: *Woody Ornamentals for Deep South Gardens.*

Voss, Gilbert: *Coral Reefs of Florida.*

Watkins, John and Thomas Sheehan: *Florida Landscape Plants.*

Watkins, John and Herbert Wolfe: *Your Florida Garden.*

Winsberg, Morton: *Florida Weather.*

# INDEX